Interpersonal behavior and administration

Interpersonal behavior

ARTHUR N. TURNER AND

Professor of Business Administration / Graduate School of Business Administration / Harvard University

The Free Press, New York / *Collier-Macmillan*

and administration

GEORGE F. F. LOMBARD

Louis E. Kirstein Professor of Human Relations / Senior Associate Dean for Educational Affairs / Graduate School of Business Administration / Harvard University

Limited, London

Collier-Macmillan Canada, Ltd., Toronto, Ontario

Library of Congress Catalog Card Number: 69–11486

First Printing

TO F.J.R.
with affection and gratitude

Contents

Preface

This book focuses on the processes by which one person fails or succeeds in understanding another person when there is some shared responsibility between them for accomplishing a task within an organization. The subject matter might be called "dyadic (two-person) communication in formal organizations."

The authors take the view that efficient inter-personal communication is a prerequisite to effective organizational administration. Consequently this book is for those who are willing to learn that it is both very important and very difficult for a person in a position of responsibility in an organization to improve his understanding of what takes place when he tries to talk with, listen to, and understand another person from the other person's point of view. This book tries to describe why this is an important and difficult process.

In one sense what we are trying to set forth can be stated simply, but in another sense we can never state adequately what we are driving at. In one sense we are all experts at understanding and communicating with other people. ("What's so complicated about that?") In another sense our objective can never be reached. ("Interpersonal understanding—how can that be *taught*?") So we are caught in the dilemma that what we are attempting sometimes seems either unnecessary or impossible, or both. And yet we are convinced that it is neither. Much needs to be learned about improving our ability to understand each other, and much can be learned, but gradually, at times circuitously, and always one small step at a time.

The effectiveness with which any organization of people

accomplishes its prescribed tasks while satisfying the needs of its members is greatly affected by the efficiency of communication between them. Directions and policies need to be understood if they are to be followed with enthusiasm. Communication is sometimes conceived as a process simply of speaking and writing clearly. But the ability to understand what another person is trying to communicate is as important as the ability to transmit one's own thought. The effectiveness of communication in organizational relationships depends in large part upon the skill with which responsible members listen with understanding to the perceptions, assumptions, and feelings of those with whom they interact in the process of accomplishing the organizational purpose.

This book is concerned with ways of practicing and improving this skill. Thus it is addressed to all who need to listen more usefully, not only to the words, but to the meaning and feeling behind the words, of the persons they must interact with in order for the prescribed work to be performed effectively and with satisfaction. Unless we know what the people we talk with are saying to us it is difficult if not impossible to know what to say to them, or how. For this reason it seems useful to concentrate on the receiving rather than on the transmitting end of the communication process, especially because, for most of us, it is more difficult to learn how to listen than to learn how to talk.

This is *not* a book that sets forth some model of approved managerial behavior. We are not interested in trying to inculcate a particular way of behaving. We are interested in encouraging the reader to work at improving his understanding of the interpersonal events in which he is involved, so that his subsequent behavior may result in fewer unanticipated consequences. This is what we mean by the phrase "learning ways of learning"; this is the sense in which we mean that this book does not espouse a particular managerial style. It espouses rather what is to us the most relevant skill for any useful participation in human interaction: understanding the other person's point of view. What is done with that understanding remains a personal choice that cannot be taught, although we believe that increased interpersonal understanding will, in time, result in increased productiveness as well as increased satisfaction in organizational behavior.

For whom is the present volume intended? Primarily, as we have already indicated, for students and practitioners of organizational administration who are in or aspire to positions of responsibility which require them to understand and communicate with other persons at work. For this reason most of the cases and much of the other material in the book are taken from formal organizational contexts. Anyone in a position of leadership has a particular responsibility to interact skillfully with others, which means to understand points of view which may be very different from his own.

But we believe the knowledge and the opportunities to use it which this book provides have also a wider relevance. For example, many selling activities require, we believe, an understanding of interpersonal relations as conceived in this book. And a wide range of professions, including medicine and law, depend in part on the practitioner's ability to understand his client's point of view. In fact in all walks of life, off the job as well as at work, there is clearly a need for more conscious, systematic attention to not just surface verbal behavior, but to the personal meaning and feeling that are so imperfectly symbolized by most of the words that people exchange with each other every day. We happen to have developed this approach within the context of a graduate school of business administration. But if we had wanted it to stay there, we would not have tried to put it between the covers of this book.

The book consists of three kinds of material: cases, introductory and explanatory material as aids in studying the cases, and articles or chapters reproduced from the writings of behavioral scientists and others who have contributed useful knowledge and understanding about the process of person-to-person communication.

The cases are accurate descriptions of events that took place, usually within a business organization. Most of the cases involve two principal persons whose prescribed behavior requires them to communicate with each other. Often at least one is having some difficulty understanding what the other is saying to him. The purpose of these cases is to provide opportunities for analyzing an interpersonal relationship in a particular setting and for deciding what behavior on the part of at least one of the persons involved would result in improved understanding between them. The particular situation within which the interpersonal behavior occurs, the organizational requirements and restraints, will always be an important influence on the behavior which is described, as well as on whatever alternate patterns of behavior might be suggested. That is, the cases are instances of interpersonal behavior within a particular organizational context, not in a vacuum.

At the beginning and end of each of the five main parts of the book, we have inserted some of our own attempts to help students understand what the objectives of the section are and how a given group of cases can be made useful by applying to them various conceptual approaches and modes of analysis. Some readers may prefer to analyze a case on their own, as an introduction to one of the parts, before turning to the authors' attempt to prepare the ground. These ten chapters have been written out of our own experience in helping students work constructively with these cases.

The third type of material in the book consists of papers reproduced, with permission, from previously published books and articles. Some of the papers report research results, but most of them present ideas and concepts which have proved to be useful. The ideas and concepts are primarily from general semantics, individual and clinical psychology, and psychotherapy. Some of the papers were originally addressed to a practice-oriented, others to a more academic, audience. All have been found useful aids to our students in helping them develop the analytical tools and underlying point of view necessary to understanding interpersonal behavior at more than just a surface level. In addition to the writings reproduced in this book, reference is frequently made to other books which our students have found useful in understanding our material. These additional references are listed and discussed in the "Readings" sections of Parts II through V. Several of them are strongly recommended for study.

Part I of the book contains one case and two chapters which serve as an introduction to the rest of the book. Part II gives examples of misunderstanding in organizations and relates them to certain assumptions about organizational behavior and about the use of words which frequently interfere with effective communication. Part III concentrates on ways of understanding another person from his point of view. Part IV turns to cases in which there is an intention not only to understand but also to help another person, and draws its conceptual framework primarily from the "client-centered" psychotherapy of Carl Rogers. In Part V the focus shifts back to more customary types of organizational relationships, in order to test out the extent to which the approaches learned in the preceding parts can be useful in such contexts as superior–subordinate, staff–line, and consultant–client relationships, especially in situations in which there is a need to improve the existing pattern of communication in these settings. Part V also offers some materials to introduce the reader to the problems of applying what he has learned to his own future learning as a person, with emphasis on the role of the administrator as an involved and aware practitioner of interpersonal skills.

The outline of the book follows closely that of a course given in the MBA Program at the Harvard Business School, beginning in 1949. The course was first developed and taught by Professor F. J. Roethlisberger with the assistance of Paul R. Lawrence and Harriet Ronken. It was planned as a one-semester elective course in the second year to go beyond a required first-year course at that time called Administrative Practices.

Professor Roethlisberger, Professor Lawrence, and Miss Ronken gave considerable thought to the course's substantive objectives. Three of the prominent alternatives would have the course focused primarily on individual behavior, on small-group problems, or on interpersonal relations. Though there were clear overlaps between these topics, it was felt that they could be largely separate. The course as it finally evolved was intended for the general practitioner rather than the specialist in business. It was to be focused on interpersonal communication in business organizations. This topic promised to provide a focus around which relevant aspects of specialist-oriented studies in individual and group behavior might be integrated, as well as providing scope for new work in business administration itself. For these reasons, and because a relatively large amount of teaching material was available from a predecessor course given at the School before World War II, the decision was made to focus the course on interpersonal communication in organizations. From about 1952 Professor Lombard taught the course with the assistance of James Surface, Tom Miller, Ralph Lynton, Louis Barnes, James Clark, Harold Spear, Melville Steckler, Peter Vaill, and Gerald Leader. Professor Turner has continued the development of the course in recent years with the assistance of Charles Hampden-Turner, Margaret Hennig, and Craig Lundberg.

The point of view from which the materials have been selected and arranged does not encourage debates as to whether behavior can be studied systematically. Rather the book is based on the assumption that it can and that it is fruitful to do so for the development of both theory and practice. Therefore, the book is not primarily intended for use in an introductory course, where such debate frequently needs to receive appropriate attention. Though our version of the course does not aim primarily to convey systematic knowledge about interpersonal communication in organizations—and a good deal is available today—it is intended for students who are "on the fence" between belief and disbelief about whether pursuing systematic knowledge of behavior in two-person situations is worthwhile, but who, while suspending their judgments, are ready to pursue study of such situations vigorously and rigorously in an attempt to let the outcome guide the settlement of the issue.

An important reason why we think of this book as more appropriate to a second year than to an introductory course in human behavior is that the materials in it require intensive attention to what are, in the scale of events, small occurrences—conversations between two persons. When even a handful of students examine such material in a classroom (and we have frequently taught the course in sections approaching 100 students), it is sometimes difficult to keep a sense of proportion about the real events. What seems to happen is that feelings and tensions in the classroom, among students and between them and the instructor, magnify the events of the case.

But sophisticated labels frequently confuse simple events rather than clarify them. Though we welcome the student of abnormal psychology, for example, we warn him against too quickly "typing" the individual's behavior that is described as either "normal" or "abnormal," and point out that the behavior of the persons in the cases presented is that of individuals who are contributing to some organization's purpose while earning their own living. We remind the reader that though these are actual persons whose conversations we are studying, we do not have them before us. All we have are records of their talk. Professional psychologists of our acquaintance do not make responsible diagnoses of personalities—that is, diagnoses designed to lead to doing things differently than they otherwise would be done—from such data. We urge the reader to think again about how his advanced knowledge can be used relevantly to the kind of situations we are discussing.

To put the material, especially Part IV, into proper perspective nothing helps more than for each reader to conduct his own interview. Whether or not an instructor using this book asks his students to do this formally as part of the work of the course, we urge every student to practice listening to someone in the sense that the interviewer does in several of our cases. Indeed, we view an attempt to practice, to actually deal with the phenomena discussed, as essential to full understanding of the book. A reader cannot apprehend adequately the phenomena we seek to call to his attention simply by listening to others discuss them, even though he takes part in the discussions himself. Neither can he adequately dredge them up from his past experiences. He must do both these things constantly and well, but he must also look and look again with fresh eyes on new phenomena as they occur. He must himself try and try again the ways of thinking, feeling, assuming, perceiving, observing, and behaving that are being presented to him. Only then will he find his skill improving, as after trial he casts aside that which does not make sense to him and adapts and adopts that which does. Fortunately, as with all human behavior, the raw materials for practice are immediately, indeed inescapably, at hand.

Throughout the book we have been plagued with the problem of finding an appropriate sequence for the topics and the materials presented. The problem is what comes first. The ordering we have settled on is one we have used in the course for many years. We have no thought that it is a final one. Within limits, it has worked for us as teachers and for many of our students, and we would like to see it tested in a wider audience.

The fact that there is an ordering raises problems for many students. They do not see why one topic comes before another and hence why they are being asked to answer one question rather than another. In a way, of course, they cannot make sense of our ordering until they have been through the whole course. We find that this problem is particularly intense for students who like to discuss what should be done about a problem in the case early in the course. In real life a person who persistently manifests such attitudes in his behavior rapidly is placed in the role of "Mr. Fix-It" and his influence on others is walled off. Similar sanctions do not always prevail in the classroom, and even bright students sometimes persist in the belief that they can "fix" other people's lives and behavior. (Indeed such an assumption seems to us deeply implanted in much of the current literature about executive behavior.) We find it important that these views be expressed in class. If they were not, their shortcomings as general solutions could not be fully realized; hence, if they are not brought up, we may bring them up. At the same time, telling students being trained as action leaders to suspend *action* until they have acquired more *understanding* poses a dilemma for them as students as well as for us as teachers; we have no good answer for it, except to get on with the course. We ask our students to be patient. We tell them we will get to the action question eventually. We tell them this in many ways, on many occasions. We wheedle them, cajole them, and tease them into looking, listening, and thinking about the complexities of human behavior, even in simple situations as presented here, before we go on to talk about what could be done in the situations. The notion that, before reacting to puzzling interpersonal events, it is helpful to stop, look, and listen carefully to what is going on is, in our view, a very important lesson for all of us to learn.

Cambridge, Mass.

ARTHUR N. TURNER

GEORGE F. F. LOMBARD

Acknowledgments

We wish to acknowledge most gratefully the many ways in which a large number of persons have contributed to this book. The contributions of three groups are especially important.

First, we thank the authors and publishers who have given us permission to use the readings listed in the text.

Second, for permission to present the happenings described in the cases, we thank the persons who helped us to secure the material, as well as their colleagues to whom reference is made. Their willingness to let their behavior be described and studied by others contributes as importantly to this book as do the ideas of those on whose writings we have drawn.

Third, we are also most grateful to the many students in our courses who struggled with us as we sought to achieve an orderly sequence for the presentation of the ideas with which we have worked. Their questions and comments have helped us to be explicit in regard to many important points.

For the opportunity to teach the course at the Harvard Business School from which this book results, we wish to thank Deans Donald K. David, Stanley F. Teele, and George P. Baker, and Associate Dean Russell H. Hassler. Without their generous support and that of the Faculty of the School the course could not have been given nor this book written. We are especially grateful to Fritz Roethlisberger, who with Harriet Ronken and Paul R. Lawrence, as explained in the Preface, started the course from which the book results. Many other colleagues in the study of behavior in organizations at the School have contributed generously of their ideas and criticisms.

Our assistants, also named in the Preface, as well as Joseph C. Bailey, Alex Bavelas, Harriet Ronken, Vincent M. Jolivet, Thomas C. Raymond, Robert K. Ready, and William J. Dickson, helped prepare the case material. We are most grateful to them.

Andrew R. Towl, Charles N. Gebhard, Jean S. Burleson, and Eleanor F. Goodale, as they have done for so many others, processed the release for publication of the case material.

Mabel T. Gragg took charge of the manuscript and galleys at a time when one of the authors was out of the country. She completed their preparation for publication with competence and devotion "beyond the call of duty."

Jean N. Neal and Mary Thompson did the original typing and secretarial work on the manuscript. Jane Clark and Janet Weaver cheerfully assisted in the final stages.

We are grateful to our families for help and assistance of still other kinds.

For the errors of omission and commission that occur in the book in spite of this valued assistance, we are solely responsible.

PART I Communication in an organizational relationship

CHAPTER 1. Purposes and methods

The objectives of this book and the needs of those who use it require at the outset that we attempt to be as clear as possible about what our purposes are in presenting this material, what methods and procedures we propose for studying these cases, and what some of the unintended as well as intended consequences of using this book may be.

All the cases that follow illustrate the problems of interpersonal communication in the accomplishment of organizational tasks and in the satisfaction of human needs. A useful first step in analyzing these cases is to ask yourself these questions:

1. What are the *intentions* of A, B, C (specific people in the case)?

2. What is the *behavior* of these same people, and how is it related to their intentions?

3. What are the outcomes or *consequences* of this behavior, and how are they related to the intentions and behavior that has led to them?

4. What orderly patterns are there in these relations between intentions, behavior, and consequences?

These apparently simple questions illustrate the frame of mind in which we attempt to understand the processes of communication in formal organizations with which this book is concerned. We assume that whether the outcomes of interpersonal behavior are in line with the intentions that people bring to their interactions varies from one instance to another. We are mainly interested in understanding why this is so.

In this effort we try to keep our questions and concepts as simple and straightforward, as close to the "territory" of behavior, as we can, introducing more complex and subtle considerations not for the sake of theoretical eloquence but only as required for more useful understanding. So we start by proposing three simple categories for case analysis:

Intentions
Behavior
Consequences

Partly to illustrate what we mean by these three words, we shall now use them to clarify the purposes, methods, and possible results of this course.

Intentions

In general, this book provides practice in understanding what takes place when people attempt or need to communicate with each other within an organizational context. That is to say, we are concerned with understanding processes of interpersonal communication. To highlight these processes, to study them under a microscope, so to speak, we shall be concerned in particular with cases in which two people are involved in an organizational relationship and in which at least one of them feels a responsibility for improving their joint performance of some task.

An important assumption underlying our purpose has to do with the relationships between "knowledge" and "skill," and between "theory" and "practice."[1] The need for increasingly adequate knowledge and theory about interpersonal relationships is tremendous, and we hope this book contributes something to meeting it. But the major focus here will be on the exercise of skill in the utilization of knowledge, on the practice of person-to-person communication rather than on its theory. Consequently,

[1] See Joseph C. Bailey, "Introduction," in Paul R. Lawrence and John S. Seiler, *Organizational Behavior and Administration* (Homewood, Ill.: R. D. Irwin and the Dorsey Press, 1965).

this book is highly selective in the knowledge and theory with which it deals. It offers a relatively large amount of practice in utilizing a relatively small number of ideas and concepts, selected according to the following criterion: which findings and concepts of interpersonal behavior are (in our opinion) most likely to help a person in a position of responsibility in an organization acquire more skill in his relationships with others with whom he must work?

Practice in the acquisition of skillful behavior in organizational relationships is, then, a central intention underlying the design of the book. But we are well aware that the phrase *skillful behavior* is open to much misinterpretation. For us the words have a very simple meaning: behavior which results in fewer unintended consequences. As we use the word *skillful*, we do not see anything sinister or selfishly manipulative about the notion that any member of an organization who has to work with other people needs to behave *skillfully* in his relationships with them. Without some skill, in this sense, little of the world's work would get done. With more of it, we believe, most organizations could accomplish their tasks more effectively and at the same time fulfill more of the human needs and aspirations of their members. Further, for us the practice of interpersonal skill (or competence) has nothing to do with acquiring tricks or gimmicks. Following Roethlisberger, we conceive of skill as a unified pattern of response that is both appropriate to the particular situation within which an individual must behave and congruent with his concept of himself. According to this way of thinking, interpersonal skill becomes "an internal way of learning, not an external technique to be learned."[2]

The central intention that we want to keep in mind, then, is to provide practice in acquiring *useful ways of learning* about interpersonal relationships (our own as well as other people's) in organizational settings. For whom are these ways of learning intended, and in what sense are they meant to be "useful"?

In one sense, at least from the authors' point of view, the book is intended for everyone, as it is concerned with a universal

[2] See readings from F. J. Roethlisberger *et al.*, *Training for Human Relations* (Boston: Division of Research, Graduate School of Business Administration, Harvard University, 1954), reproduced in Part V.

human process, but it does concentrate, as we have said, on a more restricted setting for the study of communication, namely interpersonal relations within formal organizations. Not all interpersonal processes are studied, but mainly those which are relevant to collaborative effort in the accomplishment of organizational objectives. Human relationships *at work* are the focus of our study, although other kinds of relationships (e.g., psychological counseling) are examined for their relevance to this central interest.

Primarily but not exclusively, in other words, the book is intended for the student of the practice of administration who believes that it is important, and not easy, to increase his ability to understand the other persons with whom he will work, and to understand a little better than he now does what happens when they try to communicate with him. From his previous study of administration, he has acquired some ability to diagnose human situations and some ideas about the kinds of relationships he would like to work toward in his own organizational life. He has learned that, at least to a certain extent, effective *action* for an administrator requires skillful *interaction*, and his previous diagnoses of organizational problems have led him to want to be able to interact more effectively. He may believe that the most important and most difficult leadership challenge, when faced with behavior on the part of someone else which seems inadequate, is not so much to know how to change the behavior of the other persons as it is to examine how he himself might behave more adequately. As a consequence of beliefs and motives of this kind, our student needs to be willing to examine in microscopic detail what happens when one person tries to communicate with another because he feels that a better understanding of this process will contribute to better achievement of organizational objectives and personal needs.

Perhaps some further distinctions are in order between what the book intends, on the one hand, and what it might seem to be but isn't, on the other. It is not a study of general semantics, or psychology, or counseling; it *is* a volume that draws together from these and other disciplines certain concepts that are relevant to the interpersonal skill an administrator (or any responsible member of an organization) needs to practice. It is not a discussion of ways of judging the adequacy or inadequacy of someone else's behavior from an external frame of reference, or ways of deciding what ought to be done to someone else. For example, the discussion will not stay on the level of should Mr. B. (a person in the case) be fired, promoted, reprimanded, praised, and so on. Nor will we be too concerned with ways of altering the organizational structure, objectives, rules, or procedures in order to deal with or eliminate a particular interpersonal problem. In practice these are often very relevant questions, and they will undoubtedly be raised in discussions of many of the cases which follow, but we shall not focus on them. Instead, we shall often accept as *given* a great deal in the organizational environment of a specific two-person interaction that in real life (and certainly in fantasy) we should like to change. Then—and often this may be frustrating—we shall go on to examine in detail how, *within* these given organizational and other limits, person *A* could behave so as to improve his understanding of what takes place when he and person *B* try to communicate with each other.

In comparison with most studies in the general area of organizational behavior, human relations, or even interpersonal communication, the point of view just described may appear unduly narrow and restrictive. With so many things in the real world that need to be improved why should we accept as given so much that lies outside a particular interaction? Why should we spend so much time on what takes place within these constraints when one person tries to talk with another? Because, in a larger sense, misunderstandings between people plague our world, and the procedure proposed here is designed to achieve some improvement in our understanding of why this is so and what can be done about it, one very small step at a time. And because, in a smaller sense, most of what each of us will be able to achieve and to learn that is useful to us will come about through interacting, through listening with understanding to other people. We can sum up our intentions by asking: How else, except through person-to-person interaction, does most of the world's work get done? How else, except through improving our understanding of this process, can we learn what we need to learn from each other?

The simplification we propose in concentrating on some aspects of a situation and ignoring others is the kind of simplification necessary at the beginning of any study. To understand phenomena effectively one cannot begin by studying them in their full complexity. One abstracts tentatively, cautiously, and must never forget the limits that his abstractions impose. In saying all this, our aim is to make our intentions clear, not to offer them for debate. For us, in this book at least and in these cases, our intentions are to be tested not in debate but in the consequences of the processes of study that are to be followed.

Behavior

Intentions of the sort we have been describing do not necessarily imply only one pattern of behavior. Depending on the individual and the circumstances, there are many different kinds of activities that might be designed to meet such objectives. Some choices among the various alternatives that could be considered have already been made in the design of this book, for example in the sequence of topics and concepts which are taken up, and in the selection of cases and readings. Within these limits, we hope that instructors and students will experiment with various ways of utilizing this material. But here we would like to say something about the behavior on our readers' part which in *our* experience seems to fit most aptly the intentions we have in mind.

We hope readers of this book will take the material in it seriously enough but not too seriously. Some of the behavior described in the cases, for example, will appear ludicrous, but we will want to take it seriously, in the sense of trying to understand it, and not just laugh it away. At other times events will occur in the cases and in the discussion of them that are serious and difficult, and at these times it will be helpful not to lose our sense of humor. We want to retain our ability to be amused by what is serious and to be serious about what is amusing. Above all, whatever the topic being considered, we want to learn to interact with each other—authors with reader, instructor with student, and student with student—in ways that are mutually helpful. This means that

we hope teachers and students alike will apply to their own behavior in the classroom the ways of interacting and learning with
which this book is concerned.

What attitude is best taken toward the ideas and concepts
presented in the readings (chapters from other books, reprints, and
other textual material) that are an integral part of the book?
These ideas and concepts are intended to be *used*, but not necessarily all of them by each of us, since some of them will make more
sense to some of us than others. They should be considered carefully, not blindly accepted. Ideas and concepts in the readings
should be *applied* to the cases, and in this way given a fair trial. It
is especially important for each of us to discover his *own* ways of
utilizing (and sometimes rejecting as not useful to him) the ideas
and concepts of the book by applying them to the behavior in the
cases. And if these ideas and concepts are valid they should be
applicable to behavior in the classroom as well as to the behavior
described in the cases themselves.

Perhaps something else can usefully be said at this point
about how we would like our students to prepare for discussion of
the cases we have selected. Some overall scheme for analysis is
helpful in sorting out the relevant data in a case. The scheme we
have already presented is as good a place to start as any:

Intentions ↔ Behavior ↔ Consequences

Here we have put the three categories in a straight line with
doubleheaded arrows connecting them to indicate that what is
relevant is how they are each related to the other. Behavior may
affect intentions just as intentions affect behavior, and we view
the relationship between behavior and consequences as also a
two-way street. Also the outcomes of one set of interactions may
affect the intentions with which another is begun, so that the
pattern of the previous interactions may be repeated and reinforced in subsequent contacts.

People in the cases, as in real life, often are not clear about
their intentions, and the actual consequences are often unknown.
But it is a useful exercise to study the described behavior of the key
people carefully, note its important characteristics, *infer* back from
the described behavior what the individual's intentions seem to

have been, and *predict* what the consequences will be and how related to the intentions which have been inferred. Such a procedure will at least enable a better distinction to be made between what is known and what is not known (i.e., has to be inferred or predicted) concerning the behavior in the case. And often it may provide ideas for useful thought and discussion about what contributes to the frequent occurrence of unintended as well as intended consequences in human affairs.

But we do not intend to stay only at the level of analysis indicated by this general scheme. Other conceptual ideas and analytical approaches will be introduced as we proceed, and it is always helpful to experiment with more than one way of analyzing a particular case. Another approach, which will become familiar later on, can be simply described at the outset as follows. Most of the cases focus on the interaction of two people in a particular organizational context (see Figure 1).

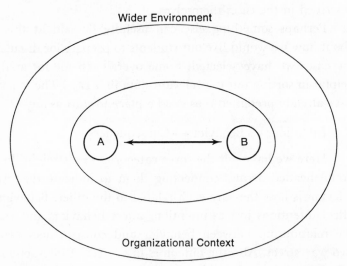

Figure 1

As indicated by the Contents and Preface, these two-person relationships will be looked at in order to discover useful answers to at least the following kinds of questions:

1. What interferes with *A* and *B* understanding each other? (Parts I and II)

2. How can *A* understand *B* better? (Part III)

Part I.   Communication in an organizational relationship

3. How can *A* help *B* to understand the situation better? (Part IV)

4. How can *A* help bring about a productive relationship with *B* within an organizational context and given a particular organizational purpose? (Part V)

5. How can *A* grow to take account more skillfully of the influence of his own involvement in the situation (e.g., of his own feelings about it) on his ability to understand it? (Part V)

As can be seen, these are progressively more complex and ambitious questions, and we will certainly not attempt to answer them all at once. We begin and stay with a central and more easily stated challenge: Can we achieve a better *understanding* of what takes place between two individuals in a particular case? In such a case we need to consider the influence on the relevant interaction between *A* and *B* of their organizational relationship and other people and pressures in the organization as a whole, as these in turn are influenced by the organization's own external environment. But primarily, as we said earlier, the focus is on the interaction between *A* and *B* that takes place within the organizational and environmental limits that are accepted as *given* for purposes of analysis. We need, then, a simple way to begin thinking about such two-person interactions, and in studying them we are always interested not only in each person's explicit behavior in relation to the other, but also in how each *perceives* the behavior. In other words we need to consider:

How person *A* views person *B*'s behavior toward *A*.
How person *B* views person *A*'s behavior toward *B*.
How each of them views his own behavior.

This way of perceiving such a two-person interaction can be diagrammed in such a way as to remind us that how *A* and *B* see and act toward each other is partially influenced by how each of them sees himself (see Figure 2). Further, as indicated by the broken diagonal arrows, the way either of them sees himself can partly be influenced directly by how the other behaves toward him, and not just through his (possibly distorted) perceptions of the other.

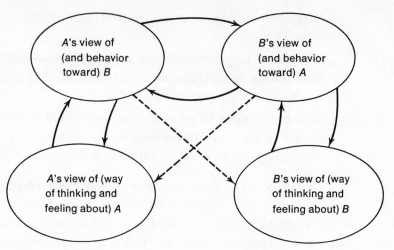

Figure 2

[*Note:* At the abstract level we are talking here, it is difficult to communicate clearly. Try working some concrete case data into this scheme and it will make more sense. For example, in Case I–1, start by simply making a list of the views of Mr. Hart and Bing about each other and about themselves. Then see how these four sets of perceptions are related to each other, noting especially how Hart's view of Bing is influenced by Hart's view of himself, and how Bing's view of Hart is influenced by Bing's view of himself. *After* conscientiously attempting this exercise you will understand, we believe, the phenomena this scheme is designed to direct your attention to.]

The purpose of sorting out (and, when necessary, making inferences about) how each person views his own and the other's participation in their relationship is to illustrate the influence on each person's behavior in the relationship of his need to maintain his beliefs about himself. There will be considerable emphasis on this process in later case discussions, since it helps to explain why the character of many interpersonal relationships tends to be self-reinforcing and thus resistant to change. A beginning toward understanding why this is so can be made by applying this simple scheme to some of the two-person relationships in the early cases.

During the discussion of these cases, it will be neither possible nor desirable to remain permanently in an analytical mood. None of us wants only to discuss why a given situation has developed. We want also a sense of more adequate control over what is happening in the present, so that our present actions may have a more dependable impact on what will happen next. We want to consider what different ways of behaving will result in different consequences from the ones we expect from our analysis of the existing behavior. We want to discuss what should be done differently, or what we would do if we were in the position of one of the people in the case. In other words, the "action question" will arise, hopefully *after* an adequate understanding of the existing situation has been achieved.

In considering these questions of "what to do" about the situation described in a case, it is important to notice the different ways in which action can be discussed. The discussion of any case may proceed on at least the following five levels, sometimes with an unfortunate lack of clarity as to which level is being used at a given time:

1. Descriptive.
2. Explanatory.
3. Predictive.
4. Normative.
5. Personal.

In other words, some of the statements made in a case discussion will be *descriptions* (with varying amounts of inference) of what took place in the case. Others will be attempts to *explain* the described behavior, or at least to understand it, e.g., by applying to the case description some more or less systematic analytical scheme. At other times the discussion may be primarily on a *predictive* level, focusing on what is likely to happen in the future, based on our understanding of what has happened so far. Discussion at this level is useful mostly as a check on previously attained understanding of the case. It sometimes throws unnoticed disagreements into prominence for further attention. However, there is a danger that *predictive* discussion will become mere idle speculation which, however enjoyable, is best cut short if the intended consequences of this book are to be avidly pursued.

Frequently the discussion may shift to a consideration of what should have been done differently in the past or ought to be done in the future in order to cope with some problem that is apparent from our analysis of the case. This is what we mean by the *normative* level: a statement not about what has happened or will happen but about what *should* be done. It is especially helpful to be aware of when a shift to a normative as distinguished from a descriptive or predictive statement has been made. Also it may be useful occasionally to ask for the origin of our ideas about what should be done, since most disagreements on normative questions arise from differences in values or assumptions about behavior that are not made explicit.

Finally there is the "personal" level of discourse in most case discussions, where what is meant is not "I believe something should be done" but rather, "If I were involved, with my values and abilities, in this case situation, here is what I would do." Such a personal frame of reference toward an action question leads away from debate concerning relatively abstract principles of behavior toward the difficult and unavoidable dilemmas of direct involvement in a concrete situation. For this reason, if no one else in a classroom situation raises a personal action question, the instructor may. But the main purpose of this distinction between the five kinds of statements that occur in a case discussion is not to compare their relative utility, since all have their place. The important point is to be aware of such differences, to be curious about which level of discourse is being used at any given time in a discussion, and to be able to ask each other, when confused, about which kind of statement is intended. By increasing our awareness of these distinctions we may increase our ability to understand and therefore learn from each other's points of view.

Consequences

The results, for any individual, of the intentions and behavior we have attempted to describe cannot be predicted with any confidence. But our experience suggests that many will eventually find that this course provides experiences that are personally valuable to them. There will be some gain in substantive knowledge about interpersonal relationships in organizations. There can be some gain in personal insight and self-understanding from the effort to understand others' efforts to communicate. And there can be a succession of steps, each small by itself but all together of real significance, in the direction of:

1. More understanding of the sources of misunderstanding between people who need to work together on a common task.

2. More appreciation of the complexity of such misunderstandings.

3. More skill in dealing with them in spite of their difficulty.

4. More ability to learn from your own interpersonal environment some useful lessons not only about others but also about yourself.

CASE I–1. Mr. Hart and Bing

[*Note on the classroom use of this case:* At least two class sessions are recommended for discussion of this short case. The case is presented in two versions, A and B. Version A presents Mr. Hart's point of view, and version B presents Bing's point of view. The instructor divides the class in half and assigns version A to one half and version B to the other. You should study only the version assigned to you, *without* reading either the other version of the case or Chapter 2, which follows it. Thus the discussion on the first day will be between the half of the class that knows only Mr. Hart's point of view and the half that knows only Bing's point of view; this may result in an instructive live case on communication between different viewpoints right in the classroom. Obviously if you should read both versions ahead of time, you would somewhat spoil the fun. For the second session we recommend you study both versions of the case and reflect on the previous class discussion. After the first or second class session on Mr. Hart and Bing, read Chapter 2, which uses an analysis of the case as a preview of the rest of the course.]

The shop situation reported in this case occurred in a work group of four men and three women who were engaged in testing and inspecting panels for electronic equipment. The employees were paid on a piecework incentive basis. The personnel organization of the company included a counselor whose duty it was to become acquainted with the workers and talk over any problems they wished to discuss with him. The following statements of the views of two men consist of excerpts from five interviews that the counselor had with each of them within a period of about two weeks.

Version A

A summarized statement of how Mr. Hart, the supervisor, felt:

> Say, I think you should be in on this. My dear little friend Bing is heading himself into a showdown with me. Recently it was brought to my attention by the Quality Control checker that Bing has been taking double and triple setup time for panels which he is actually inspecting at one time. In effect, that's cheatin', and I've called him down on it several times before. A few days ago it was brought to my attention again, and so this time I really let him have it in no uncertain terms. He's been getting away with this for too long and I'm gonna put an end to it once and for all. I know he didn't like my calling him on it because a few hours later he had the union representative breathin' down my back. But you know what talkin' to those people is like; they'll sometimes defend an employee, even though they think he's takin' advantage of the company. Well, anyway, I let them both know I'll not tolerate the practice any longer, and I let Bing know that if he continues to do this kind of thing, I'm gonna take official action with my boss to have the guy fired or penalized somehow. This kind of thing has to be curbed. Actually, I'm inclined to think the guy's mentally deficient, because talking to him has actually no meaning to him whatsoever. I've tried just

about every approach to jar some sense into that guy's head, and I've just about given it up as a bad deal. I just can't seem to make any kind of an impression upon him. It's an unpleasant situation for everyone concerned, but I'm at a loss to know what more I can do about it.

I don't know what it is about the guy, but I think he's harboring some deep feelings against me. For what, I don't know, 'cause I've tried to handle that bird with kid gloves. But his whole attitude around here on the job is one of indifference, and he certainly isn't a good influence on the rest of my group. Frankly, I think he purposely tries to agitate them against me at times, too. It seems to me he may be suffering from illusions of grandeur, 'cause all he does all day long is sit over there and croon his fool head off. Thinks he's a Frank Sinatra! No kidding! I understand he takes singin' lessons and he's working with some of the local bands in the city. All of which is OK by me; but when his outside interests start interfering with his efficiency on the job, then I've gotta start paying closer attention to the situation. For this reason I've been keepin' my eye on that bird and if he steps out of line any more, he and I are gonna part ways.

I feel quite safe in saying that I've done all I can rightfully be expected to do by way of trying to show him what's expected of him. You know there's an old saying, "You can't make a purse out of a sow's ear." The guy is simply unscrupulous. He feels no obligation to do a real day's work. Yet I know the guy can do a good job, because for a long time he did. But in recent months, he's slipped for some reason and his whole attitude on the job has changed. Why, it's even getting to the point now where I think he's inducing other employees to "goof off" a few minutes before the lunch whistle and go down to the washrooms and clean up on company time. I've called him on it several times, but words just don't seem to make any lasting impression on him. Well, if he keeps it up much longer, he's gonna find himself on the way out. He's asked me for a transfer, so I know he wants to go. But I didn't give him an answer when he asked me, 'cause I was steamin' mad at the time, and I may have told him to go somewhere else.

I think it would be good for you to talk with him frequently. It'll give him a chance to think the matter through a little more carefully. There may be something that's troubling him in his personal life, although I've made every effort to find out if there was such a thing, and I've been unsuccessful. Maybe you'll have better luck.

Version B

A summarized statement of how Bing felt:

According to the system 'round here, as I understand it, I am allowed so much "set-up" time to get these panels from the racks, carry them over here to the bench and place them in this jig here, which holds them in position while I inspect them. For convenience' sake and also to save time, I sometimes manage to carry two or three over at the same time and inspect them all at the same time. This is a perfectly legal thing to do. We've always been doing it. Mr. Hart, the supervisor, has other ideas about it, though; he claims it's cheating the company. He came over to the bench a day or two ago and let me know just how he felt about the matter. Boy, did we go at it! It wasn't so much the fact that he called me down on it, but more the way in which he did it. He's a sarcastic bastard. I've never seen anyone like him. He's not content just to say in a manlike way what's on his mind, but he prefers to do it in a way that makes you want to crawl inside a crack in the floor. What a guy! I don't mind being called down by a supervisor, but I like to be treated like a man, and not humiliated like a school teacher does a naughty kid. He's been pullin' this stuff ever since he's been a supervisor. I knew him when he was just one of us, but since he's been promoted he's lost his friendly way and seems to be havin' some difficulty in knowin' how to manage us employees. In fact, I've noticed that he's been more this way with us fellows since he's gotten married. I dunno whether there's any connection there, but I do know he's a changed man over what he used to be like when he was a worker on the bench with us several years ago.

When he pulled this kind of stuff on me the other day, I got so damn mad I called in the union representative. I knew that the thing I was doing was permitted by the contract, but I was just intent on making some trouble for Mr. Hart, just because he persists in this sarcastic way of handling me. I'm about fed up with the whole damn situation. I'm tryin' every means I can to get myself transferred out of his group. If I don't succeed and I'm forced to stay on here, I'm going to screw him every way I can. He's not gonna pull this kind of kid stuff any longer on me. When the union representative questioned him on the case, he finally had to back down, 'cause according to the contract an employee can use any timesaving method or device in order to speed up the process as long as the quality standards of the job are met. During the discussion with me and the union representative, Mr. Hart charged that it was a dishonest practice and threatened to "take it up the line" unless the union would curb me on this practice.

But this was just an idle threat, 'cause the most he can do is get me transferred out of here, which is actually what I want anyway.

You see, he knows that I do professional singing on the outside. He hears me singin' here on the job, and he hears the people talkin' about my career in music. I guess he figures I can be so cocky because I have another means of earning some money. Actually, the employees here enjoy havin' me sing while we work, but he thinks I'm disturbing them and causing them to "goof off" from their work. It's funny, but for some reason I think he's partial to the three female employees in our group. He's the same with all us guys as he is to me, but with the girls he acts more decent. I don't know what his object is. Occasionally, I leave the job a few minutes early and go down to the washroom to wash up before lunch. Sometimes several others in the group will accompany me, and so Mr. Hart automatically thinks I'm the leader and usually bawls me out for the whole thing.

So, you can see, I'm a marked man around here. He keeps watchin' me like a hawk. Naturally this makes me very uncomfortable. That's why I'm sure a transfer would be the best thing. I've asked him for it, but he didn't give me any satisfaction at the time. While I remain here I'm gonna keep my nose clean, but whenever I get the chance I'm gonna slip it to him, but good.

CHAPTER 2. Analyzing interpersonal communication — A preview

Note: This chapter is designed to be read *after* you have studied and discussed the preceding case, "Mr. Hart and Bing." The purpose of this chapter is to further illustrate the problem of achieving a useful understanding of what hinders and what facilitates interpersonal communication in administrative settings. We shall do this by reviewing the case of Mr. Hart and Bing. We intend our discussion of this case to serve as a preview of the four main topics which are considered in the remaining parts of this book: "Sources of Misunderstanding," "Understanding Another Person's Behavior," "Helping Another Person Understand His Behavior," and "Organizational Relations and Interpersonal Skill."

Like many of the cases in this book, "Mr. Hart and Bing" can be used as a basis for considering each of these four topic areas. Before using the case in this way, however, we excerpt here an analysis of the case which was written by Fritz J. Roethlisberger for The 1953 Alfred Korzybski Memorial Lecture before the Institute of General Semantics and subsequently published in the *Harvard Business Review.*

The administrator's skill: Communication[1]

... What is taking place when two people engaged in a common task interact? What do the actors involved perceive is taking place, what is

[1] Excerpted, by permission, from Fritz J. Roethlisberger, "The Administrator's Skill: Communication," *Harvard Business Review* 31, No. 6 (November–December 1953), 55–62. Copyright © 1953 by the President and Fellows of Harvard College; all rights reserved.

a useful way for the executive to think about these interpersonal proceedings in which he is engaged, and what skills can he practice which will make him more effective as an administrator of people?

In this article I want to discuss these questions in terms of a specific, down-to-earth case in an industrial plant—a case of misunderstanding between two people, a worker and a foreman. (It is not important that they happen to be foreman and worker; to all intents and purposes they might as well be superintendent and foreman or, for that matter, controller and accountant.) . . .

A CASE OF MISUNDERSTANDING

In a department of a large industrial organization there were seven workers (four men and three women) engaged in testing and inspecting panels of electronic equipment. In this department one of the workers, Bing, was having trouble with his immediate supervisor, Hart, who had formerly been a worker in the department.

Had we been observers in this department we would have seen Bing carrying two or three panels at a time from the racks where they were stored to the bench where he inspected them together. For this activity we would have seen him charging double or triple setup time. We would have heard him occasionally singing at work. Also we would have seen him usually leaving his work position a few minutes early to go to lunch, and noticed that other employees sometimes accompanied him. And had we been present at one specific occasion, we would have heard Hart telling Bing that he disapproved of these activities and that he wanted Bing to stop doing them. . . .

[After this introduction, Roethlisberger reproduces the separate points of view of Mr. Hart and Bing essentially as you have already studied them. His analysis then continues as follows.]

VIEWS OF MISUNDERSTANDING

So much for the case. Let me start with the simplest but the toughest question first: "What is going on here?" I think most of us would agree that what seems to be going on is some misunderstanding between Hart and Bing. But no sooner do we try to represent to ourselves the nature of this misunderstanding than a flood of different theories appear. Let me discuss briefly five very common ways of representing this misunderstanding: (1) as a difference of opinion resolvable by common sense, by simply referring to the facts; (2) as a clash of personalities; (3) as a conflict of social roles; (4) as a struggle for power; and (5) as a breakdown in communication. There are, of course, other theories too—for example, those of the interactionists, the field theory of Kurt Lewin, and even the widely held views of Adam Smith or Karl Marx. But for our purposes here the five I have mentioned will suffice.

● *Common Sense*

For the advocates of common sense—the first theory, though most of them would not call it that—the situation resolves itself quickly:

> Either Hart is right or Bing is right. Since both parties cannot be right, it follows that if Hart is right, then Bing is wrong; or if Bing is right, then Hart is wrong. Either Bing should or should not be singing on the job, carrying two or three panels at a time and charging double or triple setup time, and so on.

"Let us get these facts settled first," say the common-sense advocates. "Once ascertained, the problem is easily settled. Once we know who is doing what he should not be doing, then all we have to do is to get this person to do what he should be doing. It's as simple as that."

But is it? Let us look again at our case. Let us note that there are no differences of opinion between Hart and Bing about some matters. For example both would agree that Bing is taking double or triple setup time when he carries his panels two or three at a time to his bench for inspection. Both would agree that Bing sings on the job and occasionally leaves his work place a bit early for lunch.

Where they differ is in the way each *perceives* these activities. Hart perceives Bing's activities as "cheating," "suffering from illusions of grandeur," "thinking he is Frank Sinatra," "interfering with Bing's efficiency as well as the efficiency of other workers," "disturbing the other workers," "inducing them to goof off," and "influencing them against [Hart]." To Bing, on the other hand, these activities are "perfectly legal," "something we've always been doing," "something that is not disturbing the other workers," and so forth.

Among these many different conflicting claims and different perceptions, what are the facts? Many of these evaluations refer to personal and social standards of conduct for which the company has no explicit rules. Even in the case of taking double and triple setup time, there are probably no clear rules, because when the industrial engineer set the standards for the job, he did not envisage the possibility of a worker doing what Bing is now doing and which, according to Bing, is a time-saving device.

But we can waste effort on this question. For, even if it were clear that Hart is not exploring the situation, that he is not getting these important facts or rules which would settle who is right and who is wrong, it would still be true that, so far as Hart is concerned, he *knows* who is right and who is wrong. And because he *knows*, he has no reason to question the assumptions he is making about Bing's behavior.

Now this is very likely to happen in the case of advocates of the common-sense theory. Significantly, Hart himself is a good advocate of it. Does this have anything to do with the fact that he is not being very successful in getting Bing to do what he should be doing? Let us postpone this question for future consideration.

● *Clash of Personalities*

For the second school of thought, what is going on between Hart and Bing can be viewed essentially as a clash of personalities—an interaction between two particular personality structures. According to this view, what is going on cannot be known in detail until much more information about these different personality structures is secured. Hence we can only speculate that what is going on may be something of this order:

> Neither Hart nor Bing feels too sure of himself, and each seems to be suffering from feelings of inadequacy or inferiority. Being unable to recognize, admit, or accept these feelings, however, each one perceives the behavior of the other as a personal attack upon himself. When a person feels he is being attacked, he feels strongly the need to defend himself. This, then, is essentially what is taking place between Hart and Bing. Because of his feelings of inferiority, each one is defending himself against what he perceives to be an attack upon himself as a person. In psychology, the feelings of each man are conceived as being rooted somehow in his "personality."

That this theory is pointing to some very important phenomena can hardly be questioned. Certainly I will not argue its validity. I am only concerned with what it is telling us and what follows from it. As I understand it, this theory says that neither Hart nor Bing is aware of his own feelings of inadequacy and defense mechanisms. These are the important facts that each is ignoring. From this it follows that there is little hope of correcting the misunderstanding without helping Bing and Hart to become aware of these feelings and of their need to defend against them. Short of this, the solution lies in transferring Bing to a supervisor whose personality will be more compatible with Bing's, and in giving Hart a worker whose personality will be more compatible with Hart's.

● *Conflict of Social Roles*

Let us look at the third explanation. Instead of viewing the misunderstanding as an interaction between two individual personality units, it can also be viewed as an interaction between two social roles:

With the promotion of Hart to the position of a supervisor of a group in which he had been formerly a worker, a system of reciprocal expectancies has been disturbed. Bing is expecting Hart to behave toward him in the same way Hart did when Hart was a worker; but by telling Bing to stop "crooning his fool head off," for example, Hart is not behaving in accordance with the role of a friend. Similarly, Hart, as the newly appointed supervisor, is expecting that Bing should do what he tells Bing to do, but by singing Bing is not behaving in accordance with the customary role of the worker.

According to this theory, as any recent textbook on sociology will explain, when two actors in a relationship reach differing definitions of the situation, misunderstanding is likely to arise. Presumably this is what is happening between Hart and Bing. The role-expectation pattern has been disturbed. Bing views his singing as variant but permissive; Hart views it as deviant. From these differing definitions of what each other's role should be misunderstanding results. According to this view, it will take time for their new relationship to work out. In time Bing will learn what to expect from Hart now that Hart is his supervisor. Also in time Hart will define better his role *vis-à-vis* Bing.

● *Struggle for Power*

The fourth way of representing what is going on between Hart and Bing would be in terms of such abstractions as "authority" and "power":

> When Bing refuses to stop singing on the job when Hart tells him to, Bing is being disobedient to the commands or orders of a holder of power. When this occurs, Hart, who according to this theory is a "power holder," has the right to exercise or apply sanctions, such as dismissal or transfer. But the threat to exercise these sanctions does not seem to be too effective in getting Bing to stop, because Bing is a member of the union, which also has power and the right to apply sanctions. By going to his union representative, Bing can bring this power structure into play.

In other words, what is going on in the case is not merely an interaction between two individual or social personalities; it is also a struggle between two kinds of institutionalized power. It is an issue between the management and the union which may even precipitate a strike. Management will charge that it cannot have workers in the plant who are disobedient to the orders of their foremen. The union will charge that Bing is merely introducing a labor-saving device which the foreman has not enough sense to recognize. To avoid things getting to this stage, the struggle-for-power theory would recommend that if Hart and Bing between them cannot settle their differences, they should refer them to the grievance machinery set up for this purpose by union and management.

According to this theory, Hart got into trouble not because he had authority but because when he tried to exercise it and was unsuccessful, he lost it. Authority ceases to exist when it cannot be exercised successfully.[2]

● *Breakdown in Communication*

The fifth way of stating what is going on would be to say that Hart and Bing think they are talking about the same things when in fact they are not:

> Hart assumes he understands what Bing is doing and saying; Bing assumes he understands what Hart is doing and saying. In fact, neither assumption holds. From this "uncritical assumption of understanding," misunderstanding arises.
>
> Thus, when Hart tells Bing to stop "crooning his fool head off," Bing assumes that Hart is talking about Bing's singing when Hart may in fact be talking about his difficulties in maintaining his position as formal leader of the group. Hart assumes that Bing is singing deliberately to flaunt his authority, whereas in Bing's mind singing may be a way of relating himself to people and of maintaining his conceptions of himself.[3]

According to this theory, Hart and Bing are not on the same wave length, and as a result communication bypassing occurs. Each is behaving in accordance with the reality as he perceives it to be, but neither is aware of the assumptions that underlie his perceptions. Their misunderstandings arise as a result.

This theory strikes a new note that I should like to explore further.

ROOTS OF MISUNDERSTANDING

So far our theories have explained well why there is misunderstanding and conflict; they have not shown so clearly how any new behavior patterns on the part of Hart or Bing or both can emerge or be encouraged to emerge from the present ones. In them we have found no responsible actor, no learner, and no practitioner of a skill.

Could it be that what is going on between Hart and Bing results also in part from the fact that nobody is taking any responsibility for

---

[2] For an elaboration of this view see Robert Bierstedt, "An Analysis of Social Power," in *The American Sociological Review* (December 1950), 730.

[3] For an analysis of this theory see Wendell Johnson, "The Fateful Process of Mr. A Talking to Mr. B," *Harvard Business Review* (January–February 1953), 49.

what is going on? May we not assume that people can learn through experience how to determine their relationships with each other as well as be determined by them? Let us therefore look at these interpersonal proceedings from the point of view of a person who is responsibly involved in them and who may be capable of learning something from them. . . .

From now on I shall be chiefly concerned with Hart, not because I think Hart is any more or less guilty than Bing of creating misunderstanding, but because I wish to develop a useful way of thinking for persons in a position of responsibility like Hart. This way of thinking, I hope, will not be in conflict with our other theories. It will merely spell out what a supervisor must learn if he is to take into account the significant processes which these other theories say have been going on.

So, instead of viewing Hart in his dealings with Bing as a supervisor expressing his personality, playing a social role, or exercising power, let us view him as a practitioner of a skill of communication. Let us see what skills, if any, he is using. And if we find, as I fear we may, that he has not been too skillful, let us see if he can learn to become a more skillful practitioner, and how this can be done.

● *Hart's Trouble*

When we ask ourselves what Hart is doing to facilitate misunderstanding, we meet again a number of different theories. Although I am not sure that these theories are pointing to different things, each uses a slightly different terminology, so I shall state them separately:

1. *Hart is making value judgments*—According to one view, the biggest block to personal communication arises from the fact that Hart is making value judgments of Bing from Hart's point of view. Hart's tendency to evaluate is what gets him into trouble. Not only is he evaluating Bing, but he is trying to get Bing to accept his evaluation as the only and proper one. It is the orientation that angers Bing and makes him feel misunderstood.[4]

2. *Hart is not listening*—According to another and not too different view, Hart gets into trouble because he is not listening to Bing's feelings. Because he is not paying attention to Bing's feelings, he is not responding to them as such. Instead, we find him responding to the effect of Bing's feelings upon his own. Not only is he ignoring Bing's feelings, but also he is ignoring the effect of what he is saying upon

[4] See Carl R. Rogers and F. J. Roethlisberger, "Barriers and Gateways to Communication," in *Harvard Business Review* (July–August 1952), 46–50 [reproduced in Part II].

them. This kind of behavior also leads to Bing's feelings of being misunderstood.[5]

3. *Hart is assuming things that may not be so*—Still another point of view says that Hart is getting into trouble because he is making assumptions about Bing's behavior that may not be so. Hart is confusing what he sees with what he assumes and feels.

When Hart sees Bing leaving early for lunch, for example, he assumes that Bing is doing this deliberately, intentionally, and personally to discredit him and to test his authority. Because of this assumption he feels angry and his feelings of anger reinforce his assumption. Now if Bing's going to lunch a few minutes early is such an attempt to discredit him, then Hart's anger and his attempt to retaliate make sense. But if he starts with this assumption and makes no attempt to check it, then his anger makes less sense. Hart may be assuming something that is not so.

Again, Hart shows he may be making assumptions that are not so by the way he talks in trying to get Bing to stop singing at work or to stop inspecting panels two or three at a time. When he uses phrases like "crooning your fool head off" and "cheating the company," is he not assuming that Bing should feel about these activities in the same way that he himself does? And if Bing does not feel this way, then obviously, in Hart's view, Bing must be a "fool," "defective," or a "sow's ear." To Hart, Bing *is* a sow's ear. And how does one feel toward a sow's ear? Toward such an entity one must feel (by definition) helpless and hopeless. Note that Hart's assumptions, perceptions, and feelings are of a piece; each reinforces the other to make one total evaluation.

In short, all of Hart's evaluations are suspect because he confuses what he sees with what he assumes and feels. As a result, there is no way for Hart to take another look at the situation. How can Hart check his evaluations when he is not aware that he is making them? By treating inferences as facts, there is no way for him to explore the assumptions, feelings, and perceptions that underlie his evaluations.[6] For Hart, Bing *is* the way he perceives Bing to be. There is no way for him to say that "because of the assumptions I make and because of the way I feel, I perceive Bing in this way."

4. *Hart is making his false assumptions come true*—A fourth theory emphasizes still another point. This theory says that the very kind of misevaluations which our last theory says Hart is guilty of must provoke *ipso facto* the very kind of behavior on the part of Bing of which

---

[5] Ibid., pp. 50–52.
[6] For a fuller explanation see Irving Lee, *How to Talk with People* (New York: Harper & Brothers, 1953).

Hart disapproves.[7] In other words, Hart is getting into trouble because, by his behavior, he is making his assumptive world come true.

Let us examine this theory first by looking at the effect of Hart's behavior on Bing. Very clearly Bing does not like it. Bing tells us that when Hart behaves in the way Hart does, he feels misunderstood, humiliated, and treated like a child. These feelings give grounds to his perception of Hart as "a sarcastic bastard," "a school teacher" pulling "kid stuff" on him. These perceptions in turn will tend to make Bing behave in the way that will coincide more and more with Hart's original untested assumptions about Bing's behavior. Feeling like a "marked man," Bing will behave more and more like a "sow's ear." Although he will try to "keep his nose clean," he will "slip it to [Hart], but good" whenever he gets the chance.

That this kind of misevaluation on the part of Hart will tend to produce this kind of behavior on the part of Bing is, according to this view, a fact of common experience. To explain it one does not have to assume any peculiar personality structure on the part of Bing—an undue sensitivity to criticism, defensiveness, or feeling of inferiority. All one has to assume is an individual personality with a need to maintain its individuality. Therefore, any attempts on the part of Hart which will be perceived by Bing as an attempt to deny his individual differences will be resisted. What Hart says about Bing is, from Bing's point of view, exactly what he is *not*. Bing *is* what he is from his own frame of reference and from the point of view of his own feelings, background, and situation. Bing *is* what he assumes, feels, and perceives himself to be. And this is just what Hart's behavior is denying.

In spite of the different terminology and emphasis of these theories, they all seem to point to certain uniformities in the interpersonal proceedings of Hart and Bing which should be taken into account regardless of the actors' particular personalities or social roles. For the misunderstandings that arise, Hart and Bing are not to blame; the trouble resides in the process of interpersonal communication itself. . . .

● *Problem of Involvement*

So far it would seem as if we had made Hart the villain in the piece. But let us remember that although Hart has been intellectually and emotionally involved in what has been going on, he has not been aware of this involvement. All of our theories have implied this. Hart's ego has been involved; his actual group memberships have been involved;

[7] For example, see Hadley Cantril, *The "Why" of Man's Experience* (New York: The Macmillan Company, 1950).

his reference groups have been involved; his feelings, assumptions, and perceptions have been involved—but Hart is not aware of it. If any new behavior on the part of Hart is to emerge—and *all* our theories would agree to this—Hart must in some sense become aware of and recognize this involvement. Without such an awareness there can be no reevaluation or no change in perception. And without such a change no learning can take place.

How can this change be accomplished? Some theories would seem to imply that misunderstanding will be minimized only when Hart *logically understands* the nature of his involvement with Bing. Hart will learn to evaluate Bing more properly only when he understands better the personality structures of himself and Bing and the social system of which they are a part. Only by the logical understanding and critical probing of his and Bing's feelings of inadequacy and defense mechanisms can he make a proper evaluation and bring about any real change in his behavior.

But there is another view. It holds that logical understanding is not of the first importance. Rather, misunderstanding will be minimized when Hart learns to *recognize and accept* responsibility for his involvement. Better understanding will be achieved when Hart learns to recognize and accept his own and Bing's individual differences, when he learns to recognize and accept Bing's feelings as being different from his own, and when as a result he can allow Bing to express his feelings and differences and listen to them.[8]

Let me explore this second theory further, for it suggests that Hart might possibly learn to do a better job without having to become a professional social scientist or be psychoanalyzed. Moreover, it coincides with some facts of common experience.

● How Can Hart Be Helped?

Some administrators have achieved the insights of the second theory through the school of "hard knocks" rather than through the help of books or by being psychoanalyzed. So should there not be simple skills which Hart can be taught, which he can learn and practice, and which would help him to recognize and accept his involvement and to deal with it better?

Now it may be that Hart, because of certain personal deficiencies, is not able to recognize or accept his own feelings—let alone Bing's. That this holds for some supervisors goes without question. But does it apply to all? I do not think so, nor do I think it applies to Hart. Is it not possible that some supervisors may not be able to do these things because they have never learned how to do them?

[8] For a fuller explanation see Carl R. Rogers, *Client-Centered Therapy* (Boston: Houghton Mifflin, 1953).

The fact is, if our analysis up to this point is sound, that Hart does not get into trouble because he feels hopeless and helpless in the face of a worker who sings on the job, leaves early for lunch, and so on, and who refuses to stop doing these things when Hart tells him to. Any one of us who has had to deal with a worker behaving like Bing will recognize and remember feelings of inadequacy like Hart's only too well. We do not need to have very peculiar or special personality structures to have such feelings. Rather, Hart's trouble is that he assumes, and no doubt has been told too often, that he should *not* have feelings of inadequacy. It resides in the fact that he has not developed or been given a method or skill for dealing with them. As a result, these feelings are denied and appear in the form of an attribute of Bing— "a sow's ear."

In other words, I am suggesting that Hart gets into trouble partly because no one has assured him that it is normal and natural—in fact, inevitable—that he should have some feelings of inadequacy; that he cannot and *should* not try to escape from them. No one has helped him to develop a method of dealing with his own feelings and the feelings of Bing. No one has listened to him or helped him to learn to listen to others. No one has helped him to recognize the effect of his behavior on others. No one has helped him to become aware of his assumptions and feelings and how they affect the evaluations he makes.

Instead, too many training courses have told Hart what an ideal supervisor should be and how an ideal supervisor should behave. Both explicit and implicit in most of the instruction he receives is the assumption that an ideal supervisor should not become emotionally involved in his dealings with people. He should remain aloof, be objective, and deny or get rid of his feelings. But this goes against the facts of his immediate experience; it goes against everything upon which, according to our theories, his growth and development depend. Indeed, to "behave responsibly" and be "mature" in the way he is instructed to, without becoming emotionally committed, would be, to use the *New Yorker*'s phrase, "the trick of the week!"

Is it any wonder, therefore, that Hart remains immature—socially, intellectually, and emotionally? He gets no understanding of how these frustrations and misunderstandings must inevitably arise from his dealings with others; he gets no help on how to deal with them when they do arise. He probably has had many training courses which told him how to recognize and deal with workers who are sow's ears. He probably has had no training course which helped him to see how his assumptions and feelings would tend to produce sow's ears by the bushel. He has not been helped to see how this surplus of sow's ears in modern industry might be diminished through the conscious practice of a skill. Thus he has not even been allowed to become intellectually involved and intrigued in the most important problem of his job. Yet there *are* training courses designed for just such a purpose, and they have worked successfully.[9]

CONCLUSION

Am I indulging in wishful thinking when I believe that there are some simple skills of communication that can be taught, learned, and practiced which might help to diminish misunderstanding? To me it is this possibility which the recent findings of general semantics and human relations are suggesting. They suggest that although man is determined by the complex relationships of which he is a part, nevertheless he is also in some small part a determiner of these relationships. Once he learns what he cannot do, he is ready to learn what little he can do. And what a tremendous difference to himself and to others the little that he can do—listening with understanding, for example—can make!

Once he can accept his limitations and the limitations of others, he can begin to learn to behave more skillfully with regard to the milieu in which he finds himself. He can begin to learn that misunderstanding can be diminished—not banished—by the slow, patient, laborious practice of a skill.

But we can expect too much from this possibility, so let me conclude by sounding two notes of caution:

1. Although these skills of communication of which I am speaking deal in part with words, they are not in themselves words, nor is the territory to which they apply made up of words. It follows, then, that no verbal statement about these skills, however accurate, can act as a substitute for them. They are not truly articulate and never can be. Although transmissible to other persons, they are but slowly so and, even then, only with practice.

2. Let us remember that these interpersonal proceedings between Hart and Bing, or *A* and *B* whoever they may be, are extremely complex. So far as I know, there exists no single body of concepts which as yet describes systematically and completely all the important processes that our separate theories have said are taking place and how they relate to each other. Let us therefore accept gracefully and not contentiously that these interpersonal proceedings, unlike the atom, have not been as yet "cracked" by social science. Only then can we as students of human behavior live up to our responsibility for making our knowledge fruitful in practice.

[9] See Kenneth R. Andrews, "Executive Training by the Case Method," and F. J. Roethlisberger, "Training Supervisors in Human Relations," *Harvard Business Review* (September 1951), p. 58 and p. 47.—*The Editors* [*HBR*].

Reactions to this type of analysis

Before proceeding, it may be worthwhile to stop and think for a while about the differences and similarities you have noticed between your own analysis of what was going on between Hart and Bing and Professor Roethlisberger's treatment of the case. Perhaps you noticed that many of the ways of looking at the case which Roethlisberger talks about were evident when you discussed the case in class. In most class discussions considerable time is spent trying to decide who is "right" and who is "wrong" by eloquent advocates of "common sense" (or "industrial engineering" or "management theory"), without any very satisfying answers being found. Individuals with different backgrounds usually favor various other ways of conceiving the problem, such as "clash of personalities" (psychology), "conflict of social roles" (sociology), and "struggle for power" (economics or political science). Finally, expecially if some of the suggestions for analysis given in Chapter 1 have been used in preparing the case, a major portion of the discussion may stress that "the trouble resides in the process of interpersonal communication itself," and how for both Hart and Bing certain beliefs and feelings each has about himself, and certain assumptions about what is taking place, are influencing his perceptions of the other. This is, of course, the mode of analysis which is particularly emphasized both in Roethlisberger's article and in the rest of this book. But it is very important to recognize, as he does, the limitations as well as the validity of this approach. Since the processes we are examining are extremely complex, let us always be wary of using a quick and easy label like "a breakdown in communication" in order to conveniently sweep this uncomfortable complexity under the rug. The word *communication*, like many other words, can block instead of facilitate the *process* of communicating effectively with each other about what is actually taking place, unless we are careful.

A frequent reaction to Roethlisberger's article is admiration for the many facets of the case which the author clarifies at the level of *analysis*, coupled with the disappointment or frustration that the "action question" is not more clearly dealt with. Somehow it seems as though such a detailed discussion of this relatively "simple" case (but *is* it so simple?) should end up with a more definite prescription or proposed "cure" for the difficulty. We want to know more precisely what Hart should do or say differently. Or at least, we may feel, the author should have been more specific in telling us how Hart is going to acquire the more fruitful "way of thinking" about his interactions with others which, the author implies, will lead to more "skillful" behavior in the future.

These are good questions to ask at this point, but it may be premature to expect a wholly satisfying answer to them. They are not simple questions, and the rest of this book will be concerned with them, in one way or the other. In other words, we are assuming a need to work hard at *understanding* the sources of misunderstanding, and sometimes this approach may be frustrating because it seems to ask that we postpone too long our natural inclination to "do something" about the interpersonal difficulties we are being asked to understand.

As in Roethlisberger's article, so in the rest of this book, the reader will seldom be told what to do about the problems he sees; more frequently he will be asked to "stop, look, and listen," for longer than he may wish, and *then* to develop his own ideas about what *he*, in a similar situation, would do. As in the article, so in this book, we are concerned not with some theoretically optimal "solution," but with "the slow, patient, laborious practice of a skill," that is to say, a self-developed way of responding to communications problems that makes sense both in terms of the particular situation we face and in terms of what we ourselves are bringing to that situation. This is why, as in the case of Hart, neither Roethlisberger nor any other authority is going to give us answers to our "action questions"; we are going to have to find them for ourselves.

Sources of misunderstanding

In the last few paragraphs we have not only been trying to encourage more careful thought about your reactions to Roethlisberger's analysis of the Hart and Bing case (and, hopefully, more careful rereading and reconsideration of what he had to say). We have also been illustrating the major theme of Part II, "Sources of Misunderstanding." This theme is that the degree of understanding present in any communication is strongly influenced by one's pre-existing beliefs or assumptions about the purpose of that communication. For example, the reaction that any one of us has to Roethlisberger's treatment of the Hart and Bing case will depend upon our assumptions as to what the author was trying or "supposed" to communicate. A belief that communication difficulties are relatively simple (e.g., can be solved by means of speaking more logically and clearly) would make it very difficult for the reader to understand what the author was trying to say, and why. An assumption that an authority on communication problems should have the answer to a specific communication difficulty, or that being told what Mr. Hart should do will help one decide what to do in another "similar" case, will strongly affect what I perceive in the article, and may prevent me from "hearing" in it some insights which could have been more useful to me than what I thought I was looking for. Thus in Part II we shall look at cases in which the misunderstandings that exist can more easily be understood and overcome once we have identified the underlying beliefs or assumptions which one or both people are making about the nature of their relationship, about the characteristics of appropriate behavior in such a situation, and especially about the manner in which words are being (or should be) used.

As Roethlisberger points out, both Hart and Bing got into trouble with each other in no small part because of assumptions that each was making about the meaning to him of the other's words or behavior. And, as is often tragically the case, the interactions resulting from such assumptions tended not to lead to their being modified. On the contrary, not being aware of the influence of what they assumed on what they perceived, they tended to act toward each other in ways that "made their assumptions come true." The concepts of "general semantics," as developed in the writings of Korzybski, Wendell Johnson, Irving Lee, and Hayakawa, will be especially useful in analyzing the cases in Part II, because they help us examine the assumptions people trying to communicate with each other are making about their use of words.

Critics of "traditional" patterns of management behavior, such as Douglas McGregor, also help us understand these cases, because they stress the effect on communication of implicit assumptions about human motivation and about how people in a specific organizational relationship (superior–subordinate, for example) are supposed to behave in relation to each other. As has already been pointed out, there are many examples in the case of Hart and Bing of how both kinds of assumptions (about words and about organizational relationships) are difficult to challenge because they tend to produce consequences which seem to justify their validity.

Understanding another person's behavior

An obviously important aspect of the Hart and Bing case is that neither of them had a helpful way of understanding the other's behavior. Such a statement, of course, immediately raises the question, what *is* a helpful or useful way of understanding the behavior of another person with whom I have an organizational relationship, that is to say who is my subordinate, or superior, or co-worker, for example? This question is the basis for the selection of cases and readings in Part III.

The trouble with some ways of understanding other people is that they do not help us predict how the other will react to different behavior on our part, and they often make it more difficult instead of easier for us to establish effective communication with him. In this sense it is not any more useful to Hart to see Bing as "suffering illusions of grandeur" or "mentally deficient" than it is for Bing to see Hart as a "sarcastic bastard." Hart does not need more sophisticated ways of labeling or categorizing Bing. He *does* need, we claim, more ability to see Bing as Bing sees himself. Communication will be facilitated between A and B to the extent that A's view of B is more in line with B's view of himself, and vice versa.

This implies that when the objective is improvement in organizational relationships, our way of understanding another person should emphasize the attempt to see things as the other sees them, to sense what the other feels, to understand the other person from the other person's point of view. This approach to the study of individual behavior is sometimes called a *phenomenological* or *perceptual* point of view in psychology. It emphasizes understanding from an *internal*, not an *external*, frame of reference.

Two aspects of this way of trying to understand someone else are emphasized in Roethlisberger's discussion of Hart and Bing and in Part III. The first is the notion that a person has a relatively consistent way of thinking about himself, a *self-concept*, which he is strongly motivated to maintain and enhance. For example, Bing's singing, or any other element of his behavior, can be related to his need to maintain his view of himself against perceived threat, or to provide for himself opportunities for further growth and development in directions that are important to him.

The second aspect of this perceptual or internal frame of reference for understanding individual behavior which we shall emphasize is the relationship of interdependence that exists between what a person *perceives*, what he believes or *assumes*, and how he *feels*. For example, when what I see seems to violate what I believe ought to be taking place, I am likely to feel upset or defensive, and these feelings are likely to have further effects on my subsequent perceptions. Thus, "Hart's assumptions, perceptions, and feelings are of a piece; each reinforces the other. . . . As a result, . . . there is no way for him to say, 'because of the assumptions I make and because of the way I feel, I perceive Bing in this way.'" It is especially for this reason that we emphasize in Part III a point of view toward understanding individual behavior that brings out a person's need to maintain his self-concept and underlines the influence of what he assumes and feels on what he is able to perceive.

Helping another person understand his behavior

Mr. Hart's difficulty comes about, according to Roethlisberger, because "no one has listened to him or helped him to learn to listen to others." In order to understand something of how another person perceives his world and feels about himself a particularly sensitive kind of "listening" is necessary. The readings and cases in Part IV have been selected in order to illustrate what is involved in developing this kind of listening ability. In a sense we shall shift our attention from the behavior of the person who wants to be understood by someone else, to the behavior of the person who wants to understand someone else from an internal frame of reference. We shall study in some detail those ways of interacting with another person, those points of view toward the interviewing process, that have been developed specifically to facilitate such understanding. We shall see that these ways of interacting, developed primarily by counselors and psychotherapists, often have the consequence of helping the other person understand *himself* somewhat better.

Our intention in Part IV will *not* be to learn to be "amateur psychotherapists" but to learn from the counseling process an orientation that is useful to *any* person who has to interact with others from a position of some responsibility for their behavior. Such a person, like Mr. Hart, needs to listen skillfully, and, at times, he needs to be able to respond skillfully to another person who comes to him for help. Our position will be that although an administrator or leader is not and should not try to be a psychological counselor, nevertheless he can learn from the counselor's orientation and behavior some very useful lessons about two-person interaction generally, and more specifically, perhaps, about the effect of his own behavior on others. We should not all expect to agree about the applicability of counseling to administration or to ourselves personally, but we shall want to *understand* the counselor's basic orientation and to gain from our exposure to it whatever about it makes sense to us.

More simply, the purpose of Part IV is to increase the effectiveness of our study of interpersonal communication by a somewhat detailed exposure to a special setting—psychological counseling—in which the interaction process between two people attempting to communicate with each other has necessarily received more detailed attention than anywhere else. Out of this exposure we should at least learn how difficult—and instructive—it can be to really listen to another person's point of view.

Organizational relations and interpersonal skill

The purpose of Part V is to practice applying what has been learned about the sources of misunderstanding, and about the process of understanding and helping other people, to specific relationships in *organizational* settings, where a very important goal is not just to improve communication for its own sake but to contribute to greater organizational health and productiveness. At times, in previous parts of the book, we may have tended to forget temporarily, or to wonder with some frustration, what the purpose of all this communication, understanding, and listening has been. In Part V we "come down to earth," so to speak, and face the fact that the improvement of task performance by people in organizations *is* a primary purpose of the interpersonal competence with which the other parts have been concerned. In Part V, some readers may feel, we become "realistic" again.

Primarily the cases and readings concern the process of improving the effectiveness of several specific types of organizational relationships: consultant–client, staff–line, and superior–subordinate. While there are some important structural differences between these kinds of relationships, we shall be primarily interested in the uniformities we observe in the interpersonal processes involved. And in every case our most important consideration probably should be: How, very specifically, would *I* behave in this situation if I were personally involved in it, in order to apply what I have learned about interpersonal behavior appropriately, skillfully, and with understanding? Why do I think this specific behavior on my part would both facilitate communication and improve organizational performance?

In the last part of the book we focus particularly on the administrator as an *involved* practitioner of interpersonal skill. Hopefully, by this time, the importance of what Roethlisberger refers to as the "problem of involvement" will have become clear. If the administrator's goal is more accurate and constructive perception of the interpersonal events surrounding him, it becomes increasingly important for him to be aware that the involvement of his own feelings in the very events he wishes to understand is influencing his perceptions of them. Only then can he ask usefully, we maintain, what for many men of action may be the most important question they ever ask themselves: How is what is going on inside my skin influencing what I see going on outside?

As in the case of Mr. Hart and Bing, so in all the cases in the book, the "problem of involvement" will be a central concern, and the most difficult to handle. Perhaps the most fruitful arena for practicing the skill of becoming aware of the unavoidable interaction between our *own* assumptions, feelings, and perceptions will be not in the cases we study, but in our own discussion of them. In other words, the more involved you become in the discussion of these cases, as active participant *and* as sensitive listener, the more you are likely to learn of what this book is really all about.

PART II Sources of misunderstanding

CHAPTER 3. Organizational assumptions and the use of words

In this chapter we wish to develop the point that sources of inter-personal misunderstanding like those in many of the following cases are frequently to be found in certain unquestioned beliefs or untested assumptions that people make about the behavior of other people and about the meaning and use of words. Before doing so we need to recognize that these are by no means the only barriers to efficient interpersonal communication, any more than more efficient communication between men by itself will solve all of man's problems. But we can choose to direct our attention somewhat intensively to one important class of problems without implying that this is the only class of problems that needs to be studied.

Certainly many differences between people are not resolvable by improved communication between them, and many misunderstandings do not depend upon the kind of implicit assumptions we wish to examine here. Given two very different sets of values and goals, interpersonal conflict can be *increased* by improvements in communication. Misunderstandings between people can arise out of inherent biological and cultural differences, and can be caused by many things that are very difficult to change —in history, geography, uneven access to natural resources, and so forth. It is certainly not difficult to find good reasons for why people often have trouble understanding each other. The point is to devise a sensible strategy for getting to work on the problem. The strategy chosen here, though certainly not the only one, is to start with those sources of misunderstanding that reside "inside the skin" of particular people who are already at least partly aware of some need to understand each other better as a necessary (but not necessarily sufficient) condition for accomplishing what is important to them. And in so doing we shall focus, in the following cases, especially on the two classes of misunderstandings which Hayakawa (see Additional Readings) has identified as those arising from "arrogance" (thinking that you know something that you don't) and those arising from "ignorance" (not knowing something that you could). Whether or not this is the most "important" place to start, here would seem to be a problem about which much needs to be learned. We want to avoid *assuming* an inevitable conflict of interest, because sometimes with improved communication it may cease to exist. And we want to avoid *assuming* that people who think they understand each other actually do, because often, as with Hart and Bing, a major source of misunderstanding is that one person believes he knows what another person is talking about when actually he doesn't.

An example of misunderstanding

In the chapter in *Management and Morale* that he calls "Of Words and Men" (excerpts are reproduced in Reading II–2), Roethlisberger tells the following story:

> . . . The captain of a ship in the merchant marine . . . had gone to sea as a boy and had been brought up in the tradition that the captain is master of the ship: his word at sea is law. Although he was kindly toward his crew, all his reflexes had been conditioned to this tradition. As a result, for years he failed to see that his authority depended only upon the fact that his junior officers and crew also accepted and upheld the tradition. And then things at sea began to change. People who had not been so well conditioned for cooperation, and particularly for cooperation on the basis of this tradition, began to join his crew. The code began to change. The captain had to meet with his crew and listen to some of their complaints and grievances. In one instance he was confronted with a long list of complaints about the food. One item on this list was to the effect that the crew did not get "seconds on Jell-O." Now, it was at this point in the captain's story that his face became flushed and speech failed him. But his gestures of exasperation and frustration expressed only too well what he could not

say in words. Imagine him—the captain—having to deal with people who made such ridiculous charges! Moreover, the actual fact was that they *could* get "seconds on Jell-O." In the face of this problem, the captain was helpless. All his conditioned reflexes could do was to produce sputtering noises. He had no skills for handling this ridiculous situation. His sense of humor was gone; his ordinary social insight was gone. He could not remember the social mechanisms he had used when he was a boy to "get somebody's goat." In the face of this situation, the captain could only talk about "communism," "fifth-column activities," "agitators," "aliens," and then, as the story developed, get sick with a case of shingles.

This is not intended as a funny story, nor to cast any aspersions on the captain. None of us would want to be in his position. He was up against a difficult human problem, even though it manifested itself at the level of "seconds on Jell-O." The only point I want to make is to show the state of affairs into which we can get when we try to handle matters of sentiment as if they were matters of fact. For the captain, a difficult problem of human diagnosis was involved which entailed going from the symptoms to the underlying human situation among his crew. But for this he received no help; he had no skills, and his conditioned reflexes could only make matters worse both for himself and for the crew.[1]

In addition to Professor Roethlisberger's comment on this story, the following questions can be raised: Was this an example of inevitable misunderstanding? If not, was it "arrogance" or "ignorance" or both that prevented the captain from responding more skillfully to this situation? What underlying beliefs and assumptions, learned by him out of his previous experiences, contributed to his difficulty—beliefs and assumptions both about what should constitute appropriate behavior in this kind of relationship, and about how words are or should be used?

Let us consider first the questions, what did the captain think he knew that he didn't know, and what did he not know that he could have known? Among many possible answers to these questions that might be inferred, an interesting possibility is that he thought he knew what was meant by the complaint about "seconds on Jell-O," whereas he might have known that the "manifest" content of a complaint is often different from its "latent" meaning. (See Reading II–4.) The captain *was* faced

[1] F. J. Roethlisberger, *Management and Morale* (Cambridge, Mass.: Harvard University Press, 1941), 104–5. Copyright 1941 by the President and Fellows of Harvard College. Used by permission of the publishers.

with a troublesome and puzzling situation that needed to be understood, but it probably had more to do with his need to understand somewhat better how his own feelings were involved in the situation he needed to understand.

Let us look again at this example to illustrate what we mean by implicit beliefs and assumptions as sources of misunderstanding. First we should clarify that we are using the word *assumption* in Nilsen's sense, "A more or less unconscious taking for granted of certain basic but undefined conceptions of one's world." (See Reading II–3; *cf.* also Cantril, *The "Why" of Man's Experience.*)

What, then, was the captain apparently "assuming" that made it difficult for him to communicate with anyone, including himself, about what was going on? Of course we do not "know" the answer to this question. If the captain had been able to be explicit about his assumptions, they probably would not have got him in so much trouble. The existence of the kind of assumptions we are talking about almost always has to be *inferred*, and the extent to which these assumptions "impede communication" in a given case is normally a matter of judgment.[2]

So, to phrase our question more precisely, what are some useful inferences about the assumptions the captain was making, *useful* inferences in the sense that it would have helped the captain if he had considered the possibility that this was what he was doing?

The motivation is "logical"

The above heading is a somewhat misleading summary of an important cluster of ways of thinking about the behavior of other people that for the captain (or for Mr. Hart, or for many of the people in subsequent cases) can develop into a pattern of assumptions that make interpersonal understanding difficult. What we mean, primarily, is the belief (or acting as if one believed) that

---

[2] See S. I. Hayakawa, *Language in Thought and Action*, 2nd ed. (New York: Harcourt, Brace, 1964), Chapter 3, on the distinctions between "reports," "inferences," and "judgments."

human motivation is relatively simple and easy to understand rather than relatively complex and difficult. Under this general heading we would classify such notions as that the factors which motivate behavior are relatively constant and easily predicted from one time and situation to another: what motivates me motivates the other person; what motivated other people at one time and place will motivate the same or different people at other times or places. More specifically, these sorts of beliefs are reflected in the assumption that physical, physiological, and economic motivations have a constant validity, or that because some people in one situation have thought it appropriate (or expedient) to follow certain rules and procedures, other people in other situations will feel (or should feel) the same way. It would have helped the captain cope with his situation if he had been able to ask himself whether he was making assumptions of this kind about the motivations of his crew, without checking them against available evidence concerning the present situation.

It is important to recognize that if the captain *were* behaving on the basis of certain overly "logical" or static assumptions about motivation, it would not be easy for him to acknowledge that this was what he was doing. In fact the trouble with any list of the kind of assumptions we are considering (*cf.* McGregor, *The Human Side of Enterprise*, Chapter 3; Nilsen, "Some Assumptions That Impede Communication"; or the other additional readings listed under Topic A later in this Part) is that it is hard to state such assumptions in a way that the captain or anyone else would accept. The point, however, is *not* that the captain had the "wrong" theory about motivation; his ideas on the subject had probably worked well at another time and place. The important question is how aware was he of his assumptions? How able was he to say to himself, "It is not only because of how they are behaving, it is also because of what I am assuming and feeling that I perceive my crew's behavior in this way"?

In other words, it is because of the importance of being aware of one's assumptions as an influence on communication, rather than to label one set of assumptions "right" and the other "wrong," that we are urging an examination of this process in your analysis of the cases.

That organization is "rational"

Closely related to the kinds of beliefs we hold about how people are or should be motivated are our theories about how organizations are or should be structured and about what kinds of behavior are appropriate within specific organizational relationships. Obviously the crew's complaint about "seconds on Jell-O" violated some important beliefs that the captain held on this subject.

In a famous paper, Gouldner contrasted the "rational model" and the "natural-system model" of organizational analysis:

> In the rational model, the organization is conceived as an "instrument"—that is, as a rationally conceived means to the realization of expressly announced group goals. Its structures are understood as tools deliberately established for the efficient realization of these group purposes. Organizational behavior is thus viewed as consciously and rationally administered, and changes in organizational patterns are viewed as planned devices to improve the level of efficiency. . . .
>
> The natural-system model [on the other hand] regards the organization as a "natural whole" or system. The realization of the goals of the system as a whole is but one of several important needs to which organization is oriented. Its component structures are seen as emergent institutions, which can be understood only in relation to the diverse needs of the total system. The organization, according to this model, strives to survive and to maintain its equilibrium, and this striving may persist even after its explicitly held goals have been successfully attained. . . .[3]

These are clearly two different ways of thinking about what takes place within organizational relationships. Whereas the "rational model" emphasizes the behavior prescribed by the "formal organization," the "natural-system model" stresses the behavior emerging within the "informal organization." Gouldner's main point is that *both* patterns of behavior are important, and that analysis of organization should pay more attention to how they are related to each other. Nevertheless, it is relevant to consider not only which "model" is dominant in the analyses of

[3] Alwin W. Gouldner, "Organizational Analysis," in R. K. Merton, L. Broom, and L. S. Cottrell, Jr., eds., *Sociology Today: Problems and Prospects* (New York: Basic Books, Inc., 1959), 404–5.

sociologists (Gouldner's topic), but also which view of organizational life is influencing the efforts of members of an organization to communicate with each other (the topic of this chapter).

Traditionally, as has often been pointed out, management has paid more attention to the rational, formal aspects of organization than to the "nonlogical," informal patterns that inevitably emerge within the constraints of the formal structure. This is because of the necessary importance, to management, of what Roethlisberger and Dickson in *Management and the Worker* (see Reading II–4) called the "logic of cost" and the "logic of efficiency," as distinguished from the "logic of sentiment," which "represents the values residing in the interhuman relations of the different groups within the organization."[4]

Although numerous authors when discussing the Western Electric studies seem to believe that Roethlisberger and Dickson interpreted the results to mean that the logics of cost and efficiency characterize management whereas informal and nonlogical behavior is confined to workers, no such statement can be found in *Management and the Worker*. On the contrary,

> Informal organization appears at all levels, from the very bottom to the very top of the organization. Informal organization at the executive level, just as at the work level, may either facilitate or impede purposive co-operation and communication. In either case, at all levels of the organization, informal organizations exist as a necessary condition for collaboration. Without them formal organizations could not survive for long. Formal and informal organizations are interdependent aspects of social interaction.[5]
>
> * * *
>
> At first glance it might seem that the logics of cost and efficiency are the logics of management groups, whereas the logic of sentiments is the logic of employee groups. Although in one sense this may be accurate, in another sense it is an oversimplification. . . . One has only to interview a supervisor or executive to see that he has a logic of sentiments which is expressing the values residing in his personal interrelations with other

---

[4] F. J. Roethlisberger and W. J. Dickson, *Management and the Worker* (Cambridge, Mass.: Harvard University Press, 1939), 564. By the "logic of efficiency" Roethlisberger and Dickson mean a "system of ideas and beliefs" about how to secure collaboration primarily through wage payment schemes (e.g., incentives) which "is usually based upon certain assumptions about employee behavior." In other words, they are pointing to the importance of the assumptions that are made about employee motivation.
[5] *Ibid.*, 562.

supervisors or executives. Employee groups, moreover, are not unknown to apply the logic of cost.

However, it is incorrect to assume that these different logics have the same significance to different groups in an industrial plant. The logics of cost and efficiency express the values of the formal organization; the logic of sentiments expresses the values of the informal organization. To management groups and technical specialists the logics of cost and efficiency are likely to be more important than they are to employee groups.[6]

Although the "logics of cost and efficiency" and the "logic of sentiment" appear today somewhat old-fashioned and clumsy phrases, the central point of the distinction is still wholly relevant to any analysis of sources of misunderstanding in organizational relationships. As soon as an organization is conceived as a natural social system, in other words whenever one examines the organizational behavior that actually takes place as distinguished from that which is supposed to take place, the same problem is likely to appear: people with different systems of values and beliefs, with different sets of underlying assumptions about what is important and appropriate in organizational life, are having some trouble communicating with each other without understanding why. In a sense, they are "talking different languages" without knowing it. In the subsequent cases it will often be worthwhile to examine whether and in what ways this is happening.

Again let us emphasize that the point is not to decide which set of assumptions or which view of organizational life is valid in general and which is not. In any particular instance, both can be right and both can be wrong. Many organizational arrangements *are* rational, and much organizational behavior is not. In a specific case, "some of these ideas and beliefs represent more closely the actual situation than others. In all cases, however, they are abstractions from the total situation. In this respect they are to the concrete situation as maps are to the territories they represent. And like maps these abstractions may be either misleading or useful."[7] The challenge, in every case, is to examine how these

---

[6] *Ibid.*, 564–65. Citing this same passage, Gouldner (*op. cit.*) says that Roethlisberger and Dickson "maintain that the former [the logics of cost and efficiency] characterizes managerial elites, whereas the latter [the logic of sentiment] is distinctive of employee or worker echelons." This would seem an oversimplification of what Roethlisberger and Dickson actually said.

[7] Roethlisberger and Dickson, *op. cit.*, 562–63.

differing perceptions of and theories about reality are related to each other, and to be deeply concerned with how communication can be facilitated across the barriers that they create.

That words are things

In the story of the captain and his crew, what was *meant* by the words "seconds on Jell-O," that is to say what concepts, ideas, thoughts, feelings, and the like did these words symbolize—to the crew, and to the captain? In this case, as in so many others, the most basic source of misunderstanding is that when people are trying to communicate with each other they do not necessarily assign the same meanings to the same words. According to Samuel Butler, "the essence of language lies in the intentional conveyance of ideas from one living being to another through the instrumentality of arbitrary tokens or symbols agreed upon and understood by both as being associated with the particular ideas in question."[8] In most cases of breakdown in verbal communication, this is what is not being fully taken into account: that words are being used as "*arbitrary* tokens or symbols," and that a word which symbolizes one thing to one person can very easily symbolize something else to another person. Neither a dictionary nor any other universal law can tell me what will happen in my mind or in someone else's mind when a particular word is being used. But because we all tend frequently to forget this obvious (when we think about it) truth, we are constantly acting as though we assumed that words are *things* instead of arbitrarily assigned symbols, and we can frequently find ourselves, like the captain, "treating alike by words situations that [in fact] are different."[9]

In an analogy frequently used in the field of general semantics, words, like other symbols, bear the same relation to what they stand for as a map does to the territory it represents.

> What we call a map is an example of a kind of language, symbols arranged in some kind of order. Now for a map to be useful to a traveller it

[8] Samuel Butler, "Thought and Language," in Max Black, ed., *The Importance of Language* (Englewood Cliffs, N.J.: Prentice-Hall, 1962), 20.
[9] Roethlisberger, *Management and Morale*, *op. cit.*, 97.

must be coordinated with the territory. Its structure must be similar in certain respects to that of the territory it represents. The arrangement of the symbols, the dots, lines, etc., of the map must accord with the arrangement of the actual cities, roads, rivers, etc., of the territory. For example, if in the territory we find, from west to east, Denver, Omaha, Chicago, then on the map we must find these places correspondingly represented. If on the map they are represented in the order of Denver, Chicago, Omaha, the order or structure is faulty, the map is not coordinated with the territory, and the traveller who tries to follow such a map is likely to suffer consequences which may range from mere annoyance to utter calamity. Among other experiences, he will be likely to suffer shock more or less, depending upon the degree to which he maintains awareness of the difference between map and territory. If, like a savage, he scarcely recognizes any difference at all between symbol and fact—map and territory—he will be gravely confused for some time after discovering that he is in Omaha instead of Chicago. If, however, like a scientist, he has practically no tendency to identify symbol and fact, practically no readjustment at all will be required of him when he discovers that the map was wrong. He will merely change his map and go on his way. The trouble with the more primitive traveller is that he would hardly understand what was wrong. Assuming as he does that map and territory are practically identical, he places undue confidence in the map and so he is not semantically prepared to handle his difficulty with the obvious (to us) solution of changing the map. Such a solution would occur only to a person to whom map and territory were distinctly different—on different levels of abstraction—and who understood that the usefulness of a map depends precisely on the degree to which it corresponds structurally with the territory.

What we have said about map and territory can be said, also, about any symbol and whatever it is supposed to symbolize. It can be said about a statement [such as "we demand seconds on Jell-O"] and whatever it is supposed to represent. It can be said about any theory [such as McGregor's "Theory X"] and the facts it is supposed to explain and to predict. People who cling to theories that explain little and predict nothing are like the primitive who "believes in" his map even though it brings him to the wrong destinations. . . .

What is important at all times is a consciousness of abstracting, an awareness and understanding of the fact that a symbol is not the same as what it symbolizes, that the verbal and non-verbal levels are to be kept distinct and coordinated.[10]

The importance of this analogy is that, in spite of (perhaps because of) how obvious it appears at the intellectual level, it is

[10] Wendell Johnson, *People in Quandaries: The Semantics of Personal Adjustment*, 131–33. Copyright 1946 by Harper & Row, Publishers, Incorporated. Reprinted by permission of the publishers.

not easy to follow at the level of actual behavior. Certainly the captain was familiar with the relationship between maps and territories, but found it very difficult to take this same point of view toward the meaning of the words that his crew directed at him, and toward his own theory about the meaning of their behavior. If the reader watches carefully he will see many examples of confusion between verbal and nonverbal levels of abstraction in the cases. In order to understand the sources of interpersonal misunderstanding, it is advisable to examine closely the assumptions that are being made by the persons involved about the use and meaning of words. Since theories of human motivation and theories of appropriate behavior in organizational relationship are also words about behavior, "maps" that have been made to symbolize or attempt to control a concrete "territory," the most general and useful question to be asked in analyzing most of the following cases may well be "What assumptions does this person, whose behavior I want to understand, seem to be making about how people, including himself, are or should be using words?" The various Readings, especially II–5 and Hayakawa's *Language in Thought and Action* (or the other works listed under "Additional Readings," Topic B) are strongly recommended to assist in asking and answering this question. Some more specific questions for some of the cases are listed below.

Some specific questions

These questions are designed to get you started in analyzing the cases along the lines suggested in this and the previous chapter. They attempt to make more concrete the concepts and analytical schemes already introduced. They should be considered only as *examples* of the kinds of questions it may be useful for you to ask yourself about behavior in these and other cases. They are intended to start you thinking, *not* to stop you from thinking, about what questions are important to ask about the behavior described in each case in order that you may begin to improve your own behavior in organizational contexts. There is no reason to assume that we should all find the same questions useful.

1. What are some examples in this case of confusion between "reports," "inferences," and "judgments," by Baum, Norris, Harper, Finch, and McGregor? (See Hayakawa, *Language in Thought and Action*, Chapter 3.)

2. With what assumptions about behavior in an organization are the actions of Norris and the other executives consistent?

3. What assumptions by Norris about communication seem to have impeded his attempt to communicate with Baum?

4. How does Norris' view of himself and his situation apparently affect his view of Baum's behavior?

5. What are some specific examples of different meanings being assigned by different people to the same things? (For example, at various points in the case, what does Norris say to Baum, and what does Baum hear—and vice versa?)

6. Was it desirable for Norris to make Baum more "sales-minded"? If desirable, was it possible? If possible, how would you have done it?

7. If you were in Norris' position, what would you have done differently prior to the events described in the case? What would you have done differently during those events? What would you do at the end of the case?

8. To what extent is this a case of "existential" misunderstanding, and to what extent does the misunderstanding derive from "ignorance" or "arrogance"? Give one or two specific examples of how you would have behaved less "ignorantly" or less "arrogantly," as any one of the people in this case.

JOHN BYRON

1. What was Byron feeling about the situation and about Petmans? What feelings did he express? What did Petmans hear?

2. What was Petmans feeling about the situation and about Byron? What feelings did he express? What did Byron hear?

3. What seem to have been the intentions with which Byron and Petmans, respectively, entered into this conversation? How was what they each intended related to how they actually behaved?

4. What do you think were the consequences or outcomes of this conversation, in terms of

satisfaction of Byron's needs;
satisfaction of Petman's needs;
the future relationship and communication between them;
organizational purpose.

5. At the end of Petmans' first comment he asks "Now, why can't I hire that man?" If you had been in Byron's position, how would you have responded? Why?

6. Toward the end of the conversation, Byron says, "We interview about 2,500 applicants a year and we reject 20 per cent of them on the basis of physical defects. That's not easy for us to do. We're very much in this picture." How would you have responded to this statement if you had been in Petmans' position? Why?

7. Would "better communication" between Byron and Petmans have helped either or both of them? Would it have helped the organization advance its purposes? If so, how? If not, what else would be needed?

THE NIWASH DIVISION

1. What assumptions about line–staff relationships seem to underlie the behavior in Niwash? For example, what are the assumptions about the appropriate channel of communication between Tarrant and Magnus, the time-study men, and Joe Rudel and his gang?

2. What more general assumptions about human motivation and behavior in an organization would justify the apparent theory of Drake and others about communication in the line–staff relationship?

3. What do you think "really" happened? That is, was the bar "too heavy"? If you were in Drake's position, would it be important for you to find out? If so, how would you get this information, and what would you do with it?

4. How do you explain Drake's reaction to Beaubien's question, "If they [Magnus and Tarrant] knew the crane was being overloaded, why didn't they say so?"

5. Take, almost at random, any statement or action by Tarrant, Magnus, Drake, Johns, Beaubien, or Rudel and, based on your analysis of the case as a whole, explain what (and how and why) you would have done or said at that point. Upon what beliefs and organizational relationships and communication would you be basing *your* behavior?

6. How would you react in the position of Brock, Belham, or the Division Manager, if the events in this case were called to your attention? What are some of the assumptions and intentions on which you would base this reaction? (If you prefer a "normative" question, how *should* these gentlemen react, based on what assumptions and intentions?)

BOB KNOWLTON

We suggest you use this case as a detailed review of the analytical scheme, explained earlier, that stresses how *A*'s view of himself and his situation influences his view of *B* and *B*'s behavior, and that you apply this scheme both to Knowlton and Fester (a "colleague" or "rival" relationship) and to Jerrold and Knowlton (a "superior–subordinate" relationship). After you have done this you will be well equipped to ask yourself, and attempt to answer, a large number of interesting and important questions. This case also serves as a good preview of Part III, if your analysis includes a real attempt to understand the behavior of each of these three men in the light of how he sees himself, apart from how he may be perceived by the other two.

READING II–1. *Selections on the Concept of a Natural Social System*

A. R. RADCLIFFE-BROWN

[The following selections are taken from informal talks given before a faculty seminar at the University of Chicago in 1937 by the British anthropologist Radcliffe-Brown. They are reproduced here because we want to stress the importance of what Radcliffe-Brown calls "relations of interconnectedness," whether we are trying to understand an individual or a two-person relationship as a "natural system," which in turn, of course, exists within and is influenced by a series of larger social systems (small group, organization, society, and so forth). Although we shall often draw our boundaries around the smallest possible *inter*personal system, we do so because of the impossibility of studying everything at once. Personality systems and larger social systems are involved in every case, as well as interpersonal systems; but whatever the boundaries of space and time that we draw, the purpose of our analysis is to illuminate the interconnections between the elements of the "natural system" we are studying.]

A natural system . . . is a conceptually isolated portion of phenomenal reality (the system separated from the rest of the universe which is then the total environment of the system), consisting of a set of entities in such relation to one another as to make a naturally cohering unity. The constituent entities may be events, or themselves systems of events. Such a system is the solar system, an element, an atom, a horse, a falling body.

The relations *within* a natural system are relations of interdependence, but *between* natural systems there are relations of similarity, by virtue of which they can be classified into natural kinds, e.g., "the class of bodies falling toward the earth." The majority of the problems of science can be formulated as attempts to discover the essential characteristics or properties of a class or kind of natural systems.

Within the conceptual systems of abstract science the relations of interconnectedness are also logical or mathematical relationships. Thus an ellipse is a plane curve defined as the path of a point the sum of whose distances from two fixed points, the foci, is constant. This definition, however, could not be given if we had only one example of an ellipse. Those things which are unique in the universe require

Excerpted with permission of The Macmillan Company from *A Natural Science of Society* by A. R. Radcliffe-Brown, 20–22 and 43–47. © The Free Press, A Corporation, 1957.

methods of investigation other than those of science, because the essence of science is comparison. To verify our "law" of ellipses we require a *class* of systems of ellipses—of at least two ellipses, just as to establish a natural law we required a natural class of natural systems.

The distinction between class and system

To make clear the distinction between *classes* and *systems* I should like to present a little drawing. I am going to suggest that we have in these

men the members of a class, and here a class of glasses of beer. There is a very important similarity between this group of men and this group of glasses of beer. The similarity is that there are *two* of each. The term *two* is the name of a class of which this class of men is one member, and this class of glasses of beer another member; and it is also the name of every other instance of a diad. The type of relationship that exists between all instances of two members, which we may designate as "r" relationship, is the type I am talking about when I speak of relations of similarity.

Now let us suppose that you have here two *real* men and two *real* glasses of beer. You then have something quite different—a system of men drinking beer—in which there are specific relations of inter-connectedness of type "R." (The relationships would still be real, but quite different, if you had two men and one glass of beer.)

You cannot distinguish between relationships "r," those of classes, and relationships "R," those of systems, on the basis that the latter are *real*; both exist in phenomenal reality. You distinguish them as that the first are *relations of similarity*, and the relations of systems are *complex inter*relationships.

To further clarify the distinction between a class and a system, we may list their characteristics:

Class	System
("r" relations)	("R" relations)
Relations simple	Relations complex
Relations of similarity	*Relations of interconnectedness*
Mathematical relations	Spatio-temporal relations
Without form	Characteristic form
No quality of integration—coordinated by similarity	Integrated—coordinated by inter-dependence
Members may be separated without violation to them	Units violated in separation
Members may be moved about without violence to them or to class	Units may not be moved about without violence to them or to system
No cohesion between members of a class	Units cohere and thereby isolate the system from the rest of the universe
No functional relationship between members	Functional consistency
An aggregate	A genuine whole, having a structure
The sum of its parts (members)	Organic unity; not the sum of its constituent units

* * *

A social system is a natural persistent system

THE SOCIAL SYSTEM

... A natural system consists of entities that are in relations of real (existing in phenomenal reality) interconnectedness. The entities may be events or systems of events. We have to define the events.

In a social system the entities are individual human beings, in certain relations, which are differentiated from and isolated from all other relations in the universe. The individuals exist as units, but also, considered through time, are each characterized by a set of related acts of behavior which themselves constitute a system. "Tom Jones" is the name of a whole series of events, i.e., a set of acts of behavior; as such Tom Jones is a unit system in the system of society.

The relations *between* individuals in a social system are *social* relations, and these are real things, parts of phenomenal reality.

* * *

How do I meet the criticism that social science and psychology both observe the same entities, acts of behavior of individuals? If the subject matter, the data, constituted the only difference between two sciences, then there would be no difference between the sciences of the psychologist and of the sociologist. You can, however, take an act of behavior and observe it in two totally different systems. The social scientist and the psychologist are not concerned with the same system and its set of relations. The social scientist is concerned with relations he can discover between acts of diverse individuals; the psychologist with relations between acts of behavior of one and the same individual.

Psychology deals with the system we call *mind*. Mind (and this I think is the only justifiable definition) is the name of a system of mental relations, a system of which the units, individual acts of inner and outer behavior, are connected with one another by relations of interdependence. You do not have to bring in the body, which I believe exists always with the mind, Sir Oliver Lodge to the contrary. The physiologist studies the body; the psychologist, the mind; the physiological–psychologist, the system mind-and-body.

$$
\begin{array}{cc}
\underline{X} & \underline{Y} \\
a_1 & k_1 \\
a_2 & k_2 \\
a_3 & \leftrightarrow k_3 \\
a_n & k_n
\end{array}
$$

X and Y are two individuals, $a_1, a_2, a_3 \ldots a_n$ are acts of behavior in the system, individual X; a_1 is, say, an act at birth, a_n an act as an adult. The system, individual Y, is composed similarly of a set of acts of behavior, $k_1 \ldots k_n$, and relations between them. X and Y are each mental systems whose characteristics the psychologist is interested in discovering. Relations exist, however, also between acts of behavior of X and acts of behavior of Y, say between a_3 and k_3. The relations between X and Y are not psychical or mental relations. There is a relation here between two mental acts, not of one individual, but each of diverse individuals, and this relation is a social relation. Merely listening to another involves an adjustment to the interest of another. There is, in such an adjustment, interacting behavior. It is direct. There are actual relations of time and space. They constitute one kind of relation, set apart from all other relations in the universe.

The relations of a man coming into a store to buy a hat or of a woman to buy a beefsteak—with the clerk, with the cashier, with the store-owner—these are social relationships. The relationships *in* a man between coming to realize he needs a new hat and making up his mind to buy one, or *in* a woman realizing she is hungry and deciding to buy a beefsteak—these are psychological relationships. No relationship *between two persons* can by my definition be a psychological relation. The only psychological relations are those which exist within one mind —unless you admit telepathy.

If I go to school and learn geometry and later become an engineer and apply this learning, the relationship between what I learned and how I use it is specifically a psychic relationship. An exchange of ideas, on the other hand, is clearly a social relationship. The moment an exchange of symbols is involved, there is a social relation. That you are angry at a man is a psychological relation between your own mental states; but if you show your anger, swear at him—you establish a social relation. The very fact that one enters into communication with another shows that certain modifications of the interests of two people are taking place. The interest of two people may be in fighting one another; you cannot play a game of chess unless you have an opponent. An enmity of that sort is a conjunction of interests; there is a social relationship. If you are concerned with the psychological system, obviously the relations there are relations under the skin of one individual. The moment you get outside the skin of that individual, you have no longer psychological, but social, relations.

READING II–2. *Social Behavior and the Use of Words in Formal Organizations*

F. J. ROETHLISBERGER

[The following excerpts from Chapter 4 ("The Social Structure of Industry") and Chapter 6 ("Of Words and Men") of *Management and Morale* describe, as well as any of the newer writings on the same subject, the importance of and the relationship between two sets of common assumptions that influence the effectiveness of communication in organizations: assumptions about organizational relationships ("economic–technical" or "social") and assumptions about the use of words ("fact–logic" or "sentiment"). Roethlisberger's point, of course, is that *both* aspects need to be considered: social as well as economic–

Excerpted by permission of the publishers from Fritz J. Roethlisberger, *Management and Morale*, Cambridge, Mass.: Harvard University Press, 1941. Copyright 1941 by The President and Fellows of Harvard College.

technical relations are important, and language functions to communicate feelings as well as to communicate facts.]

Too frequently the human activities of industry are conceived of as essentially economic. An industrial organization is assumed to be composed of a number of individuals entering into relations of contract for the promotion of their own individual economic interests. It is not easy to explain why this conception, which runs counter to everyday experience, should be so firmly entrenched in the minds of men and why it should be so difficult to eradicate. In many of the written decisions of management it lies as an implicit premise, unchallenged and absolute. Fortunately, many executives in action are wiser than their theories and often make decisions in terms of factors not strictly economic. Yet few of them when challenged can resist the temptation to rationalize their practices in terms of this oversimplified theory of human motivation.

Social behavior

To say that a more adequate way of conceiving of the human activities of industry is to view them as essentially social brings up the question of what is meant by "social." There are few words more overworked or more shot through with different meanings. For some people the word "social" applies only to those activities enjoyed after work in the company of one's friends. It calls forth ideas of social clubs, social sets, or social circles, of people who seek diversion through association with others, and of activities pertaining essentially to the pleasure-seeking world. For others, it may bring to mind people who are sociable by nature and in habit and who have a disposition for cooperative relations with their fellow men. Those who are more serious or "socially minded" may immediately think of social problems, such as crime, suicide, and divorce, or the conditions and welfare of different groups within the community—the poor, the alien, the neglected, the maladjusted. Their thoughts then may run to social legislation, social work, social diseases, social hygiene, and social security. Another group of serious students may think of social theories or social questions pertaining to the fundamental relation between capital and labor.

But in speaking of social or socialized behavior I shall not be referring to any of these high abstractions in particular, but to far more simple matters. From experience we know that individuals interact and that the expression of that interaction is commonly recognized as social behavior. *Whenever a person is acting in accordance with the expectations and sentiments of some other person, or groups of persons, his behavior is social or socialized.* Such behavior, it is easy to see, can occur in a bread line just as well as at a fox hunt. It is manifested by the millionaire socialite owner of a factory as well as by his most lowly skilled worker. It occurs just as much at work as it does outside of working hours. In fact, there are few acts of men that are not social in the way in which I have defined the word.

* * *

The social organization of industry

... Industry has a social organization which cannot be treated independently from the technical problems of economic organization. An industrial organization is more than a plurality of individuals acting only with regard to their own economic interests. These individuals also have feelings and sentiments toward one another, and in their daily associations together they tend to build up routine patterns of interaction. Most of the individuals who live among these patterns come to accept them as obvious and necessary truths and to react as they dictate.

If one looks at a factory situation, for example, one finds individuals and groups of people associated together at work, acting in certain accepted and prescribed ways toward one another. There is not complete homogeneity of behavior between individuals or between one group of individuals and another, but rather there are differences of behavior expressing differences in social relationship. Individuals conscious of their membership in certain groups are reacting in certain accepted ways to other individuals representing another group. Behavior varies according to these stereotyped conceptions of relationship. The worker, for example, behaves toward his foreman in one way, toward his first-line supervisor in another way, and toward his fellow worker in still another. People holding the rank of inspectors expect a certain kind of behavior from the operators; the operators from the inspectors. Now, these relationships, as we all know from everyday experience, are finely shaded and sometimes become very complicated. When a person is in the presence of his boss alone, he acts quite differently from the way he acts when his boss's boss is also present. Likewise his boss acts toward him alone quite differently from the way he behaves when his own boss is also there. These subtle nuances of relationship are so much a part of our everyday life that they are commonplace. We take them for granted. We hardly realize the vast amount of social conditioning that has taken place in order that we can maneuver ourselves gracefully through the intricacies of these finely shaded social distinctions. We only pay attention to them when we blunder into new social situations where our past social training prevents us from making the necessary delicate interpretation of a given social signal and hence brings forth the socially wrong response.

* * *

Now the patterns of interaction that arise between individuals or between different groups can be graded according to the degree of intimacy involved in a relationship. Grades of intimacy or understanding can be arranged on a scale and expressed in terms of social distance. Social distance measures differences of sentiment and interest which separate individuals or groups from one another. Between the president of a company and the elevator operator, there is considerable social distance; more, for example, than between the foreman and the bench worker. Social distance is to social organization what physical distance is to physical space. However, physical and social distance do not necessarily coincide. Two people may be physically near but socially distant.

* * *

The problem of communication

In the technical organization of most companies there is very little explicit recognition given to these social distinctions. The blueprint organization plans of a company show the functional relations between working units, but they do not express these distinctions of social distance, movement, or equilibrium. This hierarchy of prestige values, which tends to make the work of men more important than the work of women, the work of clerks more important than the work at the bench, has no meaning for the technical organization. Nor does a blueprint plan show the primary groups, that is, those groups enjoying daily face-to-face relations. Logical lines of vertical and horizontal coordination of functions replace the actually existing patterns of interaction between people of different social places. From a technical standpoint, social place has no existence; only physical space exists. In place of all the sentiments of value residing in the social organization by means of which individuals and groups of individuals are differentiated, ordered, and integrated, there is substituted the logic of efficiency. Now it can be seen that this failure to recognize explicitly these human interrelations has certain consequences.

For example, the problem of communication is very important in the effective integration of any group or of a group of groups, of which industry is composed. Successful communication between individuals depends upon something more than a common language, a common set of words. People and groups with different experiences and social places, although having in common many of the same words, may vary widely in mental attitudes. These differences in modes of thought and ways of viewing things may make communication in some instances almost impossible. The trained expert with his precise and logical vocabulary has difficulty in communicating with the layman. The customary ways of thinking of the skilled toolmaker, for example, are quite different from those of the nonmachine-minded unskilled worker. They differ also from those of the engineer, the accountant, the marketing expert, the executive, or the administrator. As it is commonly expressed, people with different ways of thinking do not "get" each other.

If there is to be successful communication between the top and bottom of an industrial organization, these differences in modes of thought must be more clearly recognized. The same symbol does not necessarily have the same referent for different groups. Most symbols not only point out something, they also convey certain emotions. There is no better example than the case of the language of efficiency. The top of the organization is trying to communicate with the bottom in terms of the logical jargon and cold discriminations of the technical specialist, the engineer, the accountant, etc. The bottom of the organization, in turn, is trying to communicate with the top through its own peculiar language of social sentiments and feelings. Neither side understands the other very well. To the bottom the precise language of efficiency, instead of transmitting understanding, sometimes conveys feelings of dismay and insecurity. The bottom, in turn, instead of transmitting successfully its fears of social dislocation, conveys to the top emotional expressions of petty grievances and excessive demands.

* * *

The executive's environment is verbal

That a good portion of the executive's environment is verbal seems hardly open to question. In discussions, meetings, and conferences the verbal atmosphere is thick. The executive is dealing largely with words, symbols, and abstractions. Of course, this applies to any one of us. We are all responding to words and other stimuli involving meaning. It seems to me obvious, however, that the higher the executive goes in an organization the more important it becomes for him, if he is to handle effectively one aspect of his job, to deal competently with his verbal environment.

On the one hand, he has to become skillful in using words that will appeal to his listeners' sentiments. In trying to secure the cooperation of individuals in the common purposes of the enterprise the executive often has to practice the art of persuasion. He uses words that he hopes will produce the appropriate effects on his listeners. In statements to stockholders, employees, and customers, the executive has to resort to words, both oral and written. In handling complaints and grievances, the executive is using, as well as listening to, words.

On the other hand, the executive has to be able to interpret skillfully what people say, for in so far as his work involves the interactions of human beings his data come from what he hears as well as from what he sees and does.[1] Whether he likes it or not, he has to practice this difficult art; yet he has no explicit tools for doing it. He either picks up the skill intuitively or tries to organize his work so that the need for exercising it is at a minimum. This latter method is likely to be unsuccessful because it leads him to busy himself more and more with logical, statistical, and oversimplified abstractions or lofty principles about human motivation and conduct. In doing so he loses touch with the concrete situation before him.

In short, words play an important role in all the major functions of the executive. If this proposition is true, it seems sensible to ask what the executive needs to know about words and their functions and what skills he can explicitly develop in interpreting what people say.

The functions of language or words

Let us consider some of the different functions of language or words.[2] In the first place, words can be used to refer to events and happenings outside of our skin: this can be called the logico-experimental function of language. In this way words are used by scientists or by two or more people engaged in a discussion of matters with which they have first-hand, familiar, and intuitive acquaintance, as well as a common background of systematic knowledge. The words and symbols used by the speaker refer to events, and uniformities among events, which occur primarily outside of him or the listener, and to which they can go for observation and check in case of disagreement. Most of us spend only

---

[1] These statements are similar to those made about the social scientist by Professor L. J. Henderson in *Three Lectures on Concrete Sociology* (privately distributed), p. 13.

[2] For the purposes of this paper it would be inappropriate to discuss the many different theories of language. Only three well-recognized functions of language will be mentioned to illustrate some of the problems involved in interpreting what people say.

a very small portion of our day using words in this strict sense. We are much more likely to be engaged in less arduous and more pleasant verbal practices.

In a social conversation, for example, the situation is likely to be quite different. When two or more people are talking together, what is primarily happening is an interaction of sentiments rather than anything strictly logical. One person is using words to express certain sentiments, to which the other responds with similar or opposing sentiments; or one person tries to influence the other by using symbols that will have a favorable reaction on the latter's sentiments. This can be called the "emotive"[3] function of language, as opposed to the logico-experimental. The skillful politician is a good example of a person using words in this way.

There is a third function of language which has received considerable attention during the past two or three decades. Through words man not only communicates but satisfies his desires. I refer to the day-dreaming, revery, and air-castle building in which we all indulge and from which we obtain considerable satisfaction. A good portion of our day is spent in using words to satisfy our desires in this way.

That "Language serves a man not only to express something but also to express himself,"[4] every executive should realize and explicitly take into account. The fact that language has different functions and that these functions, except under special circumstances, are rarely distinguished complicates our problem. Words refer not only to things happening outside our skins, but also to our attitudes, feelings, and sentiments toward these objects and events. This means that many statements are expressed which have little or no meaning apart from the personal situation of the person who makes them. This not only makes the interpretation of what people say difficult, it also makes it imperative to do a skillful job, because if we refer words to a wrong context we are likely to misunderstand what a person is telling us. The channels of communication in a business organization often become clogged because words are referred to wrong contexts.

The problem would be simple if when people spoke they labeled what it was they were telling us; if, for example, they would say: "Now I am talking about simple events and uniformities among them in our common experience." "Now I am expressing my sentiments and attitude toward something." "Now I am day-dreaming and satisfying my

---

[3] Taken from C. K. Ogden and I. A. Richards, *The Meaning of Meaning* (New York: Harcourt, Brace, 1925), p. 257.

[4] *Ibid.*, p. 261 (statement by G. von der Gabelentz, quoted by Ogden and Richards).

ego." "Now I am trying to disguise my sentiments as logic." "Now I am trying to influence your sentiments by using these particular words." "Now you may think I am talking about my supervisor but really I am talking about my unhappy experiences with my father." Unfortunately (or fortunately, depending upon our point of view), this is not often true. We very seldom express our sentiments *as sentiments*. One of the most time-consuming pastimes of the human mind is to rationalize sentiments and to disguise sentiments as logic.

The skill of interpreting what people say

All I have said so far shows clearly that the interpretation of what people say is a difficult business. There is nothing to be gained by pretending that the job is simple. It is something that some people learn from experience and at which some people—physicians, lawyers, and businessmen—become exceedingly skillful. (These skillful people, however, often cannot communicate their skill.) The technique cannot be learned without practice but, again, for some people practice is not enough. No matter how much experience they have in listening to or in using words, they never acquire any great ability in this field. They continue to deal with words as constants rather than as variables, as if they had universal meanings rather than different meanings for different people under different conditions and situations. Some academic people are the worst offenders in this respect. Some scientists and engineers can never learn that words outside of the limited area of their specialty have different uses and important social functions.

Dr. Henderson has said: "Effective rules of procedure in interpreting what men say have not yet been developed . . . Therefore we are in respect of this kind of work still more or less in the master-apprentice stage."[5] However, in the past twelve years the research group with which I am associated has had considerable experience in trying to interpret what people say. It may be of some interest, therefore, if I try to state more explicitly some of the rules or discriminations which we have worked out. It may seem rather absurd to try to communicate a skill which, like any other, is in certain respects ineffable. However, inasmuch as all of us are practicing it, some more successfully than others, it can do no harm and perhaps some good to try to state more explicitly its nature. What I shall say, of course, can be only very rough, approximate, and tentative.

[5] Henderson, *Three Lectures on Concrete Sociology*, p. 19.

GETTING PEOPLE TO TALK ABOUT
MATTERS IMPORTANT TO THEM

When I am confronted with a complex situation involving the interactions of people, what people say is necessarily an important part of
the data from which I have to make a diagnosis. Therefore, my first
object is to get people to talk freely and frankly about matters which
are important to them. This situation in which I try to get people to
talk I shall call the interview. In the interview I use a number of
simple rules or ideas: I listen. I do not interrupt. I do not give advice.
I avoid leading questions. I refrain from making moral judgments
about the opinions expressed. I do not express my own opinions,
beliefs, or sentiments. I avoid argument at all cost. I do this by seeing
to it that the speaker's sentiments do not react on my own. Inasmuch
as these rules have been stated elsewhere, I shall not elaborate on them
here.[6]

ORIENTATION TO SPEAKER

Although it is sometimes difficult to get people to talk freely about
matters of importance to them, it is not nearly so difficult as the next
part of my job. While I am listening intently and sympathetically to
what the person is saying, my mind is not just a blank. I am listening
for something; there is some framework in which my thought is set. I
am oriented to the speaker in a certain way. To take an example, let
us assume that an employee in a large factory is speaking to me: he
says, "The supervisors in this company are a bunch of goddam
slavedrivers." What is my attitude toward such a remark?

First, I am not interested in the verbal definition of the word
"slavedriver." Secondly, I do not allow my sentiments to be acted
upon by this word, nor do I try to argue the speaker out of his belief.
Thirdly, I am not assuming that there exists one particular quality in
some supervisors to which this word refers; that is, I do not assume that
because there is a word "slavedriver" there is only one thing to which
it refers. Finally, I am not assuming that truth or falsity has anything
to do with the statement.[7]

How, then, am I oriented to such a remark? In the first place, I
assume that this person is expressing his feelings and sentiments. I

---

[6] These rules for interviewing are described more fully in the following publications: L. J. Henderson, "Physician and Patient as a Social System," *The New England
Journal of Medicine*, 212: 18 (May, 1935), 819–23; Elton Mayo, *The Human Problems of
an Industrial Civilization* (New York: Macmillan, 1933), pp. 91–92; F. J. Roethlisberger
and W. J. Dickson, *Management and the Worker* (Cambridge, Mass: Harvard University
Press, 1939), pp. 270–91.

[7] Perhaps I should say, "I try not to let myself take these customary attitudes
toward words," but this is often easier said than done.

assume that these feelings and sentiments are not "words," although words are being used to express them. I assume that I shall not be able to understand the feelings and sentiments expressed until I find the context to which they refer. In order to find the context, I am thinking of those events in the life of the employee to which his statement may refer, and also of the social situations in which they occurred. In other words, I am hunting for the referents of the statement. Therefore, I try to get the employee to talk about the particular supervisors (Supervisor 1, Supervisor 2, etc.) with whom he has been associated—when, where, how often, under what conditions, and so on. I am listening for what these particular supervisors did and under what conditions they did it, what meanings the employee assigned to their behavior, what the employee did and under what conditions he did it, and so on.

But more than this, I am also thinking of, and trying to get the employee to talk about, events in his previous history or in his associations with people outside the factory to which events involving interactions with people within the factory may be related *for the employee*. I do this because I assume that this particular employee's unpleasant feelings about a particular supervisor are a resultant of two sets of factors: (1) what he (the employee) is bringing to the situation in terms of hopes and expectations (sentiments), and (2) the social demands which the situation is making of him.

1. In order to find out what the employee is bringing to the situation in terms of sentiments, I need to know something about the meaningful associations he has had with other people and groups before coming to the factory. I assume that from these previous associations he has been conditioned to a certain way of life and to certain hopes, fears, and expectations. In terms of this kind of data, I can see more clearly what sentiments of the employee are being violated, disregarded, or misunderstood by a particular supervisor. I may find, for example, that the employee's attitude toward supervision is rooted somewhere in his attitude toward authority as conditioned by his early family situation; on anyone in authority he may be projecting the parental image.

2. But if I stopped here I might still be missing an important context to which his statement may refer. This worker is not an isolated individual. He has relations with other people. He is part of a social system called the factory. He is part of a smaller social system called the department. He is part of a still smaller social system called the work group—those people with whom he is associating daily at work. It may be that in the small work group this employee is an informal leader. The workers respect him as a craftsman; they go to him for help about their work; they go to him with their troubles. He instructs them about difficult jobs and he listens to their grievances. Perhaps the foreman

of his department does not recognize this employee's status in the informal work situation or, if he does, has not seen to it that his superiors also recognize it. Perhaps through ignorance of the situation he has recently promoted a younger and shorter-service man to a supervisory job in this department, a man whose efficiency record is good, and who is therefore easier to recommend to his superiors for promotion, but who is looked upon by his own work associates as a "rate buster," "chiseler," or "squealer." Perhaps it is the disturbances within this social situation to which the employee's statement, "The supervisors in this company are a bunch of goddam slavedrivers," refers.

I need not emphasize that it is important to know what a person is really complaining about before trying to act on the verbal manifestation of his complaint. Otherwise, we shall be dealing only with words, or symptoms, rather than with the situation determining the grievance.

So far, I have told you of my attitude in an interview toward a person when he is complaining about another person, but my attitude is very similar if he is complaining about nonhuman objects and events in his experience. (I say "in an interview" because this is not my ordinary social attitude.) If a person tells me, for example, that his desk is too small, I do not try to convince him that the size of his desk is sufficient for his purposes; I am thinking of the social setting in which desks appear in his work situation. What human relationship does the desk symbolize for him? It may be that in his organization the higher in the business structure the person goes, the bigger the desk becomes. It may be that the person who is talking to me is a college man with a burning desire to succeed. He may be indulging in a little wishful thinking; by getting a bigger desk he may think he is elevating himself in the company. When he complains that his desk is too small, he may really be telling me about his dissatisfaction with his advancement in the company. If so, I get him to talk about that.

Diagnosing human situations

In discussing how I interpret what people say, I have also been describing how I go about diagnosing a personal situation, that is, how I go from what people say to what their situation is. Obviously, it is the situation to which the words refer that is important and not the words themselves. *It is the situation and not the words that we want to understand.* I assume here that just as control of our physical environment came when we were able to control the objects and events to which words refer, so human control begins when we can control the human situations to which words refer.

In diagnosing human situations I try to avoid two tricks which words can play: (1) the danger of treating alike by words things that are different and unique, and (2) the danger of separating by words things that are inseparable in fact.[8]

TREATING ALIKE BY WORDS
SITUATIONS THAT ARE DIFFERENT

In our ordinary language we often use one word to refer to many unique objects in many different settings and in many different stages of process. For example, we have one word "chair" to refer to many unique objects, such as Chair 1, Chair 2, Chair 3, etc. We have one word "chair" to refer to Chair 1, which Smith 1 (the boss) occupies, and Chair 2, which Smith 2 (the secretary) occupies. The behavior of people toward the person who occupies Chair 1 is quite different from their behavior toward the person using Chair 2. The duties, obligations, and privileges of the occupant of Chair 1 are quite different from those of the occupant of Chair 2. Very seldom, at least in large business organizations, does Smith 1 sit on Chair 2. Even less often does Smith 2 sit on Chair 1, at least if Smith 1 is present; it would be considered inappropriate behavior if she did, if not by Smith 1 then by Smith 3 (Smith 1's boss). Moreover, we have the same word "chair" to refer to Chair 3 when it was in the boss's office ten years ago and Chair 3 when it has become old and dilapidated and is being used by the janitor in the basement.

Thus, our ordinary language tends to make the objects and events in our experience appear in isolation, that is, apart from their context. This is particularly true of common objects, such as chairs and desks, which occur in events involving human interactions. They appear in a certain time setting, that is, they are preceded by certain events and followed by others; moreover, they appear in a certain social setting. Therefore, if we pay exclusive attention to words and exclude the situations to which the words refer we miss very important differences of context. We fall into the error of assuming that because the same word can be applied to many different objects and events in different situations they are in some way the same. As a result, we fail to notice differences, and we read into our experience similarities where differences exist. Therefore, whenever I am concerned with overt or verbal behavior involving the interactions of human beings I am alert to differences in situation and I look for differences before I look for uniformities.
* * *

In diagnosing human situations there is also the danger of separating by words things that are inseparable in fact. It is important,

[8] For the ideas expressed in this section I am greatly indebted to A. Korzybski, *Science and Sanity* (New York: The Science Press Printing Co., 1933).

in tracing expressions of sentiment to the events in a person's experience to which they refer, to keep the events in their context; in other words, it is important to keep together those things which are together when experienced.

* * *

The exercise of human control by listening before talking

That the executive in dealing with human beings should take on some of the behavior patterns of the politician is not being suggested by these observations. Nor is it being recommended that the executive should make Fourth of July speeches, although in this connection it is interesting to note the bifurcation in our modern industrial society: on the one hand, the industrial leader is supposed to secure the loyalty of his employees by appealing to facts, while, on the other hand, the political leader is allowed to secure the loyalty of his constituents by appealing to emotion. What is being suggested is more simple and is of this order:

1. There are many words used by executives that not only communicate information, they convey sentiments.

2. The persons to whom the words are addressed also have sentiments; their sentiments vary with age, sex, personal situation, official rank, and informal position in the organization.

3. Because these sentiments in part relate to the different positions which people occupy in the organization, then it follows that some words which are very meaningful to some members, or some parts of the organization, may have little or no meaning or different meanings to other members and other parts of the organization.

4. This problem demands serious consideration. It is the problem of the effect on different members and on different parts of an organization of words used by the executive when he gives an instruction or order, when he announces a policy, or when he prepares a statement addressed to employees or to stockholders. This point is very simple. The legal jargon of a lawyer may give aesthetic satisfaction to him and his fellow brethren, but it may send shivers down the spine of the layman. The exact and precise jargon of the engineer may not be communicating "facts" to the employees who are being addressed; it may be transmitting feelings of apprehension. Sometimes also, symbols may lose their customary and traditional significance, as our example of the captain in relation to his crew well illustrated. For seamen who

demand "seconds on Jell-O" symbols evoking the traditions of the sea have lost their power to motivate.

5. Therefore, when talking to an individual or group, it is important to address oneself to their sentiments, so that on the one hand what one says will not be misunderstood, and on the other hand it will have the effect on the listeners that the speaker intends. But how does one address oneself to the listeners' sentiments? How does one know what they are? Here is where the "skill of listening" previously described comes in. This skill allows one to go from the words to the sentiments being expressed; but still more important, it allows one to go from the sentiments being expressed to the human situations underlying them. Words addressed to concrete human situations are likely to be more appropriate.

6. Therefore, it is important for the executive *to listen* before talking. By this means he comes to understand the sentiments and situations of the person or group before he practices the art of persuasion or assurance in order to secure their loyalty, confidence, and cooperation. In any large-scale organization, where many layers of supervision separate the top from the bottom, these dual skills are needed. Only when the people at the top of the organization understand better the feelings and sentiments of the people at the bottom can they communicate to the bottom what to top management is important, in a manner which will obtain the understanding and acceptance of those at the bottom. This is the exercise of human control by "understanding" and not by "verbal magic."

READING II-3. *Some Assumptions that Impede Communication*

T. R. NILSEN

[This article clearly expresses the notion that certain commonly held implicit assumptions about people and words are major sources of misunderstanding in organizational behavior. Unfortunately, such assumptions often produce consequences that appear to justify them,

Reprinted, with permission, from T. R. Nilsen, "Some Assumptions that Impede Communication," *General Semantics Bulletin*, 14 and 15 (Winter–Spring 1954), 41–44.

so that telling someone that he is evoking such an assumption on insufficient evidence is very unlikely to change his mind.]

During an extended survey of communication problems in a shoe factory and two civil service offices,[1] the importance of various assumptions on the part of the people communicating became more and more apparent. What was said, how it was said, and what was left unsaid often appeared to be a function of certain basic assumptions characterizing the communicator—assumptions about himself, other people, and his general environment. Furthermore, any significant change in attitudes toward communication problems or in the methods of communication, seemed dependent upon changes in the underlying assumptions. The present paper proposes to make explicit some of the more common assumptions and to suggest a useful classification of them and the behavior which stems from them.

By an assumption is here meant a more or less unconscious taking for granted of certain basic but undefined conceptions of one's world. Such an assumption is in a sense an "inarticulate major premise" in terms of which the individual evaluates aspects of his world. What is meant by this becomes clearer if these assumptions are distinguished from the conscious assumptions deliberately formulated to guide policy, and which are verified by, or revised in the light of, experience, and further, if these assumptions are distinguished from beliefs. The assumptions which concern us here are not consciously adopted, and are usually not revised because they have never been articulated and defined so they can be revised. They are unlike beliefs in that the latter are usually consciously held and are recognized as having alternatives. It is perhaps the explicit recognition of alternatives that most clearly distinguishes working assumptions, and beliefs, from the basic, undefined assumptions which are the subject of this paper.

People act in a particular situation in terms of the meaning they "see" in that situation; in terms of their evaluations of it. Frequently, however, these evaluations are not deliberate judgments made in terms of consciously held criteria. They are automatic judgments, the bases for which have not been examined. Perhaps the most obvious of these are moral judgments. We make most of our moral judgments not because we have carefully considered various alternatives, but because we make certain assumptions about how human beings should behave. The fact that we can point to a stated moral principle which ostensibly underlies our judgment does not invalidate the position taken here.

[1] Thomas R. Nilsen, "The Communication Survey: A Study of Communication Problems in Three Office and Factory Units," unpublished Ph.D. dissertation (Evanston, Ill.: School of Speech, Northwestern University, 1953).

The stated principle may be one the basis for which has never been examined or for which alternatives have never been considered. It is just obviously "right."

The assumptions underlying moral judgments are perhaps extreme examples of the assumptions dealt with in this paper. The former are mentioned simply to further suggest what we are trying to make clear, namely, that we often act in terms of basic orientations, unexamined concepts, or what we have called assumptions, and that these assumptions tend to result in more or less automatic patterns of behavior. We are interested here primarily in the assumptions that result in the kind of behavior that stands in the way of the most effective communication.

The assumptions people make are, of course, not observable. They are inferred from observed behavior. When patterns of behavior recur in certain situations, especially when the recurring patterns are ineffective in resolving the problems encountered, it seems evident that this behavior is a function of more or less fixed interpretations of the situations. The point of view taken in this paper is that such patterns of behavior reflect certain basic assumptions, assumptions that do not readily change but that need to be changed if the behavior is to become more adaptive and constructive.

The following examples illustrate the function of assumptions in shaping communicative behavior. In the shoe factory studied a superintendent said of his employees, "Keep them busy and let them make as much money as they can and they'll be happy." This statement seemed to suggest the assumption that economic motives are of primary importance in on-the-job behavior. Given this assumption it was not surprising that he expressed the view that the "deep-down" feelings of his supervisors or employees were no concern of his, and that he made no attempt to discover how his subordinates felt about company policies or their own jobs.

The general management of the factory stated that their problems of labor turnover and quality of production were "foreman problems." That is, the foremen lacked interest in their jobs and lacked initiative. This point of view appeared to indicate the assumption that what management was doing was right, and that the problems were "in the shop," isolated from the front office. Management, it was noted, did not seek foremen views on labor turnover or quality of production, did not examine their own relationship to the foremen, and did not re-examine their labor policies. Given the assumption that the fault lay only with the foremen, inquiry in other directions apparently did not occur to management.

In a Naval Purchasing Office there was no training or orientation program to acquaint newly promoted employees with their supervisory responsibilities. The Executive Officer frequently observed that his new supervisors did not "act like supervisors." They were too chummy with their employees and did not require the discipline and work output the Executive Officer thought warranted. Plainly he assumed that employees promoted to supervisory positions would automatically act like supervisors or, more correctly, would act as he thought supervisors should.

In a Naval Fiscal Office employees lined up at the time clock before quitting time. The office management directed supervisors to deal with the problem. There was immediate improvement and nothing more was said about it. Management was irate when a month or two later the line-ups occurred again. Their reactions seemed to reveal the assumption that when personnel problems are "solved" they should stay solved. Management had not discussed a solution to the problem with the supervisors, had made no inquiries about the policies introduced, and had not checked on the effectiveness of these policies.

In the shoe factory several of the foremen never sought suggestions from their employees or encouraged an expression of feelings. When asked, half of these foremen said they did not need to know more about what their employees thought. It seemed plain that underlying the foremen's behavior toward their employees were such assumptions as the following: that there was little or nothing any of the employees could contribute; that the attitudes of their employees were either of little importance or else of no concern to the foremen; that the foremen knew all they needed to know; or, that it was not appropriate for foremen to seek to find out more about employee thinking and feeling.

Numerous examples such as those listed above suggested the possible usefulness of a classification of such basic assumptions as appeared to impede communication. Such a classification, it is felt, might help people to make explicit their own assumptions, recognize the assumptions of others, and contribute to an understanding of the function of assumptions in communications. That this kind of awareness and understanding is important can hardly be doubted. Certainly if a supervisor assumes that he already knows enough about what operators think he will not ask for their comments with any sincerity of purpose, if he asks at all. If a supervisor assumes that the psychological needs of employees are unimportant, or of no concern to him, his talking will hardly be designed to serve or satisfy those needs. If management assumes that personnel problems once solved will stay solved, it is unlikely that management will make adequate follow-up inquiries after the corrective action has been taken. If management assumes that the foremen only are to blame for certain personnel problems, inquiry into management's own role in these problems is less likely to be made. If management assumes the primacy of economic motives, management's talking about personnel problems will hardly include adequate inquiry into the causes of these problems.

An obvious difficulty in classifying assumptions lies in their very multiplicity. Every assumption about every aspect of the environment cannot be listed, even if such a list would be useful. It does seem possible, however, roughly to delineate certain areas in which patterns of assumptions tend to exist. It is not suggested here that a one-to-one correlation exists between assumptions and the acts which stem from them. Rather, various recurring patterns of behavior imply patterns of underlying assumptions. The following classification is not intended to be exhaustive or final; it is merely suggestive. The classification is based on the behavior of people in offices and factories. The patterns of behavior listed are, of course, typical only of people in such work situations; the patterns of assumptions, however, would, with minor changes, appear to be typical of people in general.

From the point of view of the communicator we can list the areas of assumptions as follows: assumptions about (1) the communicator's own knowledge; (2) the motivations of people; (3) his own motivations; (4) the communicatee's responses; (5) the character of the general environment; (6) the process of communication itself. It will be seen that the above areas of assumptions overlap; this seems to be unavoidable. Moreover, there is a sense in which the first one includes all the others. There is value, however, in focusing attention on the various areas even though some of them could be consolidated. It will be noted also that only the communicator's assumptions are listed. The assumptions of the listener are also important, and a similar classification might be made of them.

In the following breakdown of the major areas of assumptions there are given, first, a typical pattern of assumptions within the larger area, and second, a typical pattern of behavior that tends to result. The classification includes only such assumptions as appear to impede communication. Further, the orientation of the classification is toward a supervisor as communicator, i.e., the "communicator" usually implies someone in a supervisory position talking to subordinates.

I. The communicator's assumptions about his own knowledge.

A. *Pattern of assumptions:* One assumption appears to be basic in this area, namely, that in a given situation the communicator assumes he knows enough about that situation.

B. *Pattern of behavior:*
1. The lack of inquiry into the causes of problems.

2. Avoiding group discussion of problems and issues.

3. The absence of questions to subordinates about policies adopted and decisions made or about to be made.

4. A tendency toward finality of statement.

5. A general inflexibility, or unteachability.

II. The communicator's assumptions about the motivations of people.

A. *Pattern of assumptions:*
1. The psychological needs of people are not important in the work situation.

2. The attitudes or feelings of employees are not the concern of the supervisor.

3. Men work only or primarily for economic gain.

B. *Pattern of behavior:*
1. The lack of attempts to discover how subordinates feel about their jobs or company policies.

2. The failure to structure group situations to promote member participation.

3. The failure to tell employees why work needs to be done, or why it needs to be done a particular way.

4. The failure to consult about coming policy changes with those to be affected, or a failure to give adequate advance notice.

5. In specific communication situations there is often criticism that is embarrassing, instruction that is "ego-reducing," or orders that are arbitrary.

III. The communicator's assumptions about his own motivations.

A. *Pattern of assumptions:*
1. The communicator's own psychological needs do not influence his words or actions.

2. His reasons for his behavior are "logical."

3. He is motivated only by a desire to do what is best for the company and its personnel.

B. *Pattern of behavior:*
1. Talking and acting that fails to indicate an awareness of the "meaning for me" of events.

2. The lack of awareness of his own bias.

3. In specific communication situations there is often a lack of tact and courtesy, arbitrary orders, or the withholding of information (the communicator does not recognize that such behavior on his part may be need-satisfying).

IV. The communicator's assumptions about the responses of his listeners.

A. *Pattern of assumptions:*
  1. The listener "sees" the situation the same way the speaker does.
  2. The listener understands what is said.
  3. The listener feels, or should feel, as the speaker does.
  4. The listener's responses are, or should be, "logical."

B. *Pattern of behavior:*
  1. The communicator's not checking the reception and understanding of his statements.
  2. The neglect of the listener's "meaning for me."
  3. Dealing with people as if they all see the same "facts" as facts.
  4. Failing to provide opportunities for the expression of feelings by subordinates.

V. The communicator's assumptions about the character of the environment.

In an organization such as an industry it is difficult to separate, from a policy-making point of view, the physical environment from the people working in it. Changes in the physical structure of the work situation cannot be considered apart from the effects of these changes on the personnel involved. The factors considered under the major heading of environment overlap, therefore, with assumptions about people and their responses.

A. *Pattern of assumptions:*
  1. The environment is unchanging, or ought to be.
  2. Events are fundamentally simple, not complex.
  3. Most events can be placed in one or other of two categories, e.g., "good" or "bad," "right" or "wrong."
  4. People respond the same way in different contexts or at different times.

B. *Pattern of behavior:*
  1. Treating personnel problems as if when once "solved" they will stay solved.

2. Dealing with people as if their attitudes and beliefs did not change.

3. Dealing with people the same way in different contexts and at different times.

4. Jumping to conclusions about problems.

5. Looking for *the* cause of personnel problems.

6. Not attempting to anticipate problems.

7. Not recognizing degrees of value in policies and people.

VI. The communicator's assumptions about the process of communication.

All of the above assumptions influence the process of communication. It is desirable, however, in order to throw the problems of communication into sharper relief, to focus attention on some of the assumptions about communication itself.

A. *Pattern of assumptions:*
1. The process of communication itself is not something that requires examination.

2. The communicator already knows enough about communicating.

3. The communication process in a given situation has little or no relation to other events in the same situation.

4. Communication processes are, or should be, independent of the attitudes of the people communicating.

5. The words used mean the same to the listener as to the speaker.

B. *Pattern of behavior:*
1. A failure to examine or study the communication procedures of the organization.

2. The lack of structured opportunities for personnel to express their points of view and to participate in planning.

3. The lack of verification of reception and understanding of communications.

4. The lack of consideration given to consistency between what is *said* and what is *done.*

The above classification could be extended to include more details. It does, however, include what appear to be the most common assumptions that impede communication. It should be useful in helping the individual to become more aware of his own assumptions and those of others, and how these assumptions affect communication. Further, such a classification as has been suggested should be useful to the student of communication in uncovering fundamental communication problems in situations where human interaction is unsatisfactory, and should help in avoiding the error of dealing only with communication techniques when the problems are deeper than techniques.

READING II-4. *The Analysis of Complaints: Fact vs. Sentiment*

F. J. ROETHLISBERGER
AND W. J. DICKSON

[In 1929 over 10,000 employee interviews were conducted and written up by members of the "Industrial Research Division" at the Hawthorne Works of the Western Electric Company. Since one of the purposes of this interviewing program was to discover how conditions about which employees were dissatisfied could be improved, it was necessary to develop a useful conceptual scheme for understanding the meaning of this mass of words that had been collected. The following excerpts from *Management and the Worker* describe the important distinctions that were discovered in the process of analyzing these interviews. Although these distinctions are as relevant today as when they were made some thirty-six years ago, and although they are necessary in order to interpret the meaning of almost any verbal material, they are still not well understood, unfortunately.]

For some time the investigators were baffled by the problem of analyzing the interviews. What were these interviews telling them

Excerpted by permission of the publishers from F. J. Roethlisberger and W. J. Dickson, *Management and the Worker*, Cambridge, Mass.: Harvard University Press, Chapter 12, 257–69. Copyright 1939, 1967 by the President and Fellows of Harvard College. There has been some rearrangement of the material as reproduced here but there are no substantive changes.

about the company, its supervisors, and employees? What uniformities were being revealed? They soon found that a mere statistical cataloguing of likes and dislikes was not the answer to their problem. They realized that they had been naive at first with regard to the phenomena of verbal behavior, and that the understanding of interview material, or verbal behavior, presents difficult problems which are frequently ignored. The search for uniformities among the statements made in an interview presupposes some simple conceptual framework in terms of which the interviewer can operate upon the statements made. Without such a framework, confusion is inevitable.

* * *

Three classes of complaints

These considerations prompted the following question: Did the interviews elicit from the employees many statements having characteristics essentially different from the properties which are generally associated with common facts,[1] and, if so, how were these statements to be interpreted or understood? It is apparent that even from a practical point of view the answer to this question is rather important, for if some of the complaints made by employees have properties essentially different from those of facts, it is well to discriminate such complaints from those that can be regarded as statements of fact.

To answer this question, all the complaints taken from the 1929 interviews were examined. Analysis of the comments with this question in mind showed that there are essentially three different classes of complaints. These classes can be differentiated from one another both on the basis of the kind of experiences which the statements involve and on the basis of the processes which enter into their verification.

> *Class A.* Complaints involving terms which refer to objects that can be seen and touched, and for which there exist some operations which can be agreed upon as defining them.
> *Class B.* Complaints involving terms which refer primarily to sensory experiences other than those of sight and touch, and for which there do not exist, at least in the case of one term, any operations which can be agreed upon as defining them.

[1] By a "fact" will be meant a statement from experience involving sensory processes, and physical and logical operations, such that if the statement is challenged there exist certain generally accepted procedures by means of which the statement can be tested, verified, or corroborated. For those who wish a further discussion of this definition, see L. J. Henderson, "An Approximate Definition of Fact," *University of California Publications in Philosophy*, 14 (1932), 179. The extensive use which the authors have made of this paper will be apparent to anyone who has read it.

Class C. Complaints involving terms which do not refer primarily to sensory experiences, and for which there exist no operations which can be agreed upon as defining them.

Although the formal statement of these differences seems formidable, the distinction is in fact very simple. It involves the difference between such complaints as "the doorknob is broken,"-"this machine is out of order," "this tool is not sharp," and such statements as "earnings are not commensurate with length of service," "the supervisor is unfair," "the job is too hard," "rates are too low," and "ability is not rewarded." On the basis of the kind of experiences which enter into the determination of these three classes of complaints, and consequently on the basis of means of verification, they differ as follows:

Class A complaints involve primarily sensory experiences and physical and logical operations. They are conclusions from experience about things which can be seen and touched, that is, they embody visual, tactual, and kinesthetic sensations. Physical operations, such as moving, turning, handling, lifting, assembling, as well as logical operations, such as counting, verifying, and establishing relations, enter into their determination. They involve terms which can be defined by a competent worker or engineer. Moreover, the definition implies physical procedures by means of which the statement can be tested. For example, such statements as "the tool is dull" or "the machine is out of order" involve standards that can be defined in terms of technological practice and that can be agreed upon by most people who are competent judges of such matters.

Class B complaints differ from those of *Class A* in that, although sensory experiences still play a large role, they are primarily experiences other than those of sight and touch. They involve such experiences as heat, cold, pain, nausea, thirst, and hunger, as well as sensations arising within the organism by movement or tension in its own tissues (feelings of fatigue). Moreover, such statements include terms for which no physical or logical operations exist which can be agreed upon as defining them. They are terms whose meanings are biologically or socially determined and hence vary with time, place, age, nationality, personality, social status, and temperament. Examples of such statements are: "the work is dirty," "the lockers are insanitary," "the job is dangerous," "the work is hard," and "the room is hot."

In Class C complaints sensory experience plays a small role. These comments involve the hopes and fears of the employees. Often they are reducible to verbal expressions of sentiment and reasonings in accord with sentiment. Frequently entering into their determination are such experiences as daydreaming, revery, fantasy, and preoccupation. They too contain terms whose meanings are socially determined and hence for which no physical or logical operations exist which can be agreed upon as defining them. Some examples of such complaints are: "rates are too low," "earnings are not commensurate with length of service," "ability doesn't count."

It is apparent that these three groups differ to a large extent on the question of verification. For *Class A* complaints there are certain procedures clearly defined, either explicitly or implicitly, by means of which the statement can be tested, verified, or corroborated. For the latter two groups no such clear procedures exist. In *Class A*, experiences of sight and touch can be brought in as witness; physical and logical operations can be used in verification. This possibility is not present in the case of *Class B* and *Class C* comments. If such statements are to be verified, the ambiguities of the terms require definition. But here is the difficulty: no definition can be agreed upon by all those concerned with their verification.

For example, let us take the employee who complains that piece rates are too low (*Class C*). A fair piece rate, of course, can be defined by fiat. Management assumes that a fair rate is one that is set in a systematic manner on the basis of motion and time studies and/or in accordance with rates paid by other concerns in the same territory for comparable work. But is this the definition of management or the definition of the employees? According to the employee, piece rates may be too low when the earnings therefrom are insufficient for his needs, or are not in accordance with his hopes and expectations. Depending on which definition is used, the complaint may or may not be justified. But agreement cannot be reached by logical definition. The test is very simple. Go to the employee who says his wages are too low and appeal to the fact that his rates have been set in accord with the most expert knowledge at the company's command. At the end of the discussion the employee is likely to reaffirm his statement, "the rates are too low." Where is there a court of appeal? For him the rates are too low. To him management's definition is arbitrary and management's reasoning appears equivocal.

The properties of Class B *comments*

But surely, it will be said, the statement "the room is too hot" (*Class B*) can be verified. People do agree on judgments of this kind, and it is quibbling to say that there is no definition which can be agreed upon as defining the word "hot." It may be, our dissenter continues, that a room at 68° F. is called comfortable by an Englishman, cold by an American, hot by a man who is doing muscular work, cold by a man who is sitting at a desk, cold by a hypothyroid person and hot by a hyperthyroid person, but such individual differences are not important. It still remains that for most people not doing heavy manual labor a room at 50° F. is cold and a room at 90° F. is hot.

The statement "the room is hot" still remains unverifiable. What is found from experience, however, is that a high correlation exists in many instances between the statement "the room is hot" and a set of physical conditions (temperature, humidity, and ventilation). This does not follow from definition but from the nature of the human organism as known by experience.

Let us take, as an example, three individuals who make the statement "the room is hot." In the case of A, the room is 68° F.; in the case of B, it is 72° F.; and in the case of C, it is 90° F. Let us further assume that the time of year is winter and that all three individuals are not doing heavy muscular work. It is probable that the third complaint would be considered justified, the second doubtful, and the first not justified. Note that determining the justifiability of the complaint does not change the experience of any one of the three individuals. The room still remains hot for A even though the temperature is 68° F.

But our dissenter objects. In spite of the fact that such statements are unverifiable, nevertheless they can be used by management in improving plant conditions. Should a large number of people in a room in which the temperature is 90° F. complain about the heat, the company has a basis for action. Here would be a situation in which an investigator of complaints about plant conditions could take action. But note that in such an instance action would follow not by verifying that the room is hot but by verifying the fact that when the room is 90° F. a large number of persons complain about the heat, a fact which fits in with everyday experience. In the case of a large number of similar complaints about plant conditions, a high correlation was found between the complaints and a certain set of physical circumstances. Moreover, it was assumed that by altering such physical conditions a large percentage of the complaints would be eliminated, and experience showed this assumption to be correct. However, it should be observed that action followed from treating "the room is hot" as a symptom in a way very similar to that in which a doctor handles a complaint about an ache or pain, except that the doctor refers the symptom to the organism whereas the company referred it to the physical environment. In the case of worker A, however, who complained of the heat when the room was 68° F. (and let us remember that the kind of action described above left his situation unaltered), it might be well to refer this complaint to his physical condition.

So far, then, it is clear that although *Class B* comments are not facts in the strict sense of the term, nevertheless this did not prevent their use by management within certain limits for the sufficient reason that, although they have certain properties already mentioned which differentiate them from *Class A* comments, they also have an added characteristic. Sometimes they can be referred to the relation between an organism and its physical environment, about which there is some knowledge (common and scientific facts), and in terms of such knowledge action can be taken.

The properties of Class C *comments*

Although among *Class B* statements a fairly reliable correlation can frequently be obtained between a given set of complaints and a given set of physical circumstances, this does not happen so often among *Class C* statements.

Let us take the example of worker *A* complaining about the fact that worker *B*, doing a similar job, is earning more money than he is. He says, "I have as much or more service than *B*, my efficiency is as high or higher, my potentialities are as great or greater, my attendance record is as good or better, my home responsibilities are as much or more." In short, every factor entering into the determination of wages is to *A*'s advantage. *A* concludes by saying, "This is unfair." Here we have a case in which most people would agree that *A* has a justifiable complaint. That two people doing the same work, all other things being equal, should earn the same amount would be agreed upon by management and the worker. But note that in order to obtain agreement, an *atypical* case has to be presented. Actually, there were no complaints which fulfilled the condition "all other things being equal," and there were very few which even approximated it. The situation was more frequently something like this:

Worker *A* doing (what he thinks is) a similar job to that of worker *B* might complain in the following different ways because (he thinks) *B* is earning more money than he is:

Relation of A to B	*A complains by saying*[2]
A has less service than *B*.	Earnings are not commensurate with job.
A has more service than *B*.	Service is not being rewarded.
A is a man; *B* is a woman.	Woman's place is in the home.
A is a woman; *B* is a man.	Women are being discriminated against.

[2] There is no implication from these examples that the particular condition mentioned brought forth in every case the corresponding complaint. Human situations are never quite so simple as that. All we wish to show is that factors like those illustrated influenced the reactions of the workers.

$$\left\{\begin{array}{l} A \text{ is single}; B \text{ is married.} \\ \\ A \text{ is married}; B \text{ is single.} \end{array}\right.$$

Married employees are given preference over single employees.

Home responsibilities should be taken into account by the company.

$$\left\{\begin{array}{l} A \text{ has less education than } B. \\ \\ A \text{ has more education than } B. \end{array}\right.$$

The company attaches too much importance to education.

Brains don't count.

$$\left\{\begin{array}{l} A \text{ is, or thinks he may be, less efficient than } B. \\ A \text{ is, or thinks he is, more efficient than } B. \end{array}\right.$$

Piece rates are too low.

Ability is not rewarded.

It is obvious that most of these reactions are more than simple descriptions of experience involving receptor processes and physical and logical operations. None of these conclusions follows logically from the given premises, even assuming the situation was as worker A thought. No inference can be drawn from these examples, however, about the illogicality or irrationality of employees in particular. Similar illustrations can be found in all walks of life. Even the scientist outside his laboratory is not immune from this kind of thinking.

The important thing is that these conclusions involve a logic of sentiments. They are expressions of sentiment and reasonings in accord with sentiment, which are very common phenomena in all social life. They are neither facts nor errors. They are nonfacts, involving the sentiments of individuals, and as such verification in the strict sense cannot be applied to them.

It was difficult to see just how such expressions, taken at their face value, could be used to correct conditions in the company. Differences in jobs, abilities, length of service, age, marital status, and so on, would always exist. There would always be a group of employees (generally newcomers and single) who would be opposed to having such factors as service and marital status enter into the determination of earnings. There would also be another group of employees (generally people who had long service and were married) whose sentiments would be the opposite. But that employees were not expressing facts was nothing to be deplored. This made their statements no less important or useful. Difficulty only arose if fact were not discriminated from sentiment, and the latter were taken as the former.

* * *

It should be clear that *Class C* complaints have peculiar properties which differentiate them from the other classes of comments in that:

1. They are complaints in which fact and sentiment are inextricably mixed so that verification in most cases is impossible. Any attempt

at verification involves an arbitrary definition which frequently cannot be agreed upon, so that it ends in a meaningless process (a verbal argument). The worker's complaint still remains a complaint even though it may be unjustified from a certain definition. To apply arbitrary criteria is to miss the nature of the complaint.

2. They are complaints which refer to the significant personal and social life of the worker, and apart from such a context they are meaningless. They cannot be assessed apart from the situation of the individual who makes them.[3]

It should also be clear that *Class B* comments have these properties to a lesser degree than *Class C*, and *Class A* less than *Class B*. In most cases *Class A* complaints are capable of being verified and hence are either facts or errors. Yet even in such statements there is always the possibility of a subjective reference. The complaint "the tool is dull" may be the complaint of a poor worker, as evidenced by the common saying, "a poor worker blames his tools."

Manifest vs. latent content of complaints

This study of employee comments pointed to the need for reassessing the objectives of the interviewing program. The notion that from employee comments in themselves management could obtain an accurate and correct picture of industrial conditions had to be abandoned. It would be approximately true to say that from the interviews nothing had been learned about the physical plant conditions which was not already known by those in charge of such matters. However, it was also true that although the engineers were acquainted with plant conditions they were not acquainted with the reactions of the employees to them. What the interviewing program had provided was not an exact description of plant conditions but statements of how employees felt about such conditions. And this was, for the most part, the practical way in which the employee comments functioned. They offered additional evidence on which the engineer could act.

There was another body of comments which expressed the employees' feelings toward the policies of management, supervision, and certain social conditions of work, and these comments could not be used in so simple a way as those about plant conditions. Although they gave a picture of how the employees felt about such matters, they did

[3] It would be erroneous to conclude that because of these properties there may not exist in some *Class C* statements considerable agreement among the reactions of employees to a given set of conditions (a rate, policy, etc.). To the extent that they share the same sentiments, this uniformity will appear.

not provide any immediate illumination as to why the employees felt as they did. Complaints such as these could not be handled in the simple and direct fashion considered possible in the early stages of the program, for they involved the sentiments of individuals and groups. There were no specialists in sentiments at the company to whom this material could be referred for interpretation and investigation. Of course, any skillful executive or administrator is constantly handling and manipulating such material, but his methods are largely intuitive and implicit. It was obvious that, strictly speaking, verification for this kind of material was not only impossible but irrelevant. Whether justified or not, hopes and fears, desires and sentiments, values and significances existed. To decide which were justified and which were not, to correct the former and to ignore the latter, was to lose sight of the real problem.

The difficulty lay in the reference of such complaints. To what did they refer? It was clear that frequently there was no simple and direct relation between the complaint and the object toward which the complaint was directed. This lack of relation had been noticed by the interviewers. Probably no group had become more aware of the dangers involved in a too simple acceptance of comments at their face value. Often they had good reason to believe that certain grievances, although directed toward some object or person, were not due to some deficiency in the object criticized but rather were expressions of concealed, perhaps unconscious, disturbances in the employee's situation. Such complaints had an inner as well as an outer reference, and the inner reference could be reached only by a further study of the person who made the complaint. To put it in other words, the latent content of a statement, that is, the attitude of the complainant, was, in many instances, just as important to understand as its manifest content. For example, although the manifest content of a complaint might shift and vary, sometimes being directed to this and sometimes to that object, the psychological form might remain the same. The same underlying complaining attitude might be present, even though the employee might on one occasion be complaining about smoke and fumes and on another occasion about his supervisor. Or, to cite a different example, two complaints which from the viewpoint of manifest content might appear to be the same, from the viewpoint of latent content might be quite different. Two workers might both find the same fault with the same supervisor. Yet, in one case the supervisor might be merely the object of a mild antagonism which is often present in any superior–subordinate relation and about which the worker is not greatly concerned, and in the other case the supervisor might have become an object of fear and hatred by means of which all the worker's personal failings and frustrations are expressed.

This need of differentiating the actual significance of the complaint from its manifest expression led to the first discrimination which the investigators used in studying and analyzing the interviews. This discrimination was sometimes referred to as (1) the *manifest* vs. the *latent* content of the complaint, and sometimes as (2) the *material content* vs. the *psychological form* of the complaint. A few simple illustrations will suffice to make this distinction clear.

Let us take, first, an instance which the reader may find it easy to duplicate in his own personal experience. A has an argument with his wife at the breakfast table, an argument, let us assume, in which A is worsted. Still rankling under his discomfiture, A comes to work in a surly mood. Some little thing goes wrong, something which under different circumstances A would "pass off" lightly. But this happening gives him an opportunity to "explode." Anyone or anything in the vicinity may bear the brunt of A's irritation—the temperature or stuffiness of the room, the draft from the window, the condition in which his tools have been left, the trucker who fails to arrive with the necessary piece parts, the "silly grin" of the boss, the obsequious attitude of his subordinate. In this case it can be readily seen that the irritation displayed by A at work is closely related to the argument he had with his wife.

Suppose a worker, B, complains that the piece rates on his job are too low. In the interview it is also revealed that his wife is in the hospital and that he is worried about the doctor's bills he has incurred. In this case the latent content of the complaint consists of the fact that B's present earnings, due to his wife's illness, are insufficient to meet his current financial obligations. This source of his dissatisfaction can be expressed in many different ways, one of which is to grumble about the piece rates.

The case of a worker, C, is slightly more complicated. In the interview C calls his supervisor a "bully." It is learned that C resents the fact that his supervisor passes him by in the morning without a nod of recognition. It is also apparent that this is only one of many ways in which C expresses the fact that he is sensitive about his place in the world. If he is told to do something, he interprets this as a "misuse of authority"; if he is left alone, he interprets this as a "slight" and a failure to recognize his true worth. In his preoccupations, which he begins to express freely in the interview, are to be found all sorts of fantasies about what he could have said or done or would have liked to have said or done to his boss. Under the skillful handling of the interviewer, C begins to relax and to discuss other topics not connected with the shop. He commences to talk about his family and early life. He talks a great deal about his overdominating father who brooked no insubordination on the part of his children. He relates incidents to show his father's inconsiderateness toward his mother and toward himself in particular. As the situation is gradually disclosed in the interview, a clearer picture of the real significance of C's dissatisfaction begins to emerge: it is rooted somewhere in his attitude toward authority as conditioned by the early parental situation. On anyone in a position of authority he tends to "project" the parental image.

Worker D, who complains bitterly about the temperature, ventilation, smoke, and fumes in his department, offers another example. Health is the dominating motif of the interview. This preoccupation is paramount, and a good deal of the interview is taken up with questions of diet, health, disease, and the deception of physical appearances (D is a robust, healthy-looking person). Gradually D tells about the case of his brother who had recently died from pneumonia. He compares himself to his brother: "Here I am a healthy, strapping fellow, just like my brother; yet tomorrow I too may be gone."

The first simple rule which the interviewers contributed to the analysis of complaints was this: *Consider the complaint not only in relation to its alleged object but also in relation to the personal situation of the complainant.* Only in this way is the richer significance of the complaint realized. The significance of B's grouch about piece rates is better grasped in relation to the increased financial obligation incurred by his wife's illness. C's attitude toward his boss is greatly illuminated by the experience he relates in connection with his father. D's complaint about smoke and fumes is more readily understood in relation to his fear of contracting pneumonia.

Of course, such an analysis did not settle the question of whether or not B's piece rates were "really" too low, whether or not C's boss *was* a bully, or what the "real" state of affairs with regard to smoke and fumes in D's department was. But the difficulties encountered in answering such questions, particularly the first two, have already been discussed. The investigators felt that more could be learned about the worker, his values and significances, by trying to find out more fully the emotional significance of the complaint for the complainant than by trying to judge the truth or falsity of the complaint, particularly in those cases where there was no sensory experience or common standard agreed upon by which to settle the matter. The important consideration was not whether his complaint was justified but why he felt the way he did.

This search for the latent content of the complaint afforded excellent training for the interviewers. Had this way of thinking not been developed early in the program, many interesting problems would have been overlooked, and an adequate conceptual scheme for the handling of personal dissatisfaction would not have been developed. What the interviewers found was that workers by themselves were not able to specify precisely the particular source of their dissatisfaction, but that if they were encouraged to talk freely, the effect was not merely emotional relief but also, in many instances, the revelation to the critical listener of the significance of the complaint. From a research point of view, this was the first finding of great importance which resulted from the interviewing program, and it had an important bearing on the future activities of the interviewing staff. It shifted the direction of the research from merely an exploration of industrial conditions to an exploration of human situations as well. *Certain complaints were no longer treated as facts in themselves but as symptoms or indicators of personal or social situations which needed to be explored.*

READING II-5. *Barriers and Gateways to Communication*

CARL R. ROGERS AND
F. J. ROETHLISBERGER

[This selection deals with ways of overcoming the sources of misunderstanding with which Part II is concerned, and thus serves as a bridge to Parts III and IV. Rogers' suggested test of one's ability to learn what one's "opponent" is saying can be very instructive if applied, occasionally, in the middle of a case discussion in which the participants become emotionally involved.]

Communication among human beings has always been a problem. But it is only fairly recently that management and management advisers have become so concerned about it and the way it works or

Reprinted, including editor's note, from Carl R. Rogers and F. J. Roethlisberger, "Barriers and Gateways to Communication," *Harvard Business Review*, 30, no. 4 (July–August 1952), 28–34. Copyright © 1952 by The President and Fellows of Harvard College; all rights reserved. The authors' observations are based on their contributions to a panel discussion at the Centennial Conference on Communications, Northwestern University, October 1951.

does not work in industry. Now, as the result of endless discussion, speculation, and plans of action, a whole cloud of catchwords and catch-thoughts has sprung up and surrounded it.

The Editors of the *Review* therefore welcome the opportunity to present the following two descriptions of barriers and gateways to communication, in the thought that they may help to bring the problem down to earth and show what it means in terms of simple fundamentals. First Carl R. Rogers analyzes it from the standpoint of human behavior generally (Part I); then F. J. Roethlisberger illustrates it in an industrial context (Part II).—*The Editors*

Part I

It may seem curious that a person like myself, whose whole professional effort is devoted to psychotherapy, should be interested in problems of communication. What relationship is there between obstacles to communication and providing therapeutic help to individuals with emotional maladjustments?

Actually the relationship is very close indeed. The whole task of psychotherapy is the task of dealing with a failure in communication. The emotionally maladjusted person, the "neurotic," is in difficulty, first, because communication within himself has broken down and, secondly, because as a result of this his communication with others has been damaged. To put it another way, in the "neurotic" individual parts of himself which have been termed unconscious, or repressed, or denied to awareness, become blocked off so that they no longer communicate themselves to the conscious or managing part of himself; as long as this is true, there are distortions in the way he communicates himself to others, and so he suffers both within himself and in his interpersonal relations.

The task of psychotherapy is to help the person achieve, through a special relationship with a therapist, good communication within himself. Once this is achieved, he can communicate more freely and more effectively with others. We may say then that psychotherapy is good communication, within and between men. We may also turn that statement around and it will still be true. Good communication, free communication, within or between men, is always therapeutic.

It is, then, from a background of experience with communication in counseling and psychotherapy that I want to present two ideas: (1) I wish to state what I believe is one of the major factors in blocking or impeding communication, and then (2) I wish to present what in our experience has proved to be a very important way of improving or facilitating communication.

BARRIER: THE TENDENCY TO EVALUATE

I should like to propose, as a hypothesis for consideration, that the major barrier to mutual interpersonal communication is our very natural tendency to judge, to evaluate, to approve (or disapprove) the statement of the other person or the other group. Let me illustrate my meaning with some very simple examples. Suppose someone, commenting on this discussion, makes the statement, "I didn't like what that man said." What will you respond? Almost invariably your reply will be either approval or disapproval of the attitude expressed. Either you respond, "I didn't either; I thought it was terrible," or else you tend to reply, "Oh, I thought it was really good." In other words, your primary reaction is to evaluate it from *your* point of view, your own frame of reference.

Or take another example. Suppose I say with some feeling, "I think the Republicans are behaving in ways that show a lot of good sound sense these days." What is the response that arises in your mind? The overwhelming likelihood is that it will be evaluative. In other words, you will find yourself agreeing, or disagreeing, or making some judgment about me such as "He must be a conservative," or "He seems solid in his thinking." Or let us take an illustration from the international scene. Russia says vehemently, "The treaty with Japan is a war plot on the part of the United States." We rise as one person to say, "That's a lie!"

This last illustration brings in another element connected with my hypothesis. Although the tendency to make evaluations is common in almost all interchange of language, it is very much heightened in those situations where feelings and emotions are deeply involved. So the stronger our feelings, the more likely it is that there will be no mutual elements in the communication. There will be just two ideas, two feelings, two judgments, missing each other in psychological space.

I am sure you recognize this from your own experience. When you have not been emotionally involved yourself and have listened to a heated discussion, you often go away thinking, "Well, they actually weren't talking about the same thing." And they were not. Each was making a judgment, an evaluation, from his own frame of reference. There was really nothing which could be called communication in any genuine sense. This tendency to react to any emotionally meaningful statement by forming an evaluation of it from our own point of view is, I repeat, the major barrier to interpersonal communication.

GATEWAY: LISTENING WITH UNDERSTANDING

Is there any way of solving this problem, of avoiding this barrier? I feel that we are making exciting progress toward this goal, and I should like to present it as simply as I can. Real communication occurs, and this evaluative tendency is avoided, when we listen with understanding. What does that mean? It means to see the expressed idea and attitude from the other person's point of view, to sense how it feels to him, to achieve his frame of reference in regard to the thing he is talking about.

Stated so briefly, this may sound absurdly simple, but it is not. It is an approach which we have found extremely potent in the field of psychotherapy. It is the most effective agent we know for altering the basic personality structure of an individual and for improving his relationships and his communications with others. If I can listen to what he can tell me, if I can understand how it seems to him, if I can see its personal meaning for him, if I can sense the emotional flavor which it has for him, then I will be releasing potent forces of change in him.

Again, if I can really understand how he hates his father, or hates the company, or hates Communists—if I can catch the flavor of his fear of insanity, or his fear of atom bombs, or of Russia—it will be of the greatest help to him in altering those hatreds and fears and in establishing realistic and harmonious relationships with the very people and situations toward which he has felt hatred and fear. We know from our research that such empathic understanding—understanding *with* a person, not *about* him—is such an effective approach that it can bring about major changes in personality.

Some of you may be feeling that you listen well to people and yet you have never seen such results. The chances are great indeed that your listening has not been of the type I have described. Fortunately, I can suggest a little laboratory experiment which you can try to test the quality of your understanding. The next time you get into an argument with your wife, or your friend, or with a small group of friends, just stop the discussion for a moment and, for an experiment, institute this rule: "Each person can speak up for himself only *after* he has first restated the ideas and feelings of the previous speaker accurately and to that speaker's satisfaction."

You see what this would mean. It would simply mean that before presenting your own point of view, it would be necessary for you to achieve the other speaker's frame of reference—to understand his thoughts and feelings so well that you could summarize them for him. Sounds simple, doesn't it? But if you try it, you will discover that it is one of the most difficult things you have ever tried to do. However, once you have been able to see the other's point of view, your own comments will have to be drastically revised. You will also find the emotion going out of the discussion, the differences being reduced, and those differences which remain being of a rational and understandable sort.

Can you imagine what this kind of an approach would mean if it were projected into larger areas? What would happen to a labor–management dispute if it were conducted in such a way that labor, without necessarily agreeing, could accurately state management's point of view in a way that management could accept; and management, without approving labor's stand, could state labor's case in a way that labor agreed was accurate? It would mean that real communication was established, and one could practically guarantee that some reasonable solution would be reached.

If, then, this way of approach is an effective avenue to good communication and good relationships, as I am quite sure you will agree if you try the experiment I have mentioned, why is it not more widely tried and used? I will try to list the difficulties which keep it from being utilized.

• Need for Courage

In the first place it takes courage, a quality which is not too widespread. I am indebted to Dr. S. I. Hayakawa, the semanticist, for pointing out that to carry on psychotherapy in this fashion is to take a very real risk, and that courage is required. If you really understand another person in this way, if you are willing to enter his private world and see the way life appears to him, without any attempt to make evaluative judgments, you run the risk of being changed yourself. You might see it his way; you might find yourself influenced in your attitudes or your personality.

This risk of being changed is one of the most frightening prospects many of us can face. If I enter, as fully as I am able, into the private world of a neurotic or psychotic individual, isn't there a risk that I might become lost in that world? Most of us are afraid to take that risk. Or if we were listening to a Russian Communist, or Senator Joe McCarthy, how many of us would dare to try to see the world from each of their points of view? The great majority of us could not *listen*; we would find ourselves compelled to *evaluate*, because listening would seem too dangerous. So the first requirement is courage, and we do not always have it.

• Heightened Emotions

But there is a second obstacle. It is just when emotions are strongest that it is most difficult to achieve the frame of reference of the other person or group. Yet it is then that the attitude is most needed if communication is to be established. We have not found this to be an insuperable obstacle in our experience in psychotherapy. A third party, who is able to lay aside his own feelings and evaluations, can assist greatly by listening with understanding to each person or group and clarifying the views and attitudes each holds.

We have found this effective in small groups in which contradictory or antagonistic attitudes exist. When the parties to a dispute realize that they are being understood, that someone sees how the situation seems to them, the statements grow less exaggerated and less defensive, and it is no longer necessary to maintain the attitude, "I am 100 per cent right and you are 100 per cent wrong." The influence of such an understanding catalyst in the group permits the members to come closer and closer to the objective truth involved in the relationship. In this way mutual communication is established, and some type of agreement becomes much more possible.

So we may say that though heightened emotions make it much more difficult to understand *with* an opponent, our experience makes it clear that a neutral, understanding, catalyst-type of leader or therapist can overcome this obstacle in a small group.

• *Size of Group*

That last phrase, however, suggests another obstacle to utilizing the approach I have described. Thus far all our experience has been with small face-to-face groups—groups exhibiting industrial tensions, religious tensions, racial tensions, and therapy groups in which many personal tensions are present. In these small groups our experience, confirmed by a limited amount of research, shows that this basic approach leads to improved communication, to greater acceptance of others and by others, and to attitudes which are more positive and more problem-solving in nature. There is a decrease in defensiveness, in exaggerated statements, in evaluative and critical behavior.

But these findings are from small groups. What about trying to achieve understanding between larger groups that are geographically remote, or between face-to-face groups that are not speaking for themselves but simply as representatives of others, like the delegates at Kaesong? Frankly we do not know the answers to these questions. I believe the situation might be put this way: As social scientists we have a tentative test-tube solution of the problem of breakdown in communication. But to confirm the validity of this test-tube solution and to adapt it to the enormous problems of communication breakdown between classes, groups, and nations would involve additional funds, much more research, and creative thinking of a high order.

Yet with our present limited knowledge we can see some steps which might be taken even in large groups to increase the amount of listening *with* and decrease the amount of evaluation *about*. To be imaginative for a moment, let us suppose that a therapeutically oriented international group went to the Russian leaders and said, "We want to achieve a genuine understanding of your views and, even more important, of your attitudes and feelings toward the United States. We will summarize and resummarize these views and feelings if necessary, until you agree that our description represents the situation as it seems to you."

Then suppose they did the same thing with the leaders in our own country. If they then gave the widest possible distribution to these two views, with the feelings clearly described but not expressed in name-calling, might not the effect be very great? It would not guarantee the type of understanding I have been describing, but it would make it much more possible. We can understand the feelings of a person who hates us much more readily when his attitudes are accurately described to us by a neutral third party than we can when he is shaking his fist at us.

• *Faith in social sciences*

But even to describe such a first step is to suggest another obstacle to this approach of understanding. Our civilization does not yet have enough faith in the social sciences to utilize their findings. The opposite is true of the physical sciences. During the war when a test-tube solution was found to the problem of synthetic rubber, millions of dollars and an army of talent were turned loose on the problem of using that finding. If synthetic rubber could be made in milligrams, it could and would be made in the thousands of tons. And it was. But in the social science realm, if a way is found of facilitating communication and mutual understanding in small groups, there is no guarantee that the finding will be utilized. It may be a generation or more before the money and the brains will be turned loose to exploit that finding.

SUMMARY

In closing, I should like to summarize this small-scale solution to the problem of barriers in communication, and to point out certain of its characteristics.

I have said that our research and experience to date would make it appear that breakdowns in communication, and the evaluative tendency which is the major barrier to communication, can be avoided. The solution is provided by creating a situation in which each of the different parties comes to understand the other from the *other*'s point of view. This has been achieved, in practice, even when feelings run high, by the influence of a person who is willing to understand each point of view empathically, and who thus acts as a catalyst to precipitate further understanding.

This procedure has important characteristics. It can be initiated by one party, without waiting for the other to be ready. It can even be initiated by a neutral third person, provided he can gain a minimum of cooperation from one of the parties.

This procedure can deal with the insincerities, the defensive exaggerations, the lies, the "false fronts" which characterize almost every failure in communication. These defensive distortions drop away with astonishing speed as people find that the only intent is to understand, not to judge.

This approach leads steadily and rapidly toward the discovery of the truth, toward a realistic appraisal of the objective barriers to communication. The dropping of some defensiveness by one party leads to further dropping of defensiveness by the other party, and truth is thus approached.

This procedure gradually achieves mutual communication. Mutual communication tends to be pointed toward solving a problem rather than toward attacking a person or group. It leads to a situation in which I see how the problem appears to you as well as to me, and you see how it appears to me as well as to you. Thus accurately and realistically defined, the problem is almost certain to yield to intelligent attack; or if it is in part insoluble, it will be comfortably accepted as such.

This then appears to be a test-tube solution to the breakdown of communication as it occurs in small groups. Can we take this small-scale answer, investigate it further, refine it, develop it, and apply it to the tragic and well-nigh fatal failures of communication which threaten the very existence of our modern world? It seems to me that this is a possibility and a challenge which we should explore.

Part II

In thinking about the many barriers to personal communication, particularly those that are due to differences of background, experience, and motivation, it seems to me extraordinary that any two persons can ever understand each other. Such reflections provoke the question of how communication is possible when people do not see and assume the same things and share the same values.

On this question there are two schools of thought. One school assumes that communication between *A* and *B*, for example, has failed

AUTHOR'S NOTE: For the concepts I use to present my material I am greatly indebted to some very interesting conversations I have had with my friend, Irving Lee.—
F. J. R.

when B does not accept what A has to say as being fact, true, or valid; and that the goal of communication is to get B to agree with A's opinions, ideas, facts, or information.

The position of the other school of thought is quite different. It assumes that communication has failed when B does not feel free to express his feelings to A because B fears they will not be accepted by A. Communication is facilitated when on the part of A or B or both there is a willingness to express and accept differences.

As these are quite divergent conceptions, let us explore them further with an example. Bill, an employee, is talking with his boss in the boss's office. The boss says, "I think, Bill, that this is the best way to do your job." Bill says, "Oh yeah!" According to the first school of thought, this reply would be a sign of poor communication. Bill does not understand the best way of doing his work. To improve communication, therefore, it is up to the boss to explain to Bill why his way is the best.

From the point of view of the second school of thought, Bill's reply is a sign neither of good nor of bad communication. Bill's response is indeterminate. But the boss has an opportunity to find out what Bill means if he so desires. Let us assume that this is what he chooses to do, i.e., find out what Bill means. So this boss tries to get Bill to talk more about his job while he (the boss) listens.

For purposes of simplification, I shall call the boss representing the first school of thought "*Smith*" and the boss representing the second school of thought "*Jones*." In the presence of the so-called same stimulus each behaves differently. Smith chooses to *explain*; Jones chooses to *listen*. In my experience Jones's response works better than Smith's. It works better because Jones is making a more proper evaluation of what is taking place between him and Bill than Smith is. Let us test this hypothesis by continuing with our example.

WHAT SMITH ASSUMES, SEES, AND FEELS

Smith assumes that he understands what Bill means when Bill says, "Oh yeah!" so there is no need to find out. Smith is sure that Bill does not understand why this is the best way to do his job, so Smith has to tell him. In this process let us assume Smith is logical, lucid, and clear. He presents his facts and evidence well. But, alas, Bill remains unconvinced. What does Smith do? Operating under the assumption that what is taking place between him and Bill is something essentially logical, Smith can draw only one of two conclusions: either (1) he has not been clear enough, or (2) Bill is too damned stupid to understand. So he either has to "spell out" his case in words of fewer and fewer syllables or give up. Smith is reluctant to do the latter, so he continues to explain. What happens?

If Bill still does not accept Smith's explanation of why this is the best way for him to do his job, a pattern of interacting feelings is produced of which Smith is often unaware. The more Smith cannot get Bill to understand him, the more frustrated Smith becomes and the more Bill becomes a threat to his logical capacity. Since Smith sees himself as a fairly reasonable and logical chap, this is a difficult feeling to accept. It is much easier for him to perceive Bill as uncooperative or stupid. This perception, however, will affect what Smith says and does. Under these pressures Bill comes to be evaluated more and more in terms of Smith's values. By this process Smith tends to treat Bill's values as unimportant. He tends to deny Bill's uniqueness and difference. He treats Bill as if he had little capacity for self-direction.

Let us be clear. Smith does not see that he is doing these things. When he is feverishly scratching hieroglyphics on the back of an envelope, trying to explain to Bill why this is the best way to do his job, Smith is trying to be helpful. He is a man of goodwill, and he wants to set Bill straight. This is the way Smith sees himself and his behavior. But it is for this very reason that Bill's "Oh yeah!" is getting under Smith's skin.

"How dumb can a guy be?" is Smith's attitude, and unfortunately Bill will hear that more than Smith's good intentions. Bill will feel misunderstood. He will not see Smith as a man of goodwill trying to be helpful. Rather he will perceive him as a threat to his self-esteem and personal integrity. Against this threat Bill will feel the need to defend himself at all cost. Not being so logically articulate as Smith, Bill expresses this need, again, by saying, "Oh yeah!"

WHAT JONES ASSUMES, SEES, AND FEELS

Let us leave this sad scene between Smith and Bill, which I fear is going to terminate by Bill's either leaving in a huff or being kicked out of Smith's office. Let us turn for a moment to Jones and see what he is assuming, seeing, hearing, feeling, doing, and saying when he interacts with Bill.

Jones, it will be remembered, does not assume that he knows what Bill means when he says, "Oh yeah!" so he has to find out. Moreover, he assumes that when Bill said this, he had not exhausted his vocabulary or his feelings. Bill may not necessarily mean one thing; he may mean several different things. So Jones decides to listen.

In this process Jones is not under any illusion that what will take place will be eventually logical. Rather he is assuming that what will take place will be primarily an interaction of feelings. Therefore, he cannot ignore the feelings of Bill, the effect of Bill's feelings on him, or the effect of his feelings on Bill. In other words, he cannot ignore his relationship to Bill; he cannot assume that it will make no difference to what Bill will hear or accept.

Therefore, Jones will be paying strict attention to all of the things Smith has ignored. He will be addressing himself to Bill's feelings, his own, and the interactions between them.

Jones will therefore realize that he has ruffled Bill's feelings with his comment, "I think, Bill, this is the best way to do your job." So instead of trying to get Bill to understand him, he decides to try to understand Bill. He does this by encouraging Bill to speak. Instead of telling Bill how he should feel or think, he asks Bill such questions as, "Is this what you feel?" "Is this what you see?" "Is this what you assume?" Instead of ignoring Bill's evaluations as irrelevant, not valid, inconsequential, or false, he tries to understand Bill's reality as he feels it, perceives it, and assumes it to be. As Bill begins to open up, Jones's curiosity is piqued by this process.

"Bill isn't so dumb; he's quite an interesting guy" becomes Jones's attitude. And that is what Bill hears. Therefore Bill feels understood and accepted as a person. He becomes less defensive. He is in a better frame of mind to explore and re-examine his own perceptions, feelings, and assumptions. In this process he perceives Jones as a source of help. Bill feels free to express his differences. He feels that Jones has some respect for his capacity for self-direction. These positive feelings toward Jones make Bill more inclined to say, "Well, Jones, I don't quite agree with you that this is the best way to do my job, but I'll tell you what I'll do. I'll try to do it that way for a few days, and then I'll tell you what I think."

CONCLUSION

I grant that my two orientations do not work themselves out in practice in quite so simple or neat a fashion as I have been able to work them out on paper. There are many other ways in which Bill could have responded to Smith in the first place. He might even have said, "O.K., boss, I agree that your way of doing my job is better." But Smith still would not have known how Bill felt when he made this statement or whether Bill was actually going to do his job differently. Likewise, Bill could have responded to Jones in a way different from my example. In spite of Jones's attitude, Bill might still be reluctant to express himself freely to his boss.

The purpose of my examples has not been to demonstrate the right or wrong way of communicating. My purpose has been simply to provide something concrete to point to when I make the following generalizations:

1. Smith represents to me a very common pattern of misunder-

standing. The misunderstanding does not arise because Smith is not clear enough in expressing himself. It arises because of Smith's misevaluation of what is taking place when two people are talking together.

2. Smith's misevaluation of the process of personal communication consists of certain very common assumptions, e.g., (a) that what is taking place is something essentially logical; (b) that words in themselves apart from the people involved mean something; and (c) that the purpose of the interaction is to get Bill to see things from Smith's point of view.

3. Because of these assumptions, a chain reaction of perceptions and negative feelings is engendered which blocks communication. By ignoring Bill's feelings and by rationalizing his own, Smith ignores his relationship to Bill as one of the most important determinants of the communication. As a result, Bill hears Smith's attitude more clearly than the logical content of Smith's words. Bill feels that his individual uniqueness is being denied. His personal integrity being at stake, he becomes defensive and belligerent. As a result, Smith feels frustrated. He perceives Bill as stupid. So he says and does things which only provoke more defensiveness on the part of Bill.

4. In the case of Jones, I have tried to show what might possibly happen if we made a different evaluation of what is taking place when two people are talking together. Jones makes a different set of assumptions. He assumes (a) that what is taking place between him and Bill is an interaction of sentiments; (b) that Bill— not his words in themselves—means something; (c) that the object of the interaction is to give Bill an opportunity to express freely his differences.

5. Because of these assumptions, a psychological chain reaction of reinforcing feelings and perceptions is set up which facilitates communication between Bill and him. When Jones addresses himself to Bill's feelings and perceptions from Bill's point of view, Bill feels understood and accepted as a person; he feels free to express his differences. Bill sees Jones as a source of help; Jones sees Bill as an interesting person. Bill in turn becomes more cooperative.

6. If I have identified correctly these very common patterns of personal communication, then some interesting hypotheses can be stated:

   a. Jones's method works better than Smith's, not because of any magic, but because Jones has a better map than Smith of the process of personal communication.

b. The practice of Jones's method, however, is not merely an intellectual exercise. It depends on Jones's capacity and willingness to see and accept points of view different from his own, and to practice this orientation in a face-to-face relationship. This practice involves an emotional as well as an intellectual achievement. It depends in part on Jones's awareness of himself, in part on the practice of a skill.

c. Although our colleges and universities try to get students to appreciate intellectually points of view different from their own, very little is done to help them to implement this general intellectual appreciation in a simple face-to-face relationship—at the level of a skill. Most educational institutions train their students to be logical, lucid, and clear. Very little is done to help them to listen more skillfully. As a result, our educated world contains too many Smiths and too few Joneses.

d. The biggest block to personal communication is man's inability to listen intelligently, understandingly, and skillfully to another person. This deficiency in the modern world is widespread and appalling. In our universities as well as elsewhere, too little is being done about it.

7. In conclusion, let me apologize for acting toward you the way Smith did. But who am I to violate a long-standing academic tradition!

ADDITIONAL READINGS FOR PART II

There is a very large body of research, theory, and discussion that is relevant in various ways to the topic "sources of misunderstanding," even if we confine this topic to the setting on which we focus, interpersonal relationships in formal organizations. We have narrowed the field by emphasizing two clusters of beliefs or assumptions which, when identified, help us understand the misunderstandings that frequently arise:

A. Assumptions about human motivation in general and about what kinds of behavior are appropriate in specific organizational relationships. This topic is generally dealt with in works on organizational theory and management practice. (Cf. Roethlisberger's *Management and Morale*, excerpts from which have been reproduced earlier.)

B. Notions about words and how they are used in human communication. This topic is dealt with in works on general semantics.

(This discipline is also strongly reflected in *Management and Morale*. Cf. also the article by Nilsen reproduced earlier.)

We list here our suggestions for further reading under Topic A and Topic B. We have separated each list into *required* and *recommended* as an indication of which selections we judge to fit most aptly into the design of this part of the book.

Topic A

REQUIRED

1. Douglas McGregor, *The Human Side of Enterprise*, Part I, "The Theoretical Assumptions of Management." New York: McGraw-Hill, pp. 3–57. These chapters, 1–4, or selections from them, we tend to regard as necessary background to Part II. McGregor's dichotomy, Theory X and Theory Y, has often been criticized as an "oversimplification," and we frequently outlaw the use of these labels in class discussion. But the book reflects a wide and wise experience in examining the consequences for communication of differing patterns of management thinking. Other sources for related ideas follow.

RECOMMENDED

2. Chris Argyris, *Interpersonal Competence and Organizational Effectiveness*. Homewood, Ill.: Dorsey-Irwin, 1962, pp. 15–52. Excerpted in Warren G. Bennis, *et al.*, *Interpersonal Dynamics*. Homewood, Ill.: Dorsey Press, 1964, pp. 624–38.

3. ———, *Personality and Organization: The Conflict between System and the Individual*. New York: Harper, 1957, pp. 49–75.

4. Robert Chin, "The Utility of System Models and Developmental Models in Organizational Analysis," in Warren G. Bennis, Kenneth D. Benne, and Robert Chin, eds., *The Planning of Change: Readings in the Applied Behavioral Sciences*. New York: Holt, Rinehart and Winston, 1961, pp. 201–14.

5. Alwin W. Gouldner, "Organizational Analysis," in R. K. Merton, L. Broom, and L. S. Cottrell, Jr., eds., *Sociology Today*. New York: Basic Books, 1959, pp. 400–12. Excerpted in Bennis, Benne, and Chin, *The Planning of Change*, pp. 393–99.

6. Robert L. Katz, "Toward a More Effective Enterprise," in *Harvard Business Review*, 38, No. 5 (September–October 1960), 80–102.

7. F. J. Roethlisberger and W. J. Dickson, *Management and the Worker*. Cambridge, Mass.: Harvard University Press, 1939. Chapter 24, "An Industrial Organization as a Social System," pp. 552–68.

8. Hadley Cantril, *The "Why" of Man's Experience*. New York: Macmillan, 1950. This is not a work on the consequences of particular patterns of assumptions about organizational behavior, as the other references are. Rather, it is an excellent general discussion of how assumptions, in the sense we are now using the term, are learned from past experience and influence subsequent perception and behavior in ways that tend to "make our assumptive worlds come true." Since it definitely takes a perceptual point of view toward the understanding of individual behavior, this book belongs as background reading for Part III as well as for Part II.

Topic B

REQUIRED

1. Samuel I. Hayakawa, in consultation with Leo Hamalian and Geoffrey Wagner, *Language in Thought and Action*, 2nd ed. New York: Harcourt, Brace & World, 1964. We regard Chapters 1–7, 10–14, and 16 as necessary background to Part II. Especially important: pp. 28–32, 58–62, 176–90, 214–20, 255–57, 314–16. But the whole book deserves to be read. It is available in paperback and contains an excellent bibliography. Other sources for similar ideas follow, most of which derive from Alfred Korzybski, *Science and Sanity: An Introduction to Non-Aristotelian Systems and General Semantics*, 4th ed. Lakeville, Conn.: International Non-Aristotelian Library Publishing Co., 1962 (not recommended to beginners).

RECOMMENDED

2. Max Black, ed., *The Importance of Language*. Englewood Cliffs, N. J.: Prentice-Hall, 1962 (paperback). See especially "Words and Their Meanings," by Aldous Huxley, pp. 1–12, "Thought and Language," by Samuel Butler, pp. 13–35.

3. Francis Perry Chisholm, *Introductory Lectures on General Semantics: A Transcription of a Course Given at the Institute of General Semantics*, 1945; 2nd printing, 1954.

4. Margaret Gorman, *General Semantics and Contemporary Thomism.* Lincoln, Nebraska: University of Nebraska Press, 1962.

5. William V. Haney, *Communication and Organizational Behavior*, rev. ed. Homewood, Ill.: Richard D. Irwin, Inc., 1967.

6. Samuel I. Hayakawa, *Symbol, Status, and Personality.* New York: Harcourt, Brace & World, 1963.

7. ———, ed., *The Use and Misuse of Language.* Greenwich, Conn.: Fawcett Publications, 1962.

8. Wendell Johnson, *People in Quandaries.* New York: Harper, 1946.

9. ———, "The Fateful Process of Mr. A. Talking to Mr. B," in *Harvard Business Review*, 31, No. 1 (January–February 1953), 49–56.

10. Irving J. Lee, *How to Talk with People.* New York: Harper, 1952.

11. ———, *Language Habits in Human Affairs: An Introduction to General Semantics.* New York: Harper, 1941.

12. Don Fabun, *Communication: The Transfer of Meaning.* New York: Glencoe Press, 1968.

CASE II-1. Chris Baum

Early in 1943 James Norris became the warehouse superintendent of the Star Oil Company's divisional office in Buffalo, New York (Figure 1). The Star company's head office was located in St. Louis; it distributed petroleum products throughout the country through divisional offices. To take the position, Norris, who was forty years old, resigned as division manager of a smaller and competitive oil company and replaced a man who had reached retirement age. In his new position Norris was in charge of thirty men, most of whom worked in the ware-

Case material of the Harvard Graduate School of Business Administration, prepared as a basis for class discussion. Cases are not designed to present illustrations of either correct or incorrect handling of administrative problems. All names are disguised. Copyright 1956 by the President and Fellows of Harvard College.

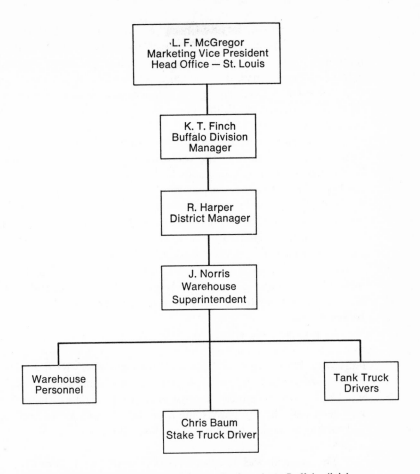

Figure 1. Star Oil Company. Partial organization chart, Buffalo division.

house. However, a few were truck drivers and salesmen who delivered the company's products to customers.

When Norris took the job, he believed there was much that could be done to improve conditions. During his first year he made several relatively small changes, generally regarded as beneficial. He felt strongly and frequently expressed the opinion that the men under his supervision should be "sales-minded," particularly the drivers who were in constant and direct contact with customers. During his second year with the company he worked especially hard on this problem.

One of the men under his supervision was Chris Baum, fifty-two years old, of German birth. A large, heavy man, he had worked for the company for nineteen years. Originally hired as a truck driver to deliver fuel oil to a section of the farming community which was predominantly German, he had since then worked both as a warehouse-man and as a driver. In recent years, Baum had served as route sales-man on a stake body truck, delivering the company's products to commercial customers, dealers' garages, and service stations. In addition to deliveries and making out invoices and daily cash reports, the work required selling ability and some knowledge of the company's products and prices.

Norris had received several complaints both from the office and from customers regarding the way in which Baum recorded his sales. Norris had spoken to him about it, but Baum had not corrected his methods. Baum's fairly heavy accent had also caused some complaints, particularly from customers whose sons were serving in the armed forces. In addition, Norris had had difficulty in getting Baum to adopt other suggestions. He had his own way of loading his truck; and when Norris had tried to get him to load it so that the weight was evenly distributed, Baum had refused, claiming that it made unloading more difficult, caused unnecessary mounting and dismounting, and tired him as well as aggravated a condition in his back which occasionally bothered him.

In pursuing his efforts to make the drivers and route salesmen more sales-minded, early in October 1944, Norris discussed his problems with Baum with his boss, a district manager, Richard Harper, and recommended that a younger man with more sales ability who would be more acceptable to customers replace Baum. Harper, who had been with the company some time but was new in his present job, was willing to make the change, provided the plant industrial council approved.

The council was a company-sponsored group, comprising two members elected by the employees and two appointed by the company with the division manager as chairman. The executives at the company's head offices were proud of these councils and insisted that they meet monthly and forward the minutes of the meetings to the head offices. The Buffalo division council and similar groups in other divisions had been effective in getting benefits for the employees. One of these was a liberal pension plan for employees at age sixty-five. An adjusted allowance was available for persons over fifty-five who for physical or other reasons could not do their work.

At the time that Baum's case came before the council, the elected members were Peter Bancroft, a tank truck salesman, and Bill Dexter, a warehouseman. Harper and Norris were the appointed members, and the division manager, K. T. Finch, was chairman. With some misgivings, these men finally agreed to put a younger man on Baum's job and to transfer Baum to the warehouse. The men realized that Baum might protest this change, because his new job would mean a $10-a-month reduction in pay. Norris felt, however, that Baum, though perhaps grudgingly, would accept the proposed job, because its fewer physical demands compensated for the drop in wages. To make it easier for Baum, the men agreed to make the less arduous work the reason for the transfer without mentioning to him the customers' complaints and the errors in his invoices.

When Norris told him of the council's decision, Baum reacted violently, claiming that it was an attempt to get rid of him. He further stated that instead of being asked to take a reduction in pay, he felt he should be allowed to become the tank truck salesman on a new delivery unit which the division was soon to add. The outcome of their talk was that Baum was to let Norris know the next day whether he would accept the transfer.

The next day Baum told Norris he had not changed his mind and that he intended to appeal to the industrial council for redress. Norris relayed this message to Harper, who with Norris spoke to Baum. Harper explained, as had Norris, that the company felt that his present job was too arduous for a man of his age and weight and that they felt the job they had in mind would be beneficial to him. Since Baum continued to hold to his opinion, a special meeting of the council was called for the next afternoon. Both Bancroft and Dexter also talked to Baum, but neither was able to persuade him to change his mind. In all their talks with Baum, none of them told him of the other reasons for his transfer.

At the council meeting, before Baum was called in, Bancroft, who was fifty-five years old and a tank truck driver, expressed a sympathetic attitude toward Baum's position. He also expressed concern that removing older men might become a company policy. Both Norris and Harper, who was chairman because Finch was away, reminded him that the company was not removing Baum because of his age, but for his unwillingness to cooperate with Norris' sales policies. The fact that they had avoided telling Baum honestly why he was to be transferred brought on a discussion in which the members decided that they should no longer hide the real reasons from him.

When Baum appeared before the meeting, he was visibly upset. He reiterated his dissatisfaction with the proposed transfer and repeated what he had previously told Norris and the others. He said that he had lost a lot of sleep over the matter and that he felt that the superintendent was prejudiced against him. He then requested that they tell him why they had taken such action, since he thought that Norris was just trying to get rid of him.

At this point Norris carefully explained that he thought the work on the stake truck was too arduous for a man as stout and old as Baum. He emphasized the hazards involved in mounting and dismounting from the back of the truck, particularly since Baum had a troublesome back. He finished by saying it was too difficult for a man as heavy as Baum to lift and carry sixty- to seventy-pound buckets of oil and deposit them in the various and often awkward places demanded by customers and the job. From then on the conversation went as follows:

HARPER: But Mr. Norris, Chris does not feel that he is incapable of performing this work in a satisfactory manner.

BAUM: That is so. I have had a little trouble with my back, but it is nothing serious and has not bothered my work. Besides, if you let me take over as tank truck salesman on the new truck, as I feel I am entitled to do, I shall not have to do any lifting. I can drive as good as any man you've got and besides, I don't want to go back into the warehouse rolling barrels with all those newer fellows.

BANCROFT: Yes, Chris discussed this with Dexter and myself and we agree with him that he has no physical incapacities which would not permit him to operate a delivery truck in a satisfactory manner.

BAUM: (Addressing Norris) You just show me where I've had any accidents. All you're trying to do is to get rid of me, so you can put one of your friends on my job.

NORRIS: That is not right. Ever since I took over at the plant here we have been very busy with additional Army and Air Force business and it has been difficult to keep our trucks in shape. I told you on several occasions not to load your truck all on one side, because the springs could not take it and were breaking, but you kept right on doing it. Not only that, you are slow getting the loads out, and you always come back a little before five o'clock with an empty truck, when I know very well that if you had worked right along and not wasted any time, several more deliveries could have been made each day.

BAUM: I have been trying to load the truck your way, but it does not work out.

NORRIS: Apart from the operation of your truck, I have had a number of complaints from customers and the office about the way you make out invoices. They can't read your writing half the time and there are plenty of mistakes. I've told you about it more than once.

BAUM: I have been making out invoices and reports for years and nobody ever complained too much before. We all make mistakes.

HARPER: Yes, Chris, but the proper handling of your invoices and reports is a very important matter, especially when we are so busy. It has much to do with our relations with customers, and as you know, we are most anxious to retain their good will.

DEXTER: If the company has definitely decided to take Baum off this truck, couldn't some inside job be found for him which would not necessitate his taking a cut in wages?

HARPER: That is not possible under our system of job evaluation, where every job has a fixed value. The only way Chris could get more would be as a foreman or a driver. Chris, you are wrong when you say we are trying to get rid of you. We have no thought of that. Mr. Norris has assured me that he can work out a position in the warehouse which will be suitable to you, but the pay will be $10 a month less because the rating does not permit more.

BANCROFT: Why don't you try the inside job for a while, Chris? It may work out better than you think.

BAUM: (with emotion) No, that is no good. Mr. Norris has got it in for me and there is no use in staying around here, no matter what job I have. Ever since I heard about this, I have been upset and not able to sleep properly. My wife and I think it's pretty rough treatment after nineteen years' service, and I might as well quit.

HARPER: Don't make a hasty decision now, Chris, which you may be sorry for later. Take a few days to think it over.

BAUM: All right. I will let you know Monday morning. (He left the meeting.)

BANCROFT: I guess that is all we can do about this case, but I'm afraid some of the older fellows in the plant are going to worry about their own security from now on.

HARPER: Peter, I would like you and Bill to reassure our older men on this point. No one will be affected as long as they are able to perform their duties in a reasonably satisfactory manner, and we want to be absolutely fair in the treatment of our employees.

The next morning, Norris received a letter from Baum in which he said that he was resigning, although he did not say when. Several days later when Mr. Finch returned to his office, he found in his mail a letter from L. F. McGregor, the company's vice president in charge of marketing in the St. Louis office, asking for a full report on Baum's case. The following letter written by Baum was enclosed:

November, 1944

Mr. L. F. McGregor
Star Oil Company
Buffalo, New York

Dear Sir:

I am writing to you to acquaint you of some facts which undoubtedly you may have heard of. About two weeks ago, Mr. Norris, our warehouse superintendent, called me into his office and told me that he thought the job I had was too hard for me and he would give me a lighter job in the warehouse. The job I have been doing was driving a stake truck and I believe I never complained that the job was too hard for me. The warehouse job would be $10 less per month, I was told.

After some discussion, I told Mr. Norris I would let him know next day if I would accept.

The next morning Mr. Norris told me that Mr. Harper (representing Mr. Finch, Buffalo manager) would see me in the afternoon.

That afternoon Mr. Harper told me in the presence of Mr. Norris that he thought when a man becomes of the age of fifty years he should not be driving a truck, on account of accidents, etc., and the nerves are not as good as a young man's. I then questioned Mr. Harper as to whether my work was not satisfactory, or whether they had anything else against me, and he replied that they had nothing against me and my work was satisfactory. I disagree with what Mr. Harper told me because there are men today still driving trucks or tank wagons who are older than I am.

When I started as an employee of the Star Oil, I was a tank wagon salesman selling gas and oil to farmers. This lasted for about 11 years, after which tank wagons were removed from the country and I was placed in the city on the stake truck, and which I have been on until the present day.

Some time ago at a meeting at which Mr. Finch presided he told all the employees that if there were any chances of a man being elevated to a higher position that the Star Oil would be pleased to do this.

Also about two months ago, Mr. Gunther retired and he drove a tank wagon to service stations. I had told Mr. Harper that if he wanted to be fair with me, he should put me on Mr. Gunther's job, to which Mr. Harper did not reply. He did say that it was the wish of the management that I be taken off the stake truck and placed in the warehouse at a reduced salary of $10 per month. The young man who was given Mr. Gunther's job had an accident sometime ago, which goes to prove that a young man is not always better than an older one. I believe that if all the employees of the Star Oil have a driving record such as I have the company would not need to have insurance on its trucks.

The next day we had another meeting with Mr. Norris and the industrial council. I explained my case to the industrial council and they felt that the job in the warehouse was not easier than the stake truck.

After thinking over the situation, I decided that the warehouse job could not be any easier for me because I would have to be on my feet all day long moving barrels and cartons from railway cars to places of storage, so I decided that if the Star Oil Company could not do any better for an employee who had worked the best years of his life in the interests of the company, then I must resign, and the next day I gave Mr. Norris my resignation.

Furthermore, I do not believe that the president of Star Oil Company would let a situation such as this go by without doing something about it.

The reason I am writing this letter is that I am not satisfied that the company would try to put a man in a lower position unless there was a better reason than the one I have received. If so, I would like to know it.

Yours very sincerely,

s/ Chris Baum

Mr. Finch asked Harper for a detailed and up-to-date record of the case and also to call a special council meeting for the next evening. In the morning before the meeting, he discussed the situation with both Harper and Norris.

Mr. Finch felt that because of Baum's long service and intense dissatisfaction with the proposed job, the company might be well advised to let Baum take over the smallest of the division's tank trucks and in that way suffer no wage cut. He felt that it was much better for the company to operate at some disadvantage than to give the employees any cause to feel that the company had treated Baum unfairly. Both Harper and Norris agreed with Mr. Finch's proposal.

That evening Mr. Finch told the council of his plan. The men unanimously agreed that it was an attractive counter-offer which

Baum would accept, since he would not have to work with junior men in the warehouse and he would not have to take a cut in wages.

The next day Finch, Harper, and Norris learned that when Bancroft and Dexter made this proposal to Baum, he insisted that since Norris was "down" on him there was no use in his trying to buck the situation. He said he was part-owner of a small grocery store and that he had decided to work there, quitting the Star Oil Company at the end of the next month.

CASE II-2. John Byron

Paul Varner and John Byron were discussing the latter's job as personnel manager of one of his company's small plants. Varner was a candidate for a doctoral degree in business administration at a local university. Byron's company manufactured electronic products. The plant where he worked was located in Eastern Pennsylvania; many of the company policies were "written" at the head offices in Kansas City and handed down to the different plants through regional and product division headquarters. The division office to which Byron's plant reported was located in Richmond, Virginia. The head office frequently consulted division personnel executives in regard to new policies but seldom went to personnel managers, particularly in the smaller plants. Typically the latter received new policies through their plant managers.

BYRON: The company has one particular hiring policy which gets us into all kinds of trouble. This policy states that we shall hire only people who are perfect physical specimens. Certainly I can read the policy no other way than that we must reject all applicants who are not perfect physical specimens; and the company doctor reads it the same way too.

Case material of the Harvard Graduate School of Business Administration, prepared as a basis for class discussion. Cases are not designed to present illustrations of either correct or incorrect handling of administrative problems. All names are disguised. Copyright 1956 by the President and Fellows of Harvard College.

Twenty per cent of all our applicants we reject because they fail to pass the rigid physical examination the doctor feels he must give them. During a year we interview about 2,500 job applicants in this office. Twenty per cent, or about 500 of them, we reject on the basis of physical defects; and one-half of those 500 are rejected for very minor physical defects. For example, we have just rejected a man because the tip of his little finger was missing. Another man was turned away because he had had an operation for hernia. He had had the operation five years ago, and, as the doctor said, in only about 5 per cent of all cases do people who have had the operation have the trouble again. But because of our rigid policy we had to reject that man. We rejected him just on the chance, 1 in 20, that maybe something could happen to him here to cause the hernia to bother him again. Management is just that worried about its workmen's compensation experience rating. They can't stand to pay workmen's compensation. This policy is to protect us at the source, I guess.

But look at the additional trouble the policy brings us. An applicant comes here, goes through the rigorous examination, and then is rejected because he isn't physically perfect. As I say, we send them away for minor things like having the tip of their little finger missing and nothing else wrong with them. Well, you can imagine what those people have to say to their friends about this company. They certainly don't build up a favorable reputation for us. This is just one of the things I've had to live with since I came here.

While Byron and Varner were still talking, Mark Petmans, superintendent of one of the manufacturing departments, walked into the former's office.

BYRON: Hi, Mark, come in.

PETMANS: (After saying hello to Paul.) John, I have a problem and I want you to give me some advice.

BYRON: Sure, I'll do what I can.

PETMANS: I want to talk about this fellow Angelo Verdini, who is applying for a job here. I was just talking to the doctor and he tells me that Verdini has to be put on limited employment. Do you know what is wrong with him? The tip of his little finger is missing. The doctor tells me he has a memorandum which he showed me from Mr. Welland [plant manager]. It says in effect, as I read it, that we hire nothing but perfect physical specimens. If this is so, this is the screwiest thing that I have ever encountered in all my life. I talked to the doctor about Angelo Verdini. He says that because the fellow is missing the tip of his little finger, he has to be rejected or put on no more than limited employment. The doctor also says that Verdini has some sort of minor nervous condition in his stomach, but from what I understand that doesn't amount to a hill of beans. In fact, neither one of his so-called defects does. Yet because this fellow is minus the tip of his little finger, we have to put him on limited employment. This is the way the doctor interprets the policy and, as a matter of fact, when he showed me the letter, that's the way I read it too. We can hire nobody but perfect physical specimens. Well, I asked the doctor, "If you were in my position, would you consider this man an accident risk?" The doctor said, "Speaking from your point of view, I think, no, I wouldn't." Well, the doctor was speaking off the record, but he said he wouldn't call the fellow an accident risk. So what I want to know is why can't I hire this man? He's a skilled employee. That's what I want. Now why can't I hire this man?

BYRON: Well, you know what the policy is and you know how dangerous it is to make exceptions.

PETMANS: What danger is there to this one? This is the damndest thing that I have ever heard of in all my life. We won't hire a man simply because he doesn't have the tip of his little finger. When it comes to the jobs I want him to do, I don't see that that hurts him at all. He can do any job I have for him to do.

BYRON: Yes, but it's making these exceptions that gets you into trouble. Now understand, I agree with you that this policy is pretty ridiculous. If you want to change the policy, see Mr. Welland, not me. But as long as this is the policy I think we have to carry it out. It is very explicitly stated, I agree, that we will hire nothing but perfect physical specimens. The doctor knows that, and that is the way he has been carrying out the policy. Twenty per cent of all job applicants we reject because of physical defects, and about 50 per cent of those we reject have minor things like the loss of a tip of the little finger.

PETMANS: Well, in this case what difference does it make that this fellow doesn't have the tip of his little finger? I think this is a pretty sad state of affairs when a fellow can't get a job because he is minus the tip of his little finger.

BYRON: Yes, but you know what happens when you make an exception. First you have a fellow who is minus the tip of the little finger; then a fellow comes in who is minus all of his little finger.

Well, you take him. Then a man comes in minus all of his fingers. Then we have an amputee, and we go on from there. You can see what happens to these things.

PETMANS: Baloney! That isn't what I mean at all and you know it isn't. I don't think it goes that way at all.

BYRON: You know that is the danger you run every time you make an exception to the rules. It will snowball every time. That is the risk you take if you go ahead and hire this man. The next thing you know everybody here will be hiring fellows first minus the tips of their fingers, then minus all of their little fingers, and then we'll have amputees and all sorts of problems on our hands. I think this rule does have a point and I'm sympathetic with it in part too, because it can be said that a fellow who has had an accident and is minus the tip of his little finger is probably a fellow who is prone to having accidents quite often.

PETMANS: This fellow didn't lose the tip of his little finger in an accident. It was from an infection.

BYRON: Well, you can see the risk, though, that you run in hiring that kind of person. Ordinarily you find that people who do have these defects from accidents are people who will generally have accidents. And those are the kind of people we don't want. We don't want to get ourselves loaded up with a lot of accident-prone employees. That just increases our experience rating for workmen's compensation, and that costs us money.

PETMANS: Yes, but this fellow didn't lose the tip of his finger in an accident. It came from an infection I told you.

BYRON: Well, how did that come about—carelessness, failure to get proper treatment?

PETMANS: I suppose the thing wasn't treated properly, but it can happen to anyone.

BYRON: No, it couldn't happen to anyone. Well, yes, in a sense it could. But you have to look out for those people. I am just saying that before I hire this fellow, I'd like to have his record all the way back to see how many times he's been to the dispensary on all his other jobs and in the services. I want to know how many accidents he has had. I want a whole record before I make the decision to hire him, because we could get ourselves in a jam. There is something else too. People with some of these so-called minor defects can have very real problems doing our work here. Take the fellow with the tip of his finger gone. A lot of our work here is very difficult and many of our jobs require hand work like lifting and counting and stacking. A person with a stump for one finger can't take it like a fellow with a whole finger. They cut off those nerves and tie them at the end, and that's more tender than the end of my finger. You see, in a sense we are doing these people a favor by not putting them to work here, because if we did it might hurt them. Take a fellow who has lost the tip of his finger. I can see that some of that lifting and stacking, constant pounding against the fingers, could aggravate that stump and make it sore. Maybe infection would spread and by all rights he could claim that this was caused on the job. So what have we done? We have hurt the employee. Not only have we increased our own experience rating for workmen's compensation, but we haven't been fair to the employee. Take another case. Suppose a coal miner came in to work here. Now a coal miner who has been breathing coal dust for a number of years is likely to have silicosis. We don't take X-rays, but if we did we could find out if he had silicosis. But we know that a lot of coal miners have silicosis and we know that the kind of dust we have in our plant aggravates silicosis. So if we bring that man in here, we don't do him a favor; we do him harm.

PETMANS: Okay, I can see that. You're not being very helpful. What about this guy who has lost the tip of his little finger? What's the matter with hiring that fellow?

BYRON: I am just trying to show you what these things can lead to. Some of these cases have cost us a lot of money. Take this Bill Sheridan case for instance. He has cost us about $1,100 in workmen's compensation. Then take the case of June Riley, the girl with the arthritic condition. She has cost us $1,900.

PETMANS: Look, if we carried this policy through completely none of us would be working here. All of us are a little reckless when we are young, a little reckless even when we are older. Who that's here now would be working in this company, if we applied this policy completely?

BYRON: Well, this is a fairly new policy. Understand, I don't agree with it either, but I am saying that I do see some reasons for it. If you want the policy changed, though, see Mr. Welland.

PETMANS: (Pause.) Look what happens, though. I've told this fellow he can't work here because he has lost the tip of his little finger. So he goes out in the community and he spreads this one around. Look what this does to the company. A fine reputation this sets for us.

BYRON: Sure, I know that happens and I know that makes a big problem. I don't like the policy either. All I'm saying is that as long as the rule is in effect, I think we ought to follow it and not make exceptions. Once you start making exceptions, you get yourself in trouble. I am also saying that I can see some rationale for it. I know this thing was thought out before it was put in, and I can see some sensible reasons for it. Don't talk to me if you don't like the rules. Go talk to Mr. Welland. He's the next man to talk to, if you want the rule changed. (Short silence.) Don't hold me responsible for the rule. I'm not to blame. If you want to change the rule, go see Mr. Welland. I can't help you on that one. What I am saying is that as long as the rule is in effect, I think we ought to follow it and not make exceptions. I am also saying that I can see that in a way we are doing the people a favor by not employing them if they do have some physical defects.

PETMANS: Well, this is the goddamndest thing I ever heard of, if you don't mind my swearing. This is completely ridiculous.

BYRON: Let's take some other cases. We don't hire men with flat feet. One of the reasons we don't is because we require all our men to wear safety shoes and a man with flat feet will have trouble wearing safety shoes because of the arch supports. Men with flat feet aren't accustomed to wearing shoes with arch supports. So we hire a man with flat feet, and put the safety shoes on him; he stands around on the floor for a couple of days, his feet start hurting him, and then we have a problem. The next thing we know we are paying workmen's compensation to him because we hired a man with flat feet.

PETMANS: Okay, I can see that one, and I can see that June Riley one; but I don't see this one with the fellow who has the tip of his finger off.

BYRON: Look, there is even something else. You know that workmen's compensation is paid according to the size of the man's family. We had one fellow here who had seven children. He had an accident and it cost us $5,500. I had a man come in here to apply for a job the other day who had nine children. It is pretty hard to think of taking a man like that. Look how much he will cost us if he gets into an accident.

PETMANS: You mean a man can't get a job because he has nine children?

BYRON: Well, you can see the risks you run if a man has an accident.

PETMANS: Ye gods, look at the risks you run with any of us. Look at the risks we're running with me. Any of us are risks if you follow that one through. You'll have nobody here at all. But I have to run this department with people.

BYRON: I'm just naming the risks that you run. If you want to take the responsibility and make an exception to the rule, okay, but you be responsible for the consequences. I say that every time you make exceptions the thing snowballs on you, and I also say that in a way you are doing a favor to these people by not hiring them.

PETMANS: Well, it is easy for you to say this, but you aren't out there in the department responsible for production. It is easy for you to talk about it when you aren't responsible for the work.

BYRON: What do you mean, I am not responsible? We interview about 2,500 applicants a year and we have to reject 20 per cent of them on the basis of physical defects. That's not easy for us to do. We're very much in this picture.

PETMANS: Well, the point is that I have lost a man and Verdini has the skill I need to replace him. I want to know how I can get him. I still say it is easier for you to talk about it. I'm the guy who is in the middle. I'm the guy who's out there and has to get out the work. I need this man.

BYRON: Well, you got yourself into this fix.

PETMANS: What would you do if you were running my department?

BYRON: I wouldn't ever let myself need a man so desperately. I'd always keep a reserve. You run your department like a company with only one boiler. Suppose the boiler broke down; the whole plant would shut down. Every company keeps an auxiliary boiler. I would do the same thing with employees. I would keep myself a cushion.

PETMANS: Well, I need an employee right now, and I want this man. I don't think you're being very helpful at all.

BYRON: You haven't done so badly about getting good employees. We have kept you supplied with people.

PETMANS: With this perfect specimen rule, I don't see how I will ever get anybody. I don't see how anybody can pass that test. I know darn well if it applied to those of us already working here none of us would be here. You have to run a department with people. I can't run this department unless I have some people in there. (Petmans headed toward the door.) I don't think we're doing so damn well with the perfect physical specimens we have here anyway. I think probably we would be better off if we had some of these amputees and people with the tips of their fingers missing. We would probably get out a lot more work and do it a lot better. (He left the office.)

CASE II–3. The Niwash Division of Allied Metals & Alloys, Inc.

On a Wednesday morning, Bill Drake, industrial engineer, was talking to his boss, Stuart Brock, the superintendent of the department:

"Stu, sometimes this job really gets me down. How can we ever get the men in the plant to follow our recommendations when we haven't got any authority? Not only that, but Bruno and Axle, my time-study men, tell me there is a feeling in the plant that we are spying. This makes their work more difficult, and they don't like it. I think Bruno is going to ask for a transfer one of these days and he's my best man."

About the same time that Drake was talking to Brock, Bruno Magnus, to whom Drake had referred, was talking with Lyn Raymond, in charge of supervisory placement in the company's headquarters personnel office. Magnus began this conversation by asking for a transfer from the industrial engineering work to which he was assigned. He continued, "I'm fed up with being looked on as a spy by the men in the operating departments. They're my friends." This was the first time Raymond and Magnus had talked.

* * *

The Niwash Division of Allied Metals & Alloys, Inc. consisted of two plants situated two miles apart in an industrial suburb of the large city where the company's central offices were located in the downtown area. Plant No. 1, constructed in 1900, was used for fabricating alloys

Case material of the Harvard Graduate School of Business Administration, prepared as a basis for class discussion. Cases are not designed to present illustrations of either correct or incorrect handling of administrative problems. All names are disguised. Copyright 1955 by the President and Fellows of Harvard College.

into wire, rod, castings, and other shapes; the administrative offices of the division were located at the plant. Plant No. 2, built in 1941, was a "producer" plant where electric furnaces were used to make alloy ingots. The two plants had separate production superintendents but operated under the same division manager and shared the same office workers and staff departments. A total of 800 workers were employed in the two plants. Figure 1 is a partial organization chart of the division.

The industrial engineering department was relatively new. It was small and the men in it worked closely with one another. Bill Drake was assigned to study special projects with particular emphasis on materials handling, an important problem in the division. These studies were undertaken at the request of the division manager, the assistant division manager, or the other superintendents or at the instigation of

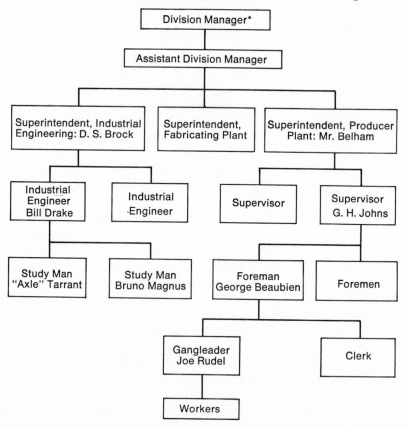

*All men from the rank of supervisor or equal and up were engineers.

Figure 1. The Niwash Division. Partial organization chart.

the department itself. Recommendations were made in the form of a report to the superintendent concerned and to the assistant division manager.

One such report recommended the use of two cranes in handling blocks of old furnace linings in Plant No. 2, if the blocks were above a certain size. These blocks were reinforced with steel bars which stuck out at regular intervals along the edge. The pieces were slung from the crane by wire-rope slings for loading on gondola railway cars to be taken outside the plant and dumped. The number of bars protruding was used as a measure of the size of the block. The specific recommendation was: "Blocks of lining containing more than twelve bars should *not* be handled by means of a single crane. It should be noted that twelve bars represent an overload of 15 to 20 per cent, and crane operators should exercise special caution." After the report was issued, a special "load beam" was provided for crane operators so that two cranes could be used in handling a heavy block of material.

Eight months after the report, two study men from the industrial engineering department, Bruno Magnus and Axle Tarrant, were making observations for a study of ingot handling in Plant No. 2. Bruno Magnus, formerly a foreman, had been with the department for a year and had participated in the survey of furnace-lining loading. Axle Tarrant was the foreman of a department which operated only during the four months of summer and worked for the industrial engineering department the rest of the year.

One Wednesday afternoon, during the course of their work, they noticed a gondola car being loaded with old furnace linings under the direction of the gangleader, Joe Rudel. One piece sixteen bars long was being carried by one crane which "grunted" as it handled the load. The men assigned to this operation were on an hourly rate. One of the regular loaders in the gang commented that the block was "a little heavy" for the crane. Bruno and Axle did not make any remarks.

Because of the intervening weekend, Bruno and Axle did not see their superior, Mr. Drake, in Plant No. 1 (see Figure 1) for five days after this. That Monday afternoon, they related the incident to him. At that time, Drake was on his way to see Mr. Johns, supervisor in Rudel's department (see Figure 1). Both Drake and Johns were engineers, war veterans in their early thirties, and with three to four years of service in the company. In the course of this conversation with Johns, Drake mentioned that he had been told about a single crane handling a heavy block of lining. Johns considered this for a moment, then replied, "Well, I don't know what the hell you can do—those guys have been told and they know they're supposed to use both cranes. . . ." Johns picked up the phone and dialed Beaubien (Rudel's foreman). "George, you busy? Can you come to my office right away?

. . . Okay." Johns replaced the receiver, and a couple of minutes later Beaubien entered Johns' office.

JOHNS: George, these big furnace-lining blocks—are you loading them with both cranes?

BEAUBIEN: Yes, they're supposed to.

DRAKE: What has happened, George, is that Tarrant and Magnus told me that the other day they watched a block with sixteen bars being loaded with only one crane. If this is true, it means an overloading of 60 per cent on the crane.

BEAUBIEN: When was this supposed to have happened?

DRAKE: I don't know exactly, but it was sometime last week.

BEAUBIEN: Well, you see, Bill, it's pretty difficult for me to do much about it now. If Magnus and Tarrant had reported the incident to me right away, I could have checked on it. As it is, if it happened last week, the gondola car has already been shipped and any evidence with it. If I were to ask Rudel or the men if they had loaded a heavy block with only one crane, they would deny it. It's their word against Magnus' and Tarrant's. (Pause.) Anyhow, they could have been mistaken about the number of bars.

DRAKE: That's possible, but I'm inclined to believe what they told me, although I wasn't there myself and can't say for sure.

BEAUBIEN: Well, anyway, you see that it's impossible for me to do anything about it now.

DRAKE: I understand that nothing can be done about this particular incident. I'm only concerned over possible accidents or damage to the cranes in the future.

BEAUBIEN: Magnus and Tarrant work for industrial engineering. If they knew the crane was being overloaded, why didn't they say so? Tell Rudel or the craneman.

DRAKE: Hang on, George. The industrial engineering department has no authority to tell those men what to do and what not to do. Bruno and Axle only noted this event as a casual observation.

BEAUBIEN: (Heatedly.) I'll tell you one thing frankly, Bill—Magnus and Tarrant are there to observe ingot handling only, not to check on the work of the cranes.

DRAKE: That's not quite right, George. It's true that that's their main concern at the moment, but I expect them to report anything which they observe which has any bearing on materials handling. I would consider that they were not doing their job well if they failed to report any such information.

BEAUBIEN: It's your department and you have the right to demand whatever information you like. Frankly, I still say it was none of their business.

DRAKE: Let's forget that part of it. I'm not interested in causing trouble for anyone. All I say is that I understand we had agreed not to load blocks of more than twelve bars with one crane.

BEAUBIEN: That's correct, and to my knowledge we have not been loading heavier blocks with one crane. I've been on the floor many times and watched large blocks being loaded with both cranes and the special load beam.

DRAKE: Well, it's some time since I've seen a car being loaded, although I know how they use the special load beam.

BEAUBIEN: Another thing, Bill, if such a block, one with sixteen bars, was loaded with one crane, it could well have been a thin block. You know, we use 1,500 pounds per bar as a rough measure, but thin blocks weigh far less than that.

At this point, the door opened and Rudel, the gangleader, walked in. He approached Beaubien directly and spoke to him about certain papers he had brought with him. This discussion took only a few seconds. Then Beaubien asked him about the oversize block. Rudel replied distinctly, "Never! . . . or if it was more than twelve bars it was a thin block." Johns intervened with a jocular remark to the effect that perhaps the ends of the reinforcing bars had been counted on both sides. Rudel then left the office, followed by Beaubien and then Drake.
* * *

The next morning (Tuesday), Drake met Magnus and Tarrant in the industrial engineering office and recounted to them the previous day's meeting in Johns' office. Magnus broke in with the remark, "Oh! So that's why Rudel is needling me so much! I was near the remelt unit yesterday afternoon and I met Rudel. He glanced at me and said, 'You're a great guy, Mr. Magnus.' I asked him what was wrong, and he replied, 'I'm too busy to talk now!' Later, I meant to ask him a few questions about ingot racks, but all he said was, 'I'm too busy to talk to you, Mr. Magnus, but you're a great guy!'"

Magnus, Tarrant and Drake then "rehashed" the whole situation. Drake conjectured on why Rudel had used only one crane and suggested that probably Rudel was trying to get the gondola car loaded before the locomotive came around on its regular afternoon schedule to pick it up and had risked loading the one large block with a single crane to save time. "That's fine, but it doesn't help us," said Tarrant. "We try to be pleasant and do our jobs, and all we get is a dirty deal. The men think that Magnus and I are spying on them."

Magnus chimed in, "They sure do and I don't like it!"

CASE II–4. Bob Knowlton

Bob Knowlton was sitting alone in the conference room of the laboratory. The rest of the group had gone. One of the secretaries had stopped and talked for a while about her husband's coming induction into the Army, and had finally left. Bob, alone in the laboratory, slid a little further down in his chair, looking with satisfaction at the results of the first test run of the new photon unit.

He liked to stay after the others had gone. His appointment as project head was still new enough to give him a deep sense of pleasure. His eyes were on the graphs before him but in his mind he could hear Dr. Jerrold, the project head, saying again, "There's one thing about this place that you can bank on. The sky is the limit for a man who can produce!" Knowlton felt again the tingle of happiness and embarrassment. Well, dammit, he said to himself, he had produced. He wasn't kidding anybody. He had come to the Simmons Laboratories two years ago. During a routine testing of some rejected Clanson components he had stumbled on the idea of the photon correlator, and the rest just happened. Jerrold had been enthusiastic; a separate project had been set up for further research and development of the device, and he had gotten the job of running it. The whole sequence of events still seemed a little miraculous to Knowlton.

He shrugged out of the reverie and bent determinedly over the sheets when he heard someone come into the room behind him. He looked up expectantly; Jerrold often stayed late himself, and now and then dropped in for a chat. This always made the day's end especially pleasant for Bob. It wasn't Jerrold. The man who had come in was a

This case was prepared by Professor Alex Bavelas, now of Stanford University, for courses in Management of Research and Development conducted at the School of Industrial Management, Massachusetts Institute of Technology, Cambridge, and is used with his permission.

stranger. He was tall, thin, and rather dark. He wore steel-rimmed glasses and had on a very wide leather belt with a large brass buckle. Lucy remarked later that it was the kind of belt the Pilgrims must have worn.

The stranger smiled and introduced himself. "I'm Simon Fester. Are you Bob Knowlton?" Bob said yes, and they shook hands. "Doctor Jerrold said I might find you in. We were talking about your work, and I'm very much interested in what you are doing." Bob waved to a chair.

Fester didn't seem to belong in any of the standard categories of visitors: customer, visiting fireman, stockholder. Bob pointed to the sheets on the table. "There are the preliminary results of a test we're running. We've got a new gadget by the tail and we're trying to understand it. It's not finished, but I can show you the section that we're testing."

He stood up, but Fester was deep in the graphs. After a moment, he looked up with an odd grin. "These look like plots of a Jennings surface. I've been playing around with some autocorrelation functions of surfaces—you know that stuff." Bob, who had no idea what he was referring to, grinned back and nodded, and immediately felt uncomfortable. "Let me show you the monster," he said, and led the way to the work room.

After Fester left, Knowlton slowly put the graphs away, feeling vaguely annoyed. Then, as if he had made a decision, he quickly locked up and took the long way out so that he would pass Jerrold's office. But the office was locked. Knowlton wondered whether Jerrold and Fester had left together.

The next morning, Knowlton dropped into Jerrold's office, mentioned that he had talked with Fester, and asked who he was.

"Sit down for a minute," Jerrold said. "I want to talk to you about him. What do you think of him?" Knowlton replied truthfully that he thought Fester was very bright and probably very competent. Jerrold looked pleased.

"We're taking him on," he said. "He's had a very good background in a number of laboratories, and he seems to have ideas about the problems we're tackling here." Knowlton nodded in agreement, instantly wishing that Fester would not be placed with him.

"I don't know yet where he will finally land," Jerrold continued, "but he seems interested in what you are doing. I thought he might spend a little time with you by way of getting started." Knowlton nodded thoughtfully. "If his interest in your work continues, you can add him to your group."

"Well, he seemed to have some good ideas even without knowing exactly what we are doing," Knowlton answered. "I hope he stays; we'd be glad to have him."

Knowlton walked back to the lab with mixed feelings. He told himself that Fester would be good for the group. He was no dunce, he'd produce. Knowlton thought again of Jerrold's promise when he had promoted him—"the man who produces gets ahead in this outfit." The words seemed to carry the overtones of a threat now.

That day Fester didn't appear until mid-afternoon. He explained that he had had a long lunch with Jerrold, discussing his place in the lab. "Yes," said Knowlton, "I talked with Jerry this morning about it, and we both thought you might work with us for awhile."

Fester smiled in the same knowing way that he had smiled when he mentioned the Jennings surfaces. "I'd like to," he said.

Knowlton introduced Fester to the other members of the lab. Fester and Link, the mathematician of the group, hit it off well together, and spent the rest of the afternoon discussing a method of analysis of patterns that Link had been worrying over for the last month.

It was 6:30 when Knowlton finally left the lab that night. He had waited almost eagerly for the end of the day to come—when they would all be gone and he could sit in the quiet rooms, relax, and think it over. "Think what over?" he asked himself. He didn't know. Shortly after 5:00 P.M. they had all gone except Fester, and what followed was almost a duel. Knowlton was annoyed that he was being cheated out of his quiet period, and finally resentfully determined that Fester should leave first.

Fester was sitting at the conference table reading, and Knowlton was sitting at his desk in the little glass-enclosed cubby that he used during the day when he needed to be undisturbed. Fester had gotten the last year's progress reports out and was studying them carefully. The time dragged. Knowlton doodled on a pad, the tension growing inside him. What the hell did Fester think he was going to find in the reports?

Knowlton finally gave up and they left the lab together. Fester took several of the reports with him to study in the evening. Knowlton asked him if he thought the reports gave a clear picture of the lab's activities.

"They're excellent," Fester answered with obvious sincerity. "They're not only good reports; what they report is damn good, too!" Knowlton was surprised at the relief he felt, and grew almost jovial as he said goodnight.

Driving home, Knowlton felt more optimistic about Fester's presence in the lab. He had never fully understood the analysis that Link was attempting. If there was anything wrong with Link's approach, Fester would probably spot it. "And if I'm any judge," he murmured, "he won't be especially diplomatic about it."

He described Fester to his wife, who was amused by the broad leather belt and the brass buckle.

"It's the kind of belt that Pilgrims must have worn," she laughed.

"I'm not worried about how he holds his pants up," he laughed with her. "I'm afraid that he's the kind that just has to make like a genius twice each day. And that can be pretty rough on the group."

Knowlton had been asleep for several hours when he was jerked awake by the telephone. He realized it had rung several times. He swung off the bed muttering about damn fools and telephones. It was Fester. Without any excuses, apparently oblivious of the time, he plunged into an excited recital of how Link's patterning problem could be solved.

Knowlton covered the mouthpiece to answer his wife's stage-whispered "Who is it?" "It's the genius," replied Knowlton.

Fester, completely ignoring the fact that it was 2:00 in the morning, proceeded in a very excited way to start in the middle of an explanation of a completely new approach to certain of the photon lab problems that he had stumbled on while analyzing past experiments. Knowlton managed to put some enthusiasm in his own voice and stood there, half-dazed and very uncomfortable, listening to Fester talk endlessly about what he had discovered. It was probably not only a new approach, but also an analysis which showed the inherent weakness of the previous experiment and how experimentation along that line would certainly have been inconclusive. The following day Knowlton spent the entire morning with Fester and Link, the mathematician, the customary morning meeting of Bob's group having been called off so that Fester's work of the previous night could be gone over intensively. Fester was very anxious that this be done and Knowlton was not too unhappy to call the meeting off for reasons of his own.

For the next several days Fester sat in the back office that had been turned over to him and did nothing but read the progress reports of the work that had been done in the last six months. Knowlton caught himself feeling apprehensive about the reaction that Fester might have to some of his work. He was a little surprised at his own feelings. He had always been proud—although he had put on a convincingly modest face—of the way in which new ground in the study of photon measuring devices had been broken in his group. Now he wasn't sure, and it seemed to him that Fester might easily show that the line of research they had been following was unsound or even unimaginative.

The next morning, as was the custom, the members of the lab, including the girls, sat around a conference table. Bob always prided himself on the fact that the work of the lab was guided and evaluated by the group as a whole and he was fond of repeating that it was not a waste of time to include secretaries in such meetings. Often, what started out as a boring recital of fundamental assumptions, to a naive listener, uncovered new ways of regarding these assumptions that would not have occurred to the researcher who had long ago accepted them as a necessary basis for his work.

These group meetings also served Bob in another sense. He admitted to himself that he would have felt far less secure if he had had to direct the work out of his own mind, so to speak. With the group-meeting as the principle of leadership, it was always possible to justify the exploration of blind alleys because of the general educative effect on the team. Fester was there; Lucy and Martha were there; Link was sitting next to Fester, their conversation concerning Link's mathematical study apparently continuing from yesterday. The other members, Bob Davenport, George Thurlow and Arthur Oliver, were waiting quietly.

Knowlton, for reasons that he didn't quite understand, proposed for discussion this morning a problem that all of them had spent a great deal of time on previously, with the conclusion that a solution was impossible, that there was no feasible way of treating it in an experimental fashion. When Knowlton proposed the problem, Davenport remarked that there was hardly any use of going over it again, that he was satisfied that there was no way of approaching the problem with the equipment and the physical capacities of the lab.

This statement had the effect of a shot of adrenalin on Fester. He said he would like to know what the problem was in detail and, walking to the blackboard, began setting down the "factors" as various members of the group began discussing the problem and simultaneously listing the reasons why it had been abandoned.

Very early in the description of the problem it was evident that Fester was going to disagree about the impossibility of attacking it. The group realized this and finally the descriptive materials and their recounting of the reasoning that had led to its abandonment dwindled away. Fester began his statement which, as it proceeded, might well have been prepared the previous night although Knowlton knew this was impossible. He couldn't help being impressed with the organized and logical way that Fester was presenting ideas that must have occurred to him only a few minutes before.

Fester had some things to say, however, which left Knowlton with a mixture of annoyance, irritation and, at the same time, a rather smug feeling of superiority over Fester in at least one area. Fester was of the opinion that the way that the problem had been analyzed was really typical of group-thinking and, with an air of sophistication which made it difficult for a listener to dissent, he proceeded to comment on the American emphasis on team ideas, satirically describing the ways in which they led to a "high level of mediocrity."

During this time, Knowlton observed that Link stared studiously at the floor, and he was very conscious of George Thurlow's and Bob Davenport's glances towards him at several points of Fester's little speech. Inwardly, Knowlton couldn't help feeling that this was one point at least in which Fester was off on the wrong foot. The whole lab, following Jerry's lead, talked if not practiced the theory of small research teams as the basic organization for effective research. Fester insisted that the problem could be approached and that he would like to study it for a while himself.

Knowlton ended the morning session by remarking that the meetings would continue and that the very fact that a supposedly insoluble experimental problem was now going to get another chance was another indication of the value of such meetings. Fester immediately remarked that he was not at all averse to meetings for the purpose of informing the group of the progress of its members—that the point he wanted to make was that creative advances were seldom accomplished in such meetings, that they were made by the individual "living with" the problem closely and continuously, a sort of personal relationship to it.

Knowlton went on to say to Fester that he was very glad that Fester had raised these points and that he was sure the group would profit by re-examining the basis on which they had been operating. Knowlton agreed that individual effort was probably the basis for making the major advances, but that he considered the group meetings useful primarily because of the effect they had on keeping the group together and on helping the weaker members of the group keep up with the ones who were able to advance more easily and quickly in the analysis of problems.

It was clear as days went by and meetings continued that Fester came to enjoy them because of the pattern which the meetings assumed. It became typical for Fester to hold forth and it was unquestionably clear that he was more brilliant, better prepared on the various subjects which were germane to the problems being studied, and that he was more capable of going ahead than anyone there. Knowlton grew increasingly disturbed as he realized that his leadership of the group had been, in fact, taken over.

Whenever the subject of Fester was mentioned, in occasional meetings with Dr. Jerrold, Knowlton would comment only on the ability and obvious capacity for work that Fester had. Somehow he never felt that he could mention his own discomforts, not only because they revealed a weakness on his own part, but also because it was quite clear that Jerrold himself was considerably impressed with Fester's work and with the contacts he had with him outside the photon laboratory.

Knowlton now began to feel that perhaps the intellectual advantages that Fester had brought to the group did not quite compensate for what he felt were evidences of a breakdown in the cooperative spirit he had seen in the group before Fester's coming. More and more of the morning meetings were skipped. Fester's opinion concerning the abilities of others of the group, with the exception of Link, was obviously low. At times, during morning meetings or in smaller discussions, he had been on the point of rudeness, refusing to pursue an argument when he claimed it was based on the other person's ignorance of the facts involved. His impatience of others led him to also make similar remarks to Dr. Jerrold. Knowlton inferred this from a conversation with Jerrold in which Jerrold asked whether Davenport and Oliver were going to be continued on; and his failure to mention Link, the mathematician, led Knowlton to feel that this was the result of private conversations between Fester and Jerrold.

It was not difficult for Knowlton to make a quite convincing case on whether the brilliance of Fester was sufficient recompense for the beginning of this breaking up of the group. He took the opportunity to speak privately with Davenport and with Oliver and it was quite clear that both of them were uncomfortable because of Fester. Knowlton didn't press the discussion beyond the point of hearing them in one way or another say that they did feel awkward and that it was sometimes difficult for them to understand the arguments he advanced, but often embarrassing to ask him to fill in the background on which his arguments were based. Knowlton did not interview Link in this manner.

About six months after Fester's coming into the photon lab, a meeting was scheduled in which the sponsors of the research were coming in to get some idea of the work and its progress. It was customary at these meetings for project heads to present the research being conducted in their groups. The members of each group were invited to other meetings which were held later in the day and open to all, but the special meetings were usually made up only of project heads, the head of the laboratory, and the sponsors.

As the time for the special meeting approached, it seemed to Knowlton that he must avoid the presentation at all cost. His reasons for this were that he could not trust himself to present the ideas and work that Fester had advanced, because of his apprehension as to whether he could present them in sufficient detail and answer such questions about them as might be asked. On the other hand, he did not feel he could ignore these newer lines of work and present only the material that he had done or that had been started before Fester's arrival. He felt also that it would not be beyond Fester at all, in his blunt and undiplomatic way—if he were present at the meeting, that is—to make comments on his [Knowlton's] presentation and reveal Knowlton's inadequacy. It also seemed quite clear that it would not be easy to keep Fester from attending the meeting, even though he was not on the administrative level of those invited.

Knowlton found an opportunity to speak to Jerrold and raised the question. He remarked to Jerrold that, with the meetings coming up and with the interest in the work and with the contributions that Fester had been making, he would probably like to come to these meetings, but there was a question of the feelings of the others in the group if Fester alone were invited. Jerrold passed this over very lightly by saying that he didn't think the group would fail to understand Fester's rather different position and that he thought that Fester by all means should be invited. Knowlton then immediately said he had thought so, too; that Fester should present the work because much of it was work he had done; and, as Knowlton put it, that this would be a nice way to recognize Fester's contributions and to reward him, as he was eager to be recognized as a productive member of the lab. Jerrold agreed, and so the matter was decided.

Fester's presentation was very successful and in some ways dominated the meeting. He attracted the interest and attention of many of those who had come, and a long discussion followed his presentation. Later in the evening—with the entire laboratory staff present—in the cocktail period before the dinner, a little circle of people formed about Fester. One of them was Jerrold himself, and a lively discussion took place concerning the application of Fester's theory. All of this disturbed Knowlton, and his reaction and behavior were characteristic. He joined the circle, praised Fester to Jerrold and to others, and remarked on the brilliance of the work.

Knowlton, without consulting anyone, began at this time to take some interest in the possibility of a job elsewhere. After a few weeks he found that a new laboratory of considerable size was being organized in a nearby city, and that the kind of training he had would enable him to get a project head job equivalent to the one he had at the lab, with slightly more money.

He immediately accepted it and notified Jerrold by a letter, which he mailed on a Friday night to Jerrold's home. The letter was quite brief, and Jerrold was stunned. The letter merely said that he had found a better position; that there were personal reasons why he didn't want to appear at the lab any more; that he would be glad to come back at a later time from where he would be, some forty miles away, to assist if there was any mixup at all in the past work; that he felt sure that Fester could, however, supply any leadership that was required for the group; and that his decision to leave so suddenly was based on some personal problems—he hinted at problems of health in his family, his mother and father. All of this was fictitious, of course.

Jerrold took it at face value but still felt that this was very strange behavior and quite unaccountable, for he had always felt his relationship with Knowlton had been warm and that Knowlton was satisfied and, as a matter of fact, quite happy and productive.

Jerrold was considerably disturbed, because he had already decided to place Fester in charge of another project that was going to be set up very soon. He had been wondering how to explain this to Knowlton, in view of the obvious help Knowlton was getting from Fester and the high regard in which he held him. Jerrold had, as a matter of fact, considered the possibility that Knowlton could add to his staff another person with the kind of background and training that had been unique in Fester and had proved so valuable.

Jerrold did not make any attempt to meet Knowlton. In a way, he felt aggrieved about the whole thing. Fester, too, was surprised at the suddenness of Knowlton's departure and when Jerrold, in talking to him, asked him whether he had reasons to prefer to stay with the photon group instead of the project for the Air Force which was being organized, he chose the Air Force project and went on to that job the following week. The photon lab was hard hit. The leadership of the lab was given to Link with the understanding that this would be temporary until someone could come in to take over.

CHAPTER 4. Improving understanding

In this chapter we look again at some of the cases already studied and discussed, in order to indicate how the topic of Part III, "Understanding Another Person's Behavior," grows out of the questions raised so far. The theme of the chapter is related to the article "Barriers and Gateways to Communication" (Reading II–5), which—as already pointed out—serves as a bridge between Part II and Part III. We shall not try to cover all the significant points illustrated by the preceding cases, or attempt to put into words what we hope has been learned from studying and discussing them. Instead we shall briefly consider *some* of the ways of thinking and behaving that seemed to make it difficult for the people in the cases to understand each other, illustrating these tendencies by referring back to specific case incidents. The main point this chapter tries to make is that in order to start to cope effectively with the various sources of interpersonal misunderstanding identified in Part II we need to develop the particular way of understanding the behavior of another individual, which is the topic of Part III.

In reviewing the cases in Part II, the following tendencies, among others, can be identified as contributing to misunderstanding and lack of communication:

1. The tendency to confuse *maps* with *territories*.

2. The tendency to perceive and deal with an *individual* as a somewhat indistinguishable member of a general *category* rather than as an unique personality with a need to be understood as himself.

3. The tendency to judge or *evaluate* before attempting to *understand*.

4. The tendency not to be aware or take account of how one's own *assumptions* and *feelings* can influence one's *perceptions* of events and other people.

5. The tendency to forget how behavior which may seem strange or bizarre from someone else's point of view becomes quite understandable and less confusing when seen from the point of view of the behaver, that is from an *internal frame of reference.*

These five tendencies, selected for illustrative purposes and not with any intention of covering fully the important points raised so far, are each considered briefly below.

Maps and territories

The notion that a map, to be useful, needs to be related sensibly to, but not identified with, the territory it represents is perhaps the most general lesson to be learned from the material in Part II. And, like many useful lessons, the fact that we already know it, that is to say that it is obvious when stated in words, does not, unfortunately, make it easy always to behave as if it were so. As used here, the map–territory analogy is applicable not only to the relationship between words (and other symbols) and the things that are being talked about but also to the manner in which our underlying assumptions or beliefs about the way people (especially in organizations) "ought to" behave affect our views of actual behavior. Just as we need to be sensitive to the various ways in which words are used, so, if we are to facilitate understanding, we need to be flexible about (willing to test) the assumptions we make about appropriate behavior in organizational relationships.

All the preceding cases illustrate this double sense in which the map–territory idea can be applied. Consider, for example, the chain of events and assumptions in the Niwash Division following the observation by Magnus and Tarrant, the time-study men, of a crane loading an ingot of "sixteen bars." At any point in this chain, the idea that it is useful to check the fit of one's map with the territory before proceeding (i.e., before building "maps on maps"), might well have resulted in a quite different outcome. And the organization chart of the Niwash Division also seems to bear a confused relationship of identity, in the executives' minds, with the territory it is designed to represent; it is as though the lines on the chart defined, for some reason, the only channels along which task-related communication could be carried out. Drake almost seems to assume that without "authority" (what is meant by this word?), as defined by the organization chart, communication is not allowed. (Here is an assumption that not only *impedes* communication but apparently seeks to *prevent* it. Does the assumption succeed, or does it merely result in changing the character of what *is* communicated between lower levels of line and staff? Such an assumption surely must perform a useful function or why else would it have been invented? What *is* its purpose, and why does it persist?)

An equally intriguing confusion between map and territory is shown in the conversation about the "perfect physical specimen" policy in the John Byron case. Apparently Byron is trying to persuade Petmans that the policy is sensible. This is difficult, especially because at another level Byron seems to be wanting Petmans to agree with him that the policy is foolish. Is Byron trying to "make the territory fit the map?" What would be the nature of a more useful conversation that the two men might have had with each other?

As we proceed into the cases in Part III, it will be important to remember that our efforts to understand another person, and the concepts used for this purpose, will always be representations of very complex phenomena. An important criterion for deciding which concepts to use in trying to understand individual behavior will be the intention to seek clear uniformities in the available data, with awareness of our own process of abstraction and inference. We need a scheme that helps us to represent to ourselves the behavior of another person in an understandable way without tempting us to assume that we know more about him than we really do. We need a map that is close to the territory without ever pretending to be identical with it, in order to avoid the extremes of "ignorance" or "arrogance" which characterize so many of our customary attempts to understand each other.

Categories and individuals

As Hayakawa points out, one of the most prevalent semantic confusions results from the tendency to forget that categories are always abstractions from phenomenal reality and to believe we have said something more useful about an individual (than we in reality have) when we label and place him in a category along with other individuals with whom he is *assumed* to share certain characteristics. Hasty classification not only often *seems* more useful than it *is*; it also tends to make us impervious to evidence about the individual with which our classification theory conflicts. Thus we perceive people as "old," "young," "men," "women," "Negro," "Protestant," "authoritarian," "introspective," "neurotic," or whatever, and often think we have said more about them than we really have when we have used these words. But: "Cow$_1$ is not cow$_2$, cow$_2$ is not cow$_3$. . . . This is the simplest and most general of the rules for extensional orientation."[1]

The people in our cases, as in real life, frequently forget this rule. The most obvious examples are seen in Chris Baum (German$_1$ ≠ German$_2$; Baum$_{1943}$ ≠ Baum$_{1924}$, etc.) and in John Byron's unhelpful classification, from Petmans' point of view, of Angelo Verdini, the tip of whose little finger is missing. Whether or not the reader has noticed other examples of this tendency in the cases, he surely has when listening to his own and others' discussions of people. In our efforts, in Part III, to reach more useful understandings of the behavior of individuals, we want to pay more attention to the concrete characteristics of the unique individual than to unprofitable debate about what category to put him in. If we have to use a label in considering an individual's behavior, at least let's try to be aware of how much the label does not say.

Evaluation and understanding

In "Barriers and Gateways to Communication," Rogers proposed "that the major barrier to mutual interpersonal communication

[1] S. I. Hayakawa, *Language in Thought and Action*, 2nd ed. (New York: Harcourt, Brace & World, 1964), 316.

is our very natural tendency to judge, to evaluate, to approve (or disapprove) the statement of the other person or the other group." In a sense this tendency is a variation or extension of the categorizing tendency just considered. It is such a universal human trait that we should not be surprised to find it in operation throughout each of the cases we have studied so far. Here we simply make two recommendations: (1) review what Rogers says about this tendency and how it might be counteracted; (2) choose almost any interpersonal exchange in any of the preceding cases and consider whether it would have helped if one of the people involved had said to himself, "Before deciding whether this other person is 'good' or 'bad' or whether or not what he is saying makes sense to me, I will try hard to understand the situation as he sees it and to sense what he means to himself by the words he is using."

In the subsequent cases we shall not eliminate the tendency to judge and evaluate other people; we are human too. But we shall urge a suspension of judgment until *after* a hard effort to understand has been made. We do not expect this to be easy, but the concepts we use for thinking about individual behavior have been chosen with this intention particularly in mind.

Assumptions, feelings, and perceptions

We have already referred several times in this book to the tendency, in these cases as in our own behavior, for our view of what is happening "outside our skin" to be influenced by what is going on inside, in ways we may not understand. We have used a general scheme for analyzing a two-person relationship which highlights the effect of "*A*'s view of *A*" on "*A*'s view of *B*," and vice versa.

Let us look at this process in the case of Bob Knowlton. Knowlton apparently *assumes* that when Jerrold says "The sky is the limit for the man who produces," Jerrold means "for the man who develops (as an individual?) important scientific innovations." Given this assumption, and his own view that his discovery of the "photon correlator" may have been a "lucky break," Knowlton may *feel* somewhat uneasy about his ability to succeed in this situation. These feelings influence his perception of Fester as a threat to his need to see himself as competent and secure. Some greater awareness by Knowlton (or by Jerrold) of how his own assumptions and feelings were interacting with his perception of Fester's behavior and its meaning to him would have prevented the development of a situation that quite quickly became intolerable to Knowlton and inexplicable to the other people involved. (There is no way of "proving" this; it just seems to us a reasonable inference, based on a more detailed analysis of the case than we have given here. All we are trying to do at this point is to make more concrete what we mean by our emphasis on the importance of considering how what a person perceives interacts with what he assumes and feels.)

The same process can be seen in the other cases. Chris Baum assumes that "Norris is out to get me" and perceives him accordingly. Norris, assuming he should make (and should be able to make) his drivers "sales-minded," may feel threatened by Baum unless he perceives him as "impossible." Both Baum and Norris then proceed to act in ways that justify their perceptions of each other and even, to a certain extent, make their assumptions come true. In somewhat the same way, John Byron and Petmans, because of the way each feels about the conflict between what they believe ought to be the policy and what they perceive the policy to be, fail to see each other as two men facing a similar situation and asking each other for help. Each of them, preoccupied with his own feelings, fails to express an understanding of how the other feels. Apparently if either had been willing to move to the other's level of abstraction and had tried to understand the other's point of view, they could have had a conversation that would have been more helpful to them and, in time, more useful to the organization as a whole.

For the reasons illustrated by these examples, we shall attempt, in the cases in Part III, to increase our ability to understand another person from his own frame of reference, and to become increasingly sensitive to the interaction of assumptions, feelings, and perceptions when people attempt to communicate with each other.

The internal frame of reference

In an earlier chapter we said that some of the behavior in these cases would at first seem strange or inexplicable. Our traditional theories about motivation and about how people ought to behave don't help us understand why many people with whom we interact behave as they do. Listening to John Byron go on about the nerves in the stub of a missing finger, miners and silicosis, June Riley's arthritis, flat feet, the man with nine children, and so forth, it is easy to agree with Petmans that "This is completely ridiculous." But if we have the humor, patience, and skill to concentrate on Byron's point of view rather than on our reaction to it, if we try to see his problem as he sees it, we begin to sense the dilemma he feels, and to see him, at least as much as Petmans, as a man who is asking for help, who needs to be understood. Even a small beginning in this way of thinking about Byron, or anyone else, can make a significant difference in the kind of conversation we might have with him.

Similarly, Fester is "surprised" when Bob Knowlton leaves for another job, and Jerrold feels "stunned," "disturbed," and "aggrieved." Yet Knowlton's departure makes perfect sense from his own frame of reference, and if Jerrold had managed to perceive the situation more nearly as Knowlton perceived it, Jerrold might have predicted or prevented Knowlton's move. In the same way, Chris Baum's letter and subsequent resignation become a sensible response to his situation *as he perceives* it, but to us this will be evident only if we have managed to some extent to interpret his behavior from an internal frame of reference. Each of these people is seen to be acting so as to preserve and give scope to his existing way of viewing himself in the light of his existing way of viewing the situation he is in. But we have to be able to achieve some feeling for how he *does* see himself and his situation in order for the resultant behavior to seem understandable to us. This is why, in the cases and readings of Part III, we concentrate on understanding another person from that other person's point of view.

PART III   Understanding another person's behavior

CHAPTER 5. A perceptual point of view

There are four cases in Part III, four individuals whose points of view we are going to try to understand. They have been selected neither because their behavior is typical of this or that category of person or type of situation nor because their problems are unusually difficult or complex. Further, most of these four cases do not seem to have an obvious bearing on issues of organizational behavior or administration as generally conceived, and the individuals (because they are being interviewed in a certain way) talk about themselves in a manner which seldom occurs in everyday organizational life. (The cases *could* be used as a basis for discussion of the behavior of the interviewer, but that is the topic of Part IV.)

Our reason for selecting these particular cases is really quite simple. Here are four individuals whose attitudes and behavior our students have enjoyed trying to understand. The fact that some of the circumstances of these individuals may seem only indirectly related to the study of business administration has not made the cases less useful for our purposes; it may have made them more interesting. In other words, partly because of the way these individuals talk about themselves, and partly because of the nature of their concerns, here are four cases with which it is relatively easy to become involved in the fascinating and instructive process of trying to understand the behavior of someone else.

To the student who still doesn't think this sounds worthwhile, we wish to address the following thought as a digression at this point from the main topic. In the conventional wisdom of the day, decision making in organizations is thought to be the perquisite of those in supervisory and management positions. March and Simon, among others however, have pointed out that all members of an organization, not only executives, make decisions that affect the organization. All members make decisions about whether they will join the organization and at what level they will produce in relation to standard. What you will be listening to as the people in these cases talk is how they made their decisions to work and produce for the organizations of which they are currently members. Though these are not—or are not solely—executive decisions, they are decisions of the greatest importance for executives. They provide the background against which the latter's decisions are received, and they have a tremendous effect on the outcomes of work. Study of these cases, therefore, has a direct connection to executives' work.

If you are to do the main job of this part of the book, you will not spend much time thinking about what these people's supervisors might do to get them to improve their output. Nevertheless, students may wish to spend some time on these questions. To help make discussion precise, think of what you would say to them if you were a supervisor wanting them to improve their output. Or what you would say to them in a conversation in the office to help them grow toward maturity in the organization in which they are now working. Or put yourself in the role of the interviewer: What do you think of his remarks? What ones would you have made? And why? Think through, from what you know about each person's situation, the consequences in his thinking of whatever it is you want to say. Think of what the person will hear as well as what you will say. In the last section of this book, we will come back to these action questions, full front and center stage; so do not spend too much time on them now.

To return to the main topic of this chapter, we not only want to enjoy discussing these people, we also want to go about understanding their behavior in a relatively disciplined way, in order to develop a procedure for thinking about the behavior of these people that can later be applied usefully to our thinking about any other individual whose behavior we may want to understand. The purpose of this chapter, and of the readings in Part III, is to develop a framework for achieving a helpful understanding of another person, however different from or similar to yourself he may at first appear to be. Before beginning we should emphasize that our objective is relatively modest; we shall be searching not for a completely adequate or scientifically accurate diagnosis of an individual's behavior, but rather for the kind of sense of another person's way of viewing, thinking about, and feeling about his world and himself that would make it easier to communicate and work with him. Not agreement about how an external authority would categorize a person and his behavior, but a sense of how the person himself looks at his behavior and at his situation—which we could check as we talked with him—is our goal, on the assumption that if *A* is to behave skillfully in relation to *B*, *A*'s view of *B* needs to be not too different from *B*'s view of himself. This is what we mean by, and why we advocate concentrating on understanding another person from, *an internal frame of reference*, or understanding another person from *the other person's point of view*.

A general framework

We recommend a careful study of Reading III–1, "A Useful Way of Thinking about Individuals in a Business Organization," as a good beginning for thinking about most of the cases that follow. Here we present a scheme for analysis which is basically an elaboration of the three questions Roethlisberger asks in Reading III–1 and a diagram of their interrelatedness.

What is the individual bringing to the work situation? How a person will react to the situation he is in obviously depends in part on certain past events in his life, not on the meaning those events might have to someone else, but on the meanings he has attributed to them himself. To the extent, then, that we learn from the person we wish to understand something of the meaning to him of past events in his life, we may be able to understand something of how he is reacting to his present circumstances. Thus, to cite a previous case, Bob Knowlton's reaction to Simon Fester's behavior is easier to understand once we know about certain of Knowlton's previous experiences *and* about the meaning Knowlton has given to those past events. (Knowing everything about Knowlton's past from an *external* frame of reference but nothing about the meaning of these events to him would not help us understand his present behavior.)

What is the situation demanding of the individual? In any situation there is obviously an important relationship between the challenges or demands on us that are inherent in the situation we are in, and the abilities, attitudes, and the like that we are bringing to it as a result of our past experience. In one sense a person's happiness, productivity, and ability to develop himself all depend upon how a balance is achieved between what is already inside of him and the external demands of the different situations in which he finds himself. But we need to consider more than the demands of the work situation. For most of us, whether on the job or not, the demands we see being placed on us by certain situations outside of work are at least as important. In other words, the balance which defines a person's present attitude can be conceived as a result of forces from three directions:

1. The meaning, to him, of past events in his life.

2. The demands of the work situation, as he perceives them.

3. The demands of the nonwork situation, as he perceives them.

What is the resulting equilibrium? A person's adjustment to the situation he perceives himself to face can be thought of as his effort to balance the three forces listed above. It is important to consider this balance *multidimensionally*, that is, not only in terms of the person's feeling of contentment or of his productivity or of some other one factor which may be of interest to us at the time. Thus one person in a certain job situation may adopt attitudes and activities which maximize his happiness but minimize his productiveness, whereas another person in the same situation may become very productive but dissatisfied. Again, one work situation may interact with my past experiences and nonwork demands in a way that makes me satisfied and productive, at least in the short run, whereas I may need a situation with greater confusion and stress if I am going to develop more of my potential capacity and achieve the growth and learning I need and want.

For these reasons, although different dimensions of this balance may be more or less relevant from one case to another, we have found it helpful to consider the outcomes of the person's relationship to his situation in terms of these three factors:

1. *Satisfaction.* How happy, content, pleased, and so forth, does the person appear to be—to others, but especially to himself?

2. *Productiveness.* How productive is this person in this situation? Sometimes there are relatively objective measures of this outcome, but it is always important to consider how productive he considers himself to be.

3. *Learning and growth.* Is this person, in this situation, learning what he may need to know to deal well with future situations? Is he growing and developing his capacity as a human being, or is his adaptation to his present environment such that he is pretty much the same person from day to day? Considerable inference or judgment may seem necessary in order to answer this kind of question for someone else, but again we want to maintain, as much as possible, the frame of reference of the person we are trying to understand.

Our modification of Roethlisberger's "useful way of thinking" about an individual in an organization can be summarized by means of a diagram, as shown in Figure 1.

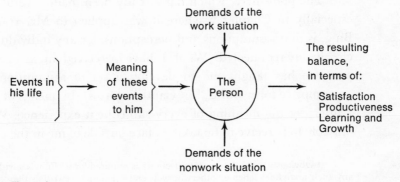

Figure 1

This scheme, like all the others in this book, is not just designed to provide a set of categories into which the data in the case can be sorted. Listing various case data under each of the diagram headings may be a good way to *start* your analysis;[1] but since we wish to encourage a *systemic* view of individual behavior (as well as of two-person relationships and other social systems), the real purpose of Figure 1 is to encourage study of the *relations of interconnectedness* that exist between these various classes of data. In other words, we draw diagrams of analytical schemes not to focus on what goes inside the circles or boxes, but to direct attention to how they are connected or related. (A student once defined what we were trying to teach as "the science of lines and circles." We didn't object too strongly, except that the "lines" are much more important to us than the "circles.")

Assumptions and perceptions

The interpretations we make of our surroundings come about through the phenomenon of perception in the light of our experiences and purposes. As Cantril puts it, "The net result of our purposive actions is that we create for ourselves a set of assumptions which serve as guides and bases for future actions. . . . The only world we know is created in terms of and by means of our assumptions. . . . —a world which we could not have at all except for our past experience in acting for the purpose of enhancing the quality of life." (See Reading III–5.)

The point here, which has already been made several times, especially in Chapter 2 where it was applied to Mr. Hart and Bing, is that assumptions and perceptions, for any individual, are closely interconnected. What I have perceived in my past experience has taught me to develop a set of assumptions (my "assumptive form world," in Cantril's terms), by means of which I interpret the meaning of every subsequent experience. What I am able to perceive to be taking place outside of me in the present

---

[1] Obviously much intelligent selectivity is required for useful work with this or any such analytical scheme; otherwise you end up simply rewriting the case, in a different order. The heart of case analysis is the art of deciding what is important.

is strongly influenced by assumptions I have learned from my interpretation of what has happened to me in the past.

These statements, about how each person thinks about and perceives reality are obvious, in one sense; yet their significance is not easily grasped. A "perception demonstration" of the kind vividly described by Cantril is the best way to learn their meaning. This *perceptual* point of view towards understanding behavior is developed much more fully in the readings of Part III. And in each of the cases there is an opportunity to study how what a person perceives in his environment is being influenced by what his past experience has led him to believe and assume about his world. We recommend that you practice identifying, for each person, some of his important underlying assumptions and perceptions, separately, and then see how they are related to each other. For example, what does Juanita Rodriguez perceive that is important to her in her present situation? What does she *not* perceive in her present situation that might be important to her if she did? What assumptions or beliefs has she learned, from contact with her parents or with José, that are influencing how she now perceives the situation she is in? (The final case in Part III, Ashok Rajguru, is especially rich in material for considering questions of this kind, and provides an interesting comparison to Juanita Rodriguez.)

Feelings

As the case of Juanita Rodriguez certainly reminds us, a person's behavior cannot be understood, from his point of view, just by focusing on what he believes and sees. What we are feeling—our emotions and sentiments—are, for most of us, equally important.[2]

[2] The reader will notice that we tend to use the words *emotion, sentiment, feeling* as roughly synonymous. In the same way we sometimes use *believe* or even *think* instead of *assume*, and *see* or *view* instead of *perceive*—mostly for stylistic variety at the expense of technical purity. Incidentally, a difficulty the reader may experience with our use of the word *feeling* is that in everyday speech *feel* is often used to refer to what we would call a perception or assumption. Thus:

"I feel teachers should insist on discipline." (Assumption.)

"I feel Miss Jones is a bad teacher." (Perception based on assumption.)

"I feel irritated at Miss Jones." (Feeling based on perception and assumption.)

Feelings are often clearly expressed when the word *feel* is not used: "I get angry when I see Miss Jones."

Further, as is emphasized by several of the authors to be read and especially by Carl Rogers (Reading III–6), just as a person can be influenced by assumptions that are not explicit, so he may not be aware of certain feelings he is experiencing. As brought out in certain of Rogers' writings that are reproduced in Part IV, feelings can be thought of as existing at one of three "levels of awareness" within a person:

1. Expression

2. Awareness

3. Experience

At the first level are those feelings that a person currently is expressing freely to himself and others, for example what he says when someone asks him, "How do you feel?" Thus at this moment, a sympathetic listener might have little trouble learning that I feel satisfied from a good breakfast, comfortable with the temperature in this room, anxious about whether I will be able to finish writing this chapter today, and so forth. However, I am also aware of other feelings within me that I am not likely to talk about. Perhaps I would feel annoyed at being interrupted by this sympathetic listener but not want to tell him so because I do not want to appear impolite. Perhaps I am worrying about some personal problem that I think of as none of his business. It can be seen that some feelings, especially negative ones, of which one may be fully aware, are not expressed openly because it does not seem appropriate to do so at a particular time or place. At another time, or talking with another person, I may speak of such feelings with no hesitation. Whether or not to express certain feelings I know I have remains a personal choice I make from one moment to another, partly governed by social codes or norms and to a large extent under my conscious control. Sometimes, of course, such control gives way, and a strong feeling of anger or joy, for example, simply bursts forth whether the person wants to express it or not. And, as is well known, a frequently discussed perception of another person is the extent to which he "controls his feelings," that is, how freely he expresses what he is aware he feels. There are interesting cultural differences in how the open expression of feeling is perceived or valued by others.

Over those feelings that I am experiencing organically—"viscerally," as Rogers puts it—but without being clearly aware of them, I have less control, because how can I *decide* whether or not to express a feeling that I don't *know* I have? For example, at this moment my mind may be clouded or my digestion upset by worry about something I have done recently and have *forgotten*. Or a person may be aware of anger when at another level he is experiencing guilt. He may express joy at a certain event and then later realize, in retrospect, that what he was *really* feeling at that time was anxiety. Thus frequently, to others or to ourselves, we make such comments as "I must have been thoroughly frightened (or some other feeling), but I didn't realize it at the time." Just as there are variations among individuals, and from one situation to another for the same individual, in the extent to which feelings at the level of awareness are expressed, so are there variations, less familiar but no less important, in the extent of awareness of feelings that are experienced. And, of course, these three "levels" —expression, awareness, experience—are not actually clear-cut; they have very fuzzy edges. Much expression of feeling is confused and unclear, and about much of what we are feeling at any time we are only dimly aware.

The last two paragraphs have been somewhat of a digression, although an important one, and a preview of ideas that will be dealt with more extensively in Part IV. The attribute of *feelings* which we particularly want to stress here is that they are interconnected with assumptions and perceptions (Figure 2). This relationship, which was illustrated in Chapter 2 by reference to the case of Mr. Hart and Bing, has been apparent in most of our cases so far. (Bob Knowlton is a good example.) In other words, how I

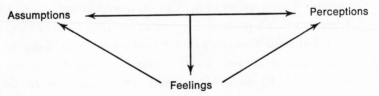

Figure 2

feel about an event is related to what I perceive in it and what I have learned from my past experience to assume about this class of event. Furthermore, the resultant feeling in turn influences (often reinforces) what I perceive and assume. Miss Jones, the teacher in our recent footnote, is perceived to be violating an important assumption about how teachers should behave. The result of this conflict between what is assumed and what is perceived is a feeling of irritation. (Other, less easily expressed feelings may be involved, such as envy—of the children who are not being "disciplined"; or threat—a belief that supports my view of myself as a good parent is being challenged.) This feeling helps me see the "bad" consequences of Miss Jones' behavior and miss any "good" consequences. As a result, my assumptions about education and discipline are reinforced and affect what I perceive and how I feel the next time I am confronted with a situation of this kind.

The self-concept

In the last paragraph we parenthetically speculated that the irritated parent might be feeling, perhaps with dim or no awareness, a threat to his view of himself as a good parent. Each of us has a set of ideas about (a system of ways of conceiving of) ourselves. Some of these concepts of self are more important, more *central* to the self, than others, and therefore more strongly defended against perceived challenge or threat. ("I am a good parent" or "I am a tolerant person" are probably more important concepts for me to maintain than "I live in the city" or "I don't like martinis." But not necessarily; often one has to listen very carefully to another person in order to get a feel for the ways of conceiving of himself that are especially important to him.) The more central of these views of self can be thought of as *systemically interrelated*, so that a perceived threat to one may seem to threaten the others as well. This central cluster of ways of conceiving of oneself constitutes what Combs and Snygg, in *Individual Behavior*, following Lecky (Reading III-2) and others, have called the "self-concept," and what Rogers (Reading III–6) calls the "self-structure."[3] As this idea of the *self-concept* is thoroughly covered in the readings, here we shall only briefly underline its importance to the problem of motivation and connect it to the previous discussion of assumptions, perceptions, and feelings.

Frequently, in the following cases as in everyday life, we see people behaving in ways that puzzle us because they are so different from how we think we would behave in a similar situation. We wonder what motivated such behavior, what need it is attempting to fill. From the perceptual point of view, there is always at least one answer: The person is behaving so as to preserve his view of himself in the light of his view of his environment. If we could see the world as he sees it *and* if we could achieve an adequate "map" of his self-concept, his behavior would no longer be puzzling. However strange to us, from *his* point of view it would make sense. Each of us acts, in other words, to fill our basic need to preserve our existing ways of thinking about ourselves, in the light of how we perceive our surroundings.

But *self-preservation* is certainly not a sufficiently inclusive explanation of human motivation. In order to maintain the *self-concept*, man will do many things which will greatly endanger his physical self, since the self-concept can include as very central elements such views of self as "enjoying risks," "brave," and "willing to sacrifice my life." Even so, a more complete explanation of motivation must include the notion that—as Rogers, Combs and Snygg, and others put it—man's basic need is not only to *maintain* but also to *enhance* his concept of himself. And, because most of us perceive the demands placed on us as changing rather than static, we believe that our selves have to grow in order to survive; maintenance and enhancement of the self are perceived as two sides of the same coin. This view of motivation is well expressed in the following passage from *Individual Behavior*, by Combs and Snygg, under the heading, "The Striving for Adequacy: The Basic Need of Human Beings." (Combs and Snygg

[3] See also Readings III–3 and III–5, as well as Allport's discussion of "The Proprium" in Reading III–4, and "Some Interpersonal Aspects of Self-Confirmation" in Warren G. Bennis, *et al.*, *Interpersonal Dynamics*, pp. 207–25.

use the term "phenomenal self" to refer to "all those perceptions which an individual has about himself irrespective of their importance to him" [p. 126], reserving "self-concept" for only the most central and important, tightly structured aspects.)

... Man lives in a changing world, a world in which the organizations of which he is composed and of which he is part are continuously changing. A changing world requires changes in the organization of the self if it is to be maintained. Each of us needs to do more than merely change with the flow of events. Because we are aware of the future and must maintain ourselves, in the future as well as in the present, it is necessary to enhance the self against the exigencies of tomorrow. The self, therefore, has to be maintained in the future, built up and enhanced so that the individual feels secure for tomorrow. And since the future is uncertain and unknown, no enhancement of the individual's experience of personal value, no degree of self-actualization, is ever enough. Human beings are, by nature, insatiable.

Thus, man seeks not merely the maintenance of *a* self but the development of an *adequate* self—a self capable of dealing effectively and efficiently with the exigencies of life, both now and in the future. To achieve this self-adequacy requires of man that he seek, not only to maintain his existing organization, but also that he build up and make more adequate the self of which he is aware. Man seeks both to maintain and enhance his perceived self.

Though the maintenance and enhancement of the self are two different words, this does not mean that man has two different needs. We express maintenance and enhancement as two different words, but both relate to exactly the same function—the production of a more adequate self. Both refer to man's striving to accomplish, like the rest of his universe, an adequate organization. I may shore up the timbers of my house to keep it from collapsing or I may plant trees to improve its looks. One activity maintains the structure, the other enhances the property. Both activities have a common result—a more adequate, better functioning dwelling for me and those important to me. In the same manner, I seek to become the most adequate person I can become in every situation in which I may find myself. I may do this by seeing my dentist to have my cavities filled, by reading a new book in my professional field, or I may seek to enhance myself by buying a new suit of clothes or by making a speech at a national convention. Whether I seek to maintain myself as I am or enhance myself against the exigencies of the future, I am always seeking to be the most adequate personality I can be.

In the previous pages we have seen: (1) that man, like the universe of which he is a part, characteristically seeks the maintenance of organization; (2) that the organization man seeks to maintain is the organization of which he is aware, namely, his phenomenal self; and (3) that, because man lives in a changing world and is aware of the future as well as of the present, maintenance of the self requires, not simply maintenance of the status quo, but an active seeking for personal adequacy.[4]

Without necessarily accepting this version of "man's basic need" as the last word on the subject (many competent psychologists take exception to it), the reader should try out for himself the extent to which such a point of view toward motivation does or does not help him to understand the behavior of the individuals in the cases in this Part.

A person's need to "maintain and enhance his self-concept" obviously influences his assumptions, perceptions, and feelings and the relationships between them. In fact the self-concept can be thought of as an integrated structure of assumptions (or beliefs) about the self, perceptions of the self, and feelings about the self, influenced by and influencing a less clearly integrated set of beliefs, views, and emotions toward the world outside the self. The notion of the self-concept, then, belongs somehow at the center of our diagram, as in Figure 3.

The use of this scheme (again focusing on the lines rather than just on the circles) can be illustrated by reference to any of the previous cases; it closely fits the analysis by Roethlisberger of Mr. Hart and Bing, given in Chapter 2. It is more useful with some cases than with others and will not make equally good sense to every student of a particular case. Above all, we must never forget that it is a highly simplified, abstract representation of the most complex imaginable set of phenomena—the personality in relation to its past and present world of experience. Nevertheless Figure 3 does point the direction to a very useful way of thinking about another person's view of himself, a view that can be checked as we talk with him, and does help give an understanding of how his ways of thinking, seeing, and feeling are interrelated in

[4] Arthur W. Combs and Donald Snygg, *Individual Behavior*, rev. ed. (New York: Harper & Row, 1959), pp. 45–46; reprinted by permission of the publishers.

On the same theme, see especially Rogers, Reading III–6 and elsewhere; Gordon Allport on "proactive behavior" and "propriate striving" in *Pattern and Growth in Personality* (New York: Holt, Rinehart and Winston, 1961), and in Reading III–4; and the very important contribution of Robert W. White, "Motivation Reconsidered: The Concept of Competence," in *Psychological Review*, 66, no. 5 (September 1959): 297–333.

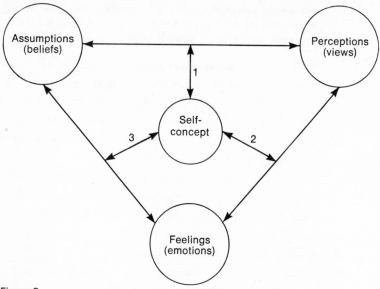

Figure 3

a pattern that tends to hold together because it makes sense to him. Let us illustrate by reference to an incident which took place one day in a classroom when one of the authors was attempting to put across the ideas presented in this chapter. At just the point when the lecture seemed to be going smoothly, as the teacher perceived it, a bright and outspoken student (Mr. Brown) interrupted, essentially as follows: "What's the point of all this? Why haven't you explained what you mean by the word 'feelings'?" During a tense moment of silence, the teacher's assumptions, perceptions, feelings, and self-concept were related to each other, from his frame of reference, somewhat as follows. (See the correspondingly numbered double-headed arrows in Figure 3.)

1. During a lecture the teacher should carefully explain and the student should carefully listen (assumption). I am a good teacher (part of self-concept). Mr. Brown has not been listening to me (perception). (Resulting possible threat to self-concept not immediately perceived.)

2. Since Mr. Brown is not stupid and I am good at explaining things clearly, Mr. Brown's question is intentionally rude. I am angry at him and am justified in feeling angry.

3. A teacher, especially in this course, should use events which occur in the classroom as an opportunity for learning, and he should be able to learn from these events as much as his students. I am not only good at explaining things, I am also good (perhaps better) at understanding and responding to the relationship between latent feeling and manifest behavior. I not only feel angry at Mr. Brown, I also feel angry with myself and somewhat anxious about whether I am as good at explaining things as I like to think. Maybe I can use my own current feelings as an illustration of what I have been talking about. "Mr. Brown, what do you think *my* 'feelings' are, right now, as a result of your question?"

Mr. Brown's reaction to this curve ball was initial bewilderment, as might be expected, but a useful discussion (at least from the teacher's point of view), in which Mr. Brown took an active role, occupied the rest of the hour.

The point of recounting this incident is not to illustrate either correct or incorrect handling of an educational situation. Certainly the teacher was not clearly aware of all he has implied was going on inside his mind. The incident is cited here simply as an illustration of what we have been talking about. Not an elaborate or adequately comprehensive theory about behavior—but practice in seeing the *relations of interconnectedness* among assumptions, perceptions, feelings, and self-concept can facilitate a response to an interpersonal event which will facilitate communication and learning for the persons involved.

READING III-1. *A Useful Way of Thinking About Individuals in a Business Organization*

F. J. ROETHLISBERGER

[In *Management and Morale*, Chapter 7, "What is Adequate Personnel Management," Roethlisberger identified and discussed three major classes of human problems that are found in any large-scale organization: "problems of communication," "problems of social balance within the organization," and "problems of individual work effectiveness." The theme of Roethlisberger's chapter is that to cope adequately with these problems it will be necessary to develop greater skill in the diagnosis of human situations. The following selection summarizes the elements of this kind of skill and presents a simple scheme for thinking about how the individual member of an organization relates his own needs to his present situation.]

There are three elements in the development of such a skill which have been well stated by Dr. L. J. Henderson.[1] He says:

> In the complex business of living as in medicine *both* theory and practice are necessary conditions of understanding, and the method of Hippocrates is the only method that has ever succeeded widely and generally. The first element of that method is hard, persistent, intelligent, responsible, unremitting labor in the sick room, not in the library: the complete adaptation of the doctor to his task, an adaptation that is far from being merely intellectual. The second element of that method is accurate observation of things and events, selection, guided by judgment born of familiarity and experience, of the salient and the recurrent phenomena, and their classification and methodical exploitation. The third element of that method is the judicious construction of a theory— not a philosophical theory, nor a grand effort of the imagination, nor a quasi-religious dogma, but a modest pedestrian affair, or perhaps I had better say, a useful walking-stick to help on the way—and the use thereof. All this may be summed up in a word: The physician must have, first,

[1] [L. J. Henderson, *Introductory Lectures*, Sociology 23, 2nd ed., revised October, 1938 (Archives, Harvard Graduate School of Business Administration), p. 6.]

intimate, habitual, intuitive familiarity with things; secondly, systematic knowledge of things; and thirdly, an effective way of thinking about things.

Let me paraphrase what Dr. Henderson says for our particular problem. In large-scale industry today adequate personnel management requires a group of people who can give their complete and uninterrupted attention to the development of a skill of handling particular human problems which arise in their particular organizations. The development of such a skill would require, first, hard, persistent, intelligent, responsible, unremitting labor in the shops among employees at the work level, not in an office on the top floor. Only in this way can be obtained an intimate, habitual, intuitive familiarity with the way workers do behave—not how they "ought to" behave or are represented as behaving by those on the top floor. The second element in the development of the skill would require a careful search for simple uniformities which may appear among the facts that are collected and roughly classified. The third step in the development of the skill would be to construct a simple way of thinking about individuals and their relations to one another in a business organization. This way of thinking would be a modest affair which would help in obtaining more facts and in making practice more effective.

This approach is no short-cut to success. It is a slow, laborious route; but it is the same route which has been followed for the past three hundred years in dealing with our physical world and which has resulted in such tremendous advances in the form of electric lights, telephones, radios, automobiles. This does not mean, however, that we in the personnel field have to wait three hundred years in order to get results. A very modest and simple beginning in the direction outlined by Dr. Henderson might bring almost at once fairly satisfying results in the three areas of human problems previously outlined. In fact it seems to me that a sufficient body of knowledge already exists in terms of which a simple theory can be constructed, the application of which would make personnel practice more effective in handling these three problems and ultimately in securing cooperation.

WHAT IS THE INDIVIDUAL BRINGING TO THE WORK SITUATION?

Probably the first step in the development of such a theory would be to have a simple way of thinking about the individuals in a business organization. In one sense, each person is unique. Each is bringing to the job situation certain attitudes, beliefs, and ways of life, as well as certain skills, technical, social, and logical. In terms of his previous experience, each person has certain hopes and expectations of his job situation.

What are some of these demands which he is making of his job? Obviously, the answer is not simple. It varies from person to person depending upon the individual's previous background and experience. Some people more than others are eager for recognition in the form of advancement. Some more than others are eager for recognition in the size of the paycheck. But most of us want social recognition in one form or another. Most of us want the satisfaction that comes from being accepted and recognized as a person of worth by our friends and associates and the feeling of security that comes from being a member of a group. We want to have a skill that is socially recognized as useful. We want tangible evidence of our importance to our fellow men. However, the particular hopes and fears, the particular social values, which each person brings to the situation vary with each individual, depending upon his background and previous experience. This is one aspect of the human organization of which any skilled administrator is aware—the particularity and uniqueness of each individual in his organization—a factor which on occasions it may be very important for him to take into account.

But to overstress the differences among the individuals who make up a business organization would be to miss some of the common ties which bind men in collaborative activity, and which, if not present, make collaboration impossible. Although, in a sense, each individual in the organization is unique and different, it is also true that each person in this country has gone through a certain cultural sieve which gives him something in common with his fellow men. Parents, particularly those who were born in this country, have transmitted the common cultural heritage of this country to their children. Through participation in common educational, religious, and political associations they have been brought up to share certain common values, to have common hopes, faiths, and standards of living. These experiences help to fit them for social living and prepare them for cooperation. Without some such common feelings and sentiments, effective cooperation is impossible. Any administrator is assuming, sometimes more than he realizes, that the people who come to his organization have already been socially conditioned in a fashion which has prepared them for cooperation. This cannot always be assumed. Sometimes more assistance than that provided by the parents or the formal educational system needs to be given after the person has gone to work.

WHAT IS THE WORK SITUATION DEMANDING OF THE INDIVIDUAL?

In developing our conception of the individual in a business organization, it is well to remember that each person not only has a past, but is also working in a present situation. He is working under particular conditions, associating with particular people. These associations are not of a hit-or-miss character. They are composed of people who have certain defined and accepted relations to one another. In his present situation, there are also certain standards to which the individual has to conform—standards of performance regarding the quantity and quality of work he does and standards of personal conduct. Pressure is put upon him to behave in a certain way, to have certain loyalties, to hold certain beliefs. Some of these pressures are in the form of law and prescribed rules of behavior; some of them are in the form of customary ways of doing things.

It is also well to remember that the individual's present situation is wider than his immediate work situation. He is also associating with people outside of work. He may have a family and belong to numerous associations in the community to which he is contributing his services, in most cases not for monetary gain. In this situation outside of work he is also submitted to pressures of one kind or another—to be a dutiful father and husband, to be a loyal citizen.

WHAT IS THE RESULTING EQUILIBRIUM?

It can be seen that a person's satisfactions or dissatisfactions are relative to (1) the demands he is bringing to the situation, and (2) the demands the situation is making of him. In order to maintain his equilibrium he has to resolve these two sets of pressures. If there is too big a gap between the social satisfaction which he is asking from his job and the social satisfaction he is getting from his job, he has a grievance. If he is bringing to his situation a demand for recognition which his present job cannot satisfy, he becomes discontented. If he is unable to fulfill the technical requirements of the job, he may become dissatisfied; then the supervisor also has a grievance. If he cannot meet the social requirements of the job and cannot adjust himself to the group, he becomes dissatisfied and often, as a result, cannot fulfill the technical requirements.

This constant adjustment between what is being asked of the individual and what he is asking of the situation is a simple framework in which our thought can be set when handling people in a business organization. Each person himself is continuously trying to resolve these two tendencies but sometimes he needs to be helped: either (1) in the direction of modifying his demands so that they can be better realized in the present situation, or (2) by changing the present situation so as to allow for the fulfillment of the normal demands he is making of his work, or (3) both.

It should be noted that this way of thinking about individuals in a business organization does not tell us in particular what any person is like or what his situation is. It only gives us a useful set of ideas—a framework in which our thought can be set—when we are confronted with a particular person and want to find out what his situation is. It suggests the kind of material that is needed, where to look, and how to go about making a diagnosis.

READING III–2. *Self-Consistency*
PRESCOTT LECKY

[Prescott Lecky's *Self-Consistency* has had a remarkable influence on American psychology. It is a very short book, based on drafts and notes which Lecky was preparing for publication at the time of his death in 1941. Because a number of the authors quoted or cited in Part II have been greatly influenced by Lecky's ideas, we have reproduced the passages which most clearly state Lecky's central theme. We have made a number of deletions, as indicated, but no substantive changes in the published text.]

Foreword

This little volume represents the distillation of some twenty years of work by Prescott Lecky in the fields of psychology, psycho-pathology, and education. His development was continuous, and his thinking both subtle and systematic. The posthumous appearance of these chapters gives the unified view of a creative thinker, whose main aim as a psychologist was to achieve that *flexibility with unity* about which he has so cogently written.

It was my privilege to know Prescott Lecky well and to learn much from him. We shared a dislike for closed and rigid systems. His development took the direction of constant and vital application to educational and to adjustment problems among his students. I had not known how mature his thinking was until some of these chapters came recently to my attention.

The fundamental idea of organic unity and of the capacity of the psychological system to maintain itself against outside pressure is one which has become increasingly familiar through the work of the Gestalt psychologists, the work of Paul Schilder, and above all, the brilliant systematic statements by Kurt Goldstein. The fact remains that Lecky had in his own way developed further than any of these the conception that the individual must *define for himself the nature of that totality which he is.* He must throughout life assimilate new experiences in such fashion

Excerpted from Prescott Lecky, *Self-Consistency: A Theory of Personality* (New York: Island Press, 1945. Copyright © 1945, by Kathryn Lecky. Used by arrangement with Archon Books/The Shoe String Press, Inc., which published *Self-Consistency* in 1961. The section on "The Theory of Self-Consistency" was Appendix 3 in the first edition; "Self-Consistency vs. the Doctrine of Specificity" was Chapter 1; "The Personality" was Chapter 4; and "Self-Consistency as a Technique" was Chapter 5. The foreword is also from the first edition.

as both to *be* and to *appear* a living unit. The practical consequence is that new habits are made, and old ones lost, not in terms of sheer conditioning or habit formation, not in terms of isolated neural bonds, but in terms of assimilation, as the individual conceives the forward step to be a continuation and fulfillment of himself.

This subtle and penetrating conception was for years applied in teaching, in clinical work, and in business situations; was tested, redrafted, and rewritten until in these present chapters, the psychology of self-consistency achieves mature expression.

The chapters as presented here have been edited by Dr. John F. A. Taylor and represent the best integration of Lecky's work which can now be achieved. The book which Lecky had for years planned was far from finished. But these chapters are offered to the reader in the hope that the emphasis upon the unity of the personality may supplement and vitalize many similar studies which come from our clinics and laboratories today.

GARDNER MURPHY,
Dept. of Psychology
College of City of New York

January 1944

The theory of self-consistency

We conceive of the mind or personality as an organization of ideas which are felt to be consistent with one another. Behavior expresses the effort to maintain the integrity and unity of the organization. The point is that all of an individual's ideas are organized into a single system, whose preservation is essential. In order to be immediately assimilated, the idea formed as the result of a new experience must be felt to be consistent with the ideas already present in the system. On the other hand, ideas whose inconsistency is recognized as the personality develops must be expelled from the system. There is thus a constant assimilation of new ideas and the expulsion of old ideas throughout life.

The nucleus of the system, around which the rest of the system revolves, is the individual's idea or conception of himself. Any idea entering the system which is inconsistent with the individual's conception of himself cannot be assimilated but instead gives rise to an inconsistency which must be removed as promptly as possible.

By way of illustration, let us consider the interpretation of why a person feels insulted or has his feelings hurt. An insult is a valuation of the individual by others which does not agree with the individual's valuation of himself. Such a contradictory valuation cannot be assimilated, and when thrust into a person's experience acts as a foreign body whose elimination is essential

The conflict provoked by the inconsistency may lead to several different kinds of behavior. The usual method of handling the problem is to strike back and try to inflict an equal injury upon the person responsible for the insult. It is necessary that the injury given be equal to the injury received if the conflict is to be dissolved completely. Ancient codes of justice emphasize this necessity—an eye for an eye, a tooth for a tooth. The demand for vengeance is especially apparent in children because of their inability to unify on any other basis. The inconsistency may also be removed by an apology, again provided that the apology be equal to the insult.

Still another method is to reinterpret the disturbing incident in such a manner that it can be assimilated. For example, a child was deeply wounded when he failed to be invited to a schoolmate's birthday party. He was asked how many children he expected to invite the next time he gave a party. Looking at the situation in this new perspective, it was apparent that since the number of guests was limited by necessity, there was no occasion to regard the omission as a personal slight. His mental suffering was thereupon relieved.

Finally, it is sometimes necessary to alter the opinion one holds of oneself. This is difficult, for the individual's conception of himself is the central axiom of his whole life theory. Nevertheless, a gradual change in the concept of self is imperative to normal development and happiness.

There is thus a constant compulsion to unify and harmonize the system of ideas by which we live. It is only when a person is unable to rid himself of inconsistencies that psychological problems arise. The difficulty is to make him realize the nature of the inconsistency. For when an inconsistency is clearly recognized, the individual can be depended upon to make the problem his own and endeavor to alter the system in such a way that consistency is restored. In constructing his personal theory of life, in other words, the individual follows the same method precisely as the scientist constructing his theory of the world. In both cases the resistance to disturbance of the existing organization is readily observable.

... The various so-called emotional states cannot be treated independently, but must be regarded as different aspects of a single motive, the striving for unity. For example, love is the emotion subjectively experienced in reference to a person or object already assimilated and serving as a strong support to the idea of the self. Grief is experienced when the personality must be reorganized due to the loss of one of its supports. Hatred is an impulse of rejection felt towards unassimilable objects. Love may turn to hate if the accepted idea of a person turns out to be false in the light of later experience, and instead of serving as a support, becomes a threat to the integrity of the organization as a whole.

The emotion of horror appears when a situation arises suddenly which we are not prepared to assimilate, such as the sight of a ghastly accident. Experiences which increase the sense of psychological unity and strength give rise to the emotion of joy. Occasionally a person's own behavior may violate his conception of himself, producing feelings of remorse and guilt. In that case, the insult to himself, as it were, may be eliminated by seeking punishment sufficient to equalize the insult. Fear is felt when no adequate solution of a problem can be found, and disorganization impends.

Of special importance from the standpoint of the school is the phenomenon of resistance. The problem of resistance has heretofore received very little attention in educational psychology, which conceives learning in terms of habit formation. In psychiatry, on the other hand, resistance is regarded as a device to protect the neurosis, and hence as belonging to abnormal psychology. Yet the very fact that we strive to be true to ourselves involves resistance to the acceptance of that which is inconsistent. Thus resistance must be recognized as normal and necessary. Indeed, a unified organization could not be maintained without it. Nevertheless, there are always present in the system a certain number of ideas accepted on insufficient evidence, whose inconsistency has not yet been demonstrated. These ideas give rise to resistances which are likely to be detrimental to the individual in the long run, and which would not be retained if carefully re-examined.

A therapeutic technique which aims to bring about the re-examination and dissolution of this type of resistance has been successfully applied in the treatment of students who encounter difficulty both in academic work and in social situations.

Sensitiveness, inability to make friends, etc. are due to definitions which are difficult to support in the existing situation. The individual's definitions often formed as the result of excessive attention in childhood, are no longer supported by the persons with whom he comes in contact. The behavior of his associates does not confirm the conception of himself which he is committed to maintain. Unconsciously demanding more recognition than he commonly receives, he feels that he is being neglected or pushed aside. Furthermore, he defines himself in passive terms, as someone whose place it is to be assisted, invited, or admired, rather than in active terms, as someone who assists, invites and admires others. To take a socially active role, even to the extent of speaking first to another person, for him is out of character.

The maintenance of such a passive definition is not, of course, an easy task in the competitive adult world. Social support is a matter of exchange, in which one receives in proportion as he gives. The therapy must therefore aim to make the subject aware of the self-valuation which prevents assimilation of the existing situation. The task is not really as difficult as it seems, for the reason that he cannot escape from his environment and is constantly having more unassimilable situations thrust upon him, and is therefore already occupied with the problem before we offer our help. His passive definition, which is the real source of his difficulties, now appears as a useless burden to be thrown off rather than an asset to be justified and retained. In order to induce the student to accept the problem as his own, of course, criticism must be carefully avoided.

Since each personality is an organized system in which every idea is related to every other, it is obvious that any attempt to force the issue and remove the resistance by attacking it misses the point completely. For this reason the consultant will probably be more successful if he does not try too hard. Parents and teachers, whose own peace of mind is affected by the child's success or failure, usually cannot set aside their personal interest in the matter and are likely to become impatient. We may with advantage remind ourselves that only the individual himself can solve his problem, and he must necessarily solve it in his own way.

Self-consistency vs. the doctrine of specificity

Conforming to the rigid determinism of the nineteenth century, the older forms of scientific psychology were committed to a causal program in which behavior was determined solely by two sets of factors, environmental and hereditary. Thus we were given to consider opposing theories of environmentally determined habits and natively determined instincts similar to the doctrines of epigenesis and preformation in early biology. In recent modifications of psychological and biological theory, however, the organism itself is beginning to appear as to some extent its own determiner. There is a coherence in the behavior of any single organism which argues against an explanation in terms of chance combinations of determiners and points to an organized dynamic system which tends toward self-determination.

* * *

The extreme positions in the controversy regarding the problem of consistency as a characteristic of behavior are represented on the one hand by psychiatry, which finds a high degree of consistency, and on the other by stimulus–response psychology, which finds almost no consistency at all. Psychiatry bases its explanations on the operation of forces located within the organism, stimulus–response psychology on forces operative in the environment.

It is quite possible to present evidence in support of either point of view. . . .

The task of adaptation must be conceived in relation to the organism and its environment jointly. The statement that the environment controls the organism is the product of a single point of view, exactly as true and as false as the view that the organism controls the environment. Both sides endeavor to alleviate the rigidity of their original positions by making concessions to common sense, but the concessions in no way change the basic framework of the two conceptions as organized structures of thought. These remain inflexible. In one respect, however, the two theories are quite similar, for both are attempts to explain human nature by means of concepts drawn from mechanics.

The psychoanalytic theory, as Lashley has pointed out, is really a theory of *psycho-hydraulics*. Simulus–response psychology is a theory of *psycho-telephonics*. Both theories represent efforts to fit the phenomena of behavior into one or the other of these familiar and simple thought–models, rather than attempts to originate a truly psychological conception. In the one case, repressed motives or instincts are thought of as liquids under pressure, exerting an outward stress which is exactly equal at all points. In the other instance, stimuli are thought of as separate and haphazard incoming messages entering an automatic telephone system.

We shall have occasion to criticize the psychiatric viewpoint on the ground that it employs the theory of instincts. But when we turn our attention to the stimulus–response hypothesis, the direction of attack must be reversed. Instead of arguing against control by internal forces, we must argue against control by external forces.

* * *

The personality

"The world hath many centers, one for each created being, and about each one it lieth in its own circle. Thou standest but half an ell from me, yet about thee lieth a universe whose center I am not but thou art."
—THOMAS MANN, *Joseph in Egypt*

. . . Until the end of the nineteenth century, the physiological theory of stimulus–response, based on the analogy between the nervous system and a telegraph system, dominated all psychological thinking. But the theory, which substituted the analogy of a hydraulic system and endeavored to conceive of mental processes in terms of the behavior of liquids under pressure, proved inadequate for clinical purposes and was challenged by psychoanalysis [sic]. It was this analogy which gave rise to such concepts as repression, emotional outlets, sublimation, drainage, equilibrium, etc. Both theories attempt by the use of these analogies to maintain the appearance of consistency with the traditions of mechanistic science.

The hydraulic analogy seemed to offer an alternative to the telegraphic concept chiefly because of its greater flexibility for dealing with problems of motivation. Instead of relying on environmental forces acting as stimuli, it postulated a group of internal forces seeking external expression. But it has never been possible to explain all behavior as the expression of the same type of energy, which would be quite necessary, of course, if the hydraulic figure were followed literally. Freud attempted to confine his theory to the single instinct of love or sex, but he was forced to recognize the so-called ego motives, and later added the death instinct, which makes for aggression and hatred. Similarly, Adler began with the aggressive striving for power or superiority, but later was obliged to admit the existence of social feeling and cooperative tendencies. Other schools recognize much longer lists of instincts. But in all cases it has been observed that motives conflict and interfere with one another, which has led to the belief that each different motive must be treated independently. The result is that the hydraulic analogy leads to a number of dynamic units, just as the telegraphic concept, with its great variety of habits and reaction patterns, leads to a number of structural units. Both theories have thus succeeded in obscuring the integral character of the organism's activity: the organization has either been divided against itself or been reduced to a loose aggregate of elements.

These mechanistic figures of speech have been useful devices for preliminary organization of the data, but they have not produced a conception of man which disinterested students of the evidence are able to accept. After fifty years of research under mechanistic auspices, psychology is more disorganized in respect of its theoretical outlook than ever before in its history.

Instead of assuming beforehand, therefore, that man is a machine which is moved by forces, a lump whose future behavior is predictable from records of its past behavior, let us assume that as long as he remains alive he must be thought of as a unit in himself, a system which operates as a whole. His behavior must then be interpreted in terms of action rather than reaction, that is, in terms of purpose.

Mechanistic theories, since they assume that activity is only an effect of some antecedent cause, must attempt to explain activity itself, and must therefore seek to define or isolate the cause of activity. The usual enunication is that the organism acts because it is stimulated. We assume, on the contrary, that every organism, as long as it remains alive, is continuously active, and hence continuously purposive. Life and activity are coexistent and inseparable. We do not have to explain why the organism acts, but only why it acts in one way rather than another. A stimulus does not initiate activity, but merely tends to modify in one or another way the activity already in progress.

Such a suggestion is by no means radical from a humanistic standpoint. Any theory which is erected on the basis of this principle of unified action, however, and any technique derived from the theory for clinical use, is automatically prohibited from assuming a plurality of purposes. One source of motivation only, the necessity to maintain the unity of the system, must serve as the universal dynamic principle. Not conflict but unity must be the fundamental postulate.

* * *

We propose to apprehend all psychological phenomena as illustrations of the single principle of unity or self-consistency. We conceive of the personality as an organization of values which are felt to be consistent with one another. Behavior expresses the effort to maintain the integrity and unity of the organization.

The point is that all of an individual's values are organized into a single system the preservation of whose integrity is essential. The nucleus of the system, around which the rest of the system revolves, is the individual's valuation of himself. The individual sees the world from his own viewpoint, with himself as the center. Any value entering the system which is inconsistent with the individual's valuation of himself cannot be assimilated; it meets with resistance and is likely, unless a general reorganization occurs, to be rejected. This resistance is a natural phenomenon; it is essential for the maintenance of individuality.

* * *

Let us think of the individual, therefore, as a unified system with two sets of problems—one the problem of maintaining inner harmony within himself, and the other the problem of maintaining harmony with the environment, especially the social environment, in the midst of which he lives. In order to understand the environment, he must keep his interpretations consistent with his experience, but in order to maintain his individuality, he must organize his interpretations to form a system which is internally consistent. This consistency is not objective, of course, but subjective and wholly individual.

The personality develops as a result of actual contacts with the world, and incorporates into itself the meanings derived from external contacts. Essentially, it is the organization of experience into an integrated whole.

Only those situations which enter into individual experience, therefore, enter into the personality and need to be provided for. Ideally, then, we should begin by determining the nature of the individual's experience, especially during the first years of life, and observing the manner in which this experience is organized. But from a practical standpoint this is impossible; instead, we have to infer the organization from the way in which present situations are dealt with. That is why mechanistic explanations are useless. We must have some means of obtaining sufficient and relevant data to work with, but the real task is to create from the data a conception of the subject which will give us insight into his behavior and reveal its coherence and purpose.

The most constant factor in the individual's experience, as we have said, is himself and the intepretation of his own meaning; the kind of person he is, the place which he occupies in the world, appear to represent the center or nucleus of the personality. The next most constant factor, as a rule, in the circle of the child's experience, and hence the next most important element in the structure of the organization, is the mother. If we think of the infant personality as made up of these two elements only, it is clear that the first major problem which the organization must face is that of assimilating the father.

This task is usually a difficult one. The father scarcely enters the child's experience until the second year, and his incorporation into the system requires that the values already established in regard to the self and the mother be altered. Consequently the entrance of the father not only means that the personality is to that extent enlarged, but also that it must undergo a process of reorganization. Nor, as a rule, can the task be avoided. The child is in somewhat the same position as Pavlov's dog in a harness; since he cannot escape from the home situation, he must learn to evaluate it more realistically (Freud's reality principle) and unify his attitude toward a larger field of experience.[1]

It is hardly necessary to point out that assimilating the father really means assimilating situations in which the father plays a part. And since some father–situations would naturally be more difficult than others to assimilate, it is obvious that the attitudes of acceptance

---

[1] We therefore fully agree with Freud that the course of future development depends upon the way in which the Oedipus situation is handled, but it seems to us that the unity theory explains the facts more convincingly than the theory of a sexual attachment to the mother. Furthermore, although it cannot be denied that the conflict is one between love and hate, it is evident that both motives are evoked in the interest of unity, and it is also clear ... that when the conflict is solved the hate is not suppressed, as psychoanalysis maintains, but the love motive unified. Otherwise, by definition, the conflict would not be solved.

and rejection would be likely to fluctuate somewhat. In this way we obtain what seems to be a reasonable explanation of the so-called "ambivalence" of the attitude toward the father. Ambivalence then must be attributed not to the failure of repression, but to the variability of the father's behavior; he is accepted when he behaves in one way, rejected when he behaves in another.

Indeed, we often notice a similar ambivalence in the attitude toward the brothers and sisters. A new baby particularly, as Adler has shown, deprives the older children of the mother's attention and often meets with a hostile reception from them for that reason. When assimilation begins, however, the attitude changes back and forth until acceptance predominates. The Oedipus situation is thus not different in kind from other problem situations, and in fact cannot be treated as an isolated problem in itself; though the nature of the adjustment which is made to this first problem will naturally have important consequences.

By the time the child is five years old, according to psychoanalysis, the hatred of the father has been suppressed and the conscious attitude is one of love. At this point the latency period begins, and the libido subsides to reawaken at the onset of puberty. Anna Freud writes, "Instead of keeping pace with the further development of the child, the sexual impulses now gradually lose their energy, their libido, as psychoanalysis calls it. The struggle for pleasure recedes more and more to the background." Yet it seems more reasonable to suppose that after five years the child has succeeded in assimilating the most frequent and typical father–situations, and hence has achieved his freedom from conflict and emotion by virtue of continuous learning. The change in behavior can be explained without resort to the theory of a mysterious but temporary loss of sexual energy. From our standpoint, such a change is a matter of necessity, for if the attitude of rejection originally taken toward the father were unified, it would involve everything associated with the father, including the mother also.

But if the age of four or five marks the end of the task of assimilating customary home situations, it also sees the beginning of a new task. The child now begins to make the acquaintance of children of its own age outside of the home. Its circle of experience widens to include situations in the school and on the playground, especially social situations, which present additional difficulties.[2] Friendships are formed,

---

[2] With regard to the task of "adaptation" the least mistaken hypothesis, it seems to me, is Adler's view that the needs of society count as heavily as those of the individual, and that social interest and cooperation are as necessary to normal development as a favorable environment. In any case, there can be little doubt that the problems set by the environment are primarily social.

new persons incorporated into the organization, and corresponding adjustments called for in the values given to the self and the parents. This period seems to have the function of preparing the child for social cooperation. The personality is consolidated and strengthened, and new supports developed outside of the family. Thus it is the beginning of independence of the family.

With adolescence, however, a change of such crucial difficulty and importance occurs in the structure of the organization that emotional crises similar to those of early childhood frequently reappear. This change, which usually requires several years to accomplish, and sometimes, indeed, is not accomplished, is the displacement of the parents from their former position by a member of the opposite sex. Occasionally there is open rebellion against the authority of the parents, who in turn are called upon to make adjustments on their own account. During this period of instability and reorganization, when the adolescent is revising his earlier values and changing his whole outlook on life, the need of unity is most acute. This may be seen in the growth of religious interests, idealism, and the desire for membership in social groups.

For the present this brief sketch must suffice. We shall now attempt graphically to represent the developing organization of values as a definite conceptual structure. Let its form be represented as a sphere, with the concept of the self or ego in the center, the concept of the parents near the center, and close friends, relatives and acquaintances arranged in order toward the periphery. This is the typical arrangement during childhood. After puberty there is typically an alteration of the original relationships, with the parents being gradually displaced from their central position by a newcomer into the organization, a member of the opposite sex, who is usually regarded first as acquaintance and friend, but finally is accepted as mate. Thus a new constellation of values is established with the husband or wife and children as the primary supports of the organization. Pets, toys, possessions, etc., and

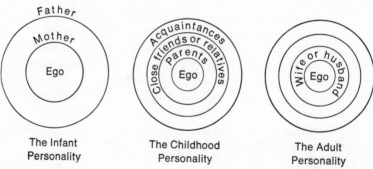

The Infant Personality

The Childhood Personality

The Adult Personality

Figure 1.

familiar stimuli in general also enter into the child's organization, though they are not represented [in Figure 1]. The complication of relationships in the adult personality can be specified only with difficulty by such diagrammatic devices.

We shall define the personality, then, as a unified scheme of experience, an organization of values that are consistent with one another. And we shall conceive the study of human beings as the study of personalities. The organization must be thought of, moreover, not merely as a figure of speech, but as in some sense a reality. Whether the interpretations of behavior which are based on this conception should be regarded as true or not will depend to some extent on how one chooses to define truth. The mechanist also believes that his explanations are true. But so far as we are concerned, our search is simply for an explanation that will prove to be illuminating and fruitful.

We believe that all behavior must be explained in terms of this system. It is too early to attempt an exhaustive treatment, but some of the more familiar phenomena of psychology are interpreted as follows.

Identification represents the effort of the child to bring his ideas of himself and his parents into more unified relationship. He not only imitates his parents, but adopts their views and opinions as his own. His parents' religion becomes his religion, their standards become his standards. In this way differences are eliminated, and the bonds of relationship strengthened by increasing the "consciousness of kind." Assimilation and identification go hand in hand; the child's weak ego, having originally no values of its own, is readily adaptable and takes on those values which aid in unifying the system as a whole.

An excellent illustration of the alteration of values which accompanies identification is found in the Book of Ruth, I, 16–17: "For whither thou goest, I will go; and where thou lodgest, I will lodge: thy people shall be my people, and thy God my God: where thou diest will I die, and there will I be buried; the Lord do so to me, and more also, if aught but death part thee and me."

Most parents identify themselves with the child to some extent, and try as it were to make themselves more assimilable by taking over some of the child's standards. Such identification also occurs between lovers. When the process is carried to sentimental extremes, however, as when the parents talk baby talk, it is obvious that the child will base its own values on unsound premises. There may be differences of opinion as to the desirability of some values, but it can hardly be of assistance to the child to derive its standards from the observation of childish behavior, whether on the part of its parents or other children.

This point, it seems to us, is overlooked by those modern theorists who would abolish the home altogether and segregate the children into child communities under scientific management where attachments to adults will not be formed. For it cannot be assumed that adult values are innate or instinctive in the child; and if they are not to be obtained by identification with adults, it is difficult to see from what other source they could be expected to arise. It is easy enough to construct utopias where behavior is conceived as the automatic performance of mechanical habits, but the problem of establishing in the child a conception of life which will work to his benefit cannot be approached so optimistically.

Resistance is the opposite of assimilation and learning, and represents the refusal to reorganize the values, especially the ego values. With age, of course, the values become more firmly established, and adaptability decreases. To the psychiatrist, the striving of the patient to maintain his organization appears as a symptom of perversity. To the educator it appears as an obstacle to learning. But if we would really understand these resistances, we must see them not as neurotic or abnormal manifestations, but as wholly natural devices for avoiding reorganization. If a person were able to adapt himself as readily as is sometimes expected, he would have no personality.

Whether resistance be thought of as desirable or undesirable, therefore, is wholly a matter of the point of view. The loyalty to individual values may interfere with efforts to change them, but this loyalty is also the source of honesty and integrity.

The following instance will illustrate that resistance to learning also has its favorable side. For years the deficiency of boys in reading, as compared with girls who receive the same instruction, has been widely recognized, particularly in elementary courses. We have discovered that this difference is due not to a lack of ability on the part of the boys, but to a lack of reading material which is suitable for boys. The boy from six to eight years old, just beginning to learn to read, is mainly concerned with maintaining the conception of himself as manly. He likes to play cowboy, G-man and Indian. He tries not to cry when he gets a bump. Yet this boy, when the reading lesson begins, must stand up before his companions and read that "the little red hen says 'Cluck! Cluck! Cluck!'"—or something equally inconsistent with his standards of how he should behave. To be obliged to read such material aloud, especially in the presence of others, is not consistent with his view of masculine values. If a boy is trying to maintain a standard of manliness on the playground, he does not abandon that standard merely because he walks from the playground into the classroom. When books on railroads and airplanes are provided, they serve to support these values and are assimilated eagerly. The point is, of course, that the assumed defect in reading never was a defect except from the standpoint of an unenlightened school system, but on the contrary was a manifestation of a wholesome, normal, and desirable resistance.

In the Freudian scheme, resistance is interpreted as the patient's desire to retain his neurosis, whereas we interpret it as the desire to maintain his personality. This enables us to point out that what the psychoanalyst calls a neurosis and what we call the personality are virtually identical. The patient is seeking to defend not a mental disease which the analyst is trying to remove, but a scheme of life which the analyst is trying to change. Many analysts admit this freely. While we may think of a person's scheme of life as unconscious in the sense that it has not been consciously formulated as a whole, however, we could scarcely attribute the unconsciousness to the mechanism of repression.

*   *   *

The Freudian theory of *repression*, which is regarded as the cornerstone of psychoanalytic theory, has undergone so many revisions that the exact present meaning of the concept is somewhat in doubt. The general idea seems to be, however, that emotions which are denied expression are suppressed into the unconscious, from which thereafter they continually seek some means of escape. There is no doubt that in certain cases this explanation seems quite plausible, but inasmuch as it presupposes the existence of emotion as a separate entity, we are forced to reject the theory of repression and seek to reinterpret the phenomena from the standpoint of organization.

Let us take, for example, the psychological problem raised when a person feels insulted. This means that there has been thrust into his experience a value of himself or or someone with whom he is identified which he cannot assimilate. This inconsistency is a source of disturbance, and unless the person responsible "takes back" the insult the disturbance continues. If he refuses to "take it back," there is an impulse to retaliation. That is, the low value seems to be eliminated by hurling it back upon its author.

But suppose that, for reasons of expediency, it cannot be hurled back; what then? Shall we say with Freud that the energy (death instinct) has undergone repression into the reservoir of the *Id*, to seek expression later when the life instinct is less active, or shall we rather say that the organization continues to strive to remove the inconsistency and unify itself?

To answer this question, let us turn to the evidence of primitive behavior to which Freud himself so often appeals. How would the repression theory account for the exact balance between injury and reprisal provided for in primitive codes of vengeance, or the conception that justice has not been done unless the punishment inflicted is consistent with the crime? Obviously, the motive is to correct the situation and make it more assimilable. We quote an illustration from the ancient Hebrew law as given in Leviticus, XXIV, 18–20: "And he that killeth a beast shall make it good; beast for beast. And if a man cause a blemish in his neighbor; as he hath done, so shall it be done to him; breach for breach, eye for eye, tooth for tooth; as he has caused a blemish in a man, so shall it be done to him again. And he that killeth a beast, he shall restore it; and he that killeth a man, he shall be put to death."

The impulse to retaliation aroused when a person has been insulted or treated unjustly is therefore not an accumulation of energy waiting to be discharged, but a purposive effort of the organization to rid itself of inconsistency.

Self-consistency as a technique

The crucial problem for all personality theories is the theoretical basis of therapy, for the true significance of a system emerges only when it meets a problem.

* * *

[For example,] the greatest handicap to constructive action in education is the well-entrenched dogma that learning is the direct result of teaching, a mechanical reaction to the school environment instead of a purposive achievement. Learning cannot be understood as a process of forming separate habits, but only in terms of the development of the entire personality. When one value has been accepted, it opposes the acceptance of other values which are not consistent with it. Hence resistance must be accepted as a normal and necessary aspect of learning. Indeed, a unified organization could not be maintained without it. Early impressions are important not only in themselves, but because they set the conditions for rejection of other values, whatever their nature, which would tend to precipitate a conflict.

Nevertheless, since the experience of everyone is more or less haphazard from an educational standpoint, there are always present in the system a certain number of values accepted on insufficient evidence. These values, whose retention depends entirely upon the success with which they can be rationalized and made to seem consistent, or at any rate not inconsistent, give rise to resistances which are likely to be detrimental to the individual.

The clinical technique which follows from the theoretical conception of the problem must therefore aim to bring about in the subject a re-examination of those values which block his development. Academic difficulties and social maladjustments are both conceived of as due to resistances arising from the subject's conception of himself. If a student shows resistance toward a certain type of material, this means that from his point of view it would be inconsistent for him to learn it. If we are able to change the self-conception which underlies this viewpoint, however, his attitude toward the material will change accordingly.

Let us take the case of an intelligent student who is deficient, say, in spelling. In almost every instance poor spellers have been tutored and practiced in spelling over long periods without improvement. For some reason such a student has a special handicap in learning how to spell, though not in learning the other subjects which are usually considered more difficult. This deficiency is not due to a lack of ability, but rather to an active resistance which prevents him from learning how to spell in spite of the extra instruction. The resistance arises from the fact that at some time in the past the suggestion that he is a poor speller was accepted and incorporated into his definition of himself, and is now an integral part of his total personality. A standard is a conception that a person maintains because he has accepted it as a part of his personality. Standards need not be admirable, even from the standpoint of the person who maintains them, so long as he believes them to be valid. As in the present instance, he may accept as his standard the conception of his own inferiority in some particular respect. His difficulty is thus explained as a special instance of the general principle that a person can only be true to himself. If he defines himself as a poor speller, the misspelling of a certain proportion of the words which he uses becomes for him a moral issue. He misspells words for the same reason that he refuses to be a thief. That is, he must endeavor to behave in a manner consistent with his conception of himself.

A study of the spelling behavior of these students shows that each individual seems to have a definite standard of poor spelling which he unconsciously endeavors to maintain. If his spelling test is cut in two, it will be found that each half contains approximately the same number of misspelled words. If we study his letters or written theses, there is likewise a striking consistency in the number of misspelled words per page. Strange to say, the spelling of foreign languages seems to be impaired very little if at all, showing clearly that the difficulty cannot be attributed to eye movements, left-handedness, or other mechanical inteferences. Evidently the conception of one's self as a poor speller usually has reference to one's native language only.

The clincial technique consists in first finding several strong values apparently unrelated to the value in question which can be used as levers, so to speak, and then demonstrating the inconsistency between these values and the one responsible for the deficiency. Almost every student considers himself independent and self-reliant, for example. On the other hand, it can readily be shown that the poor speller expects his defect to be condoned and treated sympathetically; that, in effect, he has his hand out, begging for indulgence. If the contradiction can be demonstrated from his own viewpoint, a reorganization becomes compulsory. His definition of himself as a poor speller is vigorously rejected and a determined effort made to establish the opposite definition.

It is significant that not only poor spellers, but stammerers and others with similar defects, freely admit as a rule that they accept themselves as they are and make no effort to change. This is an excellent defense, of course, for they feel no inconsistency, once the definition has been accepted. And they often attempt to avoid the effort of maintaining a more useful definition by referring the defect to heredity or neuromuscular maladjustment.

Those who claim that they "do not have a mathematical mind" are likewise victims of their own resistance. Such a student may have defined himself in childhood as the exact opposite of some unassimilable companion who had been held up as a shining example of mathematical proficiency. In other cases, remarks by parents or teachers that the child was lacking in aptitude for mathematics seem to be the explanation. The suggestion was accepted and is now a part of the student's conception of himself. In one instance, a student who despised mathematics in high school and during his freshman year acquired a sudden attachment for the subject and became a professional statistician. This boy's older brother was proficient in mathematics, and the two had been in conflict for years.

So-called laziness, lack of concentration, etc., are due to the acceptance of definitions at cross purposes with one another. Such individuals cannot act in consistency with one definition without being inconsistent with another. For example, a student may define himself as intelligent, but poor in mathematics. To maintain the first definition, he should make high grades in mathematics, but to maintain the second he should fail. However, since he must act, as long as he is playing both roles at once he is forced to compromise. His grades in mathematics will split the difference somewhere near the passing mark, and the teacher will characterize him as lazy. For his own part, he will claim that he cannot concentrate, and the claim will be perfectly true. This seems to be the explanation of the characteristic level of performance already noted in regard to spelling. As long as the definitions remain unchanged, the characteristic rate or grade of activity tends to remain constant.

The remedy is not to be found by means of tests which reveal the specific weaknesses, therefore, or in persistent drilling on the fundamentals, but only in changing the definition. Energetic concentration simply means that a person is free from conflicts and able to bring his united efforts to focus on the task in hand.

What a person is able or unable to learn, in other words, depends, to a large extent at least, upon what he has already learned, and especially upon how he has learned to define himself. Differences in native ability cannot be summarily dismissed, but at present this explanation is frequently dragged in simply to serve as an alibi, both for the school and for the individual.

It should be repeated in this connection that a person may accept any definition whatsoever if nothing has been learned to the contrary to interfere with its acceptance, while a contrary definition provides a sort of immunity. We have an instance of a very slow boy who characterized himself as "the slow one" and his brother as "the quick one." He felt so guilty when working too rapidly that he had developed a large repertory of devices to use up the necessary amount of time in order to be true to his role. Attempts to teach him rapid methods of work naturally met with complete failure as long as the original definition was retained. Very often a troublesome child has unwittingly been cast in that part by the criticism of parents or teachers. A boy who has previously defined himself as "good" would vigorously resist, of course, the suggestions that he is "bad." If his definition in this respect has not yet been strongly established, however, he may accept the role and consider the question closed. Thereafter he endeavors to perfect himself in the part to which he has been assigned, and grows more and more unmanageable the more his behavior is condemned. Youths who are placed in reformatories usually emerge not reformed, but confirmed in their self-definition as social outcasts and potential criminals.

* * *

. . . But no matter how undesirable a given definition may be from a social standpoint, it will not be rejected unless it seems inconsistent from the subject's standpoint. We do not aim at consistency with the demands of society, but only at self-consistency. Social ends must be approached indirectly. In other words, if the personal problem is solved and unity of action achieved, the social problem disappears.

Everyone's behavior is logical from his own point of view. If another person's behavior seems illogical to us, the reason is that we do not understand it, not that he is irrational.

The behavior of others seems irrational and incomprehensible only when the definitions they are striving to maintain bear too little resemblance to our own. The behavior of those whose definitions are similar to ours, on the other hand, seems quite rational and natural; it is understandable for the simple reason that we would behave that way ourselves.

READING III-3. *The Self, Its Derivative Terms, and Research*

ARTHUR W. COMBS AND
DANIEL W. SOPER

[The following article presents a more technical discussion of the self-concept and some related terms. Although addressed primarily to fellow research psychologists, the paper helps clarify for our purposes the different ways in which a person may think and talk about himself and the influence of these different kinds of views of self on his behavior.]

With the increasing tendency of social scientists to be "self-oriented" in their study of human behavior, a large number of terms had been developed for use in describing and studying the phenomenon of self. Some of these terms are: "self," "concepts of self," "self concept," "self-ideal," "self-adequacy," "self-acceptance," etc. As these terms have become adopted and used by an increasing number of people from a wide variety of theoretical frames of reference, the literature dealing with them has become more and more confused. This paper attempts to re-examine conceptual bases, to point up ambiguities and problems which exist, and to arrive at definitions of these terms consistent with a "self" frame of reference and capable of providing a more adequate base for the planning of research, and thus to facilitate communication among workers in this area. . . .

Self and real self

The word "self" is a generic term referring to a specific human personality and has been indispensable in the historical development of man as a conscious and thinking entity. The assertion that a "self" exists may involve only the assumption that for a given human being, there exist identity (uniqueness) and consciousness of self and environment. If, however, we wish to go beyond this point and describe the

Excerpted, by permission, from Arthur W. Combs and Daniel W. Soper, "The Self, Its Derivative Terms, and Research," in the *Journal of Individual Psychology*, 13, no. 2 (November 1957), 134–44. Several paragraphs, referring to specific research studies, and most of the references have been deleted.

characteristics and attributes of a given self, the job becomes a more complex and difficult one, for the self can be observed from many different frames of reference. It may be described from the point of view of innumerable observers, including the individual himself.

No one can ever observe a "real" self—his own or someone else's—directly. It can only be approached through the perceptions of someone. An individual attempting to describe *his own self*, can provide only an approximation of his "real" self; at any given time, only a part of the "real" self is "visible" to the individual. Another person attempting to describe *someone else's self*, can only approximate the "real" self through inferences based on observed behavior.

Fortunately, it is not necessary to cope with the question of the "real" self, for its very existence is a philosophical question. It is sufficient that the ways in which the self is *perceived* can be studied. This, we think, *is* necessary; for these perceptions are among the most important determinants of behavior.

Concepts of self

The number of ways in which the self may be perceived are practically limitless. Individuals may see themselves as men or women, children or adults, Republicans or Democrats. More specifically, a particular individual may see himself as John Smith, owner of a 1956 Dodge, who lives at 627 Edgemere Street, St. Albans, Utah. Descriptions like these serve to distinguish the self as unique from all other selves. But self-description does not stop with this. We are seldom content with description alone. Thus, even more important are the values the individual places upon his various qualities of self. People do not regard themselves as fathers or mothers only, but as "good" fathers and mothers or "bad" ones. They see themselves, not simply as people, but as attractive or ugly, pleasant or unpleasant, fat or thin, happy or sad, adequate or inadequate people.

Each individual, within a comparatively short time after birth, has developed a large number of perceptions about himself. These more or less separate perceptions of self might be termed "concepts of self." They are more or less discrete perceptions of self which the individual regards as part or characteristic of himself. They include all the self-perceptions which the individual has differentiated as descriptive of the self he calls "I" or "me". These concepts are not of equal importance in the peculiar economy of a human being. They vary in at least two important respects.

1. Some are more central, such as conceiving of self as man or

woman, and are more resistant to change. Other concepts of self are less strongly defended because they do not seem quite so important in a particular organization, such as being the driver of a 1956 Dodge.

2. Concepts of self will also vary in sharpness or clarity. At any moment we observe a human being, we will find the concepts of self which he holds to vary from those in clear, sharp figure to those so vague and fuzzy as to be inexpressible even by the person himself. The mother in the psychological clinic, for example, may be quite certain that she is Jimmy's mother. Whether she is a "good" mother is a perception far less clear to her. Indeed, it may be this very confusion that causes her difficulty.

The self concept

Whereas the "concepts of self" about which we have just been speaking describe isolated aspects of the person, the "self concept" is the organization of all that the individual refers to as "I" or "me." It is himself from his own point of view. The self concept is not a mere conglomeration or addition of isolated concepts of self, but a patterned interrelationship or gestalt of all these. Like many of the concepts of which it is composed, the self-concept has a degree of stability and consistency which gives predictability to the individual and his behavior.

The perceptual field of an individual includes much more than his perceptions of self. It includes, for example, perceptions of the objects and events in the world about him, perceptions of his physical being, the goals and values he has differentiated as means of achieving need satisfaction, the techniques which have come to seem appropriate ways of reaching his goals, and perceptions of abstract ideas and concepts. These perceptions, in the same fashion as perceptions of self, will also vary in importance and clarity.

The perceptual field which includes all of an individual's perceptions may be represented by a large circle, A. Within this perceptual field we may think of a second and smaller circle, B, which includes all those perceptions which the person holds about himself, irrespective of their importance or clarity to him at any particular moment. Snygg and Combs [in *Individual Behavior*] have called this the "phenomenal self." Within the phenomenal field we may think of a third, still smaller circle, C, which includes only those aspects which are important or vital to the self. This is the self-concept. It is a stable, important and characteristic organization composed of those perceptions which seem to the individual preeminently himself.

Inferential nature of the self

Both the self concept and concepts of self are inferences about the self. They are sheer abstractions, or interpretations useful in helping us understand ourselves and to make communication possible. The self as a discrete entity does not exist. Allport warns against reifying the self, making it into a homunculus to solve all problems without in reality solving any.[1] Like the concept of the atom or of electricity, the self-concept is an inference which enables us to deal with a complex function not directly observable. The fact that it is a product of inference does, however, not make it invalid. To the individual, his perceptions of self, like all his other perceptions, have the feeling of reality. His self concept seems to him to be truly what he is.

The self concept is created by the individual's inferences from his unique experiences. It is derived from observations about his own behavior and the behavior of other people toward him. The child who perceives adults push him away may come to perceive himself as un-liked or unwanted. The adult observing himself to be badly winded while playing with his young son may revise his self concept with the perception that he no longer has the old pep. Whatever self concept the individual holds has been acquired from the data of his own observations of behavior.

The outsider hoping to understand the self concept of another individual also attempts to assess it through inference. If each individual behaves in terms of his self concept, then it should be possible for an outsider, by observing the behavior of an individual, to infer the nature of the self concept. This is what each of us does quite auto-matically in dealing with other people. We infer, from the behavior we see, what other people are thinking and feeling, and adjust our own behavior accordingly. What the layman does as a matter of "common sense," the behavioral scientist seeks to do more exactly and more precisely. The data used by the psychologist in studying the self-concept are exactly the same as those used in studying any other human characteristic, namely, the observed behavior of the subject.

The self report

The self report is the individual's self-description; it represents what the individual *says* he is. Like any other act, the self report is a *behavior* revealing in larger or smaller degree what is going on within the

[1] [See G. W. Allport, *Becoming* (New Haven: Yale University Press, 1955), p. 54.]

organism. The self report and the self concept, although often confused, are by no means synonymous. One is a behavior, the other, a perception or inference made from behavior. To treat the two as synonymous is to introduce into our research a large and unknown degree of error.

The self report is valuable as a means of exploring the self concept. Like any other behavior, the self report is a product of the individual's *total* perceptual field. It is a product of *both* the subject's perceptions of self and of not-self, without having a one-to-one relationship to the self concept. Confusion of the self report with the self concept in research has led to similar confusion in thinking and research results, making communication extremely difficult. . . .

For research purposes we must know the degree to which the self report can be relied upon as an indication of the self concept. This will depend on at least the following factors:

1. *Clarity of the subject's awareness.* We have already seen that the self concept varies in degrees of clarity, and that some concepts of self at any moment are in clear figure while others may be immersed in ground. Whether or not they may be reported to others will depend in some measure on whether they can truly be called into clear figure at the moment they are asked for. Lack of clarity may also be of a more permanent character; some concepts of self may exist at very low levels of awareness for most of our lives. These correspond to the so-called "unconscious," and attempts to report them to others may be impossible.

2. *Lack of adequate symbols for expression.* Closely related to the problem of clarity is the question of the possession of the necessary symbols in which self concepts may be adequately expressed. Self descriptions can only be reported in words. But words are notoriously inadequate, and may not mean the same things to others as they mean to us. The degree to which the self report approaches the self concept is thus open to all the errors of any human communication.

3. *Social expectancy.* In our society it is customary, indeed practically necessary, for the individual to hide his true concepts of self even if he is able to report them accurately. Though a person may think of himself as very charming or as very stupid, he certainly would be most unlikely to express such feelings even under the most favorable circumstances. We can never quite escape the effects of our society, no matter how hard we may try. We are always aware of the expectancies of others toward us, and the things we say about ourselves are always more or less affected by this fact. Perhaps in psychotherapy, when a strong relationship with an accepting counselor has developed, the client may be able to

report his feelings and attitudes toward himself with a lower degree of distortion. This seldom occurs elsewhere in life, however.

4. *Cooperation of the subject.* The accuracy of the self report depends greatly on the motivation of the subject. If he wishes to hide an aspect of self, he can well do so. He does not even have to reveal his lack of cooperation, if indeed he is aware of a decision not to cooperate. But even with the best of intentions to cooperate, a subject may be quite unable to give the desired information accurately for reasons of which he himself is not clearly aware.

5. *Freedom from threat and personal adequacy.* In general, the more adequate the individual feels, the more likely his self report will approach an accurate description of the self concept, other factors being equal. The more threatened, inadequate, or maladjusted the individual, the more vulnerable will be his concepts of self and the greater the necessity for him to defend the self.

* * *

The self ideal

It has become generally accepted that an individual's perception of himself as an adequate or inadequate person—his confidence in his own ability to satisfy his basic needs—is extremely important in determining his reaction to people and situations. At first glance the fact that an individual may see himself as inadequate would seem to require that he have differentiated certain goals for himself which he defines as "adequate" and "satisfactory." The aggregate of these characteristics of self which the person feels are necessary to attain adequacy (sometimes, perhaps unfortunately, perfection) has been termed the "self ideal," and it has been assumed that the discrepancy between a person's "self concept" and his "self ideal" would provide a relatively objective measure of "adequacy" or "inadequacy."
* * *

Description of the self ideal runs into much the same difficulties as the self report. It cannot be accepted at face value. We must try to find out not only *what* the individual says, but *why* he says it under the conditions of the specific observation. Acceptance of a person's responses at face value can quickly lead to misinformation, ambiguous research findings, and further confusion. . . .

Another difficulty is that the individual may never have formulated a clear self ideal. When we ask him to report his self ideal, we may thus be forcing him to invent for us a concept which does not normally exist in his economy in a meaningful way. A person may learn to see himself as very inadequate without ever developing a clear picture of what constitutes adequacy. Indeed, this would seem to be true of most persons who suffer from strong feelings of basic inadequacy. Their inability to differentiate clear and realistic goals is familiar to clinicians and counselors everywhere. Much of the distress of the client in psychotherapy seems to occur precisely because of this inability. He feels that what he *is*, is unsatisfactory; his attempts to define criteria of satisfaction for himself reveal less a self ideal than confusion and lack of clear differentiation.

Finally, an individual's perception of himself as adequate or inadequate, and his differentiation of the qualities which would be ideal for him, involves a great deal more than static or cross-sectional descriptions of self and ideal. Adequacy is a dynamic function. The apparent difference between an individual's self concept and his self ideal, statically described, may be less important than his satisfaction with his current movement toward improvement and his confidence in being able to bridge the gap between "what is" and "what should be." It is quite possible, for example, that two individuals might describe their selves and ideals in very similar terms, yet would differ greatly in their feelings of adequacy to progress toward their goals. Both may see themselves as lacking in a particular area; one may consider this an exciting problem to be solved; the other, a forbidding and insurmountable obstacle. These differences are *perceived* distances between self and ideal. They are distances as the behaver, rather than the observer, sees them; they are "psychological" distances. The observer can only make inferences about these "perceived distances" from the behavior which he observes. He cannot subtract the one set of statements from the other!

The use of the term self ideal, then, and attempts to arrive at objective measurement of this concept, are subject to a number of limitations which have not always been observed. The self ideal involves important dynamic as well as static elements, and can only be studied under the conditions which are common to all phenomenological observations. The term must be recognized as referring to a highly abstract construct, which may or may not have its counterpart in the perceptual field of the individual.

The self and adjustment

A large number of terms have been developed to indicate good adjustment from various points of view. "Self-acceptance," "self-adequacy," and "the nonthreatened personality" are perhaps the most representative.

Unfortunately, these terms are sometimes used to refer to an individual as *totally* self-acceptant, or *totally* adequate, or *completely* non-threatened, conditions which represent ultimate desirable goals along various dimensions of self-perception. These ultimate goals, like most ultimates, represent static conditions which can *never be achieved*. Life is a dynamic process, and individuals continue to strive for growth and self-enhancement. Allport has expressed this function as follows:

> Here seems to be the central characteristic of propriate striving: its goals are, strictly speaking, unattainable. Propriate striving confers unity upon personality, but it is never the unity of fulfillment, or repose, or of reduced tension. The devoted parent never loses concern for his child; the devotee of democracy adopts a lifelong assignment in his human relationships. The scientist, by the very nature of his commitment, creates more and more questions, never fewer. Indeed the measure of our intellectual maturity, one philosopher suggests, is our capacity to feel less and less satisfied with our answers to better and better problems.[2]

Furthermore, the terms *self-acceptant, adequate,* and *nonthreatened* are used in so many ways as to be more confusing than helpful. Actually each describes the same state, yet stresses a different aspect of the field. Let us look at each term briefly.

Self-acceptance. This term . . . refers to the ability of the individual to accept into awareness facts about himself with a minimum of defense or distortion. It is related to the *accuracy* of observation and self-awareness, and does not imply approval or disapproval of self. Thus, a well-adjusted, self-accepting individual may be able to say of himself, "Yes, indeed, I have a very bad habit of interrupting people sometimes," and this unflattering judgment can be made without the necessity for defending himself or denying the existence of the perception. . . .

Self-adequacy. This is another characteristic of the individual self-concept. It is an over-all evaluation of self, at all levels of awareness. It is the individual's judgment of his present and future ability to achieve basic need–satisfaction. An individual always has as a goal a greater degree of adequacy—this is part of the dynamic process of living. To the degree that he sees himself as adequate, however, he can select among the goals he perceives, or reject them, or try and fail, without disorganization and self-defeating reactions. He feels adequate to achieve enhancement through goals which are realistically available in terms of immediate or predicted situations. His feeling of adequacy, then, does not depend on the restrictions of his immediate environment.

Objective appraisal of an individual's success as culturally defined —or his brilliance in contributing to art, science, or literature—does

[2] [*Ibid.*, p. 67.]

not provide in itself satisfactory evidence of an individual's self-adequacy. Adequacy is an attribute of his own perception of himself. Two people may be equally convinced that they are unable to deal with mathematical problems; for one, this is a realistic and matter-of-fact situation which he can use effectively in decision-making, and has relatively little relevance to his feeling of worth-whileness; for the other, it may be further evidence of personal inadequacy, a weakness which is not acceptable to him. Adequacy or inadequacy are *personal* perceptions of events.

Nonthreatened personality. Generally speaking, the "adequate" person is also "nonthreatened." There is a reciprocal relationship between self-adequacy and perceived threat on the part of an individual. Threat occurs when a person sees himself as basically inadequate to satisfy need. The result is a narrowing and distortion of perception so that he is not able to admit into clear awareness those aspects of self and environment which contribute to the threat, nor to relate these meaningfully and realistically to other perceptions of self and environment. Threat produces defense. The self-concept, as it exists at the time, is defended more vigorously and is less capable of change and growth. To speak of a nonthreatened person, then, is another way of referring to one who is self-acceptant and who perceives himself as a basically adequate person.

* * *

Phenomenological research

Phenomenological research, like any other research, begins with careful observation. From such observations it developes inferences as to the perceptions of the subject, which inferences are checked against further observations of behavior. By such a repeated process of observation, inference, prediction, observation, inference, etc., the psychologist using a perceptual frame of reference is able to explore the dynamics of the subject's behavior. Phenomenological research, however, involves the observer in a much more active role than traditional approaches. In perceptual research, he is not a passive but an active instrument of observation. This more active role affords vast opportunities to explore the private world of the behaver, on the one hand, but calls for far greater control and discipline of the observer himself, on the other hand.

The first essential to moving forward in this type of research, it seems to us, is to achieve clarity and precision of our fundamental concepts. Confusion in our concepts can only lead to similar confusion

in our research endeavors. Without clear understanding of the problems we seek to explore, we run the risk of becoming the victims of our
own perceptions.

READING III-4. *The Proprium*
GORDON ALLPORT

[Allport's work on personality has probably had as much influence as
that of any modern psychologist. In 1954 he delivered the Terry
Lectures at Yale, which were subsequently published in a very important little book, *Becoming: Basic Considerations for a Psychology of
Personality*. The following selection from this book is reproduced here
because it is a distinguished, balanced, and eclectic treatment of our
central concern in Part III: the individual personality's *concept of self*.
Allport's basic motivational concept, "propriate striving," is especially relevant to our purposes.]

Personality includes . . . habits and skills, frames of reference,
matters of fact and cultural values, that seldom or never seem warm
and important. But personality includes what is warm and important
also—all the regions of our life that we regard as peculiarly ours, and
which for the time being I suggest we call the *proprium*. The proprium
includes all aspects of personality that make for inward unity.

Psychologists who allow for the proprium use both the terms *self*
and *ego*—often interchangeably; and both terms are defined with
varying degrees of narrowness or of comprehensiveness. Whatever
name we use for it, this sense of what is "peculiarly ours" merits close
scrutiny. The principal functions and properties of the proprium need
to be distinguished.

* * *

Reprinted by permission of the publisher from Gordon W. Allport, *Becoming: Basic
Considerations for a Psychology of Personality* (New Haven: Yale University Press,
1955), 40–56.

Bodily sense

The first aspect we encounter is the bodily *me*. It seems to be composed of streams of sensations that arise within the organism—from viscera, muscles, tendons, joints, vestibular canals, and other regions of the body. The technical name for the bodily sense is *coenesthesis*. Usually this sensory stream is experienced dimly; often we are totally unaware of it. At times, however, it is well configurated in consciousness in the exhilaration that accompanies physical exercise, or in moments of sensory delight or pain. The infant, apparently, does not know that such experiences are "his." But they surely form a necessary foundation for his emerging sense of self. The baby who at first cries from unlocalized discomfort will, in the course of growth, show progressive ability to identify the distress as his own.

The bodily sense remains a lifelong anchor for our self-awareness, though it never alone accounts for the entire sense of self, probably not even in the young child who has his memories, social cues, and strivings to help in the definition. Psychologists have paid a great deal of attention, however, to this particular component of self-awareness, rather more than to other equally important ingredients. One special line of investigation has been surprisingly popular: the attempt to locate self in relation to specific bodily sensations. When asked, some people will say that they *feel* the self in their right hands, or in the viscera. Most, however, seem to agree with Claparède that a center midway between the eyes, slightly behind them within the head, is the focus. It is from this cyclopean eye that we estimate what lies before and behind ourselves, to the right or left, and above and below. Here, phenomenologically speaking, is the locus of the ego.[1] Interesting as this type of work may be, it represents little more than the discovery that various sensory elements in the coenesthetic stream or various inferences drawn from sensory experience may for certain people at certain times be especially prominent.

How very intimate (propriate) the bodily sense is can be seen by performing a little experiment in your imagination. Think first of swallowing the saliva in your mouth, or do so. Then imagine expectorating it into a tumbler and drinking it! What seemed natural and "mine" suddenly becomes disgusting and alien. Or picture yourself sucking blood from a prick in your finger; then imagine sucking

---

[1] E. Claparède, "Note sur la localisation du moi," *Archives de psychologie, 19* (1924), 172–82.

Another school of thought has placed considerable stress upon the total body-image. Its variations are said to mark changes in the course of development. Schilder, for example, points out that in experience of hate the body-image itself contracts; in experience of love it expands, and even seems phenomenally to include other beings. See P. Schilder, *The Image and Appearance of the Human Body*, Psyche Monograph (London: K. Paul, Trench, Trubner Co., 1935), p. 353.

blood from a bandage around your finger! What I perceive as belonging intimately to my body is warm and welcome; what I perceive as separate from my body becomes, in the twinkling of an eye, cold and foreign.

Certainly organic sensations, their localization and recognition, composing as they do the bodily *me*, are a core of becoming. But it would be a serious mistake to think, as some writers do, that they alone account for our sense of what is "peculiarly ours."

Self-identity

Today I remember some of my thoughts of yesterday; and tomorrow I shall remember some of my thoughts of both yesterday and today; and I am subjectively certain that they are the thoughts of the same person. In this situation, no doubt, the organic continuity of the neuromuscular system is the leading factor. Yet the process involves more than reminiscence made possible by our retentive nerves. The young infant has retentive capacity during the first months of life but in all probability no sense of self-identity. This sense seems to grow gradually, partly as a result of being clothed and named, and otherwise marked off from the surrounding environment. Social interaction is an important factor. It is the actions of the other to which he differentially adjusts that force upon a child the realization that he is not the other, but a being in his own right. The difficulty of developing self-identity in childhood is shown by the ease with which a child depersonalizes himself in play and in speech.[2] Until the age of four or five we have good reason to believe that as perceived by the child personal identity is unstable. Beginning at about this age, however, it becomes the surest attest a human being has of his own existence.

Ego-enhancement

We come now to the most notorious property of the proprium, to its unabashed self-seeking.[3] Scores of writers have featured this clamorous trait in human personality. It is tied to the need for survival, for it is

[2] Cf. G. W. Allport, *Personality. A Psychological Interpretation* (New York: Henry Holt, 1937), pp. 159–65.

[3] The term *proprium* was a favorite of Emanuel Swedenborg. He used it, however, in the narrow sense of selfishness and pride, a meaning that corresponds here fairly closely to "ego-enhancement." See his *Proprium*, with an introduction by John Bigelow (New York: New Church Board of Publication, 1907). I am grateful to Professor Howard D. Spoerl for his clarification of this matter.

easy to see that we are endowed by nature with the impulses of self-assertion and with the emotions of self-satisfaction and pride. Our language is laden with evidence. The commonest compound of self is *selfish*, and of ego *egoism*. Pride, humiliation, self-esteem, narcissism are such prominent factors that when we speak of ego or self we often have in mind only this aspect of personality. And yet, self-love may be prominent in our natures without necessarily being sovereign. The proprium, as we shall see, has other facets and functions.

Ego-extension

The three facets we have discussed—coenesthesis, self-identity, ego-enhancement—are relatively early developments in personality, characterizing the whole of the child's proprium. Their solicitations have a heavily biological quality and seem to be contained within the organism itself. But soon the process of learning brings with it a high regard for possessions, for loved objects, and later, for ideal causes and loyalties. We are speaking here of whatever objects a person calls "mine." They must at the same time be objects of *importance*, for sometimes our sense of "having" has no affective tone and hence no place in the proprium. A child, however, who identifies with his parent is definitely extending his sense of self, as he does likewise through his love for pets, dolls, or other possessions, animate or inanimate.

As we grow older we identify with groups, neighborhood, and nation as well as with possessions, clothes, home. They become matters of importance to us in a sense that other people's families, nations, or possessions are not. Later in life the process of extension may go to great lengths, through the development of loyalties and of interests focused on abstractions and on moral and religious values. Indeed, a mark of maturity seems to be the range and extent of one's feeling of self-involvement in abstract ideals.

Rational agent

The ego, according to Freud, has the task of keeping the organism as a whole in touch with reality, of intermediating between unconscious impulses and the outer world. Often the rational ego can do little else than invent and employ defenses to forestall or diminish anxiety. These protective devices shape the development of personality to an extent unrealized sixty years ago. It is thanks to Freud that we understand the strategies of denial, repression, displacement, reaction formation, rationalization, and the like better than did our ancestors.

We have become so convinced of the validity of these defense mechanisms, and so impressed with their frequency of operation, that we are inclined to forget that the rational functioning of the proprium is capable also of yielding true solutions, appropriate adjustments, accurate planning, and a relatively faultless solving of the equations of life.

Many philosophers, dating as far back as Boethius in the sixth century, have seen the rational nature of personality as its most distinctive property. (*Persona est substantia individua rationalis naturae.*) It may seem odd to credit Freud, the supreme irrationalist of our age, with helping the Thomists preserve for psychology the emphasis upon the ego as the rational agent in personality, but such is the case. For whether the ego reasons or merely rationalizes, it has the property of synthesizing inner needs and outer reality. Freud and the Thomists have not let us forget this fact, and have thus made it easier for modern cognitive theories to deal with this central function of the proprium.

Self-image

A propriate function of special interest today is the self-image, or as some writers call it, the phenomenal self. Present-day therapy is chiefly devoted to leading the patient to examine, correct, or expand this self-image. The image has two aspects: the way the patient regards his present abilities, status, and roles; and what he would like to become, his *aspirations* for himself. The latter aspect, which Karen Horney calls the "idealized self-image,"[4] is of especial importance in therapy. On the one hand it may be compulsive, compensatory, and unrealistic, blinding its possessor to his true situation in life. On the other hand, it may be an insightful cognitive map, closely geared to reality and defining a wholesome ambition. The ideal self-image is the imaginative aspect of the proprium, and whether accurate or distorted, attainable or unattainable, it plots a course by which much propriate movement is guided and therapeutic progress achieved.

There are, of course, many forms of becoming that require no self-image, including automatic cultural learning and our whole repertoire of opportunistic adjustments to our environment. Yet there is also much growth that takes place only with the aid of, and because of, a

[4] Karen Horney, *Neurosis and Human Growth: The Struggle Toward Self-realization* (New York: Norton, 1950).

self-image. This image helps us bring our view of the present into line with our view of the future. Fortunately the dynamic importance of the self-image is more widely recognized in psychology today than formerly.

Propriate striving

We come now to the nature of motivation. Unfortunately we often fail to distinguish between propriate and peripheral motives. The reason is that at the rudimentary levels of becoming, which up to now have been the chief levels investigated, it *is* the impulses and drives, the immediate satisfaction and tension reduction, that are the determinants of conduct. Hence a psychology of opportunistic adjustment seems basic and adequate, especially to psychologists accustomed to working with animals. At low levels of behavior the familiar formula of drives and their conditioning appears to suffice. But as soon as the personality enters the stage of ego-extension, and develops a self-image with visions of self-perfection, we are, I think, forced to postulate motives of a different order, motives that reflect propriate striving. Within experimental psychology itself there is now plenty of evidence that conduct that is "ego involved" (propriate) differs markedly from behavior that is not.[5]

Many psychologists disregard this evidence. They wish to maintain a single theory of motivation consistent with their presuppositions. Their preferred formula is in terms of drive and conditioned drive. Drive is viewed as a peripherally instigated activity. The resultant response is simply reactive, persisting only until the instigator is removed and the tension, created by the drive, lessened. Seeking always a parsimony of assumptions, this view therefore holds that motivation entails one and only one inherent property of the organism: a disposition to act, by instinct or by learning, in such a way that the organism will as efficiently as possible reduce the discomfort of tension. Motivation is regarded as a state of tenseness that leads us to seek equilibrium, rest, adjustment, satisfaction, or homeostasis. From this point of view personality is nothing more than our habitual modes of reducing tension. This formulation, of course, is wholly consistent with empiricism's initial presupposition that man is by nature a passive being, capable only of receiving impressions from, and responding to, external goads.

The contrary view holds that this formula, while applicable to segmental and opportunistic adjustments, falls short of representing the

[5] Cf. G. W. Allport, "The Ego in Contemporary Psychology," *Psychological Review*, 50 (1943), 451–78.

nature of propriate striving. It points out that the characteristic feature of such striving is its resistance to equilibrium: tension is maintained rather than reduced.

In his autobiography Raold Amundsen tells how from the age of fifteen he had one dominant passion—to become a polar explorer. The obstacles seemed insurmountable, and all through his life the temptations to reduce the tensions engendered were great. But the propriate striving persisted. While he welcomed each success, it acted to raise his level of aspiration, to maintain an over-all commitment. Having sailed the Northwest Passage, he embarked upon the painful project that led to the discovery of the South Pole. Having discovered the South Pole, he planned for years, against extreme discouragement, to fly over the North Pole, a task he finally accomplished. But his commitment never wavered until at the end he lost his life in attempting to rescue a less gifted explorer, Nobile, from death in the Arctic. Not only did he maintain one style of life, without ceasing, but this central commitment enabled him to withstand the temptation to reduce the segmental tensions continually engendered by fatigue, hunger, ridicule, and danger.[6]

Here we see the issue squarely. A psychology that regards motivation exclusively in terms of drives and conditioned drives is likely to stammer and grow vague when confronted by those aspects of personality—of every personality—that resemble Amundsen's propriate striving. While most of us are less distinguished than he in our achievements, we too have insatiable interests. Only in a very superficial way can these interests be dealt with in terms of tension reduction. Many writers past and present have recognized this fact and have postulated some principles of an exactly opposite order. One thinks in this connection of Spinoza's concept of conatus, or the tendency of an individual to persist, against obstacles, in his own style of being. One thinks of Goldstein's doctrine of self-actualization, used also by Maslow and others, or McDougall's self-regarding sentiment. And one thinks too of those modern Freudians who feel the need for endowing the ego not only with a rational and rationalizing ability but with a tendency to maintain its own system of productive interests, in spite of the passing solicitations of impulse and environmental instigation. Indeed the fortified ego, as described by neo-Freudians, is able to act contrary to the usual course of opportunistic, tension-reducing, adaptation.

Propriate striving distinguishes itself from other forms of motivation in that, however beset by conflicts, it makes for unification of personality. There is evidence that the lives of mental patients are marked by the proliferation of unrelated subsystems, and by the loss of

[6] Raold Amundsen, *My Life as an Explorer* (Garden City, N.Y.: Doubleday, Doran, 1928).

more homogeneous systems of motivation.[7] When the individual is dominated by segmental drives, by compulsions, or by the winds of circumstance, he has lost the integrity that comes only from maintaining major directions of striving. The possession of long-range goals, regarded as central to one's personal existence, distinguishes the human being from the animal, the adult from the child, and in many cases the healthy personality from the sick.

Striving, it is apparent, always has a future reference. As a matter of fact, a great many states of mind are adequately described only in terms of their futurity. Along with *striving*, we may mention *interest*, *tendency*, *disposition*, *expectation*, *planning*, *problem solving*, and *intention*. While not all future-directedness is phenomenally propriate, it all requires a type of psychology that transcends the prevalent tendency to explain mental states exclusively in terms of past occurrences. People, it seems, are busy leading their lives into the future, whereas psychology, for the most part, is busy tracing them into the past.

The knower

Now that we have isolated these various propriate functions—all of which we regard as peculiarly ours—the question arises whether we are yet at an end. Do we not have in addition a cognizing self—a knower, that transcends all other functions of the proprium and holds them in view? In a famous passage, William James wrestles with this question, and concludes that we have not. There is, he thinks, no such thing as a substantive self distinguishable from the sum total, or stream, of experiences. Each moment of consciousness, he says, appropriates each previous moment, and the knower is thus somehow embedded in what is known. "The thoughts themselves are the thinker."[8]

Opponents of James argue that no mere series of experiences can possibly turn themselves into an awareness of that series as a unit. Nor can "passing thoughts" possibly regard themselves as important or interesting. To whom is the series important or interesting if not to *me*? I am the ultimate monitor. The self as *knower* emerges as a final and inescapable postulate.

It is interesting to ask why James balked at admitting a knowing self after he had so lavishly admitted to psychology with his full approval material, social, and spiritual selves. The reason may well

[7] Cf. L. McQuitty, "A Measure of Personality Integration in Relation to the Concept of the Self," *Journal of Personality*, 18 (1950), 461–82.

[8] [William James, *Principles of Psychology* (New York: Henry Holt, 1890), I, Chapter 10.]

have been (and the reason would be valid today) that one who laboriously strives to depict the nature of propriate functions on an empirical level, hoping thereby to enrich the science of psychology with a discriminating analysis of self, is not anxious to risk a return to the homunculus theory by introducing a synthesizer, or a self of selves.

To be sure, the danger that abuse might follow the admission of a substantive knower into the science of psychology is no reason to avoid this step if it is logically required. Some philosophers, including Kant, insist that the pure or transcendental ego is separable from the empirical ego (i.e., from any of the propriate states thus far mentioned).[9] Those who hold that the knowing itself is not (as James argued) merely an aspect of the self as known, but is "pure" and "transcendental," argue, as Kant does, that the texture of knowledge is quite different in the two cases. Our cognition of our knowing self is always indirect, of the order of a presupposition. On the other hand, all features of the *empirical self* are known directly, through acquaintance, as any object is known which falls into time and space categories.[10]

While their metaphysical positions are directly opposed, both Kant and James agree with their illustrious predecessor, Descartes, that the knowing function is a vital attribute of the self however defined. For our present purpose this is the point to bear in mind.

We not only know *things*, but we know (i.e., are acquainted with) the empirical features of our own proprium. It is I who have bodily sensations, I who recognize my self-identity from day to day; I who note and reflect upon my self-assertion, self-extension, my own rationalizations, as well as upon my interests and strivings. When I thus think about my own propriate functions I am likely to perceive their essential togetherness, and feel them intimately bound in some way to the knowing function itself.

Since such knowing is, beyond any shadow of doubt, a state that is peculiarly ours, we admit it as the eighth clear function of the proprium. (In other words, as an eighth valid meaning of "self" or "ego.") But it is surely one of nature's perversities that so central a function should be so little understood by science, and should remain a perpetual bone of contention among philosophers. Many, like Kant, set this function (the "pure ego") aside as something qualitatively apart from

[9] Kant's position on this matter is summarized in the following pronouncement: "One may therefore say of the thinking I (the soul), which represents itself as substance, simple, numerically identical in all time, and as the correlative of all existence, from which in fact all other existence must be concluded, that it *does not know itself through the categories*, but knows the *categories* only, and through them all objects, in the absolute unity of apperception, *that is through itself.*" *Critique of Pure Reason*, trans. M. Müller (London: Macmillan, 1881), p. 347.

[10] For a fuller discussion of this matter see F. R. Tennant, *Philosophical Theology* (Cambridge: University Press, 1928), 1, Chapter 5.

other propriate functions (the latter being assigned to the "empirical me"). Others, like James, say that the ego *qua* knower is somehow contained within the ego *qua* known. Still others, personalistically inclined, find it necessary to postulate a single self as knower, thinker, feeler, and doer—all in one blended unit of a sort that guarantees the continuance of all becoming.[11]

We return now to our unanswered question: Is the concept of self necessary in the psychology of personality? Our answer cannot be categorical since all depends upon the particular usage of "self" that is proposed. Certainly all legitimate phenomena that have been, and can be ascribed, to the self or ego must be admitted as data indispensable to a psychology of personal becoming. All eight functions of the "proprium" (our temporary neutral term for central interlocking operations of personality) must be admitted and included. In particular the unifying act of perceiving and knowing (of comprehending propriate states as belonging together and belonging to me) must be fully admitted.

At the same time, the danger we have several times warned against is very real: that a homunculus may creep into our discussions of personality, and be expected to solve all our problems without in reality solving any. Thus, if we ask "What determines our moral conduct?" the answer may be "The self does it." Or, if we pose the problem of choice, we say "The self chooses." Such question-begging would immeasurably weaken the scientific study of personality by providing an illegitimate regressus. There are, to be sure, ultimate problems of philosophy and of theology that psychology cannot even attempt to solve, and for the solution of such problems "self" in some restricted and technical meaning may be a necessity.

But so far as psychology is concerned our position, in brief, is this: all psychological functions commonly ascribed to a self or ego must be admitted as data in the scientific study of personality. These functions are not, however, coextensive with personality as a whole. They are rather the special aspects of personality that have to do with warmth, with unity, with a sense of personal importance. In this exposition I have called them "propriate" functions. If the reader prefers, he may call them self-functions, and in this sense self may be said to be a necessary psychological concept. What is unnecessary and inadmissible is a self (or soul) that is said to perform acts, to solve problems, to steer conduct, in a trans-psychological manner, inaccessible to psychological analysis.

[11] P. A. Bertocci, "The Psychological Self, the Ego, and Personality," *Psychological Review*, 52 (1954), 91–99.

Once again we refer to Adler's contention that an adequate psychology of life-style would in effect dispense with the need for a separate psychology of the ego. I believe Adler's position, though unelaborated, is essentially the same as the one here advocated. An adequate psychology would in effect *be* a psychology of the ego. It would deal fully and fairly with propriate functions. Indeed, everyone would assume that psychology was talking about self-functions, unless it was expressly stated that peripheral, opportunistic, or actuarial events were under discussion. But as matters stand today, with so much of psychology preoccupied (as was Hume) with bits and pieces of experience, or else with generalized mathematical equations, it becomes necessary for the few psychologists who are concerned with propriate functions to specify in their discourse that they are dealing with them. If the horizons of psychology were more spacious than they are, I venture to suggest that theories of personality would not need the concept of self or of ego except in certain compound forms, such as *self-knowledge, self-image, ego-enhancement, ego-extension.*

READING III–5. *Assumptions, Perceptions, and the Self*

HADLEY CANTRIL

[All of Hadley Cantril's book *The "Why" of Man's Experience* is highly relevant to the main themes of this volume. Here we have only excerpted certain paragraphs that highlight our concern in Part III with the interactions among what a person assumes, what he perceives, and how he conceives of himself. We have not included most of the illustrative material with which Cantril elaborates and makes concrete these ideas.]

Excerpted from Hadley Cantril, *The "Why" of Man's Experience* (New York: Macmillan, 1950). Copyright 1950 by The Macmillan Company.

Creating a meaningful environment

All of life's activities are carried on in an "environment" which includes objects of nature, artifacts man has produced, other human beings, and their institutions and ideologies. Man's only contact with the environment in which he is born is through his senses. The impressions given man by his senses are meaningless until they become functionally related to his purposes. These sense impressions are like cryptograms or the writings in some queer cypher or code which are completely incomprehensible until we learn some clues. It is out of what Einstein has called the "rabble of the senses" that man must create for himself some sort of world in which he can act effectively, a world which will take on a degree of order or system or meaning. For this is the only kind of world in which man can act effectively.

While psychologists, beginning especially with Helmholtz, have had a great deal to say so far about the role of past experience in determining what we are aware of and how we act, no account so far seems to stress sufficiently the way in which past experience determines the significance which things in the environment "out there" assume for us as we go about the business of living. The significance anything in our environment has for us originates in some personal experience. Every perception we have is conceived and given birth in some purposeful activity. The meaning we relate to any sense impression is derived only *through* our past experience as we have tried to carry out our purposes. The whole psychology of learning and conditioning might usefully be oriented to study the learning process as an instrument man uses in acquiring his sense of what is significant for his purposive behavior. After reviewing a wide range of experimental evidence, Hebb has recently concluded that the "apparent simplicity" of a perception "is only the end result of a long learning process."

* * *

The processes man uses in building up his assumptions have a striking similarity to the process involved in scientific inquiry. In many ways the method of scientific inquiry appears to be an unconscious imitation of those age-old processes man has used in his common-sense solutions of problems. In common-sense judgments, the assumptions and awarenesses upon which man depends for effective action are the hypotheses he has established after many experiences: the weighted averages he unconsciously uses to increase the likelihood that a certain action will be effective. Since we can only exercise "common sense" in those areas of life where we have had experience, we must go to someone who has had experience or to science to get reliable assumptions and to increase the effectiveness of our action in areas where we have had no experience ourselves. Thus the average man or woman who drives an automobile or listens to the radio does not have sufficiently adequate assumptions concerning the mechanical interactions involved in these two complicated mechanisms in order to know what to do when something goes wrong with them. If he is unable to find someone else to repair the mechanism, then he must himself learn from scientific literature something about the assumptions of science on the basis of which automobile engines or radios are constructed.

There are, however, certain important differences between the process we label "common sense" and the steps involved in pursuing scientific inquiry. One important difference is that in common sense we usually are quite unaware of the assumptions on which our decisions are based, whereas in the world of science we make every effort to become intellectually aware of the assumptions on which we are operating. Another important difference between common sense and scientific inquiry is the fact that in using scientific inquiry, man is the operator who decides upon what he is going to operate and how, whereas in everyday life situations where common sense is involved, man is not only the operator but is also being operated upon and must carry out his activities in the midst of the situation itself. In everyday life situations we try to overcome the obstacles we meet with various guesses that will make for effective action: we test these guesses in a more or less insightful, more or less conscious way. In scientific inquiry, on the other hand, we test guesses by highly controlled experiments and deliberately attempt to intellectualize all the processes involved.

*   *   *

Most people tend to think and act as though the characteristics they see in things and people are characteristics of those things or people *irrespective of* the function served in carrying out their purposes. People forget that a baseball or a cigarette or a house is seen by them as being of a certain constant "size" because they have built up through past experience with such objects certain assumptions that they are the size they are. The constancy of the size of objects, the fact that we do not see a man changing his size as he approaches us on the sidewalk, is due to an assumption we have built up in our past experience with other men.

*   *   *

Social perception

The significances we learn to attach to various aspects of our social environment are built up through experience in exactly the same way and for the same reason as the significances we learn to attach to aspects of our physical environment. The only distinction to make—and it is an important distinction—is that in social situations we are dealing with people who, like ourselves, have purposes of their own which we must take into account if our action is to be effective. We learn through experience that the purposes of other people can affect us and that through our own actions, we can affect their purposes. Our social awarenesses have in them, then, a new factor not generally involved in our awareness of inanimate objects.

The result is that our awareness of another individual, another group, another nation, is an awareness of the bearing the purposes of that other individual, group, or nation, may have on our own purposes. We may see another person as a rival for the affection of someone we love; we may see him as someone who can help us get a better job or as one whose friendship we should "cultivate" because we feel his companionship would enrich our experience.

*   *   *

The assumptive form world

The net result of our purposive actions is that we create for ourselves a set of assumptions which serve as guides and bases for future actions. These assumptions are standards which we have "taken up, or into" ourselves as the dictionary definition of "assume" implies. From this point of view, action is the process involved in building up assumptions or in checking those we have. On each specific occasion of life we draw upon certain patterns of the total set of assumptions we have stored up.

The only world we know is created in terms of and by means of our assumptions. It is the world which provides what constancy there is in our environment; the world which gives our experience its consistency. And it *is* a world of assumptions—a world which we could not have at all except for our past experience in acting for the purpose of enhancing the quality of life.

This assumptive form world of ours is composed of many different assumptions. As described already, we build up the assumption that similar things are identical; that certain aspects of the environment belong together and constitute "wholes"; that certain "things" or "objects" have certain constant significances, certain constant characteristics such as color or size. We build up certain assumptions concerning people and groups of people, institutions and ideologies: we assume that most men are honest or dishonest, that a certain political party is best or that members of a certain "race" or nation have certain characteristic traits. Such assumptions as these are generally subconscious. We become aware of them only if we try to account for illusions or paradoxes we may encounter or mistakes we may make because the assumptions do not prove as reliable as they have in the past.

*   *   *

Similarities and differences in assumptive worlds

. . . It has been stressed here repeatedly that every occasion of life is unique; that situations never repeat themselves identically. In each occasion of life a different pattern of assumptions is involved in the weighing and integrating process called forth. Any action, therefore, is always unique and specific to a particular individual at a particular time and in a particular place.

Yet many of the assumptions men everywhere use are so common that they may be termed almost universal. They are common and universal because they are necessary assumptions all people must use in the process of survival and adjustment. People everywhere seem to act on the basis of assumptions that similar things are identical; that there is a relative constancy of size for each "object" in their environment; that certain "objects" are relatively permanent and so on. These assumptions are independent of any specific reference in space or time. Like maps that describe a particular geographical area, they are standards we can use when and where we want to and that do not depend in any way for their reliability on when and where we look at them.

But by no means are all of our assumptions common and universal. The similarity of our assumptive worlds depends upon the similarity of our experience. The extent to which we see and share the same world depends upon the extent to which we have acquired similar assumptions in carrying out our purposes. People are united in any group because of their common background of experience which has proved effective for carrying out their purpose. It is stupendously important in this day and age of technological advance to understand why we are not all living in one and the same world and how we can achieve greater overlapping of the various assumptive worlds that individuals and groups of individuals create.

Summary

A person can participate in the process of living only through some kind of action. Only through action can he maintain and carry out his purposes. Only through action can he build up reliable suppositions for future action and test those he already has. Our awareness of how reliable our assumptions are for meeting new contingencies as they arise gives us our sense of sureness or unsureness. A most important consequence of any action is its resulting effect upon us.

Our assumptive form world consists of the total set of assumptions which we build up on the basis of past experience in carrying out our purposes. Many of the assumptions which compose it are entirely subconscious; others are intellectual abstractions; others concern the value attributes of experiences. Those expectancies that serve as bases for future action are an important aspect of our assumptive form world.

The assumptive form world is the only world we know and it differs for each one of us. Similarities between the assumptive form worlds of different people depend upon the similarities of past experiences in carrying out common purposes.

* * *

Your awareness of what is "you," like all the awarenesses of your assumptive world, is built up only through experience: experience in overcoming obstacles and in meeting hitches that must be resolved if you are to have any sense of satisfaction. The effects of action are effects on you, and experience is always personal. What "you" are depends in large part upon the identifications and loyalties you acquire and through which you can experience emerging value attributes.

The extent to which your assumptive world is similar to that of other people depends on the similarity of the identifications, the loyalties, the expectancies, and purposes which have become a part of you. You and others are "we" in so far as you and others have common assumptions and purposes and in so far as you and others share in the pursuit of the resolution of difficulties which are both individual and common. Only under such circumstances are individual assumptive form worlds modified in common ways both with respect to their relevance and reliability for action and their creation of enhanced value.

READING III–6. *A Theory of Personality and Behavior*

CARL R. ROGERS

[In the last chapter of *Client-Centered Therapy*, Carl Rogers presented in considerable detail his progress (as of 1951) toward the development of a general theory of personality consistent with his experience as a psychotherapist and with certain research findings. Since Rogers' formulation of the process of therapy will be the basic conceptual material of Part IV of this book, this whole chapter is recommended as outside reading, although parts of it are quite technical, admittedly tentative, and have been somewhat modified in Rogers' own later writings. The more important concepts of the theory are summarized in a "schematic presentation," which we reproduce. Before presenting this final selection of the chapter, some excerpts from the material which precedes it may be helpful. The theory itself consists of nineteen carefully worded propositions, the meaning and significance of each of which is explained and illustrated in considerable detail. We reproduce here the most relevant, for our purposes, of these propositions, along with brief excerpts from Rogers' discussion of them.]

I.   *Every individual exists in a continually changing world of experience of which he is the center.*

This private world may be called the phenomenal field, the experiential field, or described in other terms. It includes all that is experienced by the organism, whether or not these experiences are consciously perceived. . . . only a portion of that [our] experience . . . is *consciously* experienced. Many of our sensory and visceral sensations are not symbolized. . . . however, . . . a large portion of this world of experience is *available* to consciousness, and may become conscious if the need of the individual causes certain sensations to come into focus because they are associated with the satisfaction of a need [p. 483]. [Examples: only when I think about it am I aware of the pressure of my chair seat against my buttocks; only when told my face is flushed may I realize that I feel angry or embarrassed.]

II.   *The organism reacts to the field as it is experienced and perceived. This perceptual field is, for the individual, "reality"* [p. 484].

Excerpted, with permission, from Carl R. Rogers, *Client-Centered Therapy* (Boston: Houghton Mifflin, 1951), Chapter 11, 481–533.

. . . Snygg and Combs give the example of two men driving at night on a western road. . . . One of the men sees a large boulder, and reacts with fright. The other, a native of the country, sees a tumbleweed and reacts with nonchalance. Each reacts to the reality as perceived. . . . We live by a perceptual "map" which is never reality itself [p. 485]. . . . when the perception changes, the reaction of the individual changes. As long as a parent is perceived as a domineering individual, that is the reality to which the individual reacts. When he is perceived as a rather pathetic individual trying to maintain his status, then the reaction to this new "reality" is quite different [p. 486].

III. *The organism reacts as an organized whole to this phenomenal field* [p. 486].
. . . the organism is at all times a total organized system, in which alteration of any part may produce changes in any other part [p. 487].

IV. *The organism has one basic tendency and striving—to actualize, maintain, and enhance the experiencing organism* [p. 487].
. . . The organism actualizes itself in the direction of greater differentiation of organs and of function, . . . limited expansion through growth, . . . greater independence or self-responsibility. . . . increasing . . . autonomy, and . . . socialization, broadly defined [p. 488].
It would be grossly inaccurate to suppose that the organism operates smoothly in the direction of self-enhancement and growth. It would be perhaps more correct to say that the organism moves through struggle and pain toward enhancement and growth. . . . [But] given the opportunity for clear-cut choice between forward-moving and regressive behavior, the tendency will operate [pp. 490–91].

VII. *The best vantage point for understanding behavior is from the internal frame of reference of the individual himself* [p. 494].
[Rogers' comments on this proposition include some sound advice on both the advantages and the difficulties of this way of understanding a person's behavior; they are worth quoting at some length.]
If we could emphatically experience all the sensory and visceral sensations of the individual, could experience his whole phenomenal field including both the conscious elements and also those experiences not brought to the conscious level, we should have the perfect basis for understanding the meaningfulness of his behavior and for predicting his future behavior. This is an unattainable ideal. Because it is unattainable, one line of development in psychology has been to understand and evaluate and predict the person's behavior from an external frame of reference. This development has not been too satisfactory, largely because such a high degree of inference is involved. The inter-

pretation of the meaning of a given bit of behavior comes to depend upon whether the inferences are being made, say, by a student of Clark Hull or a follower of Freud. For this and other reasons, the possibility of utilizing the phenomenal field of the individual as a significant basis for the science of psychology appears promising. . . .

[However,] there are many drawbacks. For one thing, we are largely limited to gaining an acquaintance with the phenomenal field as it is experienced in consciousness. . . . Furthermore our knowledge of the person's frame of reference depends primarily upon communication of one sort or another from the individual. Communication is at all times faulty and imperfect. Hence only in clouded fashion can we see the world of experience as it appears to this individual.

We may state the whole situation logically thus:

It is possible to achieve, to some extent, the other person's frame of reference, because many of the perceptual objects—self, parents, teachers, employers, and so on—have counterparts in our own perceptual field, and practically all the attitudes toward these perceptual objects—such as fear, anger, annoyance, love, jealousy, satisfaction—have been present in our own world of experience.

Hence we can infer, quite directly, from the communication of the individual, or less accurately from the observation of his behavior, a portion of his perceptual and experiential field.

The more all his experiences are available to his consciousness, the more it is possible for him to convey a total picture of his phenomenal field.

The more his communication is a free expression, unmodified by a need or desire to be defensive, the more adequate will be the communication of the field [pp. 494–96].

VIII.   *A portion of the total perceptual field gradually becomes differentiated as the self.*
. . . gradually, as the infant develops, a portion of the total private world becomes recognized as "me," "I," "myself" . . .
. . . the development of a conscious self is . . . not necessarily coexistent with the physical organism. . . . Those elements which we control are regarded as a part of the self, but when even such an object as a part of our body is out of control, it is experienced as being less a part of the self [p. 497].

IX.   *As a result of interaction with the environment, and particularly as a result of evaluational interaction with others, the structure of self is formed—*

an organized, fluid, but consistent conceptual pattern of perceptions of charac-
teristics and relationships of the "I" or the "me," together with values attached
to these concepts [p. 498].

X. *The values attached to experiences, and the values which are a part of*
the self-structure, in some instances are values experienced directly by the organism,
and in some instances are values introjected or taken over from others, but per-
ceived in distorted fashion, as if they had been experienced directly [p. 498].
. . . As the infant interacts with his environment he gradually
builds up concepts about himself, about the environment, and about
himself in relation to the environment. . . . Intimately associated with
all these experiences is a direct organismic valuing which appears
highly important for understanding later development. The very young
infant . . . appears to value those experiences which he perceives as
enhancing himself, and to place a negative value on those experiences
which seem to threaten himself or which do not maintain or enhance
himself [p. 498–99].
There soon enters into this picture the evaluation of self by others.
"You're a good child," "You're a naughty boy"—these and similar
evaluations of himself and of his behavior by his parents and others
come to form a large and significant part of the infant's perceptual
field [p. 499]. . . . [Certain negative parental evaluations of behavior
that was experienced as pleasurable can then constitute] a deep threat
to the nascent structure of self. The child's dilemma might be schematized in these terms: "If I admit to awareness the satisfactions of these
behaviors and the values I apprehend in these experiences, then this is
inconsistent with my self as being loved or lovable."
Certain results then follow in the development of the ordinary
child. One result is a denial in awareness of the satisfactions that were
experienced. The other is to distort the symbolization of the experience
of the parents. The accurate symbolization would be: "I perceive my
parents as experiencing this behavior as unsatisfying to them." The
distorted symbolization, distorted to preserve the threatened concept
of self is: "I perceive this behavior as unsatisfying" [p. 500].
Out of these dual sources—the direct experiencing by the individual, and the distorted symbolization of sensory reactions resulting in
the introjection of values and concepts *as if* experienced—there grows
the structure of the self. Drawing upon the evidence and upon clinical
experience, it would appear that the most useful definition of the self-
concept, or self-structure, would be along these lines. The self-structure
is an organized configuration of perceptions of the self which are admis-
sible to awareness. It is composed of such elements as the perceptions
of one's characteristics and abilities; the percepts and concepts of the
self in relation to others and to the environment; the value qualities
which are perceived as associated with experiences and objects; and

the goals and ideals which are perceived as having positive or negative valence. It is, then, the organized picture, existing in awareness either as figure or ground, of the self and the self-in-relationship, together with the positive or negative values which are associated with those qualities and relationships, as they are perceived as existing in the past, present, or future [p. 501].

XI. *As experiences occur in the life of the individual, they are either (a) symbolized, perceived, and organized into some relationship to the self, (b) ignored because there is no perceived relationship to the self-structure, (c) denied symbolization or given a distorted symbolization because the experience is inconsistent with the structure of the self* [p. 503].

It is the third group of sensory and visceral experiences, those which seem to be prevented from entering awareness, which demand our closest attention, for it is in this realm that there lie many phenomena of human behavior which psychologists have endeavored to explain. In some instances the denial of the perception is something rather conscious. . . . [In other instances] it would appear that there is the organic experience, but there is no symbolization of this experience, or only a distorted symbolization, because an adequate conscious representation of it would be entirely inconsistent with the concept of self. . . . [For example,] the adolescent who has been brought up in an oversolicitous home, and whose concept of self is that of one who is grateful to his parents, may feel intense anger at the subtle control which is being exerted over him. Organically he experiences the physiological changes which accompany anger, but his conscious self can prevent these experiences from being symbolized and hence consciously perceived. Or he can symbolize them in some distorted fashion which is consistent with his structure of self, such as perceiving these organic sensations as "a bad headache" [pp. 504–5].

It should be noted that perceptions are excluded because they are contradictory, not because they are derogatory. It seems nearly as difficult to accept a perception which would alter the self-concept in an expanding or socially acceptable direction as to accept an experience which would alter it in a constricting or socially disapproved direction [p. 506].

XII. *Most of the ways of behaving which are adopted by the organism are those which are consistent with the concept of self* [p. 507].

XIII. *Behavior may, in some instances, be brought about by organic experiences and needs which have not been symbolized. Such behavior may be inconsistent with the structure of the self, but in such instances the behavior is not "owned" by the individual* [p. 509].

XIV. *Psychological maladjustment exists when the organism denies to awareness significant sensory and visceral experiences, which consequently are not symbolized and organized into the gestalt of the self-structure. When this situation exists, there is a basic or potential psychological tension* [p. 510].

To illustrate briefly the nature of maladjustment, take the familiar picture of a mother whom the diagnostician would term rejecting. She has as part of her concept of self a whole constellation which may be summed up by saying, "I am a good and loving mother." This conceptualization of herself is, as indicated in Proposition X, based in part upon accurate symbolization of her experience and in part upon distorted symbolization in which the values held by others are introjected as if they were her own experiences. With this concept of self she can accept and assimilate those organic sensations of affection which she feels toward her child. But the organic experience of dislike, distaste, or hatred toward her child is something which is denied to her conscious self. The experience exists, but it is not permitted accurate symbolization. The organic need is for aggressive acts which would fulfill these attitudes and satisfy the tension which exists. The organism strives for the achievement of this satisfaction, but it can do so for the most part only through those channels which are consistent with the self-concept of a good mother. Since the good mother could be aggressive toward her child only if he merited punishment, she perceives much of his behavior as being bad, deserving punishment, and therefore the aggressive acts can be carried through, without being contrary to the values organized in her picture of self. If under great stress, she at some time should shout at her child, "I hate you," she would be quick to explain that "I was not myself," that this behavior occurred but was out of her control. "I don't know what made me say that, because of course I don't mean it." This is a good illustration of most maladjustment in which the organism is striving for certain satisfactions in the field as organically experienced, whereas the concept of self is more constricted and cannot permit in awareness many of the actual experiences [pp. 511–12].

XV. *Psychological adjustment exists when the concept of the self is such that all the sensory and visceral experiences of the organism are, or may be, assimilated on a symbolic level into a consistent relationship with the concept of self* [p. 513].

. . . [For example] the mother who "rejects" her child can lose the inner tensions connected with her relationship to her child if she has a concept of self which permits her to accept her feelings of dislike for the child, as well as her feelings of affection and liking. . . . The cost of maintaining an alertness of defense to prevent various experiences from being symbolized in consciousness is obviously great.

. . . When the self-structure is able to accept and take account in consciousness of the organic experiences, when the organizational system is expansive enough to contain them, then clear integration and a sense of direction are achieved, and the individual feels that his strength can be and is directed toward the clear purpose of actualization and enhancement of a unified organism [pp. 513–14].

XVI. *Any experience which is inconsistent with the organization or structure of self may be perceived as a threat, and the more of these perceptions there are, the more rigidly the self-structure is organized to maintain itself* [p. 515].

This proposition is an attempt to formulate a description of certain clinical facts. If the rejecting mother previously mentioned is told that several observers have come to the conclusion that she does reject her child, the inevitable result is that she will, for the moment, exclude any assimilation of this experience. She may attack the conditions of observation, the training or authority of the observers, the degree of understanding they possess, and so forth and so on. She will organize the defenses of her own concept of herself as a loving and good mother, and will be able to substantiate this concept with a mass of evidence. She will obviously perceive the judgment of the observers as a threat, and will organize in defense of her own governing concept. The same phenomenon would be observed if the girl who regards herself as utterly lacking in ability received a high score on an intelligence test. She can and will defend her self against this threat of inconsistency. If the self cannot defend itself against deep threats, the result is a catastrophic psychological breakdown and disintegration [pp. 515–16].

XVII. *Under certain conditions, involving primarily complete absence of any threat to the self-structure, experiences which are inconsistent with it may be perceived, and examined, and the structure of self revised to assimilate and include such experiences* [p. 517].

Here an important clinical fact, attested by many therapeutic cases, is difficult to state in accurately generalized form. It is clear that self-concepts change, both in the ordinary development of the individual, and in therapy. The previous proposition formulates the facts about the defenses of the self, while this one endeavors to state the way in which change may come about.

To proceed from the more clear-cut examples to those less clear: In therapy of a client-centered form, by means of the relationship and the counselor's handling of it, the client is gradually assured that he is accepted as he is, and that each new facet of himself which is revealed is also accepted. It is then that experiences which have been denied can be symbolized, often very gradually, and hence brought clearly into conscious form. Once they are conscious, the concept of self is expanded so that they may be included as a part of a consistent total. Thus the rejecting mother, in such an atmosphere, is apt first to admit the perception of her behavior—"I suppose that at times it must seem to him that I don't like him"—and then the possibility of an experience inconsistent with self—"I suppose that at times I *don't* like him"—and gradually the formulation of a broadened concept of self: "I can admit that I like him and I don't like him and we can still get along satisfactorily." Or a woman who hates her mother and justifies the pattern of self which includes such hate, comes first to recognize that there has been other than hating behavior—"I keep cleaning up my house when she comes over, as if to show her how good I am, as if to try to win her favor"—then admits experiences directly contradictory to her concept of self—"I feel a real warmth toward her, a wholesome kind of affection"—and gradually, on the basis of trying to live by a revised concept of her self in this relationship, comes to broaden that concept to a point where tension is reduced—"I get along all right with her. It's the most wonderful thing the way I have gotten mother out of my system. I can take her or leave her without so much tension" [pp. 517–18].

XVIII.   *When the individual perceives and accepts into one consistent and integrated system all his sensory and visceral experiences, then he is necessarily more understanding of others and is more accepting of others as separate individuals* [p. 520].

While this may sound abstruse, it is corroborated by much everyday evidence, as well as by clinical experience. Who are the individuals, in any neighborhood, or in any group, that inspire confidential relationships, seem able to be understanding of others? They tend to be individuals with a high degree of acceptance of all aspects of self. In clinical experience, how do better interpersonal relationships emerge? It is on this same basis. The rejecting mother who accepts her own negative attitudes toward her child finds that this acceptance, which at first she has feared, makes her more relaxed with her child. She is able to observe him for what he is, not simply through a screen of defensive reactions. Doing so, she perceives that he is an interesting person, with bad features, but also good ones, toward whom she feels at times hostile, but toward whom she also feels at times affectionate. On this comfortable and realistic and spontaneous basis a *real* relationship develops out of her real experiencing, a satisfying relationship to both. It may not be composed entirely of sweetness and light, but it is far more comfortable than any artificial relationship could possibly be. It is based primarily upon an acceptance of the fact that her child is a separate person.

The woman who hated her mother comes, after she has accepted all her feelings of affection as well as hate, to see her mother as a person with a variety of characteristics: interesting, good, vulgar, and bad. With this much more accurate perception she understands her mother, accepts her for what she is, and builds a real rather than a defensive relationship with her [pp. 521–22].

XIX.   *As the indivudal perceives and accepts into his self-structure more of his organic experiences, he finds that he is replacing his present value system— based so largely upon introjections which have been distortedly symbolized—with a continuing organismic valuing* process [p. 522].

In therapy, as the person explores his phenomenal field, he comes to examine the values which he has introjected and which he has used as if they were based upon his own experience. (See Proposition X.) He is dissatisfied with them, often expressing the attitude that he has just been doing what others thought he should do. But what does *he* think he should do? There he is puzzled and lost. If one gives up the guidance of an introjected system of values, what is to take its place? He often feels quite incompetent to discover or build any alternative system. If he cannot longer accept the "ought" and "should," the "right" and "wrong" of the introjected system, how can he know what values take their place?

Gradually he comes to experience the fact that he is making value judgments, in a way that is new to him, and yet a way that was also known to him in his infancy. Just as the infant places an assured value upon an experience, relying on the evidence of his own senses, as described in Proposition X, so too the client finds that it is his own organism which supplies the evidence upon which value judgments may be made. He discovers that his own senses, his own physiological equipment, can provide the data for making value judgments and for continuously revising them. No one needs to tell him that it is good to act in a freer and more spontaneous fashion, rather than in the rigid way to which he has been accustomed. He senses, he feels that it is satisfying and enhancing. Or when he acts in a defensive fashion, it is his own organism that feels the immediate and short-term satisfaction of being protected and that also senses the longer-range dissatisfaction of having to remain on guard. He makes a choice between two courses of action, fearfully and hesitantly, not knowing whether he has weighed their values accurately. But then he discovers that he may let the evidence of his own experience indicate whether he has chosen satisfyingly. He discovers that he does not need to *know* what are the correct values; through the data supplied by his own organism, he can experience what is satisfying and enhancing. He can put his confidence in a valuing *process*, rather than in some rigid, introjected *system* of values [pp. 522–23].

A schematic presentation

Some of the preceding propositions, particularly from IX through XIX, may be clarified by a schematic presentation of certain of the ways in which the self functions in relation to personality. Any diagrammatic representation of complex material tends to oversimplify and to seem more complete than it actually is. The material which follows should therefore be accepted with critical caution and with an awareness of its limitations.

The accompanying diagram can be understood only by referring to the definitions of each element.

DEFINITIONS

The Total Personality. The diagram as a whole (Figures 1 and 2) is intended to focus upon the structure of personality. As drawn in Figure 1, it indicates a personality in a state of psychological tension.

Experience. This circle represents the immediate field of sensory and visceral experience. It would be comparable to the total phenomenal field of the infant. It represents all that is experienced by the individual, through all the sense modalities. It is a fluid and changing field.

Self-Structure. This circle represents the configuration of concepts which has been defined as the structure of self, or the concept of self. It includes the patterned perceptions of the individual's characteristics and relationships, together with the values associated with these. It is available to awareness.

Area I. Within this portion of the phenomenal field the concept of self and self-in-relationship is in accord with, or is congruent with, the evidence supplied by sensory and visceral experience.

Area II. This area represents that portion of the phenomenal field in which social or other experience has been *distorted* in symbolization and perceived as a part of the individual's own experience. Percepts, concepts, and values are introjected from parents and others in the environment, but are perceived in the phenomenal field as being the product of sensory evidence.

Area III. In this realm are those sensory and visceral experiences which are *denied* to awareness because they are inconsistent with the structure of the self.

SPECIFIC ILLUSTRATIONS

The letters in the circles may be regarded as elements of experience. By giving them specific content we may illustrate the functioning of personality. Let us take first a somewhat minor example as illustrated in Figure 1.

(a) "*I am utterly inadequate in dealing with mechanical things, and this is one evidence of general inadequacy.*" This is an introjected concept and its associated value, taken over by the individual from his parents. The quotation marks indicate that it is perceived *as if* it were the direct sensory experience of failure with all mechanical things, but it is not. The experience was, "My parents regard me as inadequate in the mechanical field"; the distorted symbolization is, "I am inadequate in the mechanical field." The basic reason for the distortion is to guard against losing the important part of the self-structure, "I am loved by my parents." This leads to a feeling which may be schematized thus: "I want to be acceptable to my parents and hence must experience myself as being the sort of person they think I am."

(b) *I experience failure in dealing with mechanical contrivances.* This is a direct experience which has occurred a number of times. These experiences are assimilated into the structure of self because they are consistent with it.

(c) *Experience of succeeding with a difficult mechanical operation.* This is a type of sensory experience which is inconsistent with the concept of self and hence cannot be admitted directly into awareness. The person cannot perceive that "*I experience success in mechanical operations*" because this perception would be disorganizing to the structure of the self. In such an occurrence it is almost impossible completely to deny the experience to awareness, since the sensory evidence is clear. It is, however, "pre-perceived" as threatening and admitted to awareness in a sufficiently distorted fashion to eliminate the threat to the structure of self. It therefore appears in consciousness in some such fashion as "It was just luck," "The pieces just fell into place," "I couldn't do it again in a million years." This distorted symbolization could take its place

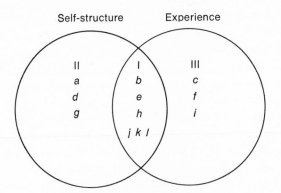

Figure 1. The Total Personality

in Area II in our diagram, since it is consistent with self. The actual experience, however, is denied to awareness in any accurately symbolized form, and hence remains in Area III.

Let us take another example, drawing this time upon the experience of Miss Har [described earlier]. . . .

(d) "*I feel nothing but hatred for my father, and I am morally right in feeling this.*" Miss Har's mother had been deserted by her husband, and it is not surprising that Miss Har had introjected this feeling, this concept of the relationship, and the value attached to it, as if they were based upon her own sensory and visceral experience.

(e) *I have experienced dislike for my father in my contacts with him.* On the few occasions when she had met her father, there were elements of his behavior which were not satisfying to her. This was first-hand sensory experience. It is congruent with the self-structure and assimilated into it. Her behavior is in accord with this total self-structure.

(f) *Experience of positive feelings toward her father.* Such experiences occurred, but were totally inconsistent with the whole structure of self. They were therefore denied to awareness. Only in the most distorted way do they appear in consciousness. She does admit the perception, "I am like my father in several ways, and this is shameful." She also overemphasizes her hatred for her father as a defense against permitting such experiences in awareness. (This is an inference from outside of her phenomenological field. It is confirmed by the fact that eventually, as described later, she can perceive this from her own internal frame of reference.)

Perhaps one other illustration may be added to indicate the introjection of values from the culture.

(g) "*I regard homosexual behavior as terrible.*" Here the experiencing of a social attitude in others is distortedly perceived as a value based upon experience.

(h) *I experience distaste for homosexual behavior.* In certain specific experiences, the sensory and visceral reactions have been unpleasant and unsatisfying. Being in accord with the self-structure, these experiences are assimilated into it.

(i) *Occasional experience of homosexual desires.* These are denied to awareness, because they would be disorganizing to self.

Many aspects of self would not exhibit the discrepancies evident in these three examples, but would be of this order:

(j) *I hear others say that I am tall, and have other evidence that they regard me as tall.* Here the attitude of others is not introjected, but is simply perceived for what it is. It is therefore in the category of sensory experience which has occurred in a social relationship, and is accurately symbolized.

(*k*) *I experience myself as tall in relation to others.*

(*l*) *Very rarely do I find myself in a group where I experience myself as shorter than others.*

j, k, l, are three different sorts of sensory evidence, all admitted to awareness. The attitudes of others are perceived as such, not as own experience. The evidence of tallness which is acquired through sensory experience is accepted into awareness. The occasional contradictory evidence is also accepted, and thus modifies the self-concept to some degree. Thus the individual has a unitary and securely founded concept of himself as taller than most people, a concept which is based upon several types of evidence, all admitted to awareness.

The picture given thus far, and the conclusion which would be based upon the diagram in Figure 1, would be that in this schematic individual there is much potential psychological tension. There is a considerable degree of incongruence between the sensory and visceral experience of the organism, and the structure of the self, the former involving much that is denied to awareness, and the latter involving an awareness of much that is not so. Whether or not this schematic individual would feel himself to be maladjusted would depend upon his environment. If his environment supported the "quasi" elements of his self-structure, he might never recognize the tensional forces in his personality, although he would be a "vulnerable" person. If the culture gave sufficiently strong support to his concept of self, he would have positive attitudes toward self. He would experience tension and anxiety, and feel maladjusted, only in so far as his culture, or overwhelming sensory evidence, gave him some vague perception of the inconsistencies within his personality. Such an awareness or anxiety might also come about if he were exposed to a highly permissive situation in which the boundaries of self-organization could be relaxed, and experiences ordinarily denied to awareness might be dimly perceived.

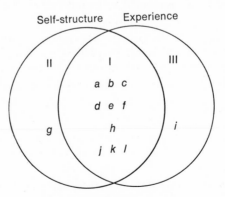

Figure 2. The Total Personality

However such anxiety or uneasiness is caused, it is in this state that he would tend to welcome psychotherapy. Let us see, diagrammatically, what occurs in therapy.

THE ALTERATION OF PERSONALITY IN THERAPY

Figure 2 shows our schematic person after successful psychotherapy. The definitions of the circles and areas remain unchanged, but it is evident that they have a different relationship to each other, the structure of self now being much more congruent with the sensory and visceral experience of the individual. The specific ways in which that relationship has changed may be illustrated by again referring to the schematic elements of experience previously described. These have now been reorganized in the perceptual field in ways which may be indicated as follows:

(*a*) *I realize my parents felt I was inadequate in mechanical things, and that this had a negative value for them.*

(*b*) *My own experience confirms this evaluation in a number of ways.*

(*c*) *But I do have some competence in this field.*

Note that experience (*c*), as previously described, has now been admitted to awareness and organized into the self-structure. Experience (*a*) is no longer perceived in distorted fashion, but it is perceived as sensory evidence of the attitude of others.

(*d*) *I perceive that my mother hates my father and expects me to do the same.*

(*e*) *I dislike my father in some ways and for some things.*

(*f*) *And I also like him in some ways and for some things, and both of these experiences are an acceptable part of me.*

Here again introjected attitudes and values are perceived for what they are, and are no longer distorted in their symbolization. Feelings formerly inconsistent with self can be integrated into the self-structure, because it has expanded to include them. Experiences are valued in accordance with the satisfactions which they bring, rather than in accordance with the views of others. It [is important] . . . to realize that the process by which this integration is achieved is a painful, vacillating one, that the acceptance of all the sensory evidence is at first a very fearful and tentative acceptance, and that keeping the locus of evaluation within oneself means that initially there is much uncertainty about values.

g, h, i. These are left unchanged. They are intended as a schematic representation of the fact that therapy never achieves complete congruence of self and experience, never clears away all introjections, never explores the entire area of denied experience. If the client has deeply learned that it is safe to accept all sensory experience into awareness without distortion, he may deal differently with his homosexual impulses (*i*) when they recur, and he may recognize the introjected cultural attitude (*g*) as being simply that. If circumstances tend to focus on this area, he may return for further therapy.

j, *k*, *l*. The individual's securely based concept of his height, and the other stable concepts of which it is representative, remain unchanged.

CHARACTERISTICS OF THE ALTERED PERSONALITY

Several of the characteristics of the personality as represented in Figure 2 may be briefly noted.

There is less potential tension or anxiety, less vulnerability.

There is a lessened possibility of threat, because the structure of the self has become more inclusive, more flexible, and more discriminating. There is therefore less likelihood of defensiveness.

Adaptation to any life situation is improved, because the behavior will be guided by a more complete knowledge of the relevant sensory data, there being fewer experiences distorted and fewer denied.

The client after therapy feels more in control of himself, more competent to cope with life. In terms of this diagram, more of the relevant experience is present in awareness, and hence subject to rational choice. The client is less likely to experience himself behaving in ways that are "not myself."

There is represented in this second diagram the basis for the "greater acceptance of self" which clients experience. More of the total experience of the organism is directly incorporated into the self; or more accurately, the self tends to be discovered in the total experience of the organism. The client feels he is his "real" self, his organic self.

The individual represented in Figure 2 would be more accepting toward another, more able to understand him as a separate and unique person, because he would have less need of being on defensive guard.

Following therapy, the individual is formulating his evaluations of experience on the basis of all the relevant data. He thus has a flexible and adaptable system of values, but one that is soundly based.

Conclusion

This chapter has endeavored to present a theory of personality and behavior which is consistent with our experience and research in client-centered therapy. This theory is basically phenomenological in character, and relies heavily upon the concept of the self as an explanatory construct. It pictures the end-point of personality development as being a basic congruence between the phenomenal field of experience and the conceptual structure of the self—a situation which, if achieved, would represent freedom from internal strain and anxiety, and freedom from potential strain; which would represent the maximum in realistically oriented adaptation; which would mean the establishment of an individualized value system having considerable identity with the value system of any other equally well-adjusted member of the human race.

It would be too much to hope that the many hypotheses of this theory will prove to be correct. If they prove to be a stimulation to significant study of the deeper dynamics of human behavior, they will have served their purpose well [pp. 524–32].

ADDITIONAL READINGS FOR PART III

Understanding another person's behavior is obviously a large topic on which many excellent books have been written. Users of this book will already have been exposed to, or have certain preferences for, some of the ways psychologists have dealt with the problem of understanding individual behavior. There will usually not be time in a course to cover even one of the various approaches to this topic that has received wide attention and certainly not enough time for adequate exposure to a *variety* of approaches. The choice between depth and breadth is particularly difficult when there is really little time for either, but, as already indicated, we have preferred to concentrate on a particular point of view in the psychology of individual behavior, one which ties in closely with the design of the rest of this book. This *perceptual* point of view, emphasizing the importance of the individual's self-concept, has been quite well represented in the readings of Part III, especially Lecky (III–2) and Rogers (III–6). For a more extended presentation of the perceptual approach we recommend:

1. Arthur W. Combs and Donald Snygg, *Individual Behavior: A Perceptual Approach to Behavior*, rev. ed. New York: Harper, 1959. See especially Chapters 1–3, 5, and 7–9.

For a more eclectic viewpoint, drawing from a wider range of theoretical approaches, yet still related to our own central framework, we include selections from four other books as required reading for Part III:

2. Gordon W. Allport, *Pattern and Growth in Personality*. New York:

Holt, Rinehart and Winston, 1961. Part V, "Understanding Personality," 497–573. See also Chapter 6, "The Evolving Sense of Self," and Chapter 8, "Culture, Situation, Role."

3. Warren G. Bennis, E. H. Schein, D. E. Berlew, and F. J. Steele, *Interpersonal Dynamics*. Homewood, Ill.: Dorsey Press, 1964. Part II, "Some Interpersonal Aspects of Self-Confirmation—Introductory Essay," 207–25.

4. Robert Ward Leeper and Peter Madison, *Toward Understanding Human Personalities*. New York: Appleton-Century-Crofts, 1959. Chapter 2, "Our Everyday Concepts about Personality," 32–53, and Chapter 6, "Personality as a Matter of How We Perceive Life Situations," 157–97.

5. Robert Tannenbaum, Irving R. Weschler, and Fred Massarik, *Leadership and Organization: A Behavioral Science Approach*. New York: McGraw-Hill, 1961. Chapter 4, "The Process of Understanding People," 52–66. Reprinted in Bennis, Schein, Berlew, and Steele, *Interpersonal Dynamics*, 725–40.

As there is some duplication of coverage among these different selections, choices can be made partly on the basis of preference for a particular style of presentation. Much the same thing could be said about the following additional readings, from which a selection can be made that would fit the purposes of Part III just as well as those we have already listed. This supplementary list does include more coverage of different views to understanding personality, including the psychoanalytic approach, which has been inadequately represented in the citations given so far.

6. Gordon W. Allport, *Becoming: Basic Considerations for a Psychology of Personality*. New Haven: Yale University Press, 1955.

7. Hadley Cantril, *The "Why" of Man's Experience*. New York: Macmillan, 1950.

8. Erik H. Erikson, "Identity and the Life Cycle," Selected Papers, in *Psychological Issues*, 1, No. 1, Monograph 1. New York: International Universities Press, 1959.

9. Saul W. Gellerman, *Motivation and Productivity*. New York: American Management Association, 1963.

10. Calvin S. Hall and Gardner Lindzey, *Theories of Personality*. New York: Wiley, 1957.

11. Don E. Hamachek, ed., *The Self in Growth, Teaching, and Learning*. Englewood Cliffs, N.J.: Prentice-Hall, 1965.

12. Alfred E. Kuenzli, ed., *The Phenomenological Problem*. New York: Harper, 1959. Includes Hadley Cantril, "Perception and Interpersonal Relations."

13. Karl Menninger *et al.*, *The Vital Balance: The Life Process in Mental Health and Illness*. New York: The Viking Press, 1964.

14. Clark E. Moustakas, ed., *The Self: Explorations in Personal Growth*. New York: Harper, 1956.

15. Anselm Strauss, *Mirrors and Masks: The Search for Identity*. New York: The Free Press, 1959.

16. Robert W. White, *Lives in Progress: A Study of the Natural Growth of Personality*. New York: Henry Holt, 1952: 2nd ed. (paperback), New York: Holt, Rinehart and Winston, 1966.

17. ———, "Motivation Reconsidered: The Concept of Competence," *Psychological Review*, 66, No. 5 (September 1959), 297–333.

18. Abraham Zaleznik and David Moment, *The Dynamics of Interpersonal Behavior*. New York: Wiley, 1964.

CASE III-1. Juanita Rodriguez

Juanita Rodriguez from Panama was graduated from boarding school in the United States at the age of sixteen and was admitted to Allegheny College at that time. Because of her age, on the advice of Allegheny, she did not enter college that fall but spent the year at home in Panama, where her father was a prominent surgeon and her mother taught Spanish literature at the University of Panama. She also visited her mother's sister's family in Spain and travelled in France and Italy with her parents. In September of that year her mother brought her to college and remained in town most of the fall.

Early in November Juanita telephoned Mr. Greene, the headmaster of her school, who had also been her teacher in chemistry for two years, and asked if he would talk to her about a problem. When she arrived in his office, Juanita chatted for a few minutes and then referred to her call.

JUANITA 1: Well, Mr. Greene, here I am back for advice again. As you must remember, I was never a really good chemistry student, and my coasting along in chem at school has caught up with me. I'm flunking Chemistry A this year. I seem to understand it when I study it, and I get along all right in the laboratory; but I just don't seem to be able to do anything on the examinations. I'm too slow. I can't manipulate the expressions fast enough. It's worse than it was in school because I'm scared in this course, and I never was in yours.

GREENE 1: What have your grades been so far?

JUANITA 2: I got 30 on the first test and 4 on the mid-semester examination. . . . I just couldn't seem to do anything on it. I couldn't get started. It was so long, and that frightened me. I couldn't decide what to do first. I think I can actually do every problem there (she handed him the examination question sheet) if I have time enough, but I can't solve the quantitative problems fast enough to do all that in one hour. Isn't that a mean exam? Nobody in the class got more than 60 except one girl who hasn't had a grade below 95 since we started. The instructor spends all his time lecturing to her, and the rest of us just pick up what we can.

GREENE 2: Hmm, it is rather a tough exam. You really have to have this stuff at your finger tips, don't you?

JUANITA 3: I did what they said about not trying to remember equations, but learning how to balance them so thoroughly that I could reconstruct any reaction in my mind in a minute or two. I can do that, but not when I'm rushed in an examination—and of course not in a minute or two either. I've studied hard, too, at least two hours on every assignment. I think I understand it until I get to class—and then he goes so fast I can't follow him.

GREENE 3: You're pretty discouraged with the whole thing.

JUANITA 4: Yes.

GREENE 4: If I can help you with tutoring or extra explanations or anything like that, I'm only too glad to do it.

JUANITA 5: I don't want to take up your time . . . It's very kind of you.

GREENE 5: I feel a certain responsibility for your chemistry because you were my pupil. Besides, I'd really enjoy helping you. It would be fun to do inorganic again—you know I'm not teaching it this year—and it would be a relief from my own work. All you have to do is give me a ring, and we can get together for an hour almost any time.

JUANITA 6: You shouldn't feel any responsibility for me; it's my own fault. If I had worked harder for speed when you tried to get me to, maybe I could solve the equations fast enough now. I didn't come to you for extra help on chemistry.

GREENE 6: No?

JUANITA 7: I want to drop chemistry. It just seems hopeless. I don't doubt that with your help I might get up to passing by the end of the semester, but just passing isn't enough. I'm so far behind now that I could never get a B.

GREENE 7: You think you have to have a B, and you don't think you could improve that much?

JUANITA 8: No. I have to have an honors record in my major if I'm to have any chance at all of getting a junior year abroad. If I follow my original plan to be a doctor, chemistry will count in my field—that's why I took it. But if I change my major to fine arts or romance languages, I won't need the chemistry and I can drop it.

GREENE 8: You want to give up medicine so you can drop chemistry?

JUANITA 9: Yes. Well, to tell the truth, I think I've been changing my mind about medicine all summer. I like the idea of helping people, and I do think I would enjoy figuring out what was the matter with someone—putting all the symptoms together to get a diagnosis—but I just can't see myself looking down people's throats or listening to their complaints day after day.

GREENE 9: You don't think you would enjoy the actual practice of medicine.

JUANITA 10: No. I don't think I'm the right type. Anyway, Dean White said it would be almost impossible for a pre-med major to get a junior year in Spain. Allegheny College doesn't have a regular arrangement for a junior year abroad, but a few girls who have special reasons, like language or fine arts majors, are sometimes granted one. In fine arts, I might get permission to go to Florence or Rome, but the only way I could be sure of going to Spain is to concentrate in romance languages with emphasis on Spanish.

GREENE 10: A junior year in Spain is very important for you?

JUANITA 11: Yes, it is. I want it very much.

GREENE 11: Going to Spain means more to you than your medical ambitions?

JUANITA 12: Yes. Well . . . lots of things seem different to me now than they did a year ago. . . . This spring my Spanish cousin introduced me to a . . . young law student . . . who lives near Madrid . . . Even when I . . . had my moments . . . at school, as you may have observed, it was nothing like this. I never felt this way about anyone else. It makes me look at everything in a different way somehow. He's very handsome and brilliant. He's only nineteen, but he's fifth in the whole law school. My family like him, too, very much. They all smile at him so. . . . I think Father and Mother and my aunt and uncle think José and I might make a good match. Of course, they don't dream, they would be shocked, that we are as serious as we are or have talked things over as far as we have . . . My cousin was very helpful . . . and discreet.

GREENE 12: You think they approve of the two of you?

JUANITA 13: I think they wouldn't mind. . . . Maybe they'd even encourage us. I've almost talked Mother into going back next summer to be with my aunt and uncle and cousin. She could take the waters again—she didn't begin to get over her illness until we went to the resort near Madrid. That's how José and I really had a chance to get to know each other—his family lives near the hotel there where we stayed.

GREENE 13: You feel that both you and your mother would benefit?

JUANITA 14: Yes, she's almost given her consent. I've tried to explain to her about the junior year abroad, too, but she isn't so agreeable about that. I could live with my cousin at Madrid, and my aunt and uncle live only thirty-five miles from there. It would cost much less than a year at Allegheny, because prices are so low in American money. My aunt and uncle owe us a debt of hospitality from the time my aunt and cousin stayed with us in Panama for three years during the Civil War. I don't mean that I'd accept money from them, but my uncle is very well-to-do, and they want very much to have me.

GREENE 14: You think it would be all right.

JUANITA 15: It could all work out beautifully . . . But it can't happen unless I get honor grades in my major, and I can't get an honor grade now in chemistry, so I want to drop it. Dean White said ordinarily a student can't drop a course just because she is failing it; otherwise what is the use of having college rules? But in my case, where I am willing to give up the pre-med course, she said maybe I could drop chemistry if I could find any other course I could begin in place of it this late in the year. If I don't find a fourth course now, I'll have to take five next term, and that will make it still harder to get honor grades. The easiest thing for me to take would be Spanish, of course, and since a freshman ought to have a language, it fits in well. Dean White suggested that I talk to the people in the Spanish Department, and I went to Professor Alvaredo and Professor Cruz. I went in and spoke to them in my best Castillian style, and they were so delighted to have someone who could speak good Spanish, especially a girl, that Professor Cruz accepted me in his Spanish poetry course. That would be very easy for me. I love to read, and I think I've already read many of the works, and the others are things I intend to read anyway. There are only twenty men in the course, and I'd be the only girl. I've been going to the classes, and it's lots of fun.

GREENE 15: You are very happy about the Spanish course.

JUANITA 16: I was until I told Mother about it. She was terribly upset and made an awful fuss about coming all the way from Panama to the United States to study Spanish, and why didn't I stay in Panama if that was what I wanted, and what would people think at home . . . We had a . . . well . . . a fight, frankly, and I left her in tears day before yesterday morning. I have to go see her again tomorrow, and . . . well, I don't know what to do. I don't know for sure if Dean White will let me drop chemistry and take Spanish, and even if she does, I don't know what to do about Mother, or what to do if I don't take Spanish. That's why I've come to you, maybe you can talk to her and get her to see it my way.

GREENE 16: You think she doesn't pay as much heed to you as she would to me.

JUANITA 17: Yes. If you talk to Mother, I know she will listen to you; she has great respect for your judgment. She hardly listens at all to me. I can't talk to her about things we disagree on. Whenever I do, I say things that hurt her, things that I don't mean, except for the argument, or that she takes in ways that I don't intend. When I argue with Father, he loses his temper too, and we have a row. But we understand each other, we get over it right away, without needing a lot of apologies and carrying hurt feelings for days afterward the way Mother does.

GREENE 17: You feel that your mother attaches more importance to an angry word in an argument than your father does, and you can't talk to her freely.

JUANITA 18: Yes. She tries to . . . to . . . not quite smother, but . . . maybe . . . hang on to me and is hurt if I don't want to do things her way. She . . . I can't be natural with her. Even when I agree to do what she wants, I don't have to like to do it that way.

GREENE 18: She makes some sort of claim or demand on you . . .

JUANITA 19: That's it, she makes me feel guilty if I don't please her. She doesn't understand that I have trouble making up my mind, and when I have to argue it all over again with her, I get excited or angry, and I don't do it convincingly—or politely . . . That's why I think, if you talk to her, she'll listen to you . . . or if you decide that I ought to do something else . . . I'll know it isn't just Mother upset because I don't speak to her sweetly enough.

GREENE 19: You feel that if I make a decision for you, both your mother and you will accept it.

JUANITA 20: Yes . . . no. Actually, I know that I have to make up my own mind—no one can do it for me. But (long pause) actually, Mother ought to be glad, because it means I'm giving up being a doctor, which she never wanted anyway, and taking languages. That's what she's wanted all along, so I could be a language teacher.

GREENE 20: You think she should be pleased with your new plan to study Spanish here.

JUANITA 21: Um-m-m, well (long pause) in a way, I suppose it does sound funny to come from Panama and Madrid to study Spanish literature in the United States. That's what Mother teaches at home, you know. . . . But Professor Alvaredo is from the University of Madrid. . . . Of course, he isn't Vasquez, that leading authority on Spanish literature, and I could work with him if I took my junior year in Spain. (Long pause, then laughs.) I suppose coming here from Panama and Spain for Spanish is like . . . carrying coals to Newcastle . . . only the opposite, somehow, I mean. (Pause.) When I think of all the people I've told about my ambition to be a doctor and my choosing Allegheny because it has such good science courses. (Long pause.) It might sound funny to some of Mother's students, too, for instance, the daughter of the cabinet minister. (Long pause.)

GREENE 21: You think it might be embarrassing to her.

JUANITA 22: Yes . . . I hadn't really thought of it that way . . . No wonder she was upset. (Long pause.) But what else am I to do?

If I don't take Spanish, I'll have to take five courses next term, and that will make it hard to get honor grades, and I might not even be able to drop chemistry. And the Spanish is only a one-semester course; I would be out of it at midyear.

GREENE 22: You think there is no way out but for you to take Spanish.

JUANITA 23: Yes. . . . I didn't tell you that when Dean White and I were talking about it first, I suggested Italian. I picked up quite a bit when we were in Italy this summer, and I am about as far along as the beginning class is now. I like Italian, and want to learn it. Mother wants me to learn Italian too. But there is a conflict. It comes at the same time as my Social Science 2. Mother suggested that I take French, I've had six years of it and passed the language requirement on my College Board. But when I was in France, I couldn't speak French freely; I was too much afraid of mispronouncing something. I knew too many rules, and the people I was with all expected me to be very good because I'd had so much French.

GREENE 23: They made you self-conscious.

JUANITA 24: Yes, I didn't want to make mistakes or mispronunciations in front of them. But with Italian, I was just learning, and I didn't mind making mistakes. None of our party knew any more Italian than I did anyway, except Father, who didn't care.

GREENE 24: You feel that they expected so much of you that you didn't want to risk making a mistake in French, but you didn't mind making mistakes where they didn't expect anything more of you.

JUANITA 25: That's right. I don't like people who expect things of you all the time. That's what Mother does; she acts like a teacher with a backward pupil. Father takes me as I am.

GREENE 25: You like your father's way better than your mother's.

JUANITA 26: I think maybe that's why I wanted to be a doctor rather than a teacher. . . . I thought it would be nice to work with Father. Going into Father's office sounded all right in Panama, and it seemed perfectly natural for me to want to be a doctor when I was in school here in the United States. But in Spain, when I said I wanted to be a doctor, they were all shocked. It wasn't a respectable occupation for a woman. The Spanish are still very strict and old-fashioned, you know. I'm afraid my American ways disturbed a good many of my uncle's friends. Even José thought it was funny I wanted to be a doctor. His mother thought it was too American.

GREENE 26: They made you wonder what they thought about you.

JUANITA 27: It frightened me a little to see how differently they thought about things. You wouldn't believe it, but my cousin, who is twenty-one, had never worn a short-sleeved dress in her life until I lent her one of mine. She had never worn a low-necked evening dress until she borrowed one of Mother's, so that all of us could go to a party when we were in Paris. Everybody could tell right away that I had spent a lot of time in the United States. . . . I had to be terribly careful to observe Spanish proprieties and not embarrass my aunt and uncle. American ways are not very popular in Spain, you know, after the way the United States has treated the government. I was glad that I had my cousin with me most of the time. There are so many things nice girls don't do in Spain that can be done in Panama and the United States.

GREENE 27: You weren't quite sure just where you were with them.

JUANITA 28: I'm not used to deferring to men the way the Spanish women do. . . . The way my uncle ignored my aunt, and the way he treated my cousin! . . . They must have been surprised at Father and me. . . . José was very nice, but even he remarked how different I was.

GREENE 28: You aren't accustomed to the Spanish attitudes toward women.

JUANITA 29: No, I'm not, and I'm not sure I can get used to the way the women are restricted there. I don't know how I'd feel if José treated me the way other Spanish men treat their wives. I might get used to it if I lived there for a while; I might find that it didn't bother me.

GREENE 29: But you worry about it just the same.

JUANITA 30: Yes. Actually, I've spent so many years in the United States, I'm more American than Panamanian. And American girls are pretty much the equals of boys. Panama seems strict and old-fashioned when I go home, but Spain is much stricter than that; the women are really kept in a subordinate position. I'm so used to the freedom American girls have, and of course Father and Mother are very liberal, I'm not sure I'd fit in a Spanish family. José is very nice and treated me more politely than an American boy would. But after all, he's an only son and has been brought up in that atmosphere of "the man first."

GREENE 30: No matter how polite he is, he may expect you to act like a Spanish woman.

JUANITA 31: Yes, besides, he's never been out of Spain, and he doesn't know what it's really like outside, and he may not like my independent ways. He was really surprised to see how Father and I argued about things. Spanish daughters aren't supposed to argue; they say "Yes, papa," and try to get their way by coaxing. That's the way my cousin does it. She asks for something, her father says "No!" in a big voice, Maria says "Yes, papa," meekly and cheerfully. Then in a day or so her mother and father say to each other, "See how cheerfully the poor child is taking it. What an obedient child she is! She should have a reward," and generally they let her do what she asked in the first place. I could never work things like that; it makes me feel funny to see Maria have to do it.

GREENE 31: You don't think you could manage to do things by indirection the way Maria does.

JUANITA 32: I'm not sure I'd want to if I could. I don't like it. Oh, dear, I didn't realize it was so late. I'm afraid I'll have to hurry to get to class on time.

Mr. Greene assured Juanita he would be glad to talk to her any time, and she promised to get in touch with him within a few days.

CASE III-2. Larry Baker

Chuck Loring, a second-year student at the Harvard Business School, conducted the following interview with Larry Baker, a first-year student, as part of an assignment for a course which Chuck was taking in Interpersonal Behavior. The purpose of the assignment was for Chuck to practice understanding another person from the other person's point of view.

Larry Baker was slightly older than most Business School students,

Case material of the Harvard Graduate School of Business Administration, prepared as a basis for class discussion. Cases are not designed to present illustrations of either correct or incorrect handling of administrative problems. All names have been disguised. Copyright © 1965 by the President and Fellows of Harvard College; revised 1967.

married, and had had both military and business experience. The two men had first become acquainted the previous summer while both of them were working for the same large manufacturing company in the Midwest. Although they had been in separate departments and buildings, their projects had overlapped to some extent, and there had been some occasion to work together. The fact that Chuck had completed one year at Harvard and Larry was just starting had naturally carried their friendship beyond the work environment. However, their contacts had been infrequent, and neither knew much about the other before the interview.

The interview time and place, which was Chuck's dormitory room, were arranged by telephone. At that time Chuck explained to Larry the nature of the assignment, that he could discuss anything he wanted, and that the object was merely that of understanding someone else's point of view—in this instance he could talk about himself, a problem, or a particular subject. As an example Chuck had suggested he talk about his business goals.

The following interview was transcribed from over two hours of tape:

LARRY 1: One of our professors posed a question to us the other day and that is what is the businessman's responsibility to society? How should he act in relation to his personal goals and goals of society. It came up in connection with a case of a lobbyist. Of course I knew that people took other people out to dinner and that favors were done. However, in this case the fellow took them out to dinner, helped the legislators, and used grassroot pressures. But yet he took exception to giving them money or women as some lobbyists seemed to do!

CHUCK 1: This seemed to bother you.

LARRY 2: Yeah, the thing that bothered me was how do you draw the line. How do you say one thing is worse than the other. Of course there is a difference of degree; I understand that, that according to society to offer them money or to cater to their whims—to offer them women—is much worse in society's eyes than to offer them a business deal or the use of a car. Yet in my mind I see these as the same things. A bribe is a bribe to me. If I take a man out to dinner, it is obvious that I am trying to get him to do something for me—that I am offering him the use of something I have control over in return for something he has—I'm bribing him same as if I handed him the money. And yet the class discussion says that favors are all right but we're to stop at money. But in relation to our employees, if I were a manager I'd use money to get things, grant favors, give status symbols, and it is all right—but when I go to someone else it isn't. I find it difficult to decide within myself which way I would go. I have the feeling I would go one way or another. At the present I just don't believe in bribes, but I interpret being nice to people just to get something for myself as a bribe too.

CHUCK 2: So you are taking this beyond mere monetary things and to your acting as a businessman and saying this is in effect a bribe and this bothers me.

LARRY 3: Yeah, this bothers me. When I get out I look upon the business world as part of a game and there seems to be varying sets and degree of rules in the game and I have to decide where I'm going to play. Uh, I have this drive—to make out if that's the expression—I want something. If I didn't I wouldn't be here. I wouldn't have gone to college in the first place. In the process of getting what I want I have to decide how I'm going to play. And uh, I've found that all the things I've done up to this point I have had a very difficult time reconciling myself to stay in the middle; I either play on one end or the other. So I would just not do favors. I would have people act because they wanted to act in my favor. I would try to convince them trying to use what I would call logical arguments, and if they can back me down—shoot holes in me—I have nothing else to stand on. I just couldn't say you're right, I'm wrong; here's a few bucks and you'll do what I want you to. I would either do this or go to the other extreme— I would just buy my way along.

CHUCK 3: So as you see it there are two means—using logic to convince people or just bribing them.

LARRY 4: Yeah, I know I could build up a credit or debt from people. I don't know quite how I feel about this myself. If I do something for someone I realize that they owe me a debt and yet I don't want people to do something for me just to repay the debt because they feel they have to. I would rather have them want to. When I do get into a work situation I would like to get in one that built up a team feeling—uh, a group feeling so that they felt that what was good for the group was good for them. And the same with me —what is good for me is good for the group rather than try to buy my way through the group or stepping on other people.

CHUCK 4: So you are trying to find some way that you can be a success and attain the things you want in business by not going to either one of these extremes.

LARRY 5: Yes! I'm trying to find a way—I suppose I'm predisposed to want to screw the system is what it amounts to. To explain this I feel that the system, and I define the system as IBM's way of doing it—the IBM look or you don't make it—you can't buck the system. Or some other places I worked where the way to get ahead is to be nice to those people who are your supervisors and it does not make any difference what kind of work you do. I don't want to operate in a system like this! I want to operate in a system where my personal characteristics are appreciated but they're not the reason why I get along. I want to get along on the type of work I do. I don't want people when they refer to me to say that he's a nice guy—he looks good. I want them to say he can do the job! The fact that his personal characteristics would enter in is incidental.

CHUCK 5: So you might say that you would rather be judged on the basis of your work—your contribution to the organization—rather than on any outside factors such as the image you project, the people that you know, the favors that you do for people, and so on.

LARRY 6: That's right, that's right! I would like to be able to say some day that I'm a success and that I don't owe anybody anything. Uh—

CHUCK 6: You would like to be independent without knowing that your success was attributable to someone's knowing you or a favor you did for someone. You would like to achieve it on your own.

LARRY 7: That's right. I want to feel, and I suppose this goes to something deeper inside, that it was me who did it and not that it was through trickery or doing personal favors or even being in the right place at the right time. I want to feel that I am where I am because I am what I am, that I've been judged on the type of work that I do and the benefit I am to whatever group I happen to be associated with and not by the fact that I'm the boss's brother-in-law or because someone likes me. I don't appreciate that position. If I were in that type of position I think I would feel that people talked among themselves and not to me that. I was one of the chosen ones. He isn't worth a damn but he is going to make out because of who he knows.

CHUCK 7: So to go back you think that this is what you would like but yet what they seem to teach you here and what society says is just the opposite—that you are going to be judged on other things besides what you contribute to the organization.

LARRY 8: Yes, uh, that is correct. This is, uh, one reason why I picked or came to the Business School was that this would be the place if any that will give me the tools that I need, will give me the confidence that I need to go out and buck the system, maybe make my own system. I think I am predisposed to want to make something of my own with a small group of people, to build an empire if you want to call it that, so that we can say we did this—we pulled each other up.

CHUCK 8: But it doesn't seem to be that way now that you're here?

LARRY 9: Well, uh, I don't know. Again in one course we had a great deal of discussion of what legislators do and why they do what they do. It seems that in every case we've considered so far that there has always been one legislator who is called unreliable, undependable, any number of derogatory names, yet he seems to be the only one in the entire group that we get to know from the case that operates according to his own convictions, who operates, at least it seems, in the manner in which he is supposed to. He takes the interest of an entire group—of the group he is supposed to represent—and considers their interests and does what he thinks he should do for them rather than casting his vote in favor of the particular pressure group or in any manner looking out for his own benefit. There seems that there is some sort of dichotomy here, that those who act like society says they should act—they don't get anywhere and yet those that do the things that everyone thinks are underhanded, unacceptable, and what have you—get somewhere!

CHUCK 9: And this is what bothers you!

LARRY 10: Yes, this bothers me.

CHUCK 10: You would like to be like the one you described where he stood for his own convictions yet you say that if you do this when you get out in the business world you may be the one, that you won't be able to achieve the things that you want.

LARRY 11: Yes, I'm afraid I'm going to dilute my character, to prostitute my ethics. I can see some inherent sort of danger that I feel that if I give a little bit one time that I'll do something a little worse the next time. I'm afraid I'll fall into some kind of a hole and maybe in effect be successful in the eyes of society or the eyes of the world but despise myself, destroy myself.

CHUCK 11: Could we say that there is an aspect of manipulating people here that you don't like?

LARRY 12: Yes! Even that word—I don't like the word *manipulating people.* I want to feel inside myself that people are doing something that I ask them to do because they want to, they want to do it for me, they want to do it for themselves, for the firm. In any case they're not being tricked or handled or pushed or walked on, and yet it seems to get ahead this is the type of thing that is done.

CHUCK 12: There doesn't seem to be any way to please both you and the people you work with at the same time. In other words, there has to be some dichotomy here where the guy that gets ahead uses the people, and the people don't get what they want, but the guy that manipulates them does get what he wants.

LARRY 13: Yes, this seems to be exactly what happens. And this is the reality but the reality is in direct opposition to what the school-books say, to what people would like to believe happens. They would like to believe that the red-blooded American boy goes out and makes good by being a Billy Budd type of character, a character who is truthful, who works hard and is sincere. And yet the people who are this way—and there's a saying that I've heard in industry that nice guys get squashed—they don't get along. Now I'm not condoning that we let people do what they want to do. I understand that there are varying degrees of responsibility of intellect and as such some people are leaders and some are followers. But I would think that the leaders making decisions and getting people to do things would consider those that are under-neath them as well as the goals that they would hope to attain. To say that the firm's goal is to make profit is all right as long as it isn't at the expense of someone who could less afford it than we can. I suppose the best example is the exploiting of labor during the Twenties. And today the exploitation of management by unions. I am directly opposed to union organizations, primarily because I think the officers of the union have their own self-interest in mind and the union itself is trying to justify its existence in the face of more benevolent management. I think they taught management a lesson.

CHUCK 13: So you would tend to avoid conflict and hurting people's goals and lives, is that it?

LARRY 14: Yes, I would tend to avoid personal conflict. I've always tried to separate my being into two entities—the academic or logical side and my emotional side. I would avoid any conflict that I would be emotionally involved in simply because I would act according to my own feelings rather than to logical thought. As far as interfering in other people's lives, I feel that every individual has a chance to do whatever he wants to do. I realize it is more difficult for some than others because there are some who are given more opportunity. But this is up to the individual. Some people say you are lucky you go to Harvard. I say I am not lucky; I got here because I wanted to be here. If you want to go somewhere like Harvard, all you have to do is want to and sit down and figure out how you are going to do it. I don't feel that I have had any special privileges.

CHUCK 14: But yet when you push this thinking that a person has a chance to make what he wants out of his life it rubs against the fact that in reality you almost have to manipulate people, and so on.

LARRY 15: Yes, I suppose that I must admit this. I must admit that in my own dealings with people I'm not so much interested in what I do as much as how other people are affected by what I do, because how they are affected determines what will happen to me. Yet I don't expect them to make any concessions for me. I do my work to the best of my ability and how this affects them is what interests me and not really what I've done. I know what kind of work I do. I know what kind of person I am. I have had occasion when I've felt that people didn't understand me, didn't know who I was. This hurts, this bothers me. I've had people misconstrue the things I say. Sometimes they think that an academic argument is insight into my emotional self and when I very coldly deny something that they think is a right of people, they think I am a calloused person. This isn't true. This is only one side of me speaking. They only saw the academic side that looks at something and gives an evaluation which has nothing to do with my personal emotions. Personally I might feel just the opposite. A case in point is the fact that we have eight girls in our class here. Two of them are in my study group. I've had numerous conversations with them and I don't feel that women have any place in business. I have this feeling not because I feel they are inferior, but I feel that they have a distinct advantage to which they are not entitled, and that is just the fact that they're women. I confronted them with this, and we argue about it. This is my logical self talking to them, but emotionally when I talk to them I can see why they're here, why they want to be here. I can see why they want to get ahead. This is the Protestant ethic that you must surge ahead. And I can see why they would be disgusted with the traditional role of a woman. Again there is this dichotomy here. I can't resolve this.

CHUCK 15: So there are really two sides here—the logical side and the emotional side, and you seem to think that your problem is re-solving them, which one of you takes the front. Can they act separately, can you get them in agreement?

LARRY 16: Yes, I think these problems—with women, legislators, my business ethics—are all basically the same. As I gain experience, I see a two-standard system in operation where people are saying something and doing something else. I can't, as you said, resolve this in my mind. I can't seem to approach a middle-of-the-road attitude. I feel that to buck the system, to act at one extreme, I'm going to end up with nothing—and if I don't buck the system I'm going to destroy some of myself, some of my feelings for people. I have had experience with people whom I thought were hard and cold and had no respect for people. I didn't like these people; I didn't like what I saw. I don't want to see myself in that position; I don't want to do that to myself. Even here at the "B" School the pressure of business contacts—I've talked to my wife and she can sense a change in my attitudes. I don't think this is bad, that I look at things from a profit-and-loss standpoint. I just see the inside of some things that I only saw the outside of before. This is the change she senses. We can see in some of the cases where people acted in a manner I don't approve of, in a manner which furthers their own interests and may well make them the most technically qualified individual in their particular area, but as a human being some of them are despicable. And I'm trying to resolve a center area for myself. I'm trying to develop some sort of attitudes so I can be firm but fair, so I can justify my moves to myself. If I had to fire someone who had worked for the company for ten, twenty years I could explain to them in logic—profit and loss—why, but in my emotional self I can understand what this person feels. I'm trying to find the middle for these two things, and I find it very difficult.

CHUCK 16: So you can see where to be a success in business is going to require a firm and harsh logical approach, but yet this gets in the way of your feelings for people and—

LARRY 17: Yeah.

CHUCK 17: And how it affects them.

LARRY 18: Yes. My family, my wife, and some of my friends think I'm foolish because I have a basic faith in people. I leave my key in my car or leave my personal things in places where people can pick them up if they want to. As far as I feel myself, I wouldn't touch something that didn't belong to me. If it's not mine, it's not mine. I realize that there are people that don't feel the way I feel. I know that I have to protect myself from people like this because they will take me for all I'm worth, but at the same time I don't feel any personal anger toward these people. If anything, I would just be further disillusioned with people. My business in the future should be an opportunity to push ahead and be perfectly honest and frank in all the dealings I have both above and below me. I am the type that can become very enthusiastic about a business development and I hope that I can communicate this to the people below me. If I ever become a business executive, I hope that I can see both the business and human sides of the business, so that I can fight off the harmful attitudes of unions or the things that make a firm inefficient. I know I can be firm and hard when I have to, because I divorce my emotional self from the other part of my character—

CHUCK 18: But you don't like to do that.

LARRY 19: But I don't like to do it, that's right, I don't like to do it. I like to feel at ease. I like to feel a serenity in both facets of my personality. Take my experience in the service as an instructor. I had occasions to fail students, and these were people of the same age as I but not with the same backgrounds. I never failed anyone without first talking to them, and at least first making them understand logically why I failed them, and I could feel some remorse on their part emotionally. I think my service experience reinforced my feeling about this reconciliation of this emotional versus the logical aspect of my personality. But I had some success with them.

CHUCK 19: But you don't know whether you can do it in business.

LARRY 20: I don't know whether I'll be successful in business. For one thing, in the service I had an absolute authority and a captive audience, and in business people have the right to turn around and walk away when I try to logically explain things. They can turn me off, and I have my doubts that I can accomplish what I want to accomplish.

CHUCK 20: So it won't be just the logical side that will be a success in business, but it will require something beyond just logically explaining—

LARRY 21: I think so, I think so. People ask me what I'm looking for and who I consider successful. And invariably I consider people successful who have made a lot of money, people who are held in high esteem, and who perhaps didn't make a lot of money. This is a personal thing. I do want to make a lot of money, although money is not my goal—my reason being simply because it has no inherent value. It's a means to an end, a way to get the things I would like to have. At the same time, I'm looking for the success that comes from being respected for who you are and what you are and not just where you are.

CHUCK 21: You don't think this will come from business?

LARRY 22: I think it can come from business, but I have some doubts if it will come within the system. My exposure, until last summer, in business had all been very distasteful simply because every job opportunity I had taken advantage of I found that I had to integrate myself into the system regardless of what I felt or thought inside—I had to outwardly appear that I was integrated into the system—before I could get anywhere, and as a result was being judged not on what I did or how I handled myself but on I suppose on what you would call my attitude.

CHUCK 22: So it almost forces you to create a system of your own rather than adapt to a new system.

LARRY 23: Yeah, this is close to being essentially true. I qualified my business experience because at the manufacturing company in the Midwest I wasn't led by the hand or watched over, and I was given a free rein to do what I chose to do. I think they were satisfied, and I don't think I integrated into their system. You didn't see the organization man there or the back-stabbers who would climb to the top over others. This is the closest I've seen of this group feeling I spoke of—what is good for me is good for the firm. They had this philosophy. For the first time in my life I felt here is a monster but I have a chance here. While in others that I worked in I didn't even want to succeed, because they weren't ethical.

CHUCK 23: So it is really a question of do I create my own system or do I find a large system that is compatible and allows me to keep my emotional values, and operate successfully.

LARRY 24: Yes, yes! This is exactly it. I have been out of high school over ten years and have had several work and military experiences, and I feel I'm perceptive. I have an inherent ability to find out what is going on so I can find out where I fit in. I have searched for the system that I would fit into and at the same time thinking in the back of my mind if that system doesn't exist, I'll create it. I have tried one business venture of my own which went in the red but that was because I lacked experience. I enjoyed it though. I came to Harvard because it should open new doors for me and I'll be able to examine new systems that I couldn't have before. Perhaps I will find this ethical situation—this logic-emotion tie I'm looking for. I think this will be available to me when I leave here. I expect to have at least three jobs after I leave here, because I will be able to inspect various systems. But then I get a little worried because, although I'm not old, I'm older than most graduates here. I realize my time is limited; I will have to pick something and do it soon. And if I can't find a system I can integrate into successfully or devise my own system, I'll have to settle for the next best thing and some way sort of adjust to fit. But yet I could never adjust to something like IBM because it is so far from myself. So I would have to go outside the job to get my satisfactions of life.

CHUCK 24: So when you add the time problem it aggravates it—the fact that you have to find a system or create your own system and do it within a reasonable amount of time.

LARRY 25: Yes! Yes, while I'm at the "B" School I'm investigating at least two opportunities to create my own business. I may have grandiose ideas but I couldn't be satisfied in IBM or with a corner grocery store. If I'm going to build something I want to build it big or at least to try to make it big. You couldn't give me something that was destined to be small.

CHUCK 25: So you want something big. It would be nice to create something big that would have your own type of system, but this takes a lot of time and risk so it would be easier to go into something that is already big provided that the system was there that agreed with you.

LARRY 26: Yeah, this is right. For this particular reason then, even though I'm predisposed to look for a business opportunity of my own, I'm more seriously looking for an opportunity in industry. In any case, if I don't find exactly what I'm looking for, I will find something that will give me enough experience to make me more valuable to someone else someday who may have the system I'm looking for. Sorta the added value theory for each year I'm with someone. I'll always look at myself as ready to go on the open market given the opportunity, given something that more closely aligns itself with my feelings, ideas.

CHUCK 26: So you don't think it does any good to adapt to a system?

LARRY 27: I find it almost impossible—I can't adapt. I sometimes wish I could. Several of my friends have successfully integrated themselves into a system and are very happy. Some are machinists and are quite happy, and I'm a little envious of them because I know they are happy. And yet I know I couldn't do what they're doing and be happy because I would want more—and not just dollars but more prestige and more value to myself. I would feel wasted. So I keep pursuing my education because I know this adds value. Just like the two months I've been here. I've learned more than I ever thought I could. (Pause.) Perhaps it has something to do with Maslow's theory of needs. I guess I'm at the level of never being satisfied with one's self. I want to leave the world better than I started. I want to give my daughter things, more than I had. To not be as disillusioned with people as I have been.

CHUCK 27: So you still come back to this basic conflict of sometimes you have certain aspirations and goals you want to achieve but there is that logical versus emotional conflict.

LARRY 28: Yes, I want to achieve these goals within my own context of values. And it seems sometimes as though it is almost impossible, and yet I have been reinforced by my constant belief that as I move, within my values I have progressed. I have been to college and through the service. Especially in the service I saw many sets of values different than mine. I compared them and our statuses and decided I couldn't go back to working in a factory as I had before—I just wouldn't be satisfied. I found at college, the white tower, this clean competition I looked for. This evaluating a person on the drive, enthusiasm, and so forth, rather than who they know. I found I could get ahead by pushing, and this is approved by society. Almost everyone approves of education, but I know there will be a difference when I get out. The system will be different.

CHUCK 28: And this is what worries you.

LARRY 29: This is a basic worry or problem. Maybe I have the whole thing colored because my first business experiences were disappointing. But my summer job was encouraging, and Harvard, I think, opened that door. (At this point the tape had to be changed and he commented: Boy, I sure am doing a lot of talking; I'm sure opening up. Don't let me down now.)

CHUCK 29: We were at the point where you were saying that you have your own system of values, your emotional and logical. You've had some experiences in business; your job last summer where this has worked out. But there is still that question that whether when you graduate from here, although it has been ideal for you in education because you can seem to operate successfully and be judged on your logical and not your side values—the people you know, and so forth—you will really find it in business out of here. Someplace where you can operate within your own values but yet achieve the things you would like to.

LARRY 30: Yes, yes, this is exactly it! I suppose some of my experience in college and business have disillusioned me, that I couldn't reconcile in my mind. I had difficulty in fitting my values to what happened. A particular instance was in college. (He relates an incident where a student tried to sell him a final and he refused and was graded on a curve with those who had seen it and hence missed an A. He said he hurt himself because he did right. Then he goes on to tell about taking a job after telling himself that he could do it. He found he couldn't, but the company, rather than telling him, just delegated to him less and less until he quit. He wished they had been frank with him and told him.)

CHUCK 30: So you like to know how you stand.

LARRY 31: That's right. I know who I am; I want to know what other people think I am. I want to know where I am all the time. I don't think I could run my life unless I did. (He then digresses on to the "B" School situation and how he stands.)

CHUCK 31: So you work hardest when there is an objective end and not a subjective end.

LARRY 32: Yes, yes that's right. I wouldn't have come here if someone had told me that Harvard professors grade you on what they thought of you. I would rather have people judge me on how well I operate—do my work—rather than how well they like me. Some people just won't like me because of the way I look or something. I wouldn't want to be judged on that basis, nor would I ever want to judge anyone else that way. Nevertheless, I realize that there are some people here at School whom I like better than others and some of those I like are not as competent as those I don't like.

CHUCK 32: So nevertheless there is still this subjective side.

LARRY 33: Oh, yes. There has to be; this is necessarily so. But I still would definitely prefer to look objectively at such things as making decisions. To look at them as a cold entity. Since my emotional values are so closely connected to my logical values, I would prefer to detach my emotional values and keep them out of my business dealings.

CHUCK 33: You would rather keep personal feelings out.

LARRY 34: I feel that they don't have any place in business. I feel I have to disconnect my personal self from my business life, otherwise I will tend to do that which will be unfair—that I wouldn't do objectively but I would do personally. I wish I could make an analogy. (Pause.) Take the girls in our class. (He goes back over the girls situation, then expands to tests in school as not being a really adequate means of evaluation.) There are many things that enter in that tests can't do.

CHUCK 34: So you can see where the emotional is important. In other words tests would be a very objective means of looking at things so there is a use for subjective evaluation.

LARRY 35: Yes, in particular instances, because in the course of our conversation here I have said that I do care for people and that I care for their feelings. But I don't like to have this color my judgment. In other words I suppose if you want to assign some rank order to these things, first, comes my objective feeling and second, comes the modifying factor—my personal feelings. In regard to raising my daughter—(goes on to relate an incident here). I really like one of the courses here because they discuss this very thing—values—and what you want to achieve and how you're going to get there.

CHUCK 35: This again is your problem then—what values do you set up, how do you achieve the things you're after, utilizing these values without bending them or losing them somewhere along the line.

LARRY 36: That's right. I really think I could destroy myself in the process of becoming successful, I could get to a point where the world would say there is a self-made man, and inside of myself I would be saying this is a man who destroyed himself. I just chipped away at my foundation until it was gone. This is one of my fears about the business world. How do I compete with someone who doesn't feel as I do. How do I compete with someone who bribes, etc. How am I going to cope with forces that oppose my foundation.

CHUCK 36: So you realize there is going to be plenty of opportunity in the reality of the business world where this will become a conflict.

LARRY 37: I think constantly. I think I'll be constantly challenged. I think my own personal measure of success will be how well I can withstand these things and still get ahead. I want to maintain a system and still be successful, of course with some compromise, but only slight. If I can't, then my picture of disillusionment will be complete and I suppose I'll retreat or get out someway. I won't shovel sand against the tide—if it's impossible I'll look for some way to escape.

CHUCK 37: So you will try to find a system to match yours, but you will only go to the point where if it's impossible you will get away someway—

LARRY 38: Yes, yes.

CHUCK 38: Changing jobs, careers, or something.

LARRY 39: Yes, even though job changing is frowned upon and job changers are looked upon as misfits. I suppose that's what I'll be —a misfit—if I can't find the right system. But I'll always keep looking for my place when I say I'll escape.

CHUCK 39: Always looking for the right system.

LARRY 40: That's right.

CHUCK 40: But you won't try to say this is my system, it doesn't seem to be getting me anywhere, so maybe I had better change it or look at it to see if it's right.

LARRY 41: I've done that—I'm continually evaluating my system. It would be ridiculous not to say it hasn't changed over the years. But it is a change of degree and not of kind—not direct change- over but a modification from experience and learning.

CHUCK 41: So you do recognize that your values will change over time.

LARRY 42: Oh, yes. But some things to me are despicable and they always will be, but over the years I have been able to at least live with these things. (He recites incident about friend who changed.) Of course his friendship meant a lot to me. It's like when I was a kid. You know how kids get the gang instinct. Well, I would often find myself faced with a decision of either dropping out of the gang or modifying my behavior. I usually dropped out and found another group to fit my system. (He cites example of being in service where he sought out a group of friends.) So I've always managed to find some system somewhere. And even though I feel a little apprehensive about my business career, I do have the feeling it will work out because it always has in the past. I didn't have to deviate. I could have; some things would have been easier, but I still got the same places without modifying. And I think I can in the business world. When I say modifying I mean radically.

CHUCK 42: So you think you can find that peace—that rationale—that you're looking for.

LARRY 43: Yes, I think it's there! I think my system exists, but I'll just have to find it. But I am smart enough to realize I might not, so I think ahead as to what I would do. I know what I'll do. I refuse to force myself into mental slavery to appease anyone else when I feel that, given time, I can find something that will be compatible to me.

CHUCK 43: So there is really that question of whether you will find the system, whether you will be able to attain your goals without giving up your values. But yet you feel that in the past you always found a group or someone with a system such as you have had, and you have been able to change from one group to another. So therefore, even though the possibility does exist, you feel you'll be able to work it out.

LARRY 44: I think so, yes, I do think so. Some people may frown upon what I do. I have friends who don't approve of my going to college. But this is what I want to do. (Pause.) Some people feel they can get along without others. I can't; I'm gregarious. I realize I can't get along completely alone. (He relates experience in California where he had no friends and so moved back to Ohio.)

CHUCK 44: So on the one hand you want to be independent but yet you recognize that you have a definite need for association with other people, and that's what makes it hard.

LARRY 45: Yes! Yes! I have to, uh—

CHUCK 45: You have to have people around you that accept you and like you for what you are.

LARRY 46: That's right. I want to be able to pick and choose the people I associate with. But I don't want to be forced into relationships, like some companies do. For instance, in the service I loved my job but I wanted to get out. My friends asked me why and I told them it was because of the uniform. They couldn't understand this, but it was because I had to wear it. That's what bothered me.

CHUCK 46: You don't like to have things forced on you.

LARRY 47: That's right, that's right. They say that's not a big thing, but I say maybe you can wear it but I can't. And in the same sense I can't wear a blue suit for IBM. Here I suppose I look the same as any other Harvard Business School student, but it's because I want to—I chose to be that way. I don't have to. If they said for everyone to wear Ivy League clothes, I would probably seek some way to get away from it.

CHUCK 47: Just don't force me.

LARRY 48: Yes, just don't force! Let me decide for myself; let me do what I want to do. And most times I'll conform. This is probably a basic reaction. If I am left alone I work harder, if I'm not pushed or watched over. I guess I'm sorta like the workers on the assembly line, I restrict my output if I'm pushed. I do a much better job if I'm left to my own devices. I expect people to trust me and give me responsibility.

CHUCK 48: So you're afraid that when you get out in business you'll have things forced on you.

LARRY 49: Well, I understand there are some things I must do. But there are things I couldn't live with without changing. I think change is basic to my nature. I couldn't just look forward to putting cards in an IBM machine all my life. Some men can do this and compensate by enjoying their leisure hours. I can't; I have to enjoy my job, because I can always control my leisure so I will enjoy it, but my job is more difficult. I realize I'll have duties, etc., to do. So I'll have to find something that fits into my system.

CHUCK 49: All right. Well, this has been interesting. Ah, have you throughout all of this discussion, has it clarified in your mind any of your own beliefs and resolved any of the conflicts? Or are you still in the same position you were in when we started?

LARRY 50: I think an extensive conversation like this where I could sit and talk for over an hour (it had been two hours) helps clarify things. I seldom get the chance. Yes, I think it has. It's crystallized a whole system for me while before I had just been considering these things. Through this monologue I think I see more clearly how the whole thing fits into my previous experience and what I expect in the future. I think it's been a benefit to me, I really do.

CHUCK 50: Do you see any new light now, that there is hope in this problem, that things will turn out?

LARRY 51: Well, I always believed they would. Otherwise I would give up. I think I have seen throughout the monologue clearly how it will work out and have made it more evident to myself.

CHUCK 51: Were you aware that it was becoming a monologue?

LARRY 52: Yes, I suppose it's because I'm a vocal person. I tend to talk to myself, even, at times. At times, and I'm being quite frank, it was rather hard but other times it just flowed, it just came out.

CHUCK 52: Well, thanks a lot for helping me out this afternoon.

CASE III-3. Joe Fielden, salesman (A)

SAMPSON 1: Well, Joe, it was nice of you to agree to this interview. As I explained on the telephone, there is no set format or subject. We can discuss anything you desire. I simply want to try to understand you from your own point of view—see how you perceive things. The fact that I am the son of one of the manufacturers you represent should not hinder your freedom to say whatever you wish; I intend to keep this conversation strictly confidential—just between us, with your name disguised even on the school report if you wish. If you have any hesitancy regarding the use of the tape recorder, we can turn it off.

JOE 1: Oh no, use the recorder if you wish. The purpose of this discussion is, I take it, for your analysis of a situation. Hell, I left the letter from the factory in the car about this complaint on the Talbott business. I just got another complaint from Lincoln Hardware in Bridgeport, and I told the factory about it. I wish I had the letter from the factory with me, but it's in the car. I just got it recently. The factory said this was probably old stock from several years ago when we had trouble and that Lincoln probably doesn't rotate their stock. I am not so sure that this stock is old, although the factory claims the numbers on the container indicate

Case material of the Harvard Graduate School of Business Administration, prepared as a basis for class discussion. Cases are not designed to present illustrations of either correct or incorrect handling of administrative problems. All names have been disguised. Copyright © 1964 by the President and Fellows of Harvard College.

it was made several years ago ... (pause) Paxton Corporation. They are a local manufacturer. They've done all their experimenting, planning, and promotion right in this area. Their discounts compared to ours are fantastic. We can't even approach them because of the conservative program Sampson Brothers has always followed. I don't go against the factory, except that is one of the reasons we don't get as much of the business we should like. We have good service and products, but we don't give enough discounts. And let's face it, some of our competitors are pretty good, too.

SAMPSON 2: If I understand you correctly, you feel that competitors have similar products and much better prices so that you are at a disadvantage.

JOE 2: That's true. Particularly with the big outfits. We have had a price which, frankly between you and I, doesn't vary much between the small shop and the big volume user. Yet our competitors give the big boys extra discounts and that's what they're interested in.

SAMPSON 3: You feel that additional discounts would help you to displace this competition.

JOE 3: Yes. We must be competitive pricewise as well as productwise. Nobody ever said we have poor products or that they are merchandised badly, it's only that it's priced too high. I had one line recently that had excellent products, but the policies of the company were inflexible. In fact, some buyers called the company screwballs—they won't bend, they won't give, they just say "that is that." We gave up the line because we can find others that are more flexible and have good products.

SAMPSON 4: It is difficult working with this type of company?

JOE 4: This type of company is difficult to promote.

SAMPSON 5: Flexibility with price structures would help you promote these products?

JOE 5: Yes. But you'll never eliminate competition in a good market. If you have a good product and acceptance, someone will try to do one better. I know this happened to Paxton. With no reflection on the policies of Sampson Brothers, you will recognize the fact that they are fundamentally a conservative operation and they never move rapidly. They move deliberately and slowly. Usually their programs are strong once they get going.

(Twenty minutes of similar conversation followed with Joe

re-emphasizing the importance of flexible prices, selling chain and discount outlets, and relating the history of how other companies changed their policies.)

The jobber today is, if you don't mind my putting it on record, a prostitute. He'll go wherever he can make a dollar in spite of old ties . . . For many years you have first gained acceptance through the major machine tool companies—and it has been a good principle. It has probably sold more merchandise for you than you realize. The independent jobber himself never liked that. But he was forced into carrying your line because the machine tool manufacturers built up a demand for the products. We created a demand that way. How much further you can go on the way, I don't know.

Now on the Stickfast line we never did have great success. Hardever (a competitive product) still sells day in and day out. Why do people want Hardever? Because they advertise and have for thirty or forty years. Yet compared to ours the product is inferior. . . . But we have established some strong trademarks with our other lines, and even with trademarks you have to adapt to whomever you're selling. It all depends on whom you're selling.

SAMPSON 6: There are differences depending on whom you're selling.

JOE 6: Yes. It all depends on whom you are selling as to what approach should be used. As a manufacturer's representative I have to wheel and deal. I have to feel my way along.

SAMPSON 7: Wheel and deal?

JOE 7: We have to feel out the market. It isn't so much a matter of wheeling and dealing on price, but on their freight proposition. We have to be very careful how we lay out our orders so the man doesn't have to pay a freight proposition on expensive small items without getting freight tonnage on the bulky items. Freight today is a big factor in shipping and the jobber can easily make freight on just one product. But it isn't so profitable for the factory to ship only one line. Therefore, we have to try and work in other products. We have to think about this—it isn't just walking in and taking orders. We get hammered from both sides.

SAMPSON 8: You have to be very careful how you plan your orders to suit your customers and you must also get orders that satisfy the factory. In other words, you must please your customer and Sampson Brothers.

JOE 8: The latter is my fundamental duty.

SAMPSON 9: Your fundamental duty—but you must also wheel and deal to please your customers. . . . You're in between the factory and customer.

JOE 9: Yes. When the distribution changes were first implemented in warehouses, I was afraid of the repercussions at the jobber level. After I opened some warehouse distributors, I cut some off after the factory objected that they didn't warrant the extra discount. This cost me some business, especially in one company, but he was interested in lower quality products anyway. (Pause.) Now, what more would you like?

SAMPSON 10: We got into some interesting areas. Why don't we talk about whatever you'd like.

JOE 10: Actually, the job isn't as easy as people think. They say "Look, a manufacturer's rep works on a commission, he doesn't have any investment, no stock, doesn't carry any accounts on the books. It's a very easy job."

This is true—it has a great deal of merit especially because of the freedom it allows a man, a great deal of latitude as to when, how, or how many calls he must make. As long as he gives his factories a good share of his time, that is all a manufacturer can demand. We are entitled to the reorders which automatically come in on the area we work.

The discounts the rep gives, however, can cut into his commission because the sale is lower. (Joe elaborated for about five minutes on how discounts could result in lower commissions unless the manufacturer raises commissions.)

Today the manufacturer's representative must work on at least a 10 per cent commission because he can't travel for less. Today travelling costs, as you well realize, are far beyond what they used to be. For $25 a week you used to be able to travel, but now you can't do it for less than $75—and that doesn't include car expenses. There's depreciation and insurance so that it has become a problem to be a manufacturer's rep and we have only one thing to sell to our customers, to our factories. That is integrity.

SAMPSON 11: You see being a manufacturer's rep as being good work. Yet things have changed today and perhaps the manufacturer doesn't fully appreciate all these changes and as you said "we get hammered from both sides" but it is still a good job. Some people may not understand your problems regarding expenses, commissions, discounts, and pleasing two groups at once. Your integrity is really all you have and perhaps that isn't too tangible.

JOE 11: It's tangible in this respect. I can walk into the average jobber and they know that since my father began in 1924 we have been active in the business. His reputation preceded my entrance into the business in 1940 and my brother's in 1941. In those forty years in the trade we have seen a lot of changes—big transitions in the marketing and price structures. I, for one, never thought the old discount structure was a true picture, and I'll go into that as soon as I finish. Experience and sincerity and the fact we have never told our jobbers an untruth—these things are part of it. The fact remains that if they get service from me and my factories back me up when I make a statement—and there again I have to be very judicious in what I commit my factories to. I have to follow their policy, but there are methods of interpreting things that can either make or break an agreement with a jobber. Unfortunately, today you will find there is far less loyalty of jobber to manufacturer than manufacturer's rep to manufacturer. In other words, the jobber will change manufacturers for a few pennies difference. We have lost accounts because of the profit margin—again back to the profit margin—because it outweighs whatever they would give me because of loyalty or because we have a good product.

SAMPSON 12: The jobbers are more loyal to the dollar than to the representative?

JOE 12: The pocket book is the ruling thing.

SAMPSON 13: In spite of your integrity, your family's experience, and loyalties you have no lease on the jobber's business unless the manufacturer backs you up.

JOE 13: That's true. And, of course, unless you have some progeny to carry on the business—just like your father and uncle—if he should go and there is no one to carry on the business, there is nothing left. Many of the qualities are reflected from the person into the company. You will carry that on because of your father and your uncle, because of the way things were done. I was the same way in carrying on from my father, combined with my own innate ability to do the things I do.

I like people. I am able to sell myself. I've been a pretty good salesman over the years if I do say so myself. Things have changed and I find more buying of business—wining and dining buyers, giving gifts—which I decry. In many ways I try to fight this off because I feel the jobber buys from me to make a profit on my product—not to get a gift with some junk. I feel integrity in selling is the main thing. They respect you more if they know they can't come to you and sucker you for a contribution.

SAMPSON 14: You want to have integrity with the trade and also to have them respect you more.

JOE 14: I know this: no one can point a finger at me for having done something illegitimate or things that have caused them a loss. On some lines I have dipped into my own pocket to offset a loss to jobbers when a factory couldn't or wouldn't back me up. We have to do a lot of queer things. (Pause.)

SAMPSON 15: You mentioned sometimes you have to buy gifts even when you don't want to.

JOE 15: I'm very careful about how I do that. Occasionally you have to slip a gift here or there. These things do no harm, but I don't do it to buy business wholesale. If I give a gift I do it personally anyway, not to get business directly. Some salesmen have tremendous expenses on gifts.

SAMPSON 16: Your competitors sometimes give a lot of gifts?

JOE 16: Definitely. That's one of the things you have to put up with—that's all. I don't fool with it—never have. I work too hard for the money I get. If I want to spend it, I want to spend it on my family.

SAMPSON 17: Your family means a great deal to you?

JOE 17: Naturally. What else?

SAMPSON 18: I didn't know.

JOE 18: To be any other way with the background I've had, with the way I've lived, is impossible. Your family must mean something to you because they are all you leave after you as your memorial. The stone they put on your grave doesn't mean a thing. It really doesn't mean a thing. People can come and look at that and it's just rock. But usually they can judge a family man by the children he leaves. Only have a short space on this earth. If you build a good structure—same way with your children as with your business—you find you will have a good impression left after. Naturally, we try to improve from generation to generation and make things better for our children.

Many of these things you consider in terms of how it will affect your family.

My family is the base of my life. My business and experience come from the way I was brought up. I hope my children will have the same way I bring them up. There are certain things I tell my boy that I would want him to follow. I hope they register and that he can then learn to make his own decisions and choose the best way. These are the important things and they are just as much a part of selling as anything else. We sell from the day we are born. We try to sell ourselves, our personalities, our charm. Just as there are poor and good salesmen, so there are personalities that are poor and good.

SAMPSON 19: Everything is selling?

JOE 19: That is true.

SAMPSON 20: What do you mean "sell?"

JOE 20: You don't understand the use of the word "selling?"

SAMPSON 21: Not in the broad sense you used it—"from the day you're born you sell."

JOE 21: I say from the day you are born—of course, you understand as an infant you don't sell too much except that you are shouting because you want attention, you want someone to pay attention. The crying of a baby is a sales pitch. As you grow old people want attention—in a small child it's showing off or exhibitionism—but it's selling. They're trying to sell themselves. As you mature and go into professions you are constantly selling. It's always been annoying to me that people say "Oh, he is just a salesman." I think selling is one of the best and most difficult professions there is. Whatever you go into, it's all selling.

SAMPSON 22: You've heard people say "he's just a salesman" even though everyone is selling.

JOE 22: Sometimes—"just a peddler" is a common expression. But everybody is selling. When you go out with a girl and make an impression on her, you're selling. When she puts on her best dress and puts up her hair, she's selling. Everybody is selling. The problem is to find a good buyer at the right price.

Joe Fielden, salesman (B)

Analysis

I believe my interview with Joe Fielden was a flop as far as utilizing the Rogerian technique is concerned. Most of the difficulty lay in the relationship between Joe and myself. Joe is a manufacturer's representative for the Sampson Brothers, Inc., a small manufacturer of industrial abrasives owned by my family. Joe knows that I plan to enter the business next year. We have known each other for about twenty years. The factory and Joe enjoy cordial relationships, although differences do result occasionally of an irritating but minor nature. The factory president describes Joe as "slow to take on new ideas. He just has too much Yankee in him." Although Joe may be slow to take on some ideas, I remember that several years ago he was the first and foremost among fifty other reps at a sales meeting to object to commission revisions (i.e., cuts). The factory trusts Joe and intends to retain the Fielden organization. I think Joe knows this. With this brief background, I shall try to summarize what I believe was in my own and in Joe's mind as we sat down for the interview:

WHAT I THOUGHT

"I hope I can get a good report from Joe that will really tell me a great deal about what he thinks of himself and of Sampson Brothers. If I can make this Rogerian technique work with Joe, I think I will be able to apply it to most of the other reps when I work with them next year. Joe is so secretive and conservative that I don't really expect him to open up. He would be stupid if he did tell me anything damaging to himself, and I don't think Joe is by any means stupid. He is very crafty. I suppose the best thing I can do is tell him that the interview is not for the business but for a class report. Maybe then he will cooperate. I hope so. I also want to show my professor how adept I am at Rogers' technique. If the interview flops, I won't be completely to blame because I can point out the relationship between Joe and myself. Besides I'm really not interested in using Rogers' technique to interview strangers. I want to use it as a business tool to gather information that the company can use. It is certainly worth a try."

WHAT JOE THOUGHT

"Well, when Mr. Sampson's son asks for an interview, I don't suppose one can refuse. He says he doesn't care what we talk about, but I think he wants to talk about business. He is young so maybe he can absorb some of the ideas I think are important. If I can get him to see some of my problems maybe I can do myself some good. Yes, this gives me an opportunity to sell something and I don't mind letting him know that.

"I do have to be careful about what I say or it might get back to the factory. Even if he claims this is a school project, I know it will carry over into the business. I'll even let him know how tough competition is around here, so they know I'm doing a good job. If we aren't getting enough business, it's not my fault but the factory's because of their backward pricing policies. The factory doesn't seem to pay attention to my complaints about these policies, so maybe I can get in through the back door—persuade the boss's son. I'll make a lot more money for my family if I can get that across. Yes, maybe this interview is an opportunity rather than an obligation."

In spite of the failure to master the Rogerian technique, I believe that Joe did tell me some things I hadn't known before and also that I told myself some things I didn't fully realize.

First, I am not a very good liar. In S 8 after Joe had mentioned that he gets "hammered from both sides," I proceeded to relate this directly to Sampson Brothers which was *my* real interest in spite of my plan to let Joe choose the subject. Rather than specifically direct this to the company, I should have related Joe's statement to his job with a repetition of "hammered from both sides?" Joe, of course, realized that my interest in him was really narrower and took the opportunity in J 8 to promote himself by responding the company is "my fundamental duty."

Similarly, in J 9 Joe stopped and asked "Now, what more would you like?" which I interpret to be "How else may I please you, boss's son?" I lied that we got into some "interesting areas" in S 10. Perhaps at that point I should have paraphrased his discount argument and suggested that we cease talking about discounts. Fortunately, Joe started to open up somewhat in J 10 and discussed his concept of the job and how others view him. This soon evolved into a new sales pitch on his commissions, travelling expenses, and trade following.

Throughout the interview Joe hesitated to state criticism of the factory directly. The following excerpts suggest the various devices he used to express his awareness of a situation and indirectly communicate that awareness:

JOE 1: "I don't go against the factory except. . . ." [Joe then proceeded to tell why he did go against the factory.]

JOE 3: "In fact, some buyers called the company screwballs—they won't bend, they won't give." [This company seems to bear a close analogy to the problems Joe sees in his relationship with Sampson Brothers.]

JOE 5: "With no reflection on the policies of Sampson Brothers, you will recognize . . ." [Then Joe made an observation which was a reflection on the company's policies.]

JOE 16: "I don't fool with it [gifts]—never have." [Yet, Joe has just finished stating that he does give some gifts although he doesn't like to.]

Thus, when Joe was stating things that could get him into trouble, he felt a need to defend himself. Some of this, such as J 16, may have been to protect his own self-image, but most of the defense was aimed at the relationship structure between the interviewer and interviewee.

I think Joe also told me that he was somewhat insecure. He felt that he was not really competitive and his competition is pretty good. He wants the factory to know that he is a good salesman and if he isn't selling enough it is because of the company's policies. Therefore, he is entitled to the line. He also expressed doubt about future management in Sampson Brothers and "how much further they can go" with the Fielden's machine tool companies in J 5 and J 13. Joe realizes that the Fieldens have spent forty years building up integrity with jobbers and now these jobbers have become "prostitutes" who have no loyalty except to the dollar. He feels that times have changed and he has not been able to change with them rapidly enough. His failure to change is due to the factories partially. Yet, he subtly acknowledges that perhaps he, too, was slow to change, as in J 9 when he was "afraid of the repercussions" of a new policy that became successful. Indirectly Joe mentions his own conservative ways in J 6, J 8, J 11, and J 15 where the words "I have to feel my way, I have to be very careful, I must be very judicious" emerge. In J 6 especially an ambivalence is revealed when Joe says, "I have to wheel and deal. I have to feel my way along." Perhaps the best question of the interviewer was in S 7, "Wheel and deal?" Joe explained in effect that he really didn't want to wheel and deal at all.

In short Joe seemed to be basically satisfied with being conservative and working with a conservative company. As a salesman he felt he must sell and try to better what he was. His observation that "everybody is a salesman" seemed to justify his sales pitch, which formed the bulk of the interview.

Joe ended the interview by looking at his watch and commenting with a laugh, "The problem is to find a good buyer at the right price." The interviewer accepted Joe's gesture and suggested that it was lunch time.

Joe Fielden, salesman (C)

The preceding—Joe Fielden, Salesman (A) and (B)—was submitted as a required report in a graduate course on interpersonal relationships, for which the assignment was to conduct, reproduce, and analyze an interview for the purpose of understanding another person from the other person's point of view.

When the report was returned to the student, attached to it were extensive comments written by the research assistant and the instructor in the course. The final comment of the research assistant was as follows:

> I'm sorry about my critical comments, but you have *completely* covered poor Joe in sandpaper—from head to toe. You've examined him almost exclusively as a profit-builder for yourself. The report is shot through with judgments from *your* point of view, with regard to *your* interests.
>
> "What Joe Thought" is what you *think* he thought—there is very little analysis of his statements—although they are very rich in material—especially in the last two pages of the interview.
>
> He makes some very feeling and (to me) most moving remarks, yet you see him only through a filter of dollar signs. I'm not saying that using

this man to help your company is illegitimate. I *am* saying that you cannot *understand* him unless you *understand your own need* to use him, and how this is distorting your view of him. He is a *whole, unique person*—and you've reduced him to "an information source to help me in my Sampson Brothers career." Unless you learn to *suspend* these needs *until* you've gained an understanding you'll never see anything except your own reflection.

To this comment the instructor in the course appended the following note:

> This is pretty harsh criticism—your reader's feelings are showing and he may be distorting what you were really trying to do. But try to understand why both of us get the impression that you are not really interested in *Joe as a person.*

After the report, with these comments attached, had been returned, the student who wrote it made an appointment with the instructor. He wanted to discuss his reactions at some length.

CASE III–4. *Ashok Rajguru*

In October 1962, Donald French, a graduate student in clinical psychology at the University of Chicago, interviewed his friend, Ashok Rajguru, a doctoral candidate in theoretical physics at Northwestern University.

Ashok Rajguru had lived in Calcutta, India, until 1960, when he had received a fellowship to continue his studies in physics at Northwestern. By the fall of 1962 Ashok had completed all the requirements for the Ph.D., except for a thesis in which he hoped to make an original contribution to quantum electrodynamics. He had not been home since first coming to this country.

Donald and Ashok had first met in June 1962 as the only summer employees at an electronics company in California. They had decided to room together, and during the summer developed an affable relationship without ever becoming close friends. They had frequently talked about such topics as politics, literature, and economics, but had found that their social and recreational interests were quite different.

The interview was arranged by telephone one day in advance. Donald told Ashok that he wanted to practice understanding another person's point of view. Donald explained that this was part of a course at the University of Chicago, and that he would be graded on his ability to understand how someone else felt about things. Ashok readily agreed to help, without any apparent concern over whether his identity or the interview would be kept confidential.

On the day of the interview Donald drove out to Evanston, had lunch with Ashok, and brought him back to Chicago. After a one-hour tour of the campus, and some conversation about life at Chicago, Donald invited Ashok over to Donald's room for the interview. No one else was present. Donald set up a borrowed tape recorder in the middle of the room, explaining that he wanted to listen to the discussion again so as to improve his understanding and technique. The recorder did not appear to bother Ashok, and Donald felt that the general atmosphere was one of relaxation and mutual confidence.

DONALD 1: Well, as I explained before, the object is not to talk about something that interests me, but rather to talk about something that is on your mind currently.

ASHOK 1: I guess I have to start somewhere!

DONALD 2: Well, what have you been thinking about lately? Is there anything particularly bothering you? (Long pause.) It doesn't have to be anything very profound. Just the kinds of things you have been thinking about; how the world is impressing you.

ASHOK 2: Well the trouble is that everything I think about nowadays is connected either with physics or politics. (Pause.) But I don't really want to talk about that.

DONALD 3: You feel you don't want to talk about physics or politics?

ASHOK 3: Well there's really no reason I shouldn't want to talk about physics, but I don't know whether that would be something of interest to you. I don't mean something technical in physics, I mean things like what you can or can not do in physics, how far you can go, whether it is really worthwhile to be interested in this one thing to the extent that you have to forget everything else, and whether it is really worth it.

DONALD 4: Are you having some doubts about your real future in physics?

ASHOK 4: Yeah! I really don't know if it is worth being—it's quite clear that if you want to do something really worthwhile and creative, not merely in physics but in any field, then you have to think only of the field to the exclusion of everything else. And this somehow seems to me to be too great a price to pay.

DONALD 5: You feel like it would be too confining?

ASHOK 5: Yes. There are just too many things in this world which one should bother about, which are interesting, to which one should pay some attention, that it isn't worthwhile to exclude everything for just one thing. I have very serious doubts as to whether it is worth it. And yet, these doubts are compounded with other doubts—such thoughts probably arise because I have done nothing significantly creative and such doubts would probably no longer be there if I were to prove myself capable in any significant way.

DONALD 6: Uh huh.

ASHOK 6: So it's probably more basically a question of my capabilities in the field.

DONALD 7: You are wondering about your ability to do something significant?

ASHOK 7: Yes, significant!

DONALD 8: And you feel like you want to do something significant.

ASHOK 8: Yes. And yet it seems that, given the capabilities that I seem to have, and to do anything significant I would have to put in much too much effort—to the exclusion of everything else.

DONALD 9: You don't feel it's possible to make contributions in physics without dedicating most of your time to it.

ASHOK 9: Yes, I think it's pretty impossible. You can not do anything significant with a peripheral attachment. I think I'm pretty much convinced of it. And I . . . (pause).

DONALD 10: Somehow you are hanging back.

ASHOK 10: That's right. And it's very serious because I'm at a stage where hanging back can be absolutely fatal and I have more or less—one decides on a career long before one goes into a Ph.D. program—that is, when one decides to go into graduate school—and at this late stage of graduate school, to have such doubts when

I should be putting in all the effort that I can—this can be pretty fatal. So, it's very disturbing. I don't work as much as I should. When I do work I have my mind half on other things. Not necessarily personal things, but things that it seems very important and relevant that I should know, things like economics and politics and modern novels. (Pause.)

DONALD 11: These things seem to be diverting your attention away from physics.

ASHOK 11: Right!

DONALD 12: And you feel sort of guilty about that?

ASHOK 12: I feel very guilty about that—I mean—I go into the library and read all sorts of other things and I feel very guilty about it afterwards. And this is creating a hell of a problem for me. I just don't know what I'm going to do about it. And it's all the more painful because, after all, I've come here from another country with a specific purpose. I gave up a set of privileges which were open to me at home, I borrowed money, I came over, and made a very definite commitment.

DONALD 13: Ah yes, I see.

ASHOK 13: A very definite commitment. If I were at home at this stage I would be much freer to choose what I wanted to do. I could conceivably give this up and go into something else, but now I've more or less burned my boats—I mean my bridges—and it's very disturbing.

DONALD 14: So the thing has some family implications as well as professional?

ASHOK 14: Yes, that has some significance. I mean part of the force which compels me to keep doing what I am is the notion that if I should at any time make a very drastic change in my career—at this stage—I would be disappointing a lot of people in the family. Not because they are very bent on seeing me as a physicist but because they won't be very happy about the waste of time.

DONALD 15: You feel like they contributed something to your being able to come here and that you would sort of be letting them down to cast it aside.

ASHOK 15: Ah yes, but in a somewhat different sense. That is to say, they have contributed to my coming here only to the extent that they were willing to make certain emotional sacrifices. For instance, it is very conventional in an Indian family that if the father should die, the mother should stay with one of the sons. It is just taken for granted, there is no question about it. And when I came away here it was pretty clear that I was shirking that part of my responsibility. Clearly my mother couldn't stay with me if such circumstances should arise. And my being willing to take this advantage and my mother being willing to let me off—she couldn't actually hold me in any sense, I mean I was grown up—but her willingness to let me come reflected on her part a willingness to let me do whatever I should want to do. And if having taken this opportunity to do what I want to do, I then at a late stage decide, no—it's all a waste of time and I really didn't want to do this or I'm changing my mind, it's being capricious in a fashion which is asking too much of the other people who have made sacrifices in allowing me to do what I should want to do.

DONALD 16: So in a way, as I see it, you feel you are sort of temporarily shirking some of your responsibilities; and that this will be all right if you are able to do something successful with the time you have taken.

ASHOK 16: Right! And it would not be so good if I should have nothing to show for all this time. And I really have nothing to show, but that's probably not too relevant because at this stage probably not too many people do. But quite apart from that, in going to courses and learning what I have to learn, I have by no means devoted as much attention and got as much out of being here as I could have if I were very sincere and serious. And this seems to be such a vast waste of my capabilities, of my time, of the fellowship I'm drawing on, it's a waste of everything. (Pause.) And I feel very guilty about it. Not merely guilty about not using my capabilities but guilty about defrauding others who are making sacrifices. Someone is giving me a fellowship so that I don't have to teach and I should, therefore, study all the time.

DONALD 17: You feel that maybe someone else should have been given this opportunity who would hurl himself into it?

ASHOK 17: Yes, someone who would get much more out of it. (Pause.) It's very bad. (Pause.) It gives you very serious feelings of guilt. It's not that I haven't worked at all. That's not it. But if I look back at the kind of work I used to do at home—by the kind of work I mean the amount of time I would have put into serious work—it's clear that in my two years here I could have done much much more. That is beyond question.

DONALD 18: I see. So you really feel like there are a lot of capabilities there that you are not measuring up to?

ASHOK 18: Yes. A lot of—ah—not merely capabilities but a lot of just sheer hard work. I mean you can't do any creative work without a lot of hard work. I'm just sort of learning this and that in a peripheral way. (Pause.) This is a very big question. I feel that I've come over here at this very important period in my life and it's just being wasted. This is extremely undesirable. Now that I am here I don't know what I can do about it, apart of course from telling myself that I have to work hard—and this and that. But you can tell yourself and yet, if certain things don't work out, what can you do? Something has to be done about it.

DONALD 19: So you are fairly certain at this point that you are going to see this thing through?

ASHOK 19: Yes, if for nothing else but the fact that I am sort of trapped physically. And being trapped physically I have to make the best of it. I mean I'm certainly not at that stage of despair where people sort of throw everything to the winds. Neither am I at that state of despair nor can I give myself up to such a state. That would be accepting defeat and I'm not willing to. But what makes me sad is that I'm making the best of a bad bargain whereas this could have been such a good bargain. (Pause.) I think back as to what my picture of myself here was when I was at home—you know—you project yourself forward and you think about what you'll be doing when you get there—and . . . (pause).

DONALD 20: It hasn't measured up to your expectations.

ASHOK 20: No, it hasn't measured up at all. I compare my projections with the realities of the past two years and there is so much lacking—much too much lacking.

DONALD 21: I gather from what you were saying before that you might leave if you were not constrained by all sorts of forces like being here, your scholarship, and so on.

ASHOK 21: Yeah! I think if I were in a similar situation at home I very possibly would leave the university for a number of years. Having a Master's I could just go and teach for a while, forgetting about a Ph.D. I very possibly would have done that. And then at the end of two or three years I possibly would have realized that my interest in the subject wasn't totally dead, rather that it was a combination of circumstances which had covered it up somehow. (Pause.) And another thing which keeps bothering me is the lack of motivation. You know—when you are at school—people by and large have a desire to excel. They are in a group and they naturally want to stand out in the class, and this function with me is just as normal as anything else. I used to pay a lot of attention to it but . . . (pause).

DONALD 22: You used to be motivated but you are not now.

ASHOK 22: Now when I go to a class and have to take an exam—it just does not bother me if I am fourth in a class of seven. Whereas previously I remember—of course there were different circumstances—that if the difference between me and the second boy in the class was even close, it would keep me awake at night. And now this just doesn't bother me at all. Of course at this stage it is silly to even think in those terms. But even so, that's an important element in motivation. People around you are working or getting ahead—and learning a lot—and you want to know as much as they do. If possible, you want to know a little more. Basically, very simply, that's just ego. But nowadays that just doesn't work. I've given that up totally. Here is someone working very hard, I just say he is working hard but I'm not. So what? (Laughs.)

DONALD 23: You don't feel any competitive motivation.

ASHOK 23: Right! That has vanished absolutely. It was there very strongly till the last days when I took my Master's exam [in India]. It meant so much to me that I could come first in my Master's exam. It was one of the strongest boosts I've ever had in my life. I worked like mad for six months. I was sick, very seriously, but that didn't matter.

DONALD 24: And you were successful.

ASHOK 24: Oh, yes! All through my school and college career there has only been one exam in which another boy beat me. This was always one of the strongest elements in my motivation. I couldn't possibly sit in a class in which other people were doing better than I—any better at all. This idea was very repugnant to me. And yet I come here and give that up totally! And yet it's quite clear to me that with a moderate amount of hard work I can definitely be as good as the students I'm with now, if not a little better. It's not that there is a huge gap between them and me, I don't feel that at all.

DONALD 25: So by asserting yourself in the past, you could excel; and you still could, but for some reason you just aren't doing it.

ASHOK 25: Right. There was one course in which I did somehow assert myself. It became important for me to do well and I did. There were thirteen or fourteen people in the class, and I got either the highest or second highest mark. I don't know for what reason I did this. I think it was perhaps that I valued that one professor very much.

DONALD 26: So you still can excel if it matters.

ASHOK 26: Right; if it matters. And somehow it has ceased to matter.

DONALD 27: Somehow, beating the other guys doesn't matter any more.

ASHOK 27: It doesn't matter. And having lost this motivation I seem to have lost all motivation.

DONALD 28: I see.

ASHOK 28: Previously it was not only that I should have to beat the other guys; in the process it was also very important that I should know just for the sake of knowing. One of the strongest elements in motivation was that I should excel, but apart from that there were other relatively minor ones—that I should know, since there were so many things to be known—I couldn't be ignorant. But now having lost the motivation to excel, I seem to have lost the other ones too. It no longer is very important to me that I don't know all the details of quantum electrodynamics.

DONALD 29: Knowing for the sake of knowing has gone too.

ASHOK 29: It has gone too. And this, more than the motivation to excel, is what bothers me. This is much more important, and this is what bothers me. I open a book in physics and read five pages and find it tough going, so I just leave it.

DONALD 30: You feel that loss of the desire to know for the sake of knowing is a more serious loss.

ASHOK 30: Oh I think so. I have no illusions as to the extent of my capabilities in physics. I realized long ago that I'm not going to be one of the very top. But to be even a moderately competent physicist, you have to know. If you are very good then you make very good use of what you know, but even if you are going to be a moderately competent physicist, you have got to know. You have to have the desire to know. And if you don't have that, then you might as well go and be a clerk. I mean some place where you just do routine work; where there is no question of knowing, no question of finding out, no inquiry, no interest in what you are working at.

DONALD 31: There is a kind of feeling of despair at not being readily able to be the best physicist in the country.

ASHOK 31: Yeah! It is very difficult to know which came first: the realization that I was not going to be a Heisenberg or the realization that I just wasn't as interested in these things as I used to be. I think the other one came first, that is, I realized earlier what my limitations as a physicist were. That is, I realized what was the highest class to which I could aspire. And since then it has been— it's very difficult to say what the reasons could be.

DONALD 32: You sort of gave your all in competing with the others and went as far as you could go, as far as you felt your capabilities could carry you.

ASHOK 32: Well, yes and no. (Reluctantly.) I took my capabilities as far as they could go in exams and competing with the others, but I realize that I could take them much further in terms of being a physicist rather than in terms of excelling in exams. And it is this part which I'm not fulfilling. I have fulfilled my part in terms of taking exams and that kind of thing. I'm not fulfilling what I realize are my capabilities in being a physicist. That is, in doing some good original work.

DONALD 33: I see. You feel like you did your part as a student, but now you are sort of falling down in applying it to the profession.

ASHOK 33: Right. I did my part very well as a student, but I'm doing practically nothing to make myself into a competent physicist, beyond what is required of me as a student.

DONALD 34: So you are finding the conversion from student to physicist a painful and difficult one.

ASHOK 34: Yes, and yet these things merge so much into one another that I don't know whether I would put it in those terms. Because you continue being a student pretty late, even after your doctorate. When you are a young postdoctoral fellow you are still really a student. Young postdoctorals even have their offices with the graduate students. (Laughs.) So this business of growing from a student to a physicist is a slow and gradual process. It isn't as though there was an abrupt jump that I'm having trouble adjusting to. It's a very slow and gradual process in which a person normally should have no difficulty because he really doesn't realize himself when he has ceased to be a student and when he has become a physicist.

DONALD 35: Uh huh.

ASHOK 35: And I'm still conscious of the fact that I am a student. That is, I'm still in the process where I have more learning and less original work to do, at least for a limited period, rather than less learning and more sheer work to do. I've a lot of learning yet to do. (Pause.)

DONALD 36: So you are not sure that it is the conversion from student to physicist which is bothering you.

ASHOK 36: No, I think that it is something even more fundamental. It has to do with things like this. You have only one life to live. What is important and relevant in that life?

DONALD 37: It's more a hesitancy to commit yourself entirely to physics.

ASHOK 37: Right. (Pause.) It probably isn't that important that I should do something creative in physics. Somehow that shouldn't be and isn't an essential ingredient in my making myself happy. It is much more important that I should be happy in quite a variety of other things. Physics just isn't as important as it used to be.

DONALD 38: So you feel like there is a wider spectrum of interests that is becoming important to you.

ASHOK 38: Yes. There was a time for example when I used to think that it didn't matter at all if in the process of coming over here— in the process of pursuing physics—the family should be hurt. There was a time when I used to think that it was perfectly all right if I went ahead. Those drags from the family should not be a factor at all. But I have ceased to think in those terms! I have come to the state where I think that human relations are much more important than I used to think even two years ago.

DONALD 39: Uh huh.

ASHOK 39: And I think basically that it is this lack of fulfillment in human relations that is at the root of all this hesitancy. If I could find satisfaction in human relations, which are more important to me than they were two years ago, then that might revive my interest in things.

DONALD 40: I see.

ASHOK 40: I mean that this is my estimate of what the situation is. I have no real idea as to whether this is correct. And this is why I have the feeling that if I were at home, just because I'm so close to the family and all that, I wouldn't have felt this lack in human relations which I do feel.

DONALD 41: I see.

ASHOK 41: And that is what at home partly contributed to my serious interest in the subject. I didn't realize at that stage how much these things [human relationships] meant to me. I took them for granted because they were there and, therefore, I could be totally immersed in physics. Now I feel their lack. I realize how important they were to me, and since I can't now find fulfillment, I lack interest in other things too.

DONALD 42: I see. You feel that at home you had satisfying family and friend relationships and that this whet your appetite for life, for physics, for everything.

ASHOK 42: Right. Right. Exactly. It was important to me that I should learn not merely because I had to learn but because I could talk about it to my friends, because they would be interested in what I was learning, and it would raise me in their esteem. This is all a feedback process and the feedback circuit is now absent. (Laughs.) Essentially, I have to work now in a personal vacuum, and with the absence of the feedback it seems impossible to work up the interest that I need to. I realize more and more how important that [supportive feedback and satisfying human relationships] was, and that is why basically I have this feeling of despair because I don't see how I can radically alter the situation, given the circumstances that I have here. I have to make the best of what I have here. But it seems to me that the best I can make of the circumstances here may not turn out to be good enough. And that is where my basic hesitancy and fear arises.

DONALD 43: So flinging yourself into physics would not permit you to satisfy this need for rich human relationships.

ASHOK 43: Rather, put it the other way around. The absence of rich human relationships makes it impossible for me to fling myself!

DONALD 44: Ah! Now I understand.

ASHOK 44: And I don't see how I can correct the situation with regard to human relationships so radically here.

DONALD 45: Particularly here as opposed to home.

ASHOK 45: Yes. And this inability to correct human relationships won't permit me to devote the amount of attention to physics that I would want to.

DONALD 46: Because here there are some barriers to satisfying human relationships.

ASHOK 46: Yes. The strongest of the barriers is the absence of family ties. I mean ordinarily you anchor yourself to your home and then move out. And now I don't have the anchor so I don't move out and it all ends in a vacuum. I live by myself. Oh, of course I have casual friends, fellows in the department, but they are not of sufficient depth to assure me of happy human relationships.

DONALD 47: So the lack of the strong secure family ties in this country, here and now, is hurting your application to your work.

ASHOK 47: Yes, that is what I think. Of course, I could be very wrong. But that is what my analysis of the situation is. And if it is correct, then it seems to me to be pretty hopeless. That is why I have been thinking of a course of action which seems to me to be the best I could do. That is, there is one language exam I have to take and there is one advanced exam one has to take while working on the thesis in the specific field in which you are working; so I've been thinking of finishing the advanced exam, finishing the language exam I have to take, and then getting permission from here to go back home. I wouldn't have the direct contact with the professors here, but I have enough confidence in myself that, given some application, the aid of the professors at home, and some correspondence with the professors here, I could turn out a thesis that they would accept here. So I've sort of been toying with that idea for a while. I would finish the requirements here and then go home. I would be left with an unfinished oral exam at the end of the thesis, but that could be worked out somehow. I don't feel like submitting myself to this void long enough so that whatever lingering interest I have in the subject would die down. It might die down to the extent that you just can't rekindle it. I don't want that to happen and I have to do something before that.

DONALD 48: You are afraid that you might destroy your interest in physics permanently.

ASHOK 48: Yes permanently, because of this peculiar set of circumstances.

DONALD 49: And you think that would be a bad thing to have happen.

ASHOK 49: Yes that would be very bad because so much of my respect for myself is related to my capabilities in physics. If I should just throw in the sponge, that would very seriously hurt my esteem of myself. I couldn't do it! Well, probably if I were forced I would do it, but I wouldn't want to do it. It would be too much of a personal psychological disaster. I wouldn't want to do that at all. Of course, I've been toying with that idea. (Pause.) Hopefully, if I could somehow get going, but I don't see how I could do it, then I wouldn't have to take recourse to such a drastic step. But, if I were forced to, then I certainly would. Because I would be much more willing to take the step than to allow my interest in physics to die down totally.

DONALD 50: Uh huh. Then you don't want to let your interest in physics wane because this would damage your self-respect and that would have a detrimental effect on your whole life.

ASHOK 50: Yes, a very detrimental effect. There was a stage when I used to think that creativity was the only thing a man could live for. I have given up such a drastic view of things. I used to think that nothing else mattered. I have given up such a drastic view, but I still do place a pretty large premium on creativity. If my life were to be lived without any element of creativity, I don't think that I could make it a worthwhile life. I wouldn't have enough respect for that kind of life.

DONALD 51: So your feeling about yourself is that it is still very important to you to create.

ASHOK 51: Very important.

DONALD 52: And yet there are other things which are important too, in particular, worthwhile human relationships.

ASHOK 52: Right. And I'm realizing how much the presence or absence of these relationships interacts with creativity.

DONALD 53: You can't separate them.

ASHOK 53: You can't separate one from the other. This is something which I never realized before coming to this country, just because my need for human relationships was satisfied. And I'm beginning to see how closely they are interrelated. You can't have one without the other. You could probably have satisfying human relationships without creativity but not the other way around, at least not for me. I've known physicists who don't care if their wives divorce them, and it happens once in awhile, but I don't think that I could be that way.

DONALD 54: So you feel a need for a kind of total existence.

ASHOK 54: Right!

DONALD 55: One that is rewarding on all fronts and you can't sacrifice one for excellence in the other.

ASHOK 55: And the worst part of the present situation is that the absence of one leads to the absence of the other, so that I'm in a state of total absence. (Laughs.) And yet I feel trapped. The way of doing away with this situation seems as though it should be so simple. One should have satisfying relationships, this should allow one to work, and it all should be so simple. And yet I'm in physical circumstances such that I can't put this to the test; I can't make it work.

DONALD 56: Uh huh. So you feel that even though you have some insight into the problem, the circumstances won't let you do anything about it.

ASHOK 56: That is right. (Pause.) So the problem has now resolved itself to the point that, given the fact that the circumstances won't allow me to get the best solution, I'm wondering what is the next best thing that I can do. I should be man enough to acknowledge the fact that I have to put up with something which is not the ideal solution and make the best of it. But that takes quite awhile. It is a very difficult thing to do.

DONALD 57: It isn't a fully satisfying way out.

ASHOK 57: No. And this period in one's life could be so productive, it could be so satisfying. Here I am on the verge of doing creative work, at the end of the learning process, maturing from a student and adolescent into a man, and this could be such a satisfying and full period in one's life, and yet I'm living in a total vacuum. This is very unsatisfying.

DONALD 58: You sort of compare the reality with the potential and see a lot lacking.

ASHOK 58: Right. You compare what it could have been and what it is and there is too much lacking. Far too much!

DONALD 59: I can certainly understand that.

ASHOK 59: But I have to make a go of it. (Pause.) I have to work enough to get a decent thesis out, to learn enough to write a good thesis, and to do it fast enough so that my work will be one step ahead of the decay process. (Laughs.)

DONALD 60: Your self-respect demands that you find some way out.

ASHOK 60: Right. And my self-respect also demands that I find some way out myself. I should not have to go and seek help from other people. You know, when I talk to one or two other boys about this they say, "Your problem is psychological and you should go and see the psychological counselor." It could be psychological, but an element of my self-respect is that I should solve my problems myself. And it seems to me that I see with a fair degree of clarity just what my problems are. Half the solution to any problem lies in seeing what it is.

DONALD 61: So it's not really a question of whether he could help you or not, it's more a question of—you feel like you should be able to solve your problems yourself.

ASHOK 61: Right. And there never has been a situation in the past in which I couldn't solve my own problems, no matter what they were. So I'm not willing to accept defeat on that count.

DONALD 62: So you don't really feel like you are beaten yet.

ASHOK 62: No, certainly not! I feel that I'm down but I feel that I'll be up. (Laughs.) No, I certainly don't feel beaten at all. But I do realize that doing nothing about it for a sufficiently long time could take me to a state where I was effectively beaten because I couldn't drag myself up. But I haven't reached that state. (Pause.) I feel reasonably confident that I can drag myself up, I don't know how but . . . (pause).

DONALD 63: So you feel that at this stage of the problem, something constructive can be done, but that maybe, if you let it go on and on, it would get out of hand.

ASHOK 63: Right! Right! And I even feel that at this stage, something constructive could be done by myself alone. But I'll be damned if I know what it is. (Laughs.) There is just that vague feeling of confidence in yourself, which sometimes turns out to be wrong. You know, you always tell yourself, "Heck, I've pulled myself out of ruts before and I'll do it again." But every once in a while it doesn't happen that way, people don't pull themselves out. I only hope that I can do it but . . . (pause) I'll be damned if I know what I can do.

DONALD 64: So behind the problem you still feel adequate to deal with it but just what the solution is, you don't know yet.

ASHOK 64: Basically yes. And I don't know just what the basis of this confidence is. If someone were to ask me, "Why do you feel confident," I wouldn't be able to give an answer. I have been told by people who have known me that, from the outside, I do look self-contained, a more or less confident individual. But of course, inside one is never the way he seems to another person. Knowing yourself from the inside you are never as sure of yourself as an outsider can be. In spite of that, I feel sure of myself to a certain extent. So there is no reason that I can offer for this confidence, having known myself from the inside with all the uncertainties that I have. An outsider who has known me for a while would say, "Well of course you'll pull through, you're a more or less balanced individual, of course you'll pull yourself through." But from the inside of course, I'm not a balanced individual. No one is, if one goes deep enough. So I've no reasons to offer as to why I should feel confident except for the fact that life has gone on in such a way that nothing catastrophic has happened so far. Things seem to have worked out just right. Otherwise I can see no reason why I should feel as confident as I do.

DONALD 65: So you sort of feel that you are not as adequate to solve this thing as other people think you are, and yet you still feel that you are adequate.

ASHOK 65: Yes. I mean that other people are not willing to recognize that I do have a problem. People in the department at Northwestern, who know me fairly well, are unwilling to admit that I could have a problem—that I could be struggling this way with myself. They feel that I haven't worked hard enough in the past six months, but that this kind of thing often happens and that I'm really all right.

DONALD 66: It's sort of puzzling to you that they can't even see the war going on inside of you when it is so important.

ASHOK 66: Right. Well, I can see why that should be so. I try very strongly not to reveal too much of my interior to other people, to sort of preserve an exterior, a very conscious sort of hypocrisy. It is hypocrisy, but it is conscious, and I would acknowledge that, so it ceases to be a crime. So I can understand why people wouldn't see the thing either as existing or as being important.

DONALD 67: So maybe your self-respect sort of demands that you not show too much of what is going on inside.

ASHOK 67: Right. I think that is a very important element in my behavior. If I have problems, I feel that I should keep them to myself. I shouldn't have to go around to people and tell them that these are my problems and ask them what to do about them. And people shouldn't come to me and say, "Jesus, man, you look like a cat with a lot of problems." (Laughs.) That is something which I certainly can't stand.

DONALD 68: You wouldn't want that to happen.

ASHOK 68: I certainly wouldn't want that to happen.

DONALD 69: So you don't let them see.

ASHOK 69: Yeah! And apparently I do that well enough so that they just can't see that or believe it. They don't believe that it exists. I myself have to do something about it. And I recognize what the problems are and have to do something about them.

DONALD 70: So you feel that at least in your own mind you have made some progress in defining the problem.

ASHOK 70: Right. I think that at the end of last term I was at the stage where I didn't even know what was wrong. I was off the mark to the extent that I thought that getting away from Northwestern would be very important. You know, getting a job out someplace else. Well it was important in a very minor sense. A change of surroundings always helps. But I was foolish to think that could be important enough by itself. Toward the end of the summer and the beginning of this term it became clear that this wasn't as important as I had thought it was. So I have overcome the total ignorance of thinking that getting away from Northwestern was the solution.

DONALD 71: You tried one solution and you realize now that that wasn't the way.

ASHOK 71: Yes. That had pretty much no relevance at all. (Long pause.)

DONALD 72: So now the question in your mind is what next.

ASHOK 72: Yeah! (Pause.) Here I just don't know. (Long pause.)

DONALD 73: And yet underneath it all you feel like somehow or other you are going to work this thing out.

ASHOK 73: Right. There is a vague notion that somehow I'm going to work it out. But it is the vaguest of notions. Somehow I can't picture myself going to the dogs. I'll do something. (Laughs.) I just can't be stupid enough to allow that to happen.

DONALD 74: So in a way, this self-respect which contributes to the problem by kind of locking up your feelings inside, is also the same force which is going to work things out.

ASHOK 74: Yes, hopefully. Right. Probably a person without this feeling would have been tempted to give up at an earlier stage. A person without this feeling of confidence in himself would have been tempted to say, I'm not capable of solving this or, I must go to a third person, or I'm going to do something very drastic about it, or—I don't know. In general he might decide that he himself could not solve it. But, you are right, the very element of keeping up appearances which contributes to the problem by locking things in myself is the same element which contributes to my self-confidence. Of course, it is silly to think that self-confidence alone could pull me through because there are clear circumstances which are creating the problem. And something will have to be done about the circumstances.

DONALD 75: Uh huh. There are external forces acting on you that are contributing to this thing also.

ASHOK 75: Right. And I have to do something about them. So the problem is really deciding what I want to do about them. Then I must force myself to go through with it.

DONALD 76: So you are beginning to feel that the problem is one of adapting yourself to these external forces.

ASHOK 76: Right. Right. I must tell myself, "Look, the circumstances are such that, beyond minor alterations here and there, you can't basically alter the circumstances in which you find yourself. Therefore, rather than try to adapt the circumstances to you, now try to adapt yourself to the circumstances." This is what I have not done in these two years. I have continued to be the same individual I was when I came here. The difference in the circumstances coupled with the continuity of my "being" has caused all these difficulties. Now I realize that I can't change the circumstances—I have to do something about changing myself—at least my reaction to the circumstances. I have come to the definite realization that, "You've tried for two years and beyond such and such you cannot alter the circumstances." I cannot hope for, ask for, or expect very deep human attachments here. This is a fact I have to accept. This is a fact I did not accept in these two years. And you know, because I didn't have these attachments, I have been unhappy and this and that. But now I tell myself, "You've tried for two years, you haven't found it, you aren't going to find it. And you must somehow adapt yourself to work in these circumstances in which there will be a lack of human attachment. And you have to live with the circumstances and alter yourself, rather than alter the circumstances." But this is a pretty difficult thing to do. I'm twenty-three. I was twenty-one when I came here, and I'm pretty grown up by this time, so its difficult to change.

DONALD 77: You feel that you have reached an age and level of maturity at which it is difficult to make an alteration.

ASHOK 77: Right. I have a more or less full grown set of values. I don't feel that I have to alter those values basically but I have to adjust them to new circumstances and it is quite difficult. Very difficult, but I have to do it, and I feel vaguely confident. Of course, part of this is coupled with the fact that I like the kind of attachments I have tried to form and failed to form. I place a great premium on such attachments.

DONALD 78: That is still a basic need.

ASHOK 78: Still a basic need. And therefore to tell yourself that you have to do without them, however temporarily, is still a very difficult thing to acknowledge and work on. But it has to be done, it has to be done. People in all sorts of circumstances do it and I will have to do it too. I feel it will take a long while but—

DONALD 79: So you kind of see the problem now as one of having come into a new environment with a personality structure which was well suited to the old environment, and now here you are transplanted to a new place with new forces working on you, and it is sort of necessary to adapt but also very difficult because the old values are deeply important.

ASHOK 79: Yes, deeply important. They are deeply ingrained but more important than that, they seem to me to be the right values. If I could somehow reason myself into their inadequacy, then I would be more ready to shed them.

DONALD 80: So it is a little puzzling as to why they are not here in this new environment.

ASHOK 80: Yeah! And I somehow have to adjust. (Long pause.) The difficulty has been that all these two years I haven't made any effort to change myself. None whatsoever, and that effort has to be made.

DONALD 81: If you don't make the effort the adjustment won't happen?

ASHOK 81: No, I'm certain that it won't happen. Just by looking at the past two years. Adjustments of the type I have to make don't happen by themselves, no, you have to make a conscious effort to do it. And I just haven't made the effort at all, because I thought that the kind of personality I had was the kind of personality I would continue to like having. It fitted in pretty well with the circumstances I lived in. It seemed to me to be a personality, no part of which I would like to shed. And yet here I am and some parts of my personality just aren't relevant and have to be shed. So it's a pretty difficult process.

DONALD 82: So life was very satisfying and you were an adequate personality at home.

ASHOK 82: Right. And I've ceased to be an adequate personality.

DONALD 83: Without changing at all.

ASHOK 83: Without changing at all. And in the back of my mind there is this thing which keeps telling me, "Oh, no! You are an adequate personality. The circumstances are wrong." And yet, at some stage I have to realize that I cannot alter the circumstances. Therefore, the definition of the word *adequate* has to change. An adequate personality is one which copes with circumstances. And what was adequate there just isn't adequate here. There is no point in hanging on to things which were suited to a different environment and aren't suited here. Take some simple things, for example. In the type of family in which I was brought up it was quite a virtue to be nonaggressive. By nonaggressive I don't mean anything physical. But in everyday life just to be sort of mildly self-effacing is considered to be quite a virtue.

DONALD 84: This is the way people should behave.

ASHOK 84: This is the way my father behaved. Therefore, this is the way I learned to behave. This is the way my mother has always told me is a nice way to behave. And it has always been very adequate. That is to say, I have missed nothing because of that. I have been allowed to be happy with that kind of a personality; but that doesn't work here. And yet in the back of my mind I keep telling myself, "There was nothing wrong with that, it was quite all right, you were a decent person then, why do you have to change?" And yet circumstances are different, so I have to change. That just isn't adequate enough.

DONALD 85: So you feel that one of the ways in which you have to change is to be a little more aggressive, the way people are here.

ASHOK 85: Yes. Specifically in connection with getting to know people. At home, even by being sort of mild and self-effacing, social factors worked in such a way that you still could know a lot of people. But here, unless circumstances throw you together in a special way, you do have to go out to meet people. You have to make the effort.

DONALD 86: You have to assert yourself.

ASHOK 86: You have to assert yourself! If you are in a group of people, you have to make your presence felt. Otherwise people just won't take note of you. People will take note of the person who is making the largest effort to make his presence felt. And yet I tell myself that it is crude and vulgar to make an effort to make your presence felt.

DONALD 87: Because that is the way it was at home.

ASHOK 87: Yes. At home it was considered crude and vulgar if you tried to put yourself forward. And that isn't adequate here. The result is that I know very few people apart from those I know by force of circumstances. I don't make the effort to know more people. I have been here for two years, I eat in those dining halls, I've been eating there every day for two years now, and yet with one or two exceptions I have never made an effort by sitting at a table where I didn't already know most of the people there. Not merely girls, but even boys. There are people whom I would like to know, who seem from a distance to be very nice people, but I just won't make the effort to go and sit down with them. They would be perfectly happy to have me there I am certain because— I have some confidence that I am not an obnoxious personality.

DONALD 88: And these people seem receptive from a distance.

ASHOK 88: Yes. And yet I won't go out and make the effort.

DONALD 89: You feel that this is one of the ways in which some kind of adaptation is needed.

ASHOK 89: Right. It is very necessary. There again, with regard to girls, at home it somehow happens that you don't have to go out to meet girls, you just come to know them. Your sister knows someone, or maybe there are two or three girls who live in the neighborhood and you get to know them, or your mother knows someone. You just happen to know a set of girls who are nice and whom you can go around with and talk with, without having to make the formal effort of going out and knowing girls. And you can be a very mild and nonaggressive person and yet know a lot of girls. Here it is just the other way around. If you don't make the effort, you are out. You are just out!

DONALD 90: Getting to know girls is one of the areas in which you have to be especially aggressive.

ASHOK 90: Right. There again, you tell yourself, "God, that's crude, you can't do that. (Laughs.) I mean, that's vulgar. How can you do it?" And yet it has to be done. It isn't crude and vulgar; it may have been crude and vulgar under a different set of circumstances, but here it is just the right thing. There are no absolute norms of crudity and vulgarity. It is just a question of what the norms of that particular social set are. By the norms of my social set at home, it might have been crude and vulgar, but it isn't here. I have to tell myself that since it isn't here, I have to act differently. (Long pause.) So it's a pretty difficult course of adaptation which should have started long ago but was deferred by the illusion that circumstances could be made to change—which is pretty absurd. It's obvious that an individual can't change circumstances. That's totally beyond his control. He can only change his reaction to them. That is, he can adapt himself. That is the only thing he can do. (Pause.) I guess the realization is coming rather late, after two years.

DONALD 91: So, in a way, you are understanding what needs to be done and yet it is a very painful thing to do.

ASHOK 91: Yes, very painful. (Long pause.)

DONALD 92: And the thing has become necessary because now it is affecting your work.

ASHOK 92: Right. It is necessary because now it is affecting the whole fabric of my future. That is totally dependent on my doing these things. (Pause.)

DONALD 92a: So it seems like the alternatives are—adapt in this environment and succeed, or return home and carry on with the physics where it is not necessary to adapt—and the latter is a very distasteful thing to do.

ASHOK 92b: Right. (Pause.) Because that would cause disappointments in people in the family and disappointments in myself. And in general, for any individual, acceptance of failure is not a very happy thing.

DONALD 93: So any particular path which you choose out of this dilemma involves some kind of pain.

ASHOK 93: Right. And it seems to me that the least painful way would be the one which involved my adapting myself. For the simple reason that, once I make the initial stages of adaptation, I can get a lot of pleasure from the altered circumstances which I am missing now. I have this vague feeling and—

DONALD 94: So you think that the avenue of adapting would be the more rewarding one in the long run.

ASHOK 94: Right. More rewarding and less painful. Quite frankly, not only will I be giving pleasure to myself, it's very possible that other people could find pleasure from my company.

DONALD 95: Uh huh. It's probably a reciprocal thing.

ASHOK 95: It is certainly true that I come from different circumstances, so there might be a variety of things others would be interested in, which they could find in me and not in other people around here.

DONALD 96: So you have some evidence that when you do begin to communicate with people, that there are certain things that they respond to.

ASHOK 96: Exactly. Even in this country, whenever I have formed any acquaintances beyond the casual it has never happened that I have not been rewarded. The first boy I got to know well enough here, this Irish boy who is no longer at Northwestern, but used to be, I got to know him very well—I got to know his family, I got to know his girl friend's family very well—and they all have reciprocated in a much fuller fashion than I expected when the friendship started out. So from the scattered instances I have gathered here, there is no reason I should fear not being rewarded —on the average—as I would like to be. There is no reason why it shouldn't work out that way.

DONALD 97: So you feel that breaking down the initial barrier is the main problem.

ASHOK 97: Yes. Because where circumstances have somehow broken the barrier down, rather than myself having broken the barriers down, I have always been rewarded.

DONALD 98: Then there seem to be strong forces that make it go.

ASHOK 98: Right. So if I could break the barriers down in other cases myself, where circumstances just don't happen to work the right way, or don't happen to do all the work for me—I'm sort of waiting for circumstances to do all my work for me. (Laughs.) That can't always happen—

DONALD 99: And to do it some other way is to be "aggressive."

ASHOK 99: Right. In all the cases where I have known someone relatively well it has happened because we were thrown together. This Irish boy, I got to know him quite well because we met on registration day and then later found out that we were supposed to be in the same office with no third person. We shared the same office for a full year. So, we were thrown together and it worked out very fine.

DONALD 100: Here was just a random person, circumstances broke down the barrier, and rewarding relationship ensued.

ASHOK 100: And he is the kind of person who selects his friends very carefully. And he is also the type of person whom other people don't take to very easily. He is a cranky sort of person, very individualistic, so he formed pretty much no other attachments, with one or two possible exceptions. Later, other people shared the office and new relationships didn't work out too well for either of us. So if he is selective and yet we could develop a fruitful relationship, then I have no reason to worry too much.

DONALD 101: You feel that if it can be done under the worst circumstances it should be possible more often.

ASHOK 101: (Long pause.) And yet it requires a change in my personality which I find very difficult. (Long pause.)

DONALD 102: Well, are you in the mood for a game of ping pong?

ASHOK 102: Sure, I used to be pretty good.

CHAPTER 6. Understanding and helping

Chapter 5 and the readings of Part III have emphasized a way of understanding an individual's behavior, not of changing or influencing it. In discussing the preceding cases the question has often arisen, "What do we *do* with the understanding we have achieved?" If an individual's existing pattern of beliefs about his world and views of himself influence so strongly how he feels about and perceives other people and events, how do shifts in this self-reinforcing pattern come about? Given my need to maintain my self-concept and my tendency to react to my surroundings in ways that "make my assumptions come true," how do I develop *new* ways of thinking and perceiving, how do I learn and grow? We cannot in this chapter attempt an adequate answer to this question. Most of the readings and citations in Parts III and IV are concerned with it, in one way or another. Here we simply want to use this question of "What produces change in a stable pattern of behavior?" as a background to a quick review of the cases in Part III as preparation for Part IV. In other words, this chapter is intended to serve as a bridge between the process of *understanding* someone else and the process of *helping* him understand himself. We are beginning to shift the focus from understanding how a person *is* behaving to understanding what might help him to behave somewhat differently.

Referring to the scheme used in Chapter 5, let us look separately at the various elements—self-concept, assumptions, perceptions, and feelings. By reference to the cases in Part III,

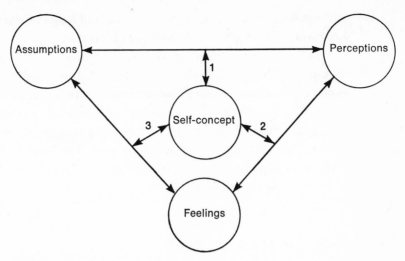

Figure 1

let us consider what might be the nature of some changes in the various elements of this scheme and how such changes might come about.

As has been seen when this scheme was applied to the cases studied so far, it directs our attention to the conflicts or incongruities that can arise between these elements and raises the possibility that a person's behavior can be understood as his attempt to balance or otherwise cope with these incongruities. For example, what does he do with feelings of confusion or threat which are the consequences of conflict between an assumption about how another person ought to behave and a perception of how he *is* behaving (1)? Or how does he cope with feelings and perceptions at variance with the sort of person he conceives himself to be (2)? Often, our cases suggest, he deals with this sort of imbalance by *misevaluating* (perceiving in a restricted or distorted way) what is outside of him or by denying to his own awareness certain feelings which he may organically experience. To us who are trying to understand him it might seem more useful (i.e., result in more skillful communication and greater learning) for the person to modify his assumptions about the world or his concept of himself, and thus to achieve a balance within which more of his real feelings were experienced with less distortion of his surroundings (3). But this kind of shift in the balance may be difficult to achieve without help. Why is this so, and what sort of help may be useful? Let us turn more specifically to some of our cases.

Before doing so, however, we want to emphasize very strongly that the following discussion is *not* intended as a substitute for exploration of the reader's *own* reaction to these cases. We are not trying to say here what should have been learned from them. We shall purposely leave out of this discussion many very important considerations, and we shall probably leave out unintentionally what to any given student of a particular case was the most important point of all.

Self-concept and assumptions

Some of our previous discussions of the self-concept, emphasizing the individual's need to maintain his existing views of himself against perceived challenge, may have given an altogether too reactive and static impression. As an individual matures, and to the extent he continues to grow as a person, new ways of conceiving the self arise and become integrated with the evolving self-structure. The personality, to use Allport's term, is a *proactive*, not just a reactive system, constantly interacting with its environment and seeking new levels of competence and actualization of its potentiality.[1] However, the articulation of new concepts of self, and their integration with the existing system of concepts, does not necessarily take place easily. Often this process involves considerable confusion and pain. This is seen most clearly, perhaps, when the adolescent or young adult finds himself wrestling with the question of who he really is.[2] Faced with new challenges and opportunities from outside and new feelings from within, it is often very difficult, from the person's own point of view, to

[1] See Gordon W. Allport, "The Open System in Personality Theory," in *Personality and Social Encounter* (Boston: Beacon Press, 1960), 39–54; and Chapter 22, "The Person in Psychology" in *Pattern and Growth in Personality* (New York: Holt, Rinehart and Winston, 1961).

[2] The "identity crisis" of adolescence and young adulthood has been a central issue in modern "ego psychology" and psychoanalytical writing. See especially E. H. Erikson, "Identity and the Life Cycle," Selected Papers, in *Psychological Issues*, 1, No. 1, Monograph 1 (New York: International Universities Press, 1959); and *Young Man Luther: A Study in Psychoanalysis and History*, 2nd ed. (New York: Norton, 1962).

achieve satisfactory answers to questions of this kind: "How can I be those other things that under these circumstances I am beginning to see in myself, and still be the person I have always thought myself to be? Can I be both? Who am I really? Under these new circumstances of my life what person am I becoming?"

These questions, the reader will have noticed, form a central theme in several of the preceding cases. Juanita Rodriguez, accustomed to thinking of herself as a good student, a Spanish-American (but mostly American) girl, a daughter who fulfills her mother's expectations, and a future doctor like her father, now finds herself failing chemistry and thinking about what it would be like to be married to José.

Ashok Rajguru's own analysis of his situation tells him that under his present circumstances he can satisfy the demands he perceives placed on him and reach his goals only by becoming more aggressive in interpersonal relationships. The situation, as he sees it, demands that he be the kind of person which his background has taught him to believe is, by definition, crude and vulgar. He knows he *ought* to change his concept of himself, yet he sees, very clearly, how difficult and painful such a change would be. The strain between his feeling of loneliness, his perception of how to overcome this feeling in his present situation, and his assumptions about how a person with his background ought to behave, results in a pattern of behavior which constitutes a deep threat to a central concept of self—his capability as a student and future physicist. Like Juanita Rodriguez, he searches for ways of seeing the situation differently as a way out of the dilemma, but he seems to sense that changing his perception of the outside world will not in fact help him to escape from his inner bind. Even during the interview, he seems to make some progress in facing up to the difficulty and pain he feels in integrating with his existing personality system some new beliefs about and views of himself.

The problem of integrating into a unified self-concept divergent views of self and assumptions about the world is also clearly illustrated in the interview with Larry Baker. In Larry's case the problem is made more apparent by the "two-valued orientation"[3]

[3] S. I. Hayakawa, *Language in Thought and Action, op. cit.*, 230–48.

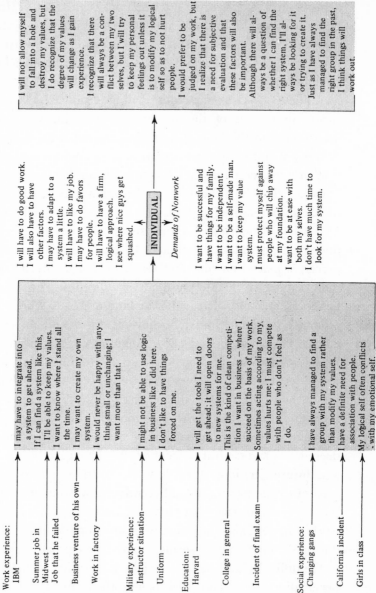

Events of His Life

Work experience:

IBM →

Summer job in Midwest →

Job that he failed →

Business venture of his own →

Work in factory →

Military experience:

Instructor situation →

Uniform →

Education:

Harvard →

College in general →

Incident of final exam →

Social experience:

Changing gangs →

California incident →

Girls in class →

Meaning of These Events to Him

I may have to integrate into a system to get ahead.

If I can find a system like this, I'll be able to keep my values.

I want to know where I stand all the time.

I may want to create my own system.

I would never be happy with anything small or unchanging; I want more than that.

I might not be able to use logic in business like I did here.

I don't like to have things forced on me.

I will get the tools I need to get ahead; it will open doors to new systems for me.

This is the kind of clean competition I want in business — where I succeed on the basis of my work.

Sometimes acting according to my values hurts me; I must compete with people who don't feel as I do.

I have always managed to find a group with my system rather than modify my values.

I have a definite need for association with people.

My logical self often conflicts with my emotional self.

Demands of Work

I will have to do good work.

I will also have to have other factors.

I may have to adapt to a system a little.

I will have to like my job.

I may have to do favors for people.

I will have to have a firm, logical approach.

I see where nice guys get squashed.

INDIVIDUAL

Demands of Nonwork

I want to be successful and have things for my family.

I want to be independent.

I want to be a self-made man.

I want to keep my value system.

I must protect myself against people who will chip away at my foundation.

I want to be at ease with both my selves.

I don't have much time to look for my system.

Resulting Balance

I will not allow myself to fall into a hole and destroy my values, but I do recognize that the degree of my values will change as I gain experience.

I recognize that there will always be a conflict between my two selves, but I will try to keep my personal feelings out unless it is to modify my logical self so as to not hurt people.

I would prefer to be judged on my work, but I realize that there is a need for subjective evaluation and that these factors will also be important.

Although there will always be a question of whether I can find the right system, I'll always be looking for it or trying to create it. Just as I have always managed to find the right group in the past, I think things will work out.

Figure 2. Larry Baker—Schematic Analysis of How a Person Views Himself and His Situation.

he displays in his view of ethics in the business world and in the conflict he sees between his "logical" and "emotional" selves. While the interview enabled him to articulate the problem that he was feeling, it probably did not help him find his "middle ground" as much as the interviewer may have hoped it had. In order to provide data for further discussion of how adequate an understanding of Larry Baker *was* achieved in this interview, we reproduce selections from the student report in which Chuck Loring presented his analysis of Larry Baker's point of view after their conversation. This report included (Figure 2) a very interesting use of the analytical scheme described in Chapter 5.

Chuck Loring, in his report, discussed Figure 2 as follows:

As shown in Figure 2, I have categorized the interview comments into the events of Larry's life, their meaning to him, and the demands of his work goals and his nonwork goals. The whole analysis follows the basic logic that, given a person's life, there are an infinite number of events that influence and shape that person's ultimate behavior. There are also certain demands that act upon the individual to further modify and determine his perception of himself.

Thus I listed all the events of his life that he discussed. I then drew from his comments what significance each particular event had for him. The only criticism of this approach is that, although the interviewee may view these events in precisely this manner, it is rather evident that his perception of all of them is not nearly so clearly organized.

I then drew from additional comments two sets of demands that he felt he was either subjected to or that he voluntarily subjected himself to. The former group I called work demands and the latter I called nonwork demands. These two lists could have been expanded to include ordinary demands made of everyone in our given society, but for purposes of simplicity and validity I confined myself to only his comments.

From all these forces which are shown acting upon the individual I then searched the interview for evidence of conclusions on his part. Part of this data came from the summaries that I made of my comments. In several instances when I tried to express my interpretation of him from his point of view he agreed with me very strongly. In some instances his indication of agreement was almost unbelievable. In these cases I felt I was justified in using my comments as material for the column, "resulting balance." Several comments used, however, are still only as he himself expressed them. The resulting balance then became the net result of all these forces that were shown acting upon him.

Although the same result would have undoubtedly been obtained by just discussing the interview, this method appears superior in presenting a clearer causal relationship diagram of not only *how* the person perceives himself but some possible reasons of *why*. Again the over-simplification of this scheme should be tempered by realizing that very likely the person's total perception of himself is not nearly so clear-cut. The important matter is that, told to reduce his perception of himself with regard to this particular situation to such an organized diagram, the interviewee could and would produce the same result.

Returning to my own point of view, I see the interviewee slightly different than he sees himself. Unfortunately, my association with him has neither been long enough nor deep enough to either repudiate or substantiate my views.

The basic difference centers about his rigorous devotion to his system of values. He claims to be deeply affected by these values and completely unwilling to change them in any great degree. Somehow I fail to see this result when he is faced with a permanent business situation in later years.

Perhaps I am saying the "map is not the territory." On the one hand he insists upon keeping his rather pure system and yet frankly admits his susceptibility to want of success and material possessions. He believes he can resolve this by being very mobile and relying on faith that his system does exist somewhere. I agree that he may ultimately find peace in a given system, but I do not believe that system will be as "pure" as the one he presently thinks he holds. As he himself points out, if a person wants something he should sit down and plan out how to get it. By deciding to further his education and come to the Business School, I believe that he will, just as he predicts, change the degree of his values. In other words, as he pursues his education to higher limits, he also intensifies the very goal which that education is based on—to be a successful businessman. Consequently, after two years here I believe he will leave with such high aspirations that the minor fact that he may have to do someone a favor or integrate into the system will no longer bother him as much. I do believe that he will always be somewhat of an individualist but that he will tend to "want to conform" to more trivial matters than he now lets himself admit. Add to this the pressures of time and status, and I believe his future self will be a bit tempered.

One comment that might be made about this analysis is that it, too, seems to leave out the "emotional side." It has more to do with assumptions and perceptions than with feelings. As a matter of fact this problem, of perceiving more clearly the *feelings* which a person experiences, is eloquently stated by Larry himself in the interview:

I know what kind of person I am. I've had occasion when I've felt that people didn't understand me, didn't know who I was. *This hurts,* this bothers me. I've had people misconstrue the things I say. *Sometimes they think that an academic argument is insight into my emotional self* and when I very coldly deny something that they think is a right of people they think I am a calloused person. This isn't true. This is only one side of me speaking. They only saw the academic side that looks at something and gives an evaluation which has nothing to do with my personal emotions. *Personally I might feel just the opposite.* [Italics added.]

One reason for emphasizing this passage is the notion, which will become more familiar with study of the material in Part IV, that it can be very valuable for a person simply to experience that his feelings are understood and accepted by someone else. This can be the experience, as it might be for Larry Baker, which helps the person to re-examine the validity of his assumptions about and perceptions of his world, and to revise accordingly, one small step at a time, his concept of himself.

Acceptance of feelings

To question a person's underlying beliefs and unstated assumptions or central aspects of his self-concept may have the consequence that he clings to them more strongly than before. In such an attempt, person A may win verbal acceptance by B of A's point of view, but not necessarily much else. A person's way of perceiving his world is also often highly resistant to change, for much the same reason. Often a perception, which seems "distorted" from an external frame of reference, can be seen from the other person's point of view to have a significant function in terms of a belief about the world which is important to him and as a way for him to maintain intact some central concept of himself.

As one example, consider Joe Fielden's perception that "everything is selling . . . the cry of a baby is a sales pitch." How does this way of seeing the world relate to Joe's concept of his career, his integrity, and his role in his family? Yet if more of Joe's strongly experienced feelings were accepted, especially perhaps certain negative feelings about himself, he might find it easier to modify somewhat his assumptions about and perceptions of other people's behavior. This, at least, is the argument we are presenting here, and we must quickly admit that in the Joe Fielden case we do not have much data to go on, since not many of such feelings were expressed and those which were do not seem to have been well understood by his "boss's son," young Sampson.

(Sampson's perception of the interview, in turn, was influenced by needs related to *his* assumptions and self-concept, and perhaps the same can be said about how Sampson's report was interpreted by the research assistant and instructor. Eventually, as it happened, Sampson did have an opportunity to express some important feelings about himself to the instructor, and as a consequence some shifts in his view of his interview with Joe Fielden did take place. But these data are not in the case.)

The process is illustrated more clearly in the cases of Juanita Rodriguez and Ashok Rajguru, and will appear again in most of the cases in Part IV, where we study in detail a way of listening to another person which facilitates the expression of his feelings about himself in an atmosphere of acceptance. What we have said here about this process is intended not to explain it adequately but to indicate why more detailed attention to it should be worthwhile. We want to end Part III with this brief consideration of the possibility that there are times when understanding a person's point of view and helping him understand himself are essentially identical processes. In this process, to the extent that a person experiences that someone else understands and accepts how he is feeling, he may find it easier to re-examine the usefulness to him of what he assumes and how he perceives.

PART IV Helping another person understand his behavior

CHAPTER 7. The counseling process—Orientation and method

In Part IV our goal is to learn about interpersonal communication generally by examining in some detail the process of psychological counseling or psychotherapy. We have already studied several cases in which person A was trying to help person B to talk about himself. We continue with the same kind of case material, but with a shift in focus. Now our major interest will be in the behavior of the interview*er*, person A, and our central question becomes: "What intentions and behavior on the part of A make it easier or more difficult for B to express clearly his thoughts and feelings about himself in relation to his situation as he sees it?" To some extent this question has arisen in previous cases; now we are ready to develop increasing competence in dealing with it. In the course of doing so we may feel ourselves at times rather far away from the world of leadership and administration in formal organizations. But when we return to Part V to more customary formal organizational relationships we hope to have developed increased skill in responding appropriately to many kinds of interpersonal situations which are quite different, at least on the surface, from the case in which B is explicitly asking A for help in understanding himself.

Our view of the relationship between "counseling" and "administration" will be developed more fully in Chapter 8. Here we want only to make a few simple statements which seem almost self-evident.

1. An administrator (a person in a position of responsibility in

relation to others at work) needs to learn through practice a way of interacting skillfully with others, that is, a way of interacting from which he will learn useful lessons about the process of facilitating communication; he needs to be able to listen for and understand the meaning to the other person of what the other person says to him.

2. Counseling or psychotherapy is a fruitful setting for the study of the process of understanding interpersonal communication, because in this rather special relationship a person who may have a hard time understanding and being understood is interacting with a person specially trained to facilitate this process.

3. From many different "schools" of psychotherapy, we have selected that approach which is particularly relevant for the roles most customarily encountered in organizational relationships, such as superior–subordinate, staff–line, consultant–client. There are several reasons for selecting "client-centered therapy" as the most promising for our purposes. First, it emphasizes as a necessary starting point the fact that the client comes for help. Whether a person is seeking help can usually be ascertained through careful listening or observation. Thus, within fairly broad limits—about which we will say more in Chapter 8—there need be no doubt in a particular situation whether lessons learned from the study of counseling are appropriate. Second, this method of counseling views the client and the resources within him as the source or locus of changes in his own behavior. The counselor's role is to facilitate those changes which the client —not the counselor—sees as desirable and possible for him. Further, this approach explicitly warns the counselor not to make interpretations of covert and hidden meanings, and to concentrate only on listening to, accepting, and clarifying the feelings which the client himself is expressing. Finally, in client-centered counseling the listener is constantly *testing*, in his reponses, the accuracy of his understanding of the meanings expressed by the client. Thus the method contains its own mechanism for correcting any errors in understanding

which the counselor may make. This emphasis on listening for the meaning which the *client* intends, with explicit avoidance of evaluation and interpretation from the *counselor's* point of view, is particularly important for practitioners in organizational settings without specialist training.

4. An additional reason for learning about this way of interacting is the fact that an individual who needs help in understanding his situation and himself will from time to time come to us with an explicit or implicit request for such help, however psychologically unsophisticated we may profess ourselves to be. Practice with the concepts and cases of Part IV should make it easier to decide how to respond when that time comes. All of us need to know more about how to hear and respond to requests for help, and also about when and how to ask for it.

These four points explain why we study the counseling process, but they do not avoid the difficulties inherent in practicing it, or make the process any less confusing or complex. This chapter will attempt to provide an introduction to and partial guide through the study of this process. It will suggest ways of applying concepts in the readings, here reproduced and cited, to the concrete behavior in the cases that follow.

Orientation and technique: philosophy and skill

As partially explained in the introduction to Reading IV–1, the orientation to interaction with another person and the method of interviewing that are of primary concern in Part IV originated in two main streams of development, which have become increasingly merged with each other over the years: employee relations research in industry (the "Hawthorne studies" conducted by representatives of the Western Electric Company and the Harvard Business School in the 1920s and 1930s) and psychological counseling (the work of Carl Rogers and his associates at Rochester, Ohio State, the Counselling Center at the University of Chicago (1945–57), and the University of Wisconsin). The manner in which this approach to interviewing developed in the Hawthorne studies is best described by Roethlisberger and Dickson in *Management and the Worker*, excerpts from which are included in this book as Readings II–4 and IV–1.[1] The most interesting account of the development of the thinking and practice of Rogers and his associates can be found in his books (both cited in full elsewhere in this volume) *Client-Centered Therapy* (especially Chapter 1, "The Developing Character of Client-Centered Therapy," pp. 3–18) and *On Becoming a Person* (especially Chapter 1, "This is Me: The Development of My Professional Thinking and Personal Philosophy," pp. 3–27).

Reading IV–1 describes the interviewing method which was developed at Hawthorne.[2] This method was originally called "indirect," an unfortunate term since to some people it implied a lack of directness, which was in fact neither intended nor in any sense a part of the method. Carl Rogers, in his early writings, introduced the word *non-directive* to describe his counseling method, and later adopted the term *client-centered* in order to emphasize that the interviewer's main intention, rather than merely to avoid directing the interviewee, was to center attention on the interviewee's own values and meanings, whatever they might be. Reading IV–2 is a condensed version of Rogers' description in *Client-Centered Therapy* of the underlying attitude and orientation of the client-centered counselor. In comparing Readings IV–1 and IV–2 it will be noticed that both descriptions place primary emphasis on the interviewer's basic orientation rather than on relatively superficial aspects of his "technique," and that the orientation described by Rogers is essentially a further and deeper development in the same direction as implied by the "Rules of Orientation" that were developed at Hawthorne.

It is especially important to notice the *relationship between orientation* and *technique*, which is implied by Roethlisberger and

---

[1] For a more recent and shorter account by an "outsider," see H. A. Landsberger, *Hawthorne Revisited* (Ithaca, N.Y.: Cornell University, 1958). For a history and evaluation of the interviewing program at Western Electric, see W. J. Dickson and F. J. Roethlisberger, *Counseling in an Organization* (Boston: Division of Research, Harvard Graduate School of Business Administration, Harvard University, 1966).

[2] A careful reading of Readings IV–1 and IV–2 is recommended before proceeding with this chapter.

Dickson and emphasized further by Rogers. The implication is that *technique* by itself will not suffice; a rather unusual attitude toward the other person and one's own relationship with him must first exist. Only then, by implication, will effective technique develop, almost as a "natural" outgrowth of the underlying orientation, and perhaps with quite different manifestations in concrete behavior for different interviewers and in different relationships. To the extent that this is true, any short exposure to this counseling method, such as we are attempting here, faces a dilemma. Here is a technique, Rogers seems to tell us, that will not be effective without a particular underlying orientation, and here is an orientation that cannot be implemented without the technique. How are we to get started? An orientation such as described by Rogers is clearly not something that can easily be taught or acquired, and yet without the orientation, what is the point of studying the technique?

However, there is no reason to become immobilized by dilemmas of this kind. *Technique* and *orientation* are not mutually exclusive goals; they are overlapping and interdependent. Balanced progress toward each can simultaneously be made, one small step at a time. Suppose we adopt, as a working hypothesis and without necessarily full conviction, some part of the orientation which Rogers describes. On the basis of this small "leap of faith" we may then begin practicing more effectively, but with limited skill, the technique of accepting and clarifying feelings which emerges from such an orientation. The consequence of this attempt, as we experience the other person's response to it, may be further confidence in the validity of the orientation, resulting in further skill with the technique. Thus, as in learning many other kinds of skills, technical competence and confidence in the underlying attitude can each contribute to the other, gradually, and we do not have to choose between complete commitment and complete rejection before starting to test out, in relatively small ways, how much of this orientation–technique makes sense for us. The first step, we suggest, is to *understand*, without necessarily having to accept fully, both the orientation and the technique, by studying the readings which are reproduced and assigned, and by discussing their relevance to the subsequent cases. During this process we will need to practice the technique in order to test out the utility of the orientation at the same time that we tentatively adopt parts of the orientation in order to practice the technique. Thus progresses the learning of any skill, as you will realize by recalling your own or another's efforts to swim, ride a bicycle, drive an automobile, sail, or ski.

The three interrelated elements of the orientation

In Rogers' more recent descriptions of the client-centered orientation, three "necessary and sufficient" conditions are emphasized:

1. "Empathic understanding."

2. "Unconditional positive regard."

3. "Congruence" (or "transparency"), in two senses:

    a. Between the level of "experience" and the level of "awareness." (To what extent is the counselor, here and now, consciously aware of the feelings he is presently experiencing?)

    b. Between the level of "awareness" and the level of "expression." (To what extent is the counselor able and willing to express the feelings of which he is presently aware?)

While Rogers sometimes uses different terms to describe these three "conditions," his explanation of the territory to which these words refer is clear and we shall not attempt to define them here. It is important to recognize the underlying hypothesis: a therapeutic relationship exists and learning and growth take place to the extent that *all three* of these conditions are both *present* within the counselor and *perceived* by the client as existing within the counselor. In other words, the counselor needs to have both an orientation that makes these conditions possible for him and the skill to communicate their existence to his client. Note also that the hypothesis is a conditional one, as indicated by the words "to the extent that." The conditions do not have to be met absolutely in order for therapy to take place; but the more they exist the more the client will be helped. Thus Rogers' hypothesis can be tested in spite of the extreme difficulty, for any of us, of actually attaining simultaneously the three conditions that it specifies.

Rogers himself makes clear that this formulation of the counselor's attitude should be seen as an ideal to work toward rather than as an attainable goal in any absolute sense. This is especially true because of the intricate relationships of interconnectedness among the three elements which become apparent as soon as one begins to understand what Rogers means by these terms. The trouble is that when we first begin to work with these concepts, to try to attain these conditions, they may sometimes seem to get in each other's way. For example, in the process of trying empathically to understand another person, I may discover that I progressively disapprove of elements in his behavior or character. I may be achieving what seems to me like understanding at the expense of what seems to him like rejection. Then this difficulty may get further compounded if I attempt not to communicate my disapproval or, even worse, if I manage not to recognize in myself the negative feelings I am experiencing toward this person I am trying to listen to. In a futile effort to hide from the other person my lack of positive regard for him (which in turn may come from my not recognizing my lack of empathic understanding), I may lose all hope of congruence.

As before, this poses a dilemma which in practice is less real than it seems when it is worked out this way on paper or in the mind of a person anticipating practice. Unconditional positive regard is not something that can be willed into existence. Congruence, which in Rogers' later writings is the key element in any "helping relationship," cannot be acquired by studying and worrying about it. Our approach in this book is to start with an effort to practice the skill of empathic understanding, on the assumption that as far as that condition really exists, the others may follow. With most of the people with whom we are likely to interact, the chances are very great that increasingly empathic understanding, an increasingly accurate sense of how things look and feel from the other person's frame of reference, will in fact lead over time to increasingly positive regard, so that the "congruence bind" described in the preceding paragraph will not arise. In this book, then, we are testing whether it makes sense to start with the hard work of increasing our ability to understand another person's point of view.

Thus in earlier cases and readings we studied instances of misunderstanding and related them to differences in assumptive frameworks and to difficulties inherent in the use of words as symbols. And we saw the relationship of congruence to communication whenever we noticed how a person's interpretation of his experience was influenced by his need to maintain his existing beliefs about himself, especially when he was not aware of this process. For example, we saw how an executive's ability to communicate effectively was hampered because he was not aware of how his feelings about himself were affecting his perception of someone else. We implied that it would be helpful for such an executive to be able to ask himself how what he could see going on "outside his skin" was being influenced by what he could not see inside. We did not imply that he should be a different person; we did imply that his ability to communicate would improve to the extent that he learned to be more aware of what it was like to be the person that he was.

Through these earlier cases a major intention was to learn more about how to practice understanding another person as the other person saw himself and the world of events and meanings in which he lived. In doing so we experienced some success in achieving the empathic understanding that Rogers describes. When this happened, we were able to sense the strain toward internal consistency which makes any person's behavior understandable. We also found that it was impossible not to revert to our *own* frame of reference when thinking about someone else and that it was useful to be aware that we were doing so.

With this background we now turn to client-centered therapy as a setting for learning more about this process, for two main reasons. *First,* here is a way of talking with and listening to another person that is uniquely designed to make it easier to sense how the world looks to someone else. Indeed, empathic understanding might be called both the principal *means* and the principal *end* of this way of interacting. *Second,* here is a way of helping another person understand himself which may serve as a model, an ideal type, that cannot be realized in settings outside psychotherapy but yet might well be *approached* in a very wide variety of other contexts within which another person asks for help.

These are our reasons for including in Part IV cases and readings which provide an opportunity to study in considerable detail the technique of client-centered interviewing, as well as to become exposed to its underlying orientation or philosophy. In doing so we shall discover that this way of interacting is a far more difficult and active process than it may at first appear.

The selectivity of client-centered interviewing

As most people being interviewed talk about more than one topic, and at more than one level, the interviewer's technique can be described in terms of the choices he makes concerning which part of his "client's" meanings to respond to.

Among other things, an interviewee may talk about (*a*) objects, events, concepts, ideas, (*b*) other people, or (*c*) himself. The client-centered interviewer, when presented with a choice among these alternatives, will respond to what the person is saying about *himself*. In doing so the interviewer has the choice of responding in terms of (*a*) advice, opinion, and the like, (*b*) interpretation of what the client has been saying, or (*c*) an acceptance or clarification of what the client has been saying from the client's own frame of reference. Again, the client-centered interviewer attempts to confine himself to the latter choice, accepting and/or clarifying what the person is saying about himself from his own point of view.

In doing this, the interviewer is presented with another choice. He can respond to the client's talk about himself at the level of (*a*) content, (*b*) expressed feeling, or (*c*) unexpressed feeling. The distinction between responding to content and responding to feeling is very central to an understanding of client-centered interviewing. It is well covered by Rogers, especially in the excerpts from *Counseling and Psychotherapy* (required additional Readings 1 and 4) listed subsequently. It is equally important to distinguish between expressed and unexpressed feeling. Client-centered therapy, unlike some other types of psychotherapy, tries to avoid responding to unexpressed feeling, on the grounds that the client himself is the best judge of at what level it will be most useful for him to talk, and that he may react with unnecessarily increased defensiveness if confronted with feelings he does not want to express, no matter how accurately the interviewer may have guessed their existence in him.

For the layman without specialized training it is especially important to avoid probing for feelings which the other person does not express. The experience that what he *does* say is understood and accepted will reinforce any previous learning from experience that he can express feelings that are difficult to talk about. This addition to his experience may lead him to risk recognizing feelings previously blocked from awareness. Though small, these additions to experience are real; they have happened—and they make a difference. But in client-centered interviewing, *especially* when attempted by most of us, it is essential to let the client decide the extent and timing of his own exploration into areas that are difficult to talk about. In the sort of interviewing we are to practice here, we should carefully avoid any attempt to deprive someone else of defenses against expression or awareness of deeper feelings; such defenses exist for reasons we probably do not understand.

Not infrequently the person interviewed expresses in one statement more than one feeling about himself, and the interviewer has to choose which expressed feeling to respond to: positive, ambivalent, or negative expressed feelings about self. As Rogers makes clear, when this choice is available, the acceptance and clarification of negative and ambivalent feelings about

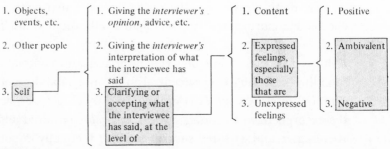

Figure 1

self is preferred as more helpful than a response to positive feelings. Those aspects of myself which I find most confusing or distasteful become easier for me to understand and accept to the extent that I see they are understood and accepted by someone else.

These various choices can be summarized in terms of a kind of "decision tree." The interviewer chooses to respond to what the interviewee says about himself in the way shown in Figure 1.

Another way of summarizing these distinctions is by means of the two-dimensional scheme depicted in Figure 2. A scheme such as this will prove useful in studying interviewer responses in the cases and in any interviews you conduct yourself, in spite of the fact that it may often be very difficult to place a given response unequivocally in a certain "box." It will be less useful to you, though no less relevant, while you are actually conducting an interview. Then too much concern for the "right" response on the part of the interviewer may block the flow of the interview. The pace of the conversation may not allow all the choices and their pros and cons to be considered and one chosen. Talk is especially sensitive to artificiality and the constraints of consciousness. In these situations it is sometimes best for he who practices to "stay loose," to let conversations flow, with techniques to be considered

	Among other possibilities, an interviewer may:				
			Clarify or accept		
	A	B	C	D	E
Among other subjects, the interviewee may talk about:	Give the interviewer's opinions, experiences, advice, etc.	Interpret what the interviewee says from the interviewer's point of view	The (intellectual) content of what the interviewee says	The interviewee's expressed feelings	The interviewee's unexpressed feelings
1. Objects, concepts, events, etc.					
2. Other people					
3. Himself					

Figure 2. A classification of an interviewer's responses.

and reconsidered at leisure, and then to practice again at another time and place, perhaps with a different person, with lessons newly learned once again transferred to the back of one's mind. Thus, again and again and again the cycle of practice and reflection in alternation becomes the proving ground for the development of competence. (For another useful classification scheme, see Reading IV–3.)

As an *example* of how the scheme may be used, consider the choices available to George, in the Edward Koch (A) case in response to Ed's initial statement of his problem. Below are listed a number of responses which George might have made at that point instead of his actual choice ("You don't like to be told what to do?"). The responses are listed under the different subjects discussed by Ed to which George might have responded. Under each subject, responses are listed which belong under one of the five ways of responding indicated by the column headings on the classification scheme in Figure 2. If the reader labels each of these responses with the number and letter indicating the appropriate "box" of the classification scheme, he will gain a better idea of how such a scheme can be used to increase his awareness of the important distinctions implicit in this way of examining interviewing technique.

Nonpersonal object: his father's house
    "In my view a father's house is not a good place for a newly-married couple to live; I think you should move away."
    "When my wife and I got married, we found my father's house was not a good place for us to live."
    "How many rooms does the house have?"

Abstract concept: harmony
    "I think harmony is important at home."
    "Let me tell you about how harmoniously my wife and I live together."
    "Why do you think living harmoniously is important to your father?"

An event: going to the wedding
    "I think going to the weddings of the children of one's parents' friends is often important socially."

"I don't like to go to such weddings myself."

"Tell me about the people who were getting married."

"You don't like to go to weddings when you don't know the people."

"You didn't like to go to the wedding because you didn't know the people."

Other people: wife, father-in-law, the people getting married

"I think a son should always do what a father wants."

"I think a wife and husband should not argue too much."

"Let me tell you about my arguments with my wife."

"What were your wife's arguments?"

"It is uncomfortable for you to take sides with your wife against your father, even when he is wrong."

Himself

"Don't let what other people say bother you so much."

"Well, here's the way I handle this kind of problem."

"Has people telling you what to do been a problem for you on other occasions?"

"What are your reasons for thinking a wife should go out of her way to please her husband?"

"You don't like to be told what to do?"

"You are worried about your marriage."

Conducting your own interview

Analyzing someone else's way of interviewing is no substitute for trying out the orientation and the technique for yourself. At some point during the study of Part IV we recommend the following assignment.

The purpose of this assignment is for you to practice understanding someone from his (or her) point of view. To complete the assignment, carry out the following steps:

1. Conduct a conversation with someone who is willing to talk with you with the above purpose in mind. During the conversation, test out, at least a little, your understanding of how he sees his situation, his problem, and/or himself.

2. Write up the conversation, or at least the most important parts of it, as nearly verbatim as you can. (If you wish, you may summarize those parts that seem less relevant to the purpose of the assignment.) The use of a tape recorder is highly recommended. You can always cut the transcript later.

3a. Using the data you have, describe your understanding of how the person views himself and his situation. (If you wish, you can make additional comments or evaluations about the person from some other point of view, for example, from your own. Keep these remarks separate, however, from the diagnosis of the person from his point of view.)

b. Analyze the interview as a case in interpersonal behavior, giving attention to how the setting and your behavior influenced what took place.

c. (Optional) Comment on anything you may have learned from this assignment about yourself and how you talk with people.

In carrying out this assignment it is best not to choose someone to interview who is a close friend or relative or a fellow student of these matters. Also it is wise to avoid selecting someone specifically because you believe he has "a lot of problems" and you think the interview will be helpful to him. This interview differs from a social conversation in that its purpose is for you to practice understanding someone else from his frame of reference, carefully putting your understanding of what he talks about to the test of his acceptance of it. It differs from a counseling interview in that it is unlikely that the person you interview will be explicitly asking for your help. (It is very important to note that in the counseling situation, as Rogers describes it, the client has already made a clear decision and gone to some trouble to come to the counselor for help. The absence of this condition creates a very different situation, in which the client-centered orientation can still be relevant provided that the interviewer stays in touch with the role the interviewee expects of him.) Remember also that even if you do not secure as "good" an interview as you would like, comments about the interview carefully related to your data can make a very interesting report and provide you with a valuable experience in understanding what takes place in an interaction in which you are highly involved.

In conducting and analyzing the interview, try to pay some but not "too much" attention to your interviewing technique as such; the important part of the assignment is to practice *understanding* what is said and heard by both persons and how the behavior of each influences the other. The most typical mistake which beginning interviewers make in analyzing their technique is to assume that they have responded to feeling when they have not. For example, consider the response, "You feel that productivity in your department is in inverse ratio to close supervision?" This is obviously *not* a response to feeling; nor do the words "You feel . . ." avoid the intellectualized discussion that is sure to follow.

As a possible aid in commenting on your interviews, here are some questions which may suggest useful areas for discussion. You should feel free *not* to answer any of these questions which seem irrelevant to you or unrelated to your data. The questions are intended only to suggest possible leads for your analysis; they are *not* intended as an imposed outline for your report. Try to keep the various topics you do discuss related to each other and to the overall purposes of the report as a whole.

A. Questions to ask about the interviewee and his (her) situation (assignment question 3a):

1. *If he expresses a complaint, problem, or dissatisfaction, what is it?*
2. *What is he asking of the situation in which he now finds himself?*
   a. What are his beliefs and assumptions about himself and his situation?
   b. How are these assumptions and beliefs related to the previous events and circumstances of his life?
3. *What is the present situation, as he sees it, asking of him?*
4. *What is the resulting balance in terms of:*
   a. His satisfactions and dissatisfactions?
   b. His productivity and nonproductivity?

c. His growth, development, learning, creativity, and their opposites?

(These may be described in a variety of ways and from more than one point of view—for example, his and yours—depending on the data available in the interview.)

B. Questions to ask about the process of the interview (assignment question 3b):

1. *What effect(s) did the circumstances under which the interview was held have on its outcome?*

    a. How was the interview arranged for and/or explained to the interviewee?

    b. How did the previous relation of the interviewer to the interviewee affect its conduct?

    c. How did the interviewer's feelings and attitudes before and during the interview affect it?

2. *How did the interviewer's questions and responses affect the interview?*

    a. Did the interviewer's response(s) help the interviewee to talk?

    b. Did the interviewer's response(s) help the interviewee to talk at the level of content or at the level of feeling?

    c. Did the response(s) help the interviewer to understand the interviewee?

    d. Did the response(s) help the interviewee to understand himself?

In thinking about this assignment, and in analyzing cases that are based on other students' past attempts to carry it out (Larry Baker, Joe Fielden, Ashok Rajguru, Donald French, John Thompson), the following questions may provide useful criteria for evaluating an interview analysis:

1. How well does the interviewer listen? How well does he understand why he doesn't listen better?

2. How well does the interviewer in his analysis present his understanding of the person interviewed from the person's own internal frame of reference? (Is there a feel for the pattern and interrelatedness of the various elements? Is it likely

to be acceptable to the interviewee as a helpful organization of those feelings and beliefs about himself of which he is aware?)

3. How well does the interviewer present his understanding of the process of the interview? (Categorization of responses, distinction between feeling and content, effect of own assumptions and feelings, proposed alternate responses at key points.)

4. What does the total report indicate has been learned? (Is there evidence of dysfunctional, neutral, or useful learning about understanding someone else or about himself.)

READING IV–1. *The Interviewing Method*

F. J. ROETHLISBERGER AND
W. J. DICKSON

[The following passages are excerpts from the chapter in *Management and the Worker* that describes the orientation and method developed at the Hawthorne Works of the Western Electric Company during the course of conducting thousands of employee interviews in 1929 and 1930. The reader will notice that this approach to interviewing, developed at a different time and place and for a different purpose, nevertheless resembles in many ways the "non-directive" or "client-centered" orientation of Carl Rogers. For our purposes the "Rules of Orientation" are more important than the "Rules for Conducting the Interview," but both sets of rules are still relevant in spite of their age (over thirty-five years). Here we have deleted some of the discussion of

Excerpted by permission of the publishers from F. J. Roethlisberger and W. J. Dickson, *Management and the Worker* (Cambridge, Mass.: Harvard University Press, 1939), 271–91. Copyright 1939, 1967 by the President and Fellows of Harvard College.

several of the "rules" (as well as certain footnotes). Later, the interested student should read the whole chapter. The most important difference to keep in mind between this description of the method of interviewing and client-centered therapy is that, in the latter case, the counselor is responding to an individual who has explicitly come to him for psychological help, whereas Roethlisberger and Dickson are describing a procedure originally developed for research as to employee opinions and attitudes. As will probably be true also in most of the interviews conducted by users of this book, the interviewee was "helping" the interviewer, not the other way around. Actually, many employees did find the process helpful, and the same underlying orientation to interviewing was continued after the purpose had shifted focus from attitude research to employee counseling.]

If the interviewers were to conduct interviews skillfully, it was necessary for them to have some simple conceptual scheme, that is, some framework in which their thought was set and by means of which they could operate on the material elicited in the interview. This conceptual scheme depended on some idea of what took place when two people were talking together, and the way in which an interview differed from an ordinary social conversation.

Rules of orientation

This conceptual scheme probably can be presented best by ... discussing separately each of the rules which the interviewers found useful for the interpretation of what took place in an interview. . . .

* * *

Rule I. The interviewer should treat what is said in an interview as an item in a context.

The relation between any item in an interview and "context" will become more clear as the following rules are discussed. It may be said here, however, that the interviewer is constantly seeking a context for every item in an interview. Although in this sense the context is that which the interviewer adds to the interview, this addition is not arbitrary. It is constantly being subjected to verification and modification as new items and interrelations appear. This first rule of interpretation has several important corollaries.

Rule IA. The interviewer should not pay exclusive attention to the manifest content of the intercourse.

This rule warns the interviewer to guard himself against falling into a common attitude that he as a human being is likely to take in a social conversation. When two people are exchanging thoughts and sharing ideas, attention is likely to be directed exclusively to the manifest content of what is being said. . . .

Here is an illustration. At an afternoon tea in New England, attended by members of both sexes, a woman made a remark to the effect that the English public school system tended to make men brutal. All in the group took sides, some agreeing and some disagreeing with the generalization. A heated and lengthy discussion followed in which the merits and demerits of the English public school system were thoroughly reviewed. In other words, the statement was taken at its face value and discussed at that level. No one, seemingly, paid attention to the fact that the woman who made the statement had married an Englishman who had received an English public school education and that she was in the process of obtaining a divorce from him. Had it occurred to the others, as it did to one person in the room, that the woman had expressed more clearly her sentiments toward her husband than she had expressed anything equally clear about the English public school system, and that the form in which she expressed her sentiments had reacted on the national and international sentiments of her audience, which they, in turn, had more clearly expressed than anything equally clear about the English public school system, such an idea would have been secretly entertained and not publicly expressed, for that is the nature of polite social intercourse.

But in an interview things are otherwise. Had this statement been made in an interview, the interviewer would not have been misled by the manifest content of the statement. He would have been on the alert for a personal reference, and, once he had learned about the woman's husband, he would have guided the conversation on this topic rather than on the English public school system. Furthermore, he would have been on his guard not to allow any sentiments which he as a social being might entertain toward the English to be acted upon by the form of the statement. This second point is of great importance . . . .

Rule IB. The interviewer should not treat everything that is said as either fact or error.

This is a favorite false dichotomy for the beginner in interviewing. He tends to be exclusively concerned with the truth or falsity of what is said in the interview. Everything for him is either fact or error. Now the majority of statements made in the interviewing program at the Western Electric Company were, strictly speaking, neither facts nor errors. They were more in the nature of nonfacts. To ask of such statements whether or not they are "true" involves a completely different kind of meaning than to ask the same question of a statement capable of verification.

For example, take three very common statements made by employees during the interviewing program:

1. My wages last month averaged only $35.00 per week. I used to make more.

2. Working in this company is like being in a jail.

3. This is the most wonderful company to work for.

If the interviewer doubts the truth of the first statement, he can easily verify it; not so with the second or third statement.

* * *

Of course, it is frequently very important for the interviewer to know what people agree and what people disagree with a nonfactual statement. But should the interviewer put such a question to himself, it is not with the purpose of establishing the truth or falsity of the statement made. He has a completely different purpose in mind, which will be discussed later. [See Rule IV.]

Rule IC. The interviewer should not treat everything that is said as being at the same psychological level.

This rule warns the beginner against another serious stumbling block. For no sooner does he stop asking of nonfactual statements whether or not they are true than he begins to ask, Is the speaker saying what he really thinks? Here again the interviewer is likely to oversimplify matters. There is always the tendency to take one of two extreme attitudes, either completely believing or completely disbelieving everything a person says. In the first case the interviewer takes everything that is said at its face value. In the other case he disbelieves everything he hears. Both attitudes arise from the fallacy of assuming that everything that is being said during the interview is at the same psychological level. This is very seldom the case. Sometimes the speaker is bored and is just making conversation. Sometimes he is poking fun at the interviewer. Sometimes he is nervous and apprehensive and therefore he is guarded in the statements he makes. Sometimes he is trying to make a favorable impression on the interviewer. At other times he is more earnest and is attending to and reflecting upon what is being said. Naturally, the meaning to be assigned to the speaker's remarks depends upon interpreting his responses in the light of the psychological context in which they occur.

The tendency completely to believe or disbelieve the speaker also arises in part from oversimplifying the relation between what the speaker says and what he thinks. It is commonly supposed, although there is very little evidence to warrant such a supposition, that there exists a simple and logical relation between what a person says and what he thinks. On this assumption, any deviation from a logically explicit statement is taken as implying a willful and conscious intent on the part of the speaker to distort and disguise what he really is thinking. Now there is the possibility that the speaker does not say what he thinks, not because he will not, but because he cannot express it. This is a very common situation and will be discussed more fully under the next rule.

. . . The difficulty which confronted the interviewers was not that of hypocrisy on the part of the worker but the achieving of a relationship to the worker which would enable him to state things in the interview which he was unable to state to himself.

Rule II. The interviewer should listen not only to what a person wants to say but also for what he does not want to say or cannot say without help.

Although there are no precise rules for the interpretation of individual responses, there are three broad categories into which the verbal behavior of a person in an interview can be placed:

1. What a person wants to say.

2. What a person does not want to say.

3. What a person cannot say without help.

During an interview the interviewer has many opportunities to note significant gaps and omissions in what a person is saying. The interviewer should note these omissions and ask himself whether these related topics have been omitted because (1) the speaker does not care to talk about them, or (2) he has never thought about them.

Things about which a person does not care to talk are often likely to be connected with unpleasant or painful experiences. . . . Such omissions are likely to indicate areas of emotional significance, which, should the opportunity arise, should be explored. These explorations cannot be rushed. The interviewer has to wait for an appropriate time to break into such critical zones. Many times the procedure has to be indirect. . . .

However, most omissions that occur in an interview involve not only things about which the speaker does not wish to talk but also things which lie so implicitly in his thinking that they have not yet become conscious discriminations. A person may not want to talk about a particular topic and yet he may not be quite clear as to why he refrains. In the case of most omissions, therefore, the interviewer is on the alert for both contexts.

* * *

For the interviewer, therefore, it is important to note what the speaker regards in his own mind as obvious and of such universal application that it has never occurred to him to doubt or question it. By listening carefully to him as he discusses a variety of topics, the interviewer can frequently detect things which underlie what is said but are themselves not expressed. These implicit assumptions are of the greatest importance in assessing a person's ultimate values and significances, for, although they cannot be expressed explicitly by the person, nevertheless for that very reason they enter into the determination of his everyday judgments and thoughts.*

Rule III. The interviewer should treat the mental contexts described in the preceding rule as indices and seek through them the personal reference that is being revealed.

* * *

For example, let us take an evaluation judgment in the form *A dislikes B because B has the characteristic x.*† There are two attitudes which can be taken toward such a statement, one of which is more common than the other. The common attitude is to look at *B* and see if *B* has the characteristic *x*. The procedure adopted is generally one of "counting noses." How many people acquainted with *B* agree with *A* in his judgment of *B*? Implicit in this procedure is the notion of assessing the correctness or incorrectness of *A*'s judgment. If most of the people acquainted with *B* agree with *A* in his judgment of *B*, *A* is considered justified in having such an opinion. If the reverse is true, *A* is not considered justified and probably is dubbed "peculiar" or "abnormal." It will be noted that this procedure reveals directly only one thing about *A*, that is, the extent to which other people agree with him in his judgment of *B*.

The other, less common, attitude is to inquire what sentiments, desires, or interests of *A* are involved in *A*'s judgment of *B*. This attitude presupposes that any evaluational judgment is a composite of two

---

* In this connection it is interesting to note that Rules IA, IB, and IC warn the interviewer against implicit assumptions frequently made by people in ordinary social intercourse.

† For those to whom this form of statement bears no resemblance to the worker as they know him in flesh and blood, let them picture a worker anxious and eager to tell the interviewer what a "helluva guy" his supervisor is and to make such statements as, "He's a bully; a slave driver; unfair; unjust; etc." The above statement is merely a formal way of expressing such remarks.

elements: (1) the total effects from the object, and (2) the reaction of the person himself. Or, to put it in another way, satisfaction or dissatisfaction is treated as relative to the demands which the person is making of his environment, and the opportunities which the environment offers for their fulfillment. Many times these demands are not precise and definite. They are only vaguely apprehended by the speaker. For this reason, it is not to be expected that they will be explicitly expressed in the statements which he makes in an interview. Rather, they take the form of implicit assumptions. Therefore, the first question the interviewer asks is, What hopes and expectations on the part of the speaker does his evaluational judgment imply? The statement *A dislikes B because B has the characteristic x* is translated into the form:

1. *A* has such and such expectations of *B*, or *A* has such and such sentiments toward *B*.

2. *B* fails to come up to these expectations, or violates these sentiments of *A*.

3. Therefore, *A* dislikes *B*.

Such a translation is, of course, in many instances not easy to make. It demands a constant probing on the part of the interviewer for a detailed account by *A* of his many unpleasant experiences with *B* and other similar experiences.

Rule IV. The interviewer should keep the personal reference in its social context.

This rule warns the interviewer against considering the sentiments, desires, or interests of an individual as things in themselves. It cautions him to remember that he is looking at a person who has a past history and that here and now in the interview he is observing an end product of a particular historical route. That is to say, the interviewee has had particular experiences which, in turn, have aroused particular preoccupations. During the formative period of his childhood he has lived in a particular family which, in turn, has had particular social relations with the wider community. In terms of such factors the individual has been conditioned to a particular way of looking at and feeling about things.

But not only does the speaker have a social past; he is also enjoying a social present. Here and now he is having social relations with other people and groups of people. Moreover, these social relations are not of a chance character but for the most part are controlled by the codes, customs, and conventions of the community to which the individual belongs. If a person's feelings and sentiments are to be understood, they have to be related to his present social reality.

* * *

Rule IVA. The interviewer should remember that the interview is itself a social situation and that therefore the social relation existing between the interviewer and the interviewee is in part determining what is said.

This rule is implicitly recognized by most interviewers, and many of the practical rules of conducting the interview, which will be discussed later, follow from it. However, unless the beginner realizes explicitly certain consequences of this rule he is likely to fall into common misunderstandings of what frequently takes place in his relation to the person being interviewed.

* * *

As the interview progresses, an informal and sometimes quite unique social relation may develop between the interviewer and the person being interviewed. Although this social relation is more conspicuous in prolonged interviewing where a therapeutic element is involved than in the case of the single interview, it may take place in some degree even in the case of the latter, and it is important that the interviewer should be aware of this possibility. The interview is quite different from an ordinary social conversation or discussion. The interviewer is sympathetically listening to the person in a way that seldom occurs in an ordinary conversation. Nothing that the speaker says is too slight or too trivial for his attention. Moreover, the social personality of the interviewer, if he follows the rules prescribed, is quite different from that to which the interviewee is generally accustomed. The interviewer is not exercising authority in its many subtle forms. He is not ordering, advising, criticizing, interrupting, or in any fashion attempting to force his set of values and significances upon the interviewee. As a result, a relation develops which is quite different from any relation which the interviewee has ever experienced. The interviewee finds himself not only saying things which he never said to anyone else but in many instances saying things which he has not been able to express explicitly to himself.

Sometimes this relation becomes extremely trying to the interviewer, for the interviewer becomes an object ideally suitable to the speaker for the projection of his most deeply rooted hopes, fears, and expectations. What happens sometimes is that the interviewee begins to project on the interviewer that complex of sentiments related to authority to which he has been previously conditioned by his early training and experience. He constantly tries to force the interviewer into a position of authority, either by asking him his advice about this and that, or in a countless number of other ways. Unless the interviewer is dealing with a very neurotic person, these complications are not likely to arise in a single interview. If they do, such cases are better handled by specialists.

* * *

In the second place, it is well to remember that the relation between interviewer and interviewee is reciprocal. What the interviewer says and does affects the speaker, and what the speaker says and does affects the interviewer. This second relation is so frequently misunderstood that it deserves a special rule.

Rule IVA$_1$. The interviewer should see to it that the speaker's sentiments do not act on his own.

To the layman it may seem that the interviewer is advised to be a very superior person, devoid of all social sentiments. This is not so, for the interviewer is also a social being, with a social past and a social present. If he is to guard against mistakes, it is important that he does not pretend to be otherwise. The only way in which the interviewer can guard against having his own sentiments acted upon is not by denying their existence but by admitting and understanding them. Anyone who has had experience in interviewing realizes that often he learns more about himself than about the person being interviewed. Frequently he finds himself becoming irritated and annoyed at what a person is saying. It is not sufficient to brush these moods lightly aside; he must ask himself what sentiments of his own are involved. Otherwise, in a quite unexpected fashion, he may find himself doing and saying things which may evoke the very attitude on the part of the speaker that he is trying to avoid. The interview might then become a battle of opposing sentiments.

Rules for conducting the interview

The rules of orientation with which we have been concerned may be applied by the field worker in social anthropology as well as by the clinical psychologist or the social caseworker. They can be used by the personnel manager of a large industrial corporation in his daily activities as well as in the more formal industrial relations interviewing. With regard to the rules for conducting the interview, however, this possibility of general application no longer holds, for they vary with the kind of personal and social situations being explored. It is evident that the interviewing of a child, a psychoneurotic, a native of a primitive community, or the normal adult of a civilized community involves different modifications in the way the interview takes place. For this reason, then, in discussing the rules of performance we shall limit ourselves to those rules which were found helpful in interviewing industrial workers.

There is always the danger for the beginner that he attach a significance to the rules of performance that they do not have. He tends to treat them as absolute prescriptions which should never be violated, and he tends to multiply them without end. This fetish about the rules of performance arises in part from a failure to understand the rules of orientation; ritualistic rules for conducting the interview are substituted for understanding. The rules of performance should play a secondary role to the rules of orientation. If the interviewer understands what he is doing and is in active touch with the actual situation, he has extreme latitude in what he can do. Whether or not the interviewee faces the light is not of first importance. What is important is that his rules of procedure should take into account the considerations discussed under Rule IVA. For if the interview is a social situation, involving a relation between two people in a particular social setting, the rules of performance must address themselves to that situation.

The interviewers formulated five rules for the conduct of interviews, to which they tried to adhere fairly closely. These were as follows:

* * *

Rule 1. The interviewer should listen to the speaker in a patient and friendly, but intelligently critical, manner.

The attitude of the interviewer should be one of patiently listening to what the speaker has to say before making any comment himself. He should listen and not talk until the person has made a complete statement. Probably the quickest way to stop a person from sufficiently expressing himself is to interrupt. No matter how irrelevant the material may seem to be to the interviewer, he must remember that the person being interviewed probably cannot easily state what is really important to him. Of course, it follows that, besides actively listening and not interrupting, the interviewer should try to understand what is being said. Nothing irritates a person more than the feeling that he is misunderstood. Moreover, the interviewer should show his interest in what is being said. His attitude should be more than a pretense of being interested; he should be really interested.

Rule 2. The interviewer should not display any kind of authority.

The interviewer should do everything to help the worker to feel at ease. There are many different ways of accomplishing this end, but most of them are corollaries of the above rule.

* * *

There are two forms of expressing authority which should be particularly avoided. They will be stated, therefore, as separate rules.

Rule 3. The interviewer should not give advice or moral admonition.

The interviewer must not suggest or imply judgments of value or of morals concerning the worker's overt or verbal behavior. If the worker says, "This is a hell of a company, and my supervisors are 'goddam' slave drivers," the attitude of the interviewer should not be, "Tut-tut, my good man, you are not displaying the proper spirit." Instead, he should prevail upon the worker to express himself more fully by asking such questions as, "Why do you feel this way?" or "Tell me more about this." In this manner the interviewer allows the person to express his opinions more frankly and in greater detail.

Rule 4. The interviewer should not argue with the speaker.

. . . The best way for the interviewer to avoid argument is for him to see that the speaker's sentiments do not react upon his own. The interviewer should not defend or justify himself. If the speaker criticizes him, he must be ready to ask, "Why do you think this?" For this reason more than any other, the interviewer should be aware of his own sentiments, for, otherwise, he is in a position of having them at times painfully violated.

Rule 5. The interviewer should talk or ask questions only under certain conditions.

a. To help the person talk. The main objective of the interview is to get the speaker to talk freely and frankly about himself and his environment, and there are a number of stock phrases that can be used for this purpose, such as, "Isn't that interesting?" "What do you mean?" "Why?" "Isn't that curious?" "For example?" and "Tell me more about it."

It has been said that the consistent use of three expressions, "Why?" "For example?" and "Define," can stop any conversation. Now, although this applies to the interview as well as to social intercourse, the interviewer sometimes can with discretion use two of these expressions, namely "Why?" and "For example?" In this way, generalizations can sometimes be brought to a more concrete level.

b. To relieve any fears or anxieties on the part of the speaker which may be affecting his relation to the interviewer.

* * *

c. To praise the interviewee for reporting his thoughts and feelings accurately. Although in general it is wise for the interviewer not to operate on the speaker's sentiments, there is one sentiment which he can use in order to facilitate the interviewing process, and that is to praise the speaker for trying to express freely and frankly what he regards as important.

d. To veer the discussion to some topic which has been omitted or neglected. Many times the interviewer would like to direct the discussion to a certain topic which has either been neglected or omitted by the speaker. In a fairly long interview opportunities sometimes arise which allow the interviewer to break into such critical zones. No specific rules can be stated. The more training an interviewer has, the more skill he develops in this direction.

e. To discuss implicit assumptions, if this is advisable. During an interview the interviewer frequently has occasion to note an assumption which underlies the conversation but which itself is not expressed. Sometimes it is helpful in stimulating further discussion to bring to the interviewee's attention such an assumption. In doing this, the interviewer has to exercise discretion. If calling forth such an assumption is likely to embarrass the speaker, it is, of course, better not to do it. But many times the person welcomes such a restatement of his thinking, and the interview starts out again with renewed vigor at a new level.

Summary

Perhaps a few words should be said about the abilities required of the interviewer. To some readers it may seem that the practice of the interviewing method requires unusual perspicacity, in fact, almost superhuman abilities. Although it is true that certain skills are demanded of the interviewer, it would be incorrect to suppose that these skills are acquired and developed differently from the way skills are developed by a competent worker in any scientific area. It is obvious, of course, that such a method cannot be applied by anyone, anywhere, and at any time. The interviewer needs to have a certain amount of intelligence, knowledge, training, and experience. But similar requirements apply to any person who wishes to become proficient in a particular technique or method.

The interviewer should be seriously and sincerely interested in human situations. At times he needs to exercise a certain amount of intelligence. But just as in a chemical laboratory there are some good technicians unable to state explicitly the grounds of their skill, so in the interviewing field there are some successful interviewers who would be unable to formulate a conceptual scheme. Equally important to the interviewer are training and experience. Several years of training at actual interviewing are almost essential before a person can become proficient. But, even though an interviewer may become very proficient in interviewing a certain class or group of people, the more experience he has with different kinds of personal and social contexts, the more proficient he becomes as an interviewer. Any successful executive, administrator, or politician implicitly makes use of many of the rules of orientation which we have more explicitly stated. Many of these rules are merely a more explicit statement of a point of view that persons who have to deal with people unconsciously take. It is not an opinion but an induction from experience that many people of moderate ability acquire considerable skill as interviewers.

READING IV–2. *The Attitude and Orientation of the Counselor*

CARL R. ROGERS

[The following reading is taken from the first part of Chapter 2 in Rogers' book, *Client-Centered Therapy*. The chapter itself is a revision and extension of an article which first appeared in the *Journal of Consulting Psychology* in April 1949. From the chapter we have excerpted only what we believe to be most relevant to our present purposes, leaving out Rogers' discussions of a number of very important related issues and of his testing of his "basic hypothesis" against available research in psychotherapy as well as in other fields such as leadership, organizational behavior, and education. The entire chapter, in fact the whole book, is strongly recommended as additional reading. What follows, then, is the clearest available statement of what is central to the "client-centered" viewpoint, selected to stimulate discussion, thought, and, when time permits, a more detailed examination.]

In any psychotherapy, the therapist himself is a highly important part of the human equation. What he does, the attitude he holds, his basic concept of his role, all influence therapy to a marked degree. Differing therapeutic orientations hold differing views on these points. At the very outset of our discussion, therefore, it seems appropriate to consider the therapist as he functions in client-centered counseling.

Reprinted with permission from Carl R. Rogers, *Client-Centered Therapy* (Boston: Houghton Mifflin, 1951), 19–29, 32–36, 40–41.

A general consideration

It is common to find client-centered therapy spoken of as simply a method or a technique to be used by the counselor. No doubt this connotation is due in part to the fact that earlier presentations tended to overstress technique. It may more accurately be said that the counselor who is effective in client-centered therapy holds a coherent and developing set of attitudes deeply imbedded in his personal organization, a system of attitudes which is implemented by techniques and methods consistent with it. In our experience, the counselor who tries to use a "method" is doomed to be unsuccessful unless this method is genuinely in line with his own attitudes. On the other hand, the counselor whose attitudes are of the type which facilitate therapy may be only partially successful, because his attitudes are inadequately implemented by appropriate methods and techniques.

Let us, then, consider the attitudes which appear to facilitate client-centered therapy. Must the counselor possess them in order to be a counselor? May these attitudes be achieved through training?

The philosophical orientation of the counselor

Some workers are reluctant to consider the relationship of philosophical views to scientific professional work. Yet in therapeutic endeavor this relation appears to be one of the significant and scientifically observable facts that cannot be ignored. Our experience in training counselors would indicate that the basic operational philosophy of the individual (which may or may not resemble his verbalized philosophy) determines, to a considerable extent, the time it will take him to become a skillful counselor.

The primary point of importance here is the attitude held by the counselor toward the worth and the significance of the individual. How do we look upon others? Do we see each person as having worth and dignity in his own right? If we do hold this point of view at the verbal level, to what extent is it operationally evident at the behavioral level? Do we tend to treat individuals as persons of worth, or do we subtly devaluate them by our attitudes and behavior? Is our philosophy one in which respect for the individual is uppermost? Do we respect his capacity and his right to self-direction, or do we basically believe that his life would be best guided by us? To what extent do we have a need and a desire to dominate others? Are we willing for the individual to select and choose his own values, or are our actions guided by the conviction (usually unspoken) that he would be happiest if he permitted us to select for him his values and standards and goals?

The answers to questions of this sort appear to be important as basic determiners of the therapist's approach. It has been our experience that individuals who are already striving toward an orientation which stresses the significance and worth of each person can learn rather readily the client-centered techniques which implement this point of view. . . .

Even this statement of the situation gives a static impression which is inaccurate. One's operational philosophy, one's set of goals, is not a fixed and unchanging thing, but a fluid and developing organization. Perhaps it would be more accurate to say that the person whose philosophical orientation has tended to move in the direction of greater respect for the individual finds in the client-centered approach a challenge to and an implementation of his views. He finds that here is a point of view in human relationships which tends to carry him further philosophically than he has heretofore ventured, and to provide the possibility of an operational technique for putting into effect this respect for persons, to the full degree that it exists in his own attitudes. The therapist who endeavors to utilize this approach soon learns that the development of the way of looking upon people which underlies this therapy is a continuing process, closely related to the therapist's own struggle for personal growth and integration. He can be only as "nondirective" as he has achieved respect for others in his own personality organization.

Perhaps it would summarize the point being made to say that, by use of client-centered techniques, a person can implement his respect for others only so far as that respect is an integral part of his personality make-up; consequently the person whose operational philosophy has already moved in the direction of *feeling* a deep respect for the significance and worth of each person is more readily able to assimilate client-centered techniques which help him to express this feeling.

The therapist's hypothesis

The question may well arise, in view of the preceding section, as to whether client-centered therapy is then simply a cult, or a speculative philosophy, in which a certain type of faith or belief achieves certain results, and where lack of such faith prevents these results from occurring. Is this, in other words, simply an illusion which produces further illusions?

Such a question deserves careful consideration. That observations to date would seem to point to an answer in the negative is perhaps most strikingly indicated in the experience of various counselors whose initial philosophic orientation has been rather distant from that described as favorable to an optimum use of client-centered techniques. The experience of such individuals in training has seemed to follow something of a pattern. Initially there is relatively little trust in the capacity of the client to achieve insight or constructive self-direction, although the counselor is intrigued intellectually by the possibilities of nondirective therapy and learns something of the techniques. He starts counseling clients with a very limited hypothesis of respect, which might be stated somewhat in these terms: "I will hypothesize that the individual has a limited capacity to understand and reorganize himself to some degree in certain types of situations. In many situations and with many clients, I, as a more objective outsider, can better know the situation and better guide it." It is on this limited and divided basis that he begins his work. He is often not very successful. But as he observes his counseling results, he finds that clients accept and make constructive use of responsibility when he is genuinely willing for them to do so. He is often surprised at their effectiveness in handling this responsibility. Against the less vital quality of the experience in those situations where he, the counselor, has endeavored to interpret, evaluate, and guide, he cannot help but contrast the quality of the experience in those situations where the client has learned significantly for himself. Thus he finds that the first portion of his hypothesis tends to be proved beyond his expectations, while the second portion proves disappointing. So, little by little, the hypothesis upon which he bases all his therapeutic work shifts to an increasingly client-centered foundation.

This type of process, which we have seen repeated many times, would appear to mean simply this: that the attitudinal orientation, the philosophy of human relationships which seems to be a necessary basis for client-centered counseling, is not something which must be taken "on faith," or achieved all at once. It is a point of view which may be adopted tentatively and partially, and put to the test. It is actually an hypothesis in human relationships, and will always remain so. Even for the experienced counselor, who has observed in many cases the evidence which supports the hypothesis, it it still true that, for the new client who comes in the door, the possibility of self-understanding and intelligent self-direction is still—for this client—a completely unproved hypothesis.

It would seem justifiable to say that the faith or belief in the capacity of the individual to deal with his psychological situation and with himself is of the same order as any scientific hypothesis. It is a positive basis for action, but it is open to proof or disproof. If, for example, we had faith that every person could determine for himself whether he had incipient cancer, our experience with this hypothesis would soon cause us to revise it sharply. On the other hand, if we have faith that warm maternal affection is likely to produce desirable personal reactions and personality growth in the infant, we are likely to find this hypothesis supported, at least tentatively, by our experience.

Hence, to put in more summarized or definitive form the attitudinal orientation which appears to be optimal for the client-centered counselor, we may say that the counselor chooses to act consistently upon the hypothesis that the individual has a sufficient capacity to deal constructively with all those aspects of his life which can potentially come into conscious awareness. This means the creation of an interpersonal situation in which material may come into the client's awareness, and a meaningful demonstration of the counselor's acceptance of the client as a person who is competent to direct himself. The counselor acts upon this hypothesis in a specific and operational fashion, being always alert to note those experiences (clinical or research) which contradict this hypothesis as well as those which support it.

Though he is alert to all the evidence, this does not mean that he keeps shifting his basic hypothesis in counseling situations. If the counselor feels, in the middle of an interview, that this client may not have the capacity for reorganizing himself, and shifts to the hypothesis that the counselor must bear a considerable responsibility for this reorganization, he confuses the client, and defeats himself. He has shut himself off from proving or disproving either hypothesis. This confused eclecticism, which has been prevalent in psychotherapy, has blocked scientific progress in the field. Actually it is only by acting *consistently* upon a well-selected hypothesis that its elements of truth and untruth can become known.

The specific implementation of the counselor's attitude

Thus far the discussion has been a general one, considering the counselor's basic attitude toward others. How does this become implemented in the therapeutic situation? Is it enough that the counselor hold the basic hypothesis we have described, and that this attitudinal orientation will then inevitably move therapy forward? Most assuredly this is not enough. It is as though a physician of the last century had come to believe that bacteria cause infection. Holding this attitude would probably make it inevitable that he should obtain somewhat better results than his colleagues who looked upon this hypothesis with contempt. But only as he implemented his attitude to the fullest extent with appropriate techniques would he fully experience the significance of his hypothesis. Only as he made sterile the area around the incision, the instruments, the sheets, the bandages, his hands, the hands of his assistants—only then would he experience the full meaning and full effectiveness of this tentative hypothesis which he had come to hold in a general way.

So it is with the counselor. As he finds new and more subtle ways of implementing his client-centered hypothesis, new meanings are poured into it by experience, and its depth is seen to be greater than was first supposed. As one counselor-in-training put it, "I hold about the same views I did a year ago, but they have so much more meaning for me."

It is possible that one of the most significant general contributions of the client-centered approach has been its insistence upon investigating the detailed implementation of the counselor's point of view in the interview itself. Many different therapists from a number of differing orientations state their general purposes in somewhat similar terms. Only by a careful study of the recorded interview—preferably with both the sound recording and transcribed typescript available— is it possible to determine what purpose or purposes are actually being implemented in the interview. "Am I actually doing what I think I am doing? Am I operationally carrying out the purposes which I verbalize?" These are questions which every counselor must continually be asking himself. There is ample evidence from our research analyses that a subjective judgment by the counselor himself regarding these questions is not enough. Only an objective analysis of words, voice and inflection can adequately determine the real purpose the therapist is pursuing. . . .

Note that in discussing this point the term "technique" has been discarded in favor of "implementation." The client is apt to be quick to discern when the counselor is using a "method," an intellectually chosen tool which he has selected for a purpose. On the other hand, the counselor is always implementing, both in conscious and nonconscious ways, the attitudes which he holds toward the client. These attitudes can be inferred and discovered from their operational implementation. Thus a counselor who basically does not hold the hypothesis that the person has significant capacity for integrating himself may think that he has used nondirective "methods" and "techniques," and proved to his own satisfaction that these techniques are unsuccessful. A recording of such material tends to show, however, that in the tone of voice, in the handling of the unexpected, in the peripheral activities of the interview, he implements his own hypothesis, not the client-centered hypothesis as he thinks.

It would seem that there can be no substitute for the continual checking back and forth between purpose or hypothesis and technique or implementation. This analytical self-checking the counselor may verbalize somewhat as follows: As I develop more clearly and more fully the attitude and hypothesis upon which I intend to deal with the client, I must check the implementation of that hypothesis in the interview material. But as I study my specific behaviors in the interview I detect implied purposes of which I had not been aware, I discover areas in which it had not occurred to me to apply the hypothesis, I realize that what was for me an implementation of one attitude is perceived by the client as the implementation of another. Thus the thorough study of my behavior sharpens, alters, and modifies the attitude and hypothesis with which I enter the next interview. A sound approach to the implementation of an hypothesis is a continuing and a reciprocal experience.

Some formulations of the counselor's role

As we look back upon the development of the client-centered point of view, we find a steady progression of attempts to formulate what is involved in implementing the basic hypothesis in the interview situation. Some of these are formulations by individual counselors, whereas others have been more generally held. Let us take a few of these concepts and examine them, moving through them to the formulation which appears to be most commonly held at the present time by therapists of this orientation.

In the first place, some counselors—usually those with little specific training—have supposed that the counselor's role in carrying on nondirective counseling was merely to be passive and to adopt a laissez-faire policy. Such a counselor has some willingness for the client to be self-directing. He is more inclined to listen than to guide. He tries to avoid imposing his own evaluations upon the client. He finds that a number of his clients gain help for themselves. He feels that his faith in the client's capacity is best exhibited by a passivity which involves a minimum of activity and of emotional reaction on his part. He tries "to stay out of the client's way."

This misconception of the approach has led to considerable failure in counseling—and for good reasons. In the first place, the passivity and seeming lack of interest or involvement is experienced by the client as a rejection, since indifference is in no real way the same as acceptance. In the second place, a laissez-faire attitude does not in any way indicate to the client that he is regarded as a person of worth. Hence the counselor who plays a merely passive role, a listening role, may be of assistance to some clients who are desperately in need of emotional catharsis, but by and large his results will be minimal, and many clients will leave both disappointed in their failure to receive help and disgusted with the counselor for having nothing to offer.

Another formulation of the counselor's role is that it is his task to clarify and objectify the client's feelings. The present author, in a paper given in 1940 stated, "As material is given by the client, it is the therapist's function to help him recognize and clarify the emotions which he feels." This has been a useful concept, and it is partially descriptive of what occurs. It is, however, too intellectualistic, and if taken too literally, may focus the process in the counselor. It can mean that only the counselor knows what the feelings are, and if it acquires this meaning, it becomes a subtle lack of respect for the client.

Unfortunately, our experience in conveying subtleties of emotionalized attitude is so limited, and the symbols of expression so unsatisfactory, that it is hard accurately to convey to a reader the delicate attitudes involved in the therapist's work. We have learned, to our dismay, that even the transcripts of our recorded cases may give to the reader a totally erroneous notion of the sort of relationship which existed. By persistently reading the counselor responses with the wrong inflection, it is possible to distort the whole picture of the relationship. Such readers when they first hear even a small segment of the recording itself, often say, "Oh, this is entirely different from the way I understood it."

Perhaps the subtle difference between a declarative and an empathic attitude on the part of the counselor may be conveyed by an example. Here is a client statement: "I feel as though my mother is always watching me and criticizing what I do. It gets me all stirred up inside. I try not to let that happen, but you know, there are times when I feel her eagle eye on me that I just boil inwardly."

A response on the counselor's part might be: "You resent her criticism." This response may be given empathically, with the tone of voice such as would be used if it were worded, "If I understand you correctly, you feel pretty resentful toward her criticism. Is that right?" If this is the attitude and tone which is used, it would probably be experienced by the client as aiding him in further expression. Yet we have learned, from the fumblings of counselors-in-training, that "You resent her criticism" may be given with the same attitude and tone with which one might announce "You have the measles," or even with the attitude and tone which would accompany the words "You are sitting on my hat." If the reader will repeat the counselor response in some of these varying inflections, he may realize that when stated empathically and understandingly, the likely attidudinal response on the part of the client is, "Yes, that is the way I feel, and I perceive that a little more clearly now that you have put it in somewhat different terms." But when the counselor statement is declarative, it becomes an evaluation, a judgment made by the counselor, who is now telling the client what his feelings are. The process is centered in the counselor, and the feeling of the client would tend to be, "I am being diagnosed."

In order to avoid this latter type of handling, we have tended to give up the description of the counselor's role as being that of clarifying the client's attitudes.

At the present stage of thinking in client-centered therapy, there is another attempt to describe what occurs in the most satisfactory therapeutic relationships, another attempt to describe the way in which the basic hypothesis is implemented. This formulation would state that it is the counselor's function to assume, in so far as he is able, the internal frame of reference of the client, to perceive the world as the client sees it, to perceive the client himself as he is seen by himself, to lay aside all perceptions from the external frame of reference while doing so, and to communicate something of this empathic understanding to the client.

* * *

The difficulty of perceiving through the client's eyes

This struggle to achieve the client's internal frame of reference, to gain the center of his own perceptual field and see with him as perceiver, is rather closely analogous to some of the *Gestalt* phenomena. Just as, by active concentration, one can suddenly see the diagram in the psychology text as representing a descending rather than an ascending stairway or can perceive two faces instead of a candlestick, so by active effort the counselor can put himself into the client's frame of reference. But just as in the case of the visual perception, the figure occasionally changes, so the counselor may at times find himself standing outside the client's frame of reference and looking as an external perceiver at the client. This almost invariably happens, for example, during a long pause or silence on the client's part. The counselor may gain a few clues which permit an accurate empathy, but to some extent he is forced to view the client from an observer's point of view, and can only actively assume the client's perceptual field when some type of expression again begins.

The reader can attempt this role in various ways, can give himself practice in assuming the internal frame of reference of another while overhearing a conversation on the streetcar, or while listening to a friend describe an emotional experience. Perhaps something of what is involved can even be conveyed on paper.

To try to give you, the reader, a somewhat more real and vivid experience of what is involved in the attitudinal set which we are discussing, it is suggested that you put yourself in the place of the counselor, and consider the following material, which is taken from complete counselor notes of the beginning of an interview with a man in his thirties. When the material has been completed, sit back and consider the sorts of attitudes and thoughts which were in your mind as you read.

CLIENT: I don't feel very normal, but I want to feel that way. . . . I thought I'd have something to talk about—then it all goes around in circles. I was trying to think what I was going to say. Then coming here it doesn't work out. . . . I tell you, it seemed that it would be much easier before I came. I tell you, I just can't make a decision; I don't know what I want. I've tried to reason this thing out logically—tried to figure out which things are important to me. I thought that there are maybe two things a man might do; he might get married and raise a family. But if he was just a bachelor, just making a living—that isn't very good. I find myself and my thoughts getting back to the days when I was a kid and I cry very easily. The dam would break through. I've been in the Army four and a half years. I had no problems then, no hopes, no wishes. My only thought was to get out when peace would come. My problems, now that I'm out, are as ever. I tell you, they go back to a long time before I was in the Army. . . . I love children. When I was in the Philippines—I tell you, when I was young I swore I'd never forget my unhappy childhood—so when I saw these children in the Philippines, I treated them very nicely. I used to give them ice cream cones and movies. It was just a period—I'd reverted back—and that awakened some emotions in me I thought I had long buried. (*A pause. He seems very near tears.*)

As this material was read, such thoughts as the following would represent an external frame of reference in you, the "counselor."

I wonder if I should help him get started talking.
Is this inability to get under way a type of dependence?
Why this indecisiveness? What could be its cause?
What is meant by this focus on marriage and family?
He seems to be a bachelor. I hadn't known that.
The crying, the "dam," sound as though there must be a great deal of repression.
He's a veteran. Could he have been a psychiatric case?
I feel sorry for anybody who spent four and one-half years in the service.

Some time he will probably need to dig into those early unhappy experiences.
What is this interest in children? Identification? Vague homosexuality?

Note that these are all attitudes which are basically sympathetic. There is nothing "wrong" with them. They are even attempts to "understand," in the sense of "understanding about," rather than "understanding with." The locus of perceiving is, however, outside of the client.

By way of comparison, the thoughts which might go through your mind if you were quite successful in assuming the client's internal frame of reference would tend to be of this order:

You're wanting to struggle toward normality, aren't you?
It's really hard for you to get started.
Decision-making just seems impossible to you.
You want marriage, but it doesn't seem to you to be much of a possibility.
You feel yourself brimming over with childish feelings.
To you the Army represented stagnation.
Being very nice to children has somehow had meaning for you.
But it was—and is—a disturbing experience for you.

As pointed out before, if these thoughts are couched in a final and declarative form, then they shift over into becoming an evaluation from the counselor's perceptual vantage point. But to the extent that they are attempts to understand, tentative in formulation, they represent the attitude we are trying to describe as "adopting the client's frame of reference."

The rationale of the counselor's role

The question may arise in the minds of many, why adopt this peculiar type of relationship! In what way does it implement the hypothesis from which we started? What is the rationale of this approach?

In order to have a clear basis for considering these questions, let us attempt to put first in formal terms and then in paraphrase a statement of the counselor's purpose when he functions in this way. In psychological terms, it is the counselor's aim to perceive as sensitively and accurately as possible all of the perceptual field as it is being experienced by the client, with the same figure and ground relationships, to the full degree that the client is willing to communicate that perceptual field; and having thus perceived this internal frame of reference of the other as completely as possible, to indicate to the client the extent to which he is seeing through the client's eyes.

Suppose that we attempt a description somewhat more in terms of the counselor's attitudes. The counselor says in effect, "To be of assistance to you I will put aside myself—the self of ordinary interaction —and enter into your world of perception as completely as I am able. I will become, in a sense, another self for you—an alter ego of your own attitudes and feelings—a safe opportunity for you to discern yourself more clearly, to experience yourself more truly and deeply, to choose more significantly."

The counselor's role as implementation of an hypothesis

In what ways does this approach implement the central hypothesis of our work? It would be grossly misleading to say that our present method or formulation of the method grew out of the theory. The truth is that, as in most similar problems, one begins to find on the basis of clinical intuition that certain attitudes are effective, others are not. One tries to relate these experiences to basic theory, and thus they become clarified and point in the direction of further extension. It is thus that we have arrived at the present formulation, and this formulation will undoubtedly change as we solve some of the perplexities stated at the end of this chapter.

For the present, it would appear that for me, as counselor, to focus my whole attention and effort upon understanding and per- ceiving as the client perceives and understands, is a striking operational demonstration of the belief I have in the worth and the significance of this individual client. Clearly the most important value which I hold is, as indicated by my attitudes and my verbal behavior, the client himself. Also the fact that I permit the outcome to rest upon this deep understanding is probably the most vital operational evidence which could be given that I have confidence in the potentiality of the in- dividual for constructive change and development in the direction of a more full and satisfying life. As a seriously disturbed client wrestles with his utter inability to make any choice, or another client struggles with his strong urges to commit suicide, the fact that I enter with deep understanding into the desperate feelings that exist but do not attempt to take over responsibility, is a most meaningful expression of basic confidence in the forward-moving tendencies in the human organism.

We might say then, that for many therapists functioning from a client-centered orientation, the sincere aim of getting "within" the attitudes of the client, of entering the client's internal frame of reference, is the most complete implementation which has thus far been formulated, for the central hypothesis of respect for and reliance upon the capacity of the person.

* * *

A theory of the therapist's role

. . . [A] possible psychological explanation of the effectiveness of the counselor's role might be developed in these terms. Psychotherapy deals primarily with the organization and the functioning of the self. There are many elements of experience which the self cannot face, cannot clearly perceive, because to face them or admit them would be inconsistent with and threatening to the current organization of self. In client-centered therapy the client finds in the counselor a genuine alter ego in an operational and technical sense—a self which has temporarily divested itself (so far as possible) of its own selfhood, except for the one quality of endeavoring to understand. In the therapeutic experience, to see one's own attitudes, confusions, ambivalences, feelings, and perceptions accurately expressed by another, but stripped of their complications of emotion, is to see oneself objectively, and paves the way for acceptance into the self of all these elements which are now more clearly perceived. Reorganization of the self and more integrated functioning of the self are thus furthered.

Let us try to restate this idea in another way. In the emotional warmth of the relationship with the therapist, the client begins to experience a feeling of safety as he finds that whatever attitude he expresses is understood in almost the same way that he perceives it, and is accepted. He then is able to explore, for example, a vague feeling of guiltiness which he has experienced. In this safe relationship he can perceive for the first time the hostile meaning and purpose of certain aspects of his behavior, and can understand why he has felt guilty about it, and why it has been necessary to deny to awareness the meaning of this behavior. But this clearer perception is in itself disrupting and anxiety-creating, not therapeutic. It is evidence to the client that there are disturbing inconsistencies in himself, that he is not what he thinks he is. But as he voices his new perceptions and their attendant anxieties, he finds that this acceptant alter ego, the therapist, this other person who is only partly another person, perceives these experiences too, but with a new quality. The therapist perceives the client's self as the client has known it, and accepts it; he perceives the contradictory aspects which have been denied to awareness and accepts those too as being a part of the client; and both of these acceptances have in them the same warmth and respect. Thus it is that the client, experiencing in another an acceptance of both these aspects of himself, can take toward himself the same attitude. He finds that he too can accept himself even with the additions and alterations that are necessitated by these new perceptions of himself as hostile. He can experience himself as a person having hostile as well as other types of feelings, and can experience himself in this way without guilt. He has been enabled to do this (if our theory is correct) because another person has been able to adopt his frame of reference, to perceive with him, yet to perceive with acceptance and respect.

READING IV-3. *Categories of Counselor and Client Responses*

WILLIAM U. SNYDER

[One of the most important contributions of Carl Rogers and the other therapists associated with him has been to pioneer in the recording and publication of counseling interviews, so that the process of psychotherapy became available for detailed comparative study. Snyder's *Casebook of Non-directive Counseling* was an early and important example. (See also the case of Herbert Bryan in Rogers' *Counseling and Psychotherapy*, pp. 261–437.) As an appendix to his casebook, Snyder described a system for categorizing responses in non-directive (or "client-centered") interviews which had been developed in early research with this material. Our students have found Snyder's explanation of his categories, especially of the *counselor's* responses, useful in analyzing the cases in Part IV as well as in understanding the behavior of both persons in the interviews they conducted themselves. However, the

Reproduced, by permission of author and publisher, from William U. Snyder, *Casebook of Non-Directive Counseling* (Boston: Houghton Mifflin, 1947), Appendix B.

reader should remember the particular purpose for which these categories were designed (early research on non-directive psychotherapy), and he should also bear in mind the danger, stressed in the previous two readings, of being overly preoccupied with technique.]

In order to make more understandable the type of statements of both client and counselor in a non-directive counseling situation, a system of categories was devised by which the various statements might be classified. The statements of counselors seemed to be classifiable into one of thirteen general categories, as determined by their subject matter. It will be noted that the last category is termed "miscellaneous." This category includes such statements as friendly conversation, responses which bring the contact or the series of contacts to a close, and unclassifiable statements. It is possible that the individual who is trying the non-directive technique for the first few times may find in analyzing his responses that the categories listed below are not inclusive enought for his material. Often such a counselor may have made a number of directive statements, perhaps using persuasion, disapproval, or criticism, or possibly proposal of some activity which the counselor feels the client should carry out. In such a case it would be wise to extend the list of categories to cover such different situations, rather than to attempt to force the classification into the categories given below.

Perhaps the counselor statements which are most difficult to classify are those called "restatement of content," "clarification of feeling," and "interpretation," because these three categories differ only in the degree to which the counselor recognizes the feeling of the client. In the first category, restatement of content, the counselor tries to clarify the feeling but succeeds only in repeating what the client has said, perhaps doing so in slightly different words. Perhaps, in general, it might be said that those counselor responses in which the phrase "you think" appears or might be substituted for some other wording are likely to be restatement of content. An illustration of this situation is given below:

s. I had an operation. It's just a very natural nervous reaction.

c. You think it's the natural aftermath of your operation.

It is the goal of the non-directive counselor, whenever possible, to *clarify* the feelings of the client. Clarification of feeling differs from restatement of content in that the counselor responds to the true feeling the client has expressed by putting the client's feeling in a clearer and more recognizable form. This often means that he uses different words than the client has used, and it always means that the counselor is responding to the *feeling* rather than to the *content* of the client's remarks. For example, the counselor must take particular care not to try to respond to the ideas of someone the client is discussing, such as his mother, wife, or friend; rather, the counselor should attempt to clarify the client's feeling toward those ideas. In the excerpt given below the counselor responds to the client's feeling rather than to her friend's ideas:

s. I remember about the end of last semester I was working on exams and I stayed up late with another girl. We got to talking about my hand. She asked me to tell her what I thought about it, so I did. I really thought I'd like to tell her about it, but I really didn't want to. She told me I oughtn't to hide it—she said that all the girls knew about it anyhow. I think that I was a little bit shocked at that. It kind of set me back. She told me, too, that no one dislikes me for it.

c. You found that hiding was no help, most people found out anyhow. That shocked you somewhat.

Another point to be remembered regarding clarification of feeling is that a counselor response which actually names an emotion, such as "you hated," "you were annoyed," or "you felt happy," is very likely to be a clarification of feeling. For example:

s. I'd just like to have it go for a week with her making meals on time. It's only one meal a day that I eat at home. I don't ask her in the morning to get up and get my breakfast; I do it myself, and I eat my noon meal downtown. But that one meal I eat at home, I feel ought to be done—and on time for me to eat when I get home. If for no other reason than to win the battle with me. And yet, I've said little about it. I've kept it pretty much to myself.

c. It burns you up, but you haven't said much about it.

The counselor is using interpretation when he goes beyond the feelings the client has expressed, when he points out patterns and relationships in the material presented of which the client may not yet have expressed awareness. Usually, interpretation is very difficult for the client to accept, and resistance is encountered when the counselor attempts it. Interpretation is a semi-directive technique, and on the whole the non-directive counselor attempts to keep it at a minimum. The following passage illustrates interpretation by the counselor:

s. There is another situation that bothers me. My father is an amateur magician. He often entertains with his tricks. When the family is all together they like to have him perform. Everybody always says, "Edith, can you do it?" I say, "No," even if I do know how—I just shy away from things that bring it into view.

c. Above all, you feel no one must see this.

s. I've always felt that way.

c. Escape at any cost.

In analyzing statements made by the client or subject, it was found that a two-dimensional classification was useful. First, there was a "content" attribute, i.e., relating to subject matter. Secondly, it was noted that with many statements considerable feeling was expressed or clearly inferred. For example, in a statement like, "I hated her. I wished she would die," the client was stating a problem and was also expressing a negative feeling toward her mother. Consequently, it was decided to construct a two-dimensional type of classification for the client responses. In the first dimension, that of the content of the material, eight categories seemed appropriate. In the second, or "emotions" dimension, three categories were decided upon. These are used when statements indicate positive, negative, or ambivalent attitudes as expressed toward the self, the counselor, or the counseling process, or toward external objects or persons. It should be remembered that, while all client statements obviously have "content" characteristics, only a part of them contain a noticeable expression of feeling. Therefore, client statements may be classified either in the one dimension or in both dimensions. The "miscellaneous" category in the client-content categories includes such responses as friendly discussion, material not related to the problem, statements ending the contact or the series of contacts, and unclassifiable material.

Definitions of counselor categories[1]

Structuring. Statements which explain the counseling procedure; responses which state the expected outcome of the treatment, or the limitations of time, or the responsibilities of the counselor or client. Examples: "I'm not interested in the least in either asking, suggesting, or telling you to do something that you really fundamentally may not want to do. I am interested, however, in talking and thinking these things through with you so that *you* feel what you are doing is really

[1] W. U. Snyder, "An Investigation of the Nature of Non-directive Psychotherapy," *Journal of General Psychology*, 33 (1945), pp. 193–223.

what you want to do." "Through talking these things over together, we may be able to find some new ways of dealing with these things. Just feel perfectly free to talk about anything you like." "You'd find that you would be free to talk about most anything you wanted to, and that I'd scarcely ever even ask you questions. . . . Now if you'd like to try that sort of thing, I believe we could arrange for regular meetings at this hour on Wednesdays and Fridays."

Direct Question. Questions in which the counselor asks for specific information; a directive technique. Examples: "Do you think you would want to go ahead with counseling on that basis?" "When did you first start having these feelings?" Not included are expressions in the form of a question which really only clarify or restate the previous expression of the client. Examples: "This seems to be a battle that you must carry out yourself, is that it?" "You think that is what you should do?" "Do you mean that you feel a situation in which you got caught might be of sufficient intensity to *make* you quit your escapades?"

Forcing Client Responsibility. Attempts by the counselor to redirect to the client the responsibility for selecting the topic to be discussed; a directive technique. Examples: "Well, how do *you* feel about that?" "You feel that's the problem?"

Non-directive Leads. Responses of the counselor which elicit further statement by the client of his problem. These responses are planned in such a manner as to avoid limiting the nature of the discussion to any narrow topic. Examples: "What's on your mind today?" "How are things going?" "Do you want to tell me more about that?" Responses which are less non-directive are these: "You mentioned that you felt your inferiority feelings are partly a result of your school experiences. Do you want to carry that further?" "You traced that back somewhat last time, didn't you?"

Acceptance. Simple agreement; statements that indicate understanding or assent, but do not imply approval or disapproval. Examples: "Yes." "M-hm." "I see." "No" (following a negative statement).

Restatement of Content. Repetitions of the idea expressed by the client which do not reorganize the statement in such a manner as to reveal more clearly the client's feelings; those statements which reflect more of the intellectual aspect of what the client has said than of the feeling tone. A counselor response can be classified as restatement of content only when the classifier is aware of the client statement which has preceded it. Examples:

s: This is one of the things he said indicated that I was upset about something. (*Sniffs, blows nose, wipes eyes, cries.*)

c: The doctor felt that the tears were caused by some emotional disturbance.

s: (*Blubbering.*) For no reason at all I cry. I just feel like crying and never stop crying. I don't know why.

c: You don't know why you get those feelings that you never can stop crying.

s: I really can't decide if I'm right or wrong. If it is wrong, I think I'd try to break it. I do it so completely automatically that I really don't have any time to think about it.

c: You can't quite decide which is right, or which is wrong.

Clarification of Feeling. Responses by the counselor which reorganize or synthesize the feelings expressed by the client. The mere changing of the client's wording does not necessarily constitute clarification of feeling. As with restatement of content, counselor responses can be classified as clarification of feeling only when the classifier is aware of the client statement which has preceded it. Examples:

s: There's one thing that I can't quite make up my mind—I've tried to figure it out—well, what is it, when I get into a rut like this, what is it that I really want? And when I examine myself I can't figure out what I really want. It's only by looking at what other people want that I think, well, maybe that's what I want. It's a very odd thing, and I don't like it. That's what makes me feel— that it's—a—that I can't do what I want to do because I don't really know what I want.

c: You feel that so far the best you have been able to achieve along that line is just to take a goal that seems to be good for somebody else. But that you don't feel that there's any real gain that you are sure *you* want.

s: The point is if I wanted to do something great, or what I consider to be great—actually I don't have the qualifications for it because you have to build up to it. So that sort of—(*laughs*) well, of course I don't seem to be willing to do the first thing.

c: You feel that you're not quite willing to set the lower intermediate goals and still you know you are not really equipped to reach some high up or far off goals. Is that it?

Interpretation. Counselor responses which indicate causal relation-ships, or which respond to feelings that have not been expressed by the client. These statements frequently represent the counselor's interjection of his "diagnostic" concepts into the interview, and they are semi-directive in character. Interpretation, like restatement of content and clarification of feeling, can be classified as such only when the classifier is aware of the client statement which preceded the counselor response. What may be in one situation a clarification of feeling, may in another context represent interpretation or restatement of content. Examples of interpretation:

s: And little quirks bother me, too. Some colors offend me more. Violet and blue depress me and yellow makes me feel self-conscious. Green makes me feel swell and red makes me mad, anything with red in it. All the colors have some effect. Red makes me feel depressed, then it's that feeling of wanting to let off steam and just blow up.

c: Even colors tend to symbolize these various frustrations and annoyances.

s: I expect it goes back to the fact that I can't respond wholly under the present situation. The fact that the intrigue of marriage begins to wear off after awhile has contributed some to the problems, too. You know, like you have a real craving for ice cream, but, after about three dishes, you don't want any more.

c: Sometimes you find yourself getting tired of the routine of marriage.

Approval. Counselor statements which evaluate the client or his ideas in terms of the counselor's own attitudes in such a manner as to provide emotional support; a semi-directive technique. Examples: "That's right." "That's a very interesting comment and may well be worth considering again." "I believe that's a good rule of personality."

Reassurance. Counselor statements which encourage the client, which are intended to raise the client's self-esteem or self-assurance, or which imply sympathy; a semi-directive technique. Examples: "I can see how you feel." "You know that I will be glad to help if I can." "And it's really not unusual; that sort of thing happens a good bit."

Information. Statements supplying factual data or the expression of an opinion; a directive counseling technique. Example: "My telephone number is 3892." "Yes, I think the registrar would know about that."

Miscellaneous. Statements which are not described by the other categories. This includes friendly conversation, ending of the contact or of the series of interviews, and so on. Examples: "Well, I see our time is up for today." "Hello." "Isn't this miserable weather?"

Client–content categories

Problem. Statements indicating areas of concern to the client, or revealing symptoms of maladjustment or dissatisfaction, or statements which report situations or incidents relating to the client's problem. Examples: "After I had become pretty well settled on the job, I think it was about then I began to dabble at work." "They think it's wrong to talk about my handicap to anyone." "You see my life has been really intense hell. You can't imagine how I had to live as a child." "I'm always worrying about some things—not big things, just little things." "I'm afraid even to be a failure."

Asking for Information. Any questions of the client which request a factual reply from the counselor. These frequently include requests for advice or for reassurance. Examples: "Once you know your problem, what are you supposed to do about it?" "Would you mind giving me your telephone number in case something else should come up, and I should want to see you again?"

Disagreement. Rejection of, or reluctance to accept, any statement of the counselor. Examples: "That's not always true." "Well, it's not exactly that." "Not symbolize, but just different colors have various effects."

Answering Questions. A reply to a direct question. Simple acceptance of a counselor's clarification of feeling is not included. Examples of answers: "Yes, I would like to go ahead with counseling." "No, no, I don't."

Agreement. Simple acceptance of a counselor's clarification of feeling. "Yes." "M-hm." "That's exactly it."

Insight. Statements by the client indicating a recognition of the causes of his behavior or revealing a reorganization in his understanding of himself. This does not include rationalizations. Examples: "I've used the 'sour grapes' policy. Always, I only wanted to do what I could be the best in." "I find a great deal of the things I do with a group are only to cover up." "There's nothing that can be done unless I do it myself. It lies within me to correct the situation." "Perhaps my trouble is I am afraid of being hurt." "Maybe my other feelings are blocked because I still feel repelled by it; I still want to push it away from me." "But you see—it's just occurred to me, really right now, that I'm big enough to live and let live." "But I am that way, and I like to be that way, and I expect it will be my life-pattern." "I like people, perhaps because I want to be liked."

Planning. Statements revealing the client's decisions regarding future actions or intentions to change his attitudes. Discussions of previous plans are excluded. Examples: "I *am* happier with Marie. And since I am willing to bring it out for discussion, it implies a willingness to continue it still further on my part." "Even if we find we can't build the house now, I *want* to go through with these other things whether the house goes through or not." "I know now what I'm going to do." "I'm going to accept it though." "I'm gonna carry out my program of finding out what Robert Winslow Smith, the fourth, really is. I'm gonna find out the ways that I can better him instead of tearing him down as I have been." "I'm gonna think it over over the week-end. Maybe I'll have the answer next week." "I'm not going to let the army get me down; at least, they're going to have a hard time trying."

Miscellaneous. Statements which are not described by the other categories. This includes friendly conversation, ending of the contact or of the series of interviews, etc. Examples: "Boy, am I miserable today. I have a cold." "Well, I'll not be back. Thanks so much for your time." "Goodbye."

Client–feeling categories

Positive Attitudes. Statements which reveal approval and acceptance of the client himself, the counselor or the counseling process, or other persons, objects, or situations. Examples: "I am really greatly improved. I'm greatly elated." "Talking it out with you has helped." "I feel that I'm really accomplishing something. Your shrewd method of leading me or helping me to lead myself is wonderful." "Every time I come here, when I go home I feel more relaxed, more at peace with people. I guess it's just because I've had this chance of letting off steam."

Negative Attitudes. Statements which reveal disapproval or rejection of the client himself, the counselor, or the counseling process, or other persons, objects, or situations. Examples: "This is all perfectly silly, but the doctor *insisted* that I come in and see you." "They still think of me as—that they have to do everything for me. We just clash. We clash because I want more independence." "I just haven't given Marie the kind of responses that will make her happy and she isn't getting the responses outside of the home either." "I always felt that other fellows could always do things, but I could never come up to the other group." "If there were two of me I'd punch myself right in the nose just for the fun of it."

Ambivalent Attitudes. Statements which reveal the concurrent existence of favorable and unfavorable attitudes toward the client himself, the counselor, or the counseling process, or other persons, objects, or situations. Examples: "I want to find out but I'm afraid to." "She can take a home and decorate it well, but on the fundamentals she was a little lax and still is." "She's so gentle, precious, kind. Fundamentally she's a snob, but it doesn't show through."

READING IV–4. *The Process of Therapy*

CARL R. ROGERS

[The following selections are from Chapter 4, "The Process of Therapy," of *Client-Centered Therapy*. In this chapter Rogers summarized the then available research and clinical evidence concerning changes observed in the client's behavior during and after the course of therapy and covering the apparent reasons for these changes under the client-centered approach. Some of the types of changes described may be summarized very briefly as follows: from focus on "problems" to "insight" into new ways of behaving; from "symptons" to "self"; from "past" to "present." Selections from the chapter dealing with such changes follow.]

IN PERCEPTION OF AND ATTITUDE TOWARD SELF

He perceives himself as a more adequate person, with more worth and more possibility of meeting life. He permits more experiential data to enter awareness, and thus achieves a more realistic appraisal of himself, his relationships, and his environment. He tends to place the basis of standards within himself, recognizing that the "goodness" or "badness" of any experience or perceptual object is not something inherent in that object, but is a value placed on it by himself   [p. 139].

Reprinted with permission from Carl R. Rogers, *Client-Centered Therapy* (Boston: Houghton Mifflin, 1951), Chapter 4.

IN THE MANNER OF PERCEPTION

Characteristically the client changes from high-level abstractions to more differentiated perceptions, from wide generalizations to limited generalizations closely rooted in primary experiences. . . . [p. 143].
. . . we may say that the client has been living by a map. In therapy he discovers first of all that the map is not the territory—that the experiential territory is very different, and far more complex. . . .

Using other semantic terminology, one may say that the client . . . moves toward a more extensional type of reaction. This may be defined as the tendency to see things in limited, differentiated terms, to be aware of the space–time anchorage of facts, to be dominated by facts, not by concepts, to evaluate in multiple ways, to be aware of the different levels of abstraction, to test his inferences and abstractions by reality, insofar as possible [p. 144].

Thus Snygg and Combs state, "we might, therefore, define psychotherapy from a phenomenological point of view as: the promotion of experience whereby the individual is enabled to make more adequate differentiation of the phenomenal self and its relationship to external reality. If such differentiations can be made, the need of the individual for maintenance and enhancement of the phenomenal self will do the test" [p. 146].

TOWARD AWARENESS OF DENIED EXPERIENCE

. . . successful therapy seems to entail the bringing into awareness, in adequately differentiated and accurately symbolized way, those experiences and feelings which are currently in contradiction to the client's concept of self [pp. 148–49].

IN THE VALUING PROCESS

In client-centered therapy . . . one description of the counselor's behavior is that he consistently keeps the locus of evaluation with the client. Some of this is evident in the way he phrases his responses. "you're angry at—"; "You're confused by—"; "It seems to you that —"; "You feel that—"; "You think you're bad because you—." In each of these responses the attitude as well as the phrasing is such as to indicate that it is the *client's* evaluation of the situation which is being accepted. Little by little the client finds that it is not only possible but satisfying and sound to accept the locus of evaluation as residing within himself. When this experience becomes internalized, values are no longer seen as fixed or threatening things. They are judgments made by the individual, based upon his own experience, and they are also alterable if and when new experience gives new and altered evidence [pp. 150–51].

[Under the heading "Characteristic Changes in Behavior," Rogers reported that the available evidence, admittedly not entirely convincing because of serious problems of measurement, pointed to changes in such directions as: more maturity, more self-direction, less defensiveness, less tension, more inner calm when faced with new stresses (p. 186). After acknowledging the gaps and weaknesses in the state of knowledge about the process he had just reported, and which has been briefly summarized in the preceding passages, Rogers concluded the chapter with an attempt to pull together various tendencies in a theoretical statement which was in line with available evidence and which also reflected something of "the dynamic and moving quality which accompanies the experiences of therapy" (p. 187). His statement follows.]

A coherent theory of the process of therapy

Can we formulate a theory of therapy which will take into account all the observed and verified facts, a theory which can resolve the seeming contradictions that exist? The material which follows is such an attempt, beginning with the personality as it exists before a need for therapy develops, and carrying it through the changes which occur in client-centered therapy. As has been mentioned before, the theory is the fluctuating and evanescent generalization. The observed phenomena of therapy are the more stable elements around which a variety of theories may be built.

Let us begin with the individual who is content with himself, who has no thought at this time of seeking counseling help. We may find it useful to think of this individual as having an organized pattern of perceptions of self and self-in-relationship to others and to the environment. This configuration, this gestalt, is, in its details, a fluid and changing thing, but it is decidedly stable in its basic elements. It is, as Raimy says, "constantly used as a frame of reference when choices are to be made. Thus it serves to regulate behavior and may serve to account for observed uniformities in personality." This configuration is, in general, available to awareness.

We may look upon this self-structure as being an organization of hypotheses for meeting life—an organization which has been relatively effective in satisfying the needs of the organism. Some of its hypotheses may be grossly incorrect from the standpoint of objective reality. As long as the individual has no suspicion of this falsity, the organization may serve him well. As a simple example, the star student in a small-town high school may perceive himself as an outstandingly brilliant person, with a mind excelled by none. This formulation may serve him quite adequately as long as he remains in that environment. He may have some experiences which are inconsistent with this generalization, but he either denies these experiences to awareness, or symbolizes them in such a way that they are consistent with his general picture.

As long as the self-gestalt is firmly organized, and no contradictory material is even dimly perceived, then positive self-feelings may exist, the self may be seen as worthy and acceptable, and conscious tension is minimal. Behavior is consistent with the organized hypotheses and concepts of the self-structure. An individual in whom such conditions exist would perceive himself as functioning adequately.

In such a situation, the extent to which the individual's perceptions of his abilities and relationships were incongruent with socially perceived reality would be a measure of his basic vulnerability. The extent to which he dimly perceives these incongruences and discrepancies is a measure of his internal tension, and determines the amount of defensive behavior. As a parenthetical comment, it may be observed that in highly homogeneous cultures, where the self-concept of the individual tends to be supported by his society, rather grossly unrealistic perceptions may exist without causing internal tension, and may serve throughout a lifetime as a reasonably effective hypothesis for meeting life. Thus the slave may perceive himself as less worthy than his master, and live by this perception, even though, judged on a reality basis, it may be false. But in our modern culture, with its conflicting subcultures, and its contradictory sets of values, goals, and perceptions, the individual tends to be exposed to a realization of discrepancies in his perceptions. Thus internal conflict is multiplied.

To return to our individual, who is not yet ready for therapy: It is when his organized self-structure is no longer effective in meeting his needs in the reality situation, or when he dimly perceives discrepancies in himself, or when his behavior seems out of control and no longer consistent with himself, that he becomes "ripe," as it were, for therapy. As examples of these three conditions, we might mention the "brilliant" small-town high school student who no longer finds himself effective in the university, the individual who is perplexed because he wants to marry the girl yet does not want to, and the client who finds that her behavior is unpredictable, "not like myself," no longer understandable. Without a therapeutic experience, planned or accidental, such conditions are likely to persist because each of them involves the perception of experiences which are contradictory to the current organization of the self. But such perception is threatening to the structure of the self and consequently tends to be denied or distorted, to be inadequately symbolized.

But let us suppose that our individual, now vaguely or keenly disturbed and experiencing some internal tension, enters a relationship with a therapist who is client-centered in his orientation. Gradually he experiences a freedom from threat which is decidedly new to him. It is not merely that he is free from attack. This has been true of a number of his relationships. It is that every aspect of self which he exposes is equally accepted, equally valued. His almost belligerent statement of his virtues is accepted as much as, but no more than, his discouraged picture of his negative qualities. His certainty about some aspects of himself is accepted and valued, but so are his uncertainties, his doubts, his vague perception of contradictions within himself. In this atmosphere of safety, protection, and acceptance, the firm boundaries of self-organization relax. There is no longer the firm, tight gestalt which is characteristic of every organization under threat, but a looser, more uncertain configuration. He begins to explore his perceptual field more and more fully. He discovers faulty generalizations, but his self-structure is now sufficiently relaxed so that he can consider the complex and contradictory experiences upon which they are based. He discovers experiences of which he has never been aware, which are deeply contradictory to the perception he has had of himself, and this is threatening indeed. He retreats temporarily to the former comfortable gestalt, but then slowly and cautiously moves out to assimilate this contradictory experience into a new and revised pattern.

Essentially this is a process of disorganization and reorganization, and while it is going on it may be decidedly painful. It is deeply confusing not to have a firm concept of self by which to determine behavior appropriate to the situation. It is frightening or disgusting to find self and behavior fluctuating almost from day to day, at times being largely in accord with the earlier self-pattern, at times being in confused accord with some new, vaguely structured gestalt. As the process continues, a new or revised configuration of self is being constructed. It contains perceptions which were previously denied. It involves more accurate symbolization of a much wider range of sensory and visceral experience. It involves a reorganization of values, with the organism's own experience clearly recognized as providing the evidence for the valuations. There slowly begins to emerge a new self, which to the client seems to be much more his "real" self, because it is based to a much greater extent upon all of his experience, perceived without distortion.

This painful dis- and re-organization is made possible by two elements in the therapeutic relationship. The first is the one already mentioned, that the new, the tentative, the contradictory, or the previously denied perceptions of self are as much valued by the therapist as the rigidly structured aspects. Thus the shift from the latter to the former becomes possible without too disastrous a loss of self worth, nor with too frightening a leap from the old to the new. The other element in the relationship is the attitude of the therapist toward the newly discovered aspects of experience. To the client they seem threatening, bad, impossible, disorganizing. Yet he experiences the therapist's attitude of calm acceptance toward them. He finds that to a degree he can introject this attitude and can look upon his experience as something he can own, identify, symbolize, and accept as a part of himself.

If the relationship is not adequate to provide this sense of safety, or if the denied experiences are too threatening, then the client may revise his concept of self in a defensive fashion. He may further distort the symbolization of experience, may make more rigid the structure of self, and thus achieve again positive self-feelings and a somewhat reduced internal tension—but at a price of increased vulnerability. Undoubtedly this is a temporary phenomenon in many clients who are undergoing considerable reorganization, but the evidence suggests the possibility that an occasional client may conclude his contacts at such a juncture, having achieved only an increasingly defensive self.

Where the client does face more of the totality of his experience, and where he adequately differentiates and symbolizes this experience, then as the new self-structure is organized, it becomes firmer, more clearly defined, a steadier, more stable guide to behavior. As in the state in which the person felt no need of therapy, or in the defensive reorganization of self, positive self-feelings return, and positive attitudes predominate over negative. Many of the outward manifestations are the same. From an external point of view the important difference is that the new self is much more nearly congruent with the totality of experience—that it is a pattern drawn from or perceived in experience, rather than a pattern imposed upon experience. From the client's internal point of view, the new self is a more comfortable one. Fewer experiences are perceived as vaguely threatening. There is consequently much less anxiety. There is more assurance in living by the new self, because it involves fewer shaky high-level generalizations, and more of direct experience. Because the values are perceived as originating in self, the value system becomes more realistic and comfortable and more nearly in harmony with the perceived self. Valued goals appear more achievable.

The changes in behavior keep pace with the changes in organization of self, and this behavior change is, surprisingly enough, neither as painful nor as difficult as the changes in self-structure. Behavior continues to be consistent with the concept of self, and alters as it alters. Any behavior which formerly seemed out of control is now experienced as part of self, and within the boundaries of conscious control. In general the behavior is more adjustive and socially more sound, because the hypotheses upon which it is based are more realistic.

Thus therapy produces a change in personality organization and structure, and a change in behavior, both of which are relatively permanent. It is not necessarily a reorganization which will serve for a lifetime. It may still deny to awareness certain aspects of experience, may still exhibit certain patterns of defensive behavior. There is little likelihood that any therapy is in this sense complete. Under new stresses of a certain sort, the client may find it necessary to seek further therapy, to achieve further reorganization of self. But whether there be one or more series of therapeutic interviews, the essential outcome is a more broadly based structure of self, an inclusion of a greater proportion of experience as a part of self, and a more comfortable and realistic adjustment to life.

Underlying this entire process of functioning and of change are the forward-moving forces of life itself. It is this basic tendency toward the maintenance and enhancement of the organism and of the self which provides the motive force for all that we have been describing. In the service of this basic tendency the pretherapy self operates to meet needs. And because of this deeper force the individual in therapy tends to move toward reorganization, rather than toward disintegration. It is a characteristic of the reformulated self which is achieved in therapy that it permits a fuller realization of the organism's potentialities, and that it is a more effective basis for further growth. Thus the therapeutic process is, in its totality, the achievement by the individual, in a favorable psychological climate, of further steps in a direction which has already been set by his growth and maturational development from the time of conception onward   [pp. 190–96].

ADDITIONAL READINGS FOR PART IV

As has already been made abundantly clear, we have concentrated almost exclusively on one approach to the problem of helping another person understand his behavior; namely, the client-centered therapy of Carl Rogers. In this section are listed selections from two of his books that we recommend as "required" reading. Other writings by Rogers, and by other authors, could well be used, and some sources for ideas similar to and different from Rogers' formulations are listed under "Recommended Further References."

We have organized these selections under three headings, depending upon whether the emphasis is primarily on the counselor's underlying orientation and intentions, on his resulting specific behavior during the interview, or on some of the consequences and wider applications of this approach to the helping process. Some readers may prefer to concentrate first on *Counseling and Psychotherapy*, published in 1942, before taking up Rogers' later book, *On Becoming a Person*, a collection of papers written between 1951 and 1961. There are a number of shifts in emphasis in Rogers' thinking over the years. The term *nondirective* does not appear in the more recent writings, for example, and there is increasing stress over the years on "congruence" as a central concept. The earlier book is important for our purposes because it teaches clearly what is meant by responding at the level of feeling as distinguished from responding at the level of content and because it applies more obviously to cases of the sort we are likely to be faced with than do some of Rogers' later writings, in which psychotherapy with more seriously disturbed clients is used for illustrative material. On the other hand, many of the papers in *On Becoming a Person* are addressed to our main concern; namely, the applicability of a way of listening and interacting in a wide range of different "helping relationships." Perhaps it does not oversimplify too drastically the history of the "Rogerian" approach to say that in the course of some twenty-five years this approach has moved progressively toward both greater depth psychologically and greater breadth of applicability. In choosing the following selections we were looking for breadth rather than depth. But many who pick up these books will find themselves reading more than the pages we have indicated here, and we certainly have no objections to that.

Required readings

THE COUNSELOR'S ORIENTATION AND INTENTIONS

1. C. R. Rogers, *Counseling and Psychotherapy*. Boston: Houghton Mifflin, 1942. Chapter 1, "The Place of Counseling," and Chapter 2, "Old and New Viewpoints . . .," 3–47.

2. ———, *On Becoming a Person*. Boston: Houghton Mifflin, 1961. Chapter 2, "Some Hypotheses Regarding the Facilitation of Personal Growth," 31–38; Chapter 3, "The Characteristics of a Helping Relationship," 39–58; and Chapter 18, "A Tentative Formulation of a General Law of Interpersonal Relationships," 338–46.

3. ——— and B. F. Skinner, "Some Issues Concerning the Control of Human Behavior," in Don E. Hamachek, ed., *The Self in Growth, Teaching, and Learning*, 94–119. Englewood Cliffs, N.J.: Prentice-Hall, 1965.

4. *Counseling and Psychotherapy*, Chapter 5, "The Directive Versus the Non-Directive Approach," 115–28; and Chapter 6, "Releasing Expression," 131–73.

SOME CONSEQUENCES AND APPLICATIONS

5. *Counseling and Psychotherapy*, Chapter 4, "Is a Therapeutic Relationship Compatible with Authority?" 108–13; and "Summary" of Chapter 4, 113–14.

6. *On Becoming a Person*, Chapter 13, "Personal Thoughts on Teaching and Learning," 273–78. The other papers in Part VI, "What Are the Implications for Living?" (including, especially, "A Tentative Formulation of a General Law of Interpersonal Relationships," listed earlier) belong equally well under this heading.

7. Nicholas Hobbs, "Sources of Gain in Psychotherapy," *American Psychologist*, 17 (1962), 741–47. (Reprinted in Bennis, Schein, Berlew, and Steele, *Interpersonal Dynamics* [Homewood, Ill.: Dorsey Press, 1964], 474–86.) This stimulating paper uses a somewhat different vocabulary to discuss the same process, questions the value of "insight" as such, stresses the importance of communication and intimacy in the therapeutic relationship, and places the Rogerian approach within a wider context of psychotherapy generally.

Recommended further references

The works listed here are intended as *examples* of where to look for answers to a question frequently raised by exposure to the client-centered approach to psychotherapy: How does the Rogerian point of view compare with other approaches to the process of helping an individual understand his behavior? Some of these books were written for a relatively unsophisticated audience (e.g., Walker) whereas others are quite technical (e.g., Glover). These selections are *not* addressed to what may be a more significant question to most users of this book: How does the client-centered point of view relate to the process of communication and administration in organizations? This will be a central topic in Part V. In other words, this somewhat arbitrary list is our only attempt, in this book, to indicate where the central concepts of Part IV belong in the broad field of psychotherapy, whereas in Part V we relate Part IV to interpersonal relations in formal organizations.

Because the following list is somewhat peripheral to our central concern in this book, we shall not use space to attempt to justify our selections. If asked which of these works the average user of this book would most enjoy reading, our answer is Frank's *Persuasion and Healing* and Berne's *Games People Play*. Both are relatively short and easy to read; both authors are psychiatrists with a fresh and challenging point of view toward psychotherapy as traditionally defined and practiced.

ADDITIONAL EXAMPLES OF THE CLIENT-CENTERED APPROACH

1. Carl R. Rogers, *Client-Centered Therapy*. Boston: Houghton Mifflin 1951. See especially Chapter 5, "Three Questions Raised by Other Viewpoints: Transference, Diagnosis, Applicability," 197–231.

2. ———, "The Interpersonal Relationship: The Core of Guidance," *Harvard Educational Review*, 32, No. 4 (Fall 1962), 416–29.

3. ———, "The Necessary and Sufficient Conditions of Psycho-therapeutic Personality Change," *Journal of Consulting Psychology*, 21 (1957), 95–103.

4. ———, "A Theory of Therapy, Personality, and Interpersonal Relationships, as Developed in the Client-centered Framework," in Sigmund Koch, ed., *Psychology: A Study of a Science*, Study 1, Vol. 3, 184–256, New York: McGraw-Hill, 1959.

5. ——— and R. F. Dymond, eds., *Psychotherapy and Personality Change*. Chicago: University of Chicago Press, 1954.

6. Julius Seeman, "Perspectives in Client-centered Therapy," in Benjamin B. Wolman, ed., *Handbook of Clinical Psychology*, 1215–29. New York: McGraw-Hill, 1965.

COMPARISONS OF DIFFERENT APPROACHES TO PSYCHOTHERAPY

7. Bernard G. Berenson and Robert R. Carkhuff, eds., *Sources of Gain in Counseling and Psychotherapy*. New York: Holt, Rinehart and Winston, 1967.

8. Laurence M. Brammer and Everett L. Shostrum, *Therapeutic Psychology: Fundamentals of Counseling and Psychotherapy*. Englewood Cliffs, N. J.: Prentice-Hall, 1960.

9. Donald H. Ford and Hugh B. Urban, *Systems of Psychotherapy: A Comparative Study*. New York: Wiley, 1963.

10. Jerome D. Frank, *Persuasion and Healing: A Comparative Study of Psychotherapy*. Baltimore: The Johns Hopkins Press, 1961; New York: Schocken Books, 1963 (paperback).

11. Robert A. Harper, *Psychoanalysis and Psychotherapy: Thirty-six. Systems.* Englewood Cliffs, N.J.: Prentice-Hall, 1959 (paperback).

12. Erwin Singer, *Key Concepts in Psychotherapy.* New York: Random House, 1965.

13. Nigel Walker, *A Short History of Psychotherapy in Theory and Practice.* New York: Noonday Press, 1959.

14. John G. Watkins, "Psychotherapeutic Methods," in Benjamin B. Wolman, ed., *Handbook of Clinical Psychology*, 1143–67.

15. Andras Angyal, *Neurosis and Treatment: A Holistic Theory*, edited by E. Hanfmann and R. M. Jones. New York: Wiley, 1965.

16. Eric Berne, *Games People Play: The Psychology of Human Relationships.* New York: Grove Press, 1964.

17. Edward Glover, *The Technique of Psychoanalysis.* New York: International Universities Press, rev. ed., 1958.

18. Karl Menninger, *The Theory of Psychoanalytic Technique.* New York: Science Editions, 1961.

19. Jurgen Ruesch, *Therapeutic Communication.* New York: Norton, 1961.

CASE IV–1. Donald French

As an assignment for a course he was taking at the University of Chicago, Donald French wrote the following analysis "Understanding Another Person From His Own Point of View," of an interview he had recently conducted with Ashok Rajguru, a graduate student in physics at Northwestern University.*

* See Case III–4 for the actual interview upon which this analysis is based.

Introduction

The preceding interview is a dynamic, changing, flowing view of a personality. It is not possible to describe Ashok's view of himself without participating in the flow. I believe he sees himself differently at different stages of the interview. Therefore, a reasonable approach is to pass through the discussion taking "snapshots" of his feelings as we go. Each "snapshot" will be a paraphrased summary of some phase in the development of his view of himself and his situation.

How he sees himself

Initially, Ashok expresses a general dissatisfaction with his life at present, particularly with his academic performance. He finds himself unable to apply his capabilities to his work. He is easily distracted by side interests. He begins to wonder about his real capabilities in physics. Ashok worries about his lack of motivation. Also, he feels guilty about not working harder and about failing to take advantage of his opportunity.

> I'm hanging back. I'm not working as hard at physics as I should. I feel guilty about not working harder. I lack motivation. The desire to excel is gone. I realize my limitations as a physicist but I'm not even measuring up to the potential I do have. I'm not taking advantage of my opportunity here.

These feelings of frustration are enhanced by the notion that he is trapped in a web of circumstances beyond his control.

> I'm trapped physically, so I have to make the best of a bad bargain. I have a definite commitment to live up to.

Amidst these negative feelings there is some evidence of determination.

> I'm not willing to accept defeat yet. I could still excel if it mattered.

Beginning about A 36, Ashok takes a deeper look at his troubles. He acknowledges that his loneliness is interfering with his work. He accepts the fact that physics by itself can't make him happy. He realizes that he was happy at home because his belonging need was satisfied automatically there. Furthermore, he feels a little desperate because he doesn't know what to do.

> The real problem has to do with: What is important in life? Human relations are more important than I used to think. Lack

of fulfillment in human relations is the cause of loss of motivation. This wasn't a problem at home. Now I live in a vacuum. I'm all alone without the support of friends and family. I feel despair because I don't know how to alter the situation. It is all pretty hopeless.

In A47 Ashok outlines a possible course of action which he has been driven to think about. To me, it amounts to a retreat from the problem with minimum loss of face. However, as Ashok sees it, it is a way of avoiding permanent deterioration of his interest in physics. He feels that he couldn't bear to lose his interest in physics permanently because this would seriously damage his self-respect.

I have to do something before my interest in physics dies out completely. If I lost my interest in physics, I'd lose my self-respect.

Ashok can't give up physics altogether, nor can he reject his old value "creativity." However, he feels he can't be creative without first satisfying his belonging need and this he doesn't know how to do. Hence, he returns once again to the desperate feelings of being trapped and living in a vacuum.

I don't have satisfying human relationships, I don't have creativity now and I can't do anything about it because I'm trapped by circumstances. There is so much lacking in my life. I'm living in a vacuum.

As happened earlier, just when his mood is darkest and most desperate, some positive feelings come forth. In particular, he expresses determination to work things out himself. His self-respect generally won't permit him to reveal these deep troubles to others.

I have to find some way out myself. I'm not willing to accept defeat. I try very strongly not to reveal too much of my interior to other people. I'll do something but I don't know what. Something will have to be done about the circumstances.

We now have arrived at what I regard as a crucial stage in the interview and in Ashok's thinking. My response in D76 seems to hit the nail on the head. He responds enthusiastically and surges on to a new level of insight. He seems to realize, possibly for the first time, that he can't change the circumstances and must adapt himself to them instead.

I can't change the circumstances. I have to change the way I react to them. I've been unhappy without human attachments—I *must learn to work without them*—but it is difficult to change. I still have a basic need for these attachments—but I have to get along without them.

In A 79 through A 82, Ashok expresses his view as to why he hasn't made any effort to adapt before. At home he was an adequate personality and the old values still seem right. In my view, his concept of himself as an adequate person was threatened by his experience of being unable to satisfy his belonging needs in the new environment. Hence, he warded off this threat by continuing to regard himself as adequate and blaming his loneliness on circumstances beyond his control. At last he comes to accept himself as inadequate and begins to look at some of the reasons. He expresses the following feelings.

> The old values seem right. I haven't made the effort to adapt because I like my old personality. I was adequate at home. But I've ceased to be an adequate personality without changing at all. However, there is this thing which keeps telling me—oh, no! You are an adequate personality. The circumstances are wrong—. But an adequate personality *copes* with circumstances. At home it is a virtue to be self-effacing and nonaggressive. I was happy with that. Here it doesn't work. I have to change.

From A 85 onward the interview takes a more positive and optimistic tone. He seems to realize that the problem is not completely beyond solution. He begins to wonder if it might not be possible for him to make new friends, even at Northwestern. He understands how his old values have contributed to the problem. Also, he understands that his situation won't improve unless he makes an effort to change.

> You have to make an effort here to know people—it wasn't required at home. Here you have to assert yourself—but at home, that was crude and vulgar. Here I haven't asserted myself so I don't know anyone except by chance. I would like to know people. I'm not an obnoxious personality. At home you can know girls without being aggressive—here you are just out. You have to be aggressive—but that's crude and vulgar—but it isn't crude and vulgar here—so I have to adapt. I should have realized this before. I might even begin to enjoy it here—others might even enjoy me. Even here—relationships beyond the casual have been rewarding. There's no reason why this should not be so. I wait for circumstances to break down the barriers, but that can't always happen. For me to break them down requires a change in my personality which I find very difficult.

Clearly there is some change in the way in which he perceives his situation as the interview progresses. We might summarize briefly the terms in which he perceives his situation in the early part of the interview (up to about D 76) as follows:

Satisfaction—Very Low
    1. No fulfillment in human relationships.
        a. No family ties to serve as an anchor.
        b. Only a few casual friends. (One close friend gone.)
        c. No girl friends. (Although he doesn't mention this till late in the interview, I'm sure he is quite aware of it all along.)

    2. Not enjoying the work. No interest or motivation.

Productivity—Quite Low
    1. Negligible progress compared with real potential, as measured by past performance. (An added source of dissatisfaction.)

    2. Done nothing creative yet, although at this stage probably not many people have.

    3. Not really keeping up with the others and the field.

Development—Low
    1. Not learning enough. Others learning more.

    2. Being diverted by other interests and feel guilty about it.

    3. Failing to take advantage of opportunity to study.

    4. Not turning into a competent physicist like I could and should.

Toward the end of the interview he sees himself as a frozen personality; one which has failed to develop by adapting to the new environment. He also feels that he has failed to partake of potentially satisfying human relationships by refusing to break down social barriers.

Furthermore, at the start, he felt there was no opportunity for him to improve his satisfaction, productivity, or development. He was trapped by circumstances beyond his control. Later, he realizes that there is opportunity for improvement in all these areas. There is some hope, but things will still be difficult.

Influence of background and social factors

The influence of Ashok's background on his view of himself and his current problem is quite strong. He analyzes some of the factors himself. It is intriguing to speculate about his view of himself and his situation before he came to this country. I can piece quite a bit of that together from his comments in the interview plus my previous knowledge of him. *My interpretation* of his views and values of two years ago runs as follows:

I am very close to my whole family, particularly to my mother. This gives me a feeling of security and confidence. Now that father is dead, my brothers and I have to look after mother. I accept this responsibility since I'm pretty grown-up and mature. Besides, it is expected of a good son.

Mother wants me to go into the Civil Service, and be like father was, but I'm much more interested in physics. I would like to do some really creative work in physics. Creativity is the most important thing in life. Therefore, I must pursue my career in physics no matter what effect it has on mother. She can't hold me back. She will let me do what I want to if I insist on it.

I may not be a Heisenberg, I may not win a Nobel prize, but I'm sure that with effort I can be a really competent physicist. I believe I can do creative work. After all, only one boy has ever beaten me in an exam and I came first in my Master's Exam. Of course, I had to work like mad, but I did excel. I'm a pretty bright young man. It is really important to me to continue to excel. My family and friends will be proud of me when I do something creative.

I am an adequate personality and I like myself the way I am. Other people like me too. I read about many things and people enjoy hearing about them. I particularly enjoy discussing physics with my friends. I know lots of nice people, including some girls. I get to know them here and there in a pretty natural way without being one of those crude and vulgar, aggressive kind of people. I wouldn't want to be that

Table 1

Need hierarchy	Two years ago in India	Now at Northwestern
Self-actualization	A	B
Status–Prestige	A	B
Self-esteem (self-respect)	S	B
Membership (belonging)	S	U
Safety	S	S
Physiological (discounting sex, of course)	S	S

Key—S Satisfied
U Unsatisfied
A Actively working toward fulfillment
B Blocked. Unable to work toward fulfillment

way. Father wasn't like that and mother wouldn't want me to be like that either.

I have a lot of respect for and confidence in myself. My ability in physics contributes to this feeling. Furthermore, I've never run into a problem which I couldn't solve by myself. I doubt if I ever will. I wouldn't want to turn to others for help.

This interpretation of his former life gives us some perspective in viewing the changes which have occurred. One can view these changes in Ashok's life in terms of the need hierarchy concept as shown in Table 1. At home his membership and self-esteem needs were essentially satisfied. This freed him to apply himself to his needs for status and self-fulfillment. At Northwestern his belonging need is largely unsatisfied. This blocks him from application toward fulfillment of his higher needs.

Data from the interview to support the need hierarchy classifications follow:

Self-Fulfillment

India

    At home I was totally immersed in physics.   A 41

    I used to think that creativity was everything.   A 50

Northwestern

    I'm not fulfilling my capabilities.   A 32

    It probably isn't that important that I should do something creative in physics.   A 37

Status–Prestige

India

    At home I could talk about what I learned to my friends and it would raise me in their esteem.   A 42

    Coming first in my Master's Exam was my biggest boost.   A 23

    I used to work like mad to excel in school.   A 23

Northwestern

    but now I've given it up totally.   A 24

Self-Respect

India

    My self-respect is related to my capabilities in physics.   A 49

    At home I flung myself into physics. (Therefore he could respect himself at home.)   A 41

My self-respect demands that I find a way out myself.   A 60
In the past I could solve things myself.   A 61

Northwestern

My respect for myself is related to my work in physics.   A 49
Here, I hang back.   A 10
My self-respect demands that I find a way out myself.   A 60
But I don't know what to do.   A 18   A 63
I can't respect a life without creativity.   A 50
Here, I have done nothing creative.   A 5

Membership (Belonging)

India

At home I wouldn't have felt this lack in human relations which
I do feel.   A 40

Northwestern

I think basically it is this lack of fulfillment in human relations
which is at the root of all this hesitancy.   A 39
The absence of rich human relationships makes it impossible for
me to fling myself into physics.   A 43

There is more data in the interview to support the need hierarchy
view, but I believe that the evidence given is pretty convincing. The
portions labeled "India" support my earlier interpretation of his views
back home.

It appears that Ashok's unsatisfied belonging need has much to do
with his present problems. It is fairly clear why Ashok has failed to
satisfy this need at Northwestern. At home his very strong family ties
were just taken for granted. Social norms permitted him to be a nice,
self-effacing young man and still know a lot of people. He was able to
win friends without effort. There were no cultural or ethnic barriers
within his own caste and religion.

Upon coming to this country he naively assumed that things would
pretty much continue as before. At Northwestern there are very few
other Indians. The racial, religious, and cultural differences between
Ashok and the others are quite large. The family ties are far away. He
has made no real effort to bridge the social barriers because:

1. He lacks the security and confidence his family gave him.

2. He didn't realize immediately that an effort was required.

3. His culture and parents taught him that nice people aren't
   aggressive or forward.

Knowing Ashok for some time, I realize that he is somewhat introspective. He seems very shy to strangers. His exceptional mind automatically sets him apart. He is not an ordinary person, even in India. All these things contribute to his isolation. The problem is compounded by the facts that he is rooming alone and his one good friend—the Irish boy in the interview—has graduated. Furthermore, he isn't taking any courses this year. He just works alone on his thesis. Finally, but not least, he has no American-style dating experience whatsoever. Now we begin to understand what he means by "Life in a personal vacuum."

How I see him

In my opinion, this is a remarkable interview! In it we are given the unusual opportunity of listening in while a powerful and sophisticated intellect analyzes its own emotional and behavioral problems. In this interview, Ashok sometimes talks as though he were two people. One of the people is a dispassionate intellect who can back away and view the other and the circumstances in the cold light of reason. The second person is a feeling being who is deeply involved in the problems. This second person is encumbered with old introjected values which make adaptation to the new environment quite difficult.

Some evidence for this *hypothesis* follows. In A 74, Ashok refers to an outsider as a third person. I grant that this could be a slip of the tongue or a misinterpretation on my part, but I don't think so! In A 76, Ashok has finally understood much of his problem and the "intellect" begins to talk to the "feeling being" to straighten him out. "Look, you can't change the circumstances! Now try to adapt yourself to them." Later the intellect talks to the feeling being again and says, "You've tried for two years, but you haven't found it [satisfying human relationships] and you aren't going to find it so you must change." The feeling being responds, "But this is a pretty difficult thing to do."

Later, in A 83, we get another glimpse of the feeling being objecting to the analysis of the intellect. Ashok reports that there is this thing in the back of his mind which keeps telling him, "Oh, no! You are an adequate personality. The circumstances are wrong." Again in A 84 he reports another conversation in the back of his mind in which he (the feeling being) asks himself (the intellect): "You were a decent person before; why do you have to change?"

The intellect observes that it is necessary to be more aggressive and outgoing if one is to meet girls. In A 90 the feeling being objects loudly with, "God that's crude, you can't do that. I mean that's vulgar.

How can you do it?" The intellect answers that such behavior isn't crude and vulgar in this country. So there!

I could go on, but I believe the point is made. There is a lot of data to support my hypothesis. On the intellectual level Ashok is very rational and analyzes his problem thoroughly. At some deeper level he feels pain and resists change. His own analysis strongly and openly threatens his concept of himself as an adequate personality. This deeper self tries to distort his perceptions by telling him that he is adequate and the world is all wrong. But the powerful intellect, which is dedicated to truth and knowledge for its own sake, will not permit such a distortion to continue. The self-concept of adequacy can no longer be defended by a distortion of perceptions. The result is painful. There is no easy way out, but there is much hope.

In this interview we see Ashok's self-concept threatened in two major ways. As explained, his early concept of himself as an adequate personality is threatened by his failure to satisfy his belonging need. In addition his concept of himself as a competent physicist, capable of creativity, is threatened by his failure to create and his failure to apply himself to his work. The need hierarchy concept strongly suggests that the former threat is the more basic of the two. Ashok studies himself and comes to the same conclusion.

It is remarkable to me how little is denied to awareness in this interview. Rather, I should say, I'm amazed at how clearly the inner struggle goes on at the conscious level. Of course, as Ashok points out, most people are never aware of his inner struggle. He won't let them see. I shall discuss later why we are granted a good look inside.

The process of the interview

The circumstances and introduction of the interview have been described. My previous relationship to Ashok had a great influence on the outcome of the interview. A summer of sharing an apartment together built up a lot of mutual respect and mutual confidence. We got along well together. A "helping" type relationship already existed. Empathic understanding and some element of unconditional positive regard already were present on my part. My behavior toward Ashok was, I believe, perceived by him as completely congruent.

As the tale unfolded and insight deepened, my feeling of positive regard increased. This probably goes a long way toward explaining the extent to which Ashok revealed his inner self. Recall that he ordinarily hides his inner feelings quite successfully. His self-respect demands it. I'm sure that very little of the depth of this interview would have been possible without the previous establishment of much confidence.

I have already explained how the interview progressed and flowed. Ashok's view of himself and his problem actually changed, and I would be very surprised if this was not a helpful discussion for him.

During our discussion my mind kept racing ahead of his story. I already knew something about his problem, but had never seen it in such depth before. I was anxious to move on and press deeper. I had to consciously restrain myself from interrupting, particularly in the early stages of the interview. When I did speak, it was often with a built-in desire to lead on rather than just to sum up or reflect. This explains some of my statements which aren't much related to what Ashok was saying.

However, I did realize that I was sometimes disrupting his thinking by attempts to lead, and my responses became more adequate. Toward the end of the interview, when I was certain that I understood the real problem, I became anxious to press on to practical, workable conclusions. Ashok sensed this. He told me after the interview that he thought I genuinely wanted to understand, but that there were certain conclusions which he thought I wanted him to accept. He didn't really resent this because he perceived me as trying to help. He agreed with the conclusions I seemed to be encouraging. Again, without mutual confidence, the progress of the interview probably would have broken down.

Let us examine some of my responses. In D 4 and D 5 I respond fairly well to his expressed feeling. However, there is just a little too much direction in the way I phrase things. However, it doesn't bother him. He goes on. Later, D 10 catches his meaning pretty well and he makes it clear that he is upset about not working very hard. However, D 11 misses the mark and he stops rather than disagree. Then D 12 reaches out and nails one of his implied feelings. This might have derailed a discussion with a stranger. However, he responds by going deeper, even though some pain is involved.

At this stage I blunder. In D 14 I leap to the conclusion that anything connected with home must mean family. I knew beforehand that he was close to his family. Actually, in A 13, he was trying to express his feeling of being trapped by circumstances. This derails his train of thought until A 19, when he again brings up the trapped feeling. By the time we reach D 21, I fear that the interview isn't progressing and I try to get it on course again by referring back to Ashok's comments in A 13 which seemed important. After responding briefly to this digression he changes the subject and brings up his concern about loss of motivation. In D 22 I begin to respond more adequately to his expressed feelings. I realize that I have been pushing him and begin to listen more carefully. Now he moves forward on his own.

Until D 31 and D 32, I respond pretty well. In D 31 I miss the mark a bit but I'm no longer trying to steer him. He ignores this aside and carries on. I'm afraid that D 32 misses the mark enough so that he can no longer bypass my error and he corrects me.

I think that D 34 catches what Ashok says in A 33, but it sets him thinking and he eventually decides that it isn't correct. There is something more basic, as he indicates in A 36.. Now he analyzes what it is that is more basic and my responses do help him clarify his thoughts. He warms to the topic and begins to see clearly the connection between his loneliness and his inability to work hard. Response D 42 is one of my best. It sums up his new insight and he accepts it enthusiastically.

I slip up again in D 46 and go beyond what he really said. But what I say is essentially correct and he accepts it. He seems willing to be steered a little. Once more I realize that I'm pushing him and try to respond more to his expressed feelings. He responds very favorably to D 63 since it supports his more positive train of thought.

By way of A 65 and A 66 one can realize that we have progressed beyond Ashok's defenses. We are now inside with him, thinking this thing out. By A 71, Ashok seems to have bogged down. It may be that he is very close to the heart of the problem and acceptance is painful.

Responses D 72, D 73, and D 74 show that I am coaxing him along. I want him to return to his positive train of thought. To my surprise, it seems to work. By A 74 we are moving again. My response D 75 reflects what he said and it seems to encourage him to accept responsibility for a solution. The situation is ripe for progress.

I'm really proud of D 76! It triggers off a torrent of insight and self-analysis. In a way D 76 reflects what Ashok said. However the word *adapt* is mine rather than his. Partly, D 76 is my analysis. However, it is in accord with his views of the moment and he accepts it readily. Perhaps he had thought such things before but couldn't quite accept them. Now with a little support his keen mind demands acceptance of D 76, over the objections of his earlier self-concept. Whatever the explanation, D 76 is highly effective.

The momentum built up in carrying on from D 76 rolls freely right through to A 90. Toward the end of A 90, Ashok sums up his newly released insights or his new awareness pretty well. My responses along the way are fairly good. They reflect his expressed feelings adequately.

The rest of the interview is fairly directive. However, it covers some constructive ground. This is the portion in which Ashok feels that I am urging conclusions upon him. But he doesn't really resist or object. He agrees with the conclusions I seem to support.

If one compares the relative number of words spoken by Ashok and me, the ratio is sufficiently heavy in Ashok's favor to strongly suggest that this is a non-directive interview. However, as already mentioned, there are a number of points where my responses are sufficiently pointed to indicate that it wasn't non-directive throughout. For the most part, one can read Ashok's comments alone and capture the essence of the discussion with only a few logical gaps.

I think that it is very clear that this interview led both Ashok and me to understand Ashok much better. Even though we have both known him for some time, we now share a new and deeper awareness of Ashok and his problem. Ashok's fine mind and the mutual confidence built up earlier, rather than the skill of the interviewer, were responsible for this outcome.

I believe that I learned how difficult it is for me to really listen to another person. My mind grows impatient with what is being said and races on ahead and far afield. I have a tendency to be concerned with my own thoughts and ideas and to be more interested in broadcasting than receiving. I can understand expressed feelings and complex interrelationships when I really listen. My experience was that understanding does indeed enhance positive regard.

CASE IV-2. Two interviews with Miss Dvorak

Hawthorne Works, Western Electric Company

September, 1929

WORKING CONDITIONS

● *Likes*

I enjoy the noon-hour programs when I go out to hear them. It gives me something to look forward to.

I think the company's asking the employees to take shares is a very good thing. It is a very good way for me to save money because the company makes the deductions. I would like to take the Ready Money Plan, but as my wages do not permit it I have to wait until I get more money.

● *Dislikes*

I don't like the rest period. It is too early in the morning, and the washroom is entirely too crowded.

Our lockers could be in a little bit better condition. They are not kept up. There are bugs crawling around all the time.

Our washroom is very poorly ventilated.

THE JOB

● *Likes*

I like my job, but it is a man's job. I am not getting the same rate as the men are getting, and I am doing the same class of work. I get thirty-three cents an hour and the men get forty-seven cents. One of the women who did the work before me was getting a better rate than what I am getting. I give a better output than any of the others that are doing the same class of work. This I don't think is fair.

My work is interesting because there is some responsibility. It is for this reason I feel that I ought to get a better wage.

All I dislike about my job is the rate. The job is hard on my nerves. There are times when I could just scream, because if the inspection department sees a certain per cent of defective work, back comes all my work. This I don't think is fair.

SUPERVISION

● *Likes*

I like my foreman. He is sociable and friendly. I really don't know much about him because he doesn't have much to say.

● *Dislikes*

My section head never gets enough output. The more we turn out, the more he wants. He is never satisfied, and if I fail to give him the output he thinks I ought to give him, he curses at me. Maybe he doesn't mean so much by it, but I don't like to hear anyone swear right at me. I don't like to hear anybody swear around where I have to work. It is not necessary for him to use that kind of language to me at all. I do all the work I can, and more than any of the other operators, but still he wants more. There is a limit to my endurance. I cannot do any more. I was out sick and I called him up and told him I wouldn't be in. He told me over the telephone that he needed me down here. I know they do, but why don't they give me a better rate? I don't say ten words all day but just work.

September, 1931

EMPLOYEE 1: I was wondering if you weren't going to interview me, but my girl friend wasn't interviewed and she has more service than I have, so I supposed that she would be taken first.

INTERVIEWER 1: Well, I'm not taking the girls according to service. I get whatever girl the supervisor can most easily spare.

EMPLOYEE 2: Oh, is that it? This is where Dash used to work, isn't it?

INTERVIEWER 2: Yes, she did work down here.

EMPLOYEE 3: I think it was a shame that she had to be transferred back to the shop after she had an office job.

INTERVIEWER 3: Yes, it was too bad.

EMPLOYEE 4: She was just taking a course too in some kind of speed writing. I think it was a shame that she wasn't allowed to finish it. She has lost all her taste for school on account of that.

INTERVIEWER 4: I suppose one does get discouraged when something like that happens.

EMPLOYEE 5: I think I'm going to school this winter.

INTERVIEWER 5: That will be nice. What are you going to take?

EMPLOYEE 6: I think I'll take cooking. The Herald and Examiner have a cooking class downtown. Some girls I know took it and they liked it real well. It's free too. I couldn't take any course that you have to pay for because I don't have the money.

INTERVIEWER 6: Well, that sounds serious when you're taking cooking.

EMPLOYEE 7: (Laughs.) Well, perhaps it is, but I don't get much chance to cook where I am and I would like to learn how. Especially I don't want to learn Bohemian cooking. I want to know how to make salads and fancy desserts. I know enough about plain cooking. That cooking the Bohemians have, I hate that.

INTERVIEWER 7: I've eaten some Bohemian cooking that I thought was pretty good.

EMPLOYEE 8: Well, it might be all right for you to eat for a change, but if you had to eat that stuff all the time you wouldn't like it. Their favorite meat is pork, and I can't stand so much pork. The lady where I'm rooming is a wonderful woman, but I certainly couldn't stand to eat her cooking. That's the reason I don't board with her. She would like to have me board there, but I know when I'm well off. So I go out where I want to eat. I don't care to eat in those old Greek places though.

INTERVIEWER 8: You don't?

EMPLOYEE 9: No, I eat at a Bohemian-American restaurant on Blank Street.

INTERVIEWER 9: Well, you don't get away from the Bohemians do you?

EMPLOYEE 10: Well, even it's supposed to be Bohemian cooking there, it isn't like home. I hate Bohemian cooking. In fact, I hate everything Bohemian.

INTERVIEWER 10: Why?

EMPLOYEE 11: Oh, I don't know. I think Bohemians have such funny odd ideas about everything. I suppose perhaps it's on account of my family that I feel that way about things.

INTERVIEWER 11: How is that?

EMPLOYEE 12: Oh, I don't know.

INTERVIEWER 12: Does your mother feel that way too?

EMPLOYEE 13: My mother is dead, but she was just that kind of a Bohemian too. She sure was old-fashioned with all her ideas. I never had a happy home life. Some girls always talk about their childhood days, but not me. I want to forget them.

INTERVIEWER 13: So your mother is dead.

EMPLOYEE 14: Yes, she was sick for fourteen years and as I was the only girl I sure did have to work hard. Boys aren't any good for doing work around the house, so all the work fell on me. I could never go any place to have any friends because I always had to take care of one of those baby boys or else do the housework. It was one thing or the other all the time. My mother couldn't talk English either. You'd think she would have learned to talk English, but she didn't. When she married my father she was just here from Bohemia. She couldn't talk any English at all, although my father was American born. You would think, wouldn't you, that she would have learned to talk English, but she didn't. Then when my father went to get married again, sure enough he picked a Bohemian woman. The one he has now can hardly talk English. Well, I suppose that's the way he likes them.

INTERVIEWER 14: They say you can talk love in any language.

EMPLOYEE 15: Maybe that's so, but I don't think there was much love in it.

INTERVIEWER 15: So your father married again?

EMPLOYEE 16: Yes, he married, I couldn't stay home with the woman. So when they were going to move to another place, I moved next door with this lady I'm staying with now. I have two brothers and they stay home with my father. One is so young he can't help himself. He's only thirteen and has to go to school. My other brother stays with my father because he's not working and he hasn't got any other place to go. In fact, my father has to keep his job because my three stepbrothers aren't working either. So somebody has to work in the family. My father picks me up nearly every morning and drives me down to work. My stepmother doesn't know it though. She'd raise the devil if she knew that he was giving me rides, but he has to pass right by my house on his way to work so he brings me down here. Sometimes I feel sorry for him and then I don't care either. I think he's having a pretty hard time. All those boys at home eating and nobody working.

My father is only working three days a week too. He'll be lucky if he holds his job. So will I, for that matter. I'm scared I'm going to get laid off. Some days I get sick and dizzy worrying about it.

INTERVIEWER 16: Well, that's too bad. Has anybody said anything to you about being laid off?

EMPLOYEE 17: No, nobody has said a word to me. I only have three years' service though. They know that I'm self-supporting. They know that I have to take care of myself. I suppose I'm not as bad off as some of the girls. I don't have anyone dependent on me. One girl working in our gang has to support a baby. That's different from me. I don't have to support anyone else, but I wouldn't have a soul to help me out if I did lose my job. Gee, I was glad to get back here.

INTERVIEWER 17: Why, did you work here before?

EMPLOYEE 18: Yes, I worked here about five years ago and I was laid off. I sure do like this place. I wish I didn't have to worry about being laid off. There isn't a thing else that bothers me about this place. Sometimes when I wake up in the morning I can hardly wait to get down here to work. I like it so much. If I could only lose this worry about being laid off, I'd be a lot happier. It's different with girls who have parents, but the kind of a father I have doesn't do a girl any good. Do you know that he never came to see me when I was in the hospital? I wrote him three cards too to tell him I was there. My girl friend says I shouldn't bother with him. She says that he hasn't been like a father to me and I shouldn't bother with him, but you can't do that. If it's your father, it's your father. You can't just leave him out entirely. You've got to think about him. Gee, that time I was in the hospital I had so many things to think about.

INTERVIEWER 18: How is that?

EMPLOYEE 19: Well, I was in the county hospital because I didn't have any money, and then my father didn't come to see me. That was pretty tough all right. I had just got laid off. I just lost my job and my mother had died just before. Then I was just about breaking up with my boyfriend and everything together gave me a nervous breakdown. They were nice to me in the hospital but I was only there two weeks. After that I felt better. I wouldn't want to be sick for fourteen years like my mother. If I was going to be sick with heart trouble for that long, I don't know what I would do. I didn't have a nervous breakdown because I missed my mother. It was just the reaction, I guess, from all the hard work

Part IV.   Helping another person understand his behavior

I've had and all the worry—at least that's what the doctor said. Since I moved next door with our neighbor, I feel a lot better. She is wonderful to me. I call her mother and I call the man dad. They have two girls, sixteen and ten. Those girls are nice to me too. They are just like sisters to me. I sure am crazy about them.

INTERVIEWER 19: Are they Bohemian too?

EMPLOYEE 20: Yes, they are Bohemians and they have funny ideas about things too, but I like them real well. The boyfriend I go with now isn't Bohemian though.

INTERVIEWER 20: He's not?

EMPLOYEE 21: No, he's not Bohemian. He's French and German. The lady where I stay is just crazy about him and so is dad. I don't mean my father, I mean the man where I stay. Dad is always so full of fun when my boyfriend comes around and we have such a good time. I wish he had a better job. He can't work steady and so we don't go out much. We just stay home with dad and mother. I was with them when I met him.

INTERVIEWER 21: How was that?

EMPLOYEE 22: Well, the girls where I stay were in a children's concert over to the pier so we were over there one night listening to the concert and another fellow and my boyfriend came along and started talking. They asked what was the name of the piece and mother told them. So we got talking and then we introduced each other around so as to be proper and he asked us if we would like to drive home in his car. So he brought us home and then the next concert he brought us home. Then mother told me I should invite him over and I did, and he's been coming over ever since. He doesn't have much money so we stay home or play cards and fool around. He's an awfully nice fellow. We're just alike. He hasn't got anybody and neither have I.

INTERVIEWER 22: Is he an orphan?

EMPLOYEE 23: No, he isn't an orphan, but he hasn't seen his mother for three months now. He left home because he didn't like the way things were at home.

INTERVIEWER 23: How is that?

EMPLOYEE 24: Well, his mother was crazy for the Eastern Star. She wanted to go up higher and get better offices in it, I guess. She used to go spend all her time at lodge meetings, so my boyfriend got sore and left home. His mother has ideas of being a society lady. She wouldn't consider that he should go out with a working girl, but he doesn't like that class. He wants a working girl. He's a nice fellow all right. I wish he had a better job. He doesn't believe in Bohemian ideas either.

INTERVIEWER 24: You've mentioned Bohemian ideas two or three times; what do you mean?

EMPLOYEE 25: Oh, Bohemians have funny ideas about religion. I'm supposed to be Catholic and I'm not. I don't believe in anything. Then Bohemians have a funny idea that a girl should marry the first fellow she goes out with, that she shouldn't look around at any other fellow, that she ought to just marry the first one. They have such funny ideas about cooking and housekeeping too. I don't know, I just don't like them. There are some Bohemian girls down here that are all right, but I don't go with any of them if I can help it. I'd rather go with the American girls. I think my mother's death was hurried up by some fool Bohemian idea. My brother was going with a girl from down here. He wanted to marry her, and my mother wanted him to marry a Bohemian girl that she had picked out for him. He wouldn't do it though. He used to see this other girl down at work and finally they got married. She was Bohemian too, but she wasn't as Bohemian as the girl that my mother wanted him to marry. Funny, the mother of the girl that my mother had selected for my brother died about a year after my mother did. People say that they both died from a broken heart because their son and daughter didn't marry each other. My brother married somebody else and that Bohemian lady's daughter married somebody else too. So the two women were so disappointed that they died. That's just another one of those Bohemian ideas. Say, do you think this depression is nearly over?

INTERVIEWER 25: That's hard to tell.

EMPLOYEE 26: Well, I wish it would be over. I think it's terrible having to worry about your job all the time. I like sports. I like to go out and play baseball and go in for the team, but all those things cost so much money. I don't care so much for dancing or jazz. I like music. I like classical music like they have at those concerts over to the pier. They can't play baseball any more this year, can they?

INTERVIEWER 26: No, I believe the season is closed.

EMPLOYEE 27: I did want to join the girl's baseball team down here. I like to do things like that. I had a beach party for our department this summer. I arranged it all myself. We went to Crystal Lake over Saturday and Sunday, about thirty of us, but it was so much work. I couldn't get any of the girls to help me with it. Everybody chipped in fifty cents so I had to take that $15 and spend it for food and whatever we needed for the outing. Nobody wants to start anything now on account of the depression. Nobody has any money. My boyfriend can't spend much either. He's only working a day or two a week. By the time he gets his room rent paid and gets some food he's pretty nearly broke. I hope I can hold my job. I like it here at the Western better than any place I ever worked and I sure would hate it if I got laid off.

INTERVIEWER 27: Have you had lots of other experience working?

EMPLOYEE 28: Oh, yes. Since I was a little girl I've been working different places. Next to the Western the place I liked best was a Bohemian store that I worked in in Cicero. I used to wait on the trade there. We got commission. I had steady customers. Some of the women would come in and want to be waited on for big orders too, so in that way I made pretty good money there. But I wouldn't want to go back to waiting on a store now if I could stay here. I'm glad to work here too because you don't have those Bohemian ideas. Our boss isn't a Bohemian and the place is run more American. Some of those places where they have Bohemian bosses it's just like being at home. It's not like working out at all. You get all those Bohemian ideas with your work as well as when you're home.

I wish I could take up baseball. I'd like to take up bowling too and swimming. All those sports, but it costs so much. You can't afford it these days. When I went with that other boyfriend that I was telling you about that time I had the nervous breakdown, I used to go in for those things then because we were working Saturday and Sunday and I had more money to spend, but now, of course, it's different.

INTERVIEWER 28: What became of that boyfriend?

EMPLOYEE 29: Oh, we broke up. You see, he was Bohemian and he has a Bohemian mother and she didn't like me. She was always finding fault with me. She didn't like the way I dressed. She didn't like my family, and she didn't like anything about me, I guess. So we finally broke up. It's just as well though. I don't miss him at all. I like my present boyfriend much the best. He's not Bohemian and he doesn't have a lot of crazy thoughts about what one should do all the time. He's not a bit bossy. Well, I guess I'd better get back to work. I want to get rid of those things I'm working on today if I can because I think they're going to take inventory Saturday and I want to get them off my bench.

INTERVIEWER 29: What are you doing?

EMPLOYEE 30: I am just dismantling all those dirty parts. We get them from the engineering department. Some of them have two screws in and some one. We have to get all the screws out and get them all sorted out. The development department have some of them fixed one way and some another. We have to get them all straightened out before they can start working. When they take inventory Saturday, I'd like to have my bench all cleaned up. I hate to work in such a mess as I had today. Did you notice how much stuff was on my bench?

INTERVIEWER 30: No, I didn't.

EMPLOYEE 31: Well, it was stacked way up high. I'd like to get it all straightened out before Saturday if I can. Shall we go?

INTERVIEWER 31: Yes, if you're ready.

Appendix: Changes in the interviewing method

... It had [previously] been the practice of the interviewers to ask the employees about their likes and dislikes, first with regard to supervision and then with regard to working conditions and the job. In each area the interviewer had in mind certain questions to be used for the purpose of eliciting the material. Such questions, however, were never used with the definite purpose of making the interview a questionnaire procedure. For example, if it was difficult to get the employee to talk about his dislikes with regard to supervision, such questions as the following were frequently resorted to: How does your boss treat you? Does your boss ever bawl you out? Has he any favorites? Is your boss a slave driver? Do you consider your boss to be reasonable?

It was found that merely asking an employee to state his likes or dislikes with regard to his working conditions was frequently misunderstood; the employee might begin to talk about his job or something else. For this reason, the interviewer was instructed to ask specifically about the lighting system, heat, ventilation, drinking water, toilets, lockers, treatment which the employee might have received in the hospital, as well as about safety devices and accident hazards in his department. One question which was found very useful in evoking opinions about working conditions was: What do you think of the

Reprinted by permission of the publishers from F. J. Roethlisberger and W. J. Dickson, *Management and the Worker* (Cambridge, Mass.: Harvard University Press, 1939), 201–3. Copyright 1939, 1967 by the President and Fellows of Harvard College. See also Chapters 12, 13, and 14.

company as a place to work? Other questions used were: Have you ever worked in any other factory? How did the working conditions there compare with those in this plant? What do you think of the thrift plans, insurance plans, and education plans? Opinions with regard to the job were elicited by asking the worker if the job was fatiguing or dirty, if he thought he had been on the job too long, if there were prospects for advancement, if he was being paid in accordance with what he thought he was worth, and so on.

In short, it was quite clear that, although it had been the intention of the interviewers merely to invite the employee to express his opinions, nevertheless each interviewer was mentally equipped with a set of questions which he expected to have answered by everyone. He was not satisfied until he had in some way solicited some comment from each employee about his supervision, working conditions, and job. It also became clear that by this method the interviewer was recording those comments of the employee which he rather than the employee thought important. The interviewer led the conversation; the employee followed.

This realization was forced on the attention of the interviewers by a number of experiences. They found that an employee might start talking about the topic suggested, but in a short time he would be way off the subject. Feeling that this material was irrelevant, the interviewer would try to lead him back to some other point, but in a few moments the employee would be back where he was before. Regardless of what the interviewer said, the employee's thoughts tended to gravitate toward one idea. There was some one thing uppermost in his mind which completely overshadowed everything else, and it was about this that he wished to talk.

It may be interesting to describe the first occasion on which such an experience was related. At a meeting of the interviewing staff a member was berating himself for being a poor interviewer because he had been unable to keep a certain employee on the specified topics. The worker had tended to wander and to talk about his personal life, his experiences, and other "irrelevant" topics. At this meeting there were several other interviewers who immediately confessed to numerous similar experiences. They had had cases in which several subjects predominated in the mind of the employee, and any attempt to lead him away from them had been unsuccessful. In other instances the interviewers had found that a particularly reticent person became remarkably communicative if just the right topic could be touched upon in the conversation.

This conference marked a turning point in the interviewing method. It revealed certain obvious defects in the direct-question method. Such a method tended to put a person in a "yes" or "no" frame of mind. Instead of obtaining the employee's spontaneous and real convictions, it tended to arouse a reaction of antagonism or a stereotyped form of response. Frequently the questions themselves suggested the answers. And, moreover, the method elicited opinions upon topics which the interviewer thought to be important but which the employee might never have thought of before.

It was finally decided, about July, 1929, to adopt a new interviewing technique, which at that time was called the indirect approach. After the interviewer had explained the program, the employee was to be allowed to choose his own topic. As long as the employee talked spontaneously, the interviewer was to follow the employee's ideas, displaying a real interest in what the employee had to say, and taking sufficient notes to enable him to recall the employee's various statements. While the employee continued to talk, no attempt was to be made to change the subject. The interviewer was not to interrupt or try to change the topic to one he thought more important. He was to listen attentively to anything the worker had to say about any topic and take part in the conversation only in so far as it was necessary in order to keep the employee talking. If he did ask questions, they were to be phrased in a noncommittal manner and certainly not in the form, previously used, which suggested the answers.

CASE IV-3. Sylvia Holden and Jane

The personnel organization of the Canton Company included counselors who were trained on the job to do non-directive interviewing with the employees. As part of this training new counselors made written records of their interviews, which they then discussed with their supervisors.

Sylvia Holden was hired as a counselor in November 1943. After

Case material of the Harvard Graduate School of Business Administration, prepared as a basis for class discussion. Cases are not designed to present illustrations of either correct or incorrect handling of administrative problems. All names have been disguised. Copyright 1949 by the President and Fellows of Harvard College.

spending about a week in becoming acquainted with the work of the department and trying several "practice interviews," she met with the supervisors in the department to which she was assigned and began to introduce herself to the girls who worked there. The conversation which follows was the second interview for which she took a worker off the job.

COUNSELOR 1: Good morning, Jane, are you busy this morning?

JANE 1: No, I'm not.

COUNSELOR 2: Would you like to go off the job for a while so we can have a chance to get acquainted?

JANE 2: All right. (Jane left her bench and walked out with the counselor.) I've been having a hard time with these shoes lately. My foot is so sore and I don't know what I've done to it; it's so uncomfortable when I walk.

COUNSELOR 3: Have you had a chance to do anything about it yet?

JANE 3: Well, I put a powder puff under my heel; that's why that one particular heel is raised up a little bit. It seems strange that shoes should bother you after you've had them a year. These are a year old and I've been wearing them a lot during the past year. I don't know just what it is but it certainly does hurt. Every time I get up to walk around it bothers me.

COUNSELOR 4: Have you had the opportunity or occasion to see a foot doctor about it?

JANE 4: No, I haven't yet, but if it keeps up I'll probably have to do something like that. Are you going to talk to all of the girls?

COUNSELOR 5: Well, I would like to get acquainted with every single one of the girls in your section so they will feel free to call on me if they ever have anything they feel I can be of help to them with. It does take a long time to get around to everyone, but I do hope to be able to do just that.

JANE 5: Just what do we talk to you about?

COUNSELOR 6: Whatever you feel you would like to talk about, Jane. The company feels that by giving the employee someone whom they feel they can go to to discuss problems of their own they will feel happier working here.

JANE 6: Can we talk about our job, or family, or what?

COUNSELOR 7: If you want to talk about your family, fine; your supervisor, your work or anything you would like to talk about, Jane.

JANE 7: I don't quite understand what it's all about. Just what's the purpose of it all?

COUNSELOR 8: Well, the company knows that when an employee and his or her supervisor are well acquainted and understand each other, the work goes along better; they are both set and satisfied. It so happens that production, being the most important aspect of our work, is very significant; no matter what, it has to go out. Well, the pressures of production are weighing on the supervisor's shoulders; he doesn't always have time to sit down and get acquainted with his employees and help them work out their problems, whereas the employee might have to be up on his toes in getting his work out by a deadline at a certain time. He wouldn't be able to leave his work even if the supervisor was free for a few minutes. The work that he does is important to someone else's work, and he has to get it to that other person. The personnel counselor is a service that the company offers to the employee and to the supervisor who feel that they have something they'd like to talk about, something that they're interested in. They get it off their chest by talking it over with someone. They understand things for themselves in a better light and it's easier on them; they can forget about it and go on with their work. Have you ever had an occasion when you were so concerned about something that you didn't do very good work or weren't happy where you were working?

JANE 8: Yes, I do remember instances of that sort of thing. It looks like we can go to you with all of our complaints then?

COUNSELOR 9: Well, not just complaints, Jane. I'm interested in other things, too, and just everything that means a great deal to you I'd be interested in hearing about, as well as complaints. You see, whatever is brought to us by a supervisor or by an employee does not go any further. It does not go to anyone else. Whatever comes to the counselor goes no further, Jane; that's part of our job. If it did go on from us we wouldn't be here to do this job. By that, I mean it's part of our responsibility that it doesn't go further.

JANE 9: Well, I sort of know what you mean then. I can't think of any particular problem I have at present.

COUNSELOR 10: That's all right, Jane, we can talk about other things, too.

JANE 10: I have been concerned, though, about getting a few days off when my husband comes in on furlough.

COUNSELOR 11: Oh, I see. When will that be?

JANE 11: Well, it should be the first of the year or shortly after.

COUNSELOR 12: Did you talk to your supervisor about it yet?

JANE 12: No, I haven't. I'm rather afraid to.

COUNSELOR 13: Afraid to? Why do you feel afraid of it, afraid to ask him about it?

JANE 13: Well, you see, other girls have asked for leaves and haven't gotten them.

COUNSELOR 14: Why do you suppose they haven't gotten them?

JANE 14: Well, I don't know. Other girls in other departments get them, but they don't seem to give them in our department.

COUNSELOR 15: Have you any idea why that would be?

JANE 15: No, I don't, except that when I went to Mr. Black he said that one department is run one way and another is run another and the policies in the departments differ. He said, too, that he wished the departments were run in the same way so that the same policy would hold good throughout the whole company. He puts it as though it were almost like two different companies from department to department, depending on the supervision within that area.

COUNSELOR 16: You have already talked to one supervisor about it, then?

JANE 16: No, that was about another problem. When I wanted time off for my wedding I asked for three days but I only got one day. It seems that you ask for a certain length of time and you only get about half of it, if you get any at all.

COUNSELOR 17: Do you happen to know of people in other departments who have gotten the time off that they wanted?

JANE 17: Yes, I know of one girl in particular who was in that department there that we passed on the way down to the interviewing room where that new fence is, that restricted area. I saw her yesterday morning, and she said they told her she could have her time off and she was going to have her time off beginning tomorrow. Her husband is going in and she's having a week off to be with him.

COUNSELOR 18: Do you happen to know how she went about getting that?

JANE 18: No, I don't know; I didn't ask her about that part of it.

COUNSELOR 19: Do you know of anyone else who has gotten time off?

JANE 19: Well, yes, this girl happens to be in a different war plant. She said that she just went up to her boss and asked for time off and said that her husband was home on furlough, and her boss said, "I suppose that you want next week off," and she said, "Yes." He said, "All right, go ahead."

COUNSELOR 20: Do you know of any other situations here in our plant?

JANE 20: No, I don't yet, but I think I shall inquire around.

COUNSELOR 21: What is your plan now for asking? By that I mean, how would you go about asking? Are you planning to ask soon or will you wait until just before you expect him to come in?

JANE 21: Well, I don't think I should ask now because then they'll think up a lot of reasons to talk me out of it and that way I probably won't get it at all. I think I should wait until I'm real sure exactly what time he'll be coming in, and just a short time before I expect him, I'll ask about it then.

COUNSELOR 22: How will you go about asking?

JANE 22: Well, I'll go to Mr. White first.

COUNSELOR 23: What response do you suppose you'll get from him? What do you expect him to say?

JANE 23: He'll probably say, "No," but then we can see Mr. Gannon. Mr. Gannon will take it to Mr. Davis, and he'll take it up to Mr. Burke; and it goes all the way around like that, and it's such a fuss and bother I hate to cause that commotion. Everybody at home says I should just let them know that I'm going to take the time off when my husband comes in.

COUNSELOR 24: How do you feel about that?

JANE 24: I sort of hate to do it that way because they may transfer me or may tell me that my job won't be here when I come back, or something of that sort.

COUNSELOR 25: And how do you feel about that?

JANE 25: I want to hold on to my job. When one girl asked for time off, she called in and said she wanted the time off, and her supervisor said, "What's more important to you, your husband or your job?" She came down here to work. You see, they threatened her that way that she'd lose her job if she didn't come in to work.

COUNSELOR 26: Was that the way it was put to her over the phone?

JANE 26: As far as I know.

COUNSELOR 27: When the remark was put that way, did it necessarily mean that she would lose her job if she didn't come in?

JANE 27: That's the impression she got.

COUNSELOR 28: If you talked to your boss and asked for time off and that statement was put to you—which was most important, your husband or your job—what would be your answer?

JANE 28: Well, my husband is more important to me, of course, but I'd like to keep my job too.

COUNSELOR 29: Were there any other girls in your particular department who have asked for leaves and found that they weren't able to have them?

JANE 29: Yes, there have been. Mary and Fran both asked for leaves and didn't get any time off when their husbands were in.

COUNSELOR 30: You feel, then, that since they didn't get any time off, you wouldn't either.

JANE 30: That's right, unless the boss had a change of heart. If he did it for me, he may be asked to do it for others.

COUNSELOR 31: Yes, that might well be the situation; if he did it for one, he would have to do it for many. Are there very many married women in your department?

JANE 31: Well, I guess there are five or six; that's about all. That isn't so very many, and I have heard of one particular company that will permit a few days off for the girls who are married, but they won't permit a few days off for the girls who have boyfriends coming into town because there would be too much of that.

COUNSELOR 32: Yes, I imagine that might be so. That would be a good way to distinguish who was to get the time off and who wasn't. That would cut down the number of people quite a bit.

JANE 32: Yes, I believe it would. If I were to ask Mr. Gannon I'm sure he would give it to me right away, but he would say: "I'd like to give it to you, but you know what Mr. Davis will say; you know I'm not the top one here."

COUNSELOR 33: Isn't he the one that you will be asking?

JANE 33: No, my immediate supervisor is Mr. White and I will ask him and then he will go to Mr. Gannon. Mr. Gannon will go to Mr. Davis, and from there it goes to Mr. Burke. Mr. White would let me go right away if he were the only one to say anything about it. He has children of his own and he knows what it's like. I remember hearing him say once that when the girls stayed out longer on their leave than they were supposed to he would only skip it; he'd say: "I have a daughter myself and I don't blame them." You see he really understands. I'm afraid of the other bosses.

COUNSELOR 34: Why do you suppose you are afraid of them? Do you feel insecure about your job in any way? Often when we're afraid of a person it's because we're insecure in regard to that person. I recall feelings of fear for a teacher whom I had in school. When I started to think of it, I knew definitely why I was afraid of that teacher; it was because I didn't do my work properly and didn't get it done on time. Of course, then I was afraid I was going to fail and I wouldn't be ready for that exam, and consequently I feared the teacher. I felt I was afraid of her when really it was my own doing. I could have overcome that fear and felt on sure ground with her if I had worked harder and better and right along through the semester.

JANE 34: I don't feel that way about it because I feel that my work is quite all right.

COUNSELOR 35: In comparison with the work from the other girls in the department, how do you feel that your work rates?

JANE 35: Well—

COUNSELOR 36: For example, if we laid out the work from the various individuals in your group or laid out the records of their work—by this, I don't mean that any individual is better than anyone else, I just mean they are more efficient at this kind of a job. Some may be very good, some may be good, and some may be just average or just getting along in their work.

JANE 36: I feel my work is about on the top. I feel pretty capable there. I don't mean that in any snobbish way or anything like that, but I just feel that way about it.

COUNSELOR 37: Of course you don't. One can judge one's self as to how capable one is in relation to those who are working around them.

JANE 37: That's it.

COUNSELOR 38: Well, thinking of it from that light, just how valuable do you think you are in this particular department?

JANE 38: Well, I know it takes about nine months to train a girl to the point where she can do all these various operations that I'm qualified to do.

COUNSELOR 39: In other words, it might take some time to have a person fully qualified to replace you. However, the person who is next best able to do the work you're doing would replace you or take over your work immediately, while they would train someone in the beginning operations of that particular job; they would train a new person there. I was thinking of this in terms of the probability that they might in your case. They might suggest that you get along without your job, or make a choice between taking your time off or holding your job. Maybe you can answer to begin with. Would you let it stand at that? Do you feel you would have any grounds to edge you further?

JANE 39: Well, I would try to.

COUNSELOR 40: Well, what particular point or issues do you feel that you would have grounds to stand on?

JANE 40: There's that side to it, too—that I may never see my husband again. I mean that there's just that possibility.

COUNSELOR 41: Yes, that is possible in times like these, isn't it? Will he be going into combat right after that leave?

JANE 41: That I don't know.

COUNSELOR 42: Do you suppose he might be just transferred to another camp?

JANE 42: There's that possibility.

COUNSELOR 43: Would that mean that you would probably be seeing him again in a few months?

JANE 43: Perhaps.

COUNSELOR 44: How long would it be before you'd know definitely what was the situation?

JANE 44: That I couldn't say. I'd have to ask him about that himself, see what he thinks is coming.

COUNSELOR 45: Would that make any difference in asking for this particular leave?

JANE 45: No, I don't think so, because at any rate it will be all of four months before I see him again.

COUNSELOR 46: I see. How long is it now since you've seen him?

JANE 46: Well, it was last October.

COUNSELOR 47: When did he leave for camp?

JANE 47: The first part of September.

COUNSELOR 48: Will you be seeing him at all before the time he expects his leave?

JANE 48: Well, I hope to see him one day over Christmas. He expects to get a leave around Christmas time, but you never know about those things. There are so many boys expecting to get leaves that they can't all have them. When he does have his leave, he'll probably have a ten-day leave. Of course, I wouldn't necessarily have to be with him all the time, but I would like to have a week off.

COUNSELOR 49: You said before that when an employee asks for a leave, perhaps of a week, you might get a half a week. If an employee asks for a leave of three days, they may get a day and a half or just a day. In other words, they would probably be more apt to get half of the time they ask for rather than the whole time. You said you wanted a week. Would there be any relationship in what you might ask for and what you might get?

JANE 49: You mean by that that if perhaps I'd ask for two weeks I might get a week?

COUNSELOR 50: Doesn't that mean anything to you? Hasn't that possibility occurred to you before?

JANE 50: Well, I haven't particularly thought of that, but Mr. Gannon said that when I wanted to be off he just didn't want to know what it was for; I should just call up and say I was sick. I'd rather not do that; I'd be aboveboard about it. He said that he would rather not ask permission for me to get that one day off; I should just call in and say that I was ill. I don't like things when you have to do them like that. I don't care to do things that way, even if he did suggest it.

COUNSELOR 51: In regard now to the method you would use to sell your supervisors on giving you this leave, do you think of any other particular items besides the two we've already mentioned: the statement that you may not see your husband again if he goes into combat, and the fact that you feel that your work is good and they don't have any comeback for your efficiency and your ability at your job? Do you feel there are any other aspects of the total situation that you could bring up that would help you handle this the way you want to? Then, too, you did mention that it would take some time to replace one who was able in that job just as you are. There you have three items or three reasons that you may be able to use effectively. (In the conversation that followed, Sylvia and Jane singled out two additional reasons for the leave which Jane considered significant.) Do you feel that you have any better ideas now as to how to approach your supervisor with your particular problem?

JANE 51: Well, in a certain way, yes. I don't know why I've been quite so bewildered about it, but still they may not grant it to me.

COUNSELOR 52: That's very true, isn't it? You can probably see how management feels about it and what their side of the question is.

JANE 52: Yes, I can; I can see in many ways where they would not want to give it. Absenteeism is quite an issue with them. Do you feel I ought to ask now or ask later?

COUNSELOR 53: I don't know; you're the only one who could say that. Which do you feel is best? I wouldn't know your situation at all, my dear; no one would know it as well as you would yourself. Then, too, I have no right to advise you on anything. I can help you to see other sides of your particular problem or various angles of your particular situation, but I cannot give you any advice, nor would I feel qualified to do so. I don't think any individual is qualified to settle the problem that occurs in another individual's mind. Do you feel that's right? That's up to each one of us individually to make the final move and the final decisions, don't you think so?

JANE 53: I guess it is.

CASE IV–4. Chrystal Smith (A)

A large university recently held a Management Development Conference for women. The program was held at a plush resort hotel and was to last for one week. Pat Hanes, a young researcher from another university, was asked to attend this conference in order to assist in evaluating both its social and academic merits and failures.

Among the twenty-two participants was Mrs. Chrystal Smith. While most of the women were of middle management level in large hospitals and corporations, Chrystal was the Kansas City manager for a company which sold women's fashions in neighborhood hostess parties.

The biographical data supplied to the researcher indicated that Chrystal was a thirty-two year old widow forced to return to work five years previously in order to support her two young children.

On the first day of the conference all of the participants breakfasted together and proceeded to the conference room. Most of the women were gray-haired and neatly dressed in smart business suits and walking shoes. As the researcher entered the room she noticed that contrary to most of the women who were busily grouped together, chatting and getting acquainted, Chrystal had taken a seat alone, at the opposite end of the room. She was attired in a lavender satin brocade dress and a fur neckpiece and had platinum blond hair.

The researcher, realizing that Chrystal was becoming isolated from the forming group, decided to see if she could help Chrystal as well as find out why this was happening.

Case material of the Harvard Graduate School of Business Administration, prepared as the basis for class discussion. Cases are not designed to present illustrations of either correct or incorrect handling of administrative problems. All names have been disguised. Copyright © 1964 by the President and Fellows of Harvard College.

Chrystal Smith (B)

The following is the actual interview held between Chrystal Smith and Pat Hanes. Chrystal was not aware of the researcher's role at the conference other than as a participant. At a get-acquainted meeting the night before, she had revealed enough biographical data so as to allow the researcher to display some knowledge of her without arousing suspicion.

PAT 1: Hi, Chrystal, I'm Pat Hanes from State School of Business Administration.

CHRYSTAL 1: Hi, Pat, this is certainly a beautiful resort, isn't it? The grounds are lovely.

PAT 2: You've been out viewing it.

CHRYSTAL 2: I didn't sleep so well last night, you know—new bed, new place and all that—I was out walking the grounds about six this morning.

PAT 3: You enjoy walking?

CHRYSTAL 3: Well, sometimes ... but ... say, what do you do at State?

PAT 4: Oh, I'm a student and a researcher, and you work for Suburban Fashions, don't you?

CHRYSTAL 4: Yes, of course my job and my company are quite different from what the rest of you girls do.

PAT 5: Oh?

CHRYSTAL 5. Yes. You see, we don't have offices or secretaries and no big plants. We work out of our homes. Our products are low-priced women's fashions and our salespeople are ordinary housewives.

PAT 6: In other words your organization uses different skills than what you see as the typical business firm.

CHRYSTAL 6: Yes, if I were to talk about it you would probably think it sounds "corny," but it really works—the way we do things, I mean.

PAT 7: You feel that because you do things differently, this might seem corny to others—to me.

CHRYSTAL 7: Well, that, and also, we don't use any of the important organization and administrative ideas—none of us have any big educations, lots of my salesgirls didn't graduate from high school. We use common sense and regard for others as the important things in our business. We tell our girls, our salesgirls that is, that if they dress well, behave with good manners and try to be warm and friendly, then that's all they need in order to be successful with their customers. When we pick our salespeople we want to see if they run a good and attractive home. We feel that if they can manage a home they can work for us.

PAT 8: Then a college education is not necessary to get along with people and have them like you. It is not always necessary to be educated in order to be successful in business.

CHRYSTAL 8: Yes, well . . . I think so. That is, the salesgirls or demonstrators, as we call them, can get along very well with their friends and neighbors to whom they sell. When I was a demonstrator, I never had any trouble at all. Of course, since we deal in fashion—with our Suburban Fashions—like dresses and hats—it's always important for us to dress fashionably—to impress our customers that we are in good taste with what they like. Also we are always trying to recruit more salespeople so we must look successful and attractive to everyone.

PAT 9: You were a very successful demonstrator, then?

CHRYSTAL 9: Oh yes, I had the highest sales in my area. I won a mink neckpiece and a trip to Washington. Then last year our Kansas City manager was promoted and they asked me to take the job. I have two kids to support and a mortgage to pay so I couldn't turn down the money, well—the opportunity to get ahead. I want my children to go to college and to be able to get along in life.

PAT 10: You had some doubts, then, about taking the promotion?

CHRYSTAL 10: Well, not really, but—

PAT 11: You considered it carefully.

CHRYSTAL 11: Yes, that's it. I did a lot of thinking about it—you know I was really good as a demonstrator and I was making a fair salary. The promotion was, well, it meant a chance—a chance for the kids, of course, but also—well, a chance for me that would kind of scare me.

PAT 12: Uhmmmmmm. . . .

CHRYSTAL 12: You see, I didn't really know what I would have to do in the new job. Oh, I knew I could get along with the other demonstrators under me, but it was the formal part, I mean . . . and the last person, well, she was real educated. She'd been to night school and got a college degree—of course she was a single woman and had the time.

PAT 13: You feel that college would have made you more able to do the new job?

CHRYSTAL 13: Yes, well I've felt this all along. That is, if I had gotten this education then I could do things better and get ahead better in the company. But I was a good demonstrator and success was easy then. But now, well, I'm wishing I had that school.

PAT 14: You took the job then, but as you suspected, the college experience could have helped you.

CHRYSTAL 14: Yes, you see, well, my district is the top one in the country now and in order to hold that position or for me to get promoted, I've got to do even more—that's why I'm here you know. Most of the others had their way paid by their companies but I've got to pay my own way—I really want to get educated. Say! I hear they give you a degree with your name on it at the end of the week. I want to get a school charm for my bracelet; all the girls at the home office have their college charms.

PAT 15: Then you have been successful up to now in your job, but you feel you could be more comfortable and more effective in the future if you had a better education?

CHRYSTAL 15: Yes, like for example, all of you girls here, you all have so much more knowledge than I do—you speak so well, you all talk about art and music and plays like they were everyday things —well I don't know anything, I guess, 'cause I don't know about these things. I feel, well—I think—

PAT 16: It's important to you to be able to talk about these things, to know about these things.

CHRYSTAL 16: Yes, I've only been here a while but I can see how much I don't know. Half of the time, well, I don't know how to talk to most of you—that is—it's easy to talk to *you*, but we're alone and we're talking about things I understand—this happens to me at the home office too. I want to make a good impression on my superiors but when I go, I know that once we leave the subject of business I won't have anything to say. When I get there I seem to make a mess of the whole thing—talking about business too. Probably they wonder what's wrong with me—I'm probably a mystery woman because I do so well in my territory but when I get to the home office, I can't even tell them how I do it. They would be crazy to promote me—if I can't explain why I am successful. What good is what I am doing, what good am I if I can't tell people?

PAT 17: The way I understand what you are saying then, is that in order to get ahead in your job you must be able to communicate with your superiors in the home office, and when you try to do this you find you can't. And you feel that a higher education could help you to communicate better.

CHRYSTAL 17: Well, I guess the education isn't everything. I've been successful up to now without it but if I had it, I would feel more relaxed when I go to the home office or, well, even here. Like I said, I freeze up when I try to explain what I do in my territory— I sort of kill myself everytime I try. You know I want so badly to talk to those women over there (the other conferees). I could learn so much from them and perhaps I could tell them something about our business. But it's different and, well, I know I am too. It's hard for someone who is different, maybe inferior, to get the courage to pretend they aren't. I've tried it but I always kill myself when I do it.

PAT 18: You would like to get acquainted with the other participants but you are afraid that, because you see yourself as being different from them, you won't be able to get along, that you will get hurt.

CHRYSTAL 18: Yes.

PAT 19: You see yourself as different from the others in other ways than education?

CHRYSTAL 19: Yes, well, I guess the others are related to education, and, well, my job. Well, I don't look like them and I can't talk like them. I know it only so well. But what can I do? I am what I am and while I envy them, I would like to be like them, I don't know how. Maybe if I could learn to talk better—go to art museums and concerts, but I'm afraid to go alone. I wouldn't know how to act. For example, I just moved to a better neighborhood and there are lots of college people in the neighborhood. Well, they have a newcomer's party whenever a new family comes. They kept calling to ask when I could come, well, I know I was scared of them. I wanted to know them—after all, they were my neighbors—but I kept putting them off, saying my job didn't allow time. I do travel a lot, to visit all the girls in my territory. This is the happiest part of my life. These girls, well, they respect me, they tell me their troubles and their personal problems and I can talk to them, help them sometimes. Sometimes, lately, I wish I could go back where I was as a demonstrator. I never had these feelings, these worries when I was there. But then, well, I look at my kids and I know I must go on at all costs. I don't want them to end up like me.

PAT 20: If you knew how, then, you would really like to be the way you see the others as being.

CHRYSTAL 20: Yes, I might have been if my husband hadn't died. I worked for seven years to get him through college. Then the army took him before he could even work. When he came out he was mentally ill. Then he was in a mental home for several years. When he finally came home he took a manual labor type of job. Then not long after that he had a heart attack and died.

PAT 21: Then your husband was a college graduate and you were able to communicate with him before he became mentally ill?

CHRYSTAL 21: Gee, I guess I never thought of us that way. Yes, of course, I could communicate with him. I remember, in fact, helping him to study art and thinking how interesting it was. Oh, I guess the meeting is about to start, I've so enjoyed talking to you, could we talk some more tonight?

From this point, the participants spent the day in the classroom listening to a rather laborious presentation of the principles of management.

The researcher noted that by dinnertime Chrystal had introduced herself to several other participants and joined them at their table. After the meal many of the women went to the cocktail lounge and it was there that Chrystal made an attempt to continue her conversation with the researcher.

CHRYSTAL 22: I guess you noted that I had dinner with Sally and Mary and Alice. I decided I would be more miserable if I stood off all week than if I tried to force myself to get acquainted. They were very interested in my job and my company. I told them all about it and they said I certainly was enthusiastic about my work.

PAT 22: You liked them then, and they didn't cause you the discomfort you had anticipated?

CHRYSTAL 23: That's for sure. I think they liked me—in fact, they were exceptionally nice and interested in me. We laughed a whole lot, too.

PAT 23: Well it surely pleases you to feel that you can be liked by the same people that you feared would dislike you because you were different.

CHRYSTAL 24: Yes, I still think I'm different, and I would still like to be liked by them but it didn't seem so bad to be different tonight. Of course, this is just one time that things went well for me, there are still all the times that it doesn't. I don't believe in miracles and especially not here, so don't let yourself be misled by my pleasure.

PAT 24: In other words, one pleasant experience can't balance out all the bad ones you've had and expect to have.

CHRYSTAL 25: There you've hit it. I've learned that I get hurt a lot. If I prepare myself in advance for a hurt by telling myself how bad it will be or, at least, the worst it can possibly be and I convince myself that it will be as bad as the worst, then if anything less than the worst happens I can take some pleasure from it.

PAT 25: In other words, you prepare in advance for the worst as a way to protect yourself.

CHRYSTAL 26: That's right. Especially recently. You see I've been going to the home office more and more and as I told you I make a mess every time. So now I find I live in a state of misery most of the time. When I am home I am anticipating the misery of when I get there, and when I get to the home office I have the actual misery.

Chrystal Smith (C)

Following the discussion related in (B), Chrystal and Pat, during the course of the conference, held further conversations in which their positive regard for each other increased and the level of intimacy in their conversation rose markedly. By the time the conference ended, Pat was comfortably familiar with most of Chrystal's life experiences and had some idea of Chrystal's feelings about and perceptions of her life. Chrystal, therefore, wrote to Pat asking to talk with her again.

Case material of the Harvard Graduate School of Business Administration, prepared as a basis for class discussion. Cases are not designed to present illustrations of either correct or incorrect handling of administrative problems. All names have been disguised. Copyright © 1964 by the President and Fellows of Harvard College.

About a month after the conference, Pat met Chrystal in a Swedish restaurant in New York City. Even though at the conference Chrystal had constantly emphasized to Pat that she did not drink, this day she immediately suggested a cocktail. She seemed very nervous and most anxious to talk with Pat.

CHRYSTAL 1: You know, Pat, you helped me so much while we were at the conference. I was so glad to be able to get together with you today. In the last few weeks, I have been to talk with both my doctor and my pastor, and neither seemed as easy to talk with nor as understanding as you. Since I left the conference I have been having so much trouble sleeping. I don't know whether it is all the changes that have been happening in my life or whether something is really bothering me.

PAT 1: You're not sure then why you haven't been sleeping, and neither your doctor nor your pastor was too helpful.

CHRYSTAL 2: Yes, well after I came back from the conference the president of my company invited me down to the home office. She said she had been very concerned that I might come back with a swelled head. Last year one of the other managers went to a similar conference and she couldn't do her work for the next six months. Well, anyway, Mrs. Chapman and I spent two days together. She ended up telling me she was very impressed with the way I had changed since she had talked with me last.

PAT 2: Oh, she said you had changed.

CHRYSTAL 3: Yes, in fact, she said I really was the best manager she had now. I asked her why she thought I had changed. She told me I was much more company-minded now and it was this maturity that she had been waiting for before offering me a promotion. It was funny, but our relationship seemed entirely different this time. We acted like a bunch of kids, laughing and being silly a lot of the time. We didn't talk about business all the time and I enjoyed this.

PAT 3: You enjoyed this trip to the home office, then.

CHRYSTAL 4: Well, yes. Mrs. Chapman started to talk to me about opening a new territory in New England. A territory which would be all my own. I would hire and train all the demonstrators and city managers and, of course, the salary increase would be just as great as the increased responsibility.

PAT 4: The responsibilities would be great, but so would the salary.

CHRYSTAL 5: Yes, well I told her right off that I didn't know if I was capable of the job and anyway I would have to move away from Kansas City just after I have gotten myself and my kids settled. But it was her answer to this that really set me thinking. She said, "Chrystal, if you think this job would change you and make you unhappy, then we don't want you to take it. We like and respect you because you are what you are; if you changed you might not be as important to us as you are now." Then she said, "Chrystal, you have a real way with people, this is your unique ability. If something happened to this we would both be in trouble. Some of our managers are successful because they are trained business managers, others know less about this but are good with people. You are one of those. When I told you I thought you were more company-minded, I mean that now you not only had your original ability with people but you were also developing some of the business sense." I said to her, "Mrs. Chapman, I am really not that good with people either." Then she asked me the fifty-dollar question, "Chrystal," she said, "honestly, I know you went up to that conference and had no trouble at all joining in with those people and having them really like you. I know you, I bet you had a ball up there. Didn't you?" Well, Pat, what was I to answer her? If I said no, I would have to explain why and anyway I don't think she would have understood. So I said, "Oh yes, I really enjoyed myself and had no trouble in meeting the others." So I went home from the office feeling really unhappy about some of the things she had said but happy about some of the others. She's not pushing me on this promotion, but she knows and I know that I've gone as far as I can with my present job and I have to make a decision. But the job decision has so much effect on my life, too, and it's not easy to come up with an answer.

PAT 5: Right now, then, you are struggling with deciding what to do about the promotion, and perhaps even more, with what to do with your life.

CHRYSTAL 6: Right—I have several choices. I could get married again, or I could stay in my present job forever, or I could take the promotion. The way I see it, getting married again and having to stay home all day would kill me. You know coming up on the train I was reading my Sunday School lesson and it quotes from that book, *The Feminine Mystique*, and it talks about the wasted life of the housewife who never goes out of the home. Well, now that I've had the experience of working and having that kind of responsibility, I don't want to go back and I don't think I could go back. For the choice seems to be between the present job and the promotion. And really, I guess, the decision is about myself and my kids. Who am I? What do I want to do with the rest of my life?

PAT 6: You've got to decide about yourself before you can decide about the job.

CHRYSTAL 7: That's right. I guess it's really myself that's troubling me now. She thinks I'm different, I guess, but you know inside I really don't feel any different. People still worry me and I still have trouble getting along with people, at least I think I do. You remember I talked to you about needing an education. Well I still think I need that education, and I still think that it would help me to be able to talk to people better.

PAT 7: Well then, Chrystal, what I hear you saying to me is that in spite of the fact that you and Mrs. Chapman had such a good time, you still feel that you have trouble communicating with people, and that the education that we talked about before would help you to get along better.

CHRYSTAL 8: Yes, Pat, I guess that's true. Although, as I think about it, I guess Mrs. Chapman was telling me that I was able to get along with her, and I guess if I were to understand this, it would make me realize that maybe not getting along with people is somewhat in my own mind, because when people like Mrs. Chapman tell me that I get along so well, then I guess that maybe I really do. What do you think?

PAT 8: Well Chrystal, I want to give you an honest answer, but of course, I have never been to the home office with you. But from what I saw at the conference, I think you have very little difficulty in getting along with people except that you lack some self-confidence. Perhaps what you just said to me, that you were apparently underestimating yourself, and also what Mrs. Chapman said, are nearer to fact. Perhaps if you could understand this and work on this you would get along better. What do you think?

CHRYSTAL 9: Well this is what I got to thinking about when I got home. I think I sort of realized this myself. In fact the night I came home I started to cry and my nine-year-old son came in and said to me, "Mommy, what's wrong?" I was desperate to talk to somebody, so I at least had my son there and I thought I'd tell him the story. I realized, of course, that he wouldn't honestly understand what my trouble was, but at least he was somebody to talk to. After I had told him the story I finished by saying, "Well honey, the real problem I think is that now we have all moved here to Kansas City, and we just got settled and you kids have gotten friends and are used to going to school, and now I don't know whether we should move away to another city or whether we should stay here. Honey, do you think we would be happier there or do you think we should stay here?" Well Pat, then my little nine-year-old son said to me, "Mommy, we are all so proud of you, we want you to go wherever you think will be best; we know you will make the decision that will be best for all of us. Don't let anybody else try to tell you how to do it. You make the decision Mommy, because all the decisions you have made for us have been best." When my son said this to me, Pat, I knew that it was up to me, that I had to make the decision myself, and that nobody else could help me. But nevertheless, I went and talked to my pastor and my doctor and neither one of them seemed to be very helpful. That's why, as I said before, I was looking forward to talking to you. I thought that perhaps you could help me to see what decision to make.

PAT 9: Then in spite of the fact that you realized that you had to make a decision yourself, Chrystal, you still felt perhaps someone else could advise you or help you make the decision.

CHRYSTAL 10: Yes, I guess I did. But wait a minute, I guess I'm sort of fooling myself. That makes it sound as if I told myself I had to make my own decision, but I'm still trying to get someone else to make it for me. Is that what I'm doing Pat? Yes, of course, I guess that is what I'm doing. Gee, sometimes we are awfully stupid about ourselves, aren't we?

PAT 10: Well, then, Chrystal, let me see if I can summarize what you've been saying. You've been offered a promotion and the real problem this offer has created for you is whether or not you will hurt your family and yourself by moving from your physical location first. Second whether or not you yourself are capable of handling the new job. Would this be right?

CHRYSTAL 11: Yes, that's it. Now I think we've got it summarized so that perhaps we can work on it; there seem to be really those two individual problems, don't there? I guess, the most important is whether or not I myself am capable of handling the job. As I was thinking about this the other night when I was lying awake, I was able to move from my other location to Kansas City and we were able to get along fine, so I guess this problem is really not so important as whether or not I can handle the job. I know I said to you before that education is still very important to me but I think I have learned since I was at the conference that education alone isn't the thing that is completely my problem. You're right, I was able to get along fine with Mrs. Chapman and it didn't seem that education was so terribly important. And, also when I was at the conference, you remember that I was able to have dinner with the other girls and I didn't seem to have any problems. At that time I think I told you that I wasn't going to be fooled by this one experience because I knew that there would be other unhappy experiences in the same area. But that experience combined with several others I had at the conference and then my going down and meeting with Mrs. Chapman have shown me that I can get along apparently without all the education. So that the thing that is really bothering me I guess is the fact that there must be something else, there must be something behind all this that's bothering me more than any of these other little problems. I guess I thought that maybe my pastor or my doctor could help me with this, that maybe they would see the problem where I couldn't, and I guess this is why I feel they weren't very helpful to me. I don't know why I thought you could solve the problem either, because I guess it's something I've really got to find out for myself. I know I can talk to you and you're understanding, but you still can't give me the answer, can you?

PAT 11: No, Chrystal, I guess I really can't give you the answer. Sometimes things come up that we just have to solve ourselves and no matter how hard others try they can't give us the answer. We must find it ourselves but I do hope that by talking to me that perhaps you can help yourself to find it.

CHRYSTAL 12: Well, I guess this is really what I've been trying to do. When I'm not sleeping at night, I'm lying in my bed trying to figure out what's behind all of this, what's really the problem. I've gone back over the last five or six years of my life and tried to figure out what happened to me, why did I get like this. I want to tell you a story to see if you think that what I'm going to tell you might have something to do with the way I am now. When I first joined the company, I went to a sales meeting in the home office. The western manager came to the same meeting. She's a very businesslike person; she's not very outgoing, but she does a terrific job in her territory as she knows so much about business. Well the president and the eastern manager and the western manager and I all went out to dinner. After a little while, I started cutting up and I could see Mary, she's the western manager, look more and more annoyed. Finally, she asked me to go to the powder room with her. When we got there, she said to me, "Chrystal, you know you must behave as if you work for this company. Our company has to have a certain image, and a representative of the company has to behave that way. You can't go around acting like a child because when you do, it makes it seem as if the company is child-like." Well, then the next thing she did, was not to go and talk to my boss, the eastern manager about it, but she went to the president's office the next day and talked to the president about me. The president never said anything to me but my boss heard about it and she told me. Well, I had never been out in public before, and was just a stupid housewife I guess, but that was me—that was the way I acted, and I didn't know how to be anything else. Well when I went home from that meeting I said to myself, Chrystal you've got to learn how to behave. I think now as I look back on it, this is what I have been trying to do for the last four years, trying to be somebody else, to be somebody I'm not. I think when Mrs. Chapman said to me down at the home office, Chrystal we like and respect you because you are what you are, she made me try to think what I am, and this is what made me realize that I'm not myself and I'm not anybody else. I'm just a sort of a confused mess of everything. I guess what I need to do is really figure out who I am and who I'm going to be, and to stick to this way of living. I guess this is not going to be an easy thing to do, but this is what I'm going to have to do in order to be happy. Pat, I do want to thank you for letting me talk to you like this, because I know that the fact that I have been able to talk to you has just a little bit helped me to realize what this problem is. I guess that whether or not I take the new job, or whether or not we move or stay where we are, won't really solve this big problem for me, and that this big problem is going to take a lot of time and a lot of work, but I do know one thing: from now on, I'm going to be myself. So I think that I can write to Mrs. Chapman now and tell her, honestly, that I will take the new job. Because a new job and a new situation should give me a better opportunity to try to be more the person that I am inside. Well, that's enough for now; let's get on down to Macy's and see the Christmas decorations going up.

CASE IV-5. Edward Koch (A)

For several years the Hamilton Manufacturing Company had provided a counseling service as a part of its employee relations program. Each counselor was assigned to several departments where it was his responsibility to become acquainted with the employees and make himself available if they wanted to talk to him. A counselor could take no action except to help the worker to talk about his problems and express the feelings associated with them. The problems might concern either the worker's job or personal situation. Such conversations occurred either at the place of work or in the counseling room. In the latter case it was necessary to obtain the supervisor's permission to leave the department. The following conversation took place on December 2, 1946, when George, an experienced counselor, was approached by Ed Koch, a worker whom he had known for some time.

ED 1: Say, George you're not too busy right now. How about going over here and sitting down? There's a few things I'd like to talk to you about.

GEORGE 1: OK, Ed.

ED 2: Golly, George, I'm in a heck of a mess. I don't know what's the matter, but things just aren't going along too good with my wife and myself. I don't know what to do; we just can't seem to get along. Maybe you can give me some advice, tell me what to do. Golly, I don't know.

GEORGE 2: Why, what seems to be the trouble, Ed?

ED 3: Well, don't you think a wife should go a little out of her way to try to please her husband, to learn about some of the things he likes, and go out of her way to learn how to do these things? We've just been arguing back and forth at my house for a couple of weeks, and, well, the other day my father broke in. He told us that he didn't want any more of this arguing around there; he was tired of hearing it and we better learn how to get along together. Well, then she took offense to that—of him breaking in. I know he shouldn't have broken in. He wasn't right there but, after all,

Case material of the Harvard Graduate School of Business Administration, prepared as a basis for class discussion. Cases are not designed to present illustrations of either correct or incorrect handling of administrative problems. All names have been disguised. Copyright 1948 by the President and Fellows of Harvard College.

it's his house and he wants everybody to live harmoniously. He doesn't want to hear this arguing all the time, and golly, we've just been arguing back and forth. We can't seem to agree on anything.

Well, one of the things we've been arguing about was a wedding. We were supposed to go to a wedding last Saturday. Well, I didn't want to go. I told my wife I didn't want to go, but the whole darn trouble is that her father said that we should go. Well, shucks, I'm not going to let anyone tell me that I should go. I didn't know the person that was getting married and my wife didn't know the person that was getting married. Just because her father knew him—that isn't any reason why we should go to the wedding. That doesn't make any sense to me. Anyway, they told my wife that we should go. So my wife was arguing with me that we should go, and I said, "No," that I didn't want to go. What finally happened is that we didn't go, but we've sure been having a lot of arguments over it. It seems to me that we have an argument over anything we do now. My gosh, we've only been married three weeks! Two people ought to be able to get along better than that. I don't know what to do. What would you do? What do you think I should do?

GEORGE 3: You don't like to be told what to do?

ED 4: That's right! I think that the man should wear the pants in the family. My gosh, if I let them tell me what to do all the time, I wouldn't be able to do anything on my own. I think a wife should go out of her way to try to do things that her husband likes. When she gets married, her first duty should be towards her husband, not towards her folks or anything like that. A lot of little things come up, you know. We're married and living at my house right now and—well, you'd think that a person would go a little bit out of their way to learn a few things, like going down and learning how to cook certain things that I like, and how to take care of my shirts, and stuff like that. My wife doesn't do anything. She has a little job. But all she does—she comes home, we wait for her for supper, she eats and washes the dishes, and that's about all. You'd think that on Sundays she'd go down in the kitchen and watch my mother cook and learn to cook a few things. My mother told her that she would teach her anything she wanted to know, and when she came in my dad told her to just make herself right at home. Anything that she wanted to do in the house she sure could, because my folks have known her since she was a real little girl. That's the way it should be, but she doesn't do anything.

Don't you think that she should learn to cook a few things the way I like them? I was going around with a Polish girl at one time. Well, I learned how to eat the things that she knew how to cook, but I think that they should learn—maybe one day a week or something like that—to cook some of the things that I like. But my wife doesn't seem to want to do anything like that. The other day I asked her to bake me a cake, and she said that she didn't want to bake and cook in somebody else's house, that she wanted to wait until she got in her own. That's foolish, because my folks told her to do anything she wants. That's no excuse. So I don't know.

She don't seem to want to take any interest in anything around there. The trouble is her folks are always telling her this and that. Her father is always telling her what to do, and I don't know where I come in. For gosh sakes, it's no fun going on that way. There's no sense in it. Life is too short to be unhappy all the time, and what are you going to do if you have children or something like that? I sure as heck don't want to go ahead and have children when I don't know how I stand with my wife. The same with a place of our own. We're supposed to get an apartment in the near future but, well, I don't know. I don't want to go ahead and spend a lot of money on furniture and that and have everything bust up. I'd kind of like to know right now what the score is. I don't know, maybe the only way out is to get a divorce now.

Her folks are always making cracks to her about me. Like I told you last week, I just bought her a watch, and it cost me $150. Well, I paid part of it and I still have $75 to pay. Her father told her one day, he said, "Oh, I saw a watch just like yours in the jewelry store for only $55." Then she told me that. Well, she knows darn well I'm still paying on that watch and what I paid for it. Still she takes stuff like that. But her folks have always been that way. I don't know, they're just dumb. They're just a couple of dumb dagoes. You can't tell them anything, you can't sit down and talk to them. That's the trouble, if I sat down and talked to them, I'd probably get sore and have to slug the old guy or something like that. They're always wanting to argue. They are always different. Well, instead of sticking up for me, my wife always sticks up for them, too. Like just the other day, we stopped in the store to get a couple of bottles of ginger ale to fix a couple of drinks at home, and we ran into my wife's father. Well, I shook hands with him, asked him how he was—"Hi, Pop"—and all that stuff, and we got talking about cars. He said, "Just across the street is that Buick." He said that he wouldn't have any other car. "It's the best car on the street today." Well, I told him that I had a 1946 Packard, that the Packard was a better car all the way around.

You could take it part by part. It was a more expensive car, and everything else. I told him to go down here to Blake's Garage and see the number of Buicks being worked on there, and then go across the street to the Packard place and see how many Packards. Buick has always had trouble with their clutches, generators, and all that.

So then my wife pipes up and says, "Well, there's more Buicks on the streets than there are Packards." You know, taking sides with her father against me. I don't know, she doesn't seem to stick up for me in anything. It's just stuff like that that gets me. I don't know what to do. I want to do right. I want to make a go of it, but still I'm not going to give in all the time. My gosh, you give in once, and the first thing you know they take everything.

GEORGE 4: You're afraid she'll take advantage of you if you give in a little bit.

ED 5: Sure, just like my mother told me. She said that all these arguments and that, differences and that, well, that's up to us to settle; but she said that if you give a woman a foot, they'll take a yard. She said that's what she does to my father. So you see, my own mother told me that.

Another trouble is the fact that my wife's father is awfully strict that way. I think that's one reason why she's the way she is. She's seen her mother being told what to do all the time by her father. She's probably afraid that she's going to be the same way if she lets me tell her all the time what to do, because her father just put his foot down. If he didn't feel like doing something, he told his wife and that was all. I think that's the big trouble right now. She's afraid that might happen to her, and she doesn't want it; and that's why she's always trying to tell me what she wants to do. I don't know, the whole thing's a mess.

Well, just like our wedding—I didn't want a big wedding. I just wanted a little supper at some hotel downtown and have a nice quiet wedding, but her father wanted a big wedding. So, naturally, what could we do? I said, "Well, O.K., go ahead if you want to." But I told him that after we were married and settled down I was going to do what I wanted to do.

He says, "Sure, that's right, after you're married and living alone, you're the boss. Do anything you want." The trouble is that it's not that way. They're trying to influence everybody too much.

Sure. I know my father did the wrong thing when he butted in the other day, but that's his home and he wants everybody in it to get along. None of this arguing all the time. He can't take it any more. I don't know what to do. I know one of these days I'll lose my temper and beat her up. If things like this keep up—well, heck, I'd just as soon have a divorce. I'm young yet; I can marry somebody else. I'm not going to go through life this way. Divorce, though too, you don't know how much it would cost, or what it would take. I wonder if I would have to pay alimony. But then again, I probably couldn't get the divorce cause I didn't have any grounds. I don't know what grounds you need. There's something I might bring up. I know that we were married the 9th of November, and then the 21st she got a letter from some soldier. She told me about it. This letter says, "Darling, I love you and I want to marry you," and all this. Well, that was after we were married. I could tell the judge that my wife was unfaithful. I don't know just what you'd do in a case like that. That's why I don't want to have any children. If we can't get along now, there's no sense in having a family and just have to break it up. If you break it up then you've got to pay extra money to support the kids. You're losing all the way around. I want to get along with my wife, but I think she ought to do things that I like. After all, that's part of a wife's duties, don't you think, to learn to do the things your husband likes to do?

I know she wants to drive my car, and I told her she couldn't drive my car. The first thing you know she'd be using it to take her mother around all over. I can't see that stuff, either. Let her stay away from her family. I know every time I go over there I get in an argument with her old man, and I have all I can do to keep from hitting him. Maybe the only solution of it would be to quit my job here and leave town and go a thousand miles away and get a job where there wouldn't be any in-laws at all. But I don't want to do that either because we both got all our friends here, and I've got seven years service here I don't want to give up. And then, suppose I did do something like that and it still didn't work out. Where would I be? I'd be out some place. I wouldn't have a job, wouldn't have a job here, and we'd be worse off than we are now.

GEORGE 5: This way out doesn't seem to be too good.

ED 6: No, I don't want to leave here. I want to stay. If you leave town, you probably couldn't get a place to live—live in a hotel. Well, I've always had a home, and I may be funny that way, but I always wanted to have a home of my own and live in a home. This idea of living in some hotel or boarding house—I don't like that idea. I think that maybe divorce is the only way out. Maybe I could tell her that I was going to quit my job and we were going to some other town to live. Well, she'd have to follow me, wouldn't she? Doesn't the wife have to go wherever the husband wants her to go?

GEORGE 6: You think that this might be one answer?

ED 7: Yeah, but what would I do if my wife said she would go? Then what kind of a spot would I be in?

GEORGE 7: You're looking at that in terms of her refusing.

ED 8: Sure! Maybe that could be grounds for a divorce. I don't know. What if I hit her or beat her or something? I suppose they could use that as grounds for a divorce; probably get a lot of my money. I was wondering if they could take that money away from me that I got saved up. You see, I've got a couple of thousand dollars put away I thought we might build a home with. But with all this coming up I don't know. I'm kind of leary that if anything happens she's liable to get hold of it. You know, there's a young widow living down the street and, well, I could go out with her any time I'd like to. That's one thing, I haven't cheated on my wife yet. I could marry this widow and I could take over her business. I was wondering maybe they could get something like that on me. They could say they saw me in the company of another woman and build up a case like that—maybe get it to court and take all that money away from me.

GEORGE 8: You're afraid that if it went to court they might try to take all your money away from you.

ED 9: Yeah, then I wouldn't have a dime. You know it's hard enough —a guy's got to have a little extra money to buy with nowadays— just to support a family and all that. Like I say, probably the smart thing to do would be to quit my job and go to someplace else, say to New York, and get a job there. But I don't want to quit my job. George, when it comes right down to it, I think more of my job here than I do of my marriage. I figure that my dad's job here was able to support a family and a wife for thirty years, working here at the plant, and I want to stay here and make something of it too. So, I say I'd rather give up my marriage than give up my job here. You know, I can't understand the whole thing. Take when we got married, the honeymoon, and then the first week—we were so happy, everything was perfect, and now everything's the opposite. It's getting so that it's affecting my work down here. I can't work very much any more. I've got this on my mind, and I don't know what to do. I don't know just what the answer is to it.

If only her folks would quit telling her what to do, leave her alone and let me decide a few things, it would be all right. Well, like this cooking—if that was all it was, it wouldn't be bad. I can eat anything. She cooks one way. I can eat it. Well, after eating all that slop in the army for four years, I sure as heck can eat just about anything. I can overlook that. That's just a minor thing. There's just all this mother stuff. Well, just like last week her brother and her sister and a niece of hers made their confirmation, so I went and got cards, three cards for them, and I put $3 in each envelope, and I gave it to the kids. Well, then the next day her dad comes up to me and is talking about this one niece. He says, "Didn't they give you $20 when you got married, and you only gave her $3 for confirmation?" I just told him that when she got married I'd give her $20, but my gosh, this is just a confirmation and I can't afford to be giving that kind of money out. I don't know, I guess maybe he figures just because he can afford it. My goodness he's been married for thirty years. I've been married for three weeks. I don't know what he wants. That was one of the troubles. Remember, I told you I was going with this gal before and couldn't get along with her folks? Then the last minute we got together and got married. Things sure have changed. I just don't know what to do. I don't know where to turn, or what to tell her. If somebody would only tell her what to do and what to expect. (Long pause.)

GEORGE 9: (Looking at his watch) Say, Ed, we've gone right through your lunch period. When are you going to eat?

ED 10: Oh, forget about it. I don't feel much like eating. I'm not too busy around here; maybe I can grab something later.

GEORGE 10: Say, Ed, let's say we make a date for tomorrow morning, and we get together and continue this discussion.

ED 11: Sure, that's swell. There's not too much work around here now. I'll be able to get away. That's a pretty good idea. I'll be looking forward to seeing you tomorrow morning, then.

GEORGE 11: Swell, tomorrow morning, then. See you later.

Edward Koch (B)

On the day following the conversation reported in (A), George went down to the shop to meet Ed as they had agreed. At Ed's suggestion, they walked over to an empty bench which was across the room from his work group.

ED 1: I had a long talk with my wife last night.

GEORGE 1: You did?

ED 2: Yeah, I thought that that was the best thing to do. I told her that I had talked it over with my personnel man during the day, that I told him all about it, how things are going. I told her that we just sat down and talked about it, so I decided to sit down and talk with her and decide just what the score was on this whole thing. I told her that a divorce wasn't the way out of this, and I told her that if I quit work here and left town that wouldn't be the answer either, because both of us didn't want to leave our friends. I told her that we just got to learn how to get along with each other. I told her some of the things that I expected—I wanted her to do things for me—and I told her that I want to go out of my way to do things to make her happy. "Why this wedding the other night," I said, "I didn't want to go to that because, well, you wouldn't like me around there with a long, sour face on. I wouldn't have enjoyed myself." I told her I didn't think she would either if I was that way. So, I told her it was just up to the two of us to look after each other. After all it was our affair.

GEORGE 2: You thought it was something that the two of you had to work out together.

ED 3: Sure, I told her that we shouldn't pay any attention to what all these in-laws are telling us to do. I told her that she was no dummy, that she was twenty, that she had a good education, and that we're both smart enough to be able to work out something like that ourselves. I told her I'm twenty-five and I've had a lot of experience in handling money, and I know all about that stuff. But these other little things like working around the house and cooking and looking after some of my stuff, I told her that was her responsibility. I told her as soon as we could get into a place of our own, then everything would work out a lot better. You know, my dad told me that both of us had to get adjusted to one another and learn to know what each other was like. He says that sometimes it's hard to get adjusted, but almost everyone goes through that period. Yeah, he himself told me that—he himself—right after they got married there was a certain period where they had a lot of little differences. My sister and her husband had to get adjusted too. So, well, I guess it's something almost everybody goes through. We're not any different than anyone else right now and, well, we want to sit down and get to know each other better. That's what I told my wife. We've got to learn what the other person likes and know each other better, so we can work this thing out.

GEORGE 3: You've found a satisfactory way of working this thing out.

ED 4: Yes, I think everything will turn out all right. You know, another thing, when I sat down talking with her, I kept my head and was calm, like I am here with you. It was very reasonable. I didn't get angry or lose my temper. I told her that there's no sense of yelling at one another, or me losing my head and striking her. I told her that I didn't want anything like that to happen. I said I didn't want to get a divorce and I didn't think she did either, although I told her she's young and could probably get married again if anything ever did happen. And then you know, we're Catholics. Well, say we went ahead and got a divorce, and then she met another nice fellow and he'd want to marry her. His folks would say that she's a nice girl but she's been divorced. She's a Catholic and they don't recognize divorces. The same would be true from my side of the story, too. Like this widow I told you about yesterday—you know, at the Bakery Shop—I could maybe marry her and that, but our religion doesn't recognize divorces. It's just like being a marked man, like going around with a number on your back or a sign on your back—"I am divorced!" (Pause.) Say, have you heard anything about a 12½ per cent raise going through?

GEORGE 4: No, I haven't.

ED 5: Well, my dad told me something about it. He said it just went through here the last day or so. I told my wife last night. I said, "Honey, if that raise went through, I'm going out and buy you a sewing machine. That's what you always wanted." You know, she's always said that she's wanted a sewing machine, and we don't have any other debts just right now. Well, the only one we have is that watch—like I told you yesterday—but outside of that we don't have any at all. I could have paid cash for that watch, but I figured there's no sense in taking the cash out. I can have that cash on hand and pay for the watch on time. Everybody else is doing it, so I might as well do it. So, if this raise went through, I told my wife that I'd buy her the sewing machine.

She said last night, "Oh, it isn't necessary, we can wait." I told her, "No," I wanted to buy it for her if we had this extra money, 'cause I told her that I wanted her to be happy, and that I was going to try and make her happy. (Pause.)

(At this time one of the other people from the department came up to the bench to work there, so Ed and George got up.)

Say, let's get out of here. We ought to get out of the department. Just a second, I'll go over there and tell my boss that I want to go out with you.

(They walked over to the foreman and Ed asked if he could go out of the department with the counselor. The foreman agreed and kidded with them briefly. When they left, Ed decided against going to George's office because it was nearly lunchtime. Instead, they found a vacant bench in an adjoining department where they could continue their conversation without being overheard.)

Yeah, you know the way I look at it, I think that the woman should go out of her way a little bit to make her husband happy. But, too, the fellow probably owes something himself towards trying to make his wife happy. I know I've been away from home for three and a half years, and I know what it is to be away from your folks and everything. Well, like her, she's away from home, too. I can understand. I told her. I know it's hard for her to get used to living with somebody else. So I told her just as soon as we get to living alone everything would be all right. I told her until then what we would do is just to try our best to get along with each other and not pay too much attention to what the others wanted us to do. I guess it's always hard for a daughter and mother-in-law to get along. You know what I mean—with my wife trying to get along with my mother. Don't you think there's always a feeling of jealousy around there?

A lot of times things are said that really don't mean anything. I told my wife that if anybody ever says anything to her—well, I hope it don't happen, but if it ever did happen—to just forget about it. Don't say anything about it. In that way we'll get along a lot better. I told her I'd have to do the same thing. Like a lot of times, we go over to their house and I always get so burned up at her dad. He always thinks he knows everything, and I always get hot. I told her that I'd just take that stuff and I wouldn't say a word about it. That way everything is easier all the way around.

You don't hurt anybody's feelings or anything. Well, you know, living with somebody else, there's always something coming up. My mother probably feels that she wants to do these things for me. She's been doing everything for me for twenty-five years, and then to have somebody else come in the house and take care of my stuff—well, there's probably a little bit of jealousy between them, and you can't blame them. I guess all mothers are alike. Your wife and your mother probably feel the same way. There's a lot of times when they don't get along, but probably the best thing is not to say a word. Well, I suppose her mother feels the same way. She probably wonders sometimes why her daughter married a fellow like me, and I guess it's only natural. Every mother thinks that there's no fellow good enough for her daughter. I know a little thing happened around our house the other day in the bathroom. When my wife goes in the bathroom, she stays in there a little longer than usual, and she kinds of cleans up the bowls and that. Well, I guess my sister wanted to go in there, and she was waiting around instead of telling my wife to hurry up, that she wanted to go in there. She waited around, and when my wife came out my sister kind of gave her a funny look. Well, I told my wife to just forget about that—don't pay any attention to it, just to worry about me, and I'd worry about her. That's all the two of us would bother with now. So, I think after having this talk everything will turn out all right. I hope so anyway.

GEORGE 5: This makes you feel pretty good about the whole thing.

ED 6: Boy, I'll say it does. You don't know what it means to be able to kind of settle down and be able to get that stuff off your mind. I'm able to at least do some work around here now. Gee, for a couple of days I couldn't do a thing. People would come up and ask you about something, and you couldn't get your mind on your work, and you didn't know what you were doing. You know, I've got a pretty good job around here. I think I can make something out of it. I've got the reputation of being able to get the work done, and people come to me when they want to get things done right. You know, that's why I don't want to give up my job around here, because I think I've got a pretty good start and a pretty good bunch of fellows to work with. You know, I know a lot of jobs around here. If somebody comes up and asks about a job, if I don't know anything about it, I'll go up to my boss or find somebody that does know something about it. I'll always go out of my way doing that.

Well, going back to my wife, I told her the same thing. I told her that if there's anything she wants to know, that she should come up to me and ask me about it. I told her that if I couldn't tell her, that I'd find somebody that could tell her. I'd find out about it.

The only trouble here on the job now is that I got a couple of gals working for me and I'd just as soon get rid of them. One of them always seems to be telling the inspectors what's going on, you know. Every now and then if I want to get something through the inspectors, when I try to get them to pass it, she'll bring something up. Well, you know, if I get it passed, it's a credit to me, but she's always got to put her two cents in someplace. So I told my foreman that I thought it would be a good idea if he could transfer her over into one of the other sections, and he said that he'd see what he could do about it. Outside of that everything's working out pretty good. I can't complain about anything around here. Say, I guess it's pretty close to the time for lunch. Let's start heading back.

(They started back. At the corner where George turned off to his own office, Ed stopped.)

Say, George, I want to thank you for all you've done for me. You sure helped me an awful lot. If there's anything I can ever do for you, you want to let me know, because you've helped me more than my dad has. You've been more of a help to me than my parents. I don't know, there's just something about this whole thing that kept building up and building up, and I didn't know what to do. It was beginning to affect my job and everything else. It was beginning to affect my entire system. Like I said to my wife, I've seen enough excitement. I can't stand all this excitement and everything else, 'cause when I do my stomach goes bad on me. Well, gee, the last couple of days all this excitement has been building up inside of me. My whole system has been on the bum. I haven't been able to do much of anything. You've really helped me an awful lot, and I just had to get all this stuff off my chest. So, I want you to know that if there's anything I can ever do for you, I just want you to say the word.

GEORGE 6: Well, thanks, Ed, but you see that's just what I'm trying to do down here with all the fellows. A lot of fellows have things on their minds, and they just want to find somebody to talk to about it. So, I want to work that way with all the fellows. If they ever have anything, I think I can help them by their getting it off their minds, getting it out in the open so they themselves can decide what to do.

ED 7: Yeah, I think that's good. You know, there's a lot of fellows have things on their minds, and talking it over with you might make them want to do something about it then. I think that's very good. Well, I'll be seeing you around a lot. Thanks a lot!

GEORGE 7: Well, I'll see you later, Ed. So long.

CASE IV–6. John Thompson (A)

John Thompson, an executive trainee with the Q Company, was taking some graduate courses at a university near Chicago. An assignment in one of his courses, which was concerned with counseling and interpersonal communication, was to practice understanding someone, preferably someone who had a problem, from that person's point of view. Thompson had to make a written report of such a conversation and analyze it.

Thompson had some difficulty in finding a person with whom he thought he could talk in a way appropriate for this report. He mentioned his difficulty to several of his friends, including a Mr. and Mrs. Roger Samuels. Thompson and Mr. Samuels had met the previous year in a course they were both taking and had become friends. Samuels, who was currently in his second year of graduate work in political science, planned to become a teacher. Mrs. Samuels had a full-time secretarial job in one of the city's science museums; in addition, she was taking evening courses. Both she and Thompson grew up and went to school in the Southwest.

When Thompson mentioned his assignment, Mrs. Samuels volunteered to be interviewed. Thompson did not at first accept her offer, because he had talked so much to her about the assignment he was afraid their conversation would become "artificial." His report was supposed to be based on a conversation that occurred "naturally." However, when the due date of the report was close at hand and no other suitable occasion had presented itself, Thompson accepted Mrs.

Samuels' offer. He talked with her at her apartment one evening. His record of their conversation follows. For his analysis and discussion of it, see John Thompson (B).

MARY 1: Well, I hope I can be of some help to you in this.

JOHN 1: I think you will. You see, this is supposed to be merely a conversation with another person, about their job, a personal problem. . . .

MARY 2: (Somewhat eagerly.) I have a problem I'd like to talk about. It's about my not having an education, a college degree.

JOHN 2: You feel that having a degree is helpful to a person.

MARY 3: Well, it's nice if you have one. You can get a better job, and things like that. That's the reason I've been taking these courses at the university. They've really helped me, given me more confidence. That's why I like my job at the museum. I really have learned a lot there.

JOHN 3: You don't feel, then, that you could have gotten a better job had you had a degree.

MARY 4: No. I really like my job at the museum. The people in my department are all so nice. Then there's more prestige working some place like a museum. I hadn't realized that before. When you say you work for the museum, it's not like working for, say, an insurance company.

JOHN 4: You feel there's more prestige working for the museum than for a business.

MARY 5: Oh, yes. The people there are all educated. Then I get a lot of satisfaction from helping the people who come there. Especially the kids who come. It's very satisfying to know you're helping them. Some of the kids come there from all over the city, from all kinds of sections and backgrounds. They can see the exhibits we prepare and if they want to, they can enroll in the courses. It doesn't cost much, but if they can't afford to pay, some group like the League will pay for them.

JOHN 5: What is the League?

MARY 6: The City Educational League.

JOHN 6: Is that a public agency?

MARY 7: Oh, no, these are all private funds.

JOHN 7: Then you mean that at the museum you feel as if you're helping these kids to go farther in their education than they might otherwise.

MARY 8: Yes, that's right, and I get real satisfaction out of that. Then, too, the people at the museum are wonderful, especially those in my department. They're all young and intelligent. And they're all so nice. They all treat me very well and respect my opinion. When we have meetings, I speak right up, and my opinions are respected just like everyone else's, though they've all been there longer than I, and lots of my ideas are accepted.

JOHN 8: Do most of them have degrees?

MARY 9: Yes. They all do.

JOHN 9: But you don't feel that their attitudes toward you are different because you don't have a degree.

MARY 10: No, because they respect my opinions. That's why I've taken these courses. When I first came here, this problem of education was really a big thing with me. It affected my confidence. I had a real inferiority complex about it.

JOHN 10: You feel your courses have helped you gain confidence?

MARY 11: Yes, I definitely do. Now I feel I can take part in conversations and things like that.

JOHN 11: Do you plan to continue your education and perhaps get a degree?

MARY 12: Well, the degree is not so important any more. Sure, I'd like to continue to go to school, but there are other things, too. When Roger gets a job, I'd like to have a family (she smiles), and maybe I won't have time for school then. Those things take a lot of time.

JOHN 12: Having a family is more important to you now than continuing school.

MARY 13: Yes, I'd like to have a family before I'm too old. When Roger begins teaching, maybe I won't have to work, and we can start a family. Of course, if there's time, maybe I can take a couple of years off and go back to school. I'd like to get the degree now that I've gone so far. I'd like to go, if it weren't for the monetary problem.

JOHN 13: You feel it would be a shame to go this far and stop.

MARY 14: Yes, but I also think it's interesting to learn to understand people—what makes them tick. Before, I never analyzed people.

I just took them as they were. But it's really interesting to try to understand what makes them act as they do.

JOHN 14: Does that help you to understand yourself, too?

MARY 15: It really does. But it takes so long to get a degree this way. I know a fellow, though, who did. He's the Dutch consul. Now he's working on an advanced degree.

JOHN 15: You mean he's taking graduate work in evening courses?

MARY 16: Oh, no. He's in the graduate school now.

JOHN 16: Let me ask you this. If you ... (pause) do you feel that if you hadn't had to work, you would have been happier in school than at the museum?

MARY 17: Oh, no! I really enjoy my job. I really get a lot out of it.

JOHN 17: What is it that you do at your job which makes it so enjoyable?

MARY 18: Well, it's the work involved. The average person who goes to a museum doesn't realize how much work goes into it. I know I didn't myself before I had this job. The average person who comes in doesn't realize all the work involved in preparing the exhibits and everything. That's where a lot of my satisfaction comes from. There's so much to be done, especially in my department. I work in the education department. Why, they offered me a transfer once, and I just refused. It would have meant a raise, too. Of course, I've had raises since, but they were going to give me a really good promotion. When Dick Edwards, who's the supervisor, called me in and told me about it, I got all confused. Boy, that was such a feeling! When I came home that night, I was all upset. I didn't know how it would look to them if I refused. Finally, I just told Dick I didn't want the transfer.

JOHN 18: Have you ever had any regrets? I mean ...

MARY 19: None! I really like the guys in my department, and I enjoy my work there. I wouldn't leave there for anything. I've learned so much there, too. (Long pause.)

JOHN 19: Then you feel that both your job and school have helped you overcome this problem concerning your education.

MARY 20: Very definitely. When we first came here, I used to lack confidence, but now I believe I can hold my own.

JOHN 20: Do you have any idea why it was you felt this lack of confidence?

MARY 21: Well, I guess it was this environment. I wasn't used to these kinds of people. The people I had known at home were just everyday people. The girls I went around with talked about things like what color lipstick to wear and movie stars and stuff like that. They were just ordinary people.

JOHN 21: You didn't feel comfortable talking to these university people.

MARY 22: That's why I began to take these courses.

JOHN 22: You hoped they'd help you feel more comfortable?

MARY 23: Yes. Roger encouraged me a lot. He really helped me.

JOHN 23: Did you feel that the things these people were talking about were important to understand?

MARY 24: Yes. I think everybody should know what's going on around him. I wanted to know about current events, for instance.

JOHN 24: You feel that your education makes you a better citizen?

MARY 25: A better citizen and more alert generally. I'm better qualified at my job because I have taken three courses in zoology and three in biology.

JOHN 25: Then you also feel that your courses have enabled you to contribute more to your job.

MARY 26: Definitely. I think I'm more valuable than if I just typed. Just the other day at lunch Jim Dakin, he's the grandson of a famous scientist, and Mac, my boss, were kidding me. Jim said, "We'd better watch out that Mary doesn't get too intellectual." They have really encouraged me. Everybody has. It really makes the job more interesting. Now I can chip in on conversations with Roger's friends and ask intelligent questions. I guess it really has helped on the job, too.

JOHN 26: Are there any other girls with jobs similar to yours?

MARY 27: Well, there's one other girl, but her work is a little different. I guess we're interchangeable, though. We both assist in courses sometimes, but most of the time I'm busy with my other work. There are eight eager men with plenty of work for me, typing and all.

JOHN 27: Would it be fair to say, then, that you feel that in large measure you've met your education problem successfully?

MARY 28: I think so. I have a lot more confidence now.

JOHN 28: Do you feel that a degree would help still more?

MARY 29: Well, I feel a degree helps. It kind of (pause, as she seeks a word) adds authority to what a person says. (She continued in this vein for some time. Several times she referred to "authority," "respect," and the ability "to hold your own better" in connection with having a degree.)

JOHN 29: You mean you place more trust in what a person says if he has a degree?

MARY 30: I wouldn't say that. For instance, there's almost no one I respect more than the man who heads up the work on astronomy. He's a self-made man. He finished high school, but he didn't go to college. But he's a real whiz in science and higher mathematics. I've never seen anyone like him.

JOHN 30: Perhaps you feel, then, that it isn't so much a matter of a degree as of gaining the trust and respect of other people.

MARY 31: Exactly. Then, too, I think my courses have helped in other ways. They've helped my relationship with Roger and made our married life richer. Now I can talk about things which interest him. I've taken several courses in that area. You might say that whereas before I was merely a good listener, now I can pitch in. For instance, if he mentions something about Max Weber, I can give my opinion because I'm familiar with Weber's books. I think, too, that education is valuable in helping people meet problems and not turning aside from them. You learn to recognize problems for what they are.

JOHN 31: In other words, recognizing the problem is half the battle.

MARY 32: Yes, exactly. Before I didn't recognize my problems. I really enjoy my education now, and I feel I've profited. I would like to have gone to school full-time, but the important thing was to get Roger through.

JOHN 32: You mean because he was the "breadwinner."

MARY 33: Yes, at least . . . (John breaks in: Well, I mean) eventually. You see, I never realized how ignorant I was. That is the funny thing. It's like Socrates trying to define "justice." I'm reading that now, and I'm having trouble with that one, too. (Both laugh.) I really want to continue my education now.

JOHN 33: Don't you feel you may be able to do this, even if you can't go to school in the future?

MARY 34: I suppose so. There are always lots of lectures. I often listen to them on FM, too. I haven't found anything worthwhile on TV yet (laugh). Anyway, I've learned the means. A certain part of education, it seems to me, has to be guided. I think I missed that going to school at home. (Interchange about schools in small communities in the Southwest.) Now, though, I think I know how to find what I want.

JOHN 34: You feel now, then, you'd be secure in any situation. As a campus wife, for instance.

MARY 35: Definitely. Still, I'd always be striving to find out more. I believe in that respect I've profited by not going right to college. I'm not doing it because it's something expected of me, and therefore it's more valuable to me. That's where I feel I'm different from other girls I know. Some of them never read a book after leaving college. I didn't go to college when I had a chance. Neither my brother nor I did. I guess our family life was too comfortable. I didn't want to go away.

JOHN 35: You felt secure in your family.

MARY 36: Yes.

JOHN 36: But you feel you're better off having taken these courses now when you were older.

MARY 37: Yes. I feel the experience in between made me appreciate the education more. Now I don't think I'll ever stop reading and learning.

JOHN 37: You don't want to fall into a groove.

MARY 38: No. And I don't think I will now. I want to know more now. And I have confidence now.

JOHN 38: Really, then, you feel you've recognized this problem of yours and taken steps to meet it, don't you? I mean, it's hardly a problem with you any more.

MARY 39: That's right, although in a sense it's a continuing problem since education doesn't stop. (Long pause. Mary shifts around while John makes notes. John suggests that maybe they have reached the end.) I guess so—if you say. I hope you'll be able to use this all right.

John Thompson (B)

John Thompson, an executive trainee with the Q Company, was taking some graduate courses at a university near Chicago. An assignment in one of his courses, which was concerned with counseling and interpersonal communication, was to practice understanding someone, preferably someone who had a problem, from that person's point of view. Thompson had to make a written report of such a conversation and analyze it. The record he made of his conversation with Mrs. Samuels has been given in John Thompson (A). The analysis of the interview which he wrote for his report follows.

An evaluation and an explanation

The conversation was recorded from memory, but with the aid of notes, during the three hours directly following the conversation. While every word spoken could not be accurately recalled, it is believed that the transcript includes most of the conversation and captures most of its flavor.

The conversation took place on a Sunday evening. Returning from Mrs. Samuels' apartment to my own, I was conscious of a heavy feeling of disappointment. This feeling persisted even during the next three hours, in which I was intensely preoccupied with reconstructing and transcribing the conversation from my notes. It was difficult for me to specify the reasons for this feeling. There were only impressions: an impression of an artificial situation; another impression of an artificial "problem" selected for its value as a conversation piece; and a self-conscious impression of my somehow having been cheated. I had been sent on a fool's errand: to find someone with a problem about which they wanted to talk. From the beginning this had sounded a little ridiculous to me. In the counseling situation as described by Rogers, the initial circumstance was "The client comes for help." In this situation, though, it was the counselor who sought help! "Won't you help me write my term paper?" And Mary's opening remark had been, "Well, I hope I can be of some help to you in this." Dutifully, she then had ransacked her past and come up with a time-dried raisin of a problem long ago recognized and cured. What understanding could

Case material of the Harvard Graduate School of Business Administration, prepared as a basis for class discussion. Cases are not designed to present illustrations of either correct or incorrect handling of administrative problems. All names have been disguised. Copyright 1956 by the President and Fellows of Harvard College.

arise from such a situation? I knew nothing new of Mary except that she had once had a problem and had licked it. And, of course, she knew nothing more of herself.

It seemed to me that these results were predictable. For days I had postponed definitely accepting Mary's offer to talk with me about her "problem." The fact that the offer had been made during a conversation in which I was describing the nature and difficulties of the assignment had made me afraid that such a situation would be "artificial." My own friendship with Mary and her husband had caused me to doubt that an uninhibited conversation was feasible. It was only as the deadline approached and my hope faded for the fortuitous development of a chance conversation that I made a definite appointment with Mary.

My original judgment, then, was that this conversation with Mary had failed to develop significant insight into a genuine problem of hers by either of us. This appeared to be the consequence of the nature of the assignment primarily and secondarily of the fact of my friendship with Mary. These, I felt, were the causes of my disappointment. I wondered how I could write a paper about this conversation.

A further explanation

THE INTERVIEWER

On the day following my interview with Mary Samuels, an interviewing practice session was held in class. Members of the class took the role of one of the persons in the conversation we had been studying and some of the others practiced interviewing them. Perhaps because of the freshness in my mind of the conversation with Mary, I saw many similarities between my classmates' handling of this situation and my own experience. Being without personal involvement or pressure, I was able to evaluate the effectiveness of the interviewers' statements, questions, and responses, their successes and failures. As was brought out later in the students' discussion of their interviews, I could understand their anxiety to "keep the conversation going" at all costs, and at the same time I could see some of the consequences of this. Above all, I could recognize some of the basic assumptions underlying each man's approach to the person he was interviewing and observe (and to some extent, predict) what effects these would bring. For the first time I began to have a deeper understanding of concepts which I had already appreciated intellectually and to recognize a gap between my awareness of the goals and techniques of non-directive counseling and my ability to apply this knowledge.

Thus, my attention was called to a series of assumptions and attitudes which had affected my conversation with Mary and my original interpretation of it. It occurred to me that an evaluation of the conversation might be forwarded by an explicit recognition of these assumptions and feelings toward the conversation. This might open the way for a more objective interpretation of my role in the conversation and a more fruitful way of viewing the experience.

This approach led me to recognize an underlying assumption on my part that the assignment was "to hold a conversation with someone *in which you practice the techniques of non-directive counseling* in an effort to gain, and help them to gain, insight into a problem." This assumption led me to think and to speak of the assignment as "my interview." Subsequent reference to my notes taken at the time the assignment was made, and talks with other students, have revealed no mention of the portion of this "assignment" here italicized, and I have concluded that this idea was imputed to the assignment by me. It is important to note that this added portion carried certain auxiliary meanings in terms of my attitude toward the assignment.

Reflecting back to the period prior to the conversation with Mary, I believe that my basic feelings toward the assignment had been fear and apprehension. In seeking reasons why this should have been, it seemed to be partly a consequence of the very fact that this was an *assignment*, with all the overtones which this had for me. An assignment for me was related to the concept of "test" and referred to something to be accomplished within time limits. This idea appeared to me to be in conflict with the demands of what I thought of as the "counseling situation" which demanded that someone *come to me* for help; that this someone should come from outside my circle of friends in order that an uninhibited discussion might take place; and that this person should be relatively uninitiated in the area of human relations in order that I might "handle the situation." On the other hand, my feelings about an assignment demanded that, in view of the time limits, I must take the initiative in finding this person. I knew nowhere else to go but to my friends, most of whom were themselves students quite familiar with the newer concepts of counseling. (It was amusingly awkward, for instance, to think of myself interviewing a former roommate who had been a graduate student in clinical psychology.) I thought of becoming a temporary barfly in the hope of encountering a troubled bartender. When a classmate semi-seriously described his experience of "hanging around the YMCA all Sunday evening," I felt genuine sympathy.

In this way I believe my assumptions and my feelings about the assignment as I understood it had brought about a conflict–situation. The demands which I felt were being made on me by the assignment were incompatible with the demands which I was making on the situation. It was inevitable that I should have entered the conversation apprehensive and afraid. Similarly, I was prepared to be disappointed by the outcome.

THE CONVERSATION

Once I had recognized the assumptions and attitudes described above, I was prepared to attempt a re-evaluation of the conversation as a means of determining the effect of my assumptions and feelings upon its pattern as well as to gain a fresh and more accurate view of what had occurred. In this way, too, it might be determined what possibilities for insight were opened to Mary. A quick rereading of the conversation revealed the effort which I had made in keeping with my basic assumption to structure the conversation according to my concept of a counseling interview. Throughout the conversation there were almost no instances in which my responses contained more than one sentence, and the majority of these were short. A count of recorded words indicates that out of something over 1,700 words I spoke only a few over 500 or slightly less than 30 per cent. This seemed to indicate that it was my objective to listen rather than speak. Such an observation confirms my own recollection. Like one of the members of the class in the practice interviews we discussed, I felt anxious to listen and was impatient when pauses occurred. Just as he said he did, I often filled the pauses with questions or comments, the sole aim of which were to speed up resumption of conversation on Mary's part. Fortunately, Mary was more talkative than the person in the practice interview. However, had I been less anxious to avoid silences, I feel that Mary often would have continued without prompting. This actually occurred on several occasions (only one of which is recorded, M 33), when she interrupted me after only a word or two. This anxiety to listen seems to reflect my belief that the conversation should assume the character of a non-directive interview. That I was somewhat over-anxious in this regard seems more a consequence of inexperience than of a tendency to direct the interview, though, as will be seen, the latter tendency was certainly present, also.

Throughout the conversation I was conscious of tremendous difficulty in framing adequate responses to Mary's comments. From the analysis attempted in Table 1, it appears that the largest number of my responses were primarily to content, while only about one-fourth were responses to feeling. This characteristic is particularly outstanding in the early portions of the conversation in which there was no clear response to feeling until my twelfth reply. Responses J 5, J 6, and J 8 all clearly were questions seeking information about external factors mentioned by Mary. The brevity of Mary's replies demonstrates how such questions interrupted the flow of her conversation. J 7 seemed to recognize this and was an attempt to return the conversation to Mary's feelings about her job. Despite the interpretative flavor added by the last part of this statement, it succeeded in its purpose. Nevertheless, in my next response (J 8) I again interrupted this flow by asking a question demanding a factual answer. The next three responses, demanding less precise answers, finally returned the conversation to the point at which Mary had begun in M 3. It would appear that in this early portion of the conversation, I experienced great difficulty assuming a non-directive attitude and tended either to seek information or to interpret and direct the conversation (as in responses J 2, J 3, and J 7).

After this shaky start I seemed to make some progress (J 12 and J 13) in understanding Mary's feelings as she talked. My next response (J 14), however, again reveals that I was primarily concerned with leading Mary toward an evaluation of her educational process, which was my own aim rather than hers. Nothing in her prior statements had indicated that she felt that her education had advanced her own self-understanding. In M 15 she rejected my interpretation. Despite her words, "It really does," she turned to a discussion of her friend who was working for an advanced degree.

In J 16 I again recognized that my previous two content responses had halted the flow of her conversation. However, in my anxiety to get to what I assumed to be an underlying feeling, I again attempted to direct Mary (J 16), and again I was rebuffed. Here greater progress would probably have been made had I merely recognized Mary's feeling of admiration for this man's accomplishment. Though badly worded (a positive statement reflecting some of the feeling of Mary's emphatic M 17 would probably have been better), J 17 recognized Mary's genuine enjoyment of her work and so elicited the longest response of the interview (M 18). In this response, too, the strength of her feelings about her job and her co-workers is expressed, particularly

Table 1

An Analysis of John's Responses

	Number	Per cent of total
Responses defining the situation	1	2.6
Responses to the content of Mary's remarks	15	39.5

Responses to feelings
  Expressed in preceding remark: 8
  Previously expressed: 1
	9	23.6

Responses seeking to interpret or reorient the conversation	13	34.5
TOTAL	38	100.0

in her account of her feelings when a transfer threatened her happiness. Even though my question (J 18) again fails to capture her emotional tone as a positive response might have, her enthusiasm carries over into her next reply.

At this point (J 19 through M 23) I believe my responses began to reflect Mary's feelings more accurately than at any other time during the conversation. While it is true that in J 20 I put a demand upon Mary for a specification of reasons, she seems to have been prepared to move into such an area. A more productive remark here, however, might have been, "Your educational experiences have helped you feel more comfortable among your friends here." In J 23 there was more interpretation which ignored Mary's comment about her gratitude toward her husband. Here a comment such as, "You appreciated Roger's encouragement" might have opened up a new area of discussion. It is possible that my failure to explore this area was a direct consequence of my assumption previously mentioned that no uninhibited discussion of this kind of area would be possible with Mary. It now appears that such inhibitions as existed were brought to the situation by me. The same situation is repeated in J 31, where my decision to reply to the later feelings expressed in M 31 ignores this same area. In this case, my failing is more understandable considering the length of Mary's comments.

My failure in J 23 to move ahead with Mary returned the conversation to an area already fairly well covered. My failure to respond appropriately in J 26 and in J 27 may indicate an anxiety to get into a new area, and in J 28 I definitely took the initiative in this direction. In J 29 I attempted to express a meaning beyond Mary's own. Consequently, she flatly rejected my interpretation. Nevertheless, this exchange apparently had the effect of helping her to examine a possible feeling on her part which was strongly hinted at in M 29. J 30 was one of the most successful responses to Mary's feelings contained in the conversation. Accordingly, it brought a long response from Mary in which she emphasized the extent to which her courses have aided her personal relationship with her husband. It is indeed unfortunate that this lead was dropped in my response (J 31), for as I shall indicate later, this now seems to me an area of great importance to Mary.

In J 35, by choosing to pick up that part of Mary's discussion which dealt with her past, I may have failed to gain insight into another aspect of her present situation. (I seem to remember that when Mary made her comments about her family ties, the thought in my mind was, "Aha, here's the root of it all!") In general, however, I feel that by this point both parties felt ready to abandon the discussion. The repeated coverage of Mary's job and her courses (which probably could have been avoided by more adept responses) created the impression that no new ground remained. J 38 was an expression of this feeling. Mary's last comments seem to indicate that she too may have been disappointed in the interview.

A re-evaluation and an apology

Some sort of re-appraisal of the interview and its results is dictated by the preceding analysis. First of all, I am not now convinced that the conversation did not provide grounds for new understanding on my part of Mary and her problems. It seems now that in many ways Mary tried to tell me, "I think of myself as the wife of a graduate student. As such, I feel that a college education is necessary to enable me to associate comfortably with my husband's friends and to give me the common background which will help me build companionship and security into our marriage. I like my job because the people there respect me and my ability, because it helps me to gain the education I desire, and because working at a museum helps me to feel comfortable with our friends."

In the light of the foregoing analysis it now seems possible that Mary gained a new measure of insight into this personal problem. In these remarks a new dimension of her situation apparently is recognized and she seems to be saying, "I now recognize that my feelings of discomfort were a consequence of an ignorance of which I was not even aware (M 32). As a result of what I have learned, I am now able to look upon myself as an intelligent, thinking person whose opinions other intelligent people, including my husband, respect (M 31)." With this new view of her problem, Mary recognized her education as a continuing problem and identified a number of means of dealing with it in the future (M 34 and M 39). It would be easy to over-emphasize the extent of Mary's new insight into her problem. Yet these remarks near the close of the interview do suggest that some of the pessimism concerning the possibilities of continuing her education expressed earlier (M 12 and M 13) has been relieved by a more thorough examination of alternatives than had previously been made.

Perhaps in self-defense, I hasten to add that my own evaluation of the conversation does not overlook the fact that this was a problem with which Mary had made significant progress prior to our conversation. Yet it remains true that certain aspects of the situation were still ill-defined and, hence, still a problem to her. At least one of these aspects, that of future action, may have been dealt with helpfully in this conversation. On the other hand, other unresolved aspects of the problem—notably that of Mary's concern about her ability to be a good companion for her husband—might have been developed in a manner more helpful to Mary had the conversation been more adeptly conducted. Here my own "directiveness" (reflected in the high number of interpretive responses shown in Table 1) undoubtedly was a deterent to development of the free and permissive atmosphere which would have fostered such additional progress.

Here I must apologize for returning to the kind of personalized, historical discussion which has characterized so much of this paper. This approach has been necessary, however, because of my feeling that most of the failures in this experiment at understanding a person have followed from the feelings and assumptions with which I began. It was my assumption that I was to conduct a non-directive interview which led to my original disappointment in the results of the conversation. Similarly, regarding the experience as a personal test, I placed primary importance upon the business of *applying the methods and techniques I had learned*, rather than on gaining a real appreciation of Mary's feelings as she talked to me. With my primary focus thus on myself rather than on Mary, I sometimes lagged behind her, frequently leapt ahead, and repeatedly failed to respond to her feelings.

Thus I come to the conclusion that the primary benefits of this conversation have come to me in the valuable insights gained into my own personality and in the new knowledge growing out of the experience of actually practicing a concept intellectually accepted but not yet fully absorbed. This exercise in "practicing a concept" has demonstrated to me the truth of Rogers' statement that, "The counselor is always implementing, both in conscious and nonconscious ways, the attitudes which he holds toward the client."[1] Recognition of the many ways in which my attitudes revealed a brand of arrogance of which I was previously unaware has led to new feelings of humility. Perhaps the other side of this same coin is a growth of my faith in the abilities of other people to learn for themselves, aided only by a truly sympathetic listener who accepts them and their feelings without censure, approval, disapproval, or direction. For whatever Mary learned about herself in this conversation seemed to follow from behavior of this sort on my part. And when I behaved differently, Mary seems to have learned nothing.

[1] Rogers, *Client-Centered Therapy*, p. 26.

CHAPTER 8. Counseling and administration

In this chapter we give more explicit attention to the question which has frequently arisen during discussion of the previous cases and readings, namely: How is our study of counseling related to our future practice of administration or management? In Part IV we have been examining in considerable detail a particular kind of relationship, in which a person with a need to improve his understanding of himself is interacting with a person who is trying to facilitate this process of self-understanding. Sometimes a manager will find himself in this kind of relationship, but there are obvious and important differences between such a situation and most of the interactions in which a manager is involved in the course of his daily work. While we have been studying counseling, what useful lessons have we been learning about the interpersonal aspects of administration, in spite of the obvious differences between the two situations in terms of the intentions and behavior of both persons involved?

Influencing and helping

Let us first consider briefly the differences we have already encountered. It is clear that in many of his interactions the orientation of an executive is to try to influence someone else's behavior in order to accomplish something the executive wants done. For example, in Case II–1, Chris Baum, Norris was primarily concerned with influencing Baum to load his truck differently and to be more "sales-minded." But this is not the only kind of interaction in which an executive takes part in the course of his work. There are also many instances in which a person comes to an executive in connection with a problem that person is encountering, as Juanita Rodriguez came to Mr. Greene, III–1, or as Paul Varner came to John Byron, II–2.

These requests frequently occur in the form of a question. When an executive is asked a question, an organizationally sanctioned and natural response is for him to answer it. This is what he feels he is expected to do. Yet our study of counseling has indicated that to answer such a question can be less helpful than to help the person find his own answer.

Thus our first lesson for administration from our study of counseling may have been to call attention to the potential difference between two sets of interactions:

1. in which an executive is trying to influence someone else's behavior in a direction the executive desires;

2. in which another person approaches an executive in connection with a problem the other person is experiencing.

In the second situation, much more clearly than in the first, the opportunity is present for structuring a counseling relationship if the executive responds in such a way as to clarify the intentions and behavior of both himself and the person who is asking him for help.

Of course in an actual experience, the two sets of interactions, one of which we may call situations of influence and the other situations of helping, are not necessarily separate or clear. They do not present themselves to the administrator's attention as we have analytically separated them here. It requires an act of observation and judgment for both persons to know what orientation dominates the interaction.

Furthermore, it should be clear from the study we have made that the words used are not necessarily a reliable guide to the character of the interaction. Given some of the kinds of beliefs about themselves which are frequently encountered stereotypes in our culture, many subordinates, for example, will feel that they cannot ask a superior for help. Their statements, therefore, may be more or less skewed in ways to indicate that they are not doing so. Similarly, experienced persons often encounter situations in which a subordinate explicitly asks for help but is implicitly saying that that is the last thing to which he would be receptive. We need not get obsessive about the difficulty of recognizing the difference between explicit and implicit meanings. In practice it is less difficult than we might think to recognize when another person is really asking us for help. We have all had much experience in recognizing what the words people use actually mean. There are few undergraduates today, for example, who would not consider themselves expert in interpreting whether a girl's "no" means "no" or "yes" or "maybe"!

We can thus distinguish two sets of interactions in which an executive takes part, to one of which our study of counseling is more obviously relevant than it is to the other. And our practice in understanding the intentions and feelings of other people and of ourselves has increased, we hope, our ability to know in which of these two situations we may find ourselves involved.

But in a very real sense the relevance of the counseling orientation we have been studying to our interpersonal relationships is something each of us has to figure out for himself. The purpose of this chapter is not to prove this relevance, but rather to provide some additional ways of thinking about it. More specifically, we now want to draw on the cases and readings in Part IV in considering the following four propositions:

1. The underlying "client-centered" orientation we have been studying provides a challenging hypothesis about man's capacity for self-realization and growth which can be tested in many ways in working with people in organizations.

2. Because so much of the manager's job requires him to interact effectively with others, he needs to learn whatever he can from counseling about how to listen with understanding to what he and others mean when they talk.

3. More specifically, the manager can learn, from his study of

counseling, useful ways of responding, when appropriate, to any person who *does* ask for help in understanding himself.

4. There *are* real limits on the applicability of the orientation and technique we have studied which each of us has to understand and work out for himself. These limits have to do with constraints of organizational structure, availability of time, the particular circumstances of each situation, and the individual "practitioner's" own understanding of and feeling about himself. Skillful administration just as much as skillful counseling requires behavior that is both appropriate to the particular situation and congruent with the individual's concept of himself. Understood in this way, the study of counseling reminds the manager, among other things, that it would *not* be appropriate for him always to behave as if he were a counselor.

Relevance of underlying orientation

As was emphasized in Chapter 7 and explained more fully in Reading IV–2, the kind of interviewing and counseling we have been studying in Part IV is best understood not in terms of surface technique, but as the implementation of an underlying orientation toward the individual, a basic belief in his capacity to deal constructively with his situation as he sees it, to learn, to grow, to develop his potential. As Rogers repeatedly reminds us, this orientation "is not something which must be taken 'on faith,' or achieved all at once. It is a point of view which may be adapted tentatively and partially, and put to the test. It is actually an hypothesis in human relationships, and will always remain so."

Any manager concerned with the behavior of other people and their responses to various kinds of challenges is also, whether he thinks this way about it or not, acting on the basis of certain underlying assumptions or hypotheses about human capacities, motivations, and relationships.

The importance of these underlying assumptions about how people behave or should behave in organizations was illustrated in several of the readings and cases of Part II. Frequently, as we saw, management's basic assumptions about people are not made explicit, but they can be seen reflected in almost every management decision concerning organizational and job design, the sharing of responsibility and autonomy, the patterns of communication and control, and the kind of challenges to which people at all levels of an organization are expected to respond. In all these and other respects, a manager with beliefs about human capacity and motivation similar to those expressed by B. F. Skinner, for example, will lead a very different kind of organizational life from that of a manager whose beliefs are closer to the working hypotheses set forth by Carl Rogers.[1]

The important point that our study of counseling has made about assumptions of this kind is that whatever they are they can be considered as hypotheses to be tested rather than as unalterable laws to be followed. It is at least as true of the manager as of the counselor that he is engaged in a constant search for more effective ways of dealing with people, and that for this search to be fruitful he needs to become increasingly aware of how his own implicit assumptions are affecting his own behavior and his interpretations of how others respond to him. In testing out the validity of these beliefs about others, he needs to be flexible but not capricious—that is, willing to alter his beliefs when the evidence indicates he should, but equally willing to give them a fair trial. In order to interpret intelligently why others respond as they do to the trust or lack of trust he places in them, the manager, like the counselor, needs to be able to understand his own beliefs and feelings without being overly preoccupied with himself.

The preceding cases, and also your own efforts to develop interpersonal skill, have shown the value of thinking of each encounter as an opportunity to test and reformulate a set of working hypotheses about the capacity of the other person to respond in positive ways. Here we are suggesting that this same orientation, this same willingness to assume more potential in the other than at first appears, *can* be thought of as a working hypothesis for

---

[1] See the papers by Rogers and Skinner in D. E. Hamachek, ed., *The Self in Growth, Teaching, and Learning* (Englewood Cliffs, N.J.: Prentice-Hall, 1965), 94–119.

managing, an hypothesis it is possible to test not just in interviews but in every decision the manager makes that involves a prediction of how others are likely to respond. This, we believe, is the most general relevance of the study of counseling to the process of administration.

Relevance of listening with understanding

More specifically, of course, we have been studying the counseling process as a way of learning about how to understand what another person means when he talks with us, not just what he says and thinks and sees, but how he feels as well. Every manager, we believe, needs something of the counselor's way of listening to and understanding another person. As you may have discovered while discussing these cases and attempting your own interviews, most of us are not as skillful as we would like to be in understanding what the others who interact with us really mean. Yet for anyone who intends to work with other people this is an undeniably important skill. It is hoped that our exposure to the counseling process, and our somewhat detailed look at client-centered counseling orientation and technique, have helped us see how to improve our ability to achieve more useful understandings of each other.

Let us look at some of our cases with the following question in mind: To what extent would the way of understanding a person that was achieved by the interviewer have been useful to a manager? In other words, in what sense is counseling relevant to administration simply because it illustrates a way of understanding people that makes it easier to work with them?

Consider the interview which Donald French had with Ashok Rajguru. Although Ashok was a student, he—or someone like him—might very well be an employee whose behavior (decreased motivation and drive) was of concern to his colleagues and superiors. If so, we might evaluate Donald's report of the understanding he achieved of Ashok's point of view with this question in mind: Would this way of understanding Ashok help me work with him if I were his co-worker or boss?

Regardless of whether we agree with everything Donald says

about Ashok Rajguru, it still seems fairly clear that this is a *way* of understanding another person that has relevance beyond the somewhat artificial circumstances of this particular interview. After listening carefully and sensitively to Ashok talk about himself, Donald has organized the beliefs, perceptions, and feelings he received into a pattern which makes sense, and Ashok's behavior becomes more understandable. (The fact that *in this case* the "need hierarchy" concept helped Donald do this is not particularly important for our purposes. Other concepts might well have been more useful. The important point is that Donald has achieved a way of understanding Ashok's behavior from Ashok's point of view which makes it less puzzling and easier to understand than it was before.)

We claim this way of understanding another *is* useful when we have to work with him, if only because having become less puzzling and more understandable he is easier to work with. Furthermore, the understanding of Ashok that Donald achieved has obvious relevance to any attempts to motivate him more effectively. From Ashok's point of view, if his circumstances made him feel less lonely and isolated, it would become more easy to mobilize effectively his need for achievement. Understanding this, we could help Ashok feel less lonely if we were in the position of his supervisor or colleague, especially once we had discovered through a little listening to him what an interesting person he was to know better.

The same point can be made by reference to any of the other cases. To the extent that a person reveals something of his own way of seeing and feeling about his situation, he presents himself to us more as someone with whom we can effectively communicate because we know more about what is important to him.

The two interviews with Miss Dvorak illustrate nicely that this kind of understanding requires more than discovering how a person answers our questions. The first interview tells us something about Miss Dvorak. In the second interview, in contrast, she permits us to understand her more nearly as she sees herself, a person, for example, who needs to think of herself as an American, not a Bohemian, girl and whose job helps her maintain this (not altogether realistic?) picture of herself. Once we have seen something of what is most important in her view of herself, her behavior and attitudes seem less puzzling and inconsistent and she becomes a person more easy to work with helpfully.

In these cases the understanding that we claim would be useful is obtained by means of a certain kind of interview. Our attention to the specific exchanges in these interviews and to the specifics of the interviewer's behavior may have indicated that it is only through such interviewing that this kind of understanding can be achieved. However, with most of the people with whom we work we are much more likely to have a series of shorter inter-actions over a longer period of time. In total such interactions, provided we pay some attention to the feelings that are being expressed, can help us achieve something of another person's frame of reference without the need for an "interview." At this point we are not advocating that a manager interview his employees in the special way described herein in order to understand them. But we are suggesting that in the normal course of events in working with people, a manager can usefully apply the way of thinking about other people that he has acquired by the study and practice of interviewing skill. For this purpose the formal interview is primarily valuable as a setting within which to become more aware of what it means to listen with understanding to the feelings expressed in the daily actions and words of those with whom we work.

Relevance of helping

There are times, for most managers, when the interviewer's orientation and technique are highly relevant in a more narrow and specific sense, namely on those occasions when another person makes an explicit or implicit request for help in thinking through something of concern for him.

Most of us as managers would like to have the kind of relationship with a subordinate, for example, within which he will tell us when worried about something which is interfering with his work. But when this happens, it is not always easy to know how to respond. The cases we have been studying suggest that often the most helpful response is not the kind of cheerful reassurance which denies the reality of the feelings being expressed, nor advice based on one's own experience and point of view. Often this is not what the person who comes to us is really asking us to give. Instead, our cases and readings suggest that what may be in fact most helpful is for us, initially at least, to simply *listen* sensitively to what he wants to say and concentrate on facilitating the clear expression of his existing feelings about himself. This is *not* to say that the manager has to be a counselor, *or* that the resulting conversation turns into therapy, but only that the manager can sometimes be most helpful by listening skillfully, which is for most managers not an easy thing to do.

All this is not to advocate that a manager has a right or duty to pry into the personal affairs of his subordinates or colleagues, nor that he has or should have the competence to be helpful in any deep psychological sense. We simply mean that occasionally he may have to respond in one way or another to a request for help in thinking through a personal problem or relationship, and that some study of the counseling process can help him decide in a specific instance what way of responding to adopt, given his view of his own competence and interest and how he interprets the constraints of his place in the organizational structure on the particular relationship.

In these kinds of contacts one of the most interesting questions to be faced is how to respond to an explicit request for advice. Our cases give several examples of different ways of dealing with such requests. These can be examined in order to work on the question: As a manager, not as a counselor, is this the way I would have responded, and why or why not?

For example, Sylvia Holden tells Jane quite clearly, "I cannot give you any advice, nor could I feel qualified to do so." In its context at the end of an interview in which Sylvia has asked Jane many questions designed to get her to see "various angles" of her situation and has not done much real listening to Jane's own point of view, this refusal to advise may make Jane feel rejected. One gets the impression that Jane may not feel she has received from Sylvia the kinds of help she was hoping for, and that Sylvia may not realize this.

The Chrystal Smith case is especially relevant to this discussion partly because of the somewhat unusual way in which the
relationship between Chrystal and Pat developed. Some students
will feel that Pat got herself too deeply involved with Chrystal,
given the nature of their relationship. (Researcher–conference
participant, friend–friend, or implicit counselor–client?) In any
event, some of Pat's specific responses are worth careful consideration as examples of meeting the client-centered counselor's
"dilemma" of responding to direct questions outside of a formal
counseling relationship. It seems to us, for example, that Pat 8
and Pat 11 in Chrystal Smith (C), while not following the "rule"
of client-centered technique, are straightforward and helpful
responses which do not violate Pat's underlying orientation. Especially outside of a formal counseling relationship, it can be
neither polite nor "good listening" artificially to ignore an important question; Pat avoided this beginner's trap. At the same
time it can be helpful, given an opportunity, to clarify the fact
that the questioner may have ambivalent feelings about whether
he really wants his questions answered by someone else (see Pat 9,
Chrystal 10, Pat 10).

An interesting contrast to these examples of responding to
the "client's" request for advice occurs at the beginning of Ed
Koch's conversation with George. When Ed asks George, "What
do you think I should do?" George finds it unnecessary either to
answer the question or to state that he isn't supposed to give
advice. George is able to avoid either alternative because he has
been listening to all that Ed has been saying, not just to his last
question, and he has heard Ed express very strongly his view of
himself as a person who does *not* "like to be told what to do." As
a matter of fact George's ability to avoid giving advice is quite
remarkable throughout the interview. As a result, whatever one
may think about the long-term resolution of Ed's problem, Ed's
subsequent actions are based upon his own diagnosis, and his
future relationship with George has not been damaged. For our
present purposes, the important question to consider is whether
George should and could have responded in a similar way to Ed's
request for help if George had been Ed's boss.

In considering this question it is helpful not to get bogged down in debate as to whether Ed's two conversations with George are "realistic." They *are* realistic in the sense that they did happen. They also are unusual in the sense that most of us would have a hard time listening as patiently to Ed as George managed to. They can be misleading as an example of the counseling process because they give some readers the impression that tremendous progress has been made, whereas another frequent reaction is that nothing significant has happened as a result of these interviews.

(In another sense, however, these two interviews represent very accurately, in a capsulated form, many of the characteristics of the counseling process as Rogers describes it. Ed seems to have achieved an ability to pay more attention to his work and in this sense to be more productive. He seems to have increased his problem-solving ability, in the sense that in the second interview he is looking at his situation in a less confused and distorted way. In particular there has been a noticeable shift in several of his perceptions; for example, his mother-in-law, a "dumb dago" in the first interview, is later seen as a person with natural concerns about "why her daughter married a fellow like me." His concept of himself has not altered significantly, but he is expressing a different and probably more useful way of thinking about his situation.)

We do not want to say much more about the extent to which Ed's supervisor should or could have responded as George did, because we believe that this is a question that each of us can only answer by putting himself, hypothetically, into that position. But since we believe intelligent thought on this question is very important, we would like to reproduce the following description of how George himself may have interpreted the interviews. (Ed is referred to as Freddie in the quotation).

> Depending upon his age and stage of development, the reader may perceive these interviews with Freddie quite differently, from being tragic, to comic, to trivial. So let us see what the counselor heard.
>
> From his point of view he was listening to the feelings of a young man, recently married, generated by the transition from his parental family to his own and the difficulties he was having in coping with them. In the first interview Freddie keeps bemoaning the fact that his wife does not come up to his conception of an ideal wife. To Freddie it was incredible

that his young wife should not have the same concerns about him that his parents had. It sounded as if Freddie wanted his young wife to be like a mother to him, or perhaps a mother he wished he had had.

So in the first interview he toys with the ideas of divorce, quitting his job, moving out of town, cheating on his wife and thus having revenge for her maltreatment of him. He does not seem to consider seriously moving out of his parents' home. But he does think of his job. "When it comes right down to it," he says, "I think more of my job than my marriage."

But what does Freddie's job and the Company mean to him? The Company had allowed his parents to earn a living and raise a family. Shouldn't it provide him with the same opportunities (dependency needs)? He wants to live in his parents' home (dependency needs) but also wear the pants in the family (counter-dependency manifestations), and the first interview ends on the dependency note to the counselor—"If only somebody would tell her (his wife) what to do and what to expect."

There is a long pause and the counselor muses, "I wonder who that somebody will be?" But the counselor does not express his musings nor, it should be noted, does he reflect many of the implied feelings he has heard. Many of these implied feelings, if reflected too soon or too baldly, he feels might damage his relation with Freddie. So he reflects only the most obvious expressed feelings without twisting (interpreting) anything Freddie has said.

Nevertheless part of the counselor's message must have gotten through to Freddie, and in the second interview we see Freddie trying to apply it. He *tells* his wife what their relation *should* be. It does not sound as if his wife had much chance to express what she would like her relations to her new husband to be. But undaunted, Freddie keeps trying; he's not surrendering or throwing in the sponge as yet.

Still the counselor, who may have felt some slight sense of futility at this point, keeps up his basic posture. He doesn't say to Freddie, "How stupid can you get." He recognizes Freddie's striving—no matter how futilely expressed—to cope with his situation. He feels that in the main, Freddie wants to make a go of it with his new wife, but his balled up (ambivalent) feelings are making this difficult to accomplish.

So the counselor keeps trying to get these feelings out in the open where they can be looked at and coped with. But mostly Freddie keeps looking in the opposite direction, i.e., not at his ambivalent feelings but at the object of them—his wife and his job, for example. However, a few occasional notes of a different direction do creep in, such as "a fellow probably owes something himself towards trying to make his wife happy."

Obviously no great miracle occurred in these two interviews. Freddie does not come out of them a fully matured and responsible person, capable of coping fully with his dependency–independency needs. But the counselor's motto is "sufficient unto the day is the problem thereof." If Freddie has taken one small step in the direction of maturation and gotten some satisfaction from it, this, the counselor feels, might reinforce Freddie's desire to take another step in that direction again someday. Moreover, the counselor has the statement from Freddie that the interviews had helped him. How much more evidence do many doctors have for their treatments?[2]

The question of limits

Before concluding this chapter we want to approach the problem of the applicability of the counseling orientation to the manager's role in a somewhat different way, by discussing briefly some of the more obvious barriers or limits to adopting this orientation outside the formal counseling relationship.

We do not intend to define these limits for anyone else, but rather to provide some ways of thinking about them, as we believe that this is what each of us has to do for himself. Further, it is an issue on which our own position may shift—in either direction—with the benefit of added experience. (We have experienced a number of such shifts ourselves, generally in the direction of seeing a wider applicability in the underlying orientation and a narrower relevance for specific aspects of the technique.)

Our point that the applicability of this orientation to non-counseling situations is best thought of as something to be worked out over time is well illustrated by Rogers' own writings. Thus in *Counseling and Psychotherapy* Rogers strongly questioned whether a therapeutic relationship could co-exist with authority, whereas he later used his counseling orientation as a basis for tentatively formulating a "general law of interpersonal relationships." The following passage taken from Chapter 5 of *Client-Centered Therapy* is a particularly interesting discussion of the shift in Rogers' own thinking on this topic between 1942 and 1951.

> In *Counseling and Psychotherapy* the author gave certain tentative criteria which, if met, indicated that counseling was advisable [footnote citing criteria omitted]. This list of criteria has proved less than helpful. It is not so much that it is entirely incorrect . . . as that it engenders in the

[2] W. J. Dickson and F. J. Roethlisberger, *Counseling in an Organization* (Boston: Division of Research, Harvard Graduate School of Business Administration, Harvard University, 1966), 323–24. Reproduced by permission. The interview with "Freddie," as Ed Koch is called by Dickson and Roethlisberger, is one of five examples discussed in their chapter on "The Difference Counseling Can Make." These interviews all took place at the Hawthorne works of the Western Electric Company.

counselor-in-training an evaluative, diagnostic frame of mind which has not been profitable.

Present opinion on applicability must take into account our experience. A client-centered approach has been used with two-year-old children and adults of sixty-five; with mild adjustment problems, such as student study habits, and the most severe disorders of diagnosed psychotics; with "normal" individuals and those who are deeply neurotic; with highly dependent individuals and those of strong ego-development; with lower-class, middle-class, and upper-class individuals; with the less intelligent as well as the highly intelligent; with healthy individuals and those with psychosomatic ailments, particularly allergies. . . . Only two of the many types of customary classifications have not been appreciably sampled—the mental defective and the delinquent. It is unfortunate that thus far circumstances have not led to much work with this therapeutic approach in these fields.

On the basis of the foregoing experience it would be correct to say that, in each of the groupings in which we have worked, client-centered therapy has achieved noteworthy success with some individuals; with some, partial success; with others, temporary success which later suffered a relapse; while with still others failure to help has been the result. Certain trends appear to be evident, such as the lesser likelihood of deep personal reorganization in the older individual. The Haimowitz study . . . indicates tentatively that intra-punitive males may make better use of the experience of client-centered therapy than others. But on the whole, our experience does not lead us to say that client-centered therapy is applicable to certain groups and not to others. It is felt that there is no advantage to be gained by trying to set dogmatic limits to the use of such therapy. If there are certain types of individuals who do not respond, or for whom client-centered therapy is contra-indicated, then accumulating experience and additional research will indicate what these groups are.

In the meantime, the lack of definite knowledge about the groups for whom client-centered therapy is more or less successful is not a matter for serious concern, since our clinical experience would indicate that such therapy does not seem to do harm to the individual. Where a client-centered approach is consistently utilized, it is our judgment that very rarely would the client leave the experience more disturbed than when he came in. In the overwhelming majority of instances, even where the counseling experience is felt by the client to be unsuccessful, he is not more upset by his problems because of the failure. This is so primarily because of the lack of any pressure in the relationship; that is, only those elements of experience come to awareness which are not too threatening to face or tolerate. The client tends to draw back from those topics which are too dangerous or upsetting to face.

A consideration of these elements leads to the conclusion that client-centered therapy is very widely applicable—that indeed in one sense it is applicable to all people. An atmosphere of acceptance and respect, of deep understanding, is a good climate for personal growth, and as such applies to our children, our colleagues, our students, as well as to our clients, whether these be "normal," neurotic, or psychotic. This does *not* mean that it will *cure* every psychological condition, and indeed the concept of cure is quite foreign to the approach we have been considering. With some types of individuals hospital care may be necessary, or with others some type of drug therapy may be necessary, and a variety of medical aids may be utilized in psychosomatic conditions. Yet a psychological climate which the individual can use for deeper self-understanding, for a reorganization of self in the direction of more realistic integration, for the development of more comfortable and mature ways of behaving— this is not an opportunity which is of use for some groups and not for others. It would appear rather to be a point of view which might in basic ways be applicable to all individuals, even though it might not resolve all the problems or provide all the help which a particular individual needs.[3]

In the foregoing passage Rogers is primarily discussing the relevance of his point of view to various kinds of therapy. In considering its relevance for the manager, several other questions arise, such as: Is there time? Does the formal structure permit it?

These limits of time and structure cannot be discussed in terms of general rules. Obviously a manager seldom if ever has time to engage in an extensive series of client-centered interviews with all or any of the people who work with him. Equally obviously a manager needs to maximize the efficiency with which he utilizes the time he does spend communicating with others. To do this he will need at times the kind of sensitivity to expressed feelings and ability to clarify them which comprise the counselor's most important and difficult skill. There is never time to listen as well or to be as helpful as we might like, but almost always there is time to listen and help more skillfully than we usually do.

Similarly the extent to which the formal structure of a particular organizational relationship (superior–subordinate, staff– line, and the like) permits practice of a counseling orientation is of necessity worked out not according to a general law but according to how the particular situation is perceived by the particular individuals involved. If my subordinate feels it inappropriate to express to me as his boss his feelings, I would not be sensitive to his point of view if I expected him to do so. However, if I can congruently express to him my feeling of disappointment that communication between us is not more open, there is a

[3] Carl R. Rogers, *Client-Centered Therapy* (Boston: Houghton Mifflin, 1951), 228–30.

chance that he can help me understand why this situation exists and what, if anything, we can do about it.

As we shall see in Part V, the extent to which congruent expression and sensitive understanding of feeling is possible or desirable in a given organizational relationship will vary widely from case to case. Primarily we have been looking at counseling as an example of skillful interaction. To interact with skill implies behavior that is appropriate (and so perceived by both persons) to the particular situation within which the interaction takes place, including whatever constraints of time or structure are relevant. Above all, skillful interaction implies behavior that is congruent with the individual's own beliefs and feelings about himself.

The danger to be avoided is the assumption that the materials we have studied teach a particular set of behaviors as always resulting in desirable consequences:

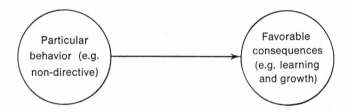

We have looked at some cases which may have seemed to be teaching this. In reality, the behavior we have tried to communicate from our study of counseling is quite different; namely, can we increase our ability to behave in ways that are both appropriate to the particular situation, whatever it may be, and congruent with our existing concepts of ourself?

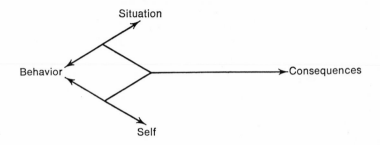

The limits we most need to pay attention to then become not those of time or structure in any absolute sense, but the limits inherent in our own developing skill of sensing what is appropriate in a particular interaction, at a particular time and place. The other person's feelings are part of that situation, and so are our own. In addition to listening to other people skillfully the manager, like the counselor, has to learn to listen to himself.

PART V Organizational relations and interpersonal skill

CHAPTER 9. Structure and self in relationships

The theme of Part IV is indicated by the diagram at the end of Chapter 8, here reproduced:

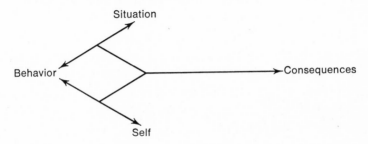

The diagram is intended as a reminder that our purpose has not been to debate the universal applicability of a certain way of behaving, but rather for each of us to develop for ourself that pattern of behavior in interpersonal relationships which is both appropriate to the particular situation and congruent with our concept of ourself. Thus in this final part of the book, as we look once again at more customary organizational interactions, we have to give particular attention to two topics:

1. What is the effect on a given interaction of the organizational *structure* of a particular relationship—superior–subordinate, staff–line, consultant–client?

2. What is the effect on my way of relating to others of my

beliefs and feelings about myself and of my ability to understand not only the situation but also the nature of my involvement in it?

In other words, when considering the applicability to my own behavior in organizations of what I have been learning about interpersonal communication, I need to be aware of two influences or constraints: those inherent in the organizational roles of myself and another person, and those inherent in my own personality and self-concept. Only by taking into account these constraints on how I apply what I have been learning will I be able to behave skillfully, i.e. appropriately and congruently.

These two topics—the influence of structure and of self on interpersonal behavior—are considered together in the following material. The cases that follow illustrate problems of interpersonal behavior and personal involvement in complex organizational settings and in three main structured relationships: superior–subordinate, staff–line, and consultant–client. The extent to which these different structural situations influence what is possible in a given relationship depends, of course, not on any law about what is permitted, but on what each person sees as appropriate to that situation. Thus, in whatever type of organizational relationship the particular interaction occurs, the same underlying skill is relevant, namely the ability to sense and respond sensitively to what the other person expects and feels, while taking into account also one's own beliefs and feelings. The skill with which we are concerned is basically the same in each of the types of organizational relationships in the following cases, and about each case we can ask the same question: To what extent is this person's interpersonal behavior sensitive not only to the other person but also to the situation he is in and to how his own feelings are involved in that situation? But our purpose will be not only to consider the behavior of the people in the cases. More importantly we need to work out for ourselves ways of behaving as administrators in formal organizations that make appropriate and congruent use of what we have been exposed to so far in this volume. The readings assigned along with the cases are selected to stimulate useful work on this personal question which, in the last analysis, each of us has to answer for himself.

Superior–subordinate relationships

In spite of the element of authority which is inevitably present in any relationship between a manager and his subordinate, the opportunities to practice the communication skill we have been considering are much greater than is often assumed. These possibilites are described in Greiner's article on "Patterns of Organization Change," which presents alternative strategies for securing changes in behavior in organizations. The article makes it clear that implementing these changes requires a high degree of interpersonal skill, including especially the ability to establish an interpersonal climate unusually free of defensiveness and artificiality. In other words, the kind of "authority" which is needed is compatible with a helping relationship.

The account by James Richard of his experience as president of Red Jacket Manufacturing Company is particularly interesting because he was consciously trying to apply the orientation and skill of client-centered therapy to his management philosophy and daily behavior (Reading V–1 and the recommended chapters from Gordon's *Group-Centered Leadership*). Richard's account is at least as valuable for its frank acknowledgment of the difficulties and limitations he discovered in his approach to administration as for its description of his successes. Also, there are in Richard's account many examples of how this kind of manager requires an unusual ability to listen with understanding not only to other people but also to himself, not only to listen sensitively to feelings but also to express them congruently. In fact, tolerance for the open expression of feeling seems to have been one of the most important values of this particular management group.

The cases on Ralph Langley and The American Radiatronics Corporation make an interesting comparison to the Red Jacket story. Whereas Richard seems to have had his greatest success working with supervisors, Langley seems to have succeeded more often with workers and to have run into some difficulty when trying to apply his approach at higher levels in the organization. The verbatim on-the-job dialogue in these cases gives us many opportunities to analyze the successes and failures which Langley and others experienced in understanding each other and to state what we would have said differently at particular points.

Having studied the A and B cases, we are in a good position to put ourselves in Langley's position and decide how we would respond to the challenge with which he was faced. Perhaps the most intriguing problem posed by the cases is to try to identify Langley's implicit as well as explicit purposes and then to analyze the effect of the larger social system and of his own feelings on his ability to accomplish what he intended. In particular it is important to try to *understand* the relationship between Langley and Brethers, the foreman, and why each of them perceived the other as he did. The cases provide good data for considering the kind of skill and self-understanding which can make it possible to overcome barriers to free communication in superior–subordinate and staff–line relationships. Above all it is important for the student to put himself into the situations, because it is easier but less useful to criticize how these people behave than to decide very specifically what you would do and say under the same circumstances at the same time and place.

The Ralph Langley cases, like some of those appearing earlier in the book, raise another important question that we have not explicitly considered before; namely, to what extent is it possible to establish a "helping relationship" with your boss?

How could Brethers have helped Langley or Langley have helped his superiors achieve a better understanding of their situation and how they were affecting it? When and how can a subordinate listen with understanding to his superior? Within the typical hierarchical relationship it is not easy for a superior to ask his subordinate for this kind of help, but certainly there are many bosses whose behavior would seem, and might in time actually become, less "unreasonable" if only we as their subordinates could find a way of making them feel their difficulties were empathically understood. Listening, in organizational relationships, is a two-way street.

Staff–line relationships

As organizations grow larger and have to adapt to increasingly complex environments a need is felt for various "service" or "staff" departments to take care of certain auxillary functions and to assist the "line" departments, such as manufacturing or sales, in accomplishing the organization's primary tasks. The distinction between *line* and *staff* and the kind of relationship which does and should exist between them become favorite topics of organizational theory and study. We do not intend to become embroiled in case topics here except to state that in our opinion much of the discussion of "staff–line relationships" at the level of organizational theory bears little relevance to what actually takes place in the interactions between members of line and staff departments. To our way of thinking the staff–line relationship in an organization is determined less by theoretical considerations of organizational structure than by the quality of the specific interpersonal communications that take place between members of different functional groups. In the previous section of this chapter we were looking at vertical communication in organizations; in this section we take up staff–line relations in particular, and other horizontal or "diagonal" relations in general, as a major setting within which the study and practice of effective interpersonal communications can be applied.

What interferes with and what facilitates applying what we know about interpersonal communication generally in the staff–line setting? The best answers to this question that we know are in the writings of Douglas McGregor (see Additional Readings for Part V). In McGregor's formulation of the problem there are obvious parallels between staff–line and counselor–client relations, especially the necessary precondition for useful collaboration, namely, that the staff person needs to be perceived by his line colleague as a source of help in achieving important goals. The extent to which this is possible depends in part, of course, on the manner in which staff groups are thought about and utilized by upper management, as well as on how the relationship is perceived by the two persons involved. When the staff function is conceived primarily in terms of providing upper management with information with which line behavior can be more effectively controlled, it becomes that much more difficult for the staff person to be perceived as helpful. As in the case of the superior–subordinate relationship, these constraints of formal structure and managerial assumptions do not mean that the sort of interpersonal skill we have been studying is irrelevant; it may be more difficult, yet at the same time more important.

Several of our earlier cases have illustrated the difficulty a staff person often experiences in being seen as helpful by his line counterpart, notably The Niwash Division in Part II. Cases of this kind not only raise important questions about what upper management could do to establish an organizational structure and climate that would promote more effective line–staff communication and collaboration. In addition such cases give us an opportunity to work on what in this book is our main concern: What could one or both of the persons involved in a specific interaction do to facilitate understanding *within the constraints* on this relationship inherent in the organizational structure and climate? Given the difficulty, what difference would more skillful interpersonal behavior make?

Our major concern in Part V also still must include how to respond skillfully in a particular interaction, because it is only through a succession of such specific responses that those structural constraints which make communication difficult can in time be changed. It is true, for example, that Drake, the industrial engineer in The Niwash Division, would find it easier for his people to be accepted by the line organization if there existed throughout management a different set of assumptions about motivation and a different theory about staff–line relationships. But it is equally true that Drake could behave more skillfully than he did without those larger changes, and that he will have to do so if he is going to exert any influence in the direction of such changes. We need to decide what we can do within the constraints imposed by the present situation before we can know how to start to do anything that might change them.

These same questions will come up with special force when you study and discuss the cases on Bruce Plastics which follow. In order to understand these cases it is important not only to analyze all the major forces that were constraining members of this organization to behave as they did but also to decide how a more helpful pattern of relationships might be promoted by upper management. It is even more important for you to decide specifically how you could have responded more congruently and appropriately to particular interactions and events if you had been in the position of Phil Hamilton or Al Lynch and thereby have exerted an influence on the total structure and climate, albeit gradually, one small step at a time.

You will also discover that in these cases as in many others it is easier to state what someone like Phil or Al is doing wrong than to understand empathically why he is behaving in this way. Yet the chances are that until someone does achieve some empathic understanding of Phil or Al, his behavior will not change. An instructive exercise is to role–play a conversation you would like to have with Phil or Al if, after studying these cases, you suddenly found yourself in the position of his boss.

More generally, it is possible to analyze the total situation described in the cases as a network of specific two-person relationships within which unrecognized assumptions and feelings are influencing interpersonal perceptions in ways which prevent open communication. Seen in this way, these are cases not of staff–line relations but of interpersonal behavior generally in organizations. This illustrates how difficult it often is in organizations to interact sensibly and congruently, and also how some slight improvements in interpersonal skill could, over time, result in very real shifts in the direction of greater productiveness, less tension, and more opportunity for personal development. Until this happens, apparently, people like Lou Lange are going to become increasingly embittered or alienated—and this is what has happened in many similar organizations. But the improvements we would like to see must start by means of someone in the system (e.g., Lynch or Fulton or Reinhold or Hamilton) becoming more aware of how his perceptions of others are being influenced by his assumptions and feelings about himself. Do not leave your study of these cases before deciding quite specifically how, if you were one of those people, you would begin in some small and concrete way to get this process of improvement started. Among other things we need the patience not to let our inability to solve all the problems we see prevent us from taking the small steps toward better understanding which we do know how to take.

The more we think about how we might behave differently in each of several of the two-person relationships in cases like Bruce Plastics, the more relevant the question becomes: What has happened to the distinction between line and staff? The interpersonal dynamics required to improve understanding turn out not to be so very different whether the relationship is horizontal, diagonal, or vertical. It is just as important, for example, for person A to understand person B's point of view sufficiently well for A to be perceived by B as a source of help when A and B are Jack Shenk and Lou Lange, or Fred Reinhold and Bob Fulton, as when they are Phil Hamilton and Al Lynch.

Furthermore, the view that the staff–line relationship is essentially different in character from other organizational relationships may well become increasingly outdated in the more fluid, adaptive, temporary "task force" types of organizational structures which future conditions will require.[1]

Consultant–client relationships

In Bruce Plastics, as well as in several other cases we have studied, the question arises of how the researcher who gathered the case material might have behaved differently if his explicit purpose was not only to understand the behavior of the people in the situation he was observing but also to help them understand and cope with it better. We have seen how a way of interacting with another person designed to increase our understanding of him can also increase his understanding of himself. The roles of "understanding" and "helping" have the same kind of "fuzzy edges" in interactions between an outside observer and an ongoing social system as in interactions between an interviewer and an individual.

For this reason our study of the relevance of the two-person counseling orientation to organizational relationships includes examples of the behavior of the organizational "change agent" (a phrase we do not intend to use again) or consultant who sees his role as facilitating the effective functioning of a total social system, which he regards as his client. He sees his role, that is, in

[1] On this topic, see W. G. Bennis, *Changing Organizations* (New York: McGraw-Hill, 1966), especially Chapter 1, or "Organizational Developments and the Fate of Bureaucracy," in *Industrial Management Review*, 7, No. 2 (Spring 1966), 41–55. For an important recent study of inter-functional (horizontal) relationships in modern organizations see Paul R. Lawrence and Jay W. Lorsh, *Organization and Environment: Managing Differentiation and Integration* (Boston: Division of Research, Graduate School of Business Administration, Harvard University, 1967).

somewhat the same way as a counselor does in relation to an individual client.

This kind of analogy between the inter-organizational consulting relationship and the interpersonal counseling relationship, like any analogy, can be misleading, but it can also be useful if we keep in mind that we are thinking primarily of a rather special kind of consulting process. Many, probably most, consultants are seen and see themselves somewhat differently (as do many counselors, for that matter); namely, as experts in a particular technique or the source of some specialized knowledge. The client pays the consultant for making available his expertise. Under this model, whether the client eventually makes good use of the consultant's advice or knowledge is not the consultant's major concern; having provided what he has been asked for, he can in good conscience look for another client who needs what he has to offer. Much useful information is obtained by means of this form of consulting, and in practice it does of course involve interpersonal communication and skill.

But our interests here are more particularly relevant to that kind of consulting process in which the consultant's avowed purpose is not so much to provide information as to help an organization as an ongoing social system function more effectively. As was true when we looked at the counseling relationship, we are interested in how the consultant's thinking and behavior affect the client's thinking and behavior, how communication between consultant and client affects the client's external and internal communication, and what sort of orientation and skill the consultant needs if he is to achieve his purpose of facilitating his client's functioning and development.

This sort of consultant may think of his client primarily as a group or social system in need of improved internal communication as a prerequisite to improved external performance. Yet in his concrete behavior the consultant has to interact skillfully with specific individual members of the client organization. In other words, at the level of underlying orientation there is an analogy between interpersonal counseling and interorganizational consulting, and at the level of skill our question once again becomes the same: How can A (in this case a consultant) increase his and

B's understanding of *B*'s behavior and situation (when in this case *B* happens to be a member of the "client organization" with whom the constultant is interacting) ? In short, we propose to study the consulting process as: (1) an example of an interorganizational relationship with some intriguing parallels to the interpersonal relationships we have studied; and (2) a setting within which two people, a consultant and an individual member of a client organization, need to improve their understanding of each other's point of view and therefore their ability to work effectively together.

Because of the wide variety in orientation and practice in organizational consulting, and because the consulting process as such has not yet received the study it deserves, we have not included any required readings on consulting. However, any of the following descriptions by consultants of their work are recommended. They show especially interesting similarities to and differences from the point of view toward the consulting process illustrated in our cases.

1. Chris Argyris, "Explorations in Consulting–Client Relationships," *Human Organization*, 20, No. 3 (Fall 1961), 121–33. (Reprinted in abridged form in W. G. Bennis *et al.*, *Interpersonal Dynamics* [Homewood, Ill.: Dorsey Press, 1964], 699–711.)

2. Richard Beckhard, "An Organization Improvement Program in a Decentralized Organization," *The Journal of Applied Behavioral Science*, 2, No. 1 (Jan.–Feb.–Mar. 1966), 3–25.

3. Ronald Lippitt, "Dimensions of the Consultant's Job," *Journal of Social Issues*, 15, No. 2 (1959), 5–12. (Excerpted in Bennis, Benne, and Chin, *The Planning of Change* [New York: Holt, Rinehart and Winston, 1961], 156–62.)

4. Cyril Sofer, *The Organization from Within*. Chicago: Quadrangle Books, 1962. (See especially Sofer's discussion of the relationship between his version of "Social Consultancy" and individual psychotherapy, 102–10.)

5. W. F. Whyte and Edith Hamilton, *Action Research for Man-*

agement. Homewood, Ill.: Irwin–Dorsey, 1964. (For a short account taken from the same consulting relationship, see W. F. Whyte, *Men at Work* [Irwin–Dorsey, 1961], 511–25.)

As is brought out in these and other descriptions of the consulting process in action, consultants who share the purpose of helping client systems to improve their performance differ at least as much as counselors in the actual strategies they use to bring about changes in their clients' behavior. An unusual and especially interesting approach is well described in the case Kestler, Dobson and Cartwright (A). Students who have studed this case usually find themselves in sharp and stimulating disagreement concerning the extent to which the underlying orientation and specific behavior of this small consulting firm is similar to the orientation of client-centered counseling. In considering this question it is important to consider both senses in which, as we have already pointed out, the analogy to individual counseling can be made: the consultant's orientation toward the total client organization as a social system, and the consultant's actual behavior in relation to specific individual members of the client organization. After studying this case you should be able to state the consultant's operating philosophy or underlying assumptions about the capacity of any organization to develop its potential. Then, having stated what seems to you the key elements of this basic orientation toward the consulting process, consider what actual behavior and interpersonal skill would be required in order to apply this orientation in a specific case. What skill would such a consultant need that is similar to a counselor's skill, and what other abilities would he need that are in large measure irrelevant in individual counseling?

The more careful your consideration of these questions, the more interesting you will find your study of Kestler, Dobson and Cartwright (B), which describes a series of interactions between the firm and members of a client organization, resulting finally in an agreement to enter into a formal and extensive consulting relationship. Which aspects of this consultant's orientation made it difficult for this client to see him as a source of help? Which elements in the consultant's actual behavior helped finally to overcome these barriers? Which specific behaviors by the consultant showed particular skill, in your opinion, and what would you have done differently at specific points in this series of events?

If is also useful to consider this case from the point of view of each of several members of the client firm. How would you have reacted to this consultant if you had been in the position of Simpson or Spinks, for example? Or as Duggan how could you have facilitated an earlier understanding by members of line management of the kind of help that this consultant had to offer? It is interesting also to note the role played by Kestler's colleague Cartwright in helping Kestler handle the relationship and, further, to raise the question of when the consulting process proper really started in spite of the fact that a formal consulting relationship was not officially established until the end of the case.

The Robertson Electric Company cases (A and B) give us a chance to observe a consultant's behavior in action and see how he responds (and might have responded differently) to specific interpersonal events as they occur. The student can put himself into Corwin's position and discover whether the concepts of this book would have helped him understand what was taking place in the superior–subordinate relationship he observes between Eaton and Denault. What are the relevant influences on Eaton's and Denault's perceptions of each other? How does the union steward, Webster, influence this relationship? By what general strategy and specific behavior can Webster help Eaton and Denault learn how to work together more effectively? Finally, how would Corwin's understanding of and possible help in this relationship be used in his work elsewhere in the organization to meet the president's request for help in improving communication among superintendents, foremen, and workers?

The relationships described in the Robertson Electric cases are especially interesting as illustrations of what is involved in asking for help and in being perceived as helpful. For example, since Eaton says he wants to help Denault, why does Denault not see Eaton as helpful? Why doesn't Eaton understand this? How could Corwin help Eaton's intention to help be seen more clearly by Denault? To what extent are both Eaton and Denault asking for help, and how would this be clarified? What specific behavior by Eaton would Denault find helpful? What specific behavior by Corwin would Eaton find helpful? Do your answers to questions of this kind help you draw some generalizations about the circumstances that can determine the readiness of people in organizations to be seen as sources of help by the persons with whom they have to work?

Dealing with one's own involvement

In considering these cases it is apparent that a very essential element of the consultant's skill is not only his ability to respond sensitively to the individuals with whom he interacts, but also his ability to relate his overall strategy to an intelligent diagnosis of the total social system within which this behavior takes place. In addition he has to be sensitive to how his own beliefs and feelings are involved in the very situation he is trying to understand and to help. The consultant cannot avoid being just as human as his clients. While not a member of his client organization, he inevitably becomes involved in it in ways that are not always easy to understand. He cannot always be as clear as he would like to be about his own implicit intentions and motivations, yet the nature of his involvement will always be influencing how he perceives the behavior he wishes to understand and influence. Such a consultant is often likely to need help from a less personally involved colleague in clarifying what he wants to accomplish and how his own intentions and feelings are affecting what he sees and does.

This problem of how the consultant handles his own involvement was present in the two previous cases and comes more clearly into focus in the Hartwell Manufacturing Company series. The A section presents a president's request for a consultant's help, and leads to the question of what will be the consultant's first steps in achieving more understanding of the situation. In B, we learn what the consultant heard when he listened to what some of the key people in the situation had to say. At the end of B, before reading C, we have a chance to decide what we would do at this point of time if we were in the consultant's position. After studying the C case, we can evaluate the usefulness of the consultant's actual diagnosis and course of action. We see him wrestling with some of the problems of involvement of which he is aware. And we can discuss what we might have done differently, why, and how, if we had been in his position. We will discover that these questions are both difficult and important and that they are relevant not only to the consulting process but also to the process by which any person in a position of influence learns how to behave skillfully and re-responsibly when asked to make decisions which strongly affect the lives of people whose behavior he has tried hard to understand.

The next cases, Ruth Haskill (A and B), are counseling rather than consulting cases, yet their real relevance, we believe, is much wider than either of these settings. The A case is the first part of a conversation between a counselor, Miss Dawes, and a supervisor, Ruth Haskill; the B case is a continuation of the same conversation. Before reading B, you should analyze carefully what has happened in A and your reaction to it. In particular, ask yourself what each person seems to be most preoccupied with and how each is dealing with these preoccupations. What feelings does each have about their organizational roles and interactions and how are these feelings affecting their conversation? What sort of help, if any, is being given and received by each person, why, and how? After making some notes on your reactions to questions of this kind based on the A case, go on to study B and then ask yourself and answer the same kind of questions. Then consider the total conversation (both parts together) as an exchange which has much to say to any practitioner of interpersonal skill on the problem of dealing with one's own involvement.

Our final case, Harris-Connor and Associates, permits us to follow the beliefs, perceptions, feelings, and consequent behavior of a recent Harvard Business School graduate during his first six years as a new member of a small consulting organization. Although consultant–client relations enter the case, the focus is on vertical and horizontal relationships within the consulting firm. In particular the case forces us to consider whether and how we can use whatever skill we have gained in our own future interactions on the job with superiors and colleagues and to meet the need to understand helpfully not only other people but also ourselves. The case closes with the sobering question: "If we can't use our own knowledge to help ourselves, isn't there something funny either with our knowledge or with the way we use it?"

READING V–1. *A President's Experience With Democratic Management*

JAMES E. RICHARD

[In a speech to a group of businessmen, James Richard, then president of the Red Jacket Manufacturing Company, described his efforts to apply to his job what he had learned as a result of exposure to the concepts of client-centered counseling. His frank account of his experiences, together with his answers to questions from his audience at the end of the talk, describe an unusual and challenging view of the management process. A more detailed account can be found in Thomas Gordon, *Group Centered Leadership*, pp. 307–53 (see Additional Readings for Part V).]

The theme proposed for my remarks today is the idea of "democracy applied in industry." My first thought was to object somewhat to this use of the word "democracy." However, my second thought was to welcome it as giving me an opportunity to make a point.

I believe that businessmen can validly object to the term "democracy in industry." In a country where private ownership of capital is the legal and practicing tradition, it can be misleading to speak of applying democracy in industry. In the political sense, we think of democracy as being a method of representation, in which the power of

University of Chicago, A. G. Bush Library of Management, Organization, and Industrial Relations, Industrial Relations Center, *Occasional Papers*, Number 18, June 1959.

control ultimately rests in the hands of the electorate. Now, can employees control? Of course, if stockholders happened to be employed in the company, some measure of control would rest with the employees. But if not, and if stockholders are to protect their equity, it surely seems to follow that it is *not* their function to put ultimate control into the hands of employees, who do not have ownership responsibilities.

In this sense of ultimate power of control, the view might well be defended that we have the very opposite of democratic conditions in business. Because we hold *being* democratic a value, we tend to overlook this very real, built-in limit upon democratic processes in business.

A dilemma for managers

With this clarification, I go on to my major point. Today we *are* concerned with twentieth century man's need to find and express himself as a particular individual in an increasingly organized and impersonal society. Ours is predominantly an industrial society, dominated by the fact of organization. So we feel an urgent need to solve the problem of the individual person in his conflict with the constrictions of formal structure.

This results in a true dilemma for managers. On the one hand, we have the force for logic, order, and control, and on the other, the need for the freely responsive, the creative, and the impulse for change.

In industry, the most immediate necessity is for logical planning, doing, and controlling. The realities of the market place demand competitively effective planning and control as a naked necessity for survival. But in a larger sense, we need the productivity and creativity of people more than ever before. There is the real question of whether our traditional practices of organization are not serving to limit and defeat the very quality of human creativity to which we aspire.

There certainly is a compelling need for logic and order, for standardization and conformity to standards. These methods have made industry exceedingly productive. And yet our ideas of organizational structure, job simplification, incentives, and employee relations, as well as our control systems, require, and tend to develop, submissive, dependent performance. Sometimes active or passive revolt is generated. More often an appalling measure of unhealthy dullness is the result.

Besides the practical management difficulties we experience, our sense of ethical and social concern is deeply distressed by the problem of the individual subordinated to the organization. I assume that it is *not* simple acquiescent, conforming, or apathetic performance we would like to see, but a lively interest and sense of excellence.

It would be absurd to deplore organization as "bad," since it is a necessity. And yet we are faced with the problem of reconciling the pressures for logic, system, order, and control with the irrepressible needs for latitude, self-expression, personal identity, and creativity.

Early experiments

In our company some years ago, we became interested in this problem, and we set out to try some experiments. From experience and by trial and error, we discovered some things that worked for us. And perhaps more important, by making mistakes we found some things that didn't work.

Our first experiment was to try to develop something in the nature of "participation" or "communication" from the bottom up. We created what we called "forums," which we held regularly on paid company time. These were conducted by top management or staff men, and we talked about company matters. We explained programs, invited comments and questions, and dealt with some controversial shop questions. We also wrote informational letters to the employees. We had open houses for the families, and the executives went out into the plant and encouraged workers to express their views. We worked hard at all this. And we did have considerable success in helping the men and women in the plant to get more representation of their needs and interests. But we unwittingly put the foremen and much of the management in a tough spot.

It seems easy to see now, looking back, but it wasn't so easy to see then. While we were *helping* the men and women in the shop, we were putting great *pressure* on the foremen and management. This hadn't been our intention. In our eager desire to alleviate our sense that workers were so completely at the bottom, we came up with an undesirable result.

Here I might make an observation. In this matter of manipulating people, of which we, as managers, are so frequently accused, I have noticed that much of our manipulation is unconscious and unintentional. This, of course, doesn't excuse it and perhaps makes it worse. But we sometimes achieve a freer situation in one place only at the expense of someone somewhere else. This is why we need to keep trying to find better ways of becoming aware of the consequences of our management actions or inactions. The true results are not always easy to foresee and not always what we hoped for.

Focusing on supervision

Our next step was to take a much keener look at the predicament of supervision, of the foremen and staff men running the plant. We realized more than we had what a difficult situation the shop foreman is in, with the pressures from the top, the controls, the limiting circumstances in which he has to work, the production schedules, and the costs he has to stick to. And yet countering these, he has the pressures from the men with all their needs and interests. His task of trying to bring together in some kind of effective way the interests and needs of the men and women in the shop with the objectives of management is considerable.

Our efforts to work things from the bottom up, with their mixture of success and undesirable consequences, made it clear that in providing a freer atmosphere for people in the organization, there is a very considerable distance from the point of being concerned about this problem to the point of taking action on it. We saw, for one thing, that to install a "participation system" or a "communication system" of one kind or another is just as bad, perhaps even worse, than installing arbitrary, top-down pressure. To insist that people participate when there may be built-in factors that make participation contrived can be manipulative, and not even as straightforward as autocratic methods.

We developed an hypothesis that went something like this. The more centralized and dominant the leadership pattern of an organization, the more rigid the organizational structure. The more rigid the organizational structure, the more imposing must be the control. When dominance and rigidity are enforced, acquiescence is required. Acquiescence spawns dependence. To the degree that people are required to be dependent, their freedom to apply ingenuity and creativity to their work is reduced. Therefore, a centralized, dominant, controlling leadership and organizational pattern tends to reduce the usefulness of employees as living, thinking, creative people.

When we recognized our bottoms-up effort for what it was, we drew back from the unnatural interference of top management's going directly to the bottom of the organization. Instead we tried to provide a freer, less controlling situation for supervision. We attempted to put as much of the decision-making, policy-making, and actual operating responsibility as we possibly could into the hands of the foremen and staff group.

The traditional role of the superintendent was radically altered. He concentrated on placing as much authority as he possibly could into the hands of supervision, as much as they could and would take. A really extensive use of consultative, collaborative practices was developed. This process, in fact, developed very far in the course of three or four years. The superintendent became so successful at it that he actually became more a part of the group than a controlling authority over it. Much of what would have been traditional controlling authority was successfully distributed to the group itself.

Our positive results

The positive effects of this were remarkable and richly rewarding. The foremen and staff men changed from passive, dependent, and acquiescent men to men who were effective, self-starting, responsible, and deeply involved. They shifted their anxious upward focus to a much more responsible attitude toward each other and toward the men and women in the plant. They developed some interesting methods of organizing themselves. They utilized the superintendent's office, which was a large working conference room, to handle their agenda in a unique way. They used a large chart pad on his wall, and maintained a completely open and accessible agenda, of which they as a group kept control.

They had previously been fed to the gills with the management literature about the conference leader—how he shuts up the noisy, brings out the reticent, and plays the whole thing like a gifted maestro. (I'll never forget the $700 we spent once for a set of little blue books, complete with conference leader's guide, and diagrams on how to arrange the chairs.) Actually, one of the best ways I know for one man to run the show is for him to seize the agenda and clutch it jealously to his breast, unfolding it, scrap by scrap. So when we say that our factory supervision as a group took over control of their own agenda, we're describing an unusual process. It is not a simple process. But when understood and done well, it can be a most efficient method.

In most cases in an operating group, there is a live agenda. But knowing what it truly is, who has it, and what allotment of time and treatment it should have takes real attention. Without claiming this to be universally true, I feel a group can draw up an agenda much more wisely than a single person.

In the course of time, this development among our plant supervisory group became extremely mature. And when the day came for the superintendent to leave his job for another, some unusual methods seemed called for to replace him. After some perplexity, this matter was resolved by the group members themselves selecting—in this case from among themselves—the man to succeed the department superintendent. That was about four years ago. The group still remains effectively intact, and more than ever it effectively utilizes its methods of collaboration and self-control.

Some problems

However, all did not end without problems for us. The first-felt ramifications were with our executive management. This whole development carried threatening implications for them. It raised such questions as: "Can managers really give up control?" "Should they give up control?" "Do people *want* more leeway?" "Should they have it?" "Will they really take it?" "Can they be trusted?" "Are they competent?" Many of these questions were answered by the responsible and disciplined performance of the foremen and the factory management staff. But some more gnawing questions were present for executives. "Isn't the manager paid more because he knows more or contributes more?" "Can a manager *afford* to give up control?" "How will he get ahead if he can't demonstrate some superiority of contribution or knowledge?"

In addition, there was the fact that some men get real satisfaction from manipulating, controlling, and guiding people. For some men there is challenge and excitement in the game of company politics. This game is looked upon as the way to get ahead. And to some, business is business, and people are paid to perform—everything else is nonsense. Sentiments like this are very common. And the whole traditional program of management rewards and status is constructed to reinforce this set of attitudes and motivations. Ours was no exception.

Thus, our well-intentioned interest in the improvement of our factory management group was welcome to them, who had nothing to lose and everything to gain, but far from welcome to the higher executive men. Some of the executives had arrived at their positions by virtue of years of energetic and intelligent response to a top-centered set of leadership values. These values were quite different from the values that seemed implicit in the position taken by the plant superintendent. (This is not to say that they did not *agree* with some of the objectives and benefits of the process.)

We tackled these natural questions. We worked on them, talked about them, and thought about them. This led us to a further question: "How can the bottling up of ideas and energy be overcome?" Granted the price paid by persons pitted against each other; granted the cost when men climb over each other in self-centered aspirations; granted also the deadly pressure of boredom, disinterest, cynicism. But *must* an executive and a natural leader become a faceless quantity and reduce himself in the interests of greater expressiveness for a lot of other people?

Freeing the manager

We worked on all of these questions. We conceived that a primary function of leadership in an organization is to provide the conditions under which people can have the maximum freedom to be responsible, interdependent, and self-controlled. Instead of acting in such a way as to reduce this freedom, the manager should have the prime responsibility for the overall vitality and health of the organization, and should be rewarded accordingly. We felt that the traditionally prime function of motivating, goading, and controlling might become a secondary function, and might conceivably, in a free organization, even disappear. We felt that if a manager did not have to be the sole judge, the evaluator, the prime controller of people in the organization, these functions might eventually be provided for in other ways. This might then free him to be creative *with* the organization rather than *for* it.

For a long time, these notions were purely hypothetical. It did seem that there might be some significant differences between the circumstances of the higher executive group and the foreman-level supervisory group. One expression of this was a tendency among the executives to be more reserved in their interpersonal relations. Perhaps they felt more responsibility for harmony. At any rate, the foremen seemed more capable of hot and direct dispute with each other. On the executive level, there was a great deal of politeness but sometimes a rather surprising lack of real exchange.

To some of the executives, the foremen seemed to be going through an undue amount of talk, and things often seemed disorganized and chaotic. Conversely, to the foremen it seemed that upper executives weren't leveling with each other, were competing, and under the surface were pulling against each other. We began to learn that some men find anything but a surface relationship very difficult. Dealing with strong feelings seems painful to them.

One natural way of dealing with these problems is the use of authority from above, or of corridor manipulations against cohorts and those below. For men of this bent, being in a situation where personal effectiveness may depend upon a high degree of exchange with others can be terribly difficult. In fact, this was so important that over a number of years the makeup of our management organization gradually changed. Managerial capacity for more than a surface relationship began to be important. With the retirement of some of the older men who were accustomed to a more inhibited way of working with each other, young men came in who had a greater capacity for informal directness. Gradually throughout the management, there developed the capacity for group processes based on a sense of informality and open exchange.

Developing group action

We grew a long way from the days of the conference leader guide, and more and more dropped controlling and restrictive techniques. We also learned how to differ constructively. We began to discover that there are different kinds of groups and group relationships, with different purposes and circumstances. At one early point, we moved to the other extreme, and went to the totally unstructured group. I smile now to remember some of the hours we spent trying to discover what we were meeting about when we first became acquainted with group-centered methods. I believe some of the older men who retired from the company about then still believe we spend most of our time in a room together trying to figure out why we are there and what to do.

However, out of all this came a very strong feeling that we liked informality. We gradually began not to want formal organization nor many, if any, permanent committees. Instead we began to depend upon the initiative of individuals or combinations of individuals to form groups as problems arose, to include any one who had an interest in the problem, and to disband whenever the problem was solved.

We found that the main requisite for this kind of natural responsiveness to situations was a climate in which people felt really involved, responsible, and interested, and where men felt self-confident, secure, and open. This kind of atmosphere really works when it exists, but much organizational growth must take place before the condition exists. Creating such an atmosphere takes time, and we found that it must mushroom slowly throughout the organization. It probably began at the top.

We became less and less inclined to try to "teach" development to people. We came to feel that when "taught," personal growth and development are somewhat like an old-fashioned mustard-plaster. It sometimes sticks to the skin and keeps in some heat, but it doesn't have any effect on the inside.

Organizational changes

We began to depend more and more on face-to-face experience and on living together. We began to stake out responsibilities for each other, but we didn't like formal or rigidly described functions. We came to feel that functions are really quite clearly discernible on a common-sense basis, and that the important thing is to develop skill at recognizing and handling together areas of overlapping interests. About the only place anything resembling an organization chart concerns us now is when some of us get together over a problem and need to set up the running plays and signals. We scarcely ever get into any of the old wrangles about whose right and responsibility it is to carry the ball. We simply have the occasional question of who does have the ball and who is blocking.

Thus we feel that we have evolved an overall management that functions in some significantly different ways from our pattern of years ago. Our management really does extend from president to foreman, and we have made some real efforts to shift the emphasis of power. Operating control has been significantly diffused from a few to many. The positive results have clearly been to relieve men of a cog-like feeling and a sense of dependency. Direct, open, straightforward relationships have become natural. Interestingly enough these include the capacity for open, direct differences, sometimes hot and heavy. We try to specialize in bringing differences into the open so that we can work them through. I believe we have developed a more mature capacity for simple live-and-let-live, based on a fundamental interest in deeper relationships.

The relevant point, to me, is that this is not a system. It is, in fact, the opposite of logically conceived and constructed organization. It is a *process* of direct, living relationships which cannot be synthesized but must be grown from the distinctively human joys and pains of life.

Difficulties and drawbacks

Accompanying our present stage of organization are some difficulties too. Reduction of centralized power and control frustrates some of the company's outside connections. Some customers, suppliers, and members of the public need to have simple points of contact which are dependable and quickly responsive. For instance, there was the letter from the marketing man of a major supplier, who wrote, "I have lost my point of contact; please tell me if I am taking my problem to the right place in your organization." And there was the salesman of another, large, aggressive supplier who was indignant, seemed to feel almost cheated, that he couldn't play purchasing, engineering, and sales off against each other, and that his divisional manager's effort to go "higher" was unfruitful. For in our company, purchasing, engineering, and marketing have close ties.

A second kind of problem is long-range planning. In the early stages of planning, we have not found a way to be very inclusive. Planning to some degree seems a special function of a few who have fewer operating responsibilities, and this tends to force structure into the organization.

Third, there is the fact that many people in the organization are deeply accustomed to a controlling, directing atmosphere. There are those who actually do need the concrete structure of organization in order to function. I'll never forget the day the switchboard operator exploded, "What this place needs is a boss!" But much more serious were the several instances of men in management who were unable to handle themselves without stern control, or who misinterpreted warmth and personal concern from cohorts. As we attempted to reduce the lines of controlling authority and put men more on their own, some transferred their dependence to cohorts for discipline or control. We have had some unhappy experiences which seem to have demonstrated that this kind of atmosphere really requires a pretty mature capacity for contribution and self-control. It can throw dependent persons into conflict.

And, finally, there is the very complicated but relevant question, "Can this approach extend beyond management? If so, how?" Granted that throughout management a broad latitude of freedom and individual responsibility can be developed and people learn how to function on an inter-dependent basis, what becomes of the people further down in the organization? As things traditionally stand, people are narrowly limited by the work processes and by systems at the worker and clerical levels. Can order and control be relaxed further downward?

We are on the edge of these questions now. We shall probably keep trying. We find it reassuring to look backward and see that we have come, according to our lights, some way forward, despite several rather startling mistakes.

Summary

In summary, I observe that to refer to "democracy" in industry can be a misnomer. The total business situation is exceedingly complex, and subject to many pressures and limitations. There are many real and practical limits in business which force us to discard perfectly good value-questions as being ill-advised or inapplicable at our present state of knowledge.

However, I believe it is practical and relevant to attempt a conceptual framework from which to derive practical applications in daily management and I believe that it is pertinent and sound for us, as managers, to concern ourselves with man's eternal struggle within himself to be free and yet to be ordered. I believe it is of special importance for us in management to attempt to rescue talented individuals from the lowered aspirations, the boredom, and the habits of mediocrity so often induced by life in an organization. I believe we should become painfully aware that we have established organizational settings in which order, harmony, and predictability have been given more emphasis than individual achievement and excellence. I believe that business management must continue to try to develop a process of life that strives for meaning and purpose, having as our goal the climate which permits every person to serve the values that have nurtured him, with the freedom of the mature and the responsible.

Question-and-answer period

Q: How long have you been working at this orbit?

A: I think about six years.

Q: How have you done financially?

A: We're making money. We're moderately profitable. It's a good question. I think that we have not done this at the expense of hard-headed business. But I'm not sure that one can say that this method helps you make more money, nor that it's done at the expense of the balance sheet.

Q: Your place in the field hasn't changed materially?

A: No, but we have great hopes for our place in the field.

Q: How do you resolve basic problems between two members of this management?

A: I think the simple answer is that we try to talk it out.

Q: It there any final say-so? Does somebody step in and say, "Joe, we're going to do it this way?" And Joe has to buckle down?

A: Sure. I'll get academic for a minute and say that I think Mary Parker Follett said a very wise thing, I guess twenty or thirty years ago: that there are three basic ways to resolve human conflict. One is by dominance, in which somebody loses and somebody wins. The second is by negotiation, in which somebody gives a little and gains a little and somebody else also gives a little and gains a little. Finally, there's resolution by integration, in which nobody loses, and everybody comes out better together. We shoot for integration, if we can, recognizing this to be an ideal. We recognize that sometimes negotiation is necessary, and sometimes dominance. Sometimes we have to pinpoint who's in charge so he can make a decision.

But commenting on this further, I personally took an interest one time in this question, and Bob Burns led me to a part of The University of Chicago called the Counseling Center where they were concerned with counseling and psychotherapy. We took a great interest in the process of counseling. Actually there are several processes of counseling. We were interested in the client-centered school. This is where there is lots of emphasis on listening of a particularly unevaluative kind. We practiced and worked, and made some horrible errors in attempting to listen. But out of this came a kind of operating notion which we have been able to adapt and use for ourselves, and it's the thought that when a person is in conflict with himself, or when two persons are in conflict with each other, another presence, of a noninterfering but really interested kind, can be helpful.

Q: Does this give some release to the manipulative instincts of your higher level management when they're called on to resolve these differences by this client-centered counseling?

A: I don't know if I follow you.

Q: Suppose you have some feelings of conflict or loss on the part of your managers. Now when they get to be expert counselors and are called upon to resolve differences, doesn't this give them a release, to be able to exercise their manipulative skills?

A: I don't want to get out on a limb here, and suggest that we all become psychotherapists or that anybody in business becomes a psychotherapist. But I do make the point that there are some things we can learn from this process. The people in our place aren't trying to counsel each other in a deep sense. I think it's more relevant to say that we use an awareness of some of the things pertaining to counseling. For example, that disharmony is permissible, that a good old straightforward battle can be a healthy thing.

We found more ways of not using political indirections on

each other. We gradually became more comfortable dealing with what had previously seemed taboo questions. The old habit was that if a fellow came up to you and said something critical, you tended to hear him say you were a drip. And frequently that's the way he said it. And then gradually we learned how to take emotion for granted, and accept it, and deal with it. A man can say he disagrees with you without your feeling he is labeling you a drip. But this is a long way around in responding to your question. I think that greater capacity for what I call deeper-than-skin-surface relationships can remove the necessity among us for manipulation. We learn how to express our strong feelings directly and how not to be upset by strong feelings in other persons.

Q: What about the selection of personnel?

A: This question is a very real problem. An organization that develops in this way becomes very closely knit, with a constructive capacity to deal with disharmony as well as harmony. So it's hard finding someone to walk into this atmosphere who's unused to the business of squaring off. It's hard to find the man who's developed a tolerance for direct contact. I'm inherently suspicious of projective testing and that kind of thing. For selection I don't know at the moment of tests that can tell me, in a way I can believe, how a man's going to be in action.

In finding persons for our management organization, we've done a lot of inquiring. We've looked into the possibility of appealing to social scientists for help, and to a number of psychologists who work on this kind of thing. To date, we've ended up doing it ourselves. Aware that we could be making a botch of it, we try to describe to a candidate what we're doing. We try to understand him as best we can in a number of direct interviews, and then we just take a chance. We've made some mistakes, and we've found some fellows that have worked out very well.

We've been doing the hiring together. I have friends who say this is a hell of a process. They say you compound all the errors of everybody. But I think our batting average has been good on making a very careful scrutiny of the man and having the whole organization meet him to try to figure out whether they like him and think he's competent. I think our successes have been greater than our failures.

There's the problem of selection and appraisal of new men, and then there's the problem of performance evaluation in the organization. That's another story, but I don't want to hold you all up.

Q: Does anyone want him to go ahead and talk about it? I think he should.

A: Well, all right. We've fired men. We've downgraded men. We've upgraded men. And we've transplanted men and reshaped functions. We've pulled some real boners. But by and large, I think we've found some effective methods.

Now this is a sophisticated process, and I'm not trying to tell myself or anyone else that it isn't. In industry we're so accustomed to not admitting that feelings are a fact. Yet feelings are as much a fact as the mixture we put in our iron. When you reach the stage where you have the capacity to accept plain, ordinary feeling and to deal with it, then you get at a lot of things that used to cause problems. Whenever it's possible to recognize that human facts are just as clearly relevant in a work situation as accountants' facts and engineers' facts, and whenever (this will be a great day) the engineers and the accountants begin to admit this too, then you reach the stage where you can really accomplish something. In such an atmosphere if a man isn't doing a job, you can talk about the fact and he can talk about it. To the extent that people in an organization can become really expressive about what they're trying to do, what they think and see and feel, performance appraisal can become a two-way integrating process rather than a top-down evaluation.

Q: I wonder if you could tell us the effect these patterns of management have had on union–management relations?

A: Well, we don't have a union. We haven't had one since 1947. We had the Farm Equipment Workers C.I.O. at the time and had a bad strike.

Q: I presume they've tried to organize since? Have your methods helped withstand unionization?

A: I don't think they have. I don't know. I'd like to say that I sure hope this line of inquiry doesn't start management thinking about it because it may appear that here's the way to keep the union off. I don't know if it does or not. But I don't think it matters whether it does or not, because I think, as Dr. Ohmann said, the union surely has a place. And one of the reasons that it's got as much place as it has is that management hasn't been in that place. Conceivably we might be able to bring this kind of give-and-take I've been discussing into the shop and get rid of the piecework system and the methods card. If we ever arrived at the point where men in the shop have a chance to do some of the planning and get their brains to work on some of the problems, this might eliminate the need for a rigidly structured union. But I'm not so sure that management can or should ever try to assume the function of doing everything.

READING V–2. *Patterns of Organization Change*

LARRY E. GREINER*

Today many top managers are attempting to introduce sweeping and basic changes in the behavior and practices of the supervisors and the subordinates throughout their organizations. Whereas only a few years ago the target of organization change was limited to a small work group or a single department, especially at lower levels, the focus is now converging on the organization as a whole, reaching out to include many divisions and levels at once, and even the top managers themselves. There is a critical need at this time to understand better this complex process, especially in terms of which approaches lead to successful changes and which actions fail to achieve the desired results.

Revolutionary process

The shifting emphasis from small- to large-scale organization change represents a significant departure from past managerial thinking. For many years, change was regarded more as an evolutionary than a revolutionary process. The evolutionary assumption reflected the view that change is a product of one minor adjustment after another, fueled by time and subtle environmental forces largely outside the direct control of management. This relatively passive philosophy of managing change is typically expressed in words like these:

> Our company is continuing to benefit from a dynamically expanding market. While our share of the market has remained the same, our sales have increased 15% over the past year. In order to handle this increased business, we have added a new marketing vice president and may have to double our sales force in the next two years.

Such an optimistic statement frequently belies an unbounding faith in a beneficent environment. Perhaps this philosophy was adequate in less competitive times, when small patchwork changes, such

Reprinted, by permission, from Larry E. Greiner, "Patterns of Organization Change," in *Harvard Business Review*, 45, No. 3 (May–June 1967), 119–28. Copyright © 1967 by the President and Fellows of Harvard College; all rights reserved.

* Author's note : This article is part of a larger study on organizational development, involving my colleagues Louis B. Barnes and D. Paul Leitch, which is supported by the Division of Research, Harvard Business School.

as replacing a manager here and there, were sufficient to maintain profitability. But now the environments around organizations are changing rapidly and are challenging managements to become far more alert and inventive than they ever were before.

Management awakening

In recent years more and more top managements have begun to realize that fragmented changes are seldom effective in stemming the underlying tides of stagnation and complacency that can subtly creep into a profitable and growing organization. While rigid and uncreative attitudes are slow to develop, they are also slow to disappear, even in the face of frequent personnel changes. Most often these signs of decay can be recognized in managerial behavior that (*a*) is oriented more to the past than to the future, (*b*) recognizes the obligations of ritual more than the challenges of current problems, and (*c*) owes allegiance more to department goals than to overall company objectives.

Management's recent awakening to these danger signs has been stimulated largely by the rapidly changing tempo and quality of its environment. Consider:

Computer technology has narrowed the decision time span.

Mass communication has heightened public awareness of consumer products.

New management knowledge and techniques have come into being.

Technological discoveries have multiplied.

New world markets have opened up.

Social drives for equality have intensified.

Governmental demands and regulations have increased.

As a result, many organizations are currently being challenged to shift, or even reverse, gears in order to survive, let alone prosper.

A number of top managements have come around to adopting a revolutionary attitude toward change, in order to bridge the gap between a dynamic environment and a stagnant organization. They feel that they can no longer sit back and condone organizational self-indulgence, waiting for time to heal all wounds. So, through a number of means, revolutionary attempts are now being made to transform their organizations rapidly by altering the behavior and attitudes of their line and staff personnel at all levels of management. While each organization obviously varies in its approach, the overarching goal seems to be the same: to get everyone psychologically redirected toward solving the problems and challenges of today's business environment. Here, for example, is how one company president describes his current goal for change:

> I've got to get this organization moving, and soon. Many of our managers act as if we were still selling the products that used to be our bread and butter. We're in a different business now, and I'm not sure that they realize it. Somehow we've got to start recognizing our problems, and then become more competent in solving them. This applies to everyone here, including me and the janitor. I'm starting with a massive reorganization which I hope will get us pulling together instead of in fifty separate directions.

STRIKING SIMILARITIES

Although there still are not many studies of organization change, the number is growing; and a survey of them shows that it is already possible to detect some striking similarities running throughout their findings. I shall report some of these similarities, under two headings:

1. *Common approaches* being used to initiate organization change.

2. *Reported results*—what happened in a number of cases of actual organization change.

I shall begin with the approaches, and then attempt to place them within the perspective of what has happened when these approaches were applied. As we shall see, only a few of the approaches used tend to facilitate successful change, but even here we find that each is aided by unplanned forces preceding and following its use. Finally, I shall conclude with some tentative interpretations as to what I think is actually taking place when an organization change occurs.

Common approaches

In looking at the various major approaches being used to *introduce* organization change, one is immediately struck by their position along a "power distribution" continuum. At one extreme are those which rely on *unilateral* authority. More toward the middle of the continuum are the *shared* approaches. Finally, at the opposite extreme are the *delegated* approaches.

As we shall see later, the *shared* approaches tend to be emphasized in the more successful organization changes. Just why this is so is an important question we will consider in the concluding section. For now, though, let us gain a clearer picture of the various approaches as they appear most frequently in the literature of organization change.

UNILATERAL ACTION

At this extreme on the power distribution continuum, the organization change is implemented through an emphasis on the authority of a man's hierarchical position in the company. Here, the definition and solution to the problem at hand tend to be specified by the upper echelons and directed downward through formal and impersonal control mechanisms. The use of unilateral authority to introduce organization change appears in three forms.

By decree: This is probably the most commonly used approach, having its roots in centuries of practice within military and government bureaucracies and taking its authority from the formal position of the person introducing the change. It is essentially a "one-way" announcement that is directed downward to the lower levels in the organization. The spirit of the communication reads something like "today we are this way—tomorrow we must be that way."

In its concrete form it may appear as a memorandum, lecture, policy statement, or verbal command. The general nature of the decree approach is impersonal, formal, and task-oriented. It assumes that people are highly rational and best motivated by authoritative directions. Its expectation is that people will comply in their outward behavior and that this compliance will lead to more effective results.

By replacement: Often resorted to when the decree approach fails, this involves the replacement of key persons. It is based on the assumption that organization problems tend to reside in a few strategically located individuals, and that replacing these people will bring about sweeping and basic changes. As in the decree form, this change is usually initiated at the top and directed downward by a high authority figure. At the same time, however, it tends to be somewhat more personal, since particular individuals are singled out for replacement. Nevertheless, it retains much of the formality and explicit concern for task accomplishment that is common to the decree approach. Similarly, it holds no false optimism about the ability of individuals to change their own behavior without clear outside direction.

By structure: This old and familiar change approach is currently receiving much re-evaluation by behavioral scientists. In its earlier form, it involved a highly rational approach to the design of formal organization and to the layout of technology. The basic assumption here was that people behaved in close agreement with the structure and technology governing them. However, it tended to have serious drawbacks, since what seemed logical on paper was not necessarily logical for human goals.

Recently attempts have been made to alter the organizational structure in line with what is becoming known about both the logics and nonlogics of human behavior, such as engineering the job to fit the man, on the one hand, or adjusting formal authority to match informal authority, on the other hand. These attempts, however, still rely heavily on mechanisms for change that tend to be relatively formal, impersonal, and located outside the individual. At the same time, however, because of greater concern for the effects of structure on people, they can probably be characterized as more personal, subtle, and less directive than either the decree or replacement approaches.

SHARING OF POWER

More toward the middle of the power distribution continuum, as noted earlier, are the shared approaches, where authority is still present and used, yet there is also interaction and sharing of power. This approach to change is utilized in two forms.

By group decision making: Here the problems still tend to be defined unilaterally from above, but lower-level groups are usually left free to develop alternative solutions and to choose among them. The main assumption tends to be that individuals develop more commitment to action when they have a voice in the decisions that affect them. The net result is that power is shared between bosses and subordinates, though there is a division of labor between those who define the problems and those who develop the solutions.

By group problem solving: This form emphasizes both the definition and the solution of problems within the context of group discussion. Here power is shared throughout the decision process, but, unlike group decision making, there is an added opportunity for lower-level subordinates to define the problem. The assumption underlying this approach is not only that people gain greater commitment from being exposed to a wider decision-making role, but also that they have significant knowledge to contribute to the definition of the problem.

DELEGATED AUTHORITY

At the other extreme from unilateral authority are found the delegated approaches, where almost complete responsibility for defining and acting on problems is turned over to the subordinates. These also appear in two forms.

By case discussion: This method focuses more on the acquisition of knowledge and skills than on the solution of specific problems at hand. An authority figure, usually a teacher or boss, uses his power only to guide a general discussion of information describing a problem situation, such as a case or a report of research results. The "teacher" refrains from imposing his own analysis or solutions on the group. Instead, he encourages individual members to arrive at their own insights, and they are left to use them as they see fit. The implicit assumption here is that individuals, through the medium of discussion about concrete situations, will develop general problem-solving skills to aid them in carrying out subsequent individual and organization changes.

By T-group sessions: These sessions, once conducted mainly in outside courses for representatives of many different organizations, are increasingly being used inside individual companies for effecting change. Usually, they are confined to top management, with the hope that beneficial spill-over will result for the rest of the organization. The primary emphasis of the T-group tends to be on increasing an individual's self-awareness and sensitivity to group social processes. Compared to the previously discussed approaches, the T-group places much less emphasis on the discussion and solution of task-related problems. Instead, the data for discussion are typically the interpersonal actions of individuals in the group; no specific task is assigned to the group.

The basic assumption underlying this approach is that exposure to a structureless situation will release unconscious emotional energies within individuals, which, in turn, will lead to self-analysis, insight, and behavioral change. The authority figure in the group, usually a professional trainer, avoids asserting his own authority in structuring the group. Instead, he often attempts to become an accepted and influential member of the group. Thus, in comparison to the other approaches, much more authority is turned over to the group, from which position it is expected to chart its own course of change in an atmosphere of great informality and highly personal exchanges.

Reported results

As we have seen, each of the major approaches, as well as the various forms within them, rests on certain assumptions about what *should* happen when it is applied to initiate change. Now let us step back and consider what actually *does* happen—before, during, and after a particular approach is introduced.

To discover whether there are certain dimensions of organization change that might stand out against the background of characteristics unique to one company, we conducted a survey of eighteen studies of organization change. Specifically, we were looking for the existence of dominant patterns of similarity and/or difference running across all of these studies. As we went along, relevant information was written down and compared with the other studies in regard to (a) the conditions leading up to an attempted change, (b) the manner in which the change was introduced, (c) the critical blocks and/or facilitators encountered during implementation, and (d) the more lasting results which appeared over a period of time.

The survey findings show some intriguing similarities and differences between those studies reporting "successful" change patterns and those disclosing "less successful" changes—i.e., failure to achieve the desired results. The successful changes generally appear as those which:

Spread throughout the organization to include and affect many people.

Produce positive changes in line and staff attitudes.

Prompt people to behave more effectively in solving problems and in relating to others.

Result in improved organization performance.

Significantly, the less successful changes fall short on all of these dimensions.

"SUCCESS" PATTERNS

Using the category breakdown just cited as the baseline for "success," the survey reveals some very distinct patterns in the evolution of change. In all, eight major patterns are identifiable in five studies reporting successful change, and six other success studies show quite similar characteristics, although the information contained in each is somewhat less complete. . . . Consider:

1. The organization, and especially top management, is under considerable external and internal pressure for improvement long before an explicit organization change is contemplated. Performance and/or morale are low. Top management seems to be groping for a solution to its problems.

2. A new man, known for his ability to introduce improvements, enters the organization, either as the official head of the organiza-

tion, or as a consultant who deals directly with the head of the organization.

3. An initial act of the new man is to encourage a re-examination of past practices and current problems within the organization.

4. The head of the organization and his immediate subordinates assume a direct and highly involved role in conducting this re-examination.

5. The new man, with top management support, engages several levels of the organization in collaborative, fact-finding, problem-solving discussions to identify and diagnose current organization problems.

6. The new man provides others with new ideas and methods for developing solutions to problems, again at many levels of the organization.

7. The solutions and decisions are developed, tested, and found creditable for solving problems on a small scale before an attempt is made to widen the scope of change to larger problems and the entire organization.

8. The change effort spreads with each success experience, and as management support grows, it is gradually absorbed permanently into the organization's way of life.

The likely significance of these similarities becomes more apparent when we consider the patterns found in the less successful organization changes. Let us briefly make this contrast before speculating further about why the successful changes seem to unfold as they do.

"FAILURE" FORMS

Apart from their common "failure" to achieve the desired results, the most striking overall characteristic of seven less successful change studies is a singular lack of consistency—not just between studies, but within studies. Where each of the successful changes follows a similar and highly consistent route of one step building on another, the less successful changes are much less orderly. . . .

There are three interesting patterns of inconsistency:

1. The less successful changes begin from a variety of starting points. This is in contrast to the successful changes, which begin from a common point—i.e., strong pressure both externally and internally. Only one less successful change, for example, began with outside pressure on the organization; another originated with the

hiring of a consultant; and a third started with the presence of internal pressure, but without outside pressure.

2. Another pattern of inconsistency is found in the sequence of change steps. In the successful change patterns, we observe some degree of logical consistency between steps, as each seems to make possible the next. But in the less successful changes, there are wide and seemingly illogical gaps in sequence. One study, for instance, described a big jump from the reaction to outside pressure to the installation of an unskilled newcomer who immediately attempted large-scale changes. In another case, the company lacked the presence of a newcomer to provide new methods and ideas to the organization. A third failed to achieve the cooperation and involvement of top management. And a fourth missed the step of obtaining early successes while experimenting with new change methods.

3. A final pattern of inconsistency is evident in the major approaches used to introduce change. In the successful cases, it seems fairly clear that *shared* approaches are used—i.e., authority figures seek the participation of subordinates in joint decision-making. In the less successful attempts, however, the approaches used lie closer to the extreme ends of the power distribution continuum. Thus, in five less successful change studies, a *unilateral* approach (decree, replacement, structural) was used, while in two other studies a *delegated* approach (data discussion, T-group) was applied. None of the less successful change studies reported the use of a *shared* approach.

How can we use this lack of consistency in the sequence of change steps and this absence of shared power to explain the less successful change attempts? In the next section, I shall examine in greater depth the successful changes, which, unlike the less successful ones, are marked by a high degree of consistency and the use of shared power. My intent here will be not only to develop a tentative explanation of the more successful changes, but in so doing to explain the less successful attempts within the same framework.

Power redistribution

Keeping in mind that the survey evidence on which both the successful and the less successful patterns are based is quite limited, I would like to propose a tentative explanatory scheme for vewing the change process as a whole, and also for considering specific managerial action steps within this overall process. The framework for this scheme hinges on two key notions:

1. Successful change depends basically on a *redistribution of power* within the structure of an organization. (By *power*, I mean the locus of formal authority and influence which typically is top management. By *redistribution*, I mean a significant alteration in the traditional practices that the power structure uses in making decisions. I propose that this redistribution move toward the greater use of *shared* power.)

2. Power redistribution occurs through a *developmental process of change*. (This implies that organization change is not a black to white affair occurring overnight through a single causal mechanism. Rather, as we shall see, it involves a number of phases, each containing specific elements and multiple causes that provoke a needed *reaction* from the power structure, which, in turn, sets the stage for the next phase in the process.)

Using the survey evidence from the successful patterns, I have divided the change process into six phases, each of them broken down

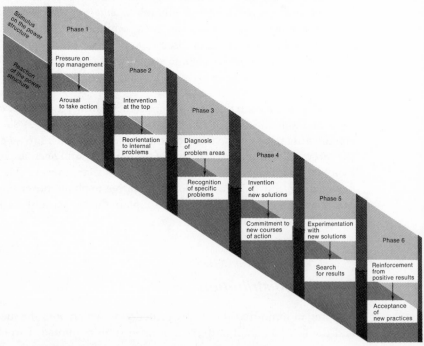

Figure 1. Dynamics of successful organizational change.

into the particular stimulus and reaction which appear critical for moving the power structure from one phase to another. Figure 1 represents an abstract view of these two key notions in operation.

Let us now consider how each of these phases and their specific elements make themselves evident in the patterns of successful change, as well as how their absence contributes to the less successful changes.

1. PRESSURE AND AROUSAL

This initial stage indicates a need to shake the power structure at its very foundation. Until the ground under the top managers begins to shift, it seems unlikely that they will be sufficiently aroused to see the need for change, both in themselves and in the rest of the organization.

The success patterns suggest that strong pressures in areas of top management responsibility are likely to provoke the greatest concern for organization change. These pressures seem to come from two broad sources: (1) serious environmental factors, such as lower sales, stockholder discontent, or competitor breakthroughs; and (2) internal events, such as a union strike, low productivity, high costs, or interdepartmental conflict. These pressures fall into responsibility areas that top managers can readily see as reflecting on their own capability. An excerpt from one successful change study shows how this pressure and arousal process began:

> "Pressure" was the common expression used at all levels. Urgent telephone calls, telegrams, letters and memoranda were being received by the plant from central headquarters. . . . Faced with an increase in directives from above and cognizant of Plant Y's low performance position, the manager knew that he was, as he put it, "on the spot."[1]

As this example points out, it is probably significant when both environmental and internal pressures exist simultaneously. When only one is present, or when the two are offsetting (e.g., high profits despite low morale), it is easier for top management to excuse the pressure as only temporary or inconsequential. However, when both are present at once, it is easier to see that the organization is not performing effectively.

The presence of severe pressure is not so clearly evident in the less successful changes. In one case, there was internal pressure for more effective working relations between top management and lower levels; yet the company was doing reasonably well from a profit standpoint. In another case, there was environmental pressure for a centralized purchasing system, but little pressure from within for such a change.

---

[1] Robert H. Guest, *Organization Change: The Effect of Successful Leadership* (Homewood, Ill.: Dorsey Press, 1962), 18.

2. INTERVENTION AND REORIENTATION

While strong pressure may arouse the power structure, this does not provide automatic assurance that top management will see its problems or take the correct action to solve them. Quite likely, top management, when under severe pressure, may be inclined to rationalize its problems by blaming them on a group other than itself, such as "that lousy union" or "that meddling government."

As a result, we find a second stage in the successful change patterns —namely, intervention by an outsider. Important here seems to be the combination of the fact that the newcomer enters at the top of the organization and the fact that he is respected for his skills at improving organization practices. Being a newcomer probably allows him to make a relatively objective appraisal of the organization; entering at the top gives him ready access to those people who make decisions affecting the entire organization; and his being respected is likely to give added weight to his initial comments about the organization.

Thus we find the newcomer in an ideal position to reorient the power structure to its own internal problems. This occurs in the successful changes as the newcomer encourages the top managers to re-examine their past practices and current problems. The effect appears to be one of causing the power structure to suspend, at least temporarily, its traditional habit of presuming beforehand where the "real" problems reside. Otherwise, we would not find top management undertaking the third stage—identifying and diagnosing organization problems. We can see how an outsider was accomplishing this reorientation in the following comment by the plant manager in one successful change study:

> I didn't like what the consultant told me about our problems being inside the organization instead of outside. But he was an outsider, supposedly an expert at this sort of thing. So maybe he could see our problems better than we could. I asked him what we ought to do, and he said that we should begin to identify our specific problems.[2]

Three of the less successful changes missed this step. Two of the three attempted large-scale changes without the assistance of an outsider, while the third relied on an outsider who lacked the necessary expertise for reorienting top management.

3. DIAGNOSIS AND RECOGNITION

Here, we find the power structure, from top to bottom, as well as the newcomer, joining in to assemble information and collaborate in seek-

[2] From my unpublished doctoral dissertation, *Organization and Development* (Harvard Business School, June 1965).

ing the location and causes of problems. This process begins at the top, then moves gradually down through the organizational hierarchy. Most often, this occurs in meetings attended by people from various organization levels.

A *shared* approach to power and change makes itself evident during this stage. Through consulting with subordinates on the nature of problems, the top managers are seen as indicating a willingness to involve others in the decision-making process. Discussion topics, which formerly may have been regarded as taboo, are now treated as legitimate areas for further inquiry. We see the diagnosis and recognition process taking place in this example from one successful change study:

> The manager's role in the first few months, as he saw it, was to ask questions and to find out what ideas for improvement would emerge from the group as a whole. The process of information gathering took several forms, the principal one being face-to-face conversations between the manager and his subordinates, supervisors on the lower levels, hourly workers, and union representatives. Ideas were then listed for the agenda of weekly planning sessions.[3]

The significance of this step seems to go beyond the possible intellectual benefits derived from a thorough diagnosis of organization problems. This is due to the fact that in front of every subordinate there is evidence that (a) top management is willing to change, (b) important problems are being acknowledged and faced up to, and (c) ideas from lower levels are being valued by upper levels.

The less successful changes all seem to avoid this step. For example, on the one hand, those top managements that took a *unilateral* approach seemed to presume ahead of time that they knew what the real problems were and how to fix them. On the other hand, those that took a *delegated* approach tended to abdicate responsibility by turning over authority to lower levels in such a non-directive way that subordinates seemed to question the sincerity and real interest of top management.

4. INVENTION AND COMMITMENT

Once problems are recognized, it is another matter to develop effective solutions and to obtain full commitment for implementing them. Traditional practices and solutions within an organization often maintain a hold that is difficult to shed. The temptation is always there, especially for the power structure, to apply old solutions to new

---

[3] Robert H. Guest, *op. cit.*, p. 50.

problems. Thus, a fourth phase—the invention of new and unique solutions which have high commitment from the power structure—seems to be necessary.

The successful changes disclose widespread and intensive searches for creative solutions, with the newcomer again playing an active role. In each instance the newcomer involves the entire management in learning and practicing new forms of behavior which seek to tap and release the creative resources of many people. Again, as in the previous phase, the method for obtaining solutions is based on a *shared* power concept. Here the emphasis is placed on the use of collaboration and participation in developing group solutions to the problems identified in Phase 3.

The potency of this model for obtaining both quality decisions and high commitment to action has been demonstrated repeatedly in research. In three successful changes, the model was introduced as a part of the Phase 3 diagnosis sessions, with the newcomer either presenting it through his informal comments or subtly conveying it through his own guiding actions as the attention of the group turned to the search for a solution. In two other studies, formal training programs were used to introduce and to help implement the model. For all successful changes, the outcome is essentially the same—a large number of people collaborate to invent solutions that are of their own making and which have their own endorsement.

It is significant that none of the less successful changes reach this fourth stage. Instead, the seeds of failure, sown in the previous phases, grow into instances of serious resistance to change. As a result, top management in such cases falls back, gives up, or regroups for another effort. Because these studies conclude their reports at this stage, we are not able to determine the final outcome of the less successful change attempts.

5. EXPERIMENTATION AND SEARCH

Each of the successful change studies reports a fifth stage—that of "reality testing" before large-scale changes are introduced. In this phase not only the validity of specific decisions made in Phase 4, but also the underlying model for making these decisions (*shared* power), falls under careful organization scrutiny. Instead of making only big decisions at the top, a number of small decisions are implemented at *all* levels of the organization. Further, these decisions tend to be regarded more as experiments than as final, irreversible decisions. People at all organization levels seem to be searching for supporting evidence in their environment—e.g., dollar savings or higher motivation—before judging the relative merits of their actions. This concern is reflected in the comment of a consultant involved in one successful change:

> As might be expected, there was something less than a smooth, un-resisted, uncomplicated transition to a new pattern of leadership and organizational activity. Events as they unfolded presented a mixture of successes and failures, frustrations and satisfactions. . . . With considerable apprehension, the supervisors agreed to go along with any feasible solution the employees might propose.[4]

This atmosphere of tentativeness is understandable when we think of a power structure undergoing change. On the one hand, lower-level managers are undoubtedly concerned with whether top management will support their decisions. If lower-level managers make decisions that fail, or are subsequently reversed by top levels, then their own future careers may be in jeopardy. Or, on the other hand, if higher-level managers, who are held responsible for the survival of the firm, do not see tangible improvements, then they may revert to the status quo or seek other approaches to change.

Thus, with these experimental attempts at change and the accompanying search for signs of payoff, there begins a final stage where people receive the results and react to them.

6. REINFORCEMENT AND ACCEPTANCE

Each of the studies of successful change reports improvements in organization performance. Furthermore, there are relatively clear indications of strong support for change from all organization levels. Obviously, positive results have a strong reinforcing effect—that is, people are rewarded and encouraged to continue and even to expand the changes they are making. We see this expansion effect occurring as more and more problems are identified and a greater number of people participate in the solution of them. Consider this comment by a foreman in one study:

> I've noticed a real difference in the hourly workers. They seem a lot more willing to work, and I can't explain just why it is, but something has happened all right. I suppose it's being treated better. My boss treats me better because he gets treated better. People above me listen to me, and I hope, at least, that I listen to my people below me.[5]

[4] S. E. Seashore and D. G. Bowers, *Changing the Structure and Functioning of an Organization* (Ann Arbor: Survey Research Center, The University of Michigan, Monograph No. 33, 1963), p. 29.
[5] Robert H. Guest, *op. cit.*, p. 64.

The most significant effect of this phase is probably a greater and more permanent acceptance at all levels of the underlying methods used to bring about the change. In each of the successful changes, the use of *shared* power is more of an institutionalized and continuing practice than just a "one shot" method used to introduce change. With such a reorientation in the decision-making practices of the power structure, it hardly appears likely that these organizations will slip back to their previous behavior.

Looking ahead

What is needed in future changes in organization is less intuition and more consideration of the evidence that is now emerging from studies in this area. While it would be unwise to take too literally each of the major patterns identified in this article (future research will undoubtedly dispel, modify, or elaborate on them), their overall import suggests that it is time to put to bed some of the common myths about organization change. As I see it, there are four positive actions called for.

   1. *We must revise our egocentric notions that organization change is heavily dependent on a master blueprint designed and executed in one fell swoop by an omniscient consultant or top manager.*
   The patterns identified here clearly indicate that change is the outgrowth of several actions, some planned and some unplanned, each related to the other and occurring over time. The successful changes begin with pressure, which is unplanned from the organization's point of view. Then the more planned stages come into focus as top management initiates a series of events designed to involve lower-level people in the problem-solving process. But, even here, there are usually unplanned events as subordinates begin to "talk back" and raise issues that top management probably does not anticipate. Moreover, there are the concluding stages of experiencing success, partly affected by conscious design but just as often due to forces outside the control of the planners.

   2. *We too often assume that organization change is for "those people downstairs," who are somehow perceived as less intelligent and less productive than "those upstairs."*
   Contrary to this assumption, the success patterns point to the importance of top management seeing itself as part of the organization's problems and becoming actively involved in finding solutions to them. Without the involvement and commitment of top management, it is doubtful that lower levels can see the need for change or, if they do, be willing to take the risks that such change entails.

3. *We need to reduce our fond attachment for both unilateral and delegated approaches to change.*

The *unilateral* approach, although tempting because its procedures are readily accessible to top management, generally serves only to perpetuate the myths and disadvantages of omniscience and downward thinking. On the other hand, the *delegated* approach, while appealing because of its "democratic" connotations, may remove the power structure from direct involvement in a process that calls for its strong guidance and active support.

The findings discussed in this article highlight the use of the more difficult, but perhaps more fruitful, *shared* power approach. As top managers join in to open up their power structures and their organizations to an exchange of influence between upper and lower levels, they may be unleashing new surges of energy and creativity not previously imagined.

4. *There is a need for managers, consultants, skeptics, and researchers to become less parochial in their viewpoints.*

For too long, each of us has acted as if cross-fertilization is unproductive. Much more constructive dialogue and joint effort are needed if we are to understand better and act wisely in terms of the complexities and stakes inherent in the difficult problems of introducing organization change.

READING V–3. *The Administrator and Behavioral Changes*

GEORGE F. F. LOMBARD

[In *Behavior in a Selling Group*, Lombard describes how a group of twenty salesgirls and the executives responsible for them accommodated to an environment in which effective vertical communication was severely limited. The last chapter, in which Lombard proposes a "Program of Training" to improve communications, concludes with the following

Reprinted with permission from George F. F. Lombard, *Behavior in a Selling Group* (Boston: Division of Research, Harvard Graduate School of Business Administration, Harvard University, 1955) 337–42.

description of the need to understand how our feelings about ourselves are involved in our perceptions of others.]

In stating in these ways the general assumptions about behavior to which our study has led us we are seeking to point to the difference that an administrator's behavior makes to persons in work groups, both in respect to the satisfaction of their needs and in respect to the accomplishment of the group's purposes. In a society where the division of labor and the differentiation of groups and individuals has become important, the collaboration of many is still necessary to carry out the varied activities of living. But a community of experience in the lives of persons prior to their association in a common task cannot be assumed. Indeed, though many of the symbols of community may remain, the community itself may be largely nonexistent. The tendencies in this direction will be particularly pronounced when social mobility and the rate of technical change is high and when education stresses specialized knowledge.[1] In such a society, the processes that maintain the behavior of the persons in adequate and mutually satisfying relations with one another rapidly attenuate. Feelings of belonging give way on a wide scale to feelings of displacement and uprootedness. Action by administrators on the assumption (1) that their chief concern is with the effectiveness of members' contributions to a group's purposes and on the assumption (2) that members' needs are for differentiation as individuals is then contrary to the demands of the situation. The situation calls for attention to the balance between the patterns of behavior that result in the purposes of the group and the ones that result in satisfying the personal needs of the members. And in the situation we have described these needs are for mutually satisfying relations with others.

Administrative action that ignores the unbalance compounds it. For the members' needs to avoid their feelings of loneliness continue and may result in a variety of behavior patterns. Some persons may avoid their feelings by identifying themselves with the norms of conduct of their group; that way the salesgirls in Department X avoided their feelings. Others may identify themselves with a set of ideals widely held in their society about what behavior ought to be; this was the way executives avoided theirs.[2]

Such compromises in a person's evaluations of himself and others are often wise in easing the difficulties he may find in living and work-

---

[1] See J. B. Conant, *Education in a Divided World* (Cambridge, Mass.: Harvard University Press, 1948); W. L. Warner, R. J. Havighurst, and M. B. Leob, *Who Shall Be Educated?* (New York: Harper and Brothers, 1944).

[2] Compare C. I. Barnard, *The Functions of the Executive* (Cambridge, Mass.: Harvard University Press), p. 89.

ing with others. Indeed, as we saw, the patterns of behavior that resulted may provide satisfactions for those concerned at a high level. But we also saw that identifications of this kind between an individual's beliefs about himself and his beliefs about others tended to lead to misevaluations of himself and his experience. Hence, our study suggests that a balance that results from misevaluations of this sort is not enough. It perpetuates the misevaluations with which it began. Learning improved ways of behaving becomes difficult, both in respect to a person's evaluations of himself and also in respect to his contributions to his group's purposes.

In this situation, the imperative need is for persons in positions of responsibility who can improve their evaluations of their own and other's behavior. The need is for persons with the capacity to understand themselves and others apart from the feelings of insecurity that their perceptions of their own and others' differences arouse in them. The task of administrators is not then to introduce changes for others to carry out, but to facilitate the processes of change that in the society we are describing are already well under way. The administrator's task is now not so much concerned with "communication to" others as with "communication among" them. His task is to facilitate the clarification and understanding of behavior patterns. Much of his work will now be in discussions with others. And since we view their capacity to change their behavior as greater than his capacity to change it, his skill must be adequate to ensure that, apart from his own feelings, he understands, at least to a first approximation, what they are telling him.

It is in discussions of this sort that an administrator's awareness of his own frames of reference is most critical. For as he listens to opinions different from his own, the maintenance of his beliefs about himself may become involved in a most personal sense. Then the problem for him of judgment under the burden of responsibility for results becomes most difficult and most delicate. For him, already differentiated from others by the nature of his work, feelings of loneliness may increase apace. The tendency for him to avoid his feelings by behaving and by believing that he should behave as though it was more important for the members to accomplish the group's task than to satisfy their personal needs is then understandable.

But however understandable, the members' needs for continued growth and development demand his re-education. For in this situation, the patterns of behavior set up between leaders and nonleaders reinforce the formers' feelings of identity with the group's task and the latters' feelings of separation from—and even behavior in opposition to—these purposes. Once this gap appears, the perceptions and feelings that leaders and nonleaders have of and about one another as they carry out their work tend to reinforce the gap without either being aware of what is happening.

Hence, a sensitive awareness of his own and others' values and an understanding of how feelings of security and insecurity arise from work with others become essential if the leader is to help in improving his own and others' evaluations of themselves and their work. Else he may without intention or understanding impose on others his need to maintain the integrity of his own beliefs and in so doing make it difficult for him and them to improve their evaluations of themselves and their contributions to their society's purposes.

Our observation that an administrator's attention to the emergent aspects of his own and others' behavior is so important is perhaps our study's greatest departure from current assumptions about behavior in work groups. Most current practice and most current theories emphasize such rational aspects of behavior as decision-making and give distinctly secondary attention to the feelings of persons that emerge from their interactions.

Yet we have found these emergent feelings and behavior patterns, unrecognized though they might be in the situations in which they occurred, our surest guide to whatever understanding of the girls' behavior we have achieved. These feelings provided us with our leads to the salesgirls' norms, to why the girls tended to stay in one place, to sell one kind of merchandise, and to have sales volume that was about the same. They helped us to understand why the behavior of most of the girls did not change and why [one salesgirl's] did when she was appointed sponsor. They helped us to understand why some customers were satisfied and others were not and why the executives found it easiest to "let the department run itself."

Thus though the group processes we studied were stubbornly persistent, they were essentially sensitive processes, governed by the needs of the persons as these needs emerged in the work situation. What we have shown is a capacity on the part of a small group to administer its affairs with a wisdom and degree of control hardly dreamed of in existing standards of administration. And our respect for the group must be even higher when we remember that the members accomplished this in a setting where the misevaluations of their behavior, though typical of many made in organizations generally, were nonetheless serious.

Some risks and safeguards

The question is not whether changes of the sort we have described should occur, but how best to facilitate them. As we see it, the major risk lies in requiring attention to patterns of behavior that have arisen spontaneously, without attention. Experience shows that there is always risk in requiring attention to that which is better managed by spontaneity. But this is an administrator's skill: by management to improve the chances for spontaneity.

Many will not agree that training administrators is the starting point for changes of the sort we have described. After all, those in positions of leadership have already received a degree of recognition that their fellows have not. To educate them in a new skill, many will hold, is to add new ways to those that already exist for their own advancement. These are real risks and must be frankly faced. But if this action be wise, to withhold it for this fear would be folly indeed. And there are, we believe, safeguards.

One is that in pointing to the training of administrators as a change from which other changes will follow, we are not denying that changes in a group's value systems may also on some occasions be necessary. The new satisfactions and growth that sometimes proceed from them have often been described in many kinds of social studes as well as in psychotherapy. What we are saying is that these changes, *unaccompanied by improved administration*, are not enough. Without the latter, the tendency will be for these other changes to be self-limiting.[3] Though a tautology, it is certainly no insult to the dignity of man to say that for improvements in his behavior he must look neither to the false simplicity of techniques nor to the verbal magic of "isms" but to improvements in his behavior itself.

Another safeguard is that the implementation of the training we have described would be slow indeed. The need broadly conceived is for re-education of many persons in many places. The resulting changes, if they come about, will do so gradually, with opportunity for further study and revision. We are not asking for a "perfect" world but for small improvements—and then more small improvements—in this. Thus we can have faith that the stubborn but sensitive group processes we have described will depose any who use new skill for themselves. And the training we see as necessary will make these results more likely, for it will facilitate the growth, development, and satisfactions not of few persons, but of many.

[3] See Crane Brinton, *The Anatomy of Revolution* (Englewood Cliffs, N.J.: Prentice-Hall, 1952).

READING V–4. *The Goals of the Program*

F. J. ROETHLISBERGER

[This is the first chapter of a study which described the Program for Advanced Training and Research in Human Relations conducted in 1951–54 at the Harvard Business School. The chapter includes the best explanation available of the point of view we have taken in this book toward the relation of knowledge to practice and toward "skill as a way of learning."]

The Program for Advanced Training and Research in Human Relations at the Harvard Business School was started in September 1951 under funds made available by the Ford Foundation. . . . The purpose of our work was to design and implement a program which would prepare people to do human relations training and research in a variety of formal organizations such as, for example, business, educational, and governmental.

In designing this program, we wished an opportunity to step back from our daily activities in human relations training and raise more fundamental questions such as, for instance: Why were we doing things the way we were? Assuming an ideal world in which we could do things the way we wanted and in light of all that we now know, what, if anything, would we do differently? What would an "ideal" training design look like? How would it have to be tailored to the realities of our situation, and to what problems would such a training be addressed?

The designing of such a program involved taking into account the problems that our previous explorations in human relations training had encountered, making a diagnosis of these problems, and deciding upon ways of dealing with them. These basic decisions determined our major activities and direction during the past three years. They gave the program its distinctive features and coloring. They involved basic assumptions (1) about the goals such a program should seek, (2) about the kinds of persons who could be helped by such a program, (3) about

Reprinted with permission from F. J. Roethlisberger *et al.*, *Training for Human Relations* (Boston: Division of Research, Harvard Graduate School of Business Administration, Harvard University, 1954), 3–29.

the skill and knowledge such persons should acquire, and (4) about the methods through which such skill and knowledge were to be obtained. These basic assumptions will be reviewed in this and the following three chapters.

In this chapter we will state the goals of the program as well as the assumptions on which they were based. In deciding upon our objectives, our conclusions on four very important matters influenced our decisions: (a) the relation of knowledge to practice, (b) the basis for the improvement of practice, (c) who the practitioner is, and (d) the function of theory for the practitioner.

In considering these questions, many Rubicons had to be crossed. Matters about which there were honest differences of outlook became no longer just matters of interesting speculation and debate. We had to make up our minds, we had to throw our weight on one side or the other, but also we wished to be as clear as we could about the assumptions upon which our major decisions were based. It will help, then, if those who read this report will keep in mind that the statements we will be making in this chapter are why *we* decided—and not how others should decide—to do things "this-a-way" rather than "that-a-way."[1]

Knowledge and practice

Although it may easily be agreed that the state of affairs in matters of human relations in most organizations can be improved, there is little agreement on how this improvement is to be reached.

To one school of thought the solution lies first in improving the content and methods of the behavioral sciences as well as the competence of behavioral scientists. Underlying such a solution is the assumption that our plight is due to ignorance, and hence what is needed is increased knowledge. At one level there can be little quarrel with this diagnosis. Both better knowledge and better scientists are highly desirable.

But is this enough and is it the first order of business? What about also improving the competence of human relations practitioners? Can

---

[1] In stating our position on these questions, it will be obvious that we are following as well as carrying forward the Mayo-Henderson tradition of "science." Much that we will be saying here has been said much better by them. Were these matters well understood there would be little need to restate them. But because it seems to us that what they were saying is even more applicable today than when they were writing, we believe it can stand repeating. Moreover, our intellectual indebtedness to them is so great that it deserves explicit acknowledgment. We are pointing to them, then, as our intellectual precursors, not as the only authorities on these matters.

it not be argued as readily that our contemporary industrial society suffers from a dearth of competent human relations practitioners as much as from a dearth of top-flight behavioral scientists? What evidence is there that knowledge *per se* changes the attitudes and behavior of people? Where is the evidence that the available knowledge about people and their relations to one another in the minds and books of scientists is affecting to any great extent the behavior of executives, supervisors, and employees in business today? And how does the scientist get his "knowledge" accepted? To a second school of thought improved knowledge must go hand in hand with improved practice. To develop one apart from the other is to perpetuate the very problem that human relations is trying to solve.

In designing our training program, this difference of emphasis could not be resolved by a mere juggling of words. It presented two quite different alternatives, involving two quite different perceptions of the human relations problem which would result in two quite different programs in terms of level of activities and direction. One perception assumes that the formulation and testing of hypotheses is the job to be done first. It assumes that better practice will result primarily from the application of better tested hypotheses and theories. The other perception assumes that better practice is not derived from experimentally tested hypotheses alone. To the contrary, it assumes that better practice is more likely to follow from better firsthand observations (and not from "controlled observations" alone), and that better firsthand observations and hypotheses are likely to follow from the conscious practice of a skill in the first instance at least.

In designing our program, we decided to choose the second road. We would start with trying to improve human relations practice; with the data that are available to the practitioner; with the skill he uses in dealing with them and with theories that might be helpful to him in his practice. In reaching this decision, we realized we might easily fall between two stools. We had chosen a "half-way-house" type of operation that would satisfy neither of two present conceptions of "knowledge."

On the one hand, the conceptual formulations of our clinical type of research would not satisfy the strict demands for experimental verification that our scientist friends thought theories required. On the other hand, the modification of behavior we sought in practitioners would not satisfy their needs for "simple and practical answers"—the kind of knowledge our business friends thought the solution of their problems required. In such a "half-way-house" kind of operation, we realized, we would be beset on all sides by extremists, faddists, and cults of one kind or another. Nevertheless, two inductions from experience reinforced our decision.

SKILL AND THE ACQUISITION OF KNOWLEDGE

In deciding to design our program at the firsthand observation–skill level, we had not abdicated any interest in improved knowledge. To the contrary, it was our belief that by starting at this level we would be on the road that might lead some day to better knowledge. Our belief was based upon certain assumptions we held about the relation of skill to knowledge. Let us review them briefly.

Although related, we assumed that there were two kinds of knowledge that needed to be differentiated. One is the kind of knowledge that is associated with the scientist who is seeking to make verifiable propositions about a certain class of phenomena. The other is the kind of knowledge that is associated with the practitioner of a skill in relation to a certain class of phenomena. This distinction is not original; it has been made over and over again by many different people. To us it still seems important and not too well understood.

The difference between these two kinds of knowledge can be readily seen by contrasting the aim of the scientist with the aim of the practitioner of a skill. The aim of the scientist is to discover and make verifiable propositions about a certain class of phenomena; the aim of the practitioner is the immediate "control" of the phenomena with which he deals. Although the "knowledge of acquaintance" which the practitioner acquires from the practice of a skill often remains intuitive and implicit, it serves his immediate purposes well. A skillful carpenter who works with many different kinds of woods, for example, has a great deal of "acquaintance with" the properties of different woods. He "knows" what different woods will and will not do under certain conditions—at least sufficient for his purposes of fashioning them into useful objects. He does not have, however, that kind of analytical *knowledge about* phenomena sought by the scientist. He does not "know" about the relative tensile strengths of different kinds of building material.

Because of a failure to distinguish between these two different kinds of knowledge, the application of knowledge is often confused with the practice of a skill. The frame in which the scientist's thought is set when applying analytical knowledge, however, is quite different from the frame in which the practitioner's thought is set when practicing a skill. Our carpenter above, for example, when designing and building a chair, is not applying "knowledge about" the tensile strength of materials. When people before Galileo designed and built pumps which raised water approximately 34 feet, they were not applying any knowledge about the weight of air; that knowledge did not exist. Nevertheless, the practitioner is capable of making firsthand observations which allow him to fashion, manipulate, and control fairly successfully the materials with which he deals in order to achieve an immediate and practical objective. A skill can be practiced with little analytical knowledge about the territory; analytical knowledge, however, cannot be applied to the territory before such knowledge is formulated.

The distinguishing features of the practice of a skill are quite different from the application of analytical knowledge. Skill is the response of a whole organism, acting as a unit, that is adequate to a particular point in a given situation. A skill is always manifested at a particular point as a complex capacity acquired by experience in responding appropriately to particular, concrete, and whole situations.[2] The applier of analytical knowledge is responding only to those observations which his specialized methods and techniques had said in advance are relevant. In differentiating skill from analytical knowledge, it does not follow that they are unrelated. It does follow that the difference between them needs to be better understood before their relation to each other can be more correctly assessed.

Our main point up to now has been that the application of better analytical knowledge can never be a substitute for skillful behavior. The relation between them is not a simple one-way street, e.g., more analytical knowledge leads directly to more skillful practice. In spite of the fact that most behavioral scientists would concede this point, nevertheless this assumption often remains unchanged in their writings, particularly in their later and concluding chapters.

In reaching our conclusions about the relation of skill to knowledge, we have attached more importance to the way scientists behave and describe their behavior than to statements by philosophers on "the scientific method"—what it is or ought to be. As the literature by scientists about the way they behave is vastly much less than the literature by philosophers on "the scientific method," our conclusions on these matters can be quickly summarized. They gave considerable support to our decision to start at the firsthand observation–skill level.

1. The successful sciences have all had a lowly and humble origin in the firsthand observations of people who were practicing a skill.

2. It has not been the observations of any layman but the firsthand observations of a skillful and responsible practitioner that have led to those ideas of wide relevance that are capable of systematic development (i.e., fruitful hypotheses).

3. For this reason not all experiments are fruitful; in the acquisition of knowledge some experiments (i.e., testing of hypotheses) are more fruitful than others. Where we saw experimental futility, we

[2] See Elton Mayo, *The Social Problems of an Industrial Civilization* (Boston: Division of Research, Harvard Business School, 1945), p. 15.

found hypotheses being tested based on observations that had little or no connection with any practice of a skill.[3]

4. In the more advanced sciences the relation between skill and knowledge becomes a two-way affair. They help each other out. The skillful practitioner reminds the scientist of what his theories have left out and provides him with new firsthand observations. The scientist's theories, in turn, help the practitioner to observe more closely and carefully. When this stage is reached, as George Homans says, "we ought to be sick and tired of boasts that one is better than the other."[4] In the acquisition of better knowledge, both are needed.

5. When this stage of progress is not reached, however (and this we believe to be the case in the behavioral sciences), skill and knowledge, instead of helping each other out, seem to have difficulty in getting together. Each cultivates its own garden; interaction diminishes, and with this decrease in interaction, as George Homan's theories have helped us to observe, negative instead of positive sentiments (all other things being equal) are more likely to develop.[5] As a result, they are prone to get "into each other's hair." . . .

SKILL AND THE ACCEPTANCE OF KNOWLEDGE

Another set of considerations also reinforced our decision to start our program at the firsthand observation–skill level. Not only in the acquisition but also in the acceptance of knowledge, skill is essential. To those who have been interested in improving human relations in industry, the gap between knowledge and practice is no fine point of theory. For the human relations "expert" who is also a practitioner, the distinction between making recommendations and getting them put into effect is only too real. It is one thing to diagnose what needs to be done; it is quite another matter to get people to do and see, as you do, the importance of what needs to be done. It is one thing to want to help people with their problems; it is quite another matter to get them to accept and perceive you as a source of help. These distinctions dig deep when so often the recommendations of the human relations expert involve a change in the behavior of others.

These distinctions bring up the difficult question of just what the relation of the human relations expert is to the organizations he studies and to the executives, supervisors, and employees who are responsible for taking action in them in respect to problems of human relations.

[3] For amplification of the above three points, see Mayo, *ibid.*, pp. 17–19.
[4] See George Homans, *The Human Group* (New York: Harcourt, Brace, 1950), p. 15.
[5] *Ibid.*, p. 112.

How does the expert establish a satisfactory relationship with them when so often the object of his endeavor is to change or modify their behavior? Is the human relations expert merely the repository of abstract knowledge, or does he too have to practice a human relations skill in getting his knowledge accepted?

The dilemma is this. Whether he likes it or not, the expert in human relations is often introduced into the organization as a means of introducing other social changes in it. He is the expert on the personal and social effects of introducing change. At the employee level he knows the effects certain technical changes have and the resistances they provoke if introduced too quickly or without understanding of their effects upon the behavior and relations of people. He realizes that certain social changes in the way management introduces these technical changes might produce more favorable responses to them. But how does he communicate these new ways of doing things to management, particularly when these changes involve important changes in management's own behavior?

He knows from his experience in studying the problems of workers with executives that telling a person the logical need for a change is not enough. How then does the expert behave in relation to the executive to gain his acceptance and understanding? The expert who behaves in relation to the executive as he sees the latter behaving in relation to his subordinates creates in management the very same anxieties and resistances which he criticizes management for creating among employees. This uniformity of response we have seen time and time again, in situation after situation, in organization after organization. It would be a sad state of affairs if the expert cannot apply to his own behavior what he has found holds true in the behavior of others. It would be curious indeed if the expert in human relations is unable to practice human relations in his face-to-face dealing with executives and policy makers.

We shall have more to say later about the problem of the expert's behavior in relation to those whom he is supposed to be helping. For the present, however, we raised it only in order to show how it reinforced our decision to design our program at the observation–skill level. Our experience showed that this level of operation was needed by the expert as well as by the practitioner.

The improvement of practice

So far we have said why we decided to design the program for the improvement of practice; we have not said, however, how we propose to do this, so let us consider it now. In exploring the relation of the expert to the practitioner, we saw how crucial to the area of human relations the problem of the relation of knowledge to practice is. For the "expert" in human relations is deeply concerned with effecting changes in individuals and their relations to each other. These changes cover many different areas—the areas of understanding, perception, sensitivity, skill, attitudes, values, and ideologies. One need only look at the literature in human relations on the applied side to find it heavily sprinkled with such recommendations as "the need to educate in more favorable attitudes," "the need to change the frames of reference of supervisors and executives," "the need to bring about more harmonious and healthy relations," and so forth.

It is this very deep concern of the expert in human relations with changes in the behavior of individuals, however, which causes so much alarm and consternation. For it raises not only the question of just how, in fact, he is going to produce such changes (the question we raised in the last section) but also the far more important question to many of just how he intends to bring these changes about. By what criteria does he assess them as "good" or "bad"? In terms of what or whose values will they be evaluated, and so forth? Around these questions, the big issues of human relations are raised. Since no one in the area can ignore them, let us consider them as simply, briefly, and clearly as possible. Since they often provide the occasion for heated charges and countercharges, of "do-goodism" on one hand and "manipulation" on the other, we shall try to discuss them in the "world of simple laughter" to which, as Mr. Welch hoped at the conclusion of the Army-McCarthy hearings, "we may someday return."

IMPROVED PRACTICE: IDEALS AND TECHNIQUES

Let us start then by correcting first a possible misunderstanding we may have unwittingly caused. Although we have said that our "expert" in human relations is deeply concerned with changes in individuals and their relations to each other, we did not wish to imply that he has any monopoly or priority in this concern. One need only look around him to see what a popular pastime for many the attempt to change behavior is. For example, one can find parents trying to change the behavior of their children, and children trying to change the behavior of their parents; employers trying to change the behavior of their employees, and employees trying to change the behavior of their employers. Similarly one can find psychiatrists and patients, Americans and Russians, line and staff people also trying to change the behavior of each other. We shall not go on with the profusion of examples that could be cited; we have only one comment to make about them. In all cases they seem to be equally unsuccessful. At this level the outlook seems dismal.

Two of the most common ways of trying to modify the behavior of others provide the two most popular conceptions (or misconceptions) of human relations. One of these ways attempts to inculcate in others the proper and correct attitudes, values, or beliefs; the other provides people with certain specific techniques by which they can get things done through others. As a result we have two popular versions of human relations. According to the first version, "human relations" is identified with "good human relations"; good human relations are associated with "ideal patterns of behavior," and hence "human relations" becomes concerned with how the practitioner should behave in order to achieve these ideals. According to the second version, "human relations" is associated with these techniques by which someone goes about getting other people to do things he wants done and in the way he wants them done, and hence "human relations" becomes concerned with providing the practitioner with more and better techniques for influencing the behavior of others in the direction he wants.

We shall say little about these two versions except to comment that alternatives such as these are likely to arise in any field when very complex matters are oversimplified for the purposes of study. Rather we should like to raise the question: Is there not perhaps another way— a more useful way—of thinking and talking about this problem of changing behavior, and, in particular, of improving practice? For example:

1. Instead of seeking for techniques by which practitioner A can influence the behavior of B, should we look first to see how in a concrete situation the behavior of A does influence the behavior of B and vice versa and how A takes this into account? Would this not be a better place at which to start?

2. Instead of trying to inculcate practitioner A with the proper attitudes, values, and beliefs, should we look first to see how in a concrete situation A deals with his own attitudes, values, and beliefs as well as those of others? How does he take these factors into account? Is there not something here that A can learn and does learn?

3. By looking at the behavior of skillful practitioners and seeing how they take into account the effect of their own behavior upon others, could we perhaps find out the uniformities that reside in and are associated with the skillful practice of human relations in concrete situations?

4. By looking at our own behavior in our own dealings with others in specific situations, could we learn to see the determinants and consequences of understanding and misunderstanding in our own daily activities and the part we may play in them? Through such an approach could we improve our practice?

This is the approach that we chose to take in designing our program to improve practice, and from it is derived our concept of human relations. It is based upon certain assumptions about skillful behavior. Let us look at them.

IMPROVED PRACTICE: SKILL AND LEARNING

According to our way of thinking most people do learn after a fashion to improve their relations to their surroundings, and so we start here. To this process by which people improve their relations to their surroundings we have given the name "skill." Perhaps this is an unfortunate choice of label for that to which we will be referring, but rather than try to coin a new word, we decided to stick with it and clarify what we mean as well as we can, whenever there is a need to do so.

● *Skill as a way of learning*

Skill, then, to us is the way an ordinary mortal goes about improving his response to an external object and situation; it is the way he learns to improve his relations to his surroundings. Let it be noted that "improvement of response" is in our conception of "skill." Therefore, what we mean by "improvement of response" is implied in what we mean by "skill" and vice versa. This circularity is to us evident and acceptable. To the reader who is bothered by it, all we can say further is this: look at those elementary forms (schemes) by which a person assimilates and orders his experience and relates himself as well as improves his relations to his surroundings. This we call "skill." Because these "schemes" do not have the clarity, lucidity, and logicality of "abstract ideas" they do not lend themselves easily to discussion and analysis. But this characteristic does not diminish their importance; so let us try— no matter how difficult—to develop a way of thinking and talking about them. Let us never forget, however, that skill as we shall be using the word, is something essentially to be practiced, not generally or easily talked about, and for which "no verbal statement, however accurate, can act as a substitute."[6] Skill precedes the more sophisticated approach called "the scientific method."

By "human relations skill" we shall mean the way Tom, Dick, and Harry learn about themselves and their relations to each other in the first instance and how they improve their understanding in the second instance. By this improvement of response on the part of an individual we shall mean an internal way of learning rather than an external technique to be learned. It involves a modification or change in himself as well as a change in his relation to his environment.

[6] See Mayo, *op. cit.*, p. 15.

It depends upon his capacity to see in a situation something different from what he customarily expects and to respond to this new and altered perception.[7]

In the process of seeking to improve our responses to other persons, there is nothing intrinsically sinister or bad. Granted that in this process one can learn the "wrong lessons," one can remain still stupid and incompetent. But so do many people in seeking to improve their relations to "things" learn the wrong lessons and remain incompetent. Not all people who use a saw or hammer and wood become skillful carpenters. And when a carpenter uses a hammer to knock someone over the head, he is not practicing his technical skill as a carpenter nor for that matter his social skill of relating himself well to others. Skill for us, then, is not something external to the user, something which he uses only for ulterior purposes. It is intrinsic to him and modifies his behavior as well as the object or situation upon which it is practiced.

● Skill as a process of balanced growth

By skill, then, we shall mean the response of the whole organism, acting as a unit, that is adequate to a particular point in a given situation.[8] The response of a total organism acting as a unit implies something quite different from a "technique." Let us therefore look more carefully at the organic character of this skilled response. Not only is the skillful person responding to an item in a context; the response that he makes is integrated. It includes not only his direct experience with the phenomena; it includes his reflective experience, his preoccupations and ways of thinking (schemes) about the phenomena as well. All these elements are of a piece; each reinforces the other to make a total evaluation.

Let us take, for example, an interview that A is having with B. A's response to what B says in this situation includes A's intuitive familiarity with the way people are expected to behave under such circumstances. It includes A's own personal standards of what the appropriate response should be. It includes his own assumptions and reflective experience about what people are doing when they speak to one another. It includes his assessment of what he believes is going on in this particular interaction. It includes his own feelings of the moment and the effect of B's comment on them, for example, as well as many other things. This capacity or lack of capacity to recognize, differentiate, and integrate as a unity these different elements of response is what makes it possible for A to be more or less adequate to a particular point in a given situation. It helps him to recognize

[7] See Mayo, *Some Notes on the Psychology of Pierre Janet* (Cambridge, Mass.: Harvard University Press, 1948), p. 56.

[8] Mayo, *The Social Problems*, p. 15.

or prevents him from recognizing, for instance, whether he is responding to his own feelings or someone else's, whether he is responding to the norms of the group or to his own personal standards.

When at a cocktail party *B* says, "Good evening," and *A* responds by saying, "I don't see anything good about it," under most conditions (not *all* conditions) we would *not* call *A*'s response a skillful one. It does not follow, however, that *A*'s response would be improved by lessons in how to behave at cocktail parties, since from our intuitive familiarity with people we have no reason to believe that *A*'s lack of social skill is restricted to cocktail parties, or that these same defects do not manifest themselves in his responses to people in other groups at work and play.

And yet in industry and elsewhere *A*'s are being taught just such lessons under the label of "skills." In some training courses, for example, foremen are being taught how to deal with "apathetic" workers, "overtalkative" or "silent" workers, "obstreperous" workers, workers with "grievances," newcomers, women, shop stewards, union officials, and so on. Such "lessons" assume separate, discrete, and special skills for particular situations.

Let it be clear that this is not our assumption about skill. For us skill is a unitary and organic phenomenon and that is why we have used the word in the singular. To break it down into separate and discrete skills is to do extreme violence to our concept. It violates the organic character of the response, the incorporation as a unit of the different elements of the response so that it will be appropriate to the personality of the responder as well as adequate to a particular point in the given situation. Too often a foreman in trying to exercise these discrete skills (more appropriately called "techniques") of responding to a particular worker feels silly. He feels that he is not being true to himself and his own immediate experience. This very feeling vitiates the effectiveness of his response. And it is this feeling of his to which his workers often respond. The total effect, far from suggesting skill, is instead tragic or comic depending on one's point of view.

Our concept of skill is a far cry from this. Instead of regarding skill as a technique to be learned, we have treated it as a way of learning; as a way one assimilates and orders experience and improves his relations to his surroundings, and therefore as something intrinsic and not sinister; as the response of a total person acting as a unit and therefore as an organic and evolving process quite different from a "technique." In short, our concept of skill has certain characteristic features which we can enumerate.

The first is the characteristic of balanced growth. On the outer side learning is the process by which the individual develops a greater complexity of relationships with things and people in the world about him. On the inner side learning is the process by which the individual develops and maintains an "organized system of capacity for response."[9] In skillful behavior we find these two processes in balance. One complements and reinforces the other. The skillful person does not complicate his thinking far beyond his knowledge of acquaintance. His encounters with the external world and his capacity for response develop together. As a result, there is a growing and developing awareness of the complexity of relationships in concrete phenomena as well as a growing and developing confidence in his capacity to deal with them.

The second feature of skillful behavior is the maintenance of balanced growth through time. The skillful practitioner realizes that his responses improve progressively through various stages of development. As Mayo points out, one learns to creep before he learns to walk; he learns to walk before he learns to run; he has to learn to speak before he can make speeches and become a politician; and he has to learn to handle a knife and fork before he can make any notable contributions to conversation at a dinner table.[10] Only by small steps and only by holding the totality in balance at each stage do we develop a greater complexity of relationships with things and people in the world about us. The human relations practitioner can ignore this characteristic of skillful behavior only at his peril.

The third feature of skillful behavior is that it is accompanied by some awareness of what is happening. It is not just a "signal" response to an external stimulus; it is the improvement of a response to a situation accompanied by awareness of what is happening. This capacity of being able to discriminate in the object or situation the relevant items for response is also a characteristic of skill. This capacity to attend, observe, and discriminate is closely related to the "organized system of capacity for response." Without the complementary development of the latter, the capacity to attend is greatly diminished. Without the capacity to attend, one cannot make adequate discriminations in the surroundings.

● *Implications for training design*

By "human relations," then, we shall mean the conscious development and practice of a skill by which one learns to relate himself better to his human, social surroundings. By "skill" we shall mean an organic, evolving, growing system of capacity for response which allows a practitioner to respond more effectively to a particular point in a given situation. By "skill" we shall refer to both an external and an internal development that go hand in hand. To develop one apart

[9] For a further elaboration of this conception, see Mayo, *Some Notes on the Psychology of Pierre Janet*, pp. 49–51.
[10] Mayo, *ibid.*, pp. 56–57.

from or beyond the other leads to unbalance and nonlearning. This conception of skill determined the initial training design of our program in three very important respects.

In the first place this conception meant that our program had to be designed in accordance with the ordinary way that people learn about themselves and others. The program would not involve—at least in the beginning—a souped-up and supercharged method of learning. Of the greatest importance was that our trainees first learn to be ordinary before they tried to be extraordinary.

In the second place this conception meant that our program would not be designed for persons who wished to change the behavior of others or their own in terms of an ideal or by means of a technique. We are not trying to give people religion and ideals of conduct, not that we felt these matters were unimportant but rather that they were not within our province; there were other and more competent persons than we concerned with them; the "cobbler sticks to his last." The way "ideals of conduct" came into our area, however, could not be ignored, and we shall have more to say about this later, after we have reported some of the experiences of our trainees who "took" the program we had designed.

In the third place this conception of skill meant that our program would be designed for persons who were seeking to improve their own practice in relation to concrete situations. The program was to be addressed to the immediate experience of the practitioner and his knowledge of acquaintance. It would raise for him such questions as the following: Are you being a competent craftsman—in the same sense that a carpenter is a competent craftsman? Do you understand the milieu in which you operate? Are you adapting yourself to the medium in which you work? Are you responding skillfully to the important factors in your situation? And is your response not adequate in general but adequate to a particular point in a given situation? How do you respond to Tom, Dick, and Harry when they say this or that in this given situation? Would you like to be more skillful? Are you willing to learn?

* * *

Theories for the practitioner

In designing our program for human relations practitioners . . . we realized we were obviously involved in matters of conceptualization. We were keying our program to people who would be interested not only in improving practice but also in making more explicit the skills which the people at the first level practiced. They would be interested in the uniformities and ways of thinking that reside in and are associated with skillful practice. They would be interested in talking about these matters. In short, they would be interested in theories.

Here again we were faced with a problem of emphasis. According to one school of thought, "it is the office of theoretical investigation to give the form in which the results of experiment may be expressed."[11] For our purposes this definition seemed too narrow. It stated well the function of the theory for the experimental scientist, ways of thinking which are useful to him in his search for "knowledge." But to make the office of theoretical investigation the concern of the experimental scientist alone perpetuated the gap between theory and practice which we were interested in trying to bridge. All our researches pointed also to the need for more useful ways of thinking for the practitioner. In fact, without such ways of thinking his skills cannot be improved and made explicit. The practitioner needs ways of thinking which will provide a form for the expression of his firsthand observations and which will allow him to make better observations to improve his competence.

Are there not also useful ways of thinking for the practitioner in his search for more effective action? Is there not also a need for theoretical investigation to provide the form in which the practitioner's thought is set for practice? We have often referred to these "useful ways of thinking" for the practitioner as "conceptual schemes." In many respects they do not differ from the conceptual schemes of the practicing rather than the talking scientist, his "useful and convenient ways of thinking about the phenomena" with which he has to deal.[12] These conceptual schemes are not subject to experimental investigation. Their test is utility and fruitfulness. For the practitioner the test of their fruitfulness in that they provide the form in which better observations can be made and practice improved. Moreover, it has always seemed to us that those ways of thinking which can be developed in the direction of both better practice and more systematic knowledge are the most fruitful.

At this point we should like to give an example of the kind of theory we have in mind, the kind of theory that is useful to the human relations practitioner and scientist as well. Example: It is fruitful and useful for the human relations practitioner and scientist each to think of the behavior of people in groups as "a system of mutually interdependent parts," "a social system," and "an organic whole surviving in an environment"[13] in which "the whole is determining the parts as well as the parts and their relations to each other are determining the

[11] Muriel Rukeyser, *Willard Gibbs* (Garden City, N.Y.: Doubleday, Doran, 1942), p. 232.

[12] Lawrence J. Henderson, *Introductory Lectures in Concrete Sociology* (unpublished, October 1938).

[13] See George Homans, *The Human Group*, p. 6.

whole."[14] To ask of this "way of thinking" whether it can be experimentally verified is a meaningless question. It is confusing two different levels of abstraction. The purpose of these abstractions, called "conceptual schemes," is their utility for practice as well as for understanding. They allow the practitioner and the scientist as well to see things which they would otherwise overlook. Thinking this way, the practitioner cannot overlook the relationships of people to each other, the effects of this piece of behavior on other pieces of behavior and on the total pattern of behavior as a whole. He cannot overlook the effect of his behavior on the behavior of the people he studies or tries to help and vice versa. He cannot study the "policies" of companies or the "logics of management" apart from the groups who have to implement these policies or logics and vice versa.

Thinking this way allows him to make a whole range of new observations, raise a whole host of new questions vital to more effective practice. It challenges a great many current assumptions about leadership, management practices, administration, control, supervision, and so forth.

To us the fruitfulness of this way of thinking is demonstrating itself. In the past twenty-five years it has produced a major revolution in administrative practice and theory. Supervisory and executive development programs—mushrooming all over the place—attest to the fact that something is brewing, a whole set of current assumptions is being challenged. Supervisors and executives are beginning to look at how they do behave and not exclusively at how they ought to behave. They are beginning to realize that all is not as yet known about matters of supervision and administration, that something more can be learned. As a result, human relations comes of age. It can no longer be relegated to the idiosyncratic level—that "people are funny." Rather, it constitutes the pervasive stuff, the hard core of the phenomena with which the administrator deals. Nothing seemed to us more important, more exciting, and more challenging than the tasks opened to us by this way of thinking.

Nevertheless, the job was admittedly pedestrian in character. It was far from being a *fait accompli*. The job still to be done did not hold the glamorous and heroic qualities that appeal to youth. We were interested in better maps for the administrator which would reflect better the important dimensions of the territory with which he had to deal. Without such a development, human relations would remain merely a fad, something "strictly for the birds." Such a development did not require persons who saw in human relations a Utopia, an end to all problems or a way of busting the union. It did require people who saw in human relations a way of presenting to practitioners a new and more exciting

[14] See *Dynamic Administration: The Collected Papers of Mary Parker Follett*, edited by Henry C. Metcalf and L. Urwick (New York: Harper & Brothers, 1940), p. 195.

set of problems to which they could give their attention. It required people who would be satisfied with the patient, laborious, unremitting practice of a skill and the associated ways of thinking that might improve that skill.

Summary of needs and goals

To summarize briefly, the needs to which our program was addressed were four in number:

1. The need for better human relations practitioners as well as the need for better behavioral scientists.

2. The need for more fruitful hypotheses derived from skill.

3. The need for more competent behavior at the level of skill at . . . human relations practice.

4. The need for more useful ways of thinking (theories) for practitioners which at the same time are also capable of systematic development.

These four needs summarized our diagnosis of the state of affairs in matters of human relations in 1951. In turn they determined the major design of our program, its direction, level, and goals. The product of our program was to be primarily a person with skill and useful ways of thinking; it was not designed for abstract knowledge *per se*.

To those *au courant* in human relations circles, it will be apparent that our design is based on observations, conclusions, assumptions, and inductions from experience (call them what you will) about which there are many honest differences of opinion. To them it will be clear that we have been "tap dancing" (not as gracefully as Fred Astaire) in and out of and roundabout many tight corners. We would have liked to avoid these "fine points." To many of our more practically minded friends who we hope will read this report, we realize that many of them may sound like "much ado about nothing." We hope this feeling will not prevent them from continuing to read further about matters which may interest them more.

In all honesty we could not avoid these questions. The "human relations approach" is not only raising basic issues for administrative practice; it is raising questions about some of the basic and traditional assumptions of "scientific method," "learning," and the relation of knowledge to practice. These questions to our more intellectually minded friends are matters of the first importance and quite rightly so. They are troublesome and disquieting questions—questions about which at some time or other those of us who are involved in them in any responsible way through teaching, research, and practice have to make up our minds.

We have tried to state, as clearly as we can, how and why we made up our minds the way we did. For any individual or group deciding on a course of action, a time comes when debate on fundamental issues must cease. Rightly or wrongly, certain assumptions must be made. If we are to start work and not remain a debating society, certain decisions involving risk have to be made. This does not mean that such assumptions are not open to question at other times. It does mean that they are not the topic of daily debate. The assumptions that we made about the methods of science and the relation of knowledge to practice are of this character. They were no longer matters of debate for us. We did not feel that our assumptions had merely come "out of the blue." To us they were inductions from experience, often bitter. We realized, however, that they were still open—and rightly so—to question and controversy. We believed that we would find out more about them by clearly making up our minds about them, taking a position and starting our program—not by debating them. But in making up our minds we are not trying to make up the minds of others. They are *our* articles of faith, *our* version of "this we believe."

READING V–5. *Learning in a Multidimensional World*

F. J. ROETHLISBERGER

[This chapter describes the kind of learning we have been concerned with in this book, its difficulties and its importance.]

. . . [In Chapter 1], it will be remembered, we stated our goal as the improvement of practice in human relations. We stated the way we

F. J. Roethlisberger *et al.*, *Training for Human Relations* (Boston: Division of Research, Harvard Graduate School of Business Administration, Harvard University, 1954) 115–42.

would proceed to achieve it as well as the assumptions we would be making along the way about both our means and our ends. In these assumptions, therefore, we have a good point of departure for evaluating our experiences. In trying to carry out these assumptions, what did we learn from and about them? This, then, will be our method of evaluation in this . . . chapter.

Problems of cultism

In implementing our program, time and again we came up against a set of difficulties we are calling the "problems of cultism." These difficulties were not new; they had been met before, but in the past they had been dealt with primarily at a name-calling level. Our critics have been prone to see in us the cults of "Mayo," the "small group," "cooperation," the "concrete" and the "practical." They saw us housed in the citadel of "capitalism," "free enterprise," and "embryonic executives," and thereby wittingly or unwittingly providing actual or would-be executives with the tools and skills of "manipulation." In turn, we have been prone to see in the activities of others the "cult of efficiency" and the "cult of science." These have been only too often the target of our attacks.

What lies beneath all this excitement? Among ourselves we have often speculated about these matters; each time we have come to the conclusion that to continue debate at this level of discourse would continue to produce more heat than light. We have never felt it would help matters to say to our accusers, "When you use these words, you'd better smile, Pardner." The recipients of our attacks have also been kind enough to allow us to "stew in our own juice" and await the outcome of our follies.

AS MANIFESTED BY THE TRAINEES

Had matters stayed at this level of "understanding," we would have decided to agree to disagree and let it go at that. But in our program . . . this problem of cultism manifested itself among our own trainees with a persistence that seemed to us at times formidable. This forced us to raise some embarrassing questions, such as, are we guilty of the same conduct as our accusers? Is it easier to see someone else's cult than one's own? Or perhaps is this problem of cultism not just an exhibition of "projection," "stereotyping," or "bad manners" but also something more basic to the problem of human relations training?

These questions, as we have said, arose first in relation to our own trainees. Probably their most recurring problem was to face up to the contradictions they felt in dealing with the multidimensional character of the situations in which they found themselves in our program. Over and over again they wished to reduce all human relations to one dimension and then became most unhappy with the contradictions into which this attempt led them. A few examples will help to make this problem more meaningful.

In the beginning, for example, some of our trainees became enamored with the "nondirective" approach.[1] Using it indiscriminately, they tried to reflect the feelings of people at all times, places, and occasions, and then were startled to find that these attempts often were not perceived by these people in the way they intended. To change their behavior they felt would involve them in becoming inconsistent with their understanding of how they ought to behave (i.e., being nondirective); on the other hand, not to change their behavior would involve them in becoming inconsistent with another principle of behavior (i.e., being scientific in the sense of looking at the facts). As a result, there was much anguish, pain, and stewing. That they might not have been too skillful in reflecting the actual feelings of the person; that they may have tried it in a situation where it was not appropriate (i.e., contrary to the norms of the group) to do so; that any tool has its limits were not for them the first matters to be considered. Instead, they held rigidly to the position that either *it* (unspecified) works or *it* doesn't.

Other beginners become enamored with being "group-centered."[2]

[1] An approach which addresses itself to the feelings of people rather than to the logical content of what they say. It responds to the feelings of people by reflecting, restating, and accepting them rather than by "interpreting" and "evaluating" them. This attitude is also called "permissive." See Carl Rogers, *Counseling and Psychotherapy* (Boston: Houghton Mifflin Co., 1942) and *Client-Centered Therapy* (Boston: Houghton Mifflin Co., 1951).

[2] "Group-centered" is much more difficult to define precisely than "nondirective." It is almost that which obtains in a group when you remove from it "the autocratic leader." In such groups "leadership" is distributed among its members. Everyone fulfills member or leadership functions depending upon the needs of the group. The "formal leader" of the group may fulfill the leadership function more often than the other members, but this is so, if it is so, only because he is a better diagnostician of the group's needs. To this "group-centered approach" the word "democratic" is often applied. To be "group-centered" is to be "democratic." In a group-centered group when a member fulfills the leadership function too frequently, it is called "bidding or vying for leadership." This is sometimes perceived as "something someone should not do." Probably the best way to think of the "group-centered approach" is to think of it as an attempt to explore new ways of leadership. This is a difficult, courageous, and very important thing to do. Like many "new things" it can be easily ridiculed. These new ways cannot be understood by defining a word such as "group-centered." Our definition thus is not intended to provide a deeper understanding of what the word stands for. Many people of different schools of thought are trying to practice what the word stands for. Other words are often given as equivalent labels for the group processes being referred to. Probably the school of thought which best exemplifies what this word stands for—and though they do not often use this particular label for it—is the Center for Group Dynamics at the University of Michigan. They have written many important books, papers, and articles about what this approach—not the word—is about. The reader may wish to look at some if he has not

They shrink from exercising any leadership or from contributing any ideas that would seem to be imposing their will on the group. The group must decide everything by itself and of course there must be unanimity. Often beginners further assume that such groups are wholly selfcontained and that there is no external environment to which they have to relate. Operating under these assumptions, again the beginner finds that often certain things happen which are not mentioned in the books about being "group-centered." The members of the group become confused and frustrated. The leader becomes immobilized. The accomplishment of the goals is in jeopardy. Negative rather than positive feelings between members of the group arise. Here again the beginner finds himself in conflict. Should he remain true to his "principles of group-centeredness" and hope that from all this confusion and frustration learning will result, or should he do something and risk the possibility of being "autocratic"?

For our trainees these problems were highlighted whenever they were in situations and groups, as members, leaders, or interviewers, where they were involved in *talking with* people. When they were just among themselves (and for the moment, at least, not concerned with their own interpersonal relations) and primarily *talking about* other people, their concepts and words seemed adequate and illuminating. They could describe well the evaluations and misevaluations, the perceptions and misperceptions of others; they could see the values and norms of behavior that the persons did or did not share, the interactions they did or did not have, the feelings they expressed or implied in their verbal and overt behavior. They even were somewhat capable of seeing these different dimensions as an "organized whole." They saw the consequences for employees of the "autocratic" or *laissez-faire* behavior of supervisors or executives. They saw the consequences for employees of having to accommodate to too-rapid technological changes required by the environment which failed to take into account their feelings and sentiments.

But when they took these diagnostic insights into situations where they were involved in *talking with* people, something happened. As observers or interviewers, the going was not too rough. But as members or leaders of groups these insights became increasingly difficult to practice. Up reared the multidimensional character of the territory with all its conflicting feelings for them and others. Should they be

---

already done so. "The Dynamics of the Discussion Group" in *The Journal of Social Issues*, 4, No. 2 (Spring 1948); Ronald Lippitt, *Training in Community Relations* (New York: Harper & Brothers, 1949); Dorwin Cartwright and Alvin Zander, *Group Dynamics* (Evanston, Ill.: Row Peterson & Company, 1953); *Explorations in Human Relations Training, 1947–1953* (Washington: National Training Laboratory on Group Development, 1953); and many others. And one which we wish we could have seen sooner—Herbert A. Thelen, *Dynamics of Groups at Work* (Chicago: University of Chicago Press, 1954).

"nondirective" and risk the chance of being regarded as "screwballs," or should they behave in accordance with the norms of the group and risk the chance of facilitating merely the expression of "superficial" feelings? Should they intrude their own opinions and feelings and risk the chance of not facilitating the "true" expression of opinions and feelings of others, or should they refrain from the expression of all feelings and opinions and arouse the suspicions (what-the-hell-is-going-on-here feeling) of others? Should they be "permissive" and how "permissive" can you be? Should they be group-centered and how group-centered can you get? And when the people who are being given permission to express their feelings and make their own decisions and formulate their own purposes do not appreciate this permissiveness but instead become bewildered, confused, angry, and will not make decisions, what then? How can this be? Why do they not appreciate our good intention? our permissiveness? The books are "screwy"; the books are not "screwy." All diagnosis is bad; no diagnosis is bad. So goes the see-saw.

At these moments books are not too helpful, primarily because the books on how to be permissive and group-centered do not go into these matters. They only tell you how *to be* these things, without saying too much what happens to people who try to be these things or often too clearly what happens to the people on whom they are being tried.

AS MANIFESTED BY OTHERS

As we looked around us, however, we found that we were not the only ones having these problems. In many places persons in positions of responsibility were trying hard to be *client-centered, employee-centered, group-centered, subordinate-centered,* and *person-centered* when they were in situations where they also had to be *organizationally-centered, production-centered, superior-centered, decision-centered,* and *task-centered.* In business and industry we had seen, to be sure, many examples of production-centered supervisors, efficiency-centered executives, and autocratic behavior. But in our reaction against these matters, were we not guilty in our training of going in the direction of another excess and over-simplification?

Let us be clear. It was not that we thought the insights to which these different kinds of "centeredness' (i.e., the "good" ones) referred were not of the greatest importance and significance. What bothered us was the lack of skill with which these insights were being practiced in groups and in face-to-face relationships. In looking at our trainees, ourselves, and others, we were appalled at the way these insights were being applied. It seemed at times as if we had lost the native intelligence with which God had endowed us as well as the elementary social skill that our parents and society had taught us. We were immersed in a sea of cults, some of which we had helped to create—the cult of the personality, the cult of the group, the cult of efficiency, and the cult of science. In trying so hard to be person-centered, democratic, purpose-centered, or scientific, we had ceased to be competent.

AS WE PERCEIVED THEM

Why then is skillful behavior in the area of human relations so difficult to learn? Why is it so easy to impede this development by escaping into cults? Were there some brute and stubborn factors which we were ignoring and which made the development of cultism almost inescapable in the area of human relations? All our experiences were forcing us to raise this question: Why is it so difficult to learn?

At one level the diagnosis is not too difficult. Looking at our trainees where we could observe this problem more microscopically and "objectively," it seemed to us the difficulty arose from three sources.

1. They were trying to apply these insights as absolute principles of behavior rather than to incorporate them first as simple guides for helping them to listen and to talk with people as members, leaders, or observers of a group.
2. They were trying to be consistent with these principles of behavior (generally derived from one important dimension of the total situation) in a situation where there were other important dimensions to be taken into account, and they were finding the "going rough."
3. They were trying so hard *to be* something or other (even trying to be themselves was tough) that they lost their capacity to observe and learn.

It is evident that for the beginner in some situations it is easier to apply principles than to practice a skill. The applier of a principle at least can appear to be consistent; he can glory in his consistency. The practitioner of a skill in a multidimensional territory has to behave inconsistently and therefore he has to learn to live with it. Through the practice of a skill he is not seeking certainty, consistency, and perfection. These are not the goals of his skill. Quite to the contrary, through the practice of a skill he learns to accept and to deal with a world of uncertainty, inconsistency, and imperfection.

Problems of learning

This, then, was the major problem to which our experience in implementing the program pointed, namely, the difficulties of learning for the practitioner in a multidimensional world. Cultism was merely one of its manifestations. In trying to carry out our assumptions we learned what a really formidable task human relations training was.

Not that we had not suspected this for, it will be remembered, in designing the program we thought we had done something about it.

Realizing that the practitioner whom we were trying to train is faced with a multidimensional situation, we had put the trainees in just such situations. We were not trying to train them to be counselors or discussion leaders of small groups as such. We were not trying to make them specialists in any one of the many dimensions with which the practitioner has to deal. We were trying to give them experiences with everyone of these dimensions as members, leaders, observers, and counselors of groups. We wanted them to see and feel the complexity of relationships in concrete phenomena and hopefully to resolve it with skill and understanding. But instead it often accentuated the very problem we were trying to solve. In getting them to face up to the complexity with all its uncertainties, imperfections, and contradictions, we unwittingly created enough anxiety, frustration, and conflict to throw them back into the security of the cults that we were hoping they would renounce.

Again it should be emphasized, however, that the problem had not been totally unanticipated by our design. We had realized that our approach to training would tend to produce a certain amount of frustration, so in the program we had provided the trainees with ample time and opportunity to work through their frustrations in individual and group conferences. We assumed that in time they would learn *to practice as a skill* the insights derived from any one dimension in a situation where other dimensions were involved, that is, to explore, test, see, and accept their limits for themselves. And . . . to a certain extent we succeeded. Nevertheless, the problem turned out to be much more formidable and time-consuming than we had anticipated. The tendency on the part of the trainees *to apply these insights as principles* —and thus to reduce human relations to the principles of one dimension—was always with us. Its tenacity, persistence, and stubbornness could not be underestimated. The practice of skill in a multidimensional world was a difficult achievement.

Was this because our assumptions were "screwy" and needed to be abandoned or at least corrected? Or rather had the attempt to carry them out helped us to find this out? And hence should we live with them a bit longer and see what more we could learn? We were inclined to take the latter position.

Let us look at these difficulties of learning for the practitioner in a multidimensional world. Without flinching (and hopefully not being seduced ourselves), let us look at this lure of the cult, these "seductive traps"[3] into which the practitioner can fall, and which

---

[3] This is a word [expression] we picked up at The National Training Laboratory for Group Development at Bethel, Maine, in the summer of 1953. We are not using the word technically so we shall not define it.

prevent him from learning and practicing a skill. Let us try to understand these problems of learning better. Why is the practitioner being
seduced over and over again? Can he never learn?

But before coming to this pessimistic conclusion, let us look also at
what, in our naïveté, perhaps, we did do, and what we could do or
might do better to help him grow stronger to resist this constant raping?
Is there another way for him to deal with his pangs of involvement?
Has skill got anything to do with it? . . .

After, and only after, we have done these things will we raise the
really tough evaluative questions. Are these problems unsurmountable?
Are these lessons the practitioner needs to learn and these distinctions
he needs to make about the multidimensional world just plain too
difficult or do they take too long to learn? Should we therefore fold up
shop and conclude that verily human relations is "strictly for the
birds"? Should we not quite reach this state of despair, we will then
raise the questions: What are the goals of our program anyway?
Can we redefine them in a way that does not make the task so formidable? How long would it take to accomplish these redefined goals?
For what individuals and groups is such training with such goals
fruitful? And what might be the next step to take in designing and
administering the program? . . .

THE MULTIDIMENSIONAL MILIEU OF THE PRACTITIONER
(WITH ITS LESSONS TO BE LEARNED AND ESCAPED)

Let us start by looking more carefully at the milieu with which the
practitioner with whom we are concerned is dealing, i.e., *an organized
human activity*.[4] What are some of the common elements of this milieu?
In dealing with it at a skill level, what important lessons does the
practitioner need to learn, what important discriminations does he
need to make about it, and what is preventing him from doing so?[5]

● *Norms of behavior*

In any organized human activity, the human relations practitioner is
faced with five quite different orders of phenomena of which one is

[4] The remarks that follow will not be restricted to those organizations whose
purposes are strictly economic but by virtue of our background and experience they
will often have such organizations in mind.

[5] The reader may wish to know why we did not do all this in the first place.
After all, he may say, "You have known for a long time that the practitioner is living
in a milieu of many dimensions." So we have. But there is a distinction between seeing
something darkly and dimly and seeing it more vividly and clearly. This part therefore
will be concerned with how what we knew in a "below-the-belt" sort of way was
catapulted into our consciousnesses by our experience in an almost blinding fashion
that can be expressed either in the form of "Eureka!" or "How stupid can one be?"

norms of behavior. In any group there are certain prescribed and customary ways of doing things, which we shall call norms of behavior. These norms are the ideas that develop in a group of how its members are expected to behave under given circumstances. Norms are not behavior itself but the ideas that govern behavior of people in groups. In terms of them, the activities of persons are evaluated. Certain activities are considered better or worse than others.

The human relations practitioner cannot ignore this dimension of human behavior. It is through this dimension that he first learns to relate himself to others. He learns the kind of behavior that is expected of him if he is to become an accepted member of the group. He also learns the kind of behavior he can expect from others. Yet in spite of the great importance of this dimension, the skill of the human relations practitioner cannot be drawn entirely from it. To do so would be to reduce social skill to the Emily Post school of thought—an elaborate set of rules of etiquette for different occasions. It would make human relations the rules and cult of conformity—a charge which has often been made against it.

The human relations practitioner improves along this dimension when he recognizes how his own behavior is determined by the norms of his group and when he can learn to differentiate the norms of behavior of his own group from the norms of behavior of other groups. His skill improves when he no longer feels compelled to evaluate the norms of others in terms of his own and when he can learn to accept their norms as something to be respected, appreciated, enjoyed, and understood rather than as something to be judged and evaluated from his point of view. Such differentiations are then incorporated in his "organized system of capacity for response" which allows him to respond as a unit (and not as an automaton) that is adequate to a particular point in a given situation. But this road of development is slow and arduous. It cannot be picked up in ten easy lessons. It involves another very important dimension of behavior which the human relations practitioner has to take into account and about which we shall talk later.

● *Ideals of behavior*

Closely allied to norms but yet of a somewhat different dimension are the *ideals of behavior* which individuals bring to work from the wider culture of which they are a part. These are the "absolute logics" of our society, our unstated assumptions, our most sacred and cherished beliefs. In our families, schools, and churches these ideals are inculcated as premises for conduct—they are what behavior ought to be regardless of time, place, and circumstances. To the members of a particular culture they are matters so obvious that they do not require explicit formulation or proof. Everyone in the society admits and accepts them even if in his daily conduct he does not act upon them.

To the human relations practitioner these ideals also cannot be ignored. Frequently and most often (unless he is dealing with a culture entirely different from his own) he holds these values in common with the people with whom he is dealing. They are his absolutes too. Again, it was our belief that in spite of the importance of these ideals and the need for certain groups in our society to keep reminding us of them, the skill of the human relations practitioner could not be derived from them alone. Human relations is not stating these ideal patterns of behavior. It would take our practitioner out of the realm of day-to-day practice and the imperfect world with which he has to deal. And this is just where we want to keep him.

In making this statement, our intent is not to be frivolous. Again and again we have been impressed with the importance of the social attitudes and beliefs of the practitioner. We have seen, for example, what persons who have faith and respect for their fellow men can often accomplish sometimes in spite of a lack of diagnostic skills. But we have also been impressed with the damage that sometimes has been done by those who have tried to implement in day-to-day behavior, and without skill, the cherished beliefs of our society.

Our human relations practitioner, like any ordinary individual, improves along this dimension when he learns to differentiate these ideals of behavior from behavior itself, when he learns to develop these ideals in relation to and not apart from the other dimensions of the milieu in which he finds himself, when he realizes the contradictions in which they sometimes lead him, and when he refuses to dogmatize about them. He is quite willing to accept that these ideals of behavior may vary from culture to culture. He is quite willing to accept that there may be some ideals which are universal and apply to all people regardless of differences of culture. About these matters his mind is open because in his day-to-day activities he does not need to close it.

● *Personality*

Still another important dimension are the individual personalities of the members of the groups with which the practitioner has to deal and, of course, his own personality too. Each person brings to work his own more personal feelings, assumptions, and perceptions of himself as developed from his past experiences and associations with other groups. These personal feelings, assumptions, and perceptions of himself constitute an organized dynamic whole—"a personality system." In terms of this conception about himself, he assimilates the happenings about him. He finds enhancing those things that tend to reinforce the pictures about himself he cherishes and likes to hold. He finds disturbing those happenings that challenge them. For example, a young supervisor may be upset when his employees do not do cheerfully and quickly what he tells them to do. He perceives in such behavior a threat to his conception of himself as a capable supervisor.

In the past fifty years since the work of Freud no dimension of human behavior has been given more attention and studied more than these "personality systems" of individuals. They have been almost the exclusive concern of psychiatrists and clinical and social psychologists. Their studies have contributed valuable and important insights to human relations practice. Yet again, in spite of its importance it seems to us unwarranted to reduce all human relations practice to this single dimension of "personality." To do so would reduce human relations to practices involving the modification of "personality" alone. Again we felt there were other groups more competent to do these things than we. Moreover, alone it would fail to throw light on some of the most important problems of the human relations practitioner.

Man not only brings to work the needs and feelings that make up that part of his personality but also some of those elements of his behavior, in conjunction with other elements of behavior found at work, tend to develop into "social systems." Sometimes these "social systems"—that important dimension of which we spoke earlier— satisfy and reinforce these initial sentiments and needs that people bring to the work place; sometimes, as we all know, they do not. Some people do not like to conform to the norms of the group. The particular personality needs they bring to work are not satisfied by the social systems of which they are members. Their particular conceptions of themselves are threatened rather than enhanced by their associations at work.

We shall not belabor this commonplace observation. All of us have had experience with these pictures of ourselves that we have to maintain and defend at all cost and to which we have to be consistent. Not only do we have to learn to live with others; we also have to be true to ourselves. Between these two forces—the need to adjust and the need to be consistent with our conceptions of ourselves—the human relations practitioner finds most of his most stubborn and baffling problems.

How does our human relations practitioner improve along this dimension? There is little question that he needs to know something about the personality structures of others; but above all he needs to know himself. Improvement along this dimension occurs when he can distinguish between his own needs and the needs of others and when he can learn that the satisfaction of his own personality needs are not *ipso facto* satisfying the needs of others. This requires self-control as well as self-understanding. And this is one of the most difficult lessons to learn. Too often we prefer to express our feelings rather than listen to the feelings of others; we prefer to maintain our pictures of ourselves even to the extent of behavior that is threatening to the self-concepts of others (e.g., bawling out a person in the presence of others).

Sometimes it would seem as if there is no road short of psycho-analysis in order to improve along this dimension. It is true that there are people with such rigid and inadequate conceptions of themselves that nothing short of a "major operation" upon this "personality" dimension seems to make it possible for them to participate congenially in an organized human activity. Yet, on the other hand, there are people whose pictures of themselves do change and become gradually more adequate and flexible through their associations with others at work. We shall speak more about this later.

● *Purpose*

There is still another dimension which the human relations practitioner has to take into account. In his multidimensional territory there exist not only norms and ideals of behavior and unique personalities but also *the consciously coordinated activities of persons*.[6] These coordinated activities have as their goal the achievement of a purpose. If the organization is to survive in its competitive environment, these purposes have to be attained. If these purposes are to be secured, the activities of persons have to be coordinated and operated efficiently toward these ends. It is for this reason that the leaders of any organized human activity must give considerable attention to the logical coordination and efficient operation of its separate job activities. From this concern ideas develop which say how matters should stand if these purposes are to be realized by rational processes alone. These ideas, stemming from science and technology, govern what the behavior and relationships of people should be, were matters ideally coordinated. As they do not coincide with behavior itself, we have called them "the logics of management."

In the past fifty years since the works of Frederick Taylor, the father of "scientific management," this dimension has also been given considerable attention and study. To it "big business" has given almost exclusive attention. It is the most articulate part of business, and many specialists have contributed to its articulation. Again the human relations practitioner can ignore this dimension only at his peril. It

[6] See Chester I. Barnard, *The Functions of the Executive* (Cambridge, Mass.: Harvard University Press, 1938), p. 73.

exists as a dominant variable in any organized human activity, big or little, articulated or not. It exists because any organized human activity has to survive in a larger environment. It comprises those essential activities that people must perform and the essential relationships that they must have in order that the purposes of the organization be secured. Yet again all human relations cannot be reduced to this dimension alone. To do so would be to reduce skill to the search for the best policies, the best methods, the best standards, the best controls, the best systems, and of course the best behavior to carry them out. It reduces human relations to what we previously referred to as "the cult of efficiency."

How does the human relations practitioner develop along this dimension? As so much of our writings have been concerned with this point, we shall be very brief. As we have pointed out again and again, this dimension has to be developed in relation to and not apart from these other dimensions that we have mentioned. The practitioner has to differentiate these "logics of management" from behavior itself. He has to learn to see that in any organized human activity the persons whose activities are being coordinated happen to be human and social as well as logical. From their loneliness and desire for intimate association with others, these persons tend to elaborate, proliferate, expand, and complicate the paucity of these essential activities, interactions, and relationships with which the logical coordination of their activities provides them. By so doing, they provide themselves with those satisfactions that no benevolent administrator can give. They elaborate their own social systems, and through them they develop their own norms in terms of which they control their own behavior. As a result, they run smack into what management often perceives as its own exclusive prerogative.

● *Science*

In the milieu of the human relations practitioner, then, we find four very important dimensions that make up his total situation. Each dimension is not behavior itself but a dominant idea that governs what the behavior of people should be.

1. There are those ideas that state what the appropriate behavior of persons in groups should be under given circumstances—what we have called "the norms of behavior."

2. There are those ideas which state the ideals of behavior—what behavior ought to be regardless of time, place, and circumstance.

3. There are those ideas which persons have about themselves and to which they have to be true and consistent.

4. There are those ideas that state the logical conditions that must obtain if the purposes of an organization are to be efficiently secured.

We have tried to show that human relations practice cannot be deduced from the principles of any one of these dimensions alone. The attempt to apply the principles of any one of these dimensions alone to the concrete human situation becomes a "cult." Each dimension can be fruitfully studied alone, but the minute the "knowledge" derived from such study is directly applied to a concrete situation, another dimension of equal importance rears its head.

As a result, the protagonist of any one of these dimensions before engaging in combat with the enemy (i.e., the concrete) often seeks alliances with other dimensions for support. Probably the most popular alliance in the world today is the one with "science." From such alliances new combinations called "schools of thought" appear such as, for example, "industrial sociology," "personality psychology," and "scientific management." We have mentioned this dimension of "science" before, but let us examine it further. Again let us remember that this dimension is not behavior itself but a dominant idea which governs what the behavior of people should be if certain things are to be accomplished.

5. It is concerned with those ideas which state what the behavior of a person should be if verifiable knowledge about the world (things and people) is to be acquired. These ideas are often referred to by different names such as, for instance, the "scientific method," the "experimental method," the "canons of induction," and "problem-solving."

There is little question that this dimension has gained increasing attention since the seventeenth century. Since this period no other ideas have so come to dominate the minds of men; no other ideas have so completely revolutionized our world.

This dimension of "science" differs from the others in certain important respects. Although we have stated it in terms of "what behavior should be," the word "should" in it refers to something different from the word "should" in our dimensions one and two (norms and ideals), for example. It does not have an ethical connotation; it is merely stating or trying to state certain uniformities in the behavior of people which produce certain results. It has considerable basis in fact about the way people acquire "knowledge" (at least a certain kind).

The ideas of this dimension of "science" differ in also another respect. Unlike those ideas in dimensions one, two, and three (norms, ideals, and personality), they dominate only a small portion of the population. No mortal escapes the first three dimensions; few escape the fourth (organizational purpose), certainly our practitioner cannot; but the fifth as a guide for behavior is primarily important only to the scientist and educator. It is the dimension that makes him conscious of his behavior and conscious of the need to observe the consequences of his behavior. It is the dimension which allows him to make more accurate and predictable propositions about the world in which he lives.

Yet again in spite of the importance of this dimension, all human relations cannot be reduced to it alone. It would identify too quickly the practices of human relations with the practices by means of which scientific knowledge is acquired. It would identify one dimension of behavior with behavior itself. In spite of its extreme importance, as we have said perhaps too often, we wish to keep it separate from behavior itself. Otherwise, it would reduce human relations to the "cult of science."

We have spoken of the affinity that some of these dimensions have for others. When we call "science" a cult, we are referring to this tendency. Its alliance with our dimesion two makes it an "ideal," an "absolute." The pragmatic "should" to which we referred above becomes a "Should with a capital S." In terms of this ideal the behavior of ordinary mortals is found wanting. From this point of view it takes only a small step to get to the injunction that for man to improve his behavior, he should become more scientific. When scientists no longer remain "scientific" about ther own "scientific behavior," we become wary.

For our ordinary human relations practitioners improvement along this dimension, like all the others, is a slow, arduous, and painful route. Through this dimension he learns to see the consequences of his behavior and why "the road to hell is paved with good intentions." He learns to listen better to others. He learns to observe better his own behavior in relation to the behavior of others. He tries to improve it —not drastically but slowly. He is searching for those *ideas which state what the behavior of a person should be if he is to continue to learn to live with himself and others in the society in which willy-nilly he has been born and has to work and live.* In this search he checks his observations and ideas with the observations and ideas of others. Some of these ideas come from religion, some from the humanities, some from psychiatry and psychoanalysis, some from the other social sciences, and even some from the physical sciences. For him there is no one repository of knowledge; no one and only way to acqure it. He finds that these ideas exist in no one book, no one bookshelf, nor even in any one library. They have not been as yet systematically developed.

Like the other dimensions, he tries to develop this dimension of "science" not apart from but in relation to the others. Through dimension one (norms of behavior) he learns what others expect from him as well as what he can expect from others, but he becomes no slave to conformity. Through dimension two (ideals of behavior) he learns the cherished beliefs of his society but realizes without bitterness that they often conflict and that they tell him little of what he should do in particular instances. Through dimension three (personality) he learns why he and others need to be true to themselves but why to do this alone would take them into mental hospitals. Through dimension four (purpose) he learns that he is determined in part by a system of relationships which he alone did not create—that social systems, just like himself, must relate themselves to an environment if they are to survive. And for this survival he learns that certain activities have to be performed and certain relationships have to be maintained for which he may have no liking. Although he learns to accept this he becomes no slave to efficiency. Through dimension five (science) he learns the most difficult lesson of all. He finds that even "knowledge" and "books" themselves can block learning and that in spite of the popular myth of his day "science" is not the only road to understanding. In a world of uncertainty, imperfection, and inconsistency he finally has to learn what his whole educational system has carefully tried to prevent him from finding out. He has to learn to live in this world and make his peace with its uncertainties, imperfections, and inconsistencies. Through this ordeal our human relations practitioner, like Christian in *Pilgrim's Progress*, has to go before he is ready to learn. As a result of trying, he may find that he is able to do through skill—and imperfectly to be sure—what those of us who have been afflicted with too much book learning cannot do through knowledge.

● *The interrelated character of these dimensions*

We have taken a long and roundabout excursion but one which we felt was necessary before we could come back to our point about the improvement of practice in human relations. Every one of these discriminations has to be made in some fashion or other by our human relations practitioner, if he is to improve his practice. Not until he can differentiate these five dimensions of the territory with which he has to deal, can he see the complexity of the problem he faces. Human relations is reduced to the cults of conformity, absolutes, personality, efficiency, or science. Until he can make these discriminations, the major problem of the human relations practitioner is escaped because he does not have to face up to the problem of how these dimensions are interrelated. None of these dimensions can be ignored; none of them can be given priority or made exclusive or separate. The overdevelopment of any one forces a counterdevelopment in the other. To develop one beyond or apart from the others creates a condition of unbalance. Merely to conform to the norms of the group can be done only at the expense of the growth of the personality. Merely to be true to oneself can be done only at the expense of learning to live with others. To supervise groups merely in terms of efficiency can be done only at the risk of losing spontaneity of cooperation; to supervise groups as if they were wholly self-contained and had no external environment to relate to (i.e., being "group-centered") can only be done at the expense of losing direction.

If these dimensions cannot be ignored, escaped, or developed separately, what is the alternative? What about trying to develop them together? This is what our program attempted to do. We realized that this attempt to develop them together would be accompanied by much groaning, sweating, and frustration. But we assumed that by this "working and sweating it through" process, "an organized system of capacity for response" could be developed which would help the practitioner to be more adequate to a point in a given situation. We assumed that this development was not only a feat of intelligence and logic; it was also a feat of the emotions. For some people it seemed to take place without "training." We assumed that training could help . . .

Problems of involvement

Let us look for a moment at the foregoing analysis of the problems of learning for the practitioner. For if it be correct, do we need to insist any further that learning in a multidimensional world is a difficult achievement and human relations training a very formidable task indeed? By the wildest stretch of the imagination, could all or most of these lessons be learned in a period of nine months, eighteen months, or indeed by many in any specified period of time at all? For what our analysis has shown is that what is preventing the practitioner from learning about himself and others in his work-a-day world is in good part the culture itself in which he lives. For look at the five injunctions these five dimensions are making to him.

1. Conform or else—

2. Hold steadfast to the eternal verities or else—

3. Be true to yourself or else—

4. Be efficient or else—

5. Be scientific; make a controlled experiment or else—

Is it not obvious that our simple injunction "Take a good look—see for yourself or else" is falling on pretty barren soil? For in the first three of the above injunctions are the conditionings of the ages; in the last two are the major precepts of the modern world; in all of them reside the most powerful sentiments of society. By violating them, not only the Junior Senator from Wisconsin but society itself will get you. Society does not approve of looking too closely at yourself and your relations to others. It has ordered these matters long ago and it wants no experimentation. There is not "gold" but "dynamite" and "sickness" in "them there hills."

* * *

Let us therefore look at our trainees again. At a simpler level of analysis, what was preventing them from learning? First, let us be clear. The trainees were not taught these discriminations that the "ideal practitioner" had to make as precepts. We did not have them recite or memorize them. Even the ideal practitioner did not learn them this way. For him they were products of living and "sweating" rather than the products of ratiocination alone. They were discriminations that resulted from learning to deal with his daily emotional encounters and involvements with the multidimensional world. They did not provide him with just intellectual *knowledge about* his complex world. They provided him with useful ways of thinking for dealing better with his feelings and emotions that resulted when he tried to cope with its complexities. It was his feelings, and in particular, his inability to cope with them, that prevented him from making these discriminations. The lessons that the "ideal practitioner" learned, then, were new ways of "controlling" his emotions and feelings that resulted from his involvements with the multidimensional; they were not just lessons about himself alone or about the territory alone, but also about his relation to it at the level of daily practice. And because his relation to it was fraught with very powerful feelings and sentiments, as the forementioned injunctions of society showed, what he needed above all was a skill of dealing with them.

In these terms the lure of the cult for the practitioner and his constant seduction by it take on a different hue. The "cult" is not something he runs to for richer and more meaningful emotional experience; it becomes a way of escaping from it. The call of the wild becomes the bleat of a sheep; the cry of a person who has no skill of dealing with learning, or getting satisfactions from his emotional involvements. In terms of our frame of reference, the cultist, in spite of all the abstract knowledge he may possess, has little skill of dealing with his involvements with the multidimensional.

And so it was with the trainees; they had little skill of dealing with these involvements. And this was what our program was about:

how do you provide them with it? This was what we were trying to help them learn; this is what they were trying to learn. As we tried to do this we found that we and they were engaged in no simple task. Had we been concerned with their involvements at the global level—their ideological beliefs and convictions—we truly would have been "sunk." But we were only concerned with their small day-to-day encounters and involvements with the concrete as observers, counselors, members, and leaders of small groups.

As they became more consciously involved in these simple daily encounters, all the dimensions we discussed previously came into play in a very simple but very central way. Their norms and ideals of behavior became involved; their conception of themselves became involved; their needs to survive in an environment became involved; their "pet theories" and assumptions became involved. And because all these matters are fraught with tremendous personal significance (this was not a matter of just putting together a jig-saw puzzle), their feelings became involved quickly and strongly but in a very simple, direct, and immediate way observable to us and to them. These feelings needed to be expressed, recognized, sorted out, and worked through. They needed to be understood and "controlled" at this simple level. Remember we were not dealing with their feelings about Republicans, Democrats, Communists, the underdog, democracy, and so forth. We were at a much lower and much more personal level. Remember we were carrying through two of our assumptions: (1) an internal development of maintaining a complexity of relationships within ourselves which must go hand in hand with the growing awareness of the complexity of relationships in concrete phenomena, and (2) it is from this process that "an organized system of capacity for response" develops and "skill" finally emerges.

As we have said before, for our trainees (and perhaps because many of them were graduate students of some social science discipline), these encounters and involvements with the multidimensional territory presented a peculiarly significant conflict for them, because they were frequently accompanied by the need to be consistent with some cherished belief or principle of what one should be or how one should behave. But let us remember that just such involvements and conflicts —often expressed, of course, in forms quite different from the way our trainees expressed them—are the natural accompaniment of living. Each person resolves them—for better or for worse—regardless of whether or not he ever heard of human relations. We had no experiences which led us to believe that only our trainees exhibited these difficulties. Our training in itself did not create them. It did make the trainees more conscious of them, and it did not allow them to escape from them too easily or quickly.

Summary

So what did we learn? What light did our assumptions throw upon our experiences? What were our experiences telling us about our assumptions?

1. Our assumptions were fruitful. They were helping us to learn and to see some things more clearly.

2. They had helped us to see that "cultism" was a manifestation of the problem of learning to live in a multidimensional world. It was like a "case of measles"—nothing to get alarmed at. What if the practitioner occasionally got seduced? *C'est la guerre.*

3. They had helped us to see that learning to live in a multidimensional world, from the point of view of skill, was a problem of learning skillfully with the conflicting and often unpleasant feelings that our encounters and involvements with it provoked.

4. This helped us to see how it was possible for many first-level practitioners with only grade school education, or less, to be able to do and in fact to be doing (i.e., dealing with the multidimensional), what according to another set of assumptions was for our trainees and us "impossible." This was both a depressing and exhilarating discovery. By the "best" processes of ratiocination we were able to give to it, our program was doomed to be a "colossal flop." It just couldn't be done. And yet here there were some Toms, Dicks, and Harrys who never went to Harvard doing it. What a bitter, bitter pill indeed to swallow! But then, looking at the matter optimistically again, how much better you feel when you've swallowed it.

And what did the trainees learn?

1. Not, of course, with such blinding clarity, but roughly and to a first approximation . . . they learned "the same things."

2. And what an "incentive" our above-mentioned point four provided! For the trainees were not going to be outdone by those lads out there and far away (shall we say Dedham, for example) who had never been even to high school, let alone a university.

ADDITIONAL READINGS FOR PART V

The readings for this last part of the book have been selected to provoke useful thought about three interrelated topics which will be central concerns in your study of the cases that follow.

1. Communication in specific organizational relationships: superior–subordinate, staff–line, consultant–client (references to the latter relationships are also given in Chapter 9).

2. Changing the pattern of relationships in organizations.

3. Involvement, skill, and personal growth.

Organizational relationships

1. "Group-Centered Leadership in an Industrial Organization," by James E. Richard and "An Evaluation of an Industrial Leader" by Thomas Gordon. Richard here explains in detail how he developed his approach to management and describes a number of events and experiences which show more specifically how he interacted with individuals and groups. Then Gordon gives the results of a follow-up study of reactions to Richard's approach. Thomas Gordon, *Group-Centered Leadership*. Boston: Houghton Mifflin, 1955, Part III, "Case Study: An Industrial Situation," pp. 307–53.

2. "Management by Integration and Self-Control," by Douglas McGregor. This chapter applies the concepts of McGregor's "Theory Y" to a specific superior–subordinate relationship, illustrating the importance of the interpersonal skill with which a manager implements this orientation. *The Human Side of Enterprise*. New York: McGraw-Hill, 1960, pp. 61–76.

3. "Staff-Line Relationships" and "Improving Staff-Line Collaboration," by Douglas McGregor. In these two chapters McGregor diagnoses and proposes a cure for the breakdown of effective lateral and diagonal communication which is often observed in large organizations. *The Human Side of Enterprise*, pp. 145–76. (See also Douglas McGregor, "The Staff Function in Human Relations," in W. G. Bennis and E. H. Schein, eds., *Leadership and Motivation*. Cambridge, Mass.: M.I.T. Press, 1966, pp. 145–71.)

4. "The Administration of Managerial Controls," by Douglas

McGregor. This chapter from McGregor's last book carries forward his ideas on staff–line relations and gives examples of several resolutions of the managerial "dilemma" cited by Richard: how to reconcile the need for order and control with the need for initiative and creativity. Warren G. Bennis and Caroline McGregor, eds., *The Professional Manager*. New York: McGraw-Hill, 1967, pp. 116–33.

Change in organizational relationships

5. "Changes in Institutions and the Role of the Change Agent," by Kenneth D. Benne. This short paper clearly describes some very important concepts derived from the work of Kurt Lewin on what facilitates behavioral change in organizations. Paul R. Lawrence and John A. Seiler, *Organizational Behavior* and Administration. Homewood, Ill.: Irwin-Dorsey, rev. ed., 1965, pp. 952–59.

6. Papers on "planned change" by W. G. Bennis, Roland Lippitt, K. D. Benne, and Kurt Lewin. From the important book of readings, *The Planning of Change*, we have selected the four papers most relevant to our purposes. W. G. Bennis, Kenneth D. Benne, and Robert Chin, eds., *The Planning of Change*. New York: Holt, Rinehart and Winston, 1961, pp. 153–62, 230–38.

7. *Changing Organizations*, by Warren G. Bennis. This book is not "required" but is strongly recommended to readers of this volume as collateral or subsequent reading. *Changing Organizations*. New York: McGraw-Hill, 1966.

Involvement, skill, and growth

8. "Toward Understanding Self," papers by Arthur T. Jersild, William C. Menninger, and Arthur W. Combs. Hamachek concludes his book of readings on "The Self" with three papers which fit in well with our purposes. These papers are primarily addressed to prospective teachers, but their emphasis on the teacher's need for self-understanding is entirely relevant to our emphasis on the administrator's ability to "listen to himself." D. E. Hamachek, ed., *The Self in Growth, Teaching*, and Learning. Englewood Cliffs, N.J.: Prentice-Hall, 1965, pp. 539–75.

9. *The Professional Manager*, by Douglas McGregor. We strongly recommend a careful reading of the whole of this, McGregor's last book.

CASE V–1. Ralph Langley and the American Radiatronics Corporation (A)

Christopher Conrad, as a casewriter from the Harvard Business School, had been at the American Radiatronics Corporation for a week in July of 1961 when Ralph Langley, the firm's manufacturing superintendent, suggested he pay particular attention in his research activities to the machine shop group. Mr. Langley revealed that he would be spending a great deal of time in the future with the machine shop. Mr. Langley told the casewriter that his superior, Larry Zeigler, the firm's manufacturing manager, had directed him to take some immediate and decisive action to improve the machine shop's productivity (see organization chart, Figure 1).

Ralph Langley

To Mr. Conrad, Ralph Langley's external appearance was in complete contrast to the stereotypical middle manager in modern American business. He wore rather plain, well-worn clothes that hung loosely on his slight frame. He was stoop-shouldered and had lost most of his hair. In ordinary conversation, he often talked in a barely audible monotone.

Mr. Langley had joined the American Radiatronics Corporation in 1958. It was one of the leading producers of specialized electronic devices. The firm had been organized several years after World War II and had experienced a very rapid growth. The history of the firm epitomized the pattern of development followed by many young companies that had taken part in the postwar electronics boom. Operations were profitable during the early 1950s, but with tightened competition losses were experienced in the two years prior to Mr. Langley's arrival and in the year following, and sales stabilized at

This case was made possible by the cooperation of an individual and a business firm that remain anonymous. It was prepared by Gerald C. Leader under the direction of George F. F. Lombard and Arthur N. Turner as the basis for class discussion. Cases are not designed to present illustrations of either correct or incorrect handling of administrative problems. All names have been disguised. Copyright 1963 by the President and Fellows of Harvard College.

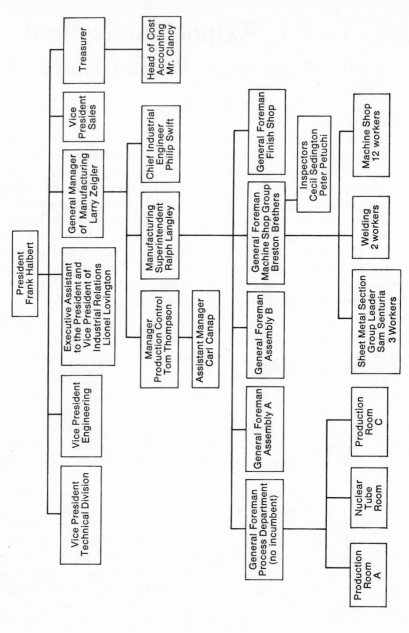

Figure 1. The American Radiatronics Corporation. Partial Organization Chart.

approximately $15 million annually. An ultramodern office and plant was located in a suburb of Baltimore, with more than 600 employees, over 50 per cent of them highly trained technical personnel.

Mr. Frank Halbert, the president in 1961, had been appointed to his office in 1958, several months before Mr. Langley joined the company. Previous to that time the Board of Directors had once before replaced the president in order to reverse the unfavorable profit trend. Upon his arrival Mr. Halbert had implemented a vast reorganization of the firm, and since then had been actively concerned with bringing the company back to profitable operations.

Mr. Langley was originally hired as an engineer for ARC, but his actual initial position with the firm was as general foreman of the Process Department, an organization of approximately twenty-four employees involved in manufacturing and assembling highly sensitive electronic tubes of a specialized design. Ralph spoke to a casewriter in 1959 about how he had acquired this job.

> I was originally hired as a senior engineer at ARC, but at that time the company wasn't making any money, and we had all kinds of production and design problems. I was asked to take over the Process Department. The job was presented to me as something the company really needed to have done. I took it on more because of the challenge involved than anything. Then, too, Frank Halbert (president of ARC) had come in, bringing with him a new management group and everything was very much up in the air. I felt that by taking the job on, it would give me an opportunity to prove to management and to myself that my approach to handling people actually would work. I had never done any production supervision prior to this date.

Although Mr. Langley at this time was in charge of the entire Process Department, which comprised three assembly rooms, he devoted a more than proportionate share of his time to one of them, the nuclear tube assembly room. This subsection of eight middle-aged women performed sequential assembly operations on a variety of nuclear tubes. The tube room activity was not directly linked with the rest of the Process Department and in fact was physically isolated in a room off the main factory floor.

As is described in the American Radiatronics case series, Mr. Langley was able to greatly increase the productivity, efficiency, and profitability of the tube room operations, as well as significantly raise the morale of the women working there. In 1961, some two years later, Mr. Langley could quote from memory percentage gains made; he talked enthusiastically about what had been accomplished.

This was dramatic proof to me that you can get people to want to do their job, because of their own interest. You have to make the job meaningful to them, to have them use their own faculties, to have responsibility toward their own job. I let them set goals for themselves. I let them decide on an action, take the action, and stand behind it themselves. The people were generally satisfied. The only problem was to keep enough work ahead of them. I found that I had pressure on me from the group, rather than I trying to pressure the group.

The results that were achieved by Mr. Langley in the Process Department were well publicized throughout ARC. Mr. Langley told the casewriter that in a conversation with the vice president of research, the latter had openly stated that the performance of the group was not only very good but extraordinary. The vice president of marketing had also indicated that the group's performance had been exceptional.

Mr. Frank Halbert, president of ARC, however, took a more modified view of Ralph's achievements. He told a casewriter in 1959, "I don't want to downgrade Ralph or anything like that—I think he has been extremely successful in what he is doing—but really that tube room is not a tough place to handle. We have got some real trouble spots in other rooms of the company. The tube room, after all, because of the kind of work done there, lends itself to the girls seeing the connection between what they do and the final product. There are opportunities there for satisfaction in the work itself that you couldn't begin to find in those other places." In the same conversation he asked the casewriter, "Do you think there is any substitute for fear as a motivation? I doubt it. Seems to me you have to step on a guy to get the best work out of him. All these fringe benefits and things don't do it."

Changes in the manufacturing organization and Mr. Langley's promotion

Late in the summer of 1959, Mr. Langley was becoming increasingly restless with his job as general foreman of the Process Department, feeling that he had accomplished all that could be done in that location. Mr. Langley said that he wanted to try his hand at "releasing some of the motivation" in technically trained personnel at ARC such as physicists and engineers. Mr. Langley had initiated talks concerning a job change with his immediate superior, the manufacturing manager whom Ralph believed to be sympathetic to his desires, but Mr. Halbert's reorganization of the manufacturing activity cut them off abruptly.

Mr. Halbert dismissed in quick succession, during the summer of 1959, both the vice president in charge of manufacturing and Ralph's boss, the manufacturing manager. Mr. Larry Zeigler, the former head of Industrial Engineering, was immediately appointed manufacturing manager, reporting directly to the president, and the vice presidential position was temporarily eliminated. On the day of this latter change, Mr. Langley was unexpectedly invited to Mr. Halbert's office; the following day Ralph described to a casewriter what had transpired in this conversation.

> Once we were seated he said, "Ralph, you are the intellectual type and with an intellectual you sometimes have to offer more explanations than you do to the other type. . . . Very frankly the manufacturing manager was let go because he wasn't doing his job—we were not making adequate progress. . . . You were not chosen as his replacement because you are not the man for the job, now let's get that clear. You have a great deal of ability and I have a high regard for you . . . (but) what we need today in ARC is an SOB who's going to be able to step in there and really give them hell. We need the top sergeant approach for a while. You know in developing an organization like ARC . . . you need a combination of the get-tough approach and the intellectual approach. Well, we've had enough of the intellectual approach and now it's time to get tough."

Ralph told the casewriter that the conversation lasted over two hours, during which time both of them presented their respective interpretations of appropriate administrative behavior, Mr. Langley using the tube room results to substantiate his argument. When the conversation turned to the subject of Mr. Langley's future work, Ralph said that Mr. Halbert had some question as to whether or not he, Ralph, had "the stomach for the things that top management needed to do."

The following day, in a move that caught everyone by surprise, Ralph was promoted to the newly created position of shop superintendent, reporting to Larry Zeigler, the manager of manufacturing, and having line responsibility for all of ARC's manufacturing and assembling activities. When questioned immediately after this appointment as to what he thought his biggest problem in his new job would be, Ralph told a casewriter:

> I know that management is going to be expecting some drastic

changes rapidly, and the big problem is going to be how to keep them happy enough so they stay off my neck, and give them the feeling that they are beginning to get what they are looking for so that they have confidence that we are going to lick the problem. This is the biggest danger area—getting stampeded in an attempt to satisfy management's urgent feelings.

Mr. Langley's thoughts in the summer of 1961

In the summer of 1961 the Process Department was operating without a formally appointed general foreman. One of the workers in each of the subsections acted as group leader reporting to Mr. Langley and handling the work assignments and administrative details.

After almost two years as manufacturing superintendent, Mr. Langley spoke to Christopher Conrad of the problems he was still facing.

My problem is, how to you get a body of foremen to believe in the same type of philosophy that I am using? What is it that influences people? How do you influence people? How do you relieve tension? These are the questions I would like to know the answer to. How do you get foremen not to push their people around? I am trying to work out a way of having the foremen learn that the most trouble comes from people resisting being pushed around and not being treated as if they were people. There is a need in people to be people. People are trying to run away from being people, to be responsible for what they are doing. The only way they can be personally satisfied is taking personal action. Exercising the ego, identifying within the framework of being a man. If we start to function under this new philosophy then the people will want to function this way. What we have to do is to overcome the inertia of their being treated as something other than people. They have to believe you are sincere. Initially they won't accept you. The history of most people is of competitiveness where they have been taken advantage of.

I am trying to get the foremen close to the people within their section. They should act as a pole around which the group can grow, a source of encouragement for them. The group needs a real live, tangible something to please . . . a focus, for what they are doing . . . something that reflects and rebounds from them, something they can satisfy, something that they can seek to satisfy . . . something that can reward them.

There are a lot of things that are preventing me from applying the same philosophy that I used in the process group to my foremen. First of all there is the structure of the organization. Secondly, there are so many things hanging on to the foremen's job. When I worked in the process room I could shut the door, I could isolate. I did things the way I wanted them to work out. I had enough confidence in what I was doing so that I didn't have to worry about extra things. Therefore, the group didn't feel threatened. I used to work with two faces, one face toward my subordinate that would reflect the philosophy that I'm working under and a second face with which I would face the rest of the organization. But now my foremen have to be worried about production control, industrial engineering, etc. They have so many things forcing them to act in the traditional organizational way.

Look at this company—600 employees and only 100 of them are direct labor. Maybe 175 of them are salesmen, engineers, and technicians, but that still leaves a lot of overhead. I told Larry Zeigler, "Why don't we throw away the production scheduling, planning, and industrial engineering, and take the money that we save and, for example, buy some machines for the machine shop?" All these services organizations are trying to scratch out an existence and they become "ends" in themselves instead of helping the productive people. They worry about their own little difficulties instead of worrying about getting the product out the door. It's no wonder that they are at each other's throat, trying to maintain their own little kingdom. Look at the foreman, he doesn't have anything to do. What we should do is give the foreman the *whole* job, let him schedule his own work, let him get his own materials, let him set up the way he wants to do the work. Let him be American Radiatronics to his subordinates, so that he won't have to go around licking the boots of these service organizations. Right now ARC is so buried down in the red tape of controlling people, we can't even get the products out of the door.

Management has seen the results of my philosophy, but they won't be shaken from their old traditional ways of acting. What do you do? How do you get them to believe what is right before their eyes? Mr. Halbert still thinks the results achieved in the tube room was because of my "Ole Black Magic." They just can't believe that if you let people develop their own potential you can get results never thought of before.

I'm just not an organized person. Sometimes I force myself to be organized; but rarely. I guess it's my little rebellion not to read two-thirds of the stuff that crosses my desk. What a bunch of junk. Most of the stuff takes care of itself without any action on my part, so why should I read it? I just let nature take its course and then if it needs a little help I do something, but not until then. You've seen the mess on my desk. I let my "In" basket fill up until it's overbrimming. I guess this is just one of my little ways of getting back at them. I don't pay any attention to routine —it's too stifling! All of this red tape is really getting me down, especially this direct labor utilization report.

I guess you would call me an experimenter. I'm an unorthodox person. I do things differently—a dreamer and an idealist. No matter where I go, people will always think I'm a little bit different and have some crazy ideas, but that's all right. I don't mind. It's all right just as long as people are allowed to become interested for their own sake and not just because someone tells them to be interested. You might say I'm trying to influence people in the direction of positive growth. I believe all people have a natural tendency for growth—of uncovering—of reaching out, but there are blocks in their way which cause them to withdraw and close up. I want to let nature take its course and then step in at the right time and influence them in the direction of positive growth.

Mr. Langley commits himself to the machine shop group

The machine shop group of ARC's manufacturing organization had for a number of years been a persistent problem to the firm's management. In July 1961, labor unrest and low "productivity" and "efficiency" performances on the direct labor utilization report had kept Mr. Zeigler, manufacturing manager, constantly urging Mr. Langley "to do something to improve the situation." The average "productivity" of the machine shop group for the last seven months was approximately 53 per cent, while the performance of the rest of the factory organization over the same period was close to 76 per cent. Of the total factory "productivity" performance, almost a quarter was made up of the "productivity" performance of the machine shop group.

Mr. Langley told Christopher Conrad that in earlier conversations with Mr. Zeigler, he had attempted to demonstrate to his superior that contrary to what might be surmised from the utilization reports the machine shop had, in the last three-quarters of a year, made significant gains. Mr. Langley had made a statistical comparison of the "productivity" performances of the machine shop group under the administration of its present foreman, Breston Brethers, and his predecessor and found them to be equal. Mr. Langley had pointed out to his superior that Mr. Brethers' results had been achieved despite the fact that 60 per cent of the personnel in the shop during his administration were new and relatively unacquainted with the specific operations required on ARC products. Moreover, Mr. Langley thought there was some evidence to show that the actual "productivity" and "efficiency" performances had increased slightly in the previous nine months but these improvements were not reflected in the percentages because of Mr. Brethers' failure to take advantage of the credits for nonrated and variance work due his organization. Mr. Brethers was known to dislike paperwork. It was also pointed out to Mr. Zeigler that there had been a noticeable improvement in the quality of the machine shop group's output. Then, too, Mr. Langley felt the industrial engineer's standards were little better than rough estimates and had been computed with no thought as to how the actual operation would have to be performed.

Mr. Zeigler informed Mr. Langley that while he was personally very sympathetic to his subordinate's arguments, their validity could not be completely substantiated with figures on paper and this was a definite requirement before anyone in top management would listen to such claims. The manufacturing manager believed that the 35 per cent "productivity" performances of the machine shop group in the previous week left him no choice other than insisting some positive action be taken immediately. He outlined several alternatives: "Weed out" all the "nonproducers" by keeping records of each worker's "productivity" and "efficiency," or, if need be, close down the machine shop completely and subcontract the work.[1] None of these possibilities was acceptable to Mr. Langley. Ralph Langley explained to Christopher Conrad the agreement he made with Mr. Zeigler and what action he planned.

> I made a deal with Larry (Zeigler) where I could have three months to get something out of the machine shop or we would go back to individual standards and start whipping the boys like we have in the past. I'm going to start working with those guys, going out on the floor and getting to know them, start telling them that they're the best. That's what they need to get them started. My one stipulation with Zeigler was that I should have my complete way in this and there would be nothing to stand in the way of putting in my philosophy. I do it my way. I want the group to grow and I'm going to push away anything, including Zeigler, that stands in the way of it.

[1] In the summer of 1961 records were not kept of individual performances, although two years previously such a system had been operating. Mr. Langley had the system abandoned upon being made superintendent.

Ralph Langley and the American Radiatronics Corporation (B)

In August 1961 Ralph Langley was doing his utmost to improve the morale and performance of the machine shop group of the American Radiatronics Corporation. He hoped to build up an enthusiastic team around the shop foreman Breston Brethers, a man of considerable technical skill and experience.

Among the workmen whose ready cooperation Ralph was seeking was Kurt Krachaleck. Ralph discussed at length with the casewriter, Christopher Conrad, his contacts with Kurt.

> Kurt is German born; he came to the United States about five years ago. He is a quiet methodical person, seems to put steady effort into a job, and wants to cooperate. A week ago on Saturday I stopped by Kurt as he worked on a drill press—"How is it going, Kurt?" He hesitated—said O.K.—then continued drilling the plate he was working on. I stood and watched. After a bit he turned and said to me, "You said you want to know our problems—what holds us back?" "That's right, Kurt, can I talk to you sometime?" "Sure, how about right now? What does a man have to do to make out? Every review I get passed by. They never give you a chance to prove what you know. Follow the sheet (pointing to the operation sheet). Lots of times they are wrong or not a good way of doing the job—the equipment and tools aren't taken into consideration. If I try to do the job the way I know how, he (Breston) gets mad—I'm not a beginner, I served apprenticeship in Germany—you can't make quality by that (pointing to the sheet again). A man should be proud of what he does; when I go home I feel empty. Sometimes I get mad and say to hell with it. I don't care whether it's right—make the time—then half the parts are rejected. He doesn't care about

This case was made possible by the cooperation of an individual and a business firm that remain anonymous. It was prepared by Gerald C. Leader and Charles M. Hampden-Turner under the direction of George F. F. Lombard and Arthur N. Turner as the basis for class discussion. Cases are not designed to present illustrations of either correct or incorrect handling of administrative problems. All names have been disguised. Copyright © 1963 by the President and Fellows of Harvard College.

the men—he thinks we're all no good, he doesn't help, he just insults. You know they put me back on the molding machine. At first I didn't mind, it was something new—but now if the shop is going to be different I want to get back here. I'm a machinist. Yesterday I asked Breston if I would get a chance to come back. 'That's up to you' he said, 'the only reason you weren't fired is because no one else knew the molding machine.' He doesn't want me. When I came to this country I couldn't speak English. Everyone acted like I was stupid. That's a bad feeling—I went to night school to learn English. Now I got the same feeling. It's bad— a man should be proud. Maybe things are done different here than in Germany—I want to learn but I want to feel that I belong. You know I know how other immigrants feel; they are completely frustrated. Everything was so different from what we were used to, we can't get started—we look very bad—I know what that does to you. Why does Breston treat the men like that?" Kurt said that these men have no pride. He told me that he went home at night and felt exhausted but it was not from feeling that he had done a good day's work. He told me, "I'm a machinist but Breston stuck me on the molding machine without any explanation." He said that wasn't what he was trained for. Then just quite recently Kurt asked Breston again about moving down to the machine shop. Breston just shrugged his shoulders, evidently, and didn't say anything to Kurt. Kurt feels rejected by the group and that there is no group feeling here.

Then I started to tell him about the way I wanted to get a group feeling here in the machine shop. I told him it was like his first coming to the United States five years ago when he couldn't speak the language and everybody gave him blank stares. I told him he had to learn the language in order to communicate. I told him that presently there wasn't any language between the foremen and the men. I told him that was why I was down here, trying to develop a communication between Breston and the rest of the workers, like Kurt. I reminded Kurt that whereas before he had become Americanized, now he had to become "Brestonized." I said that the group had to form around the foreman; he had to be the center of the group. Kurt was really enthusiastic about this idea. He kept bouncing up and down on his chair and in animated motions; I could tell that he was really sympathetic to my views. I told him that where he spoke enthusiastically of his apprenticeship training in Germany, I now wanted him to be just equally satisfied with what he was doing now and that was the reason I was down here, to make just such changes.

Next day the case writer, Christopher Conrad, was listening while Ralph quizzed Breston Brethers on Kurt's work.

LANGLEY: Say, Breston, another thing, how is Kurt doing up there on the plastic molding machine? What's his production for the week?

BRETHERS: (*Turning to his inspector and assistant, Cecil Sedington*) What about it, Cecil?

SEDINGTON: I think he's run off two batches of 200 and 300, but I don't think he's near done on the 3,000 order.

LANGLEY: I think we should better check on that. That's going to mean a lot on these productivity figures.

Christopher Conrad followed Mr. Brethers up to Krachaleck's work station, where Mr. Brethers began to quiz Kurt on the status of the 3,000-part order.

BRETHERS: When did you punch in on this job, Kurt?

KURT: Oh, let's see (pause) it was, let's see, I can't remember . . . it might have been Friday afternoon or Monday. I just don't remember when it was.

BRETHERS: Well, it couldn't have been Monday because you started another job then. The 200-unit batch. Has Bigelow from Industrial Engineering been down here doing experimental work again?

KURT: Oh no. We did the experimental work on this piece a long time ago. It was a long time ago.

BRETHERS: Then you just made the setup and started making pieces?

KURT: (Excitedly) Ya, that's right. I turn in a thousand pieces yesterday afternoon.

BRETHERS: Yes, I know. What went wrong? Did you run into any trouble?

KURT: (Pause) No, just a little. Normal trouble, you know.

BRETHERS: What is just a little?

KURT: Well, this slide started to stick a little so I had to wait a little.

BRETHERS: You never have to wait. Remember that. You come and tell me, you understand?

KURT: (Pause) Well, I didn't think anything was wrong. I didn't think it was worth calling you.

BRETHERS: I still want to know when you started the job.

KURT: (Pause) I guess it was Saturday, but I had the other job. (Goes over and shows him the 200-batch work order.)

BRETHERS: Yes, yes, I know. Look Kurt, give me a pencil. (Kurt hands him a pencil and a piece of paper.) You work nine hours a day, right?

KURT: Yah.

BRETHERS: Five days at 60-minutes an hour, that's allowing you one and one-half minutes per piece. That's what Industrial Engineering said you could do. Let's see. That's 1,800 pieces you should have produced by now. All you have to date is 1,000 plus the 200-unit batch. That comes to 1,200. You're 600 units short. What's wrong, anyway.

KURT: (Pause, shrugging his shoulders) What can I say? I don't know.

BRETHERS: They're screwing you Kurt, do you realize that? They're giving you one and one-half minutes for each one of those and giving you no time for breakdowns or if the machine sticks a little bit. (Angrily) That screws me too. I get screwed on my production time. I lose out. The whole machine shop loses out. Kurt, you just have to take the responsibility to be producing on production time. They're taking advantage of you, that's what they're doing.

KURT: I don't know, I don't know. (Pause) He wanted to set up the two-inch knobs and run them and then we got that set up and then he didn't have any material, and they needed the one-inch knobs in a hurry, so we threw out the whole gosh-darn setup and put in the one-inch setup.

BRETHERS: (Angrily) It was that damn Bigelow, wasn't it? He'll screw you every time. They get credit for developing a new process and we get screwed because our production time is used to develop it. That sneaky little rat.

KURT: (Pause) I didn't know. It was the first time I worked with him.

BRETHERS: Why didn't you come and get me when he came up here? The next time he does you be sure to run down and get me.

KURT: (Pause) I don't know. What can I tell you?

BRETHERS: Well, don't let this happen again. Our productivity this week will suffer drastically because we can't complete this job. We can't charge your time against anything worthwhile, and it's because you didn't punch out. Remember, these guys are out to take advantage of you and we suffer, and if you don't watch them closely, they'll do it again. Kurt, I don't have a chance to come up here very often and you're kind of up here in No Man's Land. You come down and see me if anything happens. But just remember to be sure you're working on production pieces when you're on production time. Come on. You don't have time to finish up this job, and I've got to complete some jobs for this week's productivity. You just got barely started on this 3,000-piece order. I've got a milling job for you. Come on down here so we can finish it up and at least get credit for that. Damn it anyway.

KURT: Just a minute. I want to close the machine down and clean up.

BRETHERS: Come on, you can do that later. We've got to get this milling job out.

KURT: I don't like this. Switching back and forth between machining and plastic molding. I don't get anything done. Somebody ought to come up here and be permanently on this job, not this back and forth stuff.

BRETHERS: Huh? Come on, we've got to get some work done today.

The next Monday morning, Christopher was standing nearby when Kurt Krachaleck approached Mr. Brethers.

KURT: What do I do now? Drill holes on the castings? I finished the milling that I started Saturday.

BRETHERS: Where's the fixture?

KURT: We can't find it. I spent about 15 minutes hunting for it.

BRETHERS: We'll finish it up later. Get me the paperwork. (Kurt goes and gets the paperwork on the milling job—shop order, and specifications—and hands them to Brethers.) Have you heated up the machine yet?

KURT: (Shakes his head, no.)

BRETHERS: You wasted all that time?

KURT: (Shrugs his shoulders.)

BRETHERS: Well, go back and get it started. (Kurt goes away. To case writer) How do you get them to learn? How do you get them to heat up a machine when they know they're going to be working on it the next morning? They'll just never learn.

The same day, several hours later, the case writer observed Brethers grinding down a tool bit for use by Ludwig Leider. Looking up, Brethers noticed Kurt Krachaleck standing beside the tool crib and motioned for Kurt to come over to where he was standing.

BRETHERS: What are you doing down here?

KURT: A fitting busted on the molding machine.

BRETHERS: Did you punch out?

KURT: No, it was my fault. I was bringing up the pressure to 18,000 pounds per square inch when it started spraying oil.

BRETHERS: What have I told you, Kurt? (Angrily) You punch out and come down and get me any time something goes wrong up there.

Brethers motioned Kurt over to the side and engaged him in a heated and animated conversation for the next thirteen minutes. Following the conversation with Breston, Kurt came over to the turret lathe where another worker, Vic Villella, was working.

KURT: That bastard has got me running around. Back to the molding machine, back to the machine shop. Why doesn't he hire a sweeping boy to do all his little odd jobs for him?

VIC: You do it just the way he wants you to. You do everything just the way he wants it. Just exactly. Then if anything goes wrong, you can always say he wanted it that way, and that it is his fault.

KURT: He wants a piece every one minute and a half. Then he figures up one and one-half minutes, forty-five hours, and comes out with 1,800 units and I've only produced 1,200 so he asks me, "Where's the 600 you little monkey?" That man. The oil leaked. It takes thirty minutes for the machine to heat up. Some of the pieces stick. Everything goes wrong, and I'm supposed to get 1,800 pieces out.

VIC: You do exactly as he wants. . . .

KURT: (Interrupting) You got to use your brain. . . .

VIC: (Breaking into Kurt) You don't think around here. You do it his way.

KURT: This is a new material—black polyethylene. So that Bigelow (the industrial engineer), he timed me on the white stuff, so I get the new material, and I'm supposed to know the exact time. I have to figure out the whole new cycle. No one knows. Breston doesn't even know how to figure out how much time for heat, press, and then cool. All I hear is one and one-half minutes. I think I'm going to quit.

Kurt angrily walked off to his plastic molding machine, at the far end of the shop, where Christopher Conrad joined him.

KURT: I don't know who he thinks I am, running up and back all the time, machining one minute down there, and then up here the next. He wants me to come and see him every time something goes wrong. Any time I'm not making a piece every one and one-half minutes. What does he know about this machine? It's ridiculous going down there every time. I was here before he came. He doesn't even know what's going on. It's ridiculous me going up to see him every time something goes wrong. It could be just the piece sticking or the pressure is down. Some little thing. No one knows anything about the machine. I know more than anybody. I call the engineers or the maintenance people and they don't know what's wrong. Every time something happens I'm supposed to call a person to fix it and go down and pitch in on machining. Why, I started this machine up. It stayed here for many years and nobody even operated it. I ordered the filament, the pressure gauges, everything. I put them on myself. This morning when I went down there to machine those things I just got down there and just got the job set up, when he sends me up here to start molding again. It takes me fifteen minutes to get the jig out of the tool bin when I go to machine. Ah, you don't get anything done. I was trying to tell him that I took my coffee break early while the machine heated up so that I wouldn't have a double wait. I don't even get to take my break with the rest of the boys when I'm up here. I'm all by myself. All I get from him is a kick in the pants, like a monkey, and told to get the pieces out. I could get so mad but that doesn't do any good. He complains about the pieces not being right. He doesn't even know the problems of this machine. I'm a machinist, not a plastic molder! But I know that plastics shrink. Oh, I don't know. Industrial engineers come up here and look at their watch and see I'm turning out a piece every one and one-half minutes, but they don't see the troubles we have sometimes of sheeting up the machine and the sticking, and the oil breaks. You go and see them and they're always sitting in their offices having coffee all the time. The job gets pretty boring with nobody up here. Look at this. I have to wait until the machine heats up before I can do anything again. I'm supposed to be producing right now. Ralph Langley should hear about this.

Kurt went over to Ralph Langley and brought him back to the plastic molding machine.

KURT: Look Ralph, this gosh darn thing. I was making pieces this morning, and I looked over and the oil pressure on it is blowed all to heck and I looked down and there is oil all over the place. It was this new job and I was trying to get the pressure up, so I called the maintenance man and we didn't all want to get shocked, and so we turned off the electricity. . . .

RALPH: (Interrupting) And now you have to reheat the machine.

KURT: Yah, dat's right. I fixed the fitting. The maintenance people ran off before they could finish it and I fixed it up. Breston was all mad about me not telling him what was wrong up here, but that's ridiculous. I can't go to him every time. They only allow me one and one-half minutes apiece.

RALPH: What's your cycle time, Kurt?

KURT: Oh, let's see, 0.58 inject, 0.60 mold and I think it's 0.20 cool. That's only for the actual operation, without the heating up and all the other things.

RALPH: What's a fair estimate of the warming-up time? That is, generally.

KURT: Oh, I would say altogether about 30 minutes. I take my coffee breaks early while the machine heats up so I won't have to close it down when the rest of the boys have theirs. Breston thinks I'm goofing off. He says I should have 1,800 units.

RALPH: Now Kurt. You were telling me all the trouble you were having.

KURT: He wants a piece every one and one-half minutes.

RALPH: That isn't right. He thinks you're doing a good job up here.

KURT: All this stuff about coming down here every time something happens.

RALPH: He knows things aren't right up here. When are you going to run another bunch of pieces?

KURT: Well, I'm waiting for the machine to heat up now. I'll be running in about ten minutes.

RALPH: All right. I'll come back up here in ten minutes and I'm going to time this operation. I'm going to see what some of your problems are. I'll time the whole thing, and then once I get a good cycle time I'll go and talk to Industrial Engineering and see if we can't do something about changing the one and one-half minutes. I'll be back, Kurt.

Mr. Langley returned to Kurt's work station several minutes later with a stop watch and notebook and timed him for approximately thirty minutes. The two worked in silence until Ralph spoke to Kurt just before leaving.

RALPH: Kurt—I'm going back and compute the time per piece. You completed thirty pieces in a total elapsed time of 32.567 minutes, with five pieces sticking and requiring extra handling. Isn't that right?

KURT: Don't forget the warm up and the breakdowns that. . . .

RALPH: Don't worry. I'll put all the allowance in, due you.

Christopher Conrad talked to Ralph Langley several hours later.

RALPH: You know I just really came in for a big surprise. Boy was I amazed. I figured out the time per piece on the molding machine for Kurt and with the allowances it came to one and one-half minutes per piece. Just exactly what the industrial engineer had computed. I guess I was a little wrong in my assumption that they were cheating him. But one thing it gives me is a little more confidence in their time standard. They had taken into account all allowances—all the allowance times, warm-up time, etc. I was very generous with the allowances on Kurt. I rated him at 110 per cent, and gave him 15 per cent for fatigue and rest—that's seventy-two minutes a day he has for all the things he wants to do besides work—going to the bathroom, coffee breaks, etc. I sure was surprised. I thought, or rather assumed, that the industrial engineers had not taken into account the warm-up time, but I guess they had, because my calculations show almost exactly the same figures as theirs. I can't figure it out. Kurt's production has been 40 per cent of the figure that it's supposed to be, and that's too gross a difference to be accounted for by errors in my calculations. I just can't understand it. When I've been around him he looks to me like he is working all right. I'm really surprised.

Mr. Langley returned to Kurt's work station and immediately began explaining the computations he had made in arriving at the standard rate of one and one-half minutes per piece. Kurt nodded in agreement throughout Ralph's presentation.

RALPH: ... So you have one and one-half minutes per piece. Is that all right?

KURT: Yah, I guess so. (Long pause) You know, I got all balled up yesterday when Breston was up here, and I just was too mad. You know all this running back and forth from machining up here, it is really bad. I told him, "Why don't you hire a permanent operator for the machine?" You know, you don't have time to start up a machine down there and finish up a job and then come up here and start molding. This running back and forth is just no good for me.

RALPH: Well, I talked to Breston about these figures and he suggested that if you have a major breakdown, that you know is going to take some time, to be sure to punch out—punch out off of production time, and go see him. He'll assign you to a production job.

KURT: Yah, that was my fault, I should have punched out on that breakdown last time, but I didn't think anything was that bad. We should have some fittings up here so that I can repair the machine when something like that happens.

RALPH: Well, you be sure to punch out when it's really a big job. I can't take the breakdowns into account in my calculations.

KURT: Oh sure. You don't know when they're going to come.

RALPH: Let's be sure. I'll figure it out for you. That's 315 pieces per day, assuming an eight-hour work day, or about forty per hour. Is that all right? Well, we'll give it a week and see how it goes.

After Ralph Langley left, Conrad asked Kurt for his reaction.

KURT: Well, at least you can talk to this guy. (Pause) You know, it took the machine twenty-five minutes to warm up this morning, and I didn't get my first good piece until 8:37. It took that long for the machine to warm up. The machine is working good today. It's not breaking down, as it usually does. Maybe it's the cool weather.

CONRAD: You mentioned that you could talk to Ralph?

KURT: Well, Breston ... I'm supposed to come and get him every time something happens. He doesn't know anything about the machine. What good would that do? He's never been up here. He doesn't know what's been going on. Ah, I don't know.

CONRAD: You'd rather be down in the machine shop?

KURT: That's my profession. I'm a machinist. (Pause) I've never been in a company that it's taken me so long to get adjusted to.

CONRAD: What's the main problem that seems to be bothering you, Kurt?

KURT: (Pause) Ah, it's the way this company is organized. You don't feel a part of it. Where I worked before in Germany at Mercedes Benz we produced so many cars per week and you had so many parts to get those cars produced. You could see the parts go over to the assembly plant. You knew if you didn't get them out, get your parts out, the whole assembly line would stop. You were given a list of how many were needed, and the foreman would leave you alone. After he got the material, and you did them, and you got them, there was no one standing over you writing in a little book. Here you look out (turns around and surveys the factory floor)—here you look out and see twenty men in white shirts tearing little pieces of paper and notebooks. We have to carry them. The production people. Oh God, the overhead is so high, and when they want to tighten, we're the ones who get pressed. Everybody turns on us. Get the work out—go faster—go faster— we get the whole organization of top of us. Look (does one of the pieces at the molding machine at an increased rate of speed) I can't do this all day. This is what they want me to do. (Pause)

CONRAD: You feel that everybody is pressing down on you.

KURT: Yah, that's right. Everybody tells us to go faster. They come up here with their little notebooks and write down how fast we should do it. They say "fine, beautiful." Sure it's fine, beautiful for them, but we got to do the work. There's too much overhead with all these people who are doing no work.

CONRAD: Do you think Ralph can do something about this?

KURT: Well, I think it's too big for him. I was telling him about the problem but, I don't know.

CONRAD: What about Breston, your foreman? What does he do?

KURT: I don't know. I don't see much of him . . . I don't think he is getting the group together. You know, so we work together. He's got so much to do. Everybody is running up to him with their problems. "How do you do this—how do you do that, Breston?"

I was a machinist down there a while and you spend so much time just getting set up. Instead of a collar for the milling machine being right there you had to go to the tool bin, and they look for it, but they don't know where it is. So much wasted time. Where I was before you had all your tools and fixtures right beside the machine. Here you're assigned a job one time and you develop a way of doing it, and the next time somebody else gets the job and they have to start all over again. You lose all the experience. Breston always has you set up this way. You don't use your brain.

CONRAD: You set up his way?

KURT: That's right. You always set up his way. You don't have a chance to use your brain. That's the fun of machining—figuring out how you're going to set it up. So maybe his way is a little better, but maybe the guy doesn't understand right off in a second, that that's the best way, Breston's way? Ah, I don't know.

Several days later Christopher Conrad again had an opportunity to speak with Kurt Krachaleck. On this occasion the latter complained bitterly that the men who had been hired by Mr. Brethers received a Class A rating and Class A pay when they had no better, or in some instances fewer, credentials than himself.

They get Class A rates of pay because they said they had apprenticeship there and there and had worked there and there. Well, I had my apprenticeship back in 1942 myself, and I've worked quite a few years since then. That's my goal in life—to be a Class A machinist, a good machinist! I should be coming up for Class A pretty soon. I'm about to the top of my grade in Class B, and they haven't had a chance to see my work. Just because I came in in the same week that the plastic machine operator quit, the foreman came up to me—the foreman that was here before Breston. He asked me if I wanted to run the plastics machine for a while. He said he wanted a good competent man that could work by himself without much supervision because he wouldn't have a chance to come up here. He wanted a man who could do a good day's work and everything would be fine. So I took the job for a while. So after that foreman was laid off and Breston came in, he comes up and tells me I'm supposed to prove to him that I'm a good machinist. Why should I prove to him that I'm a good machinist. Look—look at the work I've done (brings out from his machine box a sampling of intricate and delicate machine parts that he has done). This is close tolerance work. This shop here, they're working with fractions all the time.

I've done good work before using decimals. I can carry a piece all the way through—roughing it, milling it, drilling, finishing it—the whole works. I can do all the operations. I don't have to have anybody do anything for me. I don't like this—just doing an operation there and an operation here. I'll tell you that if anybody in the future asks me to take a job like this I'm never going to take it. I'm going to work as a machinist and stay as a machinist.

CASE V–2. **Bruce Plastics Corporation (A)**

Walter Loftus, a case writer from the Harvard Business School, spent several days one autumn visiting the main plant of the Bruce Plastics Corporation, located in the Central Atlantic States. One Wednesday afternoon, about the middle of October, Loftus was present during a conversation between Phil Hamilton and Al Lynch. Phil, in his work as employee relations manager, spent a large proportion of his time on disciplinary problems arising between workers and supervisors, including grievances over such issues raised by the union. Al was an operating supervisor in charge of quality control in the "color lab" of the department which produced "S"-type plastics (see organization chart, Figure 1).

The color lab did color matching and quality control work for this department. When making their decisions about color variance, the inspectors compared a sample from a production lot (called a "chip") with a standard chip, one of which was available for each of the several thousand formulations that S department made. The inspectors learned the acceptable limits of deviation from the standard chip

This case was made possible by the cooperation of a business firm which remains anonymous. It was prepared by Harold S. Spear under the direction of George F. F. Lombard as a basis for class discussion. Cases are not designed to present illustrations of either correct or incorrect handling of administrative problems. All names have been disguised. Copyright 1959 by the President and Fellows of Harvard College.

by consulting three notebooks which contained examples of successive degrees of color deviation for a small number of the thousands of color formulations. In time the inspectors learned how to apply the standards of deviation for the sample colors to any color currently being produced. Once the inspectors became familiar with the sample levels, they referred to the notebooks only infrequently for refresher purposes.

Almost all of the work of the color lab demanded more mental effort and less physical effort than work elsewhere in the plant. Though machines were available which aided inspectors in judging a given sample, none of them could make as accurate differentiations between slight variations in color as a trained human eye. In general, the workers in the color lab were of relatively high caliber and skill. Compared with other parts of the plant the color lab had few disciplinary cases.

On the day shift the color inspectors in the quality control part of the color lab and the color matchers in the other part of the lab did their work under separate first-line supervisors. On the night shift, however, the color inspectors were responsible to the color matching foreman. A shift foreman did not have formal authority to change an inspector's decision on a sample. This could only be done by the inspectors' higher ranking supervisors (Jack Shenk, Al Lynch, Bob Fulton, and so on), all of whom worked on the day shift. However, shift foremen had formal authority (rarely exercised), not to change, but to disregard an inspector's decision; but in doing so, they assumed personal responsibility for the acceptability of a given color being produced.

Prior to the conversation presented below, Al had phoned Phil to discuss a discipline case. Phil told Al he was unwilling to discuss a specific case over the phone and was too busy to see Al personally until later. Al said he wanted to take action before the end of the day shift, 3:00 P.M. Phil then told Al he could take action if he wished, but if it backfired or was inconsistent with plant policy, Al would be responsible. Later Al called back to say that he given Lou Lange, an inspector in the color lab, a "verbal"[1] and wished to talk with Phil to see whether he had made a mistake. Before Al arrived, Phil told Loftus the following:

PHIL: Al's a pretty new supervisor and I sort of wish he had waited and seen me before he took action. With him or any other supervisor, I'd like for them to feel they could gain by talking with me, and

[1] Company procedure called for four levels of disciplinary action, depending on the seriousness of the infraction and taking into account the employee's record. The four were: verbal warning, letter of warning, layoff without pay, and discharge.

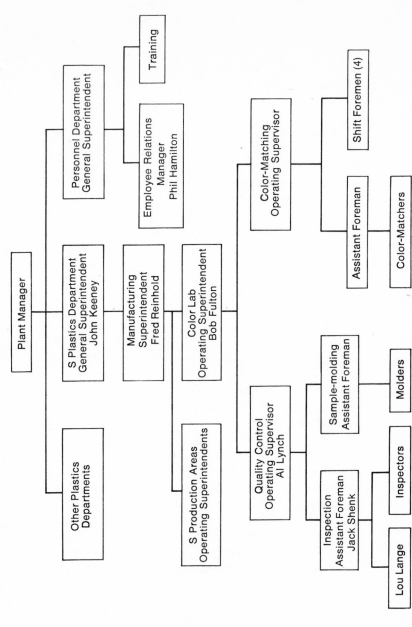

Figure 1. Bruce Plastics Corporation. Partial Organization Chart.

that they weren't coming to please me. Not that I'm an expert, but I've dealt with a lot of these problems and I sort of hope some of it can rub off. When the foremen come in to talk about a discipline infraction, they usually won't go against my recommendation. They feel that people in the personnel department are in a better position to appraise what to do; and anyhow, they know if they go and do something different from what we suggested and it fails, they'll be in much more trouble for not following our advice.

But what I try to do is to get the foremen and supervisors to think out their own problems to a conclusion. I might guide them in their thinking or interject ideas, particularly near the end of a session; but it is important that these men go through the process of working out the problem so that they can solve on-the-spot problems at other times. And the men are free to reject my recommendation, even though they usually don't. That of course depends on how often I'm right. If I were wrong fairly often, they'd stop listening. There's a lot of judgment in these kinds of problems since the union contract, legality, and things like that aren't too much help. Of course, I'm also concerned about the question of consistency. So I really do push them a little bit into seeing me before they take action, though it's still up to them as to whether they come or not.

Phil also sketched Lange's background for Loftus. Lou had been a production worker until several years previously when he fell off a tower, seriously injuring his back. At the time, the plant manager said that the "damn fool" shouldn't have been up there in the first place. There followed a long period of negotiation between the union and the personnel superintendent on the proper placement of Lou when he came back to work. Eventually, the personnel superintendent, feeling that he was getting little cooperation from the union, assigned Lou to the job of inspector in the color laboratory. The personnel superintendent thought Lou considered himself a special protégé of his. Lou came back to him several times to complain that the job was not quite right, that he couldn't get along with this or that supervisor, or that something else was wrong. In each case, the personnel superintendent told Lou that he could apply for any other job in the plant for which he was qualified, but Lou always answered, "You put me here and I'll stay here until you put me somewhere else."

Lou had other problems too, Loftus learned. His wife had been in a mental hospital several times and he spent much money on her expenses. He was about forty-five years old, a high school graduate, and had been with the company for over a dozen years.

Loftus knew that Al Lynch, about twenty-nine years old, held an undergraduate degree in chemical engineering as well as a master's degree in business administration. He had been with the company for three years, the first two as a foreman in another department and the third as operating supervisor in the color lab.

When Al Lynch came in, he immediately started talking about the case.

AL: We've had trouble with Lou Lange before. He received a letter of warning in 1955 and almost had some action taken on him last winter. Well, anyhow, in this case now, we had changed the procedures on the inspection limits a week ago and we gave him regular instructions on the new limits yesterday [Tuesday] afternoon, before he started on the late shift. And we know that he knew informally about these new limits before we formally told him. We had widened the tolerances on what would be acceptable on certain types of material and he was told this, which he understood, and he was shown two examples of what was now acceptable.

You know he has been a troublemaker. He has come in with dope, and. . . . Well, early in the evening he said he did not like the new tolerances and he threatened he would reject some lots. He threatened this to a color matcher and to the color matching shift foreman. But half the time, though, he's a loud talker and we never know whether to believe him. Well, this time, later on, he rejected a sample and this caused two production units to be stopped and the color batches in them to be pulled out. The sample chip was actually within the old limits and he agreed at the verbal session that it was within the widened tolerances. He first tried to say that he didn't understand the widened tolerances, but later he tacitly admitted that it was within the widened tolerances. One thing that complicated this situation, though, was the fact that the inspector on the next shift after Lou's also rejected some sample chips made from the very same material. This formulation was being processed in several different production units, which is why some of it did not come through until the next shift.

PHIL: What did you do about the next inspector?

AL: No action, except left a note for him. It seemed like a plain error of judgment. Furthermore, one inspector usually won't contradict a judgment of another. Six months ago we had trouble with Lou. He admitted he had done wrong that time; and we handled the situation badly so there was no verbal. But this time his action resulted in the color batch being pulled which cost $120 in down time alone.

PHIL: Why did you give him a verbal?

AL: You think it should have been stronger?

PHIL: (Laughing) No answer for now.

AL: Well, I was concerned with that inspector on the next shift.

PHIL: Why were you concerned about him?

AL: (Aside to Loftus: I guess I'm on the hot seat now.) Don't know, but he'd rejected the lot too. (Long pause) Well, we gave Lou the verbal today so he'd know what was what.

PHIL: (Long pause) Well, I have to completely disagree with you, completely disagree.

Phil then restated what Al had told him, making each aspect of Lou's behavior part of a deliberate carrying out of his threat to violate instructions.

PHIL: I don't even think you're in the ball park. We give letters of warning even for nondeliberate violations of instructions. What you did is tantamount to letting the guy do any darn thing he wants. I'd rather forget an issue altogether than just give a guy a slap on the wrist.

Phil again reviewed the seriousness (from the point of view of maintaining discipline in the plant) of Lou's threat to reject lots, of his follow-through on the threat, and of his past history as a trouble-maker.

PHIL: Just how weak can you get? That's the central question. (Al nodded his head.) I'm not trying to chew you out. (Al continued laughingly aside to Loftus: He's doing a pretty good job of that.) I'm just setting out the facts. (Long pause) Well, I guess this answers your questions on the phone about whether to wait to see me before taking action.

AL: Well, what should we do if this happens again tonight, if Lou again rejects some stuff?

PHIL: I don't know. In the usual case we would fire the guy, but now we probably couldn't fire him. I guess we'd shoot for "layoff," but expect the union to take it up to arbitration. We'd go ahead and do that, even though expecting to lose at arbitration, just so we could rebuild our position, so that the present light discipline would not become a pertinent example for the future.

AL: Well, you know there have been other cases of inspectors on the night shift fouling up where we haven't taken action but have just left notes for them.

PHIL: That's perfectly OK, if the guy had thought the stuff wasn't within the tolerances. This case with Lou is in a completely different light; it was a deliberate act; he knew what effect his action would have. You should go to a fact-finding session in a case like this. You cut short your discussion with Lou and tell him that disciplinary action is pending, then go find out just what disciplinary action would recognize the seriousness of the offense.

AL: Really? Fact-finding before the verbal session?

PHIL: Well, have you seen the latest notice with the guide to disciplinary action we are just circulating? (Al shook his head.) Well, read it when you get it. It reviews all the procedures that are relevant. (Phil then elaborated further on the need for a fact-finding session in a case like this; then with a smile) Aren't you sorry you came down? Well, act accordingly.

AL: Yeah, OK and thanks. (He left.)

After observing this conversation between Al and Phil, Loftus felt it would be useful to talk further with both Al Lynch and Lou Lange. He was particularly interested in discovering how each man viewed himself and his job. He thought this information, together with what Phil had told him, would shed light on the disciplinary problem. Lou Lange talked to Loftus as follows about himself and his job.

LOU: There can be disagreements now and then over color, but they're not really very important. Of course there's an incident now and then. There was one the other day. As a matter of fact, I was the one involved in that. Had to do with some material that . . . well, I'd rejected it. I knew it was outside the limits. I had the color matcher who worked on the batch originally and the shift foreman and the chief production foreman on nights all come in and look. The four of us all looked at that material and we all agreed that the stuff really wasn't right. I had no question. Well—next morning I was here in the lab and Jack [Shenk] had to come on duty and Jack said to me, "Come on in, we want to talk to you." We went into Al's office and then we had a long talk. We discussed . . . argued whether this stuff should or shouldn't have been adopted. It didn't really make any difference because they wanted to get someone, you know. So just as I was leaving, Al said, "You know this is a verbal." That was that, and I walked out.

You see, a lot of stuff was coming in bad from one of the molding machines out there. I found all sorts of things. When something goes wrong I have to talk to several people—foremen, operators, and such. This causes quite a lot of trouble. It was upsetting everybody, I suppose, but that's the way it had to go. I think they were afraid if I kept talking to people like this, it would get up to Keeney's level [superintendent of S department] and this would cause a lot of trouble. So they really had to have a fall guy, and they were just looking for something to get on me. Anyhow, they can't hurt me. I have a bad back from the fall I had one time. I got some home trouble, too. They can't fire me . . . if they did, I'd have to be paid compensation. But, oh well, this verbal will pass in a couple of months and then it's off the record. They needed a fall guy so they got me on whatever they could find to get me on. It isn't as if I did it deliberately. Oh, if I did that—why, they've even fired guys for doing stuff like that deliberately. [Lou then told a long story of an inspector elsewhere in the plant who had forged some test figures on some material without running the mechanical tests necessary to secure such figures.] Well, they fired that guy; boy, he was out of here like a light. This was just a verbal and it will only last a few months.

Lou also talked about some of his earlier experiences on the inspector's job. He commented, as well, on his injury and his home life.

LOU: For a while, you know, I was too eager. I was finding things that other people didn't want me to find. But I have remained on ever since, still doing the same sort of stuff. You try your best and often someone else take the credit. About ten o'clock each morning they have the color session, but I don't bother with that anymore. That's a meeting of Al, Bob, Jack, the production supervisors, the people from sales, and a couple of others to discuss any problems concerning color. Jack takes the books down and he knows the whole story so there's no need for my going.

LOFTUS: You don't any longer feel it's worthwhile, so you let Jack go. You didn't think you were getting anything out of it.

LOU: Well . . . well . . . you see, to tell the truth, they didn't want me. They didn't care what I said. Whoever has the books has the whole story, and he can tell them. I didn't care anyhow, so I don't bother with it, and Jack handles the situation. But I wouldn't want to go into color-matching. They get more money over there—fourteen cents an hour more—but over here we have the final say. They get pretty mad sometimes when we reject their stuff too. They just go by formulas, and they have to try to judge from there when it's off and put some other stuff in, but they don't have the final say. The extra money doesn't interest me. Of course, over here there's more chance to strain your eyes and there's more mental strain. But still, you know, sometimes I get cramps in my leg. I have to take codeine, you know, sometimes two or three times a month. The doctors in Delphia want to open me up again and have another go at me, but the doc here says, "You might as well leave well enough be." I've got screws holding my spine together too. An operation wouldn't be a guarantee, just a gamble. I'm not able to do much at home now. I just sit and watch TV. I used to have Cub Scouts—did a lot of stuff around the house, you know. But I'm limited now. Last year, my boy got the award for the most deserving student, in athletics that is. He's 6 foot 3 and only 15! My daughter's a stenographer here in the company, but my son—he won't have anything to do with the company.

Following this conversation with Lou Lange, Loftus spoke with Al Lynch. Al talked as follows:

AL: My main aim in this case was to take some action. I didn't care if it was a letter or a verbal or time off; that question was secondary to the one of taking action. Of course, on the other side, there was the idea of conforming to plant policy and being sure it was an appropriate action. But Lou's gotten away with murder in the past, and I didn't want him to get away with murder in the future.

He's really very odd . . . sort of a mental case in a way. His wife is in a mental institution and he has a persecution complex. After this incident he felt that everybody was jeering at him, that he had no friends anywhere, and all he had was bitter enemies. If you take strong disciplinary action with him whenever he gets out of line, then he'll keep in line and act OK. So my main concern was to take some disciplinary action on him.

A man should be disciplined for infractions. I've been there a year, but before that Lou had called people names, been insolent, no discipline . . . particularly when he was on the dark shifts. He's gotten away with murder and I just didn't want him to get away with murder this time. There was one time six months ago when he acted up almost the same way—rejecting stuff he should have accepted. Then, when we corrected him, he did just the opposite; finally he blew up at the shift foreman. So we had a meeting where Jack Shenk was in charge. It was our firm intention then to give him a verbal but Lou admitted he was wrong and wanted to be friendly; so there was just a lot of talk, and everybody was nice. From my point of view the meeting got out of hand, and we didn't give him any disciplinary action.

Now this time, I thought at least a verbal, maybe a letter, was needed. But when I found the inspector on the next shift had also rejected the lot, I was afraid Lou would point to this action as justification, or maybe he would say the sample was outside limits. So I figured a verbal was the thing to do.

About the threat Lou made . . . he dislikes so many things, threatens so much, that we're immune to his threats. I guess it just gives happiness to his own ego. I wondered if the threat was serious enough for insubordination or insolence, but his remark was too general; it wasn't directed at any one person.

My main point was to hit him cold. So when he came in I told him that this was a verbal. I said, "You'd been instructed on how to deal with the new tolerances and yet later you said you wouldn't follow them. You were even shown two samples of what was to be accepted and these were further out than the one you rejected. There's no question." But then Lou went off on all sorts of things, problems he had had with the blenders [workers in the production area] and with some of the molders and other men in the lab here. So I had to keep bringing him back to the subject, so that we could stick with the problem. At the very end, I again said it was verbal, so that he'd know it. But now that I've talked with Phil, I realize it should have been a fact-finding session, still hitting Lou cold, but not final action.

Bruce Plastics Corporation (B)

Following his observation of the conversation between Al Lynch and Phil Hamilton and his subsequent conversations with Al Lynch and Lou Lange, Walter Loftus spent several days establishing for himself the sequence of events surrounding the discipline of Lou Lange.

Loftus discovered that on the Wednesday morning in question, Jack Shenk, the assistant foreman of inspection under Al Lynch, reviewed Lou's work of the preceding night and decided Lou had acted wrongly in rejecting one sample of the material covered in the new instructions. Jack told Al, who agreed. Al gathered other information on the situation, including reports of Lou's threat to reject some lots coming within the new limits. Al talked to his superior, Bob Fulton, who was operating superintendent of the color lab. Fulton, in turn, spoke briefly to his superior, Fred Reinhold. Al then made the phone call to Phil requesting an immediate conference and reported Phil's view to Bob. Al wanted to hold the disciplinary meeting before work stopped on the day shift, so that the inspector on that shift, who had rejected a sample from another batch of the same material as Lou, would know management's view of his and Lou's action before he left for the day. Bob agreed with Al on this. Consequently, Al, with Jack present, held the disciplinary meeting with Lou right away. Later the same day, Al talked with Phil Hamilton.

The next day Al spoke to Loftus as follows:

AL: Well, I agree thoroughly with what Phil told me yesterday. Fact-finding would have been the answer. I wanted to catch Lou cold when he came in. Fact-finding would still have caught him cold but—no final action.

You see, when we discussed it up in the lab, we assumed that Lou would do something, such as deny his error; that he did not do, so our solution was based on a wrong assumption. We went in without knowing what the story was. We were afraid we might go astray. . . . We didn't think of other attitudes. . . . just not enough thought. But it seemed clear-cut enough to go ahead with the action.

I did try to check with Phil; but he was tied up, and it

seemed like a routine check. Anyhow, it had gone up as high as the manufacturing superintendent here. I guess Bob Fulton felt a little bit that bringing Phil in on it would just complicate matters further. My own experience with Phil has been fine. He was fair and objective on the one third-step grievance I was in on.

Actually, none of us in the lab have the skills for handling the situation. I'd never have thought of Phil Hamilton's fact-finding idea. But it's not just the ABC of rules, like in the pamphlet guide to discipline that Phil has just issued; it's really a whole matter of procedure. It's a question of inexperience—like me: this is only the second discipline action I've been on. If I had more experience, maybe more flexibility . . . a meeting with Phil might have helped. . . .

During the next week the men involved in the situation held further conferences. At the direction of Fred Reinhold, Phil Hamilton met with Bob Fulton; and Al Lynch and Jack Shenk discussed what they would do about Lou the next time he "acted up." Also, Lou himself decided not to appeal his "verbal" through the union grievance machinery.

Towards the end of the week, Loftus learned that Phil Hamilton and the higher ranking supervisors in the S department had come to put considerable emphasis on the fact that Lou had talked to his superiors on the night shift at the time of his rejection of the material. Loftus realized that Lou had told him this when they first talked. The significance of this was that if the case came to arbitration, an arbitrator would be unlikely to rule against an inspector whose action had had the approval of management at the time it occurred. Al Lynch spoke of this to Loftus as follows:

AL: Say, you know, that situation with Lange has become more confused than ever. When I came back from talking with Phil last week, I told Bob [Fulton] what Phil had said. Bob went off and talked with Fred, then got some more data and talked to Phil. Among other things, Bob, in order to show Phil what part judgment plays in color, brought up the fact that a color-matching shift foreman had been present and even approved of Lou's decision. Lou had brought this up at our verbal meeting, but we just told him that he knew shift foremen were instructed not to overrule inspectors. This foreman thought the sample chip was outside the old limits, but he had no idea what the new limits were. The color-matching shift foremen are continually checking to see if they can improve the color of their material, but they're instructed that they can't overrule the inspector's decision.

This complicated things, because Phil feels that whenever any member of supervision overlooks a man's wrongdoing, it means that the act has been condoned and that the arbitrator probably won't go along with any discipline in such situations. At the end, after he heard about this from Bob, Phil thought that even the verbal was on risky grounds. Phil was not even sure that a verbal could be supported beyond a second stage grievance, if it came to that.

There are more angles to this, too. Jack Shenk is very young, and he's inexperienced, particularly in disciplinary action. Six months ago when Lou had acted up, we firmly intended to give a verbal; but Jack, whom I had told to run the meeting, wasn't experienced enough; the meeting got out of hand and no disciplinary action was taken. I thought Jack by this time could run a meeting better and give the warning, but Bob wanted me to do it. Bob was afraid of what Lou might do to get around Jack; Lou may be a social misfit, but he's pretty smart. So I handled the meeting.

Anyhow, Jack feels he's been by-passed, and I think he's right. I've been trying to delegate more responsibility to Jack, and I've been working with Bob on this. Jack's in a pretty rough spot, with too many conflicting lines of authority from everybody wanting to have their say about inspection. In general, Bob's been pretty good about this delegation, and it was really my fault the way this worked out. I should have insisted with Bob that Jack was the one to do it, even though both Bob and I agree that Jack still has some experience to gain.

Lou probably feels that I'm the dirty guy and the one trying to crucify him; but even if Jack had given the verbal, Lou would have felt I was behind it. I have no ill feelings towards Lou; it's just that I wanted him to shape up a bit or else not have him around. Since the incident, he has been acting very well.

The other line executives also talked to Loftus about their responsibilities in this case. John Keeney, the general superintendent of the S department, spoke as follows.

KEENEY: I didn't get involved in this case much. I just keep tabs on such problems. This one I first heard about from Phil Hamilton, then Fred. It seems to be mainly a problem of communication through the various levels of management. I have the impression that Al was too hasty, as well as was Bob, and that all the facts didn't get to Phil, either.

I've been in here only six months, so I'm doing the same

thing you are: I'm evaluating things. I've an initial impression that people here aren't spending as much time with the people under them as they should. People are being treated too much like machines. There must be more human relations down here, more morale, and we've got to get motivation from within, not from above.

The color lab is sort of different from much of the rest of the place; it's more a high-level technical place. Because of this, I think there's been a sort of country club atmosphere. It's been more lenient that it should be. I'm not sure this is true, but it's just my initial impression.

Overall, it seems to me that things have got to be tightened up and we've got to get some work out of these people, but at the same time, we've got to move closer to them. We've got to recognize them as people and not just as numbers down there.

Fred Reinhold, the manufacturing superintendent under John Keeney, was a chemical engineer, about forty years old. He had held his present job for a few years. He related that Bob Fulton had called to ask about the case but that he (Reinhold) had firmly delegated it to Bob. The call came immediately before Bob told Al to go ahead with the discipline session. Fred also told Loftus that Bob had not had the facts on Lou from the personnel file at the time he called. Fred went on:

FRED: I feel if a person doesn't ever make mistakes, he won't learn. So I though I'd stay out of the case and I think they did learn, learn more effectively than if I had told them what to do. The net effect was that Lou got the verbal warning as he should have, Bob and Al will clear with Phil on future cases, and a big thing is that Bob's relationship with Phil has improved a lot as a result of this thing. A long-term plus and no deficits that I can see. The relationships of Al, Bob, and Phil were the key things, rather than whether an hourly employee got a discipline for a small error. Al and Bob learned about discipline, about working with Phil, and in general about how to conduct themselves in such situations. I think they'll act a little less independently and conceitedly in the future. They'll get the facts, analyze the situation, and check out the rest of it, such as how it's done in the whole plant, before taking action.

I, myself, am inclined to say to someone below, "Well, I think this is the right direction. You come back and tell me what you think." It depends on whether you want things to be done efficiently and fast, with some risk, of course, of mistakes; or whether you want your emphasis to be on developing people, with the risk that it might take longer, and so forth. I feel better with the latter view. People feel better—they feel more part of the action, and I feel better that way too.

Al's original reaction, as I interpret it now, was that the verbal warning was very important, the priority item. My reaction was that this was a small part of the total situation. Whether you do it right off or wait, what kind of action to take, and all these questions aren't as important as how your action fits the whole plant disciplinary policy and the overall situation. You make your mistakes early and so develop better judgment to take care later of things of more responsibility. Call it training or call it human relations in reverse or anything you want, but that was what was important to me.

Bob Fulton, operating superintendent of the color lab, was a chemical engineer, about thirty-one years old. He had been with the company about ten years, much of this time in the color lab of the S department. He spoke to Loftus as follows:

BOB: First off, we don't have very many problems here, maybe five in seven years. The personnel department has done a relatively good job in getting to a more standard method of operation. But in the lab here, we don't have many cases, so we haven't paid much attention. I think our philosophy is older and basically inferior to that in use elsewhere in the company. Also there's the problem of color. It's a nebulous area for management to understand and requires different areas of knowledge than usually used elsewhere in the company. There's lots of judgment involved. And there can be errors in calculation and so forth. So you can't discipline a fellow for an error *per se*.

Now to come to this incident: Lou's a pretty high-strung fellow. We haven't developed him as an individual. We could do a lot better job if his abilities were fully developed. If the assistant foreman, Jack Shenk, is out, I'd just as soon have Lou on duty; he'll do as well, maybe better, than any of the other inspectors— when he's by himself. He's high-strung and on occasion he will resent instructions from supervisors. He will say, "I can always do just as I please around here." Nevertheless, left alone, he's good.

I suppose one place we went wrong on this was in not checking with personnel, but I wasn't familiar with the idea of using the personnel department to protect oneself. But Al and I thought we should act that day. If we'd told Lou that discipline was pending, there'd have been fireworks. Maybe letting a guy stew for a while is often a useful part of discipline, but with Lou's temperament, why, boy, we'd have had trouble.

I think my big error was when I told Al to go ahead without either knowing all the facts or even bothering to find out how he really felt. One trouble is that Al is a little bit overinclined to accept instructions from above. We all have to take orders, but he carries it a little too far. So in this case, I should either have gotten all the way in or else stayed out entirely.

I think Phil feels better about the situation now. I think he believes we're willing to learn from our mistakes. I learned a lot about Phil's position and about current plant practice. Overall, I'd say that Phil shows a lot of restraint for a staff man considering that he has strong feelings and a lot of responsibility. But I'm not sure he was aware of all the facts in this case. For instance, was Lou's action deliberate? I'd say no. There was no real proof that it was deliberate. His threats were general. I told Phil it shouldn't be a question of gathering everything together—Lou's overall attitude, other events, and so forth—and then hitting him over the head with it. If he's not doing his job right, then let's get him out; if that's not the case, let's keep other factors out of it.

It's funny. Usually people in this company are pretty good about saying what they mean. But in this case when Phil talked with Al on the phone, Phil left himself the right to sort of second guess Al later. In a way, Phil told Al to do it and yet not to do it and wait. Al was sort of mousetrapped.

Bob Fulton also discussed at length his personal philosophy of management. Some of his comments to Loftus on this subject follow:

BOB: I see my job as trying to find problems, define them, and guide solutions to them but not actually to solve them myself. I've set up my day so that I have no routine job. I spend 25 per cent of my time perhaps, just communicating, 75 per cent looking for ways to improve things. The more important something is, the more I get in it. I'd like to do the job so well that really someone else could replace me. That may sound funny, but it seems to me the thing to do is develop people. I think one gets job satisfaction from being able to work near the limit of one's ability, so this means that a lot of decisions are made below. I prefer to make as few decisions as I can. The tendency usually is in tight situations for each higher person to make the next lower person's decision. But if I went into it that way, I'd be merely over-participating and messing around.

My personal ambitions are changing and growing, but I don't like to think of myself as a plant manager or division manager or something like that. I like to think mainly of the next higher job and of course, if I can't do the job I'm presently in, I can't do the next higher one. To me, my most important year is this year. I don't want to degrade the present just to look at the future.

Perhaps this applies to my age. I'm only thirty-one, and my progress I guess has been average or maybe a little bit above average. But you really have to look at a twenty-year span: I've been a little above average in the first eight years but maybe in the next twelve years I won't be. I might have some dissatisfaction if I were forty and in my present job but I hope I won't be. If I have any ability to develop, it is the one of analysis: figuring out where the lab can go, how people can operate, and so forth. I don't know what would happen in engineering or research; I'm not a professional engineer—that is, I've never taken the qualifying tests. I would take training even to be able to pass them. In the present job—and I like it—I have no intention of needing to know or wanting to know the equations.

LOFTUS: Then you'd say your main interest is in analyzing.

BOB: Yes, all sorts of situations. They can all be analyzed. The success will depend upon the analysis of individuals; of setting a course so that you'll be right, let's say, 80 per cent of the time.

Jack Shenk, about twenty-six years old, had been with the company for about eight years, for the last two of which he had been the assistant foreman in inspection. He told Loftus that he thought the company was a very fair place to work. He was pleased that despite only a high school education, he was already an assistant foreman; he hoped eventually to become a full foreman. He spoke to Loftus of his relationship with Lou.

JACK: Right now Lou is sweet as a lamb. The main thing about him is that he wants to talk. Sometimes I think that if he just finds people he can talk with, he'll be all right. A lot depends on his mood. He can do an awfully nice job. When he's been taken down a peg, he'll be nice as a lamb and go into all sorts of details and do everything, even stuff that I'd normally have to do. Then there are times that he won't take any directions whatsoever. Sometimes, though, I can give him an explanation and he'll sort of ride along. There are lots of operating changes that affect us here; most of the men, once you explain the changes to them, will go along. Lou will, too, but every now and then . . . (shrugged his shoulders).

The idea behind the changes is to keep the production units going. It's related to what the customers want, the kind of end use, how badly the material is needed and so forth. Well, most of the men realize this. But Lou's opinion is that if the color is no good, then it's no good, with no half way about it. Oh, sometimes, instead, Lou will find out before the other people of the reason behind a change, and then he'll make a big thing out of knowing such information. The others won't sit on a pedestal like he will. But of course whenever reprimanded, he keeps quiet; he really shuts up once he's had it. I bet you we won't have another problem with him for a year. As a matter of fact, right now he's accepting some stuff which is really outside of the tolerance limits. Well, once he's adjusted and knows what the limits are supposed to be like, he'll be all set. But he resists change like lots of people, I guess. I did when I was an hourly worker and maybe I even do sometimes now. Isn't it human nature? Doesn't everybody resist change?

I know he pulled this thing last week for spite; I'm positive and so are other people around here. But you can't accuse a guy of that; so what are you going to do? I can't back down; I'm supposed to be his boss; he's not supposed to be mine. So I guess the way we handled it gets more out of him than any other way.

The more I think about Lou, the more he seems like these fellows that I've read articles about: the continual gripers who always shoot off their mouths and make trouble, but when you reprimand them on something concrete, they stay in line. The more I see of him, the more I think this applies. Next time, boy, I'll nail him. I'll pull in the evidence and hit him hard on it and won't let him shoot off his mouth about it at all.

Al handled this discipline meeting with Lou, but I told Al later that Lou was my man and I should have handled it. Al agreed, and since the meeting he's left the situation all to me. If something comes up again with Lou, I think I can keep Lou in line; I can just bring up this verbal and then he'll stay in line.

Loftus also talked again with Lou Lange and Phil Hamilton. After Lange had talked again at some length about the technical aspects of the work, Loftus asked if anything new had developed about the incident of the previous week.

LOU: No, nothing. You know, that was just a verbal on that situation, so I don't care. One of those just makes you act real good for the next couple of months; I'm not even going to bother to appeal it.

Loftus also talked again with Phil Hamilton.

PHIL: The main thing I am working for is a consistent disciplinary attitude and a consistent manner for administering discipline. If it isn't consistent, you get work stoppages, lots of cases going to arbitration, and things like that. But there's lots of potential for inconsistency, since there are at least 150 men who are more or less directly involved in administering the discipline.

This thing of consistency goes beyond just discipline, too. It applies to handling any personnel situations, the handling of people, even the attitudes we have toward people. For instance, we want all the foremen in the place to respect the individual rights of their workers. This is sort of the basic fundamental of human relations. If they don't respect the individuals, they'll never get rapport.

Some companies have a completely fixed discipline system—so many days absent, a verbal; so many more, then a letter; and so forth. But there are drawbacks to this. One, it disregards the individual, a man's home troubles, things like that. Also, lots of people are willing to go right up to the edge before they'll change their behavior. So we try to fit the discipline to the situation.

My main work is advising and counseling the supervisors after the infraction has happened. The main people are the first-line supervisors, you know. They're the ones who see the infractions and have to deal with the people who commit them. I think this new guide on disciplinary procedure will help them a great deal. It tells the supervisors the things to look for, the kinds of evidence, how to handle a verbal meeting, things like that. It doesn't give any new procedures, but it brings them all together and offers some helpful questions they should answer whenever an incident occurs.

I was pretty direct with Bob Fulton [referring to the meeting held at the direction of Fred Reinhold], just as I had been with Al Lynch, perhaps more than is usually the case in a staff relationship with line supervisors. But this time there was the broader responsibility of preventing anyone from doing anything that would jeopardize the discipline program throughout the whole company. I had to call them to task, or otherwise they'd act this way again and things would get even worse. In the case of Bob Fulton, of course, my action was taken at the request of his own supervisors, Fred Reinhold and John Keeney. I spent three hours with Bob and gave him just about a lecture on the fundamentals of discipline. I think I gave him some greater insight and showed him the need for going about such things more objectively and with more planning. We attributed the mistakes to going in prematurely without all the facts. It may seem strange that two men like Fulton and Lynch could get in such a wrong position, but in highly skilled job areas like theirs, it is quite rare to get a discipline situation. And discipline is the sort of thing for which judgment comes only with experience. I was actually contributory on the problem. I presumed they knew the basic procedure on discipline, but they didn't.

On the Lange incident itself, it's now developed that the discipline action was actually not too far out of line. It turned out that a color-matching shift foreman had actually approved, or at least gone along with, Lou's rejection decision. No arbitrator would uphold our discipline once that got out. "Management must manage," they say.

CASE V-3. Kestler, Dobson and Cartwright (A)

In 1959 three consultants, who had worked together for several years as members of a larger organization, established their own independent management consulting firm, Kestler, Dobson and Cartwright. The offices were located in the suburbs of a large midwestern city. After five years the company, now consisting of five full-time consultants, had evolved an original and consistent point of view towards their practice and towards their client relationships.

In their practice, and in both their private conversations and published accounts of their work, the associates emphasized that a number of central propositions, amounting to a beginning action pro-

This case was made possible by the cooperation of members of a consulting firm which remains anonymous. It was prepared by Charles M. Hampden-Turner under the direction of Arthur N. Turner as the basis for class discussion. Cases are not designed to present illustrations of either correct or incorrect handling of administrative problems. All names have been disguised. Copyright © 1964 by the President and Fellows of Harvard College.

gram, could be applied to a client organization which was seeking help. They did not claim that a single set of principles could cure all managerial ills; but rather that there were general principles of managerial health and success, and that concentration upon these dimensions in the form of goals and overall objectives, could lead to achievement and satisfaction.

A brief outline of these operating principles is given below. These will then be illustrated and supplemented by quotations from the consultants' written accounts of their work. Finally a letter written to the case writer contains additions to this account and also illustrates some operating principles being applied to the case writer.

One principle that sharply differentiated the consultants from the majority in their field was their objection to the usual procedure of diagnosis of the clients' ills, followed by a prescription. It was argued that the whole concept of diagnosis presupposed an illness and this was a misleading analogy. Indeed the majority of clients were not "sick" at all in this sense. A better analogy might be that of an automobile, perhaps running smoothly and in good repair, but realizing only a fraction of its potential power. To focus on what was wrong with an organization was a negative approach, dispiriting to client and consultant alike. Moreover, the consultants believed that to supply a client with critical insights, from the consultant's standpoint, could often impede understanding. The client should be allowed to face problems in the way he saw them, advised and supported by the consultant. In this way problems would be recognized as and when the client felt competent to deal with them.

From this principle, emerged another, namely that a depressing diagnosis strengthened those forces that resisted change. Such a diagnosis made the environment seem more threatening and depressing and reduced the confidence of the client in his own resources for coping with his problems.

In addition, the consultants stressed that feelings of competence were an outgrowth of achievement, leading to even greater achievement, in a self-reinforcing and cumulative cycle. As managers learned to achieve the limited objectives they set for themselves, a process of increasing commitment to ever bolder and more challenging tasks would result. In this way success would breed the self-confidence, with the competence and the responsibility to tackle even bigger projects, and the unused creativity and ingenuity lying dormant within managers would be called forth as every man came to experience himself as increasingly capable and self-reliant. Such a program involved both self-discovery for the individual and growing mutual respect among participants as they demonstrated their increasing skill in assisting each other.

A further principle stressed that management should work together in goal-setting, evaluating, and planning groups, wherein individuals publicly committed themselves to objectives and deadlines, while drawing on the total resources of the group to accomplish specific goals. In this manner every resource could be mustered, needed assistance from various departments could be pledged, the interdependence of each upon the other could be dramatized, and the full weight of infectious enthusiasms and mutal support could create an environment wherein each individual felt secure enough to take initiative and aim high.

The consultants frequently stressed this necessity to aim high at "tough objectives." It was in accomplishing tough objectives by a system of "challenge and response" that managers "paced" one another. A tough, though attainable objective was really a compliment, a vote of confidence in the ability of a subordinate or colleague to master the problem. People would see themselves in the light of how others treated them. Managers who invested each other with confidence and challenge could assist each other in meeting those challenges. So could a consultant by a similar attitude to his client.

Another notable advantage of group target-setting, planning, and problem solving, included a widening of individual managers' horizons until they saw the "big picture." The contribution of a single department to an overall objective could be seen in perspective, and this helped to avoid empire building, interdepartmental strife, and defensive "department-centered" behavior. A department's contribution could be viewed as a means to an end rather than an end in itself. Every manager was obliged to consider fully the problems of others and his own contribution to solving or exacerbating these problems.

This particular type of joint planning also restricted "buck passing," as numerous responsibilities were volunteered and self-assigned, with a collective understanding of where the responsibility lay and public acceptance of such responsibility.

The very focus on "objectives," was a more powerful stimulus to action than a focus on "problems." The latter term suggested blame and guilt for some existing failure, and reeked of anxiety and defensiveness. On the other hand to focus on objectives was to see your way clear of recrimination and to explain your ideas and solutions rather than anticipate brickbats. In the very act of planning each man was gaining the chance to master his environment, and to anticipate and control events, rather than reacting to them.

Managing by total objectives, seen in this light, is essentially a program for planned change. Change is inevitable in human life and social systems. As such it may become fearful adaptation to threat and anxiety, or an exhilarating experience in mastery. Mastery is only achieved by those who know where they are, whence they wish to travel, how and when they will arrive, and their progress along the way. Men do not have a choice of whether to change but of *how* to change. They can do this purposefully, or they can *be* changed arbitrarily or accidentally. They can steer or stagger.

Untapped within the personnel of many an organization lies the creative energy and ingenuity to shape their organizational environment. Defensive reactions are nearly always limited in range, closely constrained, unthinking, unplanned and desperate. In contrast, long-range, integrated and purposeful action unlocks the courage, responsibility, and resourcefulness of those who can see clear ahead and without fear.

The key to such forward motion is to utilize rather than analyze. Many clients know what the trouble is but use this insight as a rationale for inertia. The more expert and the more vocal is their self-analysis, the more convincing becomes their excuse for inaction. They discover a unique satisfaction in being uniquely screwed up. In the consultants' view, health and growth are both confirmed and enhanced in progress towards organizational needs, rather than sitting and contemplating the enormity of one's failings.

Consultants who engage in a mammoth search for "the problem" may so frighten a client that the consultant ends by diagnosing the very rigidity and anxiety caused by his own investigation, and thus spends many well-paid months examining his own shadow.

This very brief summary of the consultants' operating principles will now be illustrated and qualified by examples from their own written accounts of their work, and other documents which molded their opinions.

Action research as an inseparable process

Crucial to the evolvement of the company's basic thinking was a speech by Nevitt Sanford which impressed James Kestler back in 1958. Talking about Freud's greatest and most lasting contribution to method, Nevitt Sanford said:

> By method I mean the whole contractual arrangement according to which both the therapist and patient become investigators, and both objects of careful observation and study; in which the therapist can ask the patient to face the truth because he, the therapist, is willing to try his best to face it himself; in which

investigation and treatment are inseparable aspects of the same humanistic enterprise. This method changed the whole conception of doctor–patient relationship, and it is in my view the best model for all those human relationships in which an expert in the psychological and social sciences undertakes in a face-to-face relationship a scientific approach to the problem of persons or groups. . . .

It is a widely held view . . . that it is impossible for the social scientist to function simultaneously as a researcher and a social therapist. In saying that the two roles cannot in fact be separated, I believe I am upholding the classical position of action research. . . .

The Cleveland Institute—A case in point

This case situation illustrates how the consultants began the improvement process in a medical institute. In this case, the management of operations was already good, better than most. The management knew, however, that in order for it to begin to plan its future development, top management time must increasingly be devoted to researching the future. To do this required placing increasingly heavy operating responsibilities on the department managers, supervisors, and employees. They would have to carry out daily operations with increasing effectiveness and control. The operations improvement program was designed to help accomplish these objectives.

There follow extracts from a joint report written by John Billings, vice president of the Cleveland Institute of Tropical Medicine, and Dick Cummings, M.B.A., of Kestler, Dobson and Cartwright. The Institute's administration had felt over-worked and over-loaded with problems of organization, morale, motivation, and efficiency. In a search for some new solution, the administration called in Kestler, Dobson and Cartwright, who introduced their concepts and operating principles in a planned program of challenge and response.

Adapted from work done by Kestler, Dobson and Cartwright in industry, the experimental approach has been put to work at the Institute in a series of projects created collaboratively by the staff and the consultants. Projects are built around assignments undertaken by managers to organize and focus the efforts of their groups in tackling some tough new jobs and getting them accomplished.

Creating and organizing projects generally involves these initial steps:

1. Interviews in the departments concerned to get everyone's ideas on where improvements are needed most.

2. Identification of some key first-step targets—changes, improvements which people believe are needed, which they should be able to accomplish in a relatively short time, and which will themselves lead to further accomplishments.

3. Assignments—to the group as a whole and to individuals—defining what needs to be done and suggesting ways of getting started.

4. A series of planning meetings in which managers and supervisors launch the work and review progress. Operations improvement projects provide a way to begin this process in an organized fashion. In essence, this approach consists of a planned series of controlled experiments in managing new kinds of effort in a department or unit, each designed to produce a specific tangible improvement in the operation and help a manager increase his competence and effectiveness.

(There followed a "reconnaissance" in which "everyone welcomed the opportunity to talk out problems and ideas.")
. . . it was clear that matters related to the work of the department, problems associated with getting it done as well as it should be done, were already of great concern:

"We're not turning out the quality of work we should. There are too many interruptions, changes and half-done jobs." "Improper and incomplete requisitions are a major problem for us. We spend too much time tracing them, trying to find out what's needed, and we fall behind on our tests."

And of course, there were gripes as well:

"Our boss never lets up. He really pours the work on. We never can get to see our boss. I've got a lot of things to talk to him about but he never seems to have time."

Most significant, however, was the wealth of ideas and positive readiness to help make changes in operations.

"We could save a lot by simplifying the file numbering system on X-rays. We could change our system to agree with account numbers and eliminate a lot of confusion."

"I've been experimenting with some ways to control the dressing sets on the floors. I haven't yet found the fool-proof method. But I know other girls have this problem and I'd like to know what they've tried and how it works."

"We could tighten up our screening procedures to prevent duplicate requisitions from getting into the work flow."

GETTING STARTED: THE WRITTEN CHARGE OF RESPONSIBILITY

The data collected in the interviews were analyzed by the department head and the consultant to identify some key targets, each in an area of work in which:

—immediate gains could be made
—there was consensus among the department heads and supervisors as to the importance of the problem
—solutions existed or were close at hand

Targets like these were chosen:

—reduction of duplication of work in Radiology
—reduction of breakage and loss in Dietary
—reduced loss of laboratory unit equipment
—streamlining of accounting operations.

In all, ten departments chose initial projects. Identification of the targets led to formulation of written assignments. For example, the Director of Research charged three day–supervisors with the responsibility for creating a joint plan for improving the control of research unit equipment so as to reduce losses. Supervision felt this was a key problem and they had some notions on how to tackle it.

(The projects were launched and reviewed by project group meetings.)

. . . there was an air of excitement . . . In many cases supervisors had done a lot of homework before coming to the meetings. They brought along written lists of ideas and descriptions of the problems.

(Upon returning to their departments the supervisors had to ask their subordinates for help). . . .

For example, in Dietary, the department manager realized that efforts to reduce the losses of silverware, and breakage of china, only scratched the surface. Great gains were also to be sought in the area of food costs. This effort required everyone's help. All employees were called to a meeting where the department manager asked for their help. They responded with enthusiasm and responsible action.

Thus, in addition to immediate steps taken by supervisors to stop silverware and china losses, workers in the canteen devised a better way to count and control chinaware. Dieticians took on some operating assignments. A supervisor and a cook were given a long-term project to review recipes. Receiving procedures have been tightened up. Work has begun on development of better control information for the department.

In each case the initial step seemed modest in itself. The point is that its achievement represented breaking out of a state of inertia—in some cases a change from a situation in which "nothing can be done" to one in which people found they could move. In other cases it represented an acceleration of pace—a change from the belief that "we're doing all we can" to "we can do more."

Step by step, the momentum is picking up. More and more people are becoming involved. The project targets are becoming more ambitious. People are shooting for bigger gains, taking on more sophisticated problems, organizing and planning work further into the future.

The problem of escapes

All the consultants in Kestler, Dobson and Cartwright were alerted to join in solving the problem of escape mechanisms whereby the manager might only pretend to confront the problem, or to hide behind pseudo-problems in order to avoid confronting the real ones. These escapes were described by Mr. Kestler as a central target of his consulting practice. His discussion of the problem follows:

ESCAPE AREA 1: ACTING OUT

A manager decides that the union leaders with whom he is dealing are unreasonable and agreement cannot be reached. He is angry and frustrated and decides that a strike is neccessary to "clear the air and bring people to their senses." This manager is achieving gratifications from what he rationalizes as being good for the company or "necessary." In fact his behavior results more from his own personality than from the needs of the situation. We said that a considerable amount of managerial energy was thus diverted. There are three ways in which this occurs. This case—in which a man clearly is working out a personal need but rationalizing it as "good for the company"—represents a category of behaviors called "Acting Out."

Aggression was used in this illustration. Preoccupation with competition between departments, sections, individuals which becomes destructive and interferes with company functioning is often described as "healthy competition." Refusal to accept the existence of a problem is another way of dealing with difficult issues. Another common example of acting out is the "nice guy," the manager who is more preoccupied with being loved than with getting a job done. He is afraid that someone will get mad at him or resent him and he spends a large portion of his managerial energies in avoiding this.

Many more examples could be given of this first area of energy dissipation, Acting Out.

This first category is unique and contrasts with the other two ways in that:

—the behavior is generally characteristic of the individual, rather than the organization, and because of this,

—it is often quite easily observed and understood by others in the organization.

Neither of these is true of the other two varieties of escapes.

ESCAPE AREA 2: BUSYNESS

("If I only had the time . . .") One of the greatest sources of frustration—as seen by managers themselves—is the burden of detail that consumes their hours. Every organization—whether moving forward with breathtaking strides or at the brink of bankruptcy—has an abundant supply of current problems, burning issues, minor conflicts, immediate decisions, and tactical issues that cry for attention. The supply is inexhaustible; organizations can always generate them faster than they can be dealt with—and the creation of more machinery or people to handle them . . . simply leads to the creation of *more* such problems and issues.

Managers claim that these trivial aspects of their job are anathema. "If I could only figure out how to get some of this nonsense off my back," they say, "I could be spending my time where I should, on planning, goal-setting, evaluating progress, long-range planning, etc."

But, alas, this is a reversed view of the situation. A man is not going to get rid of something he desperately needs. It is not that managers are forced to fill up their days with trivialities; the opposite is true; the real challenges of managing are so difficult and anxiety-provoking, that managers fill up their days (or permit them to become filled up) with detail and trivia. At least, when you've decided to buy a $20,000 machine, instead of a $22,000 machine, you've "accomplished" something tangible, real, comforting.

For some executives, the real challenges of managing are so threatening that they arrange to keep themselves frightfully busy for seventy or eighty hours a week, even more. This protects them from having even a bit of time to think about the job they are not doing. One of the most serious consequences of this form of escape is that it prevents organizations from ever solving certain problems that require long-range solutions. Conscious, planned changes in the fundamental nature of a business are much more rare than are accidental responses to changing market conditions and pressures, for example. Certain labor relations difficulties that are amenable to a five or ten year planned solution continue to fester.

We have never seen a manager who had trouble with time or with pressures or with details once he had a real grasp of the job of managing. Nor have we ever seen a manager "get rid of" the unimportant aspects of his work without learning a new approach to managing.

This form of escape, as well as the one which is discussed next, is extremely tenacious, difficult to isolate and resistant to change. First, entire groups or total organizations may unconsciously be allied in utilizing the comforts provided by busyness. Secondly, the rationalizations which justify such behavior have a power and logic difficult to cope with. (In a hospital it is the "urgent needs of very sick patients." In a newspaper it is "planning or no, the paper *must* hit the streets tonight"; in a refinery it is, "Look, we have a million gallons of oil moving through this place . . .".)

ESCAPE AREA 3: THE RITUAL OF MODERN
ORGANIZATION LIFE

Parkinson has chided organizations on ritualistic aspects of their workings: activities which seem to be nonfunctional organizationally but which perpetuate themselves and waste large amounts of organization time.

All that we can add to Parkinson is to say that even he fails to perceive by a large amount how much of organization life actually falls into this category.

Here is a random list of activities and mechanisms which frequently are used—unwittingly of course, but used nevertheless—for the excuse they offer people to pretend they are working toward organization objectives and at the same time permit them to avoid almost completely the realities associated with such a purpose: organization charts, management committees, development programs, departmental realignments, supervisory titles, manuals of procedure, and so on.

This is not an attack on these tools of management. It is simply to say that organizations have become very adept at using these tools—and practically every other management tool—in a fashion that fails to produce results.

How many management meetings serve no real purpose other than to give the participants an audience for an exhibition of their skills, cleverness and adroitness or to work off steam or to get away from the scene of real problems? How many staff man-hours have been devoted to organization studies that can never dare to confront the organization with its real conflicts and issues? And so forth.

Here again, as with the busyness syndrome, these practices resist analysis and change because:

they always appear to be very important and useful—their titles and definitions help create that illusion;

the entire organization or, at the very least, major groups in the power structure are engaged together in hiding behind these defenses.

Much of the work of Kestler, Dobson and Cartwright was seen by them as an effort to "break through" this tendency of organizations to escape from important issues. Occasionally the goal-setting procedures which the consultants introduced might themselves be subverted by a client into a new mechanism for escape, so that the consultant ran the risk of unwittingly helping the client to identify objectives which were actually irrelevant to the major issues that needed to be faced. However, in most cases in which this form of "ritual goal-setting" was encountered the process of repeatedly reviewing progress in a group setting obliged the individuals involved to face the reality of what they were doing and to account for errors. A man might seize upon a goal impulsively and charge away, but continued reality-testing would underline for everyone's benefit the emptiness of using the goal as a mere slogan.

When an early rough draft of the case material outlined above was shown to the consultants, the case writer received the following letter.

KESTLER, DOBSON AND CARTWRIGHT

Memo to: Charles Hampden-Turner, Harvard Business School
From: James Kestler and Dick Cummings

We think you've made a good beginning on the case. It's no easy job, we're sure, to try to make a cogent summary out of the mass of writing, case materials and conversations you've had to deal with. The basic approach you have chosen—citing some basic propositions on the theory of the practice and illustrating how these propositions are put to work—seems to be a sensible way to handle the material and it should make for a very interesting piece.

We believe a considerable amount of work needs to be done to develop the propositions and the example. We've jotted down some notions here for you as a kind of outline of the propositions we think should be stressed.

There are some generalizations, based on a considerable body of experience, which form the basic working hypotheses of the consultants.

1. Most organizations vastly underestimate their capacities for achievement.

2. This underestimation sets in motion a whole series of forces, expectations and demands which impose false ceilings on the levels of performance in the organization.

3. There is an enormous amount of ritual, escapism, wasted and dissipated effort in organizations which, though it keeps people busy, prevents them from focusing on the fundamental and usually most exciting issues facing the organization.

4. Most of the people in organizations have far more to offer than is ever expected or demanded of them. As a result, there is in most organizations a vast untapped reservoir of energy and talent available to be committed to making major strides forward.

5. Traditional approaches to improving organizational performance—namely, identifying problems and curing what's wrong—perpetuate the trap the organization creates for 'tself. Solving one problem after another simply keeps before the organization a depressing picture of its limitations and inadeq acies. There is no way to discover the untapped strengths in the organization and therefore no basis for building confidence, for raising aspirations, for calling upon the untapped resources which must be put to work if the organization is going to make real progress.

6. A better approach is based on assessment, exploitation and development of the strengths of the organization and its latent potentials for advancement. Investigations taken from this point of view reveal almost always a considerable amount of readiness to make advances immediately. A consulting study

should, we believe, aim to identify these positive forces and decide how to mobilize them as quickly as possible to produce some new, successful achievement. Doing this can put before the management a new perception of itself—not as an organization with innumerable difficult problems, but as an organization with unsuspected capacities. A new sense of confidence results. This leads to taking successively bolder steps. A process of successful achievement begins to build and to spread. Building step by step toward ever more ambitious achievement, the process is unending, being limited only by the imagination of the management.

7. Tough, far-reaching, inspiring goals are by far the best motivators of high performance.

8. Work toward goals like these yields satisfactions which far surpass those generally provided by "human relations" and other approaches designed to make work more palatable. Very demanding, exciting goals infuse all work with a new sense of meaning and satisfaction.

9. In order to create goals which stir men's imaginations the chief executive must set his sights on the highest possible aspirations for his organization. To create broad scale commitment to the achievement of these goals, he must share with his entire organization the job of setting and organizing to achieve these goals.

Charles, can you develop these ideas in the case? Send us the next draft and let us jot down some notes. Then we might get together to take it the next step.

We look forward to hearing from you.

June 12, 1964

Kestler, Dobson and Cartwright (B)

The following extracts from letters and internal memos were copied from the files of Kestler, Dobson and Cartwright. Outlined is the process by which the consultants set out to gain the confidence and the account of a well-known international manufacturer of foodstuffs. The short term aim of the consultants was to be employed regionally in one of the many plants of the company. From this staging post, progress in fruitful collaboration could be expanded in ever wider applications. James Kestler personally handled the protracted negotiations.

His initial contact was George Duggan, an industrial psychologist from the Houston headquarters. From this meeting and a casual exchange of letters and lunches over a period of eighteen months, Mr. Kestler learned something of the company's problems and attitudes. He explained some of his ideas to George, who seemed interested. It transpired that George was head of the management development section. With the recent formation of the consulting group under its new title of Kestler, Dobson and Cartwright, a period of more serious negotiations began.

On September 10, 1961, Charles Dobson, an associate of Mr. Kestler, wrote the following letter to the president of the manufacturing company.

Dear Mr. Hutchinson:

The greatest gratification for most company presidents comes from setting very high goals for their organizations, and then making swift, sure progress toward those goals.

Consultants may be employed when help is needed in the process. By tradition, they are expected to pinpoint weaknesses and to recommend ways of correcting them.

Our group has taken a somewhat different tack: We prefer to work with top managers who feel they *already* understand their problems, and who want help in accelerating the pace of movement toward the goals they *know* should be achieved.

Of course, major progress always requires major change,

This case was made possible by the cooperation of members of a consulting firm which remains anonymous. It was prepared by Charles M. Hampden-Turner under the direction of Arthur N. Turner as the basis for class discussion. Cases are not designed to present illustrations of either correct or incorrect handling of administrative problems. All names have been disguised. Copyright © 1964 by the President and Fellows of Harvard College.

and resistance to change exists in every organization. But in every organization there are also pressures *for* change, and *for* improvement. We work with chief executives to help find these positive pressures and put them to work.

In short, we are in business to help managers get more gratification and reward from their work—more of what they want. We find this extremely gratifying ourselves.

I would like your reaction to what I've said about our approach. Do you wonder how it actually works in practice? I'd like the opportunity to tell you, with illustrations, how it does work. I'll call to see if we can arrange an appointment.

The researcher was quite unable to trace any reply to this letter. In any event this line of communication was not continued.

EXTRACTS FROM LETTER TO GEORGE DUGGAN
FROM J. K.

October 10, 1961

Dear George:

Our group specializes in helping management devise and carry out strategies to accomplish the results they *want* to accomplish. Three features distinguish this work from that of management consultants or management engineers:

The emphasis in management consulting is on solving company problems, overcoming weaknesses or ailments. Our work concentrates, from the outset, on where management wants the company to move, and on how to get there.
The traditional consultant's value is based on his possession of special knowledge, skill, or experience, and his consequent ability to fill a gap in the company's management. The aim of our work is to find opportunities for mobilizing the abilities of the people *in* the organization, and to help create demands that call forth the full measure of these abilities.
Our assignments are defined as collaborative undertakings with our clients in the achievement of specific gains—in contrast, for example, with an assignment to analyze and report on a company situation or to make recommendations to management about what it ought to do.

In every organization there is resistance to change. But in most there are also strong forces *for* change—waiting to be discovered and put to work. And it is the methods for accomplishing this that we are now engaged in discovering. The results of our efforts have been very rewarding and gratifying.

Perhaps we can meet to talk about some of these issues. I would also enjoy becoming better informed about your recent work and some of the innovations you've been doing.

George Duggan's reply to this letter did not comment on the principles enunciated. However he suggested a lunch meeting.

EXTRACTS FROM SALES VISIT REPORT (A DIARY KEPT BY J. K.): LUNCH WITH GEORGE DUGGAN

March 1, 1962

George heads up a small group of industrial psychologists who function mostly in management development, and to a certain extent in executive selection and recruitment. Having met him in the train and having exchanged the "let's get together for lunch" remarks, I did get in touch with him, since George is a nice guy whom I like and one who moves around the executive development circuit.

It turns out that George is in the midst of a great struggle, a struggle that is most easily described by saying that he has a vague dissatisfaction with what he has been doing and is searching for a more effective approach in terms that pretty well parallel what we have been successful in doing. Because of this coincidental match between his great preoccupation and the area of our own focus and skill and experience the conversation was rather lively.

We decided to meet again to really work at some of the concepts to see if I could help him specifically with strategies and tactics. I was more than a little surprised when at the very end he said something like "when we bring in outside consultants, Jim, we have to have some pretty good documentation and I want you to be thinking in these terms between now and our next lunch." I had really rather expected just the opposite from George; namely, some apologies for helping himself to our time and ideas without being able to guarantee anything accruing to us. I wouldn't count this egg as hatched by any means but it does indicate a certain value to being able to respond to people in terms of the thing that is really on their mind.

FURTHER LUNCH MEETING WITH GEORGE DUGGAN (SALES VISIT REPORT)

April 24, 1962

George picked up immediately at the point where we had ended our last conversation. He told in some detail of his efforts to make a more substantial contribution to the goals of this organization.

Some time ago George gathered up his courage and made an appointment with the president. He went before him, with a colleague (the head of operations research, a man with whom he seems to enjoy fairly close collaborative relationships) and made a fairly lengthy presentation. But the president's response was: "You are giving me platitudes and theories and what I need are methods, approaches, and answers."

I tried to sum up the situation in these terms: "When you work at the lower levels, George, you're able to be very helpful to guys who are trying to solve specific problems. But when you get to the top of the organization you can't go very much beyond exhortation—and this is the challenge to turn exhortation into practical strategy construction." This hit the nail on the head.

Once again, toward the end of the conversation, George brought up the question of bringing consultants into the company. He said that he himself faced the question of whether to expand his own staff or to use the more flexible resources of consultants as they were needed to accomplish his purposes. He described a number of attempts he has made to bring consultants in. It is pretty much the standard routine. He introduces the consultant to a line officer who has some problems. The consultant asks some questions. The consultant writes a "proposal." Apparently this has not been very successful, since very few consultants have been hired.

I bridged the gap between the two topics of conversation in the following terms: I told George that what he was attempting to do was very challenging and stimulating to us. We believe that he is taking a pioneering step in the direction that must be the one that staff people will take in the future. Our chief interest in this situation is in trying to find a way in which we could bring our experiences and skills to bear in a way that would help him accomplish this, rather than in a parallel or independent effort. He was very pleased with this definition of approach and agreed that that made great sense. I suggested that we proceed by trying to define some specific areas of progress—and told him once again about the error reduction project and a few of the other operations improvement efforts—and that is the next task. Once such a project is defined, the potential for our participation will be evident.

Duggan will be out of town for several weeks during the rest of April and I am to contact him the first week in May.

Much encouraged by his recent meeting with George Duggan, James Kestler wrote him a long letter. The letter consisted of a determined effort to show how George's problems could be solved by the use of the general operating principles which the consultants had evolved. The letter, dated May 6, 1962, concluded with the following paragraph:

> In brief, at our meeting on the 24th you and I should concentrate (1) on discovering specific opportunities in the form of tough company jobs that need to be accomplished, and (2) on designing methods for translating those opportunities into concrete success experiences for some key executives. We should set as our own tough objective, being creative enough so that success in the initial projects will inevitably lead to subsequent, constantly broadening undertakings. Each of these will be more far-reaching in scope and time. It should not be too much to expect this process—within a few years—to result in significant advances in the methods by which corporate goals are established and a corollary heightening of productiveness throughout the organization.
>
> I look forward to seeing you next week.

J. K.'s MEETING WITH DUGGAN (SALES VISIT REPORT)

June 3, 1962

It should be noted for the record that, although George did not say so, the letter was off the target somewhat. It was aimed at operational improvements rather than at the more sophisticated problems which are concerning George and are in the nature of top level corporate goal setting, policy and organization structure and strategy. However, we weren't that far off that progress was blocked. It does emphasize again a fact noted by us in recent work that we have not yet had very much experience in dealing with corporate problems at the top level of the management ranks.

After an hour and a half or so of lunch and conversation he began to conclude our meeting by saying that after he was successful in achieving progress in the areas that we had discussed there would inevitably come a time when some consulting help would be needed to assist the divisions in carrying out the programs that resulted. At that point he wanted us to be in the wings, ready for our curtain call. I was somewhat surprised by this because I thought I had gotten across to him our desire to participate at the immediate and critical stage of the work and not at the later stages. I responded quickly by saying "That is the point at which we usually suggest to our clients that they call in special consultants" and went on to explain all that I thought I had explained in the past and what I thought had been understood, that our interest was in the creation of strategy at the corporate level—not in carrying out bits and pieces of programs.

It seemed unfortunate that this crucial point was discovered at the end of the meeting rather than at the beginning. However, I did the best I could in about fifteen or twenty minutes and emphasized very strongly that our interests and our skill all pointed to working with him immediately on the strategy questions.

He reminded me that his counterpart in the systems methods and organization structure area, Hugh Lejeune, would have to be consulted on this since the two of them had been collaborating very closely on developments to this point. I suggested a meeting, perhaps among the three of us. George said he would discuss the matter with Hugh and report the results.

As I left I was not entirely certain how convinced George was himself and had some doubts as to his salesmanship with a third party.

TELEPHONE CONVERSATION WITH GEORGE DUGGAN

June 17, 1962

It turned out that my pessimism was unfounded as was my lack of faith in George. He did a very credible job in talking with Lejeune. I will attempt to quote the conversation as I recall it in George's own terms:

"I started to chat with Hugh about many of the strategy problems that we faced together and in about ten or fifteen minutes it was quite clear that we had some very, very difficult problems to solve. When we got mired down in the complexity of it I introduced your name and our conversations. I told him about the possibility of using some consulting help on these problems. At first, Hugh's reaction was negative; if we, with all our experience in this company and our personal acquaintanceship with the key executives and our understanding of how the thing functions, etc. etc., haven't been able to make more progress, how is an outsider to come into the situation cold and do something that we have found impossible? At that point I explained to him," continued George, "that it was not your intention to come in and do it in our place, but to work with us in helping us see some new avenues and approaches. We've been going around the same old circles so many times maybe we are getting stale and maybe what we need is some fresh perspective and some new insights. At this, Hugh's attitude changed and he became quite receptive to the idea. He does want to meet you."

We talked a little bit about how to set that up and I tried to work for a two-way meeting between Lejeune and myself without actually telling Duggan I did not want him present. He must have been leaning in this direction himself, because he seized the suggestion and responded to it.

J. K.'s LUNCH MEETING WITH HUGH LEJEUNE (SALES VISIT REPORT)

July 20, 1962

Hugh's title, which I have forgotten, has words in it that seem to include manager, control, systems, procedures. That should convey the impression that his title conveyed to me. The fact of the matter is that he and George appear to be the two key staff people in the corporation and the two of them are allied in an effort to awaken top corporate management to the possibilities of new ways of managing. Lejeune's own skills and background, as well as those in the small group which he supervises, seem to focus on operations research, business mathematics and statistics, systems and procedures, and the use of computers and data processing in the work of management.

The first hour or hour and a half of conversation consisted in his talking about the company and his efforts to contribute to top management functioning. He is a rather reserved man, slow in his speech and, while one would be wrong in saying he does not have a sense of humor, there was no sign of a chuckle or a twinkle in his eye for the entire meeting. It took me some time to discover that he is a very bright, perceptive and solid citizen, one who is very sophisticated about corporate management and the facilitation of corporate change. Quite a few of his concepts and terms paralleled our own with amazing precision. He talked about such things as the unwillingness or inability of top management to put heavy enough demands on the organization, to provide goals and directions for the functioning of lower management, to provide a framework for management of the divisions and various functions. He talked about the need for much more imaginative and bold market research and market thinking. He talked about the need for looking out beyond immediate cost results.

At appropriate intervals I would try to summarize and reflect what I was hearing. I did this in terms with which our own group is very familiar and on several occasions he seemed somewhat surprised that ideas with which he has been having such a difficult time, and is not entirely certain about his ability to communicate, seem to be so well summarized by me. Thus, the conversation went for quite some time until we went to lunch.

J. K. AND GEORGE DUGGAN (SALES VISIT REPORT)

October 10, 1962

1. George was elated because a major change in the organization of the sales division is being carried out. He describes it as an intellectual brainchild of his, three years in evolution. As he describes it, it is nothing more nor less than a pure and neat example of movement toward the management by total objectives idea. (Now production managers have stakes only in sales and profit of own product. Changes will gear them to *corporation* goals and directions. I will send reprints to Duggan and Lejeune.)

2. Discussed the "task force" method of management development he's trying. The essence is to give a group of managers (from different departments) a joint problem. They work on it together to produce solution. Duggan says the change in their views during the work is amazing. I cite our own supporting evidence and theory. Both agree on need for *reality* demands on such groups—demands to produce results, not reports.

3. George messing around with use of tricky programmed learning approach: (a) to increase "skills" of men in task forces, (b) as basic training device for staff role people. I let him talk.

4. At very last possible moment—after two hours together—he lets drop that Lejeune has talked with head of manufacturing about us in connection with some specific needs. George to follow up on this.

On November 6, 1962 Mr. Kestler wrote to Mr. Lejeune and Mr. Duggan congratulating them both on the advances they were making, and drawing attention to how closely their efforts paralleled Mr. Kestler's own thinking. Each letter was accompanied by a paper entitled "Task Orientation for Managers" written by Mr. Kestler.

On December 9 Mr. Kestler again met with George Duggan. He talked for several minutes about the problem he was facing. J. K. records:

The problem is a classical one. There are a number of immediate problems always to be settled; even though many of them result from the failure to have adequate long-range plans and adequate organization arrangements to move toward the future, each of the problems is dealt with separately. While top management is aware of the need for fundamental change—in an intellectual way—when the chips are down the long-range planning is always brushed aside and assigned to a staff person while top management knuckles down to the immediate task at hand. I tried to project our participation in terms of helping George and Hugh help top management use the work they do in solving immediate problems as the base from which to construct plans which reach out further and further along the time dimension. While George appreciated this approach he was at a loss when it came to "selling" it to management. I suggested that what was needed was a specific initial assignment that was more easily described or at least concretely described than what we had agreed on so far. He called Hugh in and the three of us talked for a while. We finally agreed that the place to begin was manufacturing, working with the manufacturing vice president. Both men were careful to explain that the project, while primarily in manufacturing, would inevitably involve other divisions and the top management of the corporation. We decided that we would try to get together and meet with Mr. Spinks, head of manufacturing.

After meeting John Spinks and his second in command, Mr. Kestler wrote a letter to them on January 9, 1963, from which the following are excerpts:

> Our discussions have left little doubt about your determination to strike out for major advances in the overall performance of manufacturing. The opportunities for making a greater contribution to corporate achievement are clear, and you are going to exploit those opportunities. The question now is how to get started.

Mr. Kestler then explained how the individual problems he had discussed with them could be tackled in the form of concrete objectives and measured steps towards an agreed goal. The letter continued:

Next Steps
> The Spinney Plant has been suggested for a possible initial project. To explore this idea, I suggest the following steps:

> 1. Conversation with your managers, specifically on the topic of Spinney. Where do the opportunities for greatest progress lie? In which high-priority areas would they like to see improvements within the next three or four months?
> 2. We would work with Bill (the second in command) and with

the plant management in outlining a project aimed at translating this *readiness* for improvement into concrete, tangible gain. This project outline would be presented to top management as a proposal for action.

Your own determination to settle for nothing short of a major upgrading of performance, and your confidence that you have the resources to do it, certainly point to a bold, imaginative and successful undertaking.

MEETING BETWEEN J. K. AND BILL SIMPSON (SALES VISIT REPORT)

September 14, 1962

Bill talked for a little while and then became specific:

"What I'm wondering about is whether you people will be able to take on the assignment as we have begun to picture it —can you work in one department or do you have to start with a whole company?"

I respond with a description of our practice—and the fact that we will begin in a department if it makes sense to begin in a department. However I emphasized here—and all through the interview—that we did not consider this a "departmental assignment," that our contacts would be with the plant manager, with him, with the vice president, and so forth in the framework of total manufacturing objectives. He described the bumping situation. There is considerable fluctuation in employment levels and each time there is a change the whole plant plays musical chairs since there is plantwide seniority. About the only stability are the foremen.

* * *

"You're going to run into one hell of a lot of rationalization out there. They tend to blame everyone but themselves. 'If you guys in Houston wouldn't screw up the schedules all the time we could do a lot of improving' or 'How are we going to improve when you've taken all our clerks away on these burden reduction programs so we don't even have any records of what we're doing?''

I described how we would deal with their "rationalizations" and try to search for areas where they see opportunity to move. I went back to the question of the shifting of workers and added that to the list of rationalizations and said that what we would have to do is to work within that framework.

All through the interview ran a thread of doubt and ambivalance by Bill on this score: First, could we really produce so much progress within the framework of reality as we find it? When reassured that we could work within the ground rules, he then communicated his wish that we could get the ground rules changed through our influence as outsiders with an "objective" point of view. I tried to relate the two and show how a developing strategy would produce some immediate changes and then provide a basis for more fundamental and broader changes.

* * *

A number of times we went back to the same operations questions and I finally decided to shift gears by saying "I am not worried about our ability to go into Spinney and help the people there do some effective things about their productivity. But the details of that should come from our discussions out there, not here. What I would like to get out of this conversation is a better notion of what your mission is, what you see as your major objectives for the next couple of years and then of how our assignment fits into that framework."

Bill replied, "I feel very strongly that there is room for improvement in manufacturing, plenty of room. There's 'gold in them thar hills' and there's no question about it.

"In order to strike the gold we're going to run into a fundamental problem. When you go to people and approach them in the manner which you're outlining—and I can't quarrel with this approach at all—it has to be a two-way street. If they're going to give you suggestions you're going to have to be prepared to accept them and to do something about it." We launched into suggestions and "doing something" and I tried to steer off this course by talking about producing change and action rather than producing suggestions. Then Bill went on:

"Part of the problem is that some investment is going to have to be made. I cannot get the gold out of those hills without a pick. I need money and I need tools and the plant managers need all sorts of help." (J. K.: So that part of the purpose of the Spinney project is to produce gains, but also to produce enlightenment back in Houston about the opportunities for gain in manufacturing and the tools needed to do the job.) He agreed this was so and made the stereotyped remark about our being objective outsiders and therefore top management would listen to what we said while we might be making the same point that he has been making for some time. "A prophet is without honor in his own house." I tried to explain that we would not be working quite in the fashion he described and, when I found that he was not paying any attention, realized that he was expressing, in his own way, the desire for some solid and substantial help. I put the book down and spent the next 15 or 20 minutes trying to get a better line on the sort of help he wanted and to make sure he understood that we were going to provide that sort of help. It is clear that the nature of the problem is the lack of understanding, by those whose support is essential, of what it takes to build a modern, efficient, low-cost manufacturing function. Many of the same elements that characterize the situation at the Cleveland Inst. are present here. On a number of occasions he used expressions like this, "Damn it, Jim, we can't mine the gold until we get some tools to do it."

On the way out I spoke with Spinks, who had joined us for the last few minutes when we began to talk about arrangement for visiting the plant. He commented, "You seem to have gotten along pretty well judging by Bill's tone at the end of the meeting." Bill kidded about the fact that he had talked for the better part of two hours while I had done a lot of listening.

Throughout the entire meeting which lasted several hours, Bill Simpson made only one recorded reference to the pamphlets James Kestler had sent him.

On February 12 James Kestler sent eight papers to the president of the company.

On February 17 two excerpts from speeches were sent to Bill Simpson.

On February 22 four papers were sent to another prominent executive.

On February 26 ten papers, including duplicate copies, were mailed to another executive.

There is no record of acknowledgment in any case. However, correspondence continued with those persons whom Mr. Kestler had met and talked with.

MEETING WITH STEVE LEMON, PRODUCTION MANAGER, AND JOHN TRANSOME, PERSONNEL OFFICER (SALES VISIT REPORT)

February 21, 1963

Visit to Spinney plant

Mr. Steven Lemon is a man in his mid-fifties who has been with the company many years. He is a soft-spoken westerner with a pleasant sense of humor. He had invited John Transome to sit in on this meeting confirming one or both of the following:

1. That we are viewed as people who were sent in to help on the personnel side of things.

2. John is seen as a very important ally in the running of the plant.

I started with a pretty detailed description of our firm's contacts with the company. I described various meetings I had had with people in Houston, what my impressions were of what the manufacturing top management was trying to accomplish and how they viewed us as a possible resource.

The early part of the meeting was characterized by a gradual opening up process during which Steve became more and more free to be hostile to us. In effect he was saying, "Don't I have enough trouble around here without you? I asked for better equipment and more money and look what they send me—a consultant!"

Here are some excerpts from this part of the session:

"The more I think about your approach the more I think Spinney is not a good place for experimenting with this type of approach. We're overloaded with experiments. The market research is right in this building; naturally all of the experiments that go on, go on right there. This is especially true in foodstuffs. Sometimes I think we are nothing more than the annex of the laboratory just running a lot of tests. What do you think that does to our productivity and our costs? Nobody realizes how much time, effort and energy goes into fooling around with these experiments. All of this leads to lower productivity and higher costs."

And so on and so on. I began to shift the conversation over to what we might begin doing about all of this. With frequent references to our earlier client experience, analogous in so many ways to the situation, I began to get the conversation shifted over to initiative-taking at the plant level. The details of this part of the conversation are relatively unimportant. He was willing to accept the responsibility for further initiative-taking at his level. I was careful to explain that while our initial experiment would be limited to the ground rules as they currently exist, our ultimate sense of responsibility and mission in the company, as I perceived them at conversations in Houston, included the whole matter of upward education—helping top executives whose primary interest is not in manufacturing to permit manufacturing to make the sort of advances of which it is capable.

I was in fact surprised at the ease of transition here. He mentioned specifically two departments where productivity was a big problem and where he would like to see some gains.

Unfortunately, Transome was not going to be there the following week—on vacation—so I walked with him to his office to at least have a few minutes to chat.

There followed a list of key personnel as described by Mr. Transome. It was agreed that Mr. Kestler should have an opportunity to talk to all these men for lengthy periods, soliciting their suggestions and listening to their experience.

The next items in the files consist of bulky interviews with personnel who appear to have talked at length about their problems and possible solutions and a summary of opinions of the key employees integrated in such a way as to show common ground and congruent perspectives. From these viewpoints a specific plan of action for department managers was drawn up and sent to the plant. There, in consultation with the plant managers, the plan was reviewed and revised in a series of planning meetings.

MEETING WITH JOHN SPINKS, BILL SIMPSON, AND GEORGE DUGGAN

April 7, 1963

Bill Simpson

When I called Bill in the morning for an appointment he said that he wanted to see me before I saw Spinks. The reason for this never became clear. The first topic of conversation was the plant manager's meeting of the previous week. Two days were devoted to a sort of laboratory, home-grown, with George Duggan presiding. Bill showed me his introductory talk for those two days and it was an interesting mixture. It laid heavy emphasis on "our problems" but also challenged the group to think about solutions and steps they could take to initiate action. He thought the discussion went quite well and suggested that he felt encouraged by it. "Of course, none of the problems were really new. But we did have a chance to get them out on the table and discuss them." The more he talked about it the more clear it became that the discussions were a sort of negotiating session with Bill trying to get the group to commit themselves to produce results and the group trying to get Bill to commit himself to more help, support, money, etc. Here is a lovely example of "you first," each hesitant to be the first to change. I suggested the fact that confidence in the plant would have to be built before either he or the plant could make a strong case for more support and more autonomy.

Simpson is in conflict and I am not certain that I handled the situation as skillfully as I might have. On the one hand he has fallen into, or has never escaped from, the trap of believing that the plants are really stuck until they get a lot more help and support of various sorts. He wants us to help him prove that—and our work really will prove the need for certain kinds of help but only in the context of movement as a result of plant initiative. When we talk about the great gains that are possible even without additional help, we strike at the heart of a defense system which he has built for himself over the years.

John Spinks

I summarized our reactions and impressions of the last few weeks. The two points I emphasized were: (a) the sizable gains that could be made by the managers at Spinney and the fact that they have never really been tested as managers; (b) the fact that part of the dynamics of the situation are that Simpson seems reluctant to put very tough demands on the plant in view of his inability to provide them the kind of tools and resources he feels they should have. I then said that I was convinced that we could be of help to Spinney in moving ahead and that an essential part of this undertaking would be to work with Simpson and to help him bring into perspective the balance between expecting things from the plant and providing things for the plant.

Our analysis could not have struck the target more directly. Spinks began to describe the situation, using even language and words that we would use. For example, when I reported the word "comfortable" that had been used and that seems to characterize Spinney, he grasped that and said, "If I had to pick any single word in the English language that is the word I would pick for that plant." He also used the word "tough" and went on to explain what he meant by that in a way that made it clear that he uses it the same way we do.

For the first time he went into very frank discussion of his relationship with Simpson and his appraisal of Simpson's strengths and weaknesses. He feels that Simpson is a good technical man but as an administrator leaves much to be desired.

But Spinks was adamant about the matter of support and investment in the plant. He asserted that any investment that was adequately supported and showed a promising rate of return could expect to be favorably acted upon.

We discussed the problem of top management's confidence in the manufacturing organization and the need to build that confidence through demonstrations of forward movement. He agreed strongly with this.

I made the point several times that we considered all of these matters to be part of the subject matter of our project—that we considered that we would be working with him, with Simpson, and with the plant.

George Duggan

I spent about an hour with George and he told me about his efforts to lead the session last week—the two day "problem-solving session." He encountered the typical difficulties and resistance one meets when putting a group like this together for the first time to undertake this type of exercise. But the group did get to work. He and I smiled repeatedly as we compared "unsurmountable obstacles" which came up in the meetings. Unfortunately the situation cried out for leadership and Simpson was communicating self-doubt, pessimism, and general lack of confidence about whether they were capable of accomplishing anything as a group. "Well, it remains to be seen whether we can do anything about these things when I get back to Houston," George said, again taking personal responsibility.

TELEPHONE CONVERSATION WITH GEORGE DUGGAN

May 5, 1963

George called me at home in the evening. He announced that the whole situation was in trouble and that we must have some conversation very soon. In view of my own uneasiness following my conversation with Simpson on the previous day (see my diary notes) and the importance attaching to this account, it need hardly be said that my anxieties were aroused. Apparently Spinks had laced into Simpson on several occasions during the day and had simply exacerbated an already strained relationship. Simpson spoke openly and bitterly, saying that perhaps the next thing that is needed is Duggan's assistance in seeking a new job. It was not clear in this conversation, nor did I feel it prudent to probe, whether George's concern was about our status or whether George was simply viewing us as a colleague and collaborator working with him on a professional problem. We discussed the situation for about fifteen minutes or so and I told him about my own uneasiness that Simpson might not understand why we were restricting our efforts to progress that could be made *within* current limitations—that he might continue to believe that we saw these as desirable or permanent limitations. We decided that I would try to see Simpson the next day.

A call to Chris Cartwright, for advice and consultation, led to reconsidering those tactics. How can we expect our proposal to be considered dispassionately in this sort of environment? I questioned. Chris responded by saying perhaps the proposal itself might be viewed as a pathway out of the situation by both men. At any rate the proposal would accomplish what we wanted accomplished with much greater effectiveness than words of reassurance.

I called Duggan again, told him that I had reconsidered, and suggested that in view of the traumatic day, he, as an on-going counselor to Simpson, would be a much more appropriate person to try to deal with the situation. If it were possible, I suggested he might try to get Simpson to realize that the fact that we can have an effective relationship with Spinks is an asset and a positive value to him rather than a threat.

Two weeks later a full meeting of the management at Spinney was called. On the agenda were the proposals of Kestler, Dobson and Cartwright, and the question of whether to appoint the consultants formally. Many doubts and fears were raised, but as the discussion continued and the proposals were discussed, the fears seemed to subside. When a vote was called, the consultants were still apprehensive, but the meeting decided unanimously to launch the program in collaboration with the consultants. Once this decision had been taken, enthusiasm and optimism in the group increased markedly.

CASE V–4. The Robertson Electric Company (A)

Located on the near north side of Chicago, the Robertson Electric Company was a well established firm employing approximately 2,000 workers. The company manufactured several varieties of electrical components including radio tubes, amplifiers, speakers, automatic changers, and turntables. With the advent of high fidelity equipment the company entered this new field of production as well.

Case material of the Harvard Graduate School of Business Administration, prepared as a basis for class discussion. Cases are not designed to present illustrations of either correct or incorrect handling of administrative problems. All names have been disguised. Copyright 1954, 1956 by the President and Fellows of Harvard College.

The company was doing well financially and its products were reaching an ever-growing market.

Concurrent with this expansion the company experienced a number of administrative problems, many of which focused around the recent promotion of supervisors to positions of greater responsibilities, the enlargement of several departments, and the installation of new equipment in these departments. In the late fall of 1949 the president hired the services of Arthur Corwin, an industrial consultant in administration, to assist him in understanding some of these emerging problems.

The president believed that modern methods of production needed modern methods of supervision, and he was eager to improve both. A rise in union grievances, in absenteeism, and in labor turnover were the specific problems which the president described to Corwin in the latter's initial visits to the company. The president was interested in some of the newer views of these problems, which suggested that they could best be approached by improving the communication skills of supervisors and executives. The president hoped that after Corwin had talked with some of the company's superintendents, foremen, and workers and had some understanding of their recurring problems, a series of supervisory training meetings might result. Both men considered the use of case material resulting from Corwin's observations and interviews a possible focus for such a course.

Corwin spent his first three weeks at the company going about the different departments listening to and talking with superintendents, foremen, and workers. He explained his presence to everyone and the possibility of a training course if such meetings could be considered helpful. Corwin was most interested when talking with workers, foremen, and superintendents in the ways they described their jobs and their relations with others in their departments and divisions.

One afternoon during this three-week period, Norman Eaton, the superintendent of the radio division, invited Corwin to talk with his foremen and workers. Eaton supervised four departments. He had been promoted to his present job three years ago, a few months before the company had begun its latest expansion. He was forty-five and had worked for the company ten years, seven in the time-study and methods department before he received his promotion to the superintendency of the radio division.

In their initial discussion Eaton explained to Corwin that he had encountered a number of problems with one or two old-time foremen in his division. He described these foremen as supervisors "who had more or less been promoted to their jobs through many years of loyal service to the company." He mentioned one foreman in particular, Paul Denault, who had been with the company thirty years, ten of them as foreman of the radio turntable subassembly department. Eaton encouraged Corwin to visit all his departments and to see the situation at first hand.

Corwin accepted the invitation and for the next few days visited with two or three of Eaton's foremen. During one of his visits he met Paul Denault. After Corwin had introduced himself to Denault and explained his interests, Denault began to describe the department to him.

DENAULT: There are many things I can talk about. We've got many workers in the shop, most of them women, and of course, we have several problems. There's the shop, the product, and the girls, and so on. (Pause.) The other evening, I attended a lecture here in town that dealt with shop problems. I didn't find it too helpful. The situation described by the speaker was about two workers called Fritz and Tim.

Fritz was a German and Tim was an Irishman. They worked side by side. One day Tim walked over and knocked Fritz down. Tim said he wasn't going to work with any dirty Nazis. Now the question was: "What do you do if you're the foreman and this happens in your department?"

Well, I guess the foreman should have seen something like that coming. But, well, I don't have any Fritzes or Tims in my department. I've mostly women. My problems are just not like that. The lecture wasn't much good to me in running my department.

Now the kind of problems I have down here center around the girls and their machines. You take that worker right over there. (He pointed across the shop floor.) She doesn't watch her work carefully enough. I'm constantly afraid she will smash her hand on that press. I have to keep after her to watch her work. Several other workers aren't as careful as they might be about their machines either. I don't like to hang this sign up over their machines, but I don't know what else I can do. (He picked up a sign next to the work area by the presses which read, "Dangerous operator, do not talk to this person while she is operating the machine.") They get careless, and we can't have accidents.

And another problem that is constantly coming up is when I ask the girls to work on another machine when we need them. You see, the department is on piecework and the girls don't like to change operations. When they have to move to a strange job, their pay goes down because they aren't too used to the machine. I know they don't like to change jobs. Sometimes they refuse. They say it isn't fair, so they get mad at me. But what else can be done? We must get the products out, and sometimes I don't have enough work to keep each worker busy at her regular machine. Besides, sometimes we need to double up on certain machines.

And there's the superintendent. I guess he means well, but he's not much help. He tells me that if I let one girl refuse to work another operation and don't stop it there, others will refuse and before long no one will change jobs. In the old days we just fired workers if they refused to do what the foremen said. But not any more. The foreman is just an errand boy. He's got no place. (Pause.)

People are always coming into my department who don't tell me who they are: other supervisors, quality and cost control men, and maintenance workers. It used to be that they reported to the foreman first. Look down there right now. There's the union president talking to one of my workers. I don't know what he's talking to her about or telling her. He doesn't bother to come up here and see me to ask if he can talk to her.

Am I talking about anything that interests you?

CORWIN: Yes, I think you are, Paul. There's been quite a change.

DENAULT: The old days with Bill Yates are gone forever, I guess. Bill was the superintendent of the division for many years before he died about three years ago. Some say he killed himself working so hard here on the job. I don't know. Norman Eaton took over after Bill Yates.

I've been with Robertson nearly thirty years, twenty of them on the bench in this department. I was with them before we started manufacturing radios—before radios were ever heard of. We made equipment for electric motors in those days. I was a lead man for many years. When Bill was made superintendent, he made me foreman of this department, and in those days everything seemed to work out all right.

Now I go to hear speakers talk about problems of Fritz and Tim. They say to the foreman: "Don't get angry, don't get excited, don't blow up in front of the workers." They tell me I must handle the situation correctly, but I don't know how. In the old times we just fired the worker. I don't care what that speaker said about Fritz and Tim; it doesn't help me a bit here on the work floor. (Pause.)

You see, the workers don't come to me with their problems. They go to the chief steward here in my department. I don't know who he thinks he is. He's on piecework and he's supposed to work all the time. I bet he doesn't work twenty hours a week on his machine. He spends most of his time with grievances. But he's paid full time. Well, the workers are constantly running to the steward and they get together and go to the superintendent. I never hear about it until the problem is all settled. They are always doing something like this behind my back.

Why don't we walk around and look the department over? We can talk on the way.

CORWIN: Fine, Paul.

As they walked, Denault explained the operations to Corwin.

DENAULT: Now, Marie here is working on a stamping machine. This operation comes just before we begin to assemble the unit. Notice that the press comes down with considerable force, and it is dangerous if the workers aren't alert. . . . (The machine dropped the press hammer twice in quick succession.) What happened, Marie? The press came down twice that time and nearly caught your hand. That shouldn't happen that way.

MARIE: It wasn't the machine's fault. I didn't lift my foot off the pedal after I released the safety lever. There's nothing wrong with the machine. See, Paul. I didn't take my foot off the control pedal, that's all.

DENAULT: I want the safety device checked. You can't be too careful about safety, Marie. (Denault called the maintenance man over.) I want Marie's machine checked. The hammer came down twice. It repeated and came too close to her hand. It shouldn't do that. It might crush her hand.

JOHNNY: Sure, Paul. I'll look at it right now.

MARIE: There's really nothing wrong with the machine, Johnny. I held my foot on the pedal too long.

JOHNNY: Let's check it for safety reasons, Marie.

Marie got up from her chair while Johnny examined the major parts of the machine. In a couple of minutes he had checked the safety mechanism. He found nothing wrong.

JOHNNY: It's okay, Marie.

MARIE: I knew it all the time.

DENAULT: You've got to be careful, Marie. You must watch the press more closely.

MARIE: Sure, Paul, I will.

Denault and Corwin continued their tour of the shop.

A few days later Corwin went back to see Norman Eaton in his office. In the course of their conversation, Paul Denault's name came up. Eaton had just made the statement, "Paul Denault is one of my biggest supervisory headaches," when Max Webster, the chief steward from Denault's department, stepped into the office.

WEBSTER: I'm sorry; I didn't know you were busy, Norman.

EATON: That's all right, Max. You remember Mr. Corwin.

WEBSTER: Oh, sure, we spoke together briefly the other day when he was in the department. (Pause.) A problem has come up in the department again. I think it's urgent.

EATON: Shoot.

WEBSTER: One of the machinists just threw a paper cup in the [lubricating] oil pan on one of the drills. The sweeper, Bill Cabot, who has to keep those pans free of trash and grit so the oil flows properly, saw the machinist do it and he blew up. He says he's going for a walk. I think he plans to quit, Norman. Paul heard about the situation and went down to look things over. I got there just as Bill told Paul he was leaving for the day. You know Bill; this may be all he needs to quit.

EATON: Why would anyone throw a cup in an oil pan in the first place?

WEBSTER: Why do people throw butts on the floor? Carelessness, I guess.

EATON: Throwing a butt on the floor is perfectly normal, but throwing a paper cup in a drill press's lubricating oil isn't.

WEBSTER: I followed Bill back into the locker room. He's pretty upset. He said he had worked long and hard on the job as clean up man, but he wasn't going to take any more, particularly since he saw no future in it. He wants a machine of his own, Norman.

EATON: He's been promised one at the first opening.

WEBSTER: Has anything been done? Something I can show him?

EATON: Sure, here's the slip for his promotion as soon as there is a vacancy. (Eaton took the slip from the desk drawer and handed it to Webster.)

WEBSTER: I've talked to him, but he's pretty determined to leave. This order slip may help.

EATON: Talk to him, Max. After he calms down a little, I'll talk to him.

WEBSTER: I'll go back to him. You'll see him pretty soon?

EATON: In a few minutes, after he calms down a little, if he likes. (Webster left the room, and Eaton continued his conversation with Corwin.) Things like this are constantly coming up, and my foremen aren't too sure what to do. Bill Cabot is one of our hardest workers. I'd hate to lose him. (Pause.)

Well, we were talking about Paul Denault. He has considerable difficulty with his workers. You see, Paul is an oldtimer who believed he was cheated when management passed him up for my job. Since I've had the job as superintendent, I've tried in many ways to help him, but most of my attempts haven't been too successful. I guess, in a way, I'm waiting for his retirement. That will be in five or six years. I suppose if Bill Yates could work with him all these years, I can do the same. At times, however, the situation becomes difficult.

I've tried to get Paul to go to some supervisory discussions and demonstrations that are held periodically around here by lecturers on industrial problems. He has gone to a few, but they haven't helped him much. Dr. Everett, one of the speakers, encouraged the foremen when human situations arise on the floor to hold back and examine the problem before going off half-cocked. You know, get the facts before acting. Well, just a few weeks after this particular lecture which Paul attended, a situation almost identical to the one described by Dr. Everett came up in Paul's department. One of the girls smashed her finger on one of the presses. I was there at the time. What did Paul do? The moment it happened, he ran over to the girl and, instead of offering help, which would be the normal, natural thing to do, he stood there bawling her out for what she had done. While the girl was hurt and bleeding, he just yelled at her.

I said nothing at the time. We all tried to help the girl and calm Paul down. We got her to the dispensary and the crisis was over. About three days later I called Paul into my office and said to him: "Paul, what did Dr. Everett tell you the other week at the lecture about how to handle situations like the press accident? Didn't he say that the last thing you should do was to reprimand the worker on the spot in front of others, particularly when the worker was hurt?"

He admitted he had done wrong. I asked him, "But why do you do things like that, Paul?" To this he had no answer. So we sat down and went over the situation step by step, and we attempted to see how he might have handled the situation. He listens, but little change ever comes. The next time something like that comes up, I'm afraid it will be to do it all over again.

Let me give you another example. When I first came on the job about three years ago, Paul was known throughout the division as a "carrier of tales." The first thing I wanted to get across to my organization was the policy that I refused to listen to persons who carry tales. That is, if someone comes into my office to discuss the problems of another person with me and starts to say things about that other person, I stop the man who is reporting and say, "If I'm to hear this, I think I had better call in the man whom it concerns as well." I think people who want to talk about another should do so in front of that person, not behind his back. In that way, there will be less misunderstanding. But Paul refused to do this. So he had to learn the hard way.

One day, a year or so back, Paul came in and started to talk about his problems with Henry Benson, the foreman of radio speakers. As luck would have it, Benson just by chance walked by my office, so I called him in. I turned to Paul when Henry got in the office and said, "Paul has just been telling me about a problem he has. Would you like to continue, Paul?" Well, he didn't say a word. He got all flustered, and he stammered around. That was the last time he carried any tales to me.

And there was the situation with John Green. Denault has a number of favorites in his department and practically everyone knows it. John Green, the worker in this example, was not one of his favorites. John asked Paul some weeks ahead of time when he might take his annual two-week vacation. The date was all set, and John planned to leave at that time. Since John had planned a trip to Canada, he asked Paul for a long weekend preceding the vacation date. Not only did Paul refuse the extra days, but he told him he didn't want him to take his vacation as originally planned because the work load had piled up since their earlier discussions. John had made elaborate plans to take his family at that time and wanted very badly to go as scheduled. Paul asked him to stay on and take the vacation at another time. When John refused, Paul told him to go ahead but that he couldn't promise him that a job would be waiting when he returned.

I learned about this situation through the chief steward, Max Webster, the man you just met. Green took his vacation as originally planned, and I said nothing to Paul until it came time to discuss his three-week vacation some time later. When Paul came around, I said, "Sure, Paul, it's perfectly all right for you to take your vacation now, but I'm not sure we'll have a job for you when you come back. You see, a lot of work is coming up, and I need you badly right now." As you can imagine, Paul nearly hit the ceiling. He said that that wasn't fair. With this situation before us, I then raised the way he handled John Green some weeks back. I think this made an impression on him.

I talk to him whenever I can and try to help him, but every so often he gets so upset I recommend that he take a few days off. I give him a few days to rest up and get over his immediate problems and come to work fresh. I feel damn sorry for him, but he's got to see what he's doing to cause the division so much trouble. I think he wants to change, but his attention is constantly straying when we talk together.

Max Webster and I have talked together about Paul Denault. It's difficult not to, since most of Paul's dissatisfied workers come to Max and then to me for help. We try to work together with Paul.

I've thought several times about relieving him, but after thirty years with the company, how can I do that? If I did people would say that the other superintendent, Bill Yates, put up with him all those years, I should be able to manage a few more. (Max Webster stepped into the office).

WEBSTER: Bill is feeling better. He's calmed down considerably. He appreciated your confidence in recommending him for a position when one comes up on the machines.

EATON: You think it would help if I spoke to him?

WEBSTER: I think it might, Norman.

EATON: Max, would you keep Mr. Corwin company for a few minutes until I return? He's interested in some of the human problems we have in the division. I have spoken to him about Paul Denault.

Eaton left the office. Webster described how he saw the departments and how he, as chief steward, worked with Eaton on worker–foremen problems. Webster spoke highly of Eaton, calling him "one of the best men in the field of human relations he had ever known." He described Eaton as an "excellent superintendent, vitally interested in every worker in his division," who went out of his way to give everyone a "fair shake." Near the end of their conversation, Webster spoke directly about Paul Denault.

WEBSTER: Denault has little understanding of the workers in his department and doesn't care to have much. I think when Bill Yates was alive he had a way with Paul, but now with Yates gone, Paul has just been getting worse. Because his workers don't feel they can talk to him, they come to me and Norman for help. The two of us get together with the particular worker and attempt to arrive at some agreement. Norman has asked Paul in at these times, but he just gets so excited that Norman now feels he can handle the situation better by talking to Paul later, after the worker has gone back to his job.

Eaton returned to his office at this time and told Webster that Bill Cabot felt much better. Eaton added he had given Cabot the afternoon off, but he was confident that he would be back at his job the next day. Webster smiled in agreement and left the office.

EATON: Everyday something like this comes up. If I could just get the foremen to see the difficulties and handle them on the floor, then this job might have some peaceful moments. Like I have said before, the big problem in this division isn't the workers but the old-time foremen. (Pause.) Any ideas, Mr. Corwin?

The Robertson Electric Company (B)

About two weeks passed before Corwin saw Norman Eaton again. Corwin spent most of this time in the company's three other divisions talking with workers and supervisors about their communication problems. His interest was still to develop a training program that

Case material of the Harvard Graduate School of Business Administration, prepared as a basis for class discussion. Cases are not designed to present illustrations of either correct or incorrect handling of administrative problems. All names have been disguised. Copyright 1954, 1956 by the President and Fellows of Harvard College.

would provide supervisors and executives with an opportunity to improve their skill in communicating with others. He had made notes about a few situations he had seen during his stay at the company as possible case material for use in such a training program.

During this time, Corwin had not forgotten about Norman Eaton and Paul Denault. He wondered how he might be helpful to them, but he still had no very clear idea. Near the end of December, Corwin met Eaton at lunch. In the course of their conversation, Eaton inquired if Corwin had any ideas about the problems they had discussed two weeks before. Corwin answered that he had done some thinking about their discussions and that at Eaton's convenience he would like to talk with him again. Eaton suggested the following afternoon in his office, and Corwin agreed. Eaton began the conversation as follows.

EATON: I've done some thinking about Paul Denault and the problem of old-time foremen since we last talked together, Mr. Corwin, but frankly very little of it seems to get anywhere. I've tried to help Paul whenever I could, but there's no getting around the point that he's very difficult to change. His retirement still looks like my only solution, but that's about five or six years in the future.

He gets so excited with the workers and makes so much of such little things. I hardly know how to approach him on certain mornings. It's almost like flipping a coin: heads, he'll be all right today and I can talk with him, or tails, he'll be in one of his more disagreeable moods. I've thought several times that I might . . . (Eaton's telephone rang. He leaned forward and picked it up.)

Yes? Oh, hello, Jim. (Pause.) Well, I don't know. Day after tomorrow is Christmas Eve, as you know, and many of the workers on my day shift are talking about a party when they finish at three o'clock. Also, the second shift workers have been asking me and my foremen if the company plans to work straight through until eleven o'clock on Christmas Eve night. (Pause.) I sure would appreciate an answer as soon as possible, Jim. (Pause.) Okay, fine, Jim. I'll wait for your return call. (Eaton replaced the receiver and swung around in his chair to face Corwin.)

I'm sorry about the interruption, but the company's decision about the coming Christmas Eve is getting most of our attention around here this afternoon. The president is supposed to announce very shortly how we are to manage it. That was Jim Parks (vice president of manufacturing) just now. He phoned that he hadn't heard just what the decision is to be, but believes he should know very shortly.

My foremen and some workers have asked me if the second shift will work straight through until eleven o'clock Christmas Eve night. That shift isn't too large. In fact, at the present time, due to our seasonal slack, it's almost a skeleton crew. If the company does decide to work right through the day, I doubt if many on the second shift will do much work, particularly after the day workers throw their party. (Eaton waited a moment before continuing. Corwin thought he might talk more about Paul Denault, but Eaton spoke instead of his relationships with his superiors.)

The front office sometimes by-passes the superintendents with information. Some in top management aren't as quick as they might be in telling us when we do a good job down here. More than once I've done a good job in getting out production in my departments, but do I hear any words of praise from the fellows on top about it? Not much. . . . (Pause.) . . . Well, occasionally I hear indirectly about something I've done that pleases them.

It would take me some time to describe the conditions of the radio department before I took over three years ago. Basically, however, I managed to up production considerably in that department, while at the same time cutting our cost and waste figures. I successfully put in a new standards program where others had tried but failed to make it work. Not once have I heard any word of praise from the president about my efforts.

Oh, I hear about the praise indirectly, but that isn't quite the way I'd like it. For instance, I've done such a good job—at least, that's the way I get it from upstairs—in putting a standards system in my radio department that the president has asked Jim Parks if I could do the same thing in one of our smaller plants in Detroit. I told Jim that it all depends on the people involved at the plant.

It's hard to say just arbitrarily whether our smaller plant in Detroit could take a standards system successfully or not. You know, you can install anything if you know your people and they get behind it. If they aren't . . . well, you are sunk before you begin. So, frankly, I couldn't say whether we could put a standards system in at Detroit or not.

But that's an illustration of a typical way of hearing a note of appreciation around here. I hear in this indirect manner instead of an outright statement of praise. No one just comes out and says, "Norm, you did a fine job in your radio department. We appreciate it." Like I said, there's a lot of by-passing going on between the people upstairs in the front office and the superintendents here on the floor. They aren't in touch with us as much as they might be. (The phone range again, and Eaton answered it.)

Yes, Jim . . . Well, how about the factory workers? . . . Then it's the same for them too? Everything on Christmas Eve closes down at one o'clock in the afternoon. (Eaton smiled.) Wonderful! The workers will work right through the lunch hour, and we'll stop at one for lunch, parties—whatever they want to do. Is that right? . . . Fine. The second shift will come in the morning with the regular day workers. Swell. I'll get the word out at once. It's almost quitting time. Yeah, thanks, Jim. (Pause.) Yeah, I'm a little excited too. (Eaton rang off. He pulled his list of phone numbers out and began to call each of the departments in his division.)

You'll have to excuse me, but this is the news we've been waiting for. I want to get the foremen and workers notified before quitting time. The quitting bell is scheduled to ring any moment. (Eaton glanced at the clock on his desk as he spoke. Corwin nodded his understanding as Eaton made his first call.)

Hello, Charlie, This is Norman Eaton. The word on Christmas Eve is as follows: The workers will all come in Thursday at the regular time. That's both shifts, Charlie. (Pause.) Yeah, that's right. Both shifts will come in at seven o'clock Thursday morning. We'll work straight through the lunch hour and shut down at one o'clock for lunch or parties. And that will end work activities until the day after Christmas. (Pause.) Okay, Charlie, get the word around to the workers before quitting time if you can. (Eaton hung up and then dialed the next number.)

Hello, Stella, this is Norman Eaton. Get the word to Paul and tell the workers that we shut down at one o'clock Christmas Eve. We'll work right through the lunch hour on Thursday and then stop for lunches and parties. That's right. And, Stella, tell Paul that the second shift workers in his department will come in with the day workers Christmas Eve. There won't be any evening shift. (Pause.) Yeah, that's right. Get the word around before quitting time if you can, Stella. (Eaton cut the connection and called his other two departments. After he had passed on to each the message about Christmas Eve, he turned back to Corwin.)

Well, we have our interruptions, but that does that. I'm sure glad I got through to the departments before the quitting bell. There it goes now. Good . . . (Eaton's phone rang again. He smiled at Corwin and picked up the receiver.)

Hello. (Pause.) He did what! Now, Stella. Well, what did he say? (Pause.) Oh . . . no . . . well, I'm really sorry, Stella.

Sure, sure, I understand. He put the phone down. He looked worried when he spoke again to Corwin.

That was Stella Swanson, the timekeeper in Paul Denault's office. I gave her the message about the Christmas party when Paul didn't answer. Paul just hit the ceiling when she told him the message. Without thinking, I gave her the message, and when she told Paul, he said, "Since when did you start telling me how to run my department?" (Pause.) What have I done? (Eaton came to a stop. He tapped his desk with his fingers and got up.)

I've got to get down there right now and try to straighten this out. I've really pulled one. (He started for the door.) Come along, Mr. Corwin. Perhaps you can help.

Eaton and Corwin started for Denault's department. When they arrived, workers were pouring out the doors toward the main factory exit. Denault reached for his coat and hat when he saw Eaton coming. Eaton stopped at the door of his office.

EATON: I came down to tell you personally, Paul, about the Christmas Eve decision. I was in such a hurry to get the message out to the workers before quitting time I guess I forgot. I told Stella to tell you. (Stella Swanson was sitting at her desk in Paul's office. Paul pulled on his coat and started for the door.)

DENAULT: That's all right. We got the message around. Hello, Mr. Corwin. They shook hands. I've got to be going now, Norman. My boy is flying in from New York for the holidays, and I've got to meet the plane.

EATON: Oh, sure, Paul. Say, are you having a Christmas party in the department?

DENAULT: No, no party as far as I know. (Denault pulled on his hat and walked out of the department. The moment he left, Stella Swanson spoke to Eaton.)

STELLA: The moment after you called, Norman, I got the message to him. He was on the floor at the time. I called to him and told him what you said. He spun around and nearly bit my head off. He said, "Since when did you start giving orders in my department?" Well, you could have floored me. I never expected anything like that. I didn't see myself doing anything wrong. I just told him what you said. Well, I didn't say anything more. He got the word to the workers, I think. I'm pretty sure everyone here knows about Christmas Eve.

EATON: I see.

STELLA: Honestly, Norman, that man is the worst I've ever seen. I've never worked for anyone quite like that. It isn't right to blow up like that. He's always upset about something. You never know what's coming next or what will upset him. Why, he even gets mad occasionally when I open the office window to let in a little fresh air. If I leave the room for a minute, he'll usually close it.

EATON: It's okay, Stella. I know. Don't take it too seriously. You aren't angry with me, are you?

STELLA: Of course not, Norman. He's so touchy at times. Well, I'll see you tomorrow. (She prepared to leave as Eaton and Corwin walked back to the former's office.)

EATON: Now, I bet I'll have trouble in that department tomorrow for sure. I don't know what effect this will have on the workers, but I know Paul will be difficult tomorrow. I bet production suffers as a consequence.

CORWIN: Paul's been hurt.

EATON: Yeah, I'm afraid so. I try with that guy, but I don't know.

CORWIN: He feels misunderstood.

EATON: I think so . . . You know, I've pulled the same thing on Paul that I was just blaming the bosses upstairs for. Without thinking about the consequences of my actions or what effect it might have on Paul, I phoned Stella to relay the message about the Christmas Eve decision. I guess I thought Paul would answer the phone, but he didn't. Right then and there, though, I should have asked for him, instead of telling Stella the decision. I took something away from him, and the damndest thing was it was all unintentional on my part.

CORWIN: He wanted to tell the workers.

EATON: Sure, I see that now. That was his right. I can see it all now. It's the same thing I was talking about just a few minutes ago— about the bosses upstairs by-passing me. I by-passed Paul in the same way. It's the same thing I was talking about—when I don't get any appreciation from upstairs.

CORWIN: He heard that he wasn't important when you told Stella.

EATON: That's it, I guess. I'll have to take my share of the responsibility. I'm at fault. There's no way of getting around that one. (Eaton got up from his desk and reached for his coat. He still looked worried as he started for the door with Corwin.)

If you've got time. Mr. Corwin, I'd like to talk about this

situation further. Right now, I want to go home and think about tomorrow. I'm sure Paul's actions tomorrow will affect the workers' feelings, and I'll bet production is going to suffer as a result. I've got to be ready for it. Why don't you come around tomorrow so that we can talk some more?

CASE V–5. Hartwell Manufacturing Company (A)

On June 17, 1966, Mr. Harold Wilbur, President of the Hartwell Manufacturing Company, was concerned about rapidly rising costs in the engineering department and about falling engineering productivity and performance. Mr. Wilbur had called in Mr. Howard Elliott to discuss the problem with him and to help with his thinking. Mr. Elliott was a consultant who had served the company a number of times in the past and was very familiar with the company, its products, its operations, and its people.

The Hartwell Manufacturing Company, located in Bridgeport, Connecticut, produced and sold three major lines of products: industrial defoaming equipment (industrial line), laboratory equipment (laboratory line), and small household appliances (appliance line). The company had grown steadily since its founding, some fifty years ago, by Mr. Wilbur's father. The greatest growth, however, had occurred in the last decade with volume increasing from around $3 million to $14 million dollars per year in 1965. Two important factors had contributed to the company's growth: a strong customer-oriented marketing organization, and the continuous generation of creative product ideas.

The formal organization of the Hartwell Manufacturing Company emphasized the importance of marketing. A marketing manager was

This case was prepared by Craig E. Lundberg under the direction of Arthur N. Turner as the basis for class discussion. Cases are not designed to present illustrations of either correct or incorrect handling of administrative problems. The company name and names of individuals are disguised. Copyright © 1966 by the President and Fellows of Harvard College.

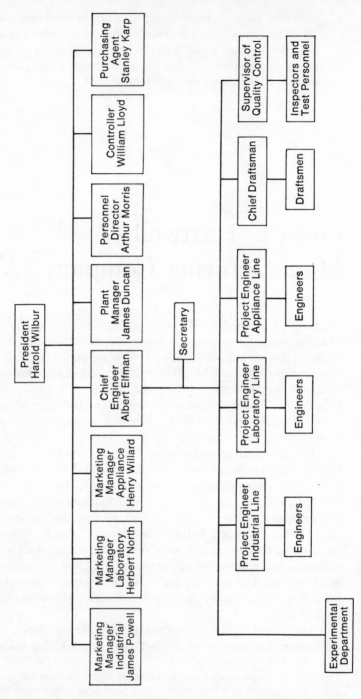

Figure 1. Partial organization chart, Hartwell Manufacturing Company.

responsible for each of the three major product lines. Each marketing manager was charged with the responsibility for planning the marketing strategy for his product line including: new product development, product improvement, sales organization, sales management, advertising, promotion, pricing, and customer service. In practice, major plans and strategies were discussed with and approved by Mr. Wilbur before being put into effect. The engineering department and the manufacturing department supported each of these marketing managers and their product lines.

The engineering department, though a central organization, was set up somewhat along product lines. Project engineers were permanently assigned to work in only one of the product line areas in order to develop specialized engineering knowhow for that product line. Project engineers reported to the chief engineer and drew on the resources provided by a central drafting pool and a central experimental department. Manufacturing, though a central organization, was also organized somewhat along product lines.

Separate assembly and test areas existed for each product line. These assembly areas were supplied with parts manufactured in central press rooms and machine shops. The process of controlling production was centralized, but within the production control department there were coordinators who specialized in planning, scheduling, and expediting for a particular product line. Other activities in the company —such as accounting, personnel, and purchasing—were totally centralized. The heads of major organizational components reported to Mr. Wilbur.

The marketing managers reported directly to Mr. Wilbur. Mr. James Powell handled the industrial line, Mr. Herbert North handled the laboratory line, and Mr. Henry Willard handled the appliance line. Also reporting to Mr. Wilbur were the controller, plant manager, personnel director, chief engineer, and purchasing agent. (An abbreviated organization chart appears as Figure 1.)

Mr. Wilbur described the current problem to Mr. Elliott as follows: "We have a rather serious problem in engineering, Howard. We are becoming increasingly concerned because our engineering costs have been rising very dramatically—much faster, in fact, than our sales—and the quality and productivity of engineering is not meeting our expectations. As you know, we hired a new chief engineer. You have met Albert Elfman, I'm sure. He was employed to replace the former chief engineer about two years ago because we didn't feel that the administration of the engineering department was being handled adequately. Al Elfman is an engineering graduate with a degree in business administration. He has held responsible engineering management jobs elsewhere and we were counting on him here. We had hoped that Mr. Elfman would be able to improve total engineering performance, but his performance, or perhaps I should say the total performance of the engineering department, has fallen far below our expectation. We are beginning to wonder if hiring Al was a mistake, even though we all like Al very much.

"Al Elfman is just the most wonderful person. He is extremely honest, and he is most pleasant and agreeable. One can discuss problems with him rationally and, I think, he has done some good work. In many important respects, however, he falls down badly. For example, I receive complaints from people on my staff that he constantly makes commitments to provide them with information— and then fails to do so. Or, he promises to issue some engineering report but forgets about it. In my own dealings with him, I find that I have to remind him again and again on requests for reports or information. When he is faced with these reminders, he readily acknowledges that he hasn't done as he promised, apologizes for his failure, gives new promises, and then fails to meet those promises.

"This is one aspect of the problem. Another part of it has to do with administration. As you know, Howard, you helped to set up a program for periodically reporting the progress and cumulative costs on engineering projects, and Al has allowed this whole system to deteriorate to the point where it is no longer effective. We no longer get monthly reports. We are fortunate to get such reports quarterly, and when we do get them, they are not accurate. I have spoken to him on a number of occasions about my interest in these reports. I know that I need something to look at for the purpose of judging engineering output and engineering productivity, and I have nothing to rely on now. In addition to these points, our marketing managers are extremely unhappy over the accomplishments in engineering.

"In our business, one key to growth and success is the development of new products and product engineering that enables us to put reliable equipment into the field. We are now faced with a severe field problem. One, I might add, that until now has received little engineering emphasis. We have several hundred of one of our major products in the field that are not performing satisfactorily. Only after considerable sales pressure did engineering tackle this problem on a priority basis. This kind of problem, added to our failure to complete development projects fast enough, leads us to take a critical look at our position here, and to try to decide what we should do about it.

"In thinking about my conversation with you, I have tried to anticipate one of your questions. How well have I informed Mr. Elfman of the things that I want him to do and the things that I expect from him? I can only say that I have done the best I can to tell him what I expect him to do. I have tried to give him a clear idea of what our objectives are in the company, where engineering fits into this picture, and what engineering should be doing in order to be making a full contribution to the growth and success of the company and, at this point, I am quite unhappy with his performance. Frankly, I doubt that he can do the job that we need. If Mr. Elfman's performance continues in the future as it has in the past, I am convinced that we will have to make a change. My reason for talking to you is to ask you if you can do anything with respect to this problem.

"My most immediate concern is with the quality of our engineering. Next, I am concerned about the excessively high cost of engineering in relation to our past experience. Our engineering costs have been going up very sharply, very much faster than our sales, and we must do something to curtail this trend. And finally, I am undecided about Al Elfman. Is there anything we can do to help him, or should he be replaced? I must confess that his personality appeals to me and he is so well liked as a person by people in our organization that I would like to be able to keep him if I can.

"I would like you to advise me on how I should deal with this problem involving the competence of the chief engineer. You might talk with Al Elfman and, as an outsider, you may be able to find out if he feels frustrated or unable to cope with this job for reasons that are unknown to me. I would then like you to review our engineering workload with Al Elfman and the marketing managers and recommend actions that will reduce costs, if this is possible."

Hartwell Manufacturing Company (B)

On June 17, 1966, Mr. Harold Wilbur, president of the Hartwell Manufacturing Company, called in Mr. Howard Elliott, a consultant who had undertaken a number of projects for the Hartwell Manufacturing Company over the past several years, to discuss an immediate

This case was prepared by Craig E. Lundberg, under the direction of Arthur N. Turner as the basis for class discussion. Cases are not designed to present illustrations of either correct or incorrect handling of administrative problems. The company name and names of individuals are disguised. Copyright © 1966 by the President and Fellows of Harvard College.

problem in their engineering department. This problem involved rapidly rising engineering costs, a general dissatisfaction with the quality of engineering work, and considerable unhappiness regarding the productivity of the engineering department. The details of the problem are described in Hartwell Manufacturing Company (A).

Following Mr. Wilbur's description of the engineering problem, Mr. Wilbur and Mr. Elliott discussed the approach Mr. Elliott would use in dealing with the engineering problem. They agreed that the first step should be for Mr. Elliott to talk with Albert Elfman, the chief engineer. Mr. Elliott would try to understand Mr. Elfman's point of view and the problems Mr. Elfman faced as chief engineer, and to act in a manner that would be most helpful to Mr. Elfman. The second step would be to interview other people in the company who interacted with the chief engineer and to elicit their opinions regarding the engineering department, the quality of its work, and its overall performance and service. The third step would involve a complete analysis of engineering workload to estimate whether engineering costs were out of line, and the final step would be for Mr. Elliott to discuss his findings and recommendations with Mr. Wilbur.

Mr. Wilbur spoke to Mr. Elfman and explained that he wanted Mr. Elliott to review the operations of engineering with Mr. Elfman. He mentioned his concern over the rising cost trend and said he thought Mr. Elliott could be helpful in reviewing the engineering operation. An appointment was arranged between Mr. Elfman and Mr. Elliott for June 21, 1966.

Mr. Elliot arrived at the office of Mr. Albert Elfman on the morning of June 21, 1966. He was met at the door by Mr. Elfman who greeted him warmly.

Mr. Elfman was a man in his early forties, heavy set, and slightly balding. One hand was deformed. His manner was relaxed and easy. He smiled often and broadly and his eyes conveyed a message of friendliness. After the exchange of pleasantries, Howard Elliott opened the discussion by asking Mr. Elfman if he would describe his view of engineering's position in the organization, its mission, and how he went about managing the engineering activity. As Elfman spoke, Howard Elliott listened carefully and tried to understand Elfman's point of view. Elliott avoided asking questions, but he tried to indicate his interest in Elfman's comments through natural nonverbal responses.

"Well, Howard," replied Mr. Elfman, "I guess you could say that my ideas about engineering's position in the company have changed rather dramatically in the two years I've been here. As you know, I've been involved in defense-type engineering where the company is primarily engineering-oriented. Here, where the emphasis is on marketing, I've found that I have to adjust my thinking drastically. My original aim was to get control of this department from an engineering point of view—to try to pin down each project with a set of specifications. Once this was done, I wanted to allow the engineers to work with as little interference and with as much freedom as possible. Periodically we planned to hold design review meetings and at these meetings to review design concepts and project progress. Between these meetings, I expected the engineers would be pretty much on their own. In practice, I find that engineering does not have as much responsibility for determining what projects should be undertaken, or what project specifications should be established, as I had foreseen. The marketing groups are constantly involved in suggesting projects and in influencing the details of engineering design. The engineers have expressed considerable resentment about the conflicting pressures they receive from marketing. We have this problem with all divisions, but it is considerably more acute with the industrial line marketing group than with the others.

"I'm sort of feeling my way along with Jim Powell, marketing manager of the industrial line. Jim is intimately familiar with the product line, the objectives of his department, and has in mind many plans for new products and product modifications. Hence, he tends to become frequently and deeply involved in engineering problems and has been quite critical of engineering. We need to get our problems out on the table. I guess I have to learn how to be a better filter between sales and engineering—not the sole filter, though, because I believe that marketing people should be able to talk directly with the men involved on engineering projects. I think I should be in a position to determine task direction and project priorities. Sometimes this is a difficult problem because the people in marketing are motivated by a variety of pressures from the field and they change the emphasis and direction of engineering work in accordance with the pressures on them. This creates some of the resentment I mentioned earlier. Yet, it is my responsibility to see that the engineering group is productive in spite of these interferences. We seem to have a lot of contact with marketing on engineering details and very little with them in the broader sense.

"I think we need to find a middle ground for engineering–marketing relationships. We must respond to marketing needs, but this must be done in an orderly way and with consideration for our capability and resources. We are expected to get the work done which requires an orderly plan, and we are expected to do the work within certain time, cost, and quality limits, which requires some emphasis on productivity and technical competence. To some extent our performance has been poor because of the lack of consistency or direction in our efforts. We face another problem—we try to do too much work in parallel and not enough in series.

"Each project engineer has five or six different projects assigned to him. In addition to these regular projects, we load each engineer with custom designs, and involve him with production problems. The result is that we fall down badly on completing some engineering projects, and we fall down a little on all of them. In our laboratory line we have done quite well, though. Most of our projects are pretty well on schedule and we have achieved fairly good control. We do fall down in the laboratory line in getting engineering specifications for our projects, but then we have that problem to an even greater extent in other areas. Our poorest performance has been with the industrial line and we've got to find ways of doing it a lot better.

"In the industrial line we have one man in engineering who has an intuitive and an experienced feel for the product line, but outside of him, Jim Powell is the only person who really understands the product objectives. It's pretty much a one man show because we don't have any long, hard sessions at the beginning of an engineering project to make sure we know where we are going. We seem to take several shots at some obscure target before we zero in on what marketing really wants and on what we should do. We do not start off with any clear ideas—and we should. We have set up some procedures to help clarify this.

"We have a design review meeting at the time engineering projects are initiated, and at various key points throughout the project. We've just got this program started and we hope that it will help us to use our time more productively. In working through our problems, I think I have come to understand engineering's role better.

"Engineering will not really initiate new product development projects. It may initiate projects to improve designs from a technical or performance point of view, but the major projects for the development of new products will come from marketing. We are a market-oriented company, and what the customer needs is probably better known by marketing than anyone else. If this is the case, and I think it is, then we must be very careful to extract all the information we can from marketing people in general, and from Jim Powell in particular, if we are to do an effective engineering job.

"Well, Howard, I've been rambling on about some of the problems. You may have some questions that you'd like to ask me."

"Yes, I would, Al," replied Howard Elliott. "Can you give me some idea about how you manage the engineering department. How do you act in order to get the engineering jobs done effectively?"

"I think I know how to manage the department," said Mr. Elfman, "but I don't think that I've done a very good job. I've seen many of the same problems that I know Jim Powell has seen: poor engineering designs, weaknesses in people, and failure to get our projects completed. I guess my first approach was to try to protect the engineers from marketing interference. I think I did this in response to the engineers' feeling that marketing's involvement in engineering affairs did more to frustrate than to help them. In some instances, this resulted in the execution of engineering work that did not help to accomplish marketing objectives and led to many complaints about engineering by marketing personnel. In response to these complaints, I tried to defend the engineering department and the engineers. I suppose this may have generated more difficulties in marketing–engineering relationships. But it seems to me that engineering has been judged too much on details and not enough on overall performance. In any event, I have responded to criticism and have tried to correct the things that seem to give people ammunition for shooting at engineering rather than working on a planned approach for engineering that would do most to help the company achieve its goals. In doing my job, I have used my time mainly to correct the immediate problems and what I have been doing is not what I would like to do, or what I believe I should do, to effectively manage engineering.

"I find I spend two-thirds of my time here in my office handling mail, dealing with people who just walk in or call in to ask questions about engineering projects, working out engineering schedules, and dealing with various administrative problems. The rest of my time is spent helping on actual project efforts, holding hands with some of the engineers, and pushing to get projects completed. I would like to spend more of my time on planning, in working with marketing in the development of project ideas, in determining project specifications, and in setting project priorities.

"You might be interested in looking at the way in which we plan engineering work," said Mr. Elfman. "I have just set up this control board."

Al Elfman reached around behind his chair and lifted a metal panel onto his desk. The names of project engineers were listed in a column at the left hand edge of the panel and the projects assigned to each engineer were designated by colored strips which were placed horizontally to the right of each engineer's name. The length of each project strip represented the amount of time estimated to complete the projects. Each project strip was of a different color so that one could easily see the number of projects assigned to an engineer and the length of time required.

"This schedule will help me to balance the work load in engineering and enable me to follow the progress on each project," Elfman explained. "I haven't started yet to indicate the progress on each project and I am not quite certain how I will do it, as each engineer has several projects that he works on in parallel. It would be fairly simple to do if each engineer performed work on only the first project, completed that, and then went on to the next, but this is not the case. We also issue reports to each division and to top management periodically."

Mr. Elfman thumbed through a large sheaf of papers scattered over his desk. After some time, he found the report he was looking for. The report, which was prepared by hand and had many notes scrawled over it, showed project number, project name, engineer assigned, estimated hours and cost to complete, hours expended to date, and a column for remarks.

Howard Elliott asked how much work remained to be done to complete each project.

"Well, we haven't made those estimates. I suppose we should since it rarely happens that engineering work is completed in exactly the amount of time we originally estimated. In fact, we are wrong on our estimates more often than we are right."

"How frequently do you issue this report, Al?" asked Howard Elliott.

"We are supposed to issue the report quarterly, but we just haven't done it. I guess I don't watch this as closely as I should, and perhaps I simply haven't organized the work so that it gets cranked out regularly. I am planning, however, to get this scheduling and reporting handled on a regular basis."

Howard Elliott then said he understood that one of the products was not performing satisfactorily in the field and was curious to know how Mr. Elfman went about handling such a problem.

Mr. Elfman replied, "We are putting great emphasis on this problem right now. It has been a very sticky situation and has severely embarrassed the company and the engineering department. Naturally, marketing is applying all the pressure they can to get us to solve the problem. The fault lies, I suppose, with engineering and stems initially from inadequate engineering and secondarily from incomplete or inadequate product testing. We think now that we have the problem licked. I have been devoting a very large part of my own time to this problem recently, and we have also assigned other engineers to work on the problem to speed the development of a solution. I'm hopeful that we will soon have the problem licked."

"Mr. Wilbur mentioned the problem of increasing engineering costs to me," said Howard Elliott. "How do you go about controlling costs in the engineering department?"

"I have spoken to Mr. Wilbur about this," said Mr. Elfman. "At the beginning of the year we set up a budget for the engineering department and, according to the reports I receive from accounting, we are operating within the budget. I submitted the budget to Mr. Wilbur at the first of the year and he approved it. Perhaps the budget was too high in relation to the expected level of sales; that I don't know. It would seem to me, if the budget was too high, Mr. Wilbur should have asked me how I could reduce it. But he didn't, and I have tried to operate within the budget we set."

Mr. Howard Elliott then asked Mr. Elfman how he measured or appraised the effectiveness of engineering personnel.

Mr Elfman said, "We just use horse sense, I guess. In the design review meetings I get a chance to evaluate their designs and progress, and, of course, I see the men from time to time when we discuss their projects out in the engineering department. I don't have any formal methods for appraisal—observation and feeling are my primary tools for evaluating performance. I know that we have two very weak men. I decided definitely a week ago that I would let one go, but I haven't taken any action yet. The other is making some contribution, but I haven't yet decided what to do about him."

In concluding the conversation with Mr. Elfman, Howard Elliott asked, "What do you consider your greatest problems in managing the engineering department and what changes, if any, would you like to bring about to make your job, or the job of the engineering department, easier to handle and more responsive to the needs of the company?"

"That's a pretty good question." said Mr. Elfman. "It seems to me that our greatest problem is in relating effectively with the marketing departments. I think we get along pretty well with the laboratory group, but we have many problems with the industrial marketing people. In particular, Jim Powell is a tough man to deal with. He is aggressive, critical, demanding, and he knows so much more about the product line, its needs, and where he wants to go than we do, that he just overwhelms us. I think one of the things that would help us to operate more productively would be to find more useful ways of doing business with the industrial marketing group—to establish a little more order and a little more consistency. Maybe we just don't understand them and they don't understand us. Another problem I have is in getting set up to really manage the engineering group.

"I think I need better methods for getting projects started, reviewing progress, and helping people to do their jobs. I think I have made some headway on this recently, but there is still a lot to be done."

Howard Elliott concluded his conversation with Mr. Elfman by offering to help in any way Mr. Elfman thought he could be useful. They also discussed the future meetings that were scheduled with the marketing managers to review the engineering project workload. Mr. Elfman accompanied Howard Elliott to the door, where they parted with a friendly handshake.

Following his conversation with Mr. Albert Elfman, the chief engineer, Mr. Elliott spoke at length with the marketing manager for each product line. In each of these interviews the subject of engineering performance came up, and in each instance the marketing managers were very critical of the engineering support given their departments. They complained about the quality of engineering designs, engineering's inability to complete projects when needed, and about Mr. Elfman's failure to do the things he promised to do. Mr. Powell, in particular, was very strong in his opinions about engineering and stated flatly that Mr. Elfman, though personally most congenial, was incompetent. Each manager presented examples of engineering's failures and spoke favorably about engineering's accomplishments. In the few days following these private conversations with the marketing managers, meetings were held to review the engineering workload.

Mr. Elliott and the chief engineer, Mr. Elfman, met with each marketing manager to review the engineering projects that were outstanding, to calculate the engineering workload, and to compare this workload with the available workforce. The results of these conversations led to the elimination of several projects, the modification of a few projects, changes in priorities, and to a determination that at least two extra people were employed in engineering that were not needed to handle the workload. It was agreed that two engineers, whose competence was doubted, would be released. Mr. Elfman made this change immediately. Mr. Elliott then turned his attention to the question of what he would say to Mr. Wilbur, what recommendations he would make, and how he would present his ideas in an effective manner.

Hartwell Manufacturing Company (C)

Howard Elliott began to assemble and classify the information received from Mr. Wilbur, from the marketing managers, from his interview with Mr. Elfman, and from his experiences in reviewing the

This case was prepared by Craig E. Lundberg under the direction of Arthur N. Turner as the basis for class discussion. Cases are not designed to present illustrations of either correct or incorrect handling of administrative problems. The company name and names of individuals are disguised. Copyright © 1966 by the President and Fellows of Harvard College.

engineering workload. It seemed to him that the evidence overwhelmingly suggested that Mr. Elfman's performance as chief engineer was inadequate. In fact, Mr. Elfman had himself agreed that his management of the engineering department had not produced the results he hoped to achieve. After two years on the job Mr. Elfman had said that he was just now beginning to get a handle on the process of planning, guiding, and reporting on engineering activities. Should it really take this long to set up an adequate process for managing engineering? Why was it that it took a severe field problem before sufficient engineering attention was applied to solve a serious product performance problem? Why was the engineering and testing on this product inadequate? Why were effective interdepartmental relationships between marketing and engineering difficult to achieve? What effect has Mr. Elfman's past view of engineering's mission had on his ability to structure effective relationships in this situation? Why is Mr. Elfman unable to follow through on specific promises he has made to people in the organization? Could Mr. Elfman be expected to alter his behavior in the future? How could he be influenced to change his behavior patterns? If he could change, would he be able to alter his behavior sufficiently to produce satisfactory engineering results, and to become recognized within the organization as a competent engineering executive? How long would this take? Could the company afford to wait this long? These questions seemed to be central to Howard Elliott's analysis:

1. Is Mr. Elfman a competent manager?

2. Is poor engineering performance a consequence of ineffective marketing–engineering relationships, and/or a consequence of incompetent engineering management?

3. What other factors might be major determinants of engineering performance?

In thinking about the global problem of engineering performance, Elliott listed the following items of information he had gathered:

1. Mr. Elfman frequently failed to return telephone calls, to respond to written inquiries, to gather and transmit information after acknowledging that he would do so.

2. Reports on engineering progress were not accurately prepared, were messy in appearance, lacked important information, and were not issued regularly.

3. A program for planning, scheduling, and controlling engineering work had not existed in the past, but was now in the process of being developed.

4. Engineering costs had increased substantially but total engineering costs were within the budgets established.

5. Misunderstandings existed between marketing and engineering about which projects were required and about project priorities.

6. The marketing managers and the chief engineer indicated they were not satisfied with existing engineering–marketing relationships.

7. Most engineering projects were not completed on schedule.

8. A very serious problem involving poor product performance exists in the field, and had existed for some time.

9. Marketing managers and the chief executive say they are not satisfied with overall engineering results.

Elliott thought the first four items were directly within the scope of or directly under the control of Mr. Elfman. To Elliott they seemed personal in the sense that Elfman could act pretty much as he chose, independently of other segments of the organization, with respect to these items. In other words, how Elfman chose to handle each of these items was a function of how important he judged them to be and was a function of his own personality, interests, or avoidances. Figure 1 sets forth a conceptual scheme which Elliott prepared in analyzing the influences that tended to shape Elfman's performance and behavior.

Elfman's failure to respond to requests for information and to do the things he promised to do seemed to Elliott to be a characteristic of Elfman's behavior that was related to his personality and his personality development. Too many people complained about this aspect of Elfman's behavior to discount the complaints as simply isolated instances of behavior that caused irritation. This behavior appeared to be a characteristic style that Elfman repeated over and over again. It did not seem reasonable to account for Elfman's failure to be responsive to requests of others by the argument that he was busy. Occasionally, a busy man might overlook commitments, but to do so repeatedly seemed more than casual forgetfulness. Elliott doubted that this aspect of Elfman's behavior could be changed by simply pointing out to Elfman that it was important for him to remember his commitments.

Engineering's failure to prepare and issue accurate, comprehensive, and timely reports may be somewhat related to Elfman's failure to do things he promised he would do. A commitment to issue a report at a given time is as much a commitment as a promise to "call you back this afternoon." Furthermore, there didn't seem to be any rational reason why engineering reports should not be accurate and complete. There

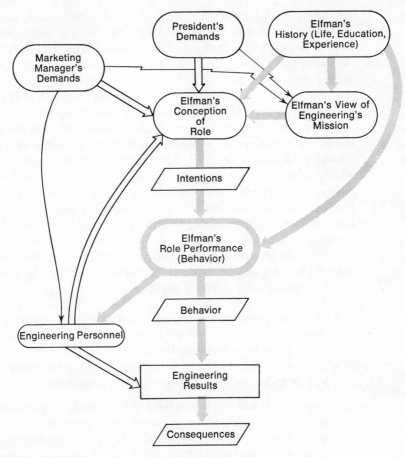

Figure 1. Hartwell Manufacturing Company.

were clerical and secretarial people in the engineering organization who could gather information and prepare reports. Elliott found it difficult to understand why Elfman had not set up an internal system for preparing and issuing reports regularly, especially since Mr. Wilbur had expressed, on a number of occasions, his interest in receiving such reports. Elfman certainly could have seen that such a system was established if he had chosen to devote the necessary time and effort to do so.

The issue of rising engineering costs did have some logical explanation. Mr. Wilbur complained about rising engineering costs, yet he had approved the engineering budget which specifically authorized increased expenditures in the engineering department. Elfman believed that he was operating within the limits of his authority with respect to engineering expenses, yet Mr. Wilbur apparently felt that Elfman should not have increased engineering expenses. Some sort of misunderstanding existed between Mr. Wilbur and Mr. Elfman on this point and Elliott decided he would speak with Mr. Wilbur about this when he next met with him. It did not seem reasonable for Mr. Wilbur to be critical of Mr. Elfman, when Mr. Elfman was acting according to pre-arranged agreements.

Howard Elliott noted, as he continued his analysis, that items 5 and 6 had to do with interdepartmental and interpersonal relationships between engineering and marketing. Neither Mr. Elfman nor the marketing managers were satisfied with engineering–marketing relationships. Marketing personnel felt they were not adequately in touch with and did not have adequate control over what was being done in engineering. They felt that engineering efforts were being wasted on fruitless investigations and that marketing ideas were not effectively incorporated into engineering designs. Engineering personnel, on the other hand, felt that attempts by marketing personnel to influence their work resulted in confusion and frustration. Effective relationships did not exist between engineering and marketing. Elliott thought that some or all of the following elements might contribute to this situation:

a. The concept of engineering's mission in the organization is not clear. Engineering personnel have one idea regarding their role which is not in accord with the idea held by marketing personnel. This basic conflict of engineering's mission may be creating problems of status, prestige, self-esteem, and competition.

b. Engineering and marketing have not developed a system of inter-action and coordination that enables each group to accomplish its goals. This may be a consequence of the lack of consistency in their views regarding engineering's role and/or simply that engineering and marketing have not interacted sufficiently, at a fundamental level, to establish a system of constructive interaction.

c. The interpersonal dynamics between Elfman and Powell may be such that mutual understanding and coordination is difficult to achieve. Conflicting personal goals and the desire for personal achievement may activate defense mechanisms that prohibit these individuals from developing an understanding and mutually helpful relationship.

d. The president's efforts to establish effective interpersonal relationships at the executive level and to establish effective interdepartmental relationships may be inadequate or ineffective. The president may not view his role as one of facilitating integration between individuals and between departments. It may be difficult, and perhaps impossible, for executives or departments to establish effective relationships without the chief executive's help. The mission of each department cannot be determined independently of other departments. Corporate objectives are achieved through coordinated efforts. Such coordination might be achieved by a logical plan for coordination, in-depth discussions with executives and other personnel to communicate the objectives of the plan, some give-and-take discussions regarding the validity or legitimacy of the plan, a feeling that a consensus has been reached, observations of the effectiveness of coordination, and reviews of the plans and practices to generate improvements over time.

e. The organization structure itself may be contributing to engineering ineffectiveness. The existing structure may be complicating the ability of marketing personnel to interact directly with the engineers who were assigned to product development and improvement projects for their product lines.

Elliott, in reviewing the situation, saw items 7, 8, and 9 as consequences of items 1 through 6. His observations and interviews convinced him that engineering's total performance was quite unsatisfactory, and that the fears and concerns of Mr. Wilbur , the president, and those of the marketing managers, were justified. Furthermore, on the basis of his interviews and observations, and his evaluation of Mr. Elfman's performance as compared with the performance of other managers that he had observed throughout his consulting experience, he concluded that Mr. Elfman was not doing an effective job, and he doubted that Mr. Elfman, even with help from Mr. Wilbur, would be able to overcome the negative opinions that others held toward him or that he would be able to do an effective job in the future. He decided to recommend that Mr. Elfman be released. Though Elliott concluded that his recommendation was sound and that he could give it ample support, he was not so sure how he should act in the future. What really were his responsibilities now? How should he act to fulfill them effectively?

It did not seem to Elliott that the mere presentation of his recommendations was sufficient. He wondered how he could discuss the Elfman episode with Mr. Wilbur in a way that would enable Mr. Wilbur to evaluate his own experience and relationship with Elfman and to learn something from it. He wondered how he might help Jim Powell to do the same. It seemed to Elliott that a conscious concern over the development of effective interpersonal and interdepartmental relationships needed to be recognized and somehow incorporated into the thoughts and actions of management people. Perhaps, in his future contacts with Mr. Wilbur and Mr. Powell, he could somehow help them to give greater consideration to these issues. Howard Elliott was also concerned over his relationship with and his responsibilities to Albert Elfman.

Elliott wondered whether he had really been of any help to Elfman. As the situation stood, he was about to recommend that Mr. Elfman be released. This recommendation might be accepted and acted upon immediately, a decision to act might be delayed, or it was possible, though Elliott thought it unlikely, that Elfman would not be released at all. In any event, whether Elfman stayed or not, Elliott felt that he should talk with him again. He felt he had some obligation to act helpfully with Elfman—either in a way that would make his further tenure at Hartwell more productive, or to help him to think about his experience with Hartwell and to learn something from it that would help him in any new situation. Elliott decided to get Mr. Wilbur's approval before talking with Elfman again, but as he thought about the conversation he planned to hold with Elfman further questions arose in his mind about his relationship with Elfman.

Would it be possible, Elliott wondered, for him to act helpfully with Elfman in view of the fact that he was going to recommend Elfman's release? Would Elfman's perceptions of Elliott, possibly including that of seeing Elliott as a threat to his security and career, prevent Elfman from gaining anything from such a conversation? How openly should Elliott discuss his own assignment in the organization, or the conclusions that he had reached? What motives and intentions stimulated him to want to talk with Elfman again?

CASE V-6. Ruth Haskill (A)

This is a report of the first part of a talk between Miss Dawes, a personnel counselor, and Ruth Haskill, the first-line supervisor of a group of fifteen girls. The girls assembled parts into a small but complex unit, at benches, where their chairs were placed about four feet apart. Miss Haskill reported to a forelady, who was one of four second-line

Case material of the Harvard Graduate School of Business Administration, prepared as a basis for class discussion. Cases are not designed to present illustrations of either correct or incorrect handling of administrative problems. All names have been disguised. Copyright 1956 by the President and Fellows of Harvard College.

supervisors in the department. The conversation took place early in 1946, at which time the company had begun its postwar reconversion program.

For some time prior to the conversation, Miss Dawes had had it in mind to talk with Miss Haskill. She had been available for counseling with the members of Miss Haskill's group for about six months, but she was not entirely satisfied with the way her relations with Miss Haskill and the girls under the latter's supervision had developed. For example, from her interviews and other contacts with them Miss Dawes had gained the impression that the girls who might benefit the most from counseling were not coming to her for help. Hence, she welcomed Miss Haskill's request to be taken off the job for a talk.

RUTH HASKILL: Hi.

MISS DAWES: Hello, Miss Haskill.

RUTH HASKILL: How are you?

MISS DAWES: Fine. How about you?

RUTH HASKILL: I'm OK.

MISS DAWES: Good.

RUTH HASKILL: When are you going to take me out?

MISS DAWES: Whenever you'd like to go out.

RUTH HASKILL: Oh, you're kidding me.

MISS DAWES: If you'd like to go, let's go.

RUTH HASKILL: Would you really take me out?

MISS DAWES: If you would like to.

RUTH HASKILL: It's been a long time since we've had a talk.

MISS DAWES: It has been.

RUTH HASKILL: When was the last time? Oh, I remember, it was when we went upstairs to see Mrs. Anderson's gift, remember? That's a long time. That's before Christmas. You've been neglecting me.

MISS DAWES: You don't think that's a good idea.

RUTH HASKILL: No, I should say I don't.

MISS DAWES: Well, would you like to go now?

RUTH HASKILL: Sure.

MISS DAWES: All right, fine. Do you want to wait just a minute until I see if the forelady can get someone to replace you here?

RUTH HASKILL: Sure, I'll wait. You see if she can get anybody. But don't tell the forelady that I asked you to take me out. You know, just tell her that you'd like to see me.

MISS DAWES: Just that I'd like to have you go out with me.

RUTH HASKILL: Yeah, that's right.

MISS DAWES: OK, just a minute.

RUTH HASKILL: All right. (The counselor walked off and returned shortly.)

MISS DAWES: It's all right, we can go. Miss Smith is coming down to replace you.

RUTH HASKILL: Oh, that's swell. Did she say anything about my being out a lot or anything?

MISS DAWES: About you being out a lot?

RUTH HASKILL: I mean about—I had my relief, or anything like that?

MISS DAWES: No, I told her that you were here and that I would like for you to go out with me if it wasn't too busy. It isn't. Here comes Miss Smith now; I think she'll replace you.

RUTH HASKILL: OK.

MISS SMITH: (As she started to take over Miss Haskill's work, she bantered with her.) So you're going out to kill time.

RUTH HASKILL: I'll say. I'm going out to pour out all my troubles to Miss Dawes.

MISS SMITH: Yeah, uh huh, that's a fine story. You're just going out for a rest.

RUTH HASKILL: Sure, Miss Dawes always comes around when I look tired.

MISS SMITH: Well, then, she ought to come all the time. Sounds like a good idea to me. Well, go ahead, I'll take over for an hour.

RUTH HASKILL: I may not be back in an hour.

MISS SMITH: Yeah, I know you. Well, have a good time.

RUTH HASKILL: Oh, we will, don't worry. (She walked out with the counselor.) Well, now that we're on our way I think that I have to have a little food before I can talk. Do you want to feed me?

MISS DAWES: Oh, there's a catch in this. You aren't just going with me for a talk. You have an ulterior motive.

RUTH HASKILL: I'll say I have. I would like to get something to eat, though. You don't mind, do you? We can go up to the cafeteria and get something to eat, and then we can talk.

MISS DAWES: All right, sure, if that's what you'd like to do.

RUTH HASKILL: Uh huh. Wait until I put this thing away (indicating a smock she was wearing), and then we can go up.

MISS DAWES: OK.

On the way up to the cafeteria they met several people with whom they chatted informally, and in the cafeteria several other girls joined them at the table, so that conversation remained general. When they had finished eating, Miss Haskill said, "Well, I guess we're all through. Where shall we go, downstairs?"

MISS DAWES: If you'd like to.

RUTH HASKILL: Yeah, I would like to. Let's go down and talk for a while.

MISS DAWES: Fine.

RUTH HASKILL: I feel a lot better now. I get so hungry about this time in the morning. I wish I could make a standing date with you to come around every morning just about this time.

MISS DAWES: Well, maybe we'd better work on that.

RUTH HASKILL: Oh, yeah, wouldn't that be fine—go out with you, so that I can get a breakfast.

MISS DAWES: I bet we'd find out other things to do besides that.

RUTH HASKILL: Yeah, I bet we would, too. (As they entered a counseling room, she commented:) Oh, the rooms are bright and shiny this morning.

MISS DAWES: Look like a good cleaning job, doesn't it?

RUTH HASKILL: Yeah, it does. Say, it's awful hot in here.

MISS DAWES: We could try the other room. (They moved next door.)

RUTH HASKILL: Oh, this is better.

MISS DAWES: You'd rather stay here?

RUTH HASKILL: Yeah, this is all right, isn't it? (She sat down.) Well, how are you doing with your nylons?[1]

MISS DAWES: How am I doing with them?

RUTH HASKILL: Yeah, did you get any?

MISS DAWES: No, did you?

RUTH HASKILL: No, but you hear about some people that have five or six pairs. Gee, I don't have any. They put them out at such funny hours that we don't have a chance to get over there.

MISS DAWES: I haven't had any luck with it, either. I never seem to be there at the right time.

RUTH HASKILL: Seems to me they could fix it up some way so that people who work will have a chance to get in there and get some. I need them, too. (She talked for several minutes about the difficulty of getting stockings. There was a short pause, which she broke, saying:) "How's your job going?"

MISS DAWES: Well, if you mean do I like my job, I like it.

RUTH HASKILL: I mean are there a lot of kids coming up and talking to you? What do they talk about; what do they say to you?

MISS DAWES: That's a pretty big question. We really talk about everything.

RUTH HASKILL: Yeah, I know, but like what things?

MISS DAWES: Well, what have we talked about before? A little bit of everything, haven't we?

RUTH HASKILL: Yeah, I guess that's right. Only, that one time I had a problem, you know. Do they all have problems?

MISS DAWES: Some do, some don't. There are all different kinds of things that we talk about. You are a supervisor; what do the girls talk to you about

RUTH HASKILL: Oh, I don't know. I don't talk to them so very much. But then, I think that's different. They feel different about talking to me.

MISS DAWES: Yes, there is definitely a difference. Here they know that they're free to talk about anything, or at least I try to tell them that, but sometimes it's a little bit difficult for the girls to understand

[1] At the time it was difficult to buy nylons in the stores.

that. Many times they'll say, "I don't have anything to talk about." We always found something.

I'm glad we had a chance to get together today, because I have been wanting to talk with some of you supervisors a little bit more. I talked with a few, but I haven't gotten around to all of them. I thought maybe we might talk a little bit more about this inasmuch as we're both doing a job, the same kind of a job; we're both there for pretty much the same reason, and I thought maybe we could sort of work on it together, and I might be able to get some suggestions about my work.

RUTH HASKILL: Yeah, yeah, I suppose that's right. We're both sort of doing the same thing.

MISS DAWES: Well, we're both working with people. You're in a little different position than I am, but I believe that is our job.

RUTH HASKILL: Yes, that right. They are the same that way. I don't know what you mean by suggestions.

MISS DAWES: Well, I've been around here now for about six months meeting the girls and talking with them. I figured that you girls, you supervisors, work about as closely with the people as anybody does. The forelady can give me suggestions as to when is the best time to come in as far as the business is concerned; but it seems to me that you supervisors work more closely with the people, and you probably know them a little bit better than the others. Maybe you could give me little pointers.

Now, for instance, it seems to me that some girls I haven't talked with yet would like to come out and talk, but I don't know about it, so I don't go up to them as quickly as I might if I knew that they wanted to come out with me. I'd get around to them eventually, but if I knew about it ahead of time I could go up a little sooner and ask them to come out. And then there may be others who don't care to have anything to do with it; I go up and ask them and it's a sort of annoyance to them. I could avoid that because I don't want any of them to feel that I'm trying to push myself on them, trying to get them to come out, even though they don't want to. I don't want them to feel pushed, you know.

RUTH HASKILL: I know what you mean. Well, I don't think I can give you any suggestions, because I don't really talk to the girls very much about this. I haven't heard them say very much about it, so I don't think that I could give you any suggestions, but I see what you mean. It would be better if you could go and get the girls that do want to come out with you.

MISS DAWES: There seems to be some holding back on asking to come out with me. The girls will ask me, well, as you did today, on the floor there, in the hall, or in the rest room some place; they'll ask me to take them out, but as far as going to the supervisor or anything of that kind, they don't seem to be interested in doing that. Unless I know that they want to come out, I don't ask them, except just as I go along, selecting people at random.

RUTH HASKILL: Sure, it would be better if they'd let you know about it. I could see how maybe the supervisor could let you know, because we do work with them more. We could probably tell you about people that we thought you might be interested in talking to.

MISS DAWES: Or, perhaps, you don't know whether someone wants to talk to me or not, but you think it would be a good idea for her to get away for a little while. You notice something about her and think maybe it would be a good chance for her to go out and talk for a while.

RUTH HASKILL: Yeah, I know, and I think we do have some that ought to get out for a while because, well, they're sort of resentful and don't do a very good job. I think, if they would get out a little bit, it would do them some good.

MISS DAWES: People who you think are pretty much confined and have things that are bothering them; but they don't say anything about it until it's affecting their job.

RUTH HASKILL: Yeah, I think so; course, I don't know. I mean, that's my own feeling about them.

MISS DAWES: Well, those are the things I'm interested in hearing about, and anytime you know of anyone like that, if you'd feel free to just mention it to me, I could get her out.

RUTH HASKILL: Yeah, uh huh. I suppose I could tell you about those cases when I think of them. I can't think of any right now.

MISS DAWES: Yes, sure. I don't suppose you do think of anything now, but maybe as you go along you'll be thinking about a little of what we've talked about. Something might occur to you, and if you sort of make a memo and tell me anytime you see me, I'd appreciate it a lot. If you speak to me about some girl, I'll go up to her the same way that I come up to you or anyone else. I'd like to talk with her and wonder if she'd like to come out. I won't ever mention that you suggested that she come, or anything of that kind.

RUTH HASKILL: Yeah, well, that would be a good idea. I'll think about it and let you know if I know of anybody. Do you think that more of the girls are coming out now?

MISS DAWES: Have you noticed that there's more interest in counseling?

RUTH HASKILL: Well, I don't know. I don't hear them talking about it so much any more. I know at first they were all talking about it. They didn't like the idea at all; they were just sure that it wasn't on the level, sort of. I mean they felt—if they went down and talked to you—the company would know about all they said, and I don't hear so much of that any more. Of course, as I say, I don't talk to them very much about it. Really, I haven't said anything to them about it. Well do they talk to you about it?

MISS DAWES: Lately I find, I think, that more of the girls are feeling free to talk to me about it or to ask questions. At first it seemed to me that they'd come out for an interview, but they were a little uneasy. I'd ask them if they had any question about it, any comments. Oh, no-no, they didn't have any; everything was fine. Well, I was pretty sure that they did have some—wondering about it, you know. Lately, however, I notice that of their own accord, without my asking them anything, they are asking questions about the counseling program.

RUTH HASKILL: What kind of questions do you mean?

MISS DAWES: One question that has come up quite a bit lately is "What is the company getting out of this? Why are they putting this in?" Well, now, to me it's interesting to have it come out that way because I see that the workers are thinking seriously about it and really wondering. As long as they tell me about it, I can answer them and have something to go on, sort of. I think for the most part when I do try to explain it to them they understand it a little bit better than they did before. Not that they understand the idea of counseling, necessarily, but why the company has put this into effect. I think in some cases I have cleared up quite a bit of wondering, and I like to see that happen.

RUTH HASKILL: Well, what do you tell them when they ask you why the company put it in?

MISS DAWES: You mean you would like to have me explain what the idea is on the part of the company?

RUTH HASKILL: Yes, I'd sort of like to know myself just what you tell them, so that if they ever ask me I can talk about it a little bit to them, too.

MISS DAWES: Sure, I think I can give you an idea of what I usually tell them. As far as the company is concerned, it's true that they're not here to take care of you and me. They're not in business to see that you and I are happy; it isn't a charitable organization.

RUTH HASKILL: How well I know!

MISS DAWES: Why, sure. And I think that's where a lot of the wondering comes in. A lot of the girls think, "Well, the company isn't getting anything out of this in black and white. Why are they bothering so much about me as an individual?"

RUTH HASKILL: Yeah, yeah, I've heard them say that, too. And you do sort of wonder about that.

MISS DAWES: Well, it seems to me that this is one more effort to make conditions as pleasant as they can for you people. Not for any unselfish motive on the part of the company, because, after all, any business is interested in profit, making as much money as they can.

RUTH HASKILL: That's right.

MISS DAWES: And our company isn't any different than any other; they want to make as much as they can. Over a period of time employers have learned that they can get more profit by making conditions for their employees as pleasant as they can, and I think every company tries to do that to a certain extent. Some may be a little more successful than others. I don't suppose there is any place where the job is just perfect and the working conditions are perfect. At least I've never heard about it.

RUTH HASKILL: No, and neither have I.

MISS DAWES: But each company does in their own way try to make things as pleasant as they can—little things I can think of, relief periods in the morning and afternoon, an hour for lunch, a cafeteria here in the building so we don't have to go outside if we don't want to. The rest room is pleasant and redecorated. They don't really know how much those things mean to us, how often we use them, how much we use them, how many of us use them; but they're trying these things, hoping that a pleasant atmosphere will make it easy for you to relax and feel better about going back to work. In the cafeteria they try to have the food as good as they can because if you have a good lunch you will probably feel better and work better.

Well, an idea like personnel counseling: the company looks it over; they're not getting anything from it in black and white, but on the other hand it might be just one more thing to make conditions more pleasant for the people. So, they think they'll try it. They put it in and have me come up here. Well, as far as the company is concerned, they aren't going to know until after a period of time whether this is really doing any good or not. If the girls want to take advantage of it, here it is; if they don't want to, all right. Well, then, the same thing with the cafeteria, relief; you're not forced to take part in any of those things if you don't want to make use of them. Well, it's the same way with me; that's why I want to be so careful not to have any of the girls feel that I'm trying to force them to come out, because it isn't that kind of a thing. If you want to use it, all right, and if you don't want to use it, all right.   It may be just one more thing in making the work more pleasant for you.

RUTH HASKILL: I see that—uh huh. I never thought of it that way before, but I suppose that is right. Well, then, they don't get anything from you. I mean, you don't make any report—you have a supervisor though; don't you have to make some kind of a report to him?

MISS DAWES: Well, yes and no. That's kind of a silly way to answer that question, but it's kind of a puzzling question. I have a record, if that's what you want to call it. Yet it isn't like what we think of when we think of reports. Well, for instance, in your department, you keep a record of how many units you make in a day. You have something in black and white down on paper that you can see.

RUTH HASKILL: Yeah, that's right. And we keep an individual record, too.

MISS DAWES: That's right, and that's what you think of when you think of reports.

RUTH HASKILL: Yes, it is.

MISS DAWES: Well, now, my record is something different from that. When I came in here I didn't have any training for this job. I'm getting my training as I go along. My training is my experience in talking to you girls. Our idea is, if someone does have something they really want very much to talk about, our place is to allow them to talk about it with as little interruption from me as possible. I try to avoid making any criticism or any kind of judgment, or try to keep from interrupting the person in allowing them to talk and find out about this thing themselves. Well, I'm pretty much like other people. I'm inclined to jump in and say, "Oh, yes, I know just what you mean. That happened to me, too." I could go off and talk about myself and prevent that girl from talking.

RUTH HASKILL: Yeah, I know. I've had that happen to me.

MISS DAWES: Surely, probably a lot of times. Maybe it isn't anything very serious at the time, but you just never know. It may be that this girl has something very important to her that she wants to talk about. Another thing I might do is appear to be shocked about something. Well, if that was the case, the girl would think, "Oh, I'm not going to say any more 'cause she thinks this is terrible."

RUTH HASKILL: Yeah. When you think somebody is kind of shocked you don't want to say any more because they'll think you're kind of funny or sort of queer. I know what you mean.

MISS DAWES: Now, I have to try to avoid that as much as possible because actually I'm interested in the person and not the things they're telling me. I'm not here for information or for facts, but rather to allow that person to examine this thing that she happens to be so much interested in at the time. Now, when I have a talk with a girl and I feel that things haven't gone too well—maybe I've cut her off in some way or I prevented her from talking as I'd like to have her talk—I go back to my office and try to put that down word for word. Well, you can imagine, I couldn't remember it entirely word for word.

RUTH HASKILL: I wouldn't think so.

MISS DAWES: It would be too difficult, but I try to get it as nearly word for word as I can and, of course, I'm especially interested in putting down what I had said, anything that I think may have interrupted her talk.

RUTH HASKILL: Yeah, I see.

MISS DAWES: When I get that down, then I go over that with my supervisor, and we talk it over, and I try to find where perhaps it would have been better if I had said something different or maybe hadn't said anything at all. But we go over it pretty thoroughly so the next time that I talk with someone—regardless if it's this person again or another person—I may be able to handle it a little differently and allow her to talk more, which is what I'm here for. I don't use any names or any information that might identify the individual. When I go over it with my supervisor, he doesn't know who the person is that I've been talking to. He isn't interested in that. That's not part of his job. He's interested in trying to help me do a little better the next time I'm talking with someone. When we're through going over this record, it's destroyed, so you see it isn't really a report. There isn't anything permanent kept on my talk with this person.

RUTH HASKILL: Oh, I see. You just don't keep anything, then.

MISS DAWES: That record is destroyed. Probably if it were seen, it wouldn't make any difference. There would be very few people who could recognize that information and know who said it; but at the same time you can't afford to take any chances like that and we don't because, if that information did get out or in the hands of the wrong person, it would simply mean that we would be all through, because then none of the girls would have any confidence in us at all, and I wouldn't blame them. But that is the only type of what you might consider a report or record that we make, and that is not permanent.

RUTH HASKILL: I see.

MISS DAWES: Now, of course, I can sit here and tell you that that record is destroyed. Well, you have no way of knowing whether it is or not. The only thing that you can do is take my word for it.

RUTH HASKILL: We'll just have faith in what you're saying.

MISS DAWES: That's about it. After I've been here for a while and the girls find that this information isn't getting back, people aren't talking about it, then I think they'll feel more free to come out and talk to me. They'll realize that I'm not repeating this information. It's not going into the company, it's not being used on any records, it's not being held against them in any way. And they'll understand a lot better. But that's something that takes sort of a long time, because I can sit here and tell you that I have no reports, but you still don't know for yourself; you haven't investigated it. The only thing I can ask you to do is to take my word for it. You can do that or not, however you feel about it.

Ruth Haskill (B)

The second part of a talk between Miss Dawes, a personnel counselor, and Ruth Haskill, a first-line supervisor, continues as follows without interruption after the first part of their talk, reported in Ruth Haskill (A).

RUTH HASKILL: I see I know about it. Well, I think that really has been the main thing with the girls. They've been wondering about that report and you know they're so conscious of it because we have so many records up there. Everything we do, practically, is put down, and now, lately, it's just getting worse than ever. They're just keeping all kinds of records, and they're getting a lot tougher with them, too. I don't know, production in our department hasn't been so good lately, and, well, there's been an awful lot of talking at the benches. That's one thing that they're not supposed to do. The girls know they're not supposed to do it, but nevertheless lately there has been an awful lot of it. We've had a lot of defective stuff returned, too, so, of course it makes the production record go down. They want to find out what's causing that. They decided to, well, get tough, and they're after them all the time now about this talking, about their conduct, and, well, it's getting kind of tight up there.

MISS DAWES: You mean it's been pretty lax, and so now it's all the harder to take this discipline, so to speak.

RUTH HASKILL: Yes, you know the girls know right along that they shouldn't talk. Not a whole lot has been done about it. Oh, we speak to them once in a while, but things were sort of let go. Well, we were so busy, and everyone was so rushed during the war, and we didn't have time to think too much about that sort of thing; but now the war is over, and they're really getting down to business. I think they call it their 1946 program, or something, but it's going to be an awful lot stricter up there, and, well, as a matter of fact the girls are getting pretty mad about it. They just resent all this close supervision, and you know I honestly think they do a better job when they let them relax a little bit, because it's awfully hard just to sit there. I know; I haven't been away from it too long. But when you're waiting for more material and you're just sitting there and there's a girl on either side of you, next to you, it's awfully hard not to talk.

MISS DAWES: When you have just nothing to do and the other girls are so close to you, it's sort of a temptation for you to talk. Is that it?

RUTH HASKILL: Well, sure, because if you just sit there and wait, or if you just make your units all day, you get so sleepy or dopey or something that—oh, I don't know—you just feel like you want to talk, and, of course, that's when you get into trouble because you lean over, sort of, to talk to the girl next to you and she leans over to talk to you, and then you both stop working, or you only half pay attention to what you're doing. Then you forget to check something and the inspector sends your work back. Well, I don't suppose they want them to just sit there and not say one word to anybody because that would be inhuman and they couldn't expect that, but I guess there's been so much of it lately, and I know there has. I've seen a lot of it myself. They just figure they've got to do something about it. That's probably one thing that's causing our low production, and so they're getting real tough about it, and they're keeping an awfully close eye on the girls. It makes them mad, and they call it spying and supervising, and everything is just like a prison. Somebody is saying, "Do this," and "Don't do that," and they resent it; and when some supervisor is with them, a lot of them won't even try; they'd rather do a good job when no one was watching over their shoulder, because they just don't like the idea of it. Well, it's just something that can't be helped, I guess. They've got to do something to bring up our production, get it back to where it used to be. But at the same time the girls just resent it so that they're not doing a good job. And I know. I have to go up to them and say, "Don't talk." Well, with some of them I could be up there every five minutes, saying it over and over again. You're supposed to only say a thing twice to them, and then if they don't do anything about it, you're supposed to report it to the forelady. Well, I don't know, I just sort of hate to do that, and oh, I suppose I should tell her and have it settled once and for all, but well, I just don't like to do it that way. The girls are—well, kind of funny about me. Some of them are awful resentful to think that I got this job, because most of them have more service than I do and they don't take things from me very well. If I say something to them, they say. "You're getting just like all the rest of them. What's the matter with you, anyway?" And you know I don't like that.

MISS DAWES: You don't want them to feel that you've changed because you have another job.

RUTH HASKILL: Yeah, that's right, and they sort of have the idea that just because I have this job now, I think I'm real good and I can come around and tell them what to do and what not to do. That isn't the idea. I've got a job, too. I've got people telling me what to do. I just don't go out and pick on somebody because I want to pick on her. Oh, I don't know, sometimes I get so fed up with it that I'd like to go back to the bench.

MISS DAWES: You're getting pressure, then, from both ways, from above and from below. You're sort of beginning to feel like you're squeezed in.

RUTH HASKILL: Yeah, that's it. The kids get mad at me if I say anything to them; and at the same time if I don't say anything to them, why, then, the forelady comes around and says, "I told you to do something about that; you go and do it," and I have to go and do it. And I sometimes think that I want to go back. (Pause.) I don't want to go back because then if I do they'll say, "Oh, she couldn't take it. She wasn't good enough." And sometimes I think I'm not good enough. I think they must have thought I had something in order to pick me for the job in the first place.

There's an awful difference in the way you tell people to do things, anyway. I know sometimes I'm not in the mood to be as nice as I should be about it. I'll go up to a girl and say, "Miss so and so just told me that you were talking and asked me to come over and ask you not to do it any more." Well, they take that pretty well, but sometimes I'm not in the mood to do it that way. I go up and say, "Stop your talking," and then they get angry. Well, I don't know; I guess I'm pretty much the same way. I don't like to have anyone tell me things to do, either, and tell it in a tone of voice like I wasn't doing what I should be doing. It just seems like there is somebody watching me all the time. I don't have any peace at all.

I like the job, the supervising; it's kind of hard standing around on my feet all the time, but it kind of seems like a step up, I guess. Heck, I don't want to go back to the bench and do the same thing all over again, just keep at it and never have any change. I think if they would just leave me alone for a while and let me do things my own way . . . I do things the way I was trained to do it, and if they don't like it they have to come up and tell me about it; but if they'd only get together. They tell me the same things, but they tell me how to go about it differently.

MISS DAWES: You're sort of betwixt and between.

RUTH HASKILL: Yeah, I don't know which to do. I know what I want to do, but it's just the way of doing it. Just yesterday I was talking to one of the other supervisors, and she was telling me about some training that she got on something the forelady gave her, and I said, "That isn't the way she told me to do it." So I told her how she told me to do it, and she said, "Oh no, you must have got it wrong." And there it is. It makes you sort of think, "My gosh, what am I here for?" I just don't seem to be doing anything the way I'm supposed to, yet who knows how I'm supposed to do it. Yesterday the forelady came up to me and told me to give a girl a certain kind of training. Well, I guess they forget sometimes that I'm new and that I haven't had all my training yet. So I told her I couldn't do that because I had never learned how, and she looked at me so disgusted and walked away. Well, what was I supposed to do? I couldn't give the girl the training because I had never learned it myself. And if they aren't going to give me the training, I certainly can't go up and ask them to give me this or that because, well, I don't even know what to ask for. Besides, that's their job, to take care the supervisors and see that they're trained on everything. Sometimes I think I'd like to quit the whole thing and get out of it. If the kids would be different about it; some of them are all right. The ones that have been here longer than I have resent me especially and yet so do some of the younger ones. You know, my forelady said to me one day, "The trouble with you is you have too many friends." And I did. I used to go around with the whole bunch of kids. You know, they were about my own age, and now that I'm a supervisor they aren't supposed to call me by my first name, and yet they do, and the other day one of the foreladies was in checking me. One of the kids signaled for me, and I went over to her bench, and she called me by my first name. Well, I don't want to correct her—oh, it didn't seem important enough— yet I was called down for it. And if I say something like that to the kids, why it just makes them all the more think that, oh, you're getting to be more like the rest of them. I don't want them to think that; I'm no different than I was before, but it does make a difference. They don't feel the same way about me, and yet when I tell them something to do, they laugh and say, "Oh, come off it now."

MISS DAWES: They don't seem to have the respect for your position that they would have if you hadn't been so friendly perhaps.

RUTH HASKILL: I think that's it. They think they know me so well that they can get away with stuff, and then when I tell them something to do—well, I'm just being—oh, you know, think I'm somebody, and that isn't it. I've got a job to do and I'm trying to do it the best way I can. I get to thinking about it and I get into such a mood that I don't do it very well, and I say things to them that I probably wouldn't say if I weren't feeling that way about it.

MISS DAWES: Well, then, your own feeling about the work seems to be getting in the way of doing an effective job.

RUTH HASKILL: Yeah, sometimes I think if I didn't feel this way about it, if I didn't get so mad inside, that I wouldn't talk to them in the way that I do and have them resent it. Lately it's been getting so that if anybody says one more thing to me I just get mad. Then I'm mad for the rest of the day. When the forelady comes around she'll say, "Smile, smile," and I don't feel like smiling and I don't want to smile. You can't go around with a grin on your face when you don't feel like it. I don't know, I guess I've got the wrong attitude. I'm just making it harder for myself by doing this because my own feelings are getting the best of me.

I think I can do the work all right if it weren't for the way these people treated me. Maybe it's me; maybe I don't treat them the way I should. You know, it wasn't so bad before. I thought I was going to like it a lot, but we've got these two new supervisors in the department, but they're people I didn't know before. Oh, sure, I knew them to say hello to—see them in the cafeteria and everything; I didn't know them to work with, you know. Well, now they come in, and they have different ideas and have different ways of doing things. Well, I'm not accustomed to that. With the others we used to have, I knew them real well and they understood. If things were wrong, I'd tell them about it and see how they would handle it if it was in their section; or if we were talking about how to do something in the department and I didn't understand what they meant, I'd say, "Wait a minute, I don't understand," and they would go over it again for me so that I would understand it. Now these two come in; I have nothing against them, but they just have a different way of doing things and telling me things, and it confuses me.

MISS DAWES: You are going through sort of an adjusting to them yet.

RUTH HASKILL: Yeah, and I suppose they are too, but they bring their ideas over here from another department and they don't try to get our ideas. They just do things just the way they've been doing things over there. We're not used to that, and that sort of takes time, and it sort of makes me mad, because I could have gotten along so well with the others. I sort of felt that they understood me. Maybe I'm the one that's making it harder for me than they are.

MISS DAWES: You think your own feelings are getting in the way, and you're not giving them a chance. You're not explaining to them that you don't understand and are really trying to find out if they would be willing to help you.

RUTH HASKILL: Maybe that's it. I honestly think that they would help me if I did tell them about it, but as soon as they say anything I just get mad right away. That's silly, I guess, because I shouldn't do that. Maybe it'll be sort of a matter of time before I get used to them and kind of get over this idea of the girls resenting me, too. I used to go with three girls—one we met this morning at the table —and we just palled around together all the time; the four of us had real good times; I liked them. After I got this job, they just changed toward me so; it wasn't my imagination, because I could tell when I was with them. They acted differently toward me and, oh, they were pleasant and nice, but we weren't together as much. One day I went down for a cigarette during my relief and two of these friends of mine were down there. They were sitting on the window sill so they didn't see me come in and, well, I just couldn't believe it. They had got talking about me, and, well, I've just never been able to feel the same toward them since, because no matter what they said or what they did or what anybody has told me about them, I couldn't believe in them again. And the things they said were so unkind and so untrue and it just made me feel terrible. Now, no matter how nice to me they are, I just can't warm up to them. It just makes me feel terrible to think that the girls all feel that way.

MISS DAWES: You're sort of becoming distrustful of all the girls, then, because these three have turned against you.

RUTH HASKILL: Yeah, and it makes me feel that when I go up to the benches, to say anything, to tell them not to do this or not to do that, they're angry, they're resentful, they'll do it more than ever just because I told them, and yet I suppose it isn't true; I know it isn't true of all of them. I've just gotten so that I'm very, very care-ful about what I say or what I do. I don't talk freely to anybody down here because I never know who's going to be listening; or if I do talk to them, I never know who they're going to tell. So, when they start to talk about someone or something I just say I don't care to discuss it and get up and walk away or just stop talking about it, because I don't take any chances around here anymore. There are people that can be very nice to your face, and behind your back, oh, it's just unbelievable. It makes me feel bad because I don't feel that I can do a good job when I know they feel that way about me.

MISS DAWES: Well, you have two things, then, that are concerning you: You have a job to do and you want to do that job to the very best of your ability, and yet you also have a desire to sort of maintain a friendship that you have with these girls. Well, you've seen some upsetting things happen, and you don't exactly want to be friends with them, maybe, but at the same time you want to feel comfortable with them. They may like you or they may have a respect for your position, and you find the two of them sort of conflicting. If you do your job well, the girls are going to resent it; but if you go in with these girls and are pleasant and let them get away with things, then your job is going to be neglected. You're sort of trying to decide which is more important to you: your job and your progress here with the company, or whether it would be more comfortable to you to go back to the bench and be with the girls on pretty much the same basis that you were before.

RUTH HASKILL: Yeah, I guess that is about it. I have my job to do. Well, I don't want to stay here forever. I'd like to do the best I can while I am here, and yet I do want to consider the girls. I don't really care, I don't want to be friends with them. I wish they would get over this feeling of resenting me. At the same time there doesn't seem to be anything I can do about that. I want to do my job and do it well.

MISS DAWES: Then part of your job is having the girls understand you.

RUTH HASKILL: It would make it a lot easier if they did understand me and if they did like me and knew that I wasn't doing that because I was trying to get even with them or because I was trying to show my authority or anything. It's part of my job, but they don't seem to understand that. But maybe if I could get over this feeling, and treat them a little differently, maybe they would understand better. You should come around more often, I think.

MISS DAWES: I think so, too. Let's do this more often.

RUTH HASKILL: Say, I'd better be going; I didn't know it was this time. I'd better get back there, don't you think?

MISS DAWES: It's up to you if you'd like to.

RUTH HASKILL: Oh, yes, I think I'd better go.

MISS DAWES: All right, but I would like to get together again. How would Monday be?

RUTH HASKILL: Monday? Sure, that's swell. Do you really mean it?

MISS DAWES: Yes, I'll look for you sometime Monday, and if you can't make it then, we'll make another date; but try and plan on Monday.

RUTH HASKILL: Oh, gee, that'll be swell. I think I'll go on my relief now. Do you think I'm entitled to a relief?

MISS DAWES: Do you want one?

RUTH HASKILL: Yeah, I think I will.

MISS DAWES: All right, sure.

RUTH HASKILL: Will you go in and tell them that I'll be down?

MISS DAWES: Yes, if you want me to, sure.

RUTH HASKILL: OK. I'll see you Monday.

MISS DAWES: Fine. Goodbye.

RUTH HASKILL: Goodbye.

CASE V-7. Harris-Connor and Associates

This case describes the relationships that existed between the members of the supervisory training section of Harris–Connor and Associates, a large and successful management consulting firm, during the six years from 1952 to 1958. The firm, located in New York, had nine separate sections and a staff of ninety people. Of these about ten were senior associates, twenty-five were junior associates, twenty were staff assistants, and the remainder were secretaries and clerical help.

Case material of the Harvard Graduate School of Business Administration, prepared as a basis for class discussion. Cases are not designed to present illustrations of either correct or incorrect handling of administrative problems. All names have been disguised. Copyright 1959 by the President and Fellows of Harvard College.

Table 1

HARRIS—CONNOR AND ASSOCIATES

Background Information on Individuals
in the Supervisory Training Section
July 1952

Name	Age	Job Title	Salary	Education	Years Seniority With Firm	Married or Single	Ethnicity and Religion
Marvin Cranshaw	39	Jr. Associate and Section Director	$30,000*	B.S.	11	M	English Protestant
Bill Shea	37	Jr. Associate	17,000*	M.S.	6	M	Irish Catholic
Paul Staples	27	Staff Assistant	6,000*	B.S.	2	M	Irish-English Catholic
Harry Blaul	23	Staff Assistant	5,300	M.B.A.	—	M	English-German Protestant
Harriet Harding	23	Secretary	2,500	Secretarial School	1	S	Scotch-English Protestant

* Including fees from outside speaking engagements and (in the case of Cranshaw and Shea) university teaching on a part-time basis.

Harry Blaul was hired as a staff assistant in 1952 after he graduated from the Harvard Business School. Blaul joined the supervisory training section with the understanding that he would probably leave the firm after two years in order to move into an industrial training position with a client company. Staff assistants employed by Harris–Connor and Associates typically spent only two or three years with the firm. Nevertheless, staff assistants' jobs were highly sought after because of Harris–Connor's excellent reputation with industry as an "advanced training ground" for business school graduates.

July 1952–July 1953

At the time Harry Blaul joined the supervisory training section, it had operated for ten years under the direction of Martin Cranshaw, a junior associate with the firm. In addition to Cranshaw, two other consultants and a secretary were members of the section. Table 1 gives background information on these four individuals and on Harry Blaul. At that time Blaul was told by Cranshaw that Blaul would report to Cranshaw and to Bill Shea. Cranshaw also explained that for the first six months Blaul would help Cranshaw, Shea, and Staples with the implementation of different industrial training programs which the section members designed and taught. After that with some guidance Blaul would begin to conduct his own training programs.

CRANSHAW: Most of these programs are built around the idea of combining the tools and techniques of industrial engineering with good sound human relations. There's no textbook for our courses, because the whole field is changing and developing so rapidly that any textbook would be obsolete before it got printed. We build our programs around the idea that the man on the job is in the best position to improve that job. He should be his own efficiency expert. And he should get the participation of his subordinates and associates. That way they won't resist the changes he wants to make or take these changes as criticism. Participation is the key to the whole thing. It ties back to the fact that two heads are better than one for ideas and the man who participates in a new idea will help to build it, not destroy it.

You haven't had any engineering or technical experience, but that's not important. We can teach you what you need to know in no time at all. The most important factor in all these programs is the human relations part. As I say, the biggest problem in getting any new idea into effect comes from the people who resist change or resent the criticism of an applied change. The answer to these problems, of course, is to get their participation in planning the change.

During his first six months at Harris–Connor, Blaul felt that he learned something about both the training programs and the men who taught them. He assisted Cranshaw and Paul Staples with two programs each and assisted Shea with one training program. In each case Blaul attempted to note what factors contributed to the strengths or weaknesses of each man's sessions. Blaul's notes with regard to sessions conducted by Cranshaw, Shea, and Staples included the following observations:

> Cranshaw relies primarily upon a well tested fund of stories, anecdotes, gadgets and gimmicks to make his points. He preaches participation, but he does 90 per cent of the talking. . . . He reaches pat answers and platitudes more often than depth in his conclusions. He avoids controversy. His second program was almost word for word identical with the first. Cranshaw begins with the interesting part that people play in any change situation, but soon focuses almost entirely upon how the gadgets and techniques can be worked into a factory setting. [Is this participation or manipulation?]
>
> Shea, though pedantic at times, has a real sensitivity for the training situation. Of the three he has the greatest talent for understanding and teaching others to understand some of the human problems involved in technical improvement and change. He lets the supervisors learn their way through the course and only becomes adamant around the crucial points when he argues like a skillful lawyer. Most important, Shea practices the participation that he preaches. His sessions are designed more around thought provoking questions, arguments, and demonstrations than around gadgets and gimmicks. Where Cranshaw will use a demonstration to make a series of pat points, Shea will use it as a springboard to challenge oversimplifications in the supervisors' thinking about human behavior.
>
> Staples, though pleasant, lacks the spark of either Cranshaw or Shea. His notes, style, jokes, and personality appear to be copied mostly from Cranshaw, but something is missing. Like Cranshaw, Staples seems to treat the human factors as necessary evils to be removed by lip service participation before the important problems of technical change and productivity are solved.

Partly because of these conclusions, Blaul tended to associate with and look to Bill Shea for guidance and advice. Unlike Cranshaw, who usually gave the impression of being too busy to discuss his sessions or Blaul's work, Shea proved very willing to discuss the sessions, the teaching material, the men in the programs, the problems that Blaul found in his work, and Shea's own problems. By late 1952, Blaul and Shea had become good friends, often seeing each other outside of work. One of the their strongest common bonds became the frustration that each felt working under Marvin Cranshaw.

Shea and Blaul felt that Cranshaw's behavior resembled that of the villains against whom he lectured so effectively. Though they admired his technical competence, both men felt that Cranshaw pyramided technical competence into a supersensitive concern for minute details. Blaul knew that Cranshaw justified this attention to detail and perfection on the grounds that the nature of the section's work required its staff to practice efficiency and constant improvement. The supervisory training section preached industrial improvement and efficiency. Therefore, reasoned Cranshaw, the section should set examples for both the firm and its clients to follow. From Cranshaw's point of view, not only the training sessions themselves, but the office procedures, work schedules, training aids, and the behavior of individuals in the section should reflect modern management thinking and a strong concern for administrative perfection.

More than once, however, Blaul felt that Cranshaw's concern for perfection resulted in his obsession with unimportant details. Within the section Cranshaw became to Blaul an efficiency expert, often forcing Blaul to undo or revise hours of work around what Blaul felt to be trivial points. Within Cranshaw's training session, Blaul found he became the motion picture projectionist, the janitor who cleaned up after training sessions, the librarian for the teaching material, and the scapegoat for any inadequacies of the program. These ranged from the blackboard's not being perfectly cleaned to a certain film's being out of stock when Cranshaw suddenly decided to use it. After most of Cranshaw's training sessions, Blaul found himself left to clean up the conference room, while Cranshaw left for lunch or cocktails with one or more of the client company's executives. On several occasions both Shea and Blaul found the office secretary, Harriet Harding, in tears over what she described as Cranshaw's thoughtlessness and his demand for picayune perfections. Under these circumstances, Blaul looked forward to the time when he could move out from his apprenticeship position under Cranshaw.

At the end of his first six months on the job, Blaul almost resigned when Cranshaw suggested that Blaul should spend the balance of his first year assisting Cranshaw, Shea, and Staples in the same capacity as during the first six months. From Blaul's point of view, this not only violated the initial agreement, but he also felt that he had learned all he could learn in the section without actually conducting his own training programs. Furthermore, on the two occasions when Blaul had substituted for Staples, the men's reactions in the class sessions had been gratifying. Shea supported Blaul's emotional reasoning, and it was finally agreed that Blaul would be given a section beginning in January 1953. From Blaul's point of view, the best feature of this arrangement lay in the fact that he would be less under Cranshaw's direction and more on his own.

During the following six months Blaul conducted a training program for supervisors in a local manufacturing plant in which Cranshaw and Shea had previously conducted sessions. With Shea's advice and help, Blaul conducted a program which seemed to be well received by the trainees and by the company's management. During this same period Blaul maintained only those contacts with Cranshaw required by the job. At the same time, Blaul and Shea continued to strengthen their friendship through frequent discussions of ways in which they could improve the training courses. Both men felt that the courses needed strengthening in order to meet the demands of their management and increased competition from other firms. Harris–Connor management had suggested to both Cranshaw and Shea that some clients had reported that they had nothing new to learn from the supervisory training section. Both Shea and Blaul felt that the section's programs should devote more effort to including new research in the behavioral sciences and less attention to selling the programs through gadgets and gimmicks.

July 1953–July 1955

By the summer of 1953, Paul Staples resigned after his two years as a staff assistant with the firm. Bill Shea told Blaul that higher management had not been impressed with Staples as a permanent member of the staff and had recommended that he accept a position open within one of Cranshaw's client companies.

Staples was replaced by Peter Mikovich, a supervisor who had been in one of Cranshaw's previous programs. Cranshaw recommended Mikovich very highly as the new staff assistant, though both Shea and Blaul had the impression that he was hot-tempered and high-strung and that his behavior was intentionally rough and outspoken. Furthermore, Shea and Blaul could not see that Mikovich strengthened any of the section's weaknesses. Mikovich was twenty-nine years old, had a B.S. degree in industrial engineering, was married, and of Slavic origin. He was hired at $5,000 a year, a decrease in salary from his previous job.

Nevertheless, Mikovich accepted the job and became, from Blaul's point of view, Cranshaw's new whipping boy. During the two years in which Mikovich was a member of the supervisory training section, Blaul experienced more and more a sense of freedom and learning as he worked on new training designs and material with both Shea and Mikovich. At the same time, according to Mikovich's own reports, he became increasingly frustrated by Cranshaw. Mikovich tended to seek sympathy from both Shea and Blaul, though neither could think of any really effective ways of easing the growing conflict. Meanwhile, Harriet Harding, the secretary, resigned; she explained to management that she did so because she could not see how anyone could work for Cranshaw. She was replaced by another secretary, who left a year later giving similar reasons.

During the spring of 1954, Shea told Blaul and Mikovich that the firm's management had asked him to take over the directorship of the supervisory training section. Management believed, said Shea, that the section was becoming less and less effective under Cranshaw's leadership and more and more bogged down in inconsequential improvements. At the same time, neither management nor Shea wanted to lose Cranshaw. They did, however, wish to move Cranshaw out of the key position in the section, where he tended to stifle both his personnel and the development of new programs. Management and Shea agreed that Cranshaw should be retained as the section's contact man, simply because Cranshaw had been in the field of supervisory training long enough to have established a national reputation. Companies which became training program clients of Harris–Connor and Associates were often attracted by Cranshaw's name and reputation. According to Shea:

> Cranshaw is our front man and whether we like it or not he's a damned good one. We need him, simply because he makes the best impressions on the men who are important to this business, the top executives in the companies. In addition, I want to put him in charge of new program design to see if we can get him out of his rut.

The switch in positions was subsequently effected by the consulting firm's management, who convinced Cranshaw that they needed more of his time and talent in customer relations for the supervisory training section. Management further explained to Cranshaw that Shea would be placed in charge of the training programs and internal administration of the section in order to release Cranshaw for customer contact work. In addition, Shea explained to Cranshaw that he hoped Cranshaw would start thinking of designs for new training programs.

Cranshaw reacted enthusiastically to his new assignment, which permitted him to spend more time with outside executives. He told Shea that the change would be to the best advantage of the section and would enable Cranshaw to do a better job of selling the section's programs to both outside executives and to Harris–Connor's increasingly skeptical management. Consequently, the switch in positions took place in the fall of 1954. Shea became director of the section. Cranshaw became assistant director in charge of new business and program planning.

Despite these changes, the relationship between Cranshaw and Mikovich became worse instead of better. Cranshaw tended to assign his administrative and sales detail work to Mikovich, who described himself as "Marv's lackey." Mikovich told Shea that he would stay with the firm until the end of his two-year contract (July 1955) only because of his respect for Shea and his friendship for Blaul.

In December of 1954 Shea and Blaul attempted to analyze what had happened within the section during recent years and, more important, what they could do about it. Both men recognized that whereas the section had once centered around Cranshaw, he was now practically an outsider to the clique comprised of Shea, Blaul, Mikovich and even the newest secretary, who resented Cranshaw's whirlwind orders and detailed demands.

SHEA: Marv is too talented to put out on a limb altogether, but I don't want to serve as the buffer between his complaints and the new staff assistant. What I'd really rather do is get above that rat race, so that I could spend some time getting a little perspective on this operation. If we are smart, we'll find a fellow to take Pete's job who can stand up to Marv without being intimidated by his gamesmanship and bluster.

With this in mind, Shea and Blaul seriously began to consider an industrial psychologist named Karl Konig as Mikovich's replacement. All four of the section's staff members had met Konig at training conferences held during the summers of both 1953 and 1954. At the first of these conferences Dr. Konig had been a delegate or student. At the second in 1954 he had served on the staff as a consultant in psychological testing and test procedures. In addition, Konig had had industrial engineering experience both during his work for a Ph.D. and in industry.

Shea and Blaul felt that, for their purposes, Konig had several strong points in his favor. First of all, Konig had a Ph.D. and knew something about the behavioral sciences and research. Secondly, Konig was 41 years old. At this age, the chances of his being intimidated by Cranshaw seemed small. Thirdly, Konig was experienced in industrial engineering as well as psychology. He had served as chief industrial engineer of a large European company just after the war. Finally, Cranshaw knew and respected Konig. Shea and Blaul thought that Konig could help move Cranshaw out of his tradition bound concepts of training programs.

SHEA: We're supposed to be able to practice this idea of creativity and industrial improvement as well as to preach it. If we can't do that, we might as well hang up. I'm hoping that Konig's age and experience will work in our favor. He should be able to help us without being pulled apart by Cranshaw. Possibly he can even help Marv see the light of day. You want to watch Karl, though. He's not only very smart, but he's very ambitious. That won't hurt us, but he'd like to have my job if he could.

July 1955–Spring 1956

Karl Konig accepted the offer of a job made by Shea in February 1955 and reported for work in August 1955. At that time the supervisory training section consisted of Shea, Cranshaw, Blaul, and Mikovich, who had remained for three months to complete an unfinished project. Table 2 presents background information on these five individuals as of August 1955. Harry Blaul, in an effort to help Shea, had agreed to remain in the section until the fall of 1956, when he planned to leave to devote full time to work on a Ph.D. in psychology at Columbia. With management approval during the summer of 1955, Blaul had also begun to do project work on a part-time basis for the psychological research section of Harris–Connor and Associates. It was planned that this would continue in 1956.

When Karl Konig reported for work in August 1955, Blaul found him extremely solicitous and polite. Inasmuch as Shea was on vacation during August, Blaul attempted to help get Konig settled on the job. At Shea's request, Blaul also attempted to explain the nature of the section's work and took Konig to several local companies where training programs were in progress. Blaul and his wife also entertained the Konigs at home.

During their frequent conversations, Konig continually expressed an interest in the nature of the training programs, in the history of the section, and in its personnel. Blaul, to begin with, said nothing about the problems and conflicts within the group, assuming that Konig would eventually reach his own conclusions. As the days went by, however, Blaul was surprised to hear Konig comment more and more favorably on Marvin Cranshaw and his contributions to the firm.

Table 2

HARRIS—CONNOR AND ASSOCIATES

Background Information on Individuals
in the Supervisory Training Section
August 1955

Name	Age	Job title	Salary	Education	Years seniority with firm	Married or single	Ethnicity and religion
Marvin Cranshaw	42	Jr. Associate	$35,000*	B.S.	14	M	English Protestant
Bill Shea	40	Jr. Associate and Section Director	29,000*	M.S.	9	M	Irish Catholic
Karl Konig	41	Jr. Associate	10,000	Ph.D.	—	M	Danish Protestant
Harry Blaul	26	Staff Assistant	8,500*	M.B.A.	3	M	English-German Protestant
Peter Mikovich	31	Staff Assistant	6,500*	B.S.	2	M	Yugoslavian Protestant

* Including fees for outside speaking engagements and conferences (about $5,000 for Shea, $12,000 for Cranshaw, $1,500 for Blaul, and $1,500 for Mikovich), and for university teaching on a part-time basis (for Shea, Cranshaw, and Blaul).

Konig's remarks disturbed Blaul, who began to feel that he should help Konig realistically recognize some of the problems that Konig would face within the group. Blaul also felt that his three years' experience within the supervisory training section had taught him something about working effectively with both Shea and Cranshaw. Blaul hoped that he could pass some of his knowledge on to Konig, in the hope that Konig could help Shea even after Blaul left Harris–Connor in the fall of 1956. It seemed to Blaul that Konig continually misevaluated the relationship between Cranshaw and Shea and Cranshaw and the firm's management. In effect, because of Cranshaw's executive-like behavior and frequent contacts with management, Konig seemed to have assumed that Cranshaw was the real operating head of the section. Shea's quieter, less flashy behavior had apparently not impressed Konig as much as Cranshaw had. In addition, other members of the firm commented to Blaul regarding Konig's evaluation of Cranshaw. The question had been put to Blaul, "Why doesn't someone set that guy [Konig] straight?"

Under these circumstances, Blaul began to wonder how he could help both the section and Konig by painting a more factual picture of conditions in the section. Blaul felt that if Konig could only understand what Blaul knew, it would help Konig to become a valuable and more productive member of the section. Consequently, after a few weeks, Blaul attempted to ask Konig for his impressions of Harris–Connor and Associates with the hope that Blaul might find some way of clarifying for Konig the actual conditions within the group.

KONIG: Well, I've been extremely impressed by the organization and by the variety of work that the firm does. I still have a great deal to learn from people like yourself, but I hope to continue to learn as I go along. I'd heard great things about Marv before I came here, so its a real pleasure to be working with a man of his reputation. Naturally I'm looking forward to my own sessions in a month or two, but I'd really rather sit in on one of Marv's sessions first, since he's such an authority in the field. Only one thing puzzles me. That's Pete Mikovich, who really seems to hold a grudge against Marv. I don't see how a fellow like Mikovich ever got a job in a group like this. He's extremely hot-tempered and unstable. I was quite disturbed at the vehemence of his comments.

BLAUL: You felt his remarks were unfair?

KONIG: Oh, definitely. I suppose it's partly his lack of confidence in himself, but his symptoms are almost those of a sick person. Marv had already told me to expect this kind of thing from Pete, but I was still surprised at the strength of Pete's emotion.

BLAUL: You haven't experienced this yet, Karl, but Pete has been pretty much involved emotionally with Marv for two years now. You know Pete came in here originally as Marv's boy. They were pretty thick at the beginning, at least until Pete began to work for Marv. But Marv has a funny way of really strangling the people who work for him. I'm farther away from real involvement now, but for the first year here, when I was low man on the totem pole, I felt just like Pete does. The only thing you can do is break away from him and go your own way. Otherwise he'll latch on to you and have you doing his dirty work as well as your own. That's OK within limits, but he keeps pushing you over the edge. He's such a stickler for insignificant detail that the edge approaches pretty fast. Pete's had Marv on his back now for two years, and Pete's gotten to the point where he avoids Marv like the plague. I think the only thing that's preserved Pete's sanity has been Bill Shea. Take one example, the motion picture attachment that Marv assigned Pete a year ago. Marv brought a picture of the attachment back from a conference and asked Pete to make one like it for him. Pete started, but the darned thing involved everything from machine shop work, which Pete did himself, to a knowledge of plastics, which he had to read up on. Then Marv didn't like the looks of the attachment and said it looked too homemade, so Pete had to start all over again. After that, Marv didn't like the way the thing balanced on the camera, so Pete had to remachine some of the parts. And finally, Marv didn't like the color Pete had painted it, but by that time Pete had deliberately painted it some bizarre color. Anyway, he had to repaint it.

In every case, though, the worst thing was that Marv, who preaches participation and human relations all over the place, just couldn't realize when he wasn't practising what he preached. He could have gotten much better results from Pete if he'd taken some of his own words to heart. Pete had some good ideas on that attachment.

Or take the case of the time that Pete, on his own, got some rubber tips put on the tripod legs, so they wouldn't slide all over the floor. That was a darned good idea that made it a lot easier for him to level the camera and get rid of that ridiculous string arrangement that held the legs. But then Marv made Pete get rid of the rubber tips and reinstate the string tying setup. I don't think Pete slept for two nights after that. He was shattered, mostly by what he called the Captain Queeg-like way in which Marv made Pete admit that he'd been pretty stupid to try rubber tips on the tripod legs. When you get right down to it, the whole thing becomes so infantile.

Fortunately, the company realizes this, I think. That's why they put Bill in the driver's seat here. He's not nearly the showman or the salesman that Marv is outside the section, but he'll help to figure out your own problems and then let you use your own head. He thinks more in terms of progress rather than maintaining the same old teaching material taught in the same old way. Really, Karl, if you want to contribute in this area, you'll find you'll almost have to go by way of Bill and drop Marv altogether.

KONIG: Well, that certainly is interesting. That's one side of the section that I haven't seen. You'll have to excuse me now, Harry. I promised Marv that I'd run an errand for him on my way downtown. We must talk more about this later sometime. I certainly want to learn about things here as soon as I can and you've been a great help.

From Konig's behavior during and after Blaul's outburst, Blaul felt that he had made no real impression on Konig. Furthermore, he felt that Konig had now mentally placed Blaul in the same category as he had placed Mikovich—hot-headed, emotional, and unreasonable. Worst of all, Blaul felt that he hadn't really helped Konig to understand the situation as it existed for Blaul. Instead, Blaul felt that he had really been trying to meet his own needs and to justify his own past behavior rather than to help Konig. In effect, Blaul felt pretty silly.

Blaul felt even worse about a week later when during a conversation with Cranshaw, Cranshaw asked Blaul whether or not he liked his job. Blaul replied that he did.

CRANSHAW: Well, I'm glad to hear that, because I knew you were leaving next year, and I've received the impression that you're dissatisfied with the job and particularly with me. That makes me feel badly, because I think you've come a long way and I'd hate to think you didn't feel the same way. I know that Pete and you are friends, but I figured that you were more mature in your outlook than he is. If you are, then you know that I'm handling him the way he should expect to be handled when he goes out into industry working for a company. I have the impression that you disapprove of the way I've handled Pete and that you've been talking about it to other people. That doesn't help our reputation as a section with the rest of the firm, you know. One of our real problems now is to sell this section to management. They expect us to be a pretty harmonious group down here, and I don't think it helps if you give the impression that we're not. Particularly now, when we're trying to bring Karl into the section, it looks bad if you insist on pointing up the difficulties rather than the strengths of the section. I feel very badly, because I always thought you and I got along without any of the friction that Pete brought to the job.

BLAUL: Well, I think we have gotten along well, but you know from our previous talks that I felt my first year was a tough year and you were a tough fellow to work for.

CRANSHAW: That's certainly understandable. You were pretty wet behind the ears when you first came down here, but I think you've developed a lot. I like to think that I've helped in that development, but I hate to be punished by you for what I've done.

Blaul felt very badly after the conversation, particularly because over the next few months Cranshaw went out of his way to be nice to Blaul. Blaul knew that everything that Cranshaw had said contained some truth, but he could not accept Cranshaw's reasoning wholeheartedly. At the same time, Blaul felt that Konig had betrayed him by recounting their conversation to Cranshaw. As soon as he could, Blaul accused Konig of betraying a confidence. Konig was very evasive on the point, but seemed to deny that he had said anything to Cranshaw that would have incriminated Blaul.

Over the next several months, Konig and Blaul became more reserved with each other, partly because Blaul felt on the defensive with Konig. Konig tried to muscle in, Blaul felt, on Blaul's work with the psychological research section even though the section's director discouraged Konig. Though Konig considered himself a psychologist, according to the director of the psychological research section, those in the section perceived him as a dyed-in-the-wool industrial engineer. Soon after, Konig began to criticize the psychological research section's work, and again Blaul felt compelled to defend the section, its work, and his own involvement in the section.

Relations within the supervisory training section developed in such a way that Blaul usually found himself either alone on program design questions and policies or siding with Bill Shea. Shea, however, tended more and more to remain above the quarrels within the group and adopted the position of letting Cranshaw, Blaul, and Konig recommend moves or policies to him. During the preliminary discussions prior to talking with Shea, Blaul usually found himself taking a minority position against Cranshaw and Konig. Concurrently, Blaul began to devote an increasing amount of time, effort, and interest to his work within the psychological research section.

Fall 1956–Spring 1958

Beginning in the fall of 1956, Blaul devoted himself almost entirely to work at Columbia on his doctoral studies in social psychology. In addition he did some special assignment work for both the supervisory training and psychological research sections of Harris–Connor and Associates. During this time he found that, though his relations with Shea and Cranshaw did not appreciably change, his relationships with Konig began to improve markedly. During 1957 and the spring of 1958, the Konigs and Blauls saw each other socially on several occasions. Konig planned to edit a book on the history, trends, and consequences of supervisory training programs and asked Blaul to contribute a chapter based upon some research Blaul had done. Konig also took what Blaul regarded as a sincere interest in Blaul's dissertation research. On one occasion Konig was able to help Blaul with a question involving psychological testing procedures.

During this time, however, Blaul noted that Konig referred to Cranshaw in increasingly bitter terms while holding Shea up as his, Konig's, ally in the section. In March 1958 Konig told Blaul that he was leaving Harris–Connor for a job in another consulting firm in Philadelphia, that he was thrilled at the prospects, and that the sooner he could get away from his unpleasant relationships with Cranshaw the better. Soon after that Konig and Blaul were at a supper party at the home of a mutual acquaintance who was seriously considering applying for a position as Cranshaw's assistant in the supervisory training section of Harris–Connor and Associates. The Blauls, and particularly Konig and his wife, began to recount stories that pointed up the problems involved in working with or for Cranshaw. The stories in retrospect provided considerable amusement, but Blaul felt that both Karl Konig and his wife were rather bitter about Cranshaw.

Several weeks later, Blaul and Konig had lunch together. The following conversation occurred:

BLAUL: Karl, I have the feeling that a great deal has happened since you came to Harris–Connor three years ago, particularly in your relations with Marv. How do you explain it?

KONIG: Oh, brother, things certainly have happened. You know you told me about some of those things when I first came to work here in New York, and I have a tape recording of another session when all four of us were together at a meeting. You said then that the firm's management was becoming more and more research-oriented and you wanted us to do and to communicate research.

I guess over the next months I began to agree with that appraisal. Then when I tried to do something about it, I ran smack into Cranshaw. After that I began to agree with your appraisal of the difficulties involved in working with him.

BLAUL: That's funny, because you know when we had that discussion where I laid my soul bare with regard to Marv, I looked back on it as being maybe an attempt on my part to exhibit and to push my superior knowledge. At any rate I felt I hadn't convinced you of a thing.

KONIG: That's hard to believe, about your trying to show superior knowledge, but you're right about my not taking what you said to heart. It did fit in with some things that Bill Shea had said about Cranshaw when he hired me, but you know I was terribly ambitious when I came to Harris-Connor. I saw no reason why I couldn't rise to the very top of that section over all three of you. I felt that I had a better theoretical background than any of the group, and I decided to just wait and see how things broke.

That didn't take too long, as it turned out. First of all, I designed a training program around psychological testing, which Marv tried to criticize apart. The result was that I was forced to drop a potentially wonderful design. After that, you know, I started to gather people together who could write a book on supervisory training. I didn't want to write it. I just wanted to put it together. When I asked Marv what he thought of the idea of the book and of his writing several of the really important chapters, I got the frozen treatment. He told me right out that I had no business writing such a book, and there were others far more qualified than I, and that he felt the field was changing so fast that no book could keep up with the trends. Hell, he knows that the field hasn't changed that much in the last ten years. He also knew that I wasn't trying to write the book, but just wanted our group to get some of the credit for all the work we've done in the past. As it is, everyone else is taking the credit.

Anyway, I still tried to sell my idea to top management at a meeting that Marv attended. He just raked me over the coals in a very supercilious fashion. He spent a good half-hour belittling any contribution that the book would make and kept challenging my right to write such a book. After that, I just plain gave up.

The final irony, of course, lies in the fact that Marv has now started out to write the book himself. He made that decision about two months ago, a full fifteen months after I tried to interest him in the idea.

Then there was the other thing that prevented me from really knowing what I was in for, when you talked to me in 1956. I thought that Marv had a great many contacts that would be extremely helpful to me. Frankly, I wanted to have those contacts, too, and getting them was a goal of sorts. Although Bill Shea was extremely likeable, I didn't see him as helping me in that respect. He didn't have nearly the influence with industry that Marv had. That's changed somewhat now. First of all, the contacts have lost their meaning for me. I don't see Marv's contacts as being important. Secondly, I believe that Bill has the intellectual scope that is much more attractive to me now. He and I became good friends, while my relationship with Marv just kept on deteriorating. (Konig also made reference to one other part of his and Blaul's conversation in 1956.)

You know you accused me of having sold you out to Marv after our talk then. That was very probably the case, because I made some pretty indiscriminate remarks about that time. I was strictly out for myself and very likely said some things to Marv that reflected upon you.

I hope you don't regard me as a despicable individual for all that I've said. As you can see, I've shown a great many weaknesses today. I feel that I learned a great deal during the last two years, but after today you would have just cause for wondering what kind of guy I was.

BLAUL: As a matter of fact, I've been wondering, especially right now, whether I shouldn't be saying the same thing to you. It seems to me that we both agree on what the situation in the section was and on what ought to have been done about it. It also seems to me that my talking to you as I did in 1956 may have delayed your reaching these conclusions. There is at least a good chance that we would both have been better off and the section also if I'd kept my big mouth shut.

KONIG: Well (he hesitated) . . . I suppose that's a possibility.

BLAUL: There's something interesting here. It relates to the business we're in. I thought I could use the knowledge I had about the relationships in our section to help you see our problems so that we could both work on them. Even though you now agree with me about the problems, I'd say what I did probably delayed rather than helped things. This ought to mean something for what we teach. If we can't use our own knowledge to help ourselves, isn't there something funny either with our knowledge or with the way we use it?

CHAPTER 10. Leadership and individual growth

While putting this book together, as whenever we teach this course, we have often wondered what we were going to say at the end of it. The book has emphasized listening to the beliefs and feelings of other people. But it has also illustrated the value of understanding sensitively and expressing congruently one's *own* beliefs and feelings. Although we may at times have given a contrary impression, our idea of an effective manager (or teacher) is not just a person skilled at listening to others but also a person in touch with and able to state clearly what he values and stands for. He is at least as concerned with developing his own effectiveness and growth as a person as with helping others develop their potential. What, then, after so much concern for what is important to others, shall we say about what is important to us?

Actually, by our selection of cases and readings, and our comments about them in previous chapters, we have stated as clearly as we could what is important to us about how an administrator needs and will need to think and behave in relation to: assumptions about motivation in organizations and the use of words, understanding the behavior of others, helping others understand their own behavior, and improving the effectiveness of organizational relationships. Rather than summarize again all of this, we would now like to state, briefly and convincingly, three things we believe an effective and responsible leader has to be able to do:

1. He has to understand and manage the translation of an

expanding body of knowledge into practical concrete behavior.

2. He has to be able to listen to himself, and see this as both more important and more difficult than listening to others.

3. He has to develop and congruently express in his behavior a central concern for every individual's potential as a human being; he has to value individual growth and development for himself and others, not as a means to other ends but as his own major purpose in life.

Knowledge and practice

A central and difficult function of leadership in any modern organization is the skillful management of the practical implementation of an ever expanding body of relevant knowledge.

> The systematic and rapid accumulation of knowledge in all the disciplines that have relevance to management is a major phenomenon of our time. Behavioral science knowledge is one example, but others are no less important. Computer technology, applied mathematics, statistics, and symbolic logic, most of which have hitherto been of relatively small concern to the manager, are becoming highly relevant. As industrial firms become international in character, they must acquire additional knowledge in political science, history, anthropology, economics, and perhaps also philosophy and ethics.[1]

In these circumstances there is a need for increasingly useful ways of thinking about the relationship between the development of systematic knowledge and its application in practice. As an instance of this general problem, the relationship between knowledge about the counseling process and skill in practicing it illustrates very clearly two important points which have a wider relevance:

a. Practice contributes to the development of knowledge at the same time that the development of knowledge contributes to the improvement of practice.

[1] Douglas McGregor, *The Professional Manager* (New York: McGraw-Hill, 1967), p. 52.

b. Knowing something about a process like counseling may be a necessary condition but is certainly not a sufficient one for practicing it successfully.

According to one view of the relation between systematic knowledge and practice, the process, in oversimplified terms, goes something like this. From an assumed existing body of knowledge (1), a great scientist develops a new theory made up of testable hypotheses (2), which lead to experiments (3), which generate findings (4), leading to methods of application (5), and finally to improved practice (6). According to this model the practitioner makes little contribution to the process of developing knowledge. He comes into the chain of events only at the end of the process and it almost seems as if it would all work better without him.

However the history of the development of the orientation we have been studying, and our own efforts to practice it, illustrate very clearly that this one-directional chain of events does not at all represent the actual development of knowledge and practice. A most accurate model of what takes place in the history of the development of any science requires a circular rather than a linear model, in which the role of the practitioner is central rather than that of a somewhat inconvenient last step. Some of the major phases of this development could be represented by Figure 1.

This conception of the development of knowledge and practice is not put forward as an adequate description of a very com-

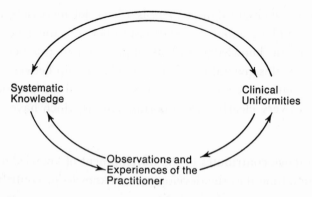

Figure 1

plex subject.[1] Its purpose is only to call attention to the probability that what we discovered in our own study and practice of interpersonal behavior may have wide relevance. The observations which come from skillful practice and the hypotheses which derive from systematic knowledge contribute to each other. The ideas which make sense at the level of clinical uniformities and at the level of theory are the same ideas which make sense to the intuitions of a skillful, responsible practitioner. For this kind of balanced progress in both theory and practice to take place, scientific and practical viewpoints must remain in effective communication with each other. To maintain and improve this communication is becoming an increasingly important management challenge.[2]

In this conception of the knowledge–practice relation, the intuitions, curiosities, and feelings of the practitioner remain important contributors to the development of systematic knowledge, which in turn is useful to the practitioner as a framework for the organization of the observations and reflections he draws from this experience. Thus any theory of human behavior is useful to a manager—not when he believes it tells him what to do, but when it helps him order the phenomena he experiences in useful ways and test out for himself the consequences of differences in his own behavior.[3] This kind of relationship between knowledge and practice requires that the practitioner remain curious about and sensitive to what he experiences when he interacts with another person. To benefit from and contribute to useful knowledge the practitioner has to learn to respond ever more skillfully to the total situation in which he is involved and to recognize that his own feelings are an unavoidable part of that situation.

[1] For readable and authoritative accounts of the relations between theory and practice in the historical development of science, see J. B. Conant, *On Understanding Science* (New Haven: Yale University Press, 1947) and *Modern Science and Modern Man* (Garden City, N.Y.: Doubleday Anchor Books, 1955).

[2] For accounts of the interplay between knowledge and practice in the historical development of non-directive counseling and client-centered interviewing, see W. J. Dickson and F. J. Roethlisberger, *Counseling in an Organization* and C. R. Rogers, *On Becoming a Person*.

[3] Thus McGregor's "Theory X" and "Theory Y" have often been misunderstood by managers. See Douglas McGregor, *The Human Side of Enterprise* and *The Professional Manager*.

Listening to oneself

This is what to us this book has really been about: the administrator's ability to increase his awareness and understanding of how he feels about events in which he is involved and other people with whom he interacts. Sometimes in the midst of my involvement, at other times when I reflect on what has taken place, I have to ask myself this question and listen with skill to my answer: How is what I am aware of experiencing outside of myself being affected by what I may not be aware of experiencing inside?

Sometimes I can ask for help on this question from colleague, friend, or counselor, but often I will have to work on it alone. If this volume has provided some additional incentive and way of learning when and how to listen to ourselves, it will have served its purpose.

Commitment to individual development

For too long, it seems to us, there has been a sort of collusion between administrator and "behavioral scientist" (a label as misfortunate in our opinion, and as fashionable, as "change agent") to avoid open and forthright expression of the central value position on which their work together is based. Thus one popular model for the development of the field of interpersonal behavior in organizations sees it as an exchange between the practitioner committed to the improvement of organizational performance and the researcher committed to the improvement of scientific knowledge about human behavior. As new "findings" are discovered they become the means by which the practitioner increases his organization's efficient production of goods and services. This model says nothing about how and by whom improved skill is to be developed, and it seems to sanction no open communication about fundamental values.

To us, increased knowledge about human behavior in organizations (improved "behavioral science") is important, and we feel equally committed to the efficient utilization of human resources in the production of material goods and services. These two goals are both important, and each contributes to the other. But they are not enough. In addition, our world needs, desperately as we see it, improved skill in applying to organizational life what is already known about human behavior (and has been known for centuries), and it needs more clear commitment to the development of those kinds of human organizations within which each member is able to realize his potential as a thinking, feeling, growing human being. This is the third purpose to the attainment of which—because it is so badly needed in the world—we hope will be dedicated whatever improved ways of understanding self in relation to others may have been learned in this study.

List of Cases

List of Readings